Lecture Notes in Computer Science 15373

Founding Editors

Gerhard Goos
Juris Hartmanis

AF167701

The series Lecture Notes in Computer Science (LNCS), including its subseries Lecture Notes in Artificial Intelligence (LNAI) and Lecture Notes in Bioinformatics (LNBI), has established itself as a medium for the publication of new developments in computer science and information technology research, teaching, and education.

LNCS enjoys close cooperation with the computer science R & D community, the series counts many renowned academics among its volume editors and paper authors, and collaborates with prestigious societies. Its mission is to serve this international community by providing an invaluable service, mainly focused on the publication of conference and workshop proceedings and postproceedings. LNCS commenced publication in 1973.

Chutiporn Anutariya · Marcello M. Bonsangue
Editors

Theoretical Aspects of Computing – ICTAC 2024

21st International Colloquium
Bangkok, Thailand, November 25–29, 2024
Proceedings

 Springer

Editors
Chutiporn Anutariya ⓘ
Asian Institute of Technology
Pathum Thani, Thailand

Marcello M. Bonsangue ⓘ
LIACS – Leiden University
Leiden, Zuid-Holland, The Netherlands

ISSN 0302-9743   ISSN 1611-3349 (electronic)
Lecture Notes in Computer Science
ISBN 978-3-031-77018-0   ISBN 978-3-031-77019-7 (eBook)
https://doi.org/10.1007/978-3-031-77019-7

This Springer imprint is published by the registered company Springer Nature Switzerland AG
The registered company address is: Gewerbestrasse 11, 6330 Cham, Switzerland

If disposing of this product, please recycle the paper.

Preface

This volume comprises the papers presented at the 21st International Colloquium on Theoretical Aspects of Computing (ICTAC 2024), held from November 25–29, 2024, in Bangkok, Thailand. The ICTAC series, established in 2003 by the United Nations University International Institute for Software Technology, is an annual event that brings together practitioners and researchers from academia, industry, and government. Its primary aim is to present research findings, exchange experiences, and foster cooperation in research and education between participants from developing and industrial regions.

For ICTAC 2024, we received 46 submissions. Each paper underwent a rigorous review process, with at least three single-blind reviews. Following these evaluations and extensive discussions, the Program Committee accepted 21 papers, the revised versions of which are included in this volume. These papers span a wide range of topics, from automata theory to algorithms, games to process calculi, and program verification to automated reasoning.

We were honored to feature four distinguished invited speakers:

Ichiro Hasuo (National Institute of Informatics, Japan), who presented his recent work on proving the safety of automated driving vehicles; Annabelle McIver (Macquarie University, Australia), who discussed probabilistic data types and their role in implementing probabilistic specifications; Alfons Laarman (Leiden University, Netherlands), who demonstrated the effectiveness of classical automated reasoning methods for computationally challenging problems in quantum computing; and Priyanka Golia (Indian Institute of Technology Delhi, India), who provided an overview of recent approaches combining formal methods and artificial intelligence to solve various automated synthesis problems.

Extended abstracts for the four invited talks, along with two related invited papers by Annabelle McIver and Alfons Laarman, are included in this volume.

The conference also featured several tutorials:

Martin Leuker (University of Lübeck, Germany) on automata learning and its application to learning and verifying recurrent neural networks; Alfons Laarman and Tim Copperman (Leiden University, Netherlands) on quantum circuit compilation using formal methods; Ichiro Hasuo (National Institute of Informatics, Japan) on lattice theory and category theory in model checking; and Uwe Nestmann and Nadine Karsten (Technische Universität Berlin, Germany) on the web application ProofBuddy for the proof assistant Isabelle.

In keeping with the tradition of previous ICTAC conferences, ICTAC 2024 hosted a Training School aimed at introducing Master's students, Ph.D. candidates, and early-stage researchers to key topics in theoretical computing:

Priyanka Golia (Indian Institute of Technology Delhi, India) introduced SAT solvers; Emil Sekerinsky (McMaster University, Canada) provided an introduction to the classical theory of program correctness; and Zhiming Liu (Southwest University, China), the founder of ICTAC, presented formal refinement of component and object systems as a framework for model-driven engineering.

The success of ICTAC 2024 was made possible by the contributions of many colleagues and friends. We extend our heartfelt thanks to all the authors who submitted their work, the Program Committee members, and the external reviewers for their thorough and constructive evaluations. We are grateful to our invited speakers for their inspiring talks, tutorials, and lectures, to the publicity chair and local organizers for their dedication to organizing the conference and the school, and to attracting high-quality submissions. Our appreciation also goes to the Steering Committee for their unwavering support.

We acknowledge the Asian Institute of Technology in Bangkok, Thailand, for hosting the conference, and EasyChair for facilitating the assignment and review process and supporting the production of the proceedings. Special thanks go to Springer for their cooperation in publishing the proceedings and sponsoring the Best Paper Award. We also thank the Leiden Institute of Advanced Computer Science (LIACS) at Leiden University in the Netherlands for the financial support for the invited talks and tutorials.

November 2024   Chutiporn Anutariya
                                                     Marcello M. Bonsangue

Organization

Steering Committee

Martin Leucker (Chair)	University of Lübeck, Germany
Zhiming Liu	Southwest University, China
Tobias Nipkow	Technische Universität München, Germany
Augusto Sampaio	Universidade Federal de Pernambuco, Brazil
Natarajan Shankar	SRI, USA
Tarmo Uustalu	Reykjavik University, Iceland

Publicity Chair

Hans-Dieter Hiep	Amazon Web Services, UK

Local Organizers

Siriporn Nanthasing	Asian Institute of Technology, Thailand
Sireekant Thanwongpan	Asian Institute of Technology, Thailand

Program Committee

Erika Abraham	RWTH Aachen, Germany
Wolfgang Ahrend	Chalmers University of Technology, Sweden
Davide Ancona	Università di Genova, Italy
Chutiporn Anutariya (Chair)	Asian Institute of Technology, Thailand
Kyungmin Bae	Pohang University of Science and Technology, South Korea
Luis Soares Barbosa	Minho University, Portugal
Filippo Bonchi	University of Pisa, Italy
Marcello Bonsangue (Chair)	Leiden University, Netherlands
Georgiana Caltais	University of Twente, Netherlands
Valentina Castiglioni	Eindhoven University of Technology, Netherlands
Corina Cirstea	University of Southampton, UK
Erik de Vink	Eindhoven University of Technology, Netherlands
Besik Dundua	Kutaisi International University, Georgia

Hadar Frenkel	CISPA Helmholtz Center for Information Security, Germany
Reiner Hähnle	Technical University of Darmstadt, Germany
Paula Herber	University of Münster, Germany
Tobias Kappé	Open University, Netherlands
Jan Kretinsky	Technical University of Munich, Germany
Frederic Mallet	Côte d'Azur University, France
Matteo Mio	CNRS/ENS-Lyon, France
Rosemary Monahan	Maynooth University, Ireland
Sophie Fortz	King's College London, UK
David Naumann	Stevens Institute of Technology, USA
Jurriaan Rot	Radboud University, Netherlands
Prakash Saivasan	Institute of Mathematical Sciences, India
Gerardo Schneider	University of Gothenburg, Sweden
Martina Seidl	Johannes Kepler University Linz, Austria
Emil Sekerinski	McMaster University, Canada
Marjan Sirjani	Mälardalen University, Sweden
Meng Sun	Peking University, China
Silvia Lizeth Tapia Tarifa	University of Oslo, Norway
Maurice ter Beek	ISTI-CNR, Italy
Andrea Turrini	Chinese Academy of Sciences, China
Tarmo Uustalu	Reykjavik University, Iceland
Heike Wehrheim	University of Oldenburg, Germany
Min Zhang	East China Normal University, China

Additional Reviewers

Anastasiadi, Elli	Masud, Abu Naser
Bargmann, Lara	Miné, Antoine
Bichhawat, Abhishek	Prokop, Maximilian
Bu, Hao	Reder, Gabriel
Bubel, Richard	Reidenbach, Daniel
Galby, Esther	Rieder, Sabine
Grobelna, Marta	Rigo, Michel
Kobialka, Paul	Romanelli, Marco
Kori, Mayuko	Simon, Sunil
Kufleitner, Manfred	Teh, Wen Chean
Källberg, Linus	Teuber, Samuel
Luan, Xiaokun	Veschetti, Adele
MacConville, Dara	Yang, Jianting

Sponsors

Asian Institute of Technology
Leiden Institute of Advanced Computer Science, Leiden University
Springer Verlag

Keynote Talks

Proving Safety of Automated Driving Vehicles

Ichiro Hasuo

National Institute of Informatics, Japan
i.hasuo@acm.org

Abstract. I will introduce our recent work on using formal logic to rigorously prove the safety of automated driving vehicles. The main challenge in such formal verification attempts for real-world systems is the absence of target system models. We follow the methodology called RSS (responsibility-sensitive safety, Shalev-Shwartz et al., 2017) that tells what to model (and what not to model) in a both technically and socially sensible way. Our formalization and extension of RSS with a Floyd–Hoare-style program logic allows us to handle complex driving scenarios compositionally, and to cover real-world scenarios such as emergency pull over for the first time. I will demonstrate the use of obtained proofs with driving simulation. Overall, the work suggests the potential of formal logic as a social infrastructure for establishing trust in novel ICT. The talk is based on the following papers:

- Ichiro Hasuo, Clovis Eberhart, James Haydon et al. Goal-Aware RSS for Complex Scenarios via Program Logic. IEEE Trans. Intelligent Vehicles, 8(4): 3040–3072 (2023)
- James Haydon, Martin Bondu, Clovis Eberhart, Jérémy Dubut, Ichiro Hasuo: Formal Verification of Intersection Safety for Automated Driving. Proc. ITSC 2023: 107–114
- Clovis Eberhart, Jérémy Dubut, James Haydon, Ichiro Hasuo: Formal Verification of Safety Architectures for Automated Driving. Proc. IV 2023: 1–8

Automated Synthesis: Fusing Formal Methods and AI

Priyanka Golia

Indian Institute of Technology Delhi, India
pgolia@iitd.ac.in

Abstract. We increasingly entrust large parts of our daily lives to computer systems, which are becoming more complex. Developing scalable and trustworthy techniques for designing, developing, and verifying these systems is crucial. In this talk, we will focus on automated synthesis, a technique that uses formal specifications to automatically generate systems (such as functions, programs, or circuits) that provably satisfy the specified requirements.

The talk will overview recent approaches that combine advances in automated reasoning, knowledge compilation, and machine learning to address a wide variety of practical automated synthesis problems. Additionally, we will introduce a state-of-the-art functional synthesis algorithm that leverages artificial intelligence to provide an initial guess for the system and then uses formal methods to repair and verify this guess, resulting in a system that is correct by construction.

Contents

Graphs and Games

Process Calculi

Verification and Reasoning

Keynote Presentations and Invited Papers

Probabilistic Datatypes

Chris Chen[1], Annabelle McIver[1(✉)], and Carroll Morgan[2]

[1] School of Computing, Macquarie University, Sydney, Australia
{chris.chen1,annabelle.mciver}@mq.edu.au
[2] University of New South Wales and Trustworthy Systems, Sydney, Australia
carroll.morgan@unsw.edu.au

Abstract. An encapsulated datatype collects related data together with the operations used to access them. Datatype refinement then provides a clear separation between the expectations of programs that call the operations (i.e. from outside the encapsulation) and the implementation of the operations themselves (inside the encapsulation), and it enforces consistency between the two.

In this paper we consider encapsulated *probabilistic* datatypes, i.e. those whose operations can "flip coins"; and we find as a result that the interface between calling programs' expectations and their encapsulated probabilistic implementations must now provide consistency not only for functional properties but also for properties related to information flow.

In this paper we use a quantitative information-flow model for programs to give a sound basis for refinement of probabilistic datatypes.

1 Introduction

A *datatype encapsulation* groups related variables—the data values—together with operations (also known as "functions", "procedures", "methods") on them. Encapsulation allows a surrounding program to use only the datatype's operations to access the datatype's variables: in general, the variables may not be accessed by the program directly.

The point of encapsulation is presentation of its variables and operations abstractly to the program containing it, as a specification: the program's operation can then be understood by referring to that specification alone. The implementation of the encapsulation however can be given concretely, possibly using more complicated but more efficient structures, and that the containing program cannot tell the difference.

In that case, we say that the abstract datatype is *refined* by the concrete datatype—just when no program using the second can detect that it is not using the first. Refinement ensures that understanding the surrounding program's operation in abstract terms corresponds with what actually happens when using the concrete implementation is run.

We summarise these ideas as follows [12]:

Definition 1. *An* encapsulated datatype *is a triple* (I, OP, F), *where* I *and* F *are two distinguished operations called respectively the* initialisation *and* finalisation, *and* OP *is an indexed set of publicly accessible operations.* [12]

C. Anutariya and M. M. Bonsangue (Eds.): ICTAC 2024, LNCS 15373, pp. 3–16, 2025.
https://doi.org/10.1007/978-3-031-77019-7_1

Refinement of datatypes is defined relative to refinement of the programs that use them; and refinement itself is dependent on the a-priori identification of (desired) properties those programs should have: in its most general sense refinement therefore means "preservation of desired properties"[1]. In particular, if *any* calling program replacing a datatype (I, OP, F) by (I', OP', F') will find all its desired properties preserved, we say that (I, OP, F) is *itself* refined by (I', OP', F'). We write $\sqsubseteq$ for the refinement relation between programs, so that $P \sqsubseteq P'$ meaning (as stated above) desired behaviours of P are preserved by P'.

Our setting is sequential programs defined by the basic program constructs: sequential composition, assignment, branching and loops, and also both demonic nondeterminism ($\sqcap$), and probabilistic choice ($_p\oplus$). There are few works on the combination of probability *and* nondeterminism for datatypes [27]; in the next section we review some known results with an example.

Definition 2. *A datatype (I, OP, F) is refined by (I', OP', F') [12] if, for every program $\mathcal{P}$ expressible using the constructs mentioned above, including calls on corresponding operators in OP and OP', we have*

$$I; \mathcal{P}(OP); F \quad \sqsubseteq \quad I'; \mathcal{P}(OP'); F' \ ,$$

where ";" indicates sequential composition.

There is a wealth of literature on verification methods for proving refinement of datatypes (Def. 2). A common method is *simulation*:

Definition 3. *We say that an operation rep is a simulation from (I, OP, F) to (I', OP', F') if—using $j \in J$ to index corresponding operations in OP and OP'—the following inequations hold [12]:*

$$
\begin{align}
I; rep \quad &\sqsubseteq \quad I' \tag{1} \\
OP[j]; rep \quad &\sqsubseteq \quad rep; OP'[j] \qquad \forall j \in J \tag{2} \\
F \quad &\sqsubseteq \quad rep; F' \tag{3}
\end{align}
$$

In order however for simulation (Def. 3) to establish refinement (Def. 2), an additional constraint is required, namely that *rep* must commute even with "intermediate" external program constructs lying between calls of the datatype's operations, i.e. ones that don't refer to the datatype at all.

2   Abstract Datatypes with Probability

Figure 1 depicts two probabilistic datatypes. The left-hand datatype Fig. 1a has a single operation Flip_A which outputs a random value. The right-hand datatype,

---

[1] For example, desired properties of sequential programs are often their *termination* and their establishment of a given *postcondition* on the program state, in both cases provided a *precondition* holds. Hoare logic, Dijkstra weakest-preconditions and the refinement calculus all derive their definition of refinement from that [6,10,16,29,32]

Fig. 1b, also outputs a random value, when its corresponding operation Flip_C is called—however the two implementations are very different.

Whereas Fig. 1a flips the coin just when it is needed, Fig. 1b flips the coin in advance and, after having delivered it, "pre-flips" to be ready for next time. That is, the initialisation I_C sets a local variable c to a random value; then when Flip_C is called, later, it assigns to coin the previously randomly chosen value c, then immediately "re-flips" c, ready for its next use. And so

the question here is whether the encapsulation, guaranteeing that variable c *cannot be accessed or observed* by the calling program, suffices for datatype $(I_A, \{\text{Flip}_A\}, F_A)$ to be refined by $(I_C, \{\text{Flip}_C\}, F_C)$ according to Def. 2, given a definition of refinement that takes the observability assumption into account.

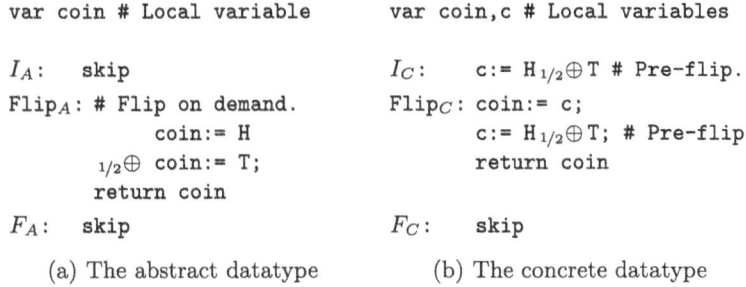

```
var coin # Local variable          var coin,c # Local variables

I_A:   skip                        I_C:   c:= H 1/2⊕ T # Pre-flip.
Flip_A: # Flip on demand.          Flip_C: coin:= c;
          coin:= H                          c:= H 1/2⊕ T; # Pre-flip.
   1/2⊕ coin:= T;                            return coin
       return coin
F_A:   skip                        F_C:   skip
```

(a) The abstract datatype   (b) The concrete datatype

Fig. 1. Abstract and concrete probabilistic datatypes

Intuitively the answer should be "yes" because, even though the random setting of c used later to assign to coin has already been resolved after initialisation, there is no way for that resolution to affect the calling program until the invocation of Flip_C, and at that point *it is as though* coin *is set randomly in exactly the same way as* Flip_A did. In fact, as shown in [27], the operation *rep* given by c:= 0 $_{1/2}⊕$ 1 satisfies (1)–(3) for the datatypes in Fig. 1a and 1b. But is this enough to prove refinement?

As we will see, it is possible to write a program where the two datatypes seemingly *are* distinguished when we define refinement using the standard semantics for probabilistic sequential programs (*pGCL* [26]) based on a Markov Decision Process Model (MDP) [15, 18, 20, 30]. We discuss that scenario in the next section.

2.1 The "Copy Rule" for MDP's and Probabilistic Datatypes

A well-known technique for establishing the meaning of procedure calls, here referred to as operations (whether encapsulated or not) is based on a version of the *Copy Rule* for the verification of procedures [4, 7], which is essentially inlining the operation's text at its point of call (taking care with variable capture), then using normal refinement rules on the resulting operation-call -free programs.

```
skip # I_A inlined.              c:= H_{1/2}⊕T # I_C inlined.
v:= H⊓T; # Program.              v:= H⊓T; # Program.
g:= H_{1/2}⊕T; # Flip_A.         g:= c; c:= H_{1/2}⊕T # Flip_C.
skip # F_A inlined.              skip # F_C inlined.
```

(a) Inlined abstract encapsulation   (b) Inlined concrete encapsulation

```
I
v:= H⊓T;
g:= Flip()    # Is this Flip_A, or Flip_C?
F             # Does it matter?
```

What is the probability that $v = g$ here?

(c) User's code

Fig. 2. Using the copy rule

It turns out that the exact interpretation of the refinement and program semantics determines whether or not this verification technique is valid within a proposed context and set of assumptions, as we now explain.

Consider the user's program in Fig. 2c that sets a global variable v nondeterministically to H or T, and subsequently sets another global variable g probabilistically via the Flip operation. (That is, neither g nor v are in the encapsulation.) The program is an example of a context $\mathcal{P}(\cdot)$ in Def. 2, and so it is reasonable to ask whether there are any differences in behaviour between the instantiation of $(I, \{\text{Flip}\}, F)$ with either $(I_A, \{\text{Flip}_A\}, F_A)$ or $(I_C, \{\text{Flip}_C\}, F_C)$. Given the comments above concerning the idea that the internals of the datatype are "not observable" wrt. the calling program at run-time, one would hope that there is no difference.

We make this precise by appealing to the Copy Rule; the result appears in Fig. 2a and 2b, for the instantiation of respectively $(I_A, \{\text{Flip}_A\}, F_A)$ versus $(I_C, \{\text{Flip}_C\}, F_C)$. Inlining in the abstract Fig. 2a, the flip is made into local variable coin but then assigned immediately to the global variable g via Flip_A's return coin statement. In Fig. 2b however it is the earlier coin flip into c, carried out during the initialisation I_C, that Flip_C assigns to g.

If refinement from abstract to concrete *does* hold, then the probability that v and g have the same value finally in Fig. 2b should be at least that for Fig. 2a[2]. Suppose now we use an MDP semantics to interpret the program fragments in Fig. 2a and 2b.

When the concrete initialisation "c := 0 $_{1/2}$⊕ 1" is copied, as in Fig. 2b, the subsequent execution of the demonic choice "v:=0 ⊓ 1" can, in the MDP interpretation, now be resolved *depending on the value of* c. The program Fig. 2a on

---

[2] In fact the probabilities will be equal, since the same argument applies to their having opposite values.

the other hand cannot do that. As a result, for Fig. 2b globals g and v can be equal with probability as low as 0, because the surrounding program's demonic choice could resolve to $v := \texttt{NOT } c$ on every run; but for Fig. 2a the equality must have probability exactly $1/2$.

And so our refinement technique must ensure that c's value is not detectable outside the encapsulation—for example by the demonic choice $v := \texttt{H} \sqcap \texttt{T}$ in the calling program. Otherwise the result of a call to $\texttt{Flip}$ could be "predicted" in the concrete case, but not the abstract.

A more succinct example of the inconvenient interaction between probability and demonic choice in an MDP interpretation is given by the failure of the following refinement:

$$v := 0 \sqcap 1; \; c := 0 \;_{1/2}\oplus\, 1 \quad \not\sqsubseteq \quad c := 0 \;_{1/2}\oplus\, 1; \; v := 0 \sqcap 1 \;. \tag{4}$$

It shows that probabilistic- and demonic assignments might not commute even when the assignments have no variables in common. Figure 3 below sketches the MDP interpretation for each fragment, with the lower sequence of transitions corresponding to the right-hand program fragment in (4), showing again that when the nondeterminsim is resolved *after* a probabilistic assignment, the assumption underlying the MDP model comes into play, resulting in more behaviours than the upper sequence (left-hand fragment) allows.

But (4) actually illustrates that even the presence of the simulation *rep* as $c := 0 \;_{1/2}\oplus\, 1$ established between Fig. 1a and 1b is insufficient to prove Def. 2 in the presence of nondeterminism in the calling program, since as (4) shows, this *rep* does not commute with the nondeterministic operator. What this tells us is that the Copy Rule is consistent with Def. 3 only when the *rep* commutes with the calling program's operators.

One option would be to ban the use of demonic nondeterminism entirely, since this seems to be the offending operator. But nondeterminism is fundamental to abstraction, and the problem here is really that the MDP model is failing to capture the intended concept of "non-observability" in the organisation of probabilistic datatypes. It therefore behoves us to look for a model that can indeed discriminate between encapsulated variables and external program variables, even in the presence of external nondeterminism. We look at this next.

3   A Quantitative Information Flow Model for Probabilistic Datatypes

It turns out that a model that does encapsulate probabilistic behaviour has the same characteristics as a model for quantitative information flow (QIF) [2,3] in terms of its distinguishing between "hidden" and "visible" state, where we now assume that the calling program cannot access any variables or state that are initialised within the datatypes, and information about what that state could be can only occur through assignments to external variables declared by the calling program. In a probabilistic semantics this means that we are interested

$$(g, v, c) \xrightarrow{\texttt{v:= 0 $\sqcap$ 1}} \{(g, 0, c), (g, 1, c)\} \xrightarrow{\texttt{c:= 0 $_{1/2}\oplus$ 1}} \left\{ \begin{array}{l} \mathsf{u}\{(g, 0, 0), (g, 0, 1)\}, \\ \mathsf{u}\{(g, 1, 0), (g, 1, 1)\} \end{array} \right\}$$

$$(g, v, c) \xrightarrow{\texttt{c:= 0 $_{1/2}\oplus$ 1}} \{\mathsf{u}\{(g, v, 0), (g, v, 1)\}\} \xrightarrow{\texttt{v:= 0 $\sqcap$ 1}} \left\{ \begin{array}{l} \mathsf{u}\{(g, 0, 0), (g, 0, 1)\}, \mathsf{u}\{(g, 1, 0), (g, 1, 1)\}, \\ \mathsf{u}\{(g, 0, 0), (g, 1, 1)\}, \mathsf{u}\{(g, 1, 0), (g, 0, 1)\} \end{array} \right\}$$

Here $\mathsf{u}(\mathcal{S})$ is the uniform distribution over the elements of the set $\mathcal{S}$.

In the first case, the demonic choice is made in ignorance of the outcome of the coin-flip, which has not yet occcured: the probability of $v{=}c$ afterwards is $1/2$. In the second case, the demonic choice "knows" the outcome of the coin-flip, because it has already happened: the $\sqcap$ can then decide to establish $v{=}c$, or $v{\neq}c$ or indeed any probabilistic outcome in between.

Fig. 3. Probabilistic simulation for program with MDP interpretation.

in how information about the encapsulated data might *leak* in terms of correlations between (hidden) encapsulated state, and visible state, and what kind of semantics could support a Copy Rule that correctly captures this assumption of non-observability of encapsulated state.

In fact QIF deals exactly with this type of analysis of information leaks from programs and, unlike an MDP model where the adversary is assumed to have complete run-time knowledge of all program state, a QIF model instead accounts for probabilistic behaviour that either has, or has not, been revealed during program execution. QIF therefore uses a partially observable Markov Decision Process (POMDP) [25].

In general we distinguish programs' *visible* state component $\mathcal{V}$ from their hidden state component $\mathcal{H}$, and the actual program state is of type $\mathcal{V}{\times}\mathbb{D}\mathcal{H}$, i.e. one in which only a *distribution* over say a hidden variable h appears, not the actual value of h itself. (In our programs of Fig. 2, the visible variables $\mathcal{V}$ are g,v and the hidden variables $\mathcal{H}$ are c,coin.)

With that model, demonic nondeterminism $\sqcap$ can be influenced only by the first component $\mathcal{V}$, essentially in ignorance of any actual value in $\mathcal{H}$. A QIF-interpretation of a program state that includes visible state $\mathcal{V}$ and hidden state $\mathcal{H}$ would be take initial states $\mathcal{V}{\times}\mathbb{D}\mathcal{H}$ to sets of final states each of type $\mathbb{D}(\mathcal{V}{\times}\mathbb{D}\mathcal{H})$, which we call "hyper-distributions".

For example, for both the program extracts in (4) where $\mathcal{V}$ is g,v and $\mathcal{H}$ is c,coin, starting from an initial state $((g, v), -)$, the nondeterminism reacts only to the first component of the triple (a pair itself), while the probabilistic update occurring within the datatype affects only the second, updating it to new *distribution* over pairs of (c,coin) values. The result is that in this more expressive POMDP interpretation, as depicted in Fig. 4, the result sets of the two program fragments (4)—right then down vs. down then right—are the same; and that is our goal, i.e. that the refinement distribute through the external program's operations:

$$((g, v), -) \quad \xrightarrow{\;\text{v}\;:=\;0 \sqcap 1\;} \quad \{((g, 0), -), ((g, 1), -)\}$$

$$\text{c}:=\;0\;{}_{1/2}\oplus 1 \Big\downarrow \qquad\qquad\qquad\qquad \Big\downarrow \text{c}:=0\;{}_{1/2}\oplus 1$$

$$((g, v), \mathsf{u}\{0, 1\}) \quad \xrightarrow{\;\text{v}\;:=\;0 \sqcap 1\;} \quad \{((g, 0), \mathsf{u}\{0, 1\}), ((g, 1), \mathsf{u}\{0, 1\})\}$$

Note that the *second* component of the state is a *distribution* (uniform u) over $\mathcal{H}$, the "hidden" c,coin, and that the nondeterministic choice of v therefore has the same overall effect irrespective of whether it precedes or follows the hidden probabilistic assignment. The diagram commutes.

Fig. 4. Probabilistic simulation for program with POMDP interpretation.

Lemma 1 ([25]**).** *Given a POMDP model for probabilistic datatypes [25], the existence of a simulation (Def. 3) which maps hidden state in in the abstract datatype (I, OP, F) to hidden state in the concrete datatype (I', OP', F'), implies that (I, OP, F) is refined by (I', OP', F').*

Proof. (Sketch) We use the assumption here that rep distributes through all program operators, including external demonic nondeterminism, of the calling program. The soundness proof of [12] completes this proof.

4   Property-Preserving Encryption as a Probabilistic Datatype

In general, property-preserving encryption preserves some properties of the original data; searchable encryption is the special case where relative order is preserved, so that comparisons can be carried out on the encrypted data, i.e. without having to decrypt them: range searches could, for example, be carried out without decryption. Order-preservation could be considered a beneficial leak; but turns out however that some *implementations* of searching with order-preserving encryption have been found to leak more than they should—and so there is interest in determining the impact of these unintentional leaks [17].

We approach the verification problem—*viz* assuring that there are no inadvertent and harmful information leaks—in terms of our QIF-setting for probabilistic datatypes. Figure 7 sets out two datatypes for access to an encrypted array: Fig. 5 is the specification for a search function, and Fig. 6 is the implementation. Notice that both initialisations I_A, I_C choose uniformly over a set $\mathcal{A}$ of potential arrays. Recall from Sect. 3 that we assume that all internal variables are hidden from the adversary, thus the random assignment models a scenario of an encrypted array A with some prior knowledge such as the adversary's knowing the kind of data that is encrypted.

The specification Search_A says that, given an (external) variable x, the value returned to the (external) calling program is either true in the case x's value occurs somewhere (encrypted) in A, or false in the case it does not. Notice in particular the expression x∈A means that *only* the information about the presence or absence of x's value being in A is reported, and *not*, for example, anything about the position where that value might occur. In comparison, Search$_C$ provides a hoped-for implementation of this: it declares a local (hidden) variable n which is used to search for x, and terminates as soon as it is found, going all the way to N, the length of A, only when x is not there. Functionally, this is indeed correct, as a standard verification can establish. But are there also any harmful leaks?

In fact it is well known that implementations such as these, which aim to perform a function as efficiently as possible, can contain a timing vulnerability. In particular the time to termination might be correlated with the location of x in A, and this correlation can be detected externally through a measurement of time taken [17]. It turns out that the QIF semantics is able to detect that information leak—its refinement relation ⊑ $_{QIF}$, in fact its failure in this case, stops one from concluding that Fig. 5 is refined by Fig. 6, exactly because of the undesirable information leak in Search$_C$. We sketch how this works for this example.

Consider the two program fragments assuming a probabilistic initialisation of a 2-valued sequence, selecting A uniformly from the two possibilities $[a, b]$ and $[b, a]$:

$$I_A; \texttt{g}:= \texttt{Search}_A(\texttt{x}); (\texttt{v}:= \texttt{0} \sqcap \texttt{1}); F_A \tag{5}$$

$$\not\sqsubseteq_{\textsf{QIF}} \quad I_C; \texttt{g}:= \texttt{Search}_C(\texttt{x}); (\texttt{v}:= \texttt{0} \sqcap \texttt{1}); F_C \quad ; \tag{6}$$

and we now ask the question "What is the probability that the external visible variable v can be set to the *position* that x's (encrypted) value appears in A?" If it is the case that Search$_A$ and Search$_C$ leak the same information about A, these probabilities will be the same. In (5), where the calling program uses Search$_A$, the answer is only $1/2$–no information about the position is mentioned in its declaration, and so no information can be leaked[3]. However the opposite is true for (6), where the calling program uses Search$_C$, since the correlation between position and final value of the local n is leaked: the probability that v can be set to x's position is 1. Thus that behaviour of (6) is not possible for (5)[4], and therefore ⊑ $_{\textsf{QIF}}$ does not hold. These differences are illustrated in Fig. 8.

Recall that the result of this situation in the HMM/POMDP semantics for QIF is $\mathbb{D}(\mathcal{G} \times \mathcal{V} \times \mathbb{D}\mathcal{A})$. Here the outer probability of the hyperdistribution ($\mathbb{D}$ applied to the whole state) models visible probabilistic behaviour, such as in our earlier example when Flip$_A$ is called in Fig. 1a. The inner probability ($\mathbb{D}$ applied to the third component only of the state) models hidden probabilistic behaviour, such as when I_C initialises A. Probabilistic behaviour can be "transferred" from hidden behaviour to visible behaviour as shown in the lower sequence in Fig. 8. This describes a scenario where first the array A was set uniformly between two possibilities drawn from $\{[a, b], [b, a]\}$, which are the same except for the positions of

---

[3] It's $1/2$ in this example because of our choice of A as one of two sequences.
[4] In simulation terms (5) cannot simulate (6).

```
                              # A is a local array with
                              # encrypted contents

# A is a local array with
# encrypted contents         I_C : A:∈ u(A)

I_A : A:∈ u(A)               Search_C(x):
                                n= 0 # n is local
Search_A(x):                    WHILE n!=N and A[n]!=x: n=n+1
   return x∈A                   return n<N

F_A : Skip                   F_C : Skip
```

Fig. 5. Abstract datatype   **Fig. 6.** Concrete datatype

Internal to both datatypes is the probabilistic uniform setting over all possible array values drawn from a given finite set $\mathcal{A}$. Internal to the concrete datatype is the local variable n; we assume for simplicity that comparisons x=A[i] within the concrete datatypes reflect the homomorphic aspect of the encryption i.e. that equality testing between encrypted values x and A[i] yields the same outcome as equality testing between their cleartexts. Similarly x∈A is true exactly when the encrypted values of x matches one of the encrypted values of A.

Fig. 7. Abstract and concrete datatypes for searching an encrypted array

$$(g, v, \mathsf{u}(\mathcal{A})) \xrightarrow{\ \mathsf{search}_A\ } \{(1, v, \mathsf{u}(\mathcal{A}))\} \xrightarrow{\ v:=\ 0\sqcap 1\ } \{\overline{(1, 0, \mathsf{u}(\mathcal{A}))}, \overline{(1, 1, \mathsf{u}(\mathcal{A}))}\}$$

$$(g, v, \mathsf{u}(\mathcal{A})) \xrightarrow{\ \mathsf{search}_C\ } \{\mathsf{u}\{(1, v, \overline{[a, b]}), (1, v, \overline{[b, a]})\}\} \xrightarrow{\ v:=\ 0\sqcap 1\ } \begin{array}{l} \{\mathsf{u}\{(1, 0, \overline{[a, b]}), (1, 0, \overline{[b, a]})\}, \\ \mathsf{u}\{(1, 0, \overline{[a, b]}), (1, 1, \overline{[b, a]})\}, \\ \mathsf{u}\{(1, 1, \overline{[a, b]}), (1, 0, \overline{[b, a]})\}, \\ \mathsf{u}\{(1, 1, \overline{[a, b]}), (1, 1, \overline{[b, a]})\}\} \end{array}$$

The result of both programs is a set of (hyper) distributions $\mathbb{D}(\mathcal{G}, \mathcal{V}, \mathbb{D}\mathcal{A})$. The set indicates a demonic external non-determinism in the calling program, the outer $\mathbb{D}$ is the observable resolution of probabilistic behaviour, and the inner $\mathbb{D}$ is encapsulated probabilistic behaviour, whose exact resolution is withheld from the calling program at run-time. Here we use $\bar{s}$ to denote the point distribution over s.

Fig. 8. HMM/POMDP interpretation for (5) and (6), with x set to a.

values a, b. Next, when Search_C is called there is an information leak in Fig. 6—the leak of the position in which x was found. In the semantics this is acccounted for by the initial state $(g, v, \mathsf{u}(\mathcal{A}))$ being converted to $\mathsf{u}\{(g, v, \bar{0}), (g, v, \bar{1})\}$, which is of type $\mathbb{D}(\mathcal{G} \times \mathcal{V} \times \mathbb{D}\mathcal{A})$. That difference indicates that the exact probabilistic setting of A has become visible to the calling program, essentially revealing x's position in A. This behaviour is explicitly disallowed by the specification datatype Fig. 5. In Appendix A we provide more details.

5   Conclusions and Related Work

In this paper we have decsribed how to use a QIF model for programs to understand how probabilistic behaviour can be "encapsulated" as an additional feature related to internal state[5]. The interface for probabilistic datatypes provides
a clear boundary between what the calling program is able to expect of the
operations processing the encapsulated data; this provides an opportunity to
determine when proposed implementations of the datatypes violate not only
functional constraints but also information theoretic constraints implied by the
specification. Future work is required ensure efficiency and mechanisable of the
refinement proofs required by the usual simulation relations.

QIF analyses of programs was first introduced by Malacaria and Hunt [9,22];
later the g-leakage framework used here was introduced by Smith [34] and Alvim
et al. [3]. These ideas were introduced independently for programs, used to define
first the HMM- [23,28] and then the POMDP model used here [25]. POMDP models
have also been used in probabilistic verification generally [8], although not for
this setting.

QIF analyses of information flow propeties for encrypted datatypes have
been introduced by Köpf et al. [5,19] and Jurado et al. [17]. A formal definition
of datatype refinement was introduced by [11] and others [33]. and the classic
technique of simulation is widely used in many areas of probabilistic formal
verification [21]. Probabilistic datatypes was first introduced by Troubitsyna et
al. [27] as a way to approach the specification challenge of a complex system [1].

A   QIF in Programming Languages

Elsewhere [24] we introduced a probabilistic semantics applicable to a small
sequential programming language. It embeds QIF ideas within a probabilistic
semantics based on the well known probability monad [14].

A.1   The Probabilistic Monad for Information Flow

Standard models of (sequential) probabilistic programs are normally based on
Markov Processes with type $\mathcal{A} \to \mathbb{D}\mathcal{A}$. In this sense programs can be thought of
as mapping a base type $\mathcal{A}$ to a probability distribution (also) over type $\mathcal{A}$. In
QIF however, the mathematical essentials for understanding information flows
are priors, posteriors and marginals. Setting $\mathcal{A}$ to $\mathbb{D}\mathcal{X}$ that gives the type of a
QIF-enabled model for programs as $\mathbb{D}\mathcal{X} \to \mathbb{D}(\mathbb{D}\mathcal{X})$, or $\mathbb{D}\mathcal{X} \to \mathbb{D}^2\mathcal{X}$.

We call an object of type $\mathbb{D}^2\mathcal{X}$ a *hyper-distribution* over $\mathcal{X}$. This is a distribution of distributions, where the (inner) distribution models the (encapsulated)
probabilistic behaviour that is not immediately observable at run-time, such as
in the initialisation of data, as in the concrete datatypes in Figs. 1b and 6; the
outer probability represents the probabilistic behaviour that is observable to the
calling program at run-time, as in the abstract datatypes at Figs. 1a and 5.

---

[5] This model allows only external nondeterminism.

The result of previous probabilistic assignments to update the state of the datatype can become apparent as a run-time observation some time later through an "information leak", and hence the semantics of such a program would result in a hyper-distribution. Recall the function $\mathtt{Search}_C(g, a)$ which produces not only whether a occurs in A, but also its position of first occurrence. When applied to the prior which initialises A to a uniform distribution π over $[a, b], [b, c], [a, a]$ (say), the semantics produces a hyper-distribution:

$$\frac{2}{3}(\pi|^B) \quad \oplus \quad \frac{1}{3}(\pi|^C) \, , \tag{7}$$

where $\pi|^B$ is the uniform distribution on $\{[a, b], [a, a]\}$ and $\pi|^C$ is the point distribution on $\{[b, a]\}$; we use the operator $\oplus$ to indicate addition at the level of $\mathbb{D}\mathcal{X}$ considered as a "vector space", so that a hyper-distribution is a weighted $\oplus$-sum of posteriors considered as individual (1-summing) vectors.

A.2 Abstract HMM Model for Programs [13, 24]

A program without nondeterminism can be modelled as an HMM, i.e. as a function $\mathbb{D}\mathcal{X} \to \mathbb{D}^2\mathcal{X}$; when we do this, it turns out that a standard Giry Monadic setting provides the basic functionality for sequencing and assignments. We summarise the semantics for three important operators here which are used to define the implementations fo the concrete datatypes above, and refer elsewhere for full details [24]. Recall the Giry Monad defined by the triple $(\mathbb{D}, \eta, \mu)$, where the type constructor $\mathbb{D}$ is a functor, η maps an object of type $\mathcal{A}$ to a point distribution in $\mathbb{D}\mathcal{A}$ and $\mu : \mathbb{D}^2\mathcal{A} \to \mathbb{D}\mathcal{A}$ takes the weighted average of a hyper-distribution, defined

$$(\mu.\Delta)_a \quad := \quad \sum_{\delta \in \mathbb{D}\mathcal{X}} \Delta_\delta \times \delta_a \, .$$

Here we use $+$ and $\sum$ to mean the normal summation between numbers.

We can interpret a programming language in terms of hyper-distributions as follows, where we use $\llbracket \cdot \rrbracket$ to map a program fragment to a function $\mathbb{D}\mathcal{X} \to \mathbb{D}^2\mathcal{X}$.

1. **Probabilistic Assignment.** Let $f : \mathcal{X} \to \mathbb{D}\mathcal{X}$ be a function that maps states in $\mathcal{X}$ to distributions over states in $\mathcal{X}$[6].

$$\llbracket \mathtt{x} := \mathtt{f(x)} \rrbracket.\pi \quad := \quad (\eta \circ \mu \circ \mathbb{D}f).\pi \, .$$

2. **Sequence.** Let P, Q be program fragments.

$$\llbracket P \sqcap Q \rrbracket.\pi \quad := \quad (\mu \circ \mathbb{D}\llbracket Q \rrbracket \circ \llbracket P \rrbracket).\pi \, .$$

3. **Print statement.** Let g be a function from $\mathcal{X}$ to $\mathcal{Y}$.

$$\llbracket \mathtt{Print} \ g \rrbracket.\pi \quad := \quad \bigoplus_y p_y(\pi|^y) \, ,$$

---

[6] This is essentially a Markov update of the state.

where $p_y := ((\mathbb{D}g).\pi)_y$, and $\pi|^y$ is the posterior probability distribution, given that y is an output of g, and $\oplus$ is the summation over 1-summing vectors described above.

The assignment statement is used to assign a value to a variable x according to a distribution, where informally we assume that the value of the variable x is value $x \in \mathcal{X}$. We use the unit of the Giry Monad to produce a point hyper-distribution. Sequence is defined in the standard monadic manner, by first applying $[\![P]\!]$ to the input and then $\mathbb{D}[\![Q]\!]$ is applied to $[\![P]\!]$'s output hyper-distribution, with a final application of μ applied to amalgamate equivalent posteriors. The action of $\mathbb{D}[\![Q]\!]$ is to apply $[\![Q]\!]$ to each of the posteriors in the output of $[\![P]\!]$. Finally, notice that the Print statement models an information leak from the a formerly probabilistic initialisation local to the datatype. In fact the semantics of conditionals means that and information leak occurs every time the loop guard is tested, and so the example at Fig. 6 is the same as:

```
Search_C(g,x):
    n= 0 // n is local
    WHILE n!=N and A[n]!=x: n=n+1
    g:= n<N
    Print(n)
```

A full description of the HMM QIF-aware program semantics (including loops and conditionals) is detailed elsewhere [24].

A.3 Abstract POMDP Model for Calling Programs [25]

In the example in Fig. 8, the calling program uses a nondeterministic assignment; unlike an MDP model, the nondeterminism simply takes the union over the outputs of the components
External Choice. Let P, Q be program fragments.

$$[\![P \sqcap Q]\!].\pi \quad := \quad cl.([\![Q]\!].\pi \bigcup [\![P]\!].\pi) \ .$$

where $cl(S)$ adds in any hyper-distribution that is formed from the convex combination of any hyper-distribution in S together with information-refinement of hyperdistributions defined elsewhere [25]. This means that if $P \ /\sqsubseteq_{\mathsf{QIF}} Q$ for two programs then there is some hyperdistribution in Q that cannot be formed from one of these closures in P. In the example given in Fig. 8, none of the hyperdistribution elements in the set listed for the calling program that uses the concrete datatype can be formed from closures of the hyperdistribution elements for the program using the abstract datatype.

References

1. Abrial, J.-R., Börger, E., Langmaak, H.: Formal Methods for Industrial Applications: Specifying and Programming the Steam Boiler Control, LNCS, vol. 1165. Springer (1996)
2. Alvim, M., Chatzikokolakis, K., McIver, A.K., Morgan, C.C., Smith, G.S., Palamidessi, C.: The science of quantitative information flow. In: Information Security and Cryptography. Springer (2020)
3. Alvim, M.S., Chatzikokolakis, K., Palamidessi, C., Smith, G.S.: Measuring information leakage using generalized gain functions. In: Proceedings of 25th IEEE Computer Security Foundations Symposium (CSF 2012), pp. 265–279 (2012)
4. Apt, K.R., Olderog, E.-R.: Fifty years of Hoare's logic. Formal Aspects Comput. **31**, 751–807 (2019)
5. Köpf, B.B., Basin, D.: An information-theoretic model for adaptive side-channel attacks. In: Proceedings of the 14th ACM Conference on Computer and Communications Security, CCS '07, pp. 286–296, New York, NY, USA. ACM (2007)
6. Back, R.-J.R., von Wright, J.: Refinement Calculus: a Systematic Introduction. Springer (1998)
7. Backus, J.W., et al.: Report on the algorithmic language ALGOL 60. Commun. ACM **3**(5), 299–311 (1960)
8. Chatterjee, K., Chmelík, M.: POMDPs under probabilistic semantics. Artif. Intell. **221**, 46–72 (2015)
9. Clark, D., Hunt, S., Malacaria, P.: Quantitative information flow, relations and polymorphic types. J. Log. Comput. **15**(2), 181–199 (2005)
10. Dijkstra, E.W.: A Discipline of Programming. Prentice-Hall (1976)
11. Gardiner, P.H.B., Morgan, C.C.: Data refinement of predicate transformers. Theor. Comput. Sci. **87**, 143–62 (1991)
12. Gardiner, P.H.B., Morgan, C.C.: A single complete rule for data refinement. Formal Aspects Comput. **5**(4), 367–82 (1993)
13. Gibbons, J., McIver, A.K., Morgan, C.C., Schrijvers, T.: Quantitative information flow with monads in Haskell. In: Barthe, A.S.G., Katoen, J.-P. (eds.) Foundations of Probabilistic Programming. CUP (2019)
14. Giry, M.: A categorical approach to probability theory. In: Categorical Aspects of Topology and Analysis, Lecture Notes in Mathematics, vol. 915, pp. 68–85. Springer (1981)
15. Gretz, F., Katoen, J.-P., McIver, A.K.: Operational versus weakest pre-expectation semantics for the probabilistic guarded command language. Perform. Eval. **73**, 110–132 (2014)
16. Hoare, C.A.R.: An axiomatic basis for computer programming. Commun. ACM **12**(10), 576–583 (1969)
17. Jurado, M., Palamidessi, C., Smith, G.S.: A formal information-theoretic leakage analysis of order-revealing encryption. In: 34th IEEE Computer Security Foundations Symposium, CSF 2021, Dubrovnik, Croatia, June 21–25, 2021, pp. 1–16. IEEE (2021)
18. Kaminski, B.L.: Advanced Weakest Precondition Calculi for Probabilistic Programs. PhD thesis, RWTH Aachen University, Germany (2019)
19. Köpf, B., Smith, G.S: Vulnerability bounds and leakage resilience of blinded cryptography under timing attacks. In: Proceedings of the 23rd IEEE Computer Security Foundations Symposium, CSF 2010, Edinburgh, United Kingdom, July 17–19, 2010, pp. 44–56 (2010)

20. Kwiatkowska, M., Norman, G., Parker, D.: Probabilistic symbolic model checking with PRISM: a hybrid approach. Int. J. Softw. Tools Technol. Transf. (STTT) **6**(2), 128–42 (2004)
21. Larsen, K.G., Skou, A.: Bisimulation through probabilistic testing. Inf. Comput. **94**(1), 1–28 (1991)
22. Malacaria, P.: Risk assessment of security threats for looping constructs. J. Comput. Secur. **18**(2), 191–228 (2010)
23. McIver, A.K.,Meinicke, L.A., Morgan, C.C.: Compositional Closure for Bayes Risk in Probabilistic Noninterference. Draft full version of [24] with appendices (2010). arXiv:1007.1054v1
24. McIver, A., Meinicke, L., Morgan, C.: Compositional closure for Bayes Risk in probabilistic noninterference. In: Abramsky, S., Gavoille, C., Kirchner, C., Meyer auf der Heide, F., Spirakis, P.G. (eds.) ICALP 2010. LNCS, vol. 6199, pp. 223–235. Springer, Heidelberg (2010). https://doi.org/10.1007/978-3-642-14162-1_19
25. McIver, A.K., Meinicke, L.A., Morgan, C.C.: A Kantorovich-monadic powerdomain for information hiding, with probability and nondeterminism. In: Processsdings of LICS 2012 (2012)
26. McIver, A.K., Morgan, C.C.: Abstraction, Refinement and Proof for Probabilistic Systems. Springer, New York (2005)
27. McIver, A.K., Morgan, C.C., Troubitsyna, E.: The probabilistic steam boiler: a case study in probabilistic data refinement. In: Grundy, J., Schwenke, M., Vickers, T. (eds.) Proceedings International Refinement Workshop, ANU, Canberra. Discrete Mathematics and Computer Science, pp. 250–65. Springer (1998)
28. McIver, A., Morgan, C., Rabehaja, T.: Abstract hidden Markov models: a monadic account of quantitative information flow. In: Proceedings of LICS 2015 (2015)
29. Morgan, C.C.: Programming from Specifications, 2nd edn. Prentice Hall (1994)
30. Morgan, C.C., McIver, A.K., Seidel, K.: Probabilistic predicate transformers. ACM Trans. Prog. Lang. Sys. **18**(3), 325–53 (1996). https://doi.org/10.1145/229542.229547
31. Morgan, C.C., Vickers, T.N. (eds.): On the Refinement Calculus. FACIT Series in Computer Science, Springer, Berlin (1994)
32. Morris, J.M.: A theoretical basis for stepwise refinement and the programming calculus. Sci. Comput. Program. **9**(3), 287–306 (1987)
33. Nipkow, T.: Non-deterministic data types: models and implementations. Acta Informatica **22**(6), 629–661 (1986)
34. Smith, G.: On the foundations of quantitative information flow. In: de Alfaro, L. (ed.) FoSSaCS 2009. LNCS, vol. 5504, pp. 288–302. Springer, Heidelberg (2009). https://doi.org/10.1007/978-3-642-00596-1_21

Disentangling the Gap Between Quantum and #SAT

Jingyi Mei, Jan Martens, and Alfons Laarman[(⊠)]

Leiden University, Leiden, The Netherlands
`a.w.laarman@liacs.leidenuniv.nl`

Abstract. Weighted model counting (#SAT) has recently been shown to deliver a promising new method for tackling core problems in quantum circuit analysis. However, the development of weighted model counting tools is currently strongly motivated by applications in the domain of probabilistic computing, where weights consist of positive probabilities. Quantum computing, on the other hand, deals with complex amplitudes, which include the negative domain and are subject to the ℓ^2 norm, contrary to the ℓ^1 norm used for probabilities. The current paper explores reductions from quantum circuit semantics to weighted model counting over the complex, real, natural and integer numbers (e.g., #SAT$_\mathbb{C}$, #SAT$_\mathbb{R}$, etc.), and various sub(semi)rings of those. This study thereby charts tradeoffs between counting over simpler algebras and the costs of the reduction. While previous works recommend the use of different (semi)rings, like those including negative numbers, we can now more precisely state the tradeoff introduced by this change as (polynomial) blowup of the length of the encoding as #SAT formula, the number of variables and the structure of the formula. Moreover, our final encoding to #SAT$_{\{0,1\}}$ (unweighted model counting) represents an exact solution, obviating the need for floating-point calculations that could potentially cause numerical instability.

1 Introduction

The analysis of quantum circuits plays a pivotal role in quantum computing and, more generally, in quantum physics. Equivalence checking of quantum circuits —which is canonical for "quantum NP" (QMA)— is at the core of many analysis tasks for quantum computing. It is the main tool used to optimize circuits for various kinds of quantum hardware currently in development. Better equivalence checking methods can, therefore, contribute to achieving quantum supremacy, roughly defined as finding a (useful) task for which a quantum computer outperforms the (largest available) classical computers. Moreover, the task of classical simulation of quantum circuits —which is canonical for "quantum P" (BQP)— *also* advances the quantum supremacy challenge more directly, by establishing regimes (in the complexity-theoretic sense) in which quantum computers cannot beat classical computers, thus focusing the search on more fruitful

C. Anutariya and M. M. Bonsangue (Eds.): ICTAC 2024, LNCS 15373, pp. 17–40, 2025.
https://doi.org/10.1007/978-3-031-77019-7_2

regimes. Third, better methods to classically simulate circuits can have implications for quantum mechanical systems more generally [48,66]. Tackling these problems remains crucial regardless of whether powerful-enough quantum computers (will) exist because they are key to core problems in material science and chemistry.

Weighted model counting, or #SAT, has recently been pioneered to solve various problems in quantum computing [46,47] and quantum physics [48]. These approaches take as input one or more quantum circuits, encode them as a weighted propositional formula —a Boolean formula in conjunctive normal form with real weights assigned to literals— and then call a #SAT solver to compute the probability of specific outcomes for measurements in the circuit or the measure to which the circuits are equivalent. The weights in these encodings were (positive and negative) real numbers; complex numbers could be avoided by moving from the computational basis to the Pauli basis [46,47]. These works offered multiple ideas to further improve #SAT tools for tackling problem instances from this novel domain, including better support from negative and complex numbers. However, they failed to address to what extent these suggested modifications are strictly necessary.

In this work, we address this shortcoming by showing how quantum circuits can be encoded as model counting instances with weights in various domains. We begin with complex weights and incrementally reduce to real and integer weights, ultimately reaching Boolean weights. The end product is a framework to encode equivalence checking and classical simulation of quantum circuits as unweighted model counting problems. The advantage over the existing methods is that the final integer and Boolean encodings are exact in that they can be implemented without the need for floating point numbers. In addition, this approach eliminates multiple prerequisites on the weighted model counters used. For example, they no longer need to support negative or real weights. Finally, this new framework allows us to compare the different encodings in terms of length, number of variables and formula structure. A natural question is whether the empirical performance of existing #SAT tools is in line with the trade-offs between the given encodings, a question we reserve for future work.

We use *algebraic model counting* [36], which allows the definition of counting problems over arbitrary semirings. For this work, the semiring operations are the natural addition and multiplication, thus inducing a counting problem that is a sum of products [23]. This leads us to adopt a notion of weighted model counting with weights from different domains similar to the one introduced in [17], which defines and relates (hard) functional counting problems like $\#SAT_\mathbb{C}$, and $\#SAT_\mathbb{R}$. We start in Sect. 3 by phrasing quantum gates as (easy) functional problems to the complex domain. Next to the Pauli basis of the original encoding from [46], we also use the computational basis for the first time. We then express the quantum circuit semantics in the usual path sum formulation, which we subsequently connect to the closure properties of #P, and related classes like GapP [25], to show that model counting can indeed compute the circuit semantics.

In Sect. 4, we gradually move to smaller domains from $\#P_{\mathbb{C}}$ via inter alia $\#P_{\mathbb{R}_{\geq 0}}$ to $\#P_{\{0,1\}} = \#P$ by reducing to corresponding #SAT instances the following figure shows. Thus no floating point number will be needed and the exact result can be obtained.

In Sect. 5, we show how this framework for encoding can be used to solve both equivalence checking and simulation. The resulting flow of reductions from algebraic model counting to these applications can be viewed as a framework for deriving and comparing different encodings. Among other observations, we find that getting rid of complex numbers merely doubles the formula length in the computational basis, whereas it only doubles the number of qubit variables in the Pauli basis. Earlier experimental results indicated that the depth of the circuit (length of the formula) is often more of a bottleneck for solvers [46].

Our work distinguishes itself from previous works in that we are not concerned with proving any new separations but rather concretely study and compare the different encodings resulting from working with different algebraic domains, which can impact the behavior of practical solvers. While a previous reduction to unweighted model counting exist [9], it starts from the domain of positive real numbers and assumes the ℓ^1 norm. Section 6 provides a detailed overview and comparison to related works.

Section 2 now first introduces the necessary notation and background information.

2 Preliminaries

2.1 Quantum Computing Notation

For an extensive introduction, including a definition of the tensor product ($\otimes$), see [49].

An amplitude α is a complex number whose modulus square is a probability: $|\alpha|^2 \in [0,1]$. An n-qubit quantum state $\vec{\varphi}$ is a column vector $[\alpha_{00...00}, \ldots, \alpha_{11...11}]^T$ of amplitudes α_b for $b \in \mathbb{B}^n$ satisfying the ℓ^2 norm: $|\alpha_{00...00}|^2 + \cdots + |\alpha_{11...11}|^2 = 1$. It can also be denoted as $|\varphi\rangle$ using Dirac notation, standard in quantum computing. Its complex adjoint $\langle\varphi|$ is a row vector with conjugated entries: $[\alpha_{00...00}^*, \ldots, \alpha_{11...11}^*]$, therefore $\langle\varphi|\varphi\rangle = 1$. We have $\langle\varphi| = |\varphi\rangle^\dagger$, where $A^\dagger$ is the conjugate and transpose of a matrix A. A state (and its adjoint) can be viewed as a pseudo-Boolean function $|\varphi\rangle: \mathbb{B}^n \to \mathbb{C}$. But instead of writing $|\varphi\rangle(b)$ for $b \in \mathbb{B}^n$, we may use braket notation $\langle b|\varphi\rangle$. An n-qubit quantum gate U is a linear map on n-qubit quantum states, which preserves the ℓ^2 norm. It follows that U is an $2^n \times 2^n$ complex matrix satisfying *unitarity*, i.e., $U^\dagger \cdot U = U \cdot U^\dagger = I^{\otimes n}$. We will consider the well-known universal gate sets Clifford $\{S, H, CX\} + T$ and the Toffoli $+ H$. For the definition of the gates please refer to Table 2.

Alternatively, we may represent a state $|\varphi\rangle$ as a density matrix $\rho = |\varphi\rangle\langle\varphi|$. The *trace* of a density matrix is 1 denoted as $\text{tr}(\rho) = 1$, where trace is defined as the sum of diagonal elements of a matrix. A density matrix can be decomposed in the Pauli basis as detailed in [47]. The Pauli matrices are $I = \left[\begin{smallmatrix} 1 & 0 \\ 0 & 1 \end{smallmatrix}\right], X = \left[\begin{smallmatrix} 0 & 1 \\ 1 & 0 \end{smallmatrix}\right], Y = \left[\begin{smallmatrix} 0 & -i \\ i & 0 \end{smallmatrix}\right], Z = \left[\begin{smallmatrix} 1 & 0 \\ 0 & -1 \end{smallmatrix}\right]$. An n-qubit *Pauli string* P is a parallel composition of n Pauli gates, so $P \in \{I, X, Y, Z\}^{\otimes n}$. Let $[n] = \{1, \dots, n\}$. The decomposition of a density matrix in this basis is as follows:

$$\rho = \sum_{j \in [4^n]} \beta_j \cdot P_j \text{ for the pauli strings } P_j \in \{I, X, Y, Z\}^{\otimes n} \qquad (1)$$

Observe that while the density matrix ρ may contain complex numbers, the basis coefficients β_i do not [47]. By encoding a Pauli matrix with two bits x, z [1], e.g., $I \equiv 00, X \equiv 10, Y \equiv 11, Z \equiv 01$, we may also view density matrices as pseudo-Boolean functions $\rho \colon \mathbb{B}^{2n} \to \mathbb{R}$ in this basis.

Applying a unitary U to a density matrix $\rho = |\varphi\rangle\langle\varphi|$ should be done through *conjugation*, i.e.: $U\rho U^\dagger = U |\varphi\rangle\langle\varphi| U^\dagger = |\psi\rangle\langle\psi|$ for $|\psi\rangle = U \cdot |\varphi\rangle$. We now show that conjugation can also be viewed as linear mapping and introduce denotation $\tilde{U}|\rho\rangle$ for the above. Let $L2V(A) := \sum_{i,j \in [n]} \langle i|A|j\rangle \cdot (|i\rangle \otimes |j\rangle)$ be the function that rearranges entries of the linear operator A as a column vector by concatenating its columns and $V2L(\vec{v}) := \sum_{i,j \in [n]} ((\langle i| \otimes \langle j|)\vec{v} |i\rangle\langle j|$ [67, (1.132)]. Here $L2V$ and $V2L$ are pronounced as "linear operator to vector" and "vector to linear operator." We denote $L2V(A)$ as $|A\rangle$ and $\langle A| = L2V(A)^\dagger$, where A is a matrix. Let $\tilde{U} \triangleq U \otimes U^*$. The conjugation $\rho' = U^\dagger \rho U$ is a linear mapping $\rho' = U^\dagger \rho U = V2L((U \otimes U^*)L2V(\rho))$, which can be written as $|\rho'\rangle = \tilde{U}|\rho\rangle$. Thus we can also rewrite the Pauli decomposition in Eq. 1 as $|\rho\rangle = \sum_j \beta_j |P_j\rangle$. Given two matrices A_1 and A_2, their inner product is defined as $\mathrm{tr}(A_1^\dagger \cdot A_2)$, which is exactly the same value as $\langle A_1|A_2\rangle$.

2.2   Functional Complexity Classes

We focus on the (semi)rings under addition and multiplication over $\mathbb{Z}$, $\mathbb{N}$, $\mathbb{Q}$, $\mathbb{R}$ and $\mathbb{C}$ or sub(semi)rings thereof. Here, we should note that we are not concerned with the representation of the algebraic numbers. For instance, the number $\sqrt{2}$ can be represented and manipulated symbolically when working in a subring over the integers with the irrational $\sqrt{2}$ and complex value i added, denoted $\mathbb{Z}[i, \sqrt{2}] \subseteq \mathbb{C}$ [29]. The class of efficiently-computable algebraic functions is defined as follows.

Definition 1 (Functional Polytime). *Given an alphabet Σ and a subset of the complex numbers $\mathcal{U} \subseteq \mathbb{C}$, $\mathsf{FP}_\mathcal{U}$ is the class of functions $f \colon \Sigma^* \to \mathcal{U}$ that are computable in polynomial time in the size of its single argument.*

We will also use $\langle O \rangle$ to denote the Σ-serialization of any mathematical object O. If one input contains multiple variables, we write $f(a, b)$ for $f(\langle a, b \rangle)$.

For a function $f \in \mathsf{FP}_\mathcal{R}$ that has arguments $a, b \in \Sigma^*$, then for $f(a, b)$, we view a as the problem description and b as its inputs or witness. For instance, if f is formula evaluation, a could be a propositional formula, as described in Sect. 2.3, and b an assignment to its variables. This is a canonical problem in

$\mathsf{FP}_{\mathbb{B}} = \mathsf{FP}$. While not all $a, b \in \Sigma^*$ represent valid formula–assignment pairs, the function f need not to be partial since, for invalid cases, the additive identity e_+ can be returned. Alternatively, a can be a description of a deterministic Turing machine while b represents the content of its input tape to model the universal Turing machine problem.

This definition of FP leads naturally to the following definition of #P. For the following definition, we follow [17].

Definition 2 (Weighted counting problem). *Given $\mathcal{U} \subseteq \mathbb{C}$, a polynomial q and a polynomially computable function $f \in \mathsf{FP}_{\mathcal{U}}$, the weighted counting problem over the subring generated by $\mathcal{U}$, denoted $\#\mathsf{P}_{\mathcal{U}}$, is to compute for an input $a \in \Sigma^*$:*

$$g(a) = \sum_{b \in \Sigma^{q(|a|)}} f(\langle a, b \rangle)$$

We define $\#\mathsf{P}_{\mathcal{U}}$ the class of weighted counting problems where the range of the functions being counted over is restricted to $\mathcal{U}$. A canonical problem is the weighted model counting problem with the weight restricted to $\mathcal{U}$, discussed in Sect. 2.3.

Analogous to many-one reductions in classical complexity, we define *metric reductions* for counting problems over semirings [17,23,24]. More intuitively, a metric reduction from $\#\mathsf{P}_A$ to $\#\mathsf{P}_B$ can be thought of as functional problem FP_B with access to an oracle machine $\#\mathsf{P}_A$ which can only be called once. This is (somewhat tediously) denoted with $\mathsf{FP}_B^{\#\mathsf{P}_A[1]}$. Hence, it can be understood as a many-one reduction from a function $f \in \#\mathsf{P}_A$ to $g \in \#\mathsf{P}_B$ with polynomial time post-processed on the result (with access to the original input for instance f).

Definition 3 (Metric reduction). *Given the sets $A, B \subseteq \mathbb{C}$, a metric reduction from a counting problem $f \in \#\mathsf{P}_A$ to the problem $g \in \#\mathsf{P}_B$ consists of two polynomial-time computable functions R, and T. The function $R : \Sigma^* \to \Sigma^*$ translates an input of problem f to an instance of problem g, and the function $T : B \times \Sigma^* \to A$ translates the result of g to the answer to f. For all inputs $a \in \Sigma^*$ it holds that $f(a) = T(g(R(a)), a)$.*

We summarize closure properties that $\#\mathsf{P}$ is well-known to possess [25], and are maintained in the weighted counting classes $\#\mathsf{P}_A$ [17].

Property 1. If $f \in \#\mathsf{P}_A$ and q is a polynomial then for the set $\mathcal{D}_a = \{b \mid b \in \Sigma^* \text{ and } |b| \leq q(|a|)\}$, the function g such that

$$g(a) = \sum_{b \in \mathcal{D}_a} f(\langle a, b \rangle)$$

is in $\#\mathsf{P}_A$.

Property 2. If $f \in \#\mathsf{P}_A$ and q is a polynomial then for the set $\mathcal{D}_a^{\log} = \{b \mid b \in \Sigma^* \text{ and } |b| \leq \log q(|a|)\}$ the function g such that

$$g(a) = \prod_{b \in \mathcal{D}_a^{\log}} f(\langle a, b \rangle)$$

is in $\#\mathsf{P}_A$.

2.3 Weighted Model Counting (#SAT)

Model counting, first studied by Valiant [63], asks the number of distinct solutions for a decision problem. Weighted model counting extends model counting, by assigning each solution a weight. Weighted model counting has applications in areas like Bayesian inference and network analysis [9,56]. These tasks can all be seen in the generalized framework of algebraic model counting [36] over arbitrary semirings.

The counting problem #SAT is the counting problem for the Boolean satisfiability problem and asks how many distinct satisfying solutions a given Boolean formula has. #SAT is complete for #P under *counting reductions* [31] (defined in Sect. 2.2).

A Boolean propositional formula F is a formula over a finite set of propositional variables V and the usual set of connectives $\{\wedge, \vee, \neg\}$, i.e., conjunction, disjunction, and negation. For notational brevity we use $\oplus$ for exclusive or, e.g. $x \oplus y \Leftrightarrow (x \vee y) \wedge (\neg x \vee \neg y)$ for all $x, y \in V$. A truth assignment τ assigns to each propositional variable a Boolean value. The formula F is said to be satisfied under a truth assignment α iff replacing all variables by their logical values leaves a valid statement. We denote $\mathrm{SAT}(F) = \{\tau \mid \tau \text{ satisfies } F\}$ the set of all satisfying assignments for F. The unweighted model counting (UMC) problem #SAT asks to compute the number of satisfying assignments $\#\mathrm{SAT}(F) = |\mathrm{SAT}(F)|$.

Given a set $\mathcal{A} \subseteq \mathbb{C}$ and a weight function, we define the weighted model counting problem $\#\mathrm{SAT}_{\mathcal{A}}$ by summing the weight of all distinct truth assignments. An instance of weighted model counting is given by a Boolean formula F over the set of variables V and a weight function $W : 2^V \to \mathcal{A}$ that associates to each truth assignment τ a value in $\mathcal{A}$. In this paper, we only use *literal-weighted* weight functions. A weight function for literals is a function $W : V \times \mathbb{B} \to \mathcal{A}$ that maps a variable and its assignment, either positive or negative, to a weight. For notational convenience we write for a variable $x \in V$, the positive weight $W(x) = W(x, 1)$ and negative $W(\bar{x}) = W(x, 0)$. Given an assignment τ, the weight of this assignment, written $W(\tau)$, is the product of the weight of each variable with its assignment $W(\tau) = \prod_{x \in V} W(x, \tau(x))$. A variable $x \in V$ is called *unbiased* if $W(x) = W(\bar{x}) = 1$. The $\#\mathrm{SAT}_{\mathcal{A}}$ problem asks the sum of all weighted satisfying assignments,

$$\#\mathrm{SAT}_{\mathcal{A}}(F, W) = \sum_{\tau \in \mathrm{SAT}(F)} W(\tau).$$

In this notation $\#\mathrm{SAT}_{\{0,1\}}$ corresponds with unweighted model counting #SAT, $\#\mathrm{SAT}_{\{-1,0,1\}}$ with function described in GapP, and $\#\mathrm{SAT}_{\mathbb{C}}$ all weighted model counting instances over the complex numbers. Each assignment will be written as a *cube* (a conjunction of literals, i.e. positive or negative variables). In the rest of the paper, we will omit the conjunctions in a cube, e.g. $a \wedge b \wedge \neg c$ will be shorten as $ab\neg c$ or $ab\bar{c}$.

In this work we often construct formulas over a sequence of given variables, we denote this in the functional approach $F(x_1, \ldots, x_n)$. For example, if we define $F(x, y) = xy \Leftrightarrow z$, then $F(x', y') = x'y' \Leftrightarrow z$. The variable z in this example, is a free variable, but it is dependent. It can be seen as an output of the Boolean formula defined on the variables x, y. For Boolean arguments b, b', we write $F(b, b')$ for the formula in which the variables are replaced with the Booleans b, b'. Given a weight function W, as short hand notation we write $[\![F(x, y)]\!]_W$ for the problem #SAT$(F(x, y), W)$, when W is clear from context we often omit it. Note that when a formula $F(x_1, \ldots, x_n)$, where all the extra free variables $y_1, \ldots, y_m$ are dependent, then for a Boolean assignment $b_1, \ldots, b_n \in \mathbb{B}^n$ to the variables $x_1, \ldots, x_n$, the value $[\![F(b_1, \ldots, b_n)]\!]_W$, becomes equal to formula evaluation and computing the weight of the unique satisfying assignment τ, $[\![F(b_1, \ldots, b_n)]\!] = W(\tau)$.

Using metric reductions, one can show that #SAT$_{\mathcal{A}}$ is not significantly harder than unweighted model counting. This is demonstrated in [9] where a metric reduction is given to show how a literal-weighted model counting instance for Bayesian inference can be translated to unweighted model counting. A more general result is achieved in [23], in which metric reductions are introduced for more generic semirings.

3   Encoding Quantum Circuit Semantics in #SAT

Here, we rephrase the Pauli-basis encoding presented in [46,47] on a more abstract level by using the path-sum formulation and the closure properties of #P$_{\mathcal{A}}$ [17]. To increase understandability, we also rephrase this encoding in the computational basis in parallel to presenting the original Pauli basis encoding.

In this section and the next (Sect. 4), we only consider computing amplitudes $\langle \vec{b}|U|\vec{b}'\rangle$ for circuits/gates U and computational basis states $|\vec{b}\rangle, |\vec{b}'\rangle$ for $\vec{b}, \vec{b}' \in \mathbb{B}^n$, or, in the Pauli basis, the coefficient of some Pauli string P' in $U^\dagger P U$, denoted as $\langle P'|\tilde{U}|P\rangle$. Here $\langle P'|\tilde{U}|P\rangle$ represents the weight with which U maps Pauli string P to P' by conjugation, analogous to the amplitude $\langle \vec{b}'|U|\vec{b}\rangle$ with which U maps computational basis state $|\vec{b}\rangle$ to $|\vec{b}'\rangle$. In Sect. 5, we then discuss how this forms a basis for applications to circuit simulation and verification.

	Computational basis	Pauli basis
Unit	Basis state $|\vec{b}\rangle$ for $\vec{b} \in \mathbb{B}^n$	Pauli string $P \in \{I, X, Y, Z\}^{\otimes n}$
Operation	$\langle \vec{b}'|U|\vec{b}\rangle$	$\langle P'|\tilde{U}|P\rangle$
Dimension	2^n	4^n

3.1   Representing Quantum States as Weighted Formulae

Table 1 summarizes the state encoding presented in this section.

For an n-qubit quantum state, we reserve propositional variables $\vec{q} = (q_1, \ldots, q_n)$ for a computational basis encoding and $\vec{q} = (x_1, z_1, \ldots, x_n, z_n)$ for the Pauli basis encoding, as done in [46,47]. The variables in $\vec{q}$ will remain unbiased. In addition, we will introduce several auxiliary variables $\vec{u}$ (one or more per gate) to represent weights introduced along computation paths. Since the assignment to these auxiliary variables is always fully determined by the assignment to $\vec{q}$, we will often omit these variables, writing $F(\vec{q})$ instead of $F(\vec{q}, \vec{u})$.

We denote with $F_{|\varphi\rangle}$ a formula encoding a state $|\varphi\rangle$ denoted $|\varphi\rangle \equiv F_{|\varphi\rangle}$. For a formula $F_{|\varphi\rangle}(\vec{q})$ and associated weight function W, we let the weight of each assignment of the variables in $\vec{q}$, written as bitstring $\vec{b} \in \mathbb{B}^{\vec{q}}$ represent the amplitudes of computational basis states: $|\varphi\rangle = \begin{bmatrix} W(00\ldots00) & \ldots & W(11\ldots11) \end{bmatrix}^T$. E.g., $F_{|00\rangle}(q_1, q_2) = \neg q_1 \wedge \neg q_2 \equiv |00\rangle$ as its unique satisfying assignment is $\overline{q_1}\overline{q_2}$. Or, the formula $F_{|+\rangle}(q_1) = h \equiv |+\rangle$ has two satisfying assignments $\overline{q_1}h$ and $q_1 h$ with weight $W(h) = 1/\sqrt{2}$.

In the Pauli basis, representing states is less intuitive because their density matrices are decomposed as a linear combination of $P_j \in \{I, X, Z, Y\}^{\otimes n}$ with coefficients β_j (see Eq. 1) in Sect. 2.1. So in this basis, we let weighted satisfying assignments represent Pauli strings. For instance, $P = -1 \cdot Z \otimes \cdots \otimes Z \equiv F_P(x_1, z_1, \ldots, x_n, z_n) = r\overline{x_1}z_1 \ldots \overline{x_n}z_n$ with $W(r) = -1$ and $W(\overline{r}) = 1$ (again, we suppress the determined auxiliary variable r).

Deep insights from stabilizer theory [1] tell us that for many interesting states at least $k = 2^n$ of those 4^n coefficients are non-zero, but that their group structure often allows representations linear in n. For instance, we have:

$$|0^n\rangle\langle 0^n| \equiv F_{|0^n\rangle\langle 0^n|}(x_1, z_1, \ldots, x_n, z_n) \qquad = \overline{x}_1\overline{x}_2 \ldots \overline{x}_n, \text{ and}$$
$$|+^n\rangle\langle +^n| \equiv F_{|+^n\rangle\langle +^n|}(x_1, z_1, \ldots, x_n, z_n) \qquad = \overline{z}_1\overline{z}_2 \ldots \overline{z}_n$$

We will not go into further details here, but refer to [46] instead.

It is now easy to show that we can encode $\langle \vec{b}|\varphi\rangle$ for $\vec{b} \in \mathbb{B}^{\vec{q}}$ as a conjunction $F_{\vec{b}} \wedge F_{|\varphi\rangle}$, which yields the amplitude $\alpha_{\vec{b}}$ in $|\varphi\rangle$ as expected. Similarly, for the Pauli basis, we can compute the coefficient of Pauli string P in state $\rho = |\varphi\rangle\langle\varphi|$, i.e., $\text{tr}(P \cdot \rho)$ as the conjunction of $F_P \wedge F_\rho$.[1]

3.2   Reducing Quantum Gates

Table 2 summarizes the gate encoding presented in this section.

As usual, we let $\vec{q}', \vec{q}_j$ denote the primed or indexed version of a sequence of variables, i.e., $\vec{q}' = (q_1', \ldots, q_n')$ and $\vec{q}_j = (q_{1,j}, \ldots, q_{n,j})$. We represent the

---

[1] The intuition here is that by multiplying ρ with the Pauli string P, we map *only* the P component in the Pauli decomposition of ρ to $I^{\otimes n}$, which happens to be the only traceless component in that decomposition. Hence, the trace operator computes the coefficient associated with P in the Pauli decomposition of ρ times $\text{tr}(I) = 2^n$.

Table 1. Overview of the encoding aspects in both bases. Without loss of generality, we may assume that one sign and factor variable r_j, h_j exists for each of the m gates in the circuit. The variables representing states are unbiased.

	Computational basis	Pauli basis
Variables	$\vec{q} = (q_1, \ldots, q_n)$	$\vec{q} = (x_1, z_1, \ldots, x_n, z_n)$
Auxiliary	$\vec{u} = (r_1, \ldots, r_m, h_1, \ldots, h_m)$	
Sign weights	$W(r_j) = -1$ and $W(\overline{r}_j) = 1$ for $j \in [m]$	
Factor weights	$W(h_j) = 1/\sqrt{2}$ and $W(\overline{h}_j) = 1$ for $j \in [m]$	
$\lvert 00 \rangle \equiv$	$F_{\lvert 00 \rangle}(q_1, q_2) = \overline{q_1 q_2}$	$F_{\lvert 00 \rangle \langle 00 \rvert}(x_1, z_1, x_2, z_2) = \overline{x_1 x_2}$
$\lvert ++ \rangle \equiv$	$F_{\lvert ++ \rangle}(q_1, q_2) = h_{j_1} h_{j_2}$	$F_{\lvert ++ \rangle \langle ++ \rvert}(x_1, z_1, x_2, z_2) = \overline{z_1 z_2}$
Inner product	$F_{\langle \psi \lvert \varphi \rangle}(\vec{q}_{\lvert \psi \rangle}, \vec{q}_{\lvert \varphi \rangle}) = F_{\langle \psi \rvert} \wedge F_{\lvert \varphi \rangle}$	$F_{\mathrm{tr}(P_1 P_2)}(\vec{q}_{P_1}, \vec{q}_{P_2}) = F_{P_1} \wedge F_{P_2}$

input quantum state of a gate as variables $\vec{q}$, and we copy the qubit variables of $\vec{q}$ to represent the output state after the gate. For instance, an n-qubit gate U will be encoded as a formula $F_U(\vec{q}, \vec{q}')$, where $\vec{q}$ acts as input state and $\vec{q}'$ denotes the output. A whole circuit $C = (U_1, \ldots, U_m)$ will be modelled as a formula $F_C(\vec{q}_0, \ldots, \vec{q}_m)$, where each state $\vec{q}_j$ represents the (intermediate) state after applying gates $U_1, \ldots, U_j$.

A local gate is a gate acting on a constant number of qubits. We consider, more generally, simple gates, which we define as $2^n \times 2^n$ matrices U whose entries $\langle \vec{b} \lvert U \rvert \vec{b}' \rangle$, $\vec{b}, \vec{b}' \in \mathbb{B}^{\vec{q}}$ can be computed efficiently (i.e., with formula evaluation in FP). These also include global gate sets found in, e.g., ion-trapped-based quantum computer designs [3, 64].[2] For this purpose, we fix the number of qubits in our quantum circuits to n, and we extend all "local" gates to n-qubit unitaries (by applying identities on all unaffected qubits). For instance, U could be the $S = \begin{bmatrix} 1 & 0 \\ 0 & i \end{bmatrix}$ on the first qubit, i.e., $U = S \otimes I^{\otimes n-1}$.

More concretely, for a simple gate U, we define the Boolean formula $F_U(\vec{q}, \vec{q}')$ and weight function W in such a way that it represents $\langle \vec{q} \lvert U \rvert \vec{q}' \rangle$. Concretely, for two quantum states $\vec{b} \in \mathbb{B}^{\vec{q}}$ and $\vec{b}' \in \mathbb{B}^{\vec{q}'}$, because U is simple, we can compute $[\![F_U(\vec{b}, \vec{b}')]\!]_W$ through formula evaluation, i.e., there is only one satisfying assignment τ of F_U with $\tau(\vec{q}) = \vec{b}$ and $\tau(\vec{q}') = \vec{b}'$ that completely determines the values for auxiliary variables $\vec{u}$:

$$[\![F_U(\vec{b}, \vec{b}')]\!]_W = W(\tau) \equiv \prod_{u \in \vec{u}} W(u, \tau(u)) \equiv \langle \vec{b} \lvert U \rvert \vec{b}' \rangle.$$

For example, in the computational we can encode the Hadamard gate $H \triangleq 1/\sqrt{2} \begin{bmatrix} 1 & 1 \\ 1 & -1 \end{bmatrix}$ as $F_H(q, q') = h \wedge (r \Leftrightarrow qq')$, where we assign q and q' unbiased weights, the auxiliary variables h, r, we assign the weight $W(h) = 1/\sqrt{2}$, $W(\overline{r}) = 1$ and $W(r) = -1$ (isolating the negative sign to an r variable for future purposes).

---

[2] Although we do not further consider global gates in the current paper, this illustrates the generality of the approach based on model counting.

Indeed, we can verify that evaluating $[\![F_H(b, b')]\!]$ yields $\langle b|H|b'\rangle$ for all $b, b' \in \mathbb{B}$. Again, in a satisfying assignment, the possible truth assignment of h, r is fully determined by the assignment of q, q'. The identity gate can be encoded as $F_I(x, y) \triangleq x \Leftrightarrow y$ where the weights of x, y are unbiased as before. For the rest of paper, we will use auxiliary variables r_j for each time step j as above to indicate if there is a change of sign in the basis by defining $W(r_j) = -1$ and $W(\bar{r}_j) = 1$. Based on the semantics of the gates, other variables will be introduced, for example, h for the coefficient $\frac{1}{\sqrt{2}}$ by defining $W(h) = \frac{1}{\sqrt{2}}$ and $W(\bar{h}) = 1$ and u for the coefficient i ($W(u) = i$ and $W(\bar{u}) = 1$). See Table 2 for the usage of these variables.

Denote the encoding of a k-qubit local gate U as $F_U(\vec{p}, \vec{p}')$, where $\vec{p}$ (resp $\vec{p}'$) is the set of the variables representing the qubit(s) to which U should be applied before (resp. after). This encoding can now be extended into a simple gate U' which has semantics for all n qubits. To achieve this in the computational basis, let $\vec{q} = (q_1, \ldots, q_n)$ (resp. $\vec{q}' = (q_1', \ldots, q_n')$) be the variables of the n qubits before (resp. after) the simple gate U', and $\vec{p} = (q_{j_1}, \ldots, q_{j_k})$ be the k variables which represent the qubit to which U should be applied, then the simple gate U' is modeled by the Boolean formula

$$F_{U'}(\vec{q}, \vec{q}') = \bigwedge_{\ell \notin \{j_1, \ldots, j_k\}} F_I(q_\ell, q_\ell') \wedge F_U(\vec{p}, \vec{p}'),$$

where $F_I(q_\ell, q_\ell') \triangleq q_\ell \Leftrightarrow q_\ell'$ in computational basis. For example, consider the simple gate for n qubits containing a Hadamard gate on the second qubit, for convenience written as $H_2 \triangleq I \otimes H \otimes I^{\otimes n-2}$, as $F_{H_2}(\vec{x}, \vec{y}) \triangleq F_I(x_1, y_1) \wedge F_H(x_2, y_2) \wedge \bigwedge_{j \in [3,n]} F_I(x_j, y_j)$, with weight function W defined for F_H before. Switching to Pauli basis, variables for representing the states are $\vec{q} = (x_{q,1}, z_{q,1}, \ldots, x_{q,n}, z_{q,n})$ and $\vec{p} = (x_{p,j_1}, z_{p,j_1}, \ldots, x_{p,j_n}, z_{p,j_k})$ and the identity gate is defined as $F_I(x, z, x', z') \triangleq x \Leftrightarrow x' \wedge z \Leftrightarrow z'$. Thus $F_{U'}(\vec{q}, \vec{q}') = \bigwedge_{\ell \notin \{j_1, \ldots, j_k\}} F_I(x_{q,\ell}, z_{q,\ell}, x_{q,\ell}', z_{q,\ell}') \wedge F_U(\vec{p}, \vec{p}')$.

In [46], we show how local gates can be encoded in the Pauli basis as formula $F_U(x, y, \ldots)$ with $x = x_1 \ldots x_n, z_1, \ldots, z_n$, $y = x_1' \ldots x_n', z_1', \ldots, z_n'$ and the dots represent any auxiliary variables. For instance, one can check that the encoding of the Hadamard gate becomes $F_H(x, z, x', z') \triangleq (r \Leftrightarrow x z) \wedge (z' \Leftrightarrow x) \wedge (x' \Leftrightarrow z)$ with weights $W(r) = -1$ and $W(\bar{r}) = 1$ (hint: consider the conjugations $HXH^\dagger$, $HYH^\dagger$ and $HZH^\dagger$).

The following Pauli-basis encoding of the T gate in this basis is a bit more involved.

$$F_T(x, z, x', z') \triangleq (r \Leftrightarrow x z \bar{z}') \wedge (x' \Leftrightarrow x) \wedge (\bar{x} \Rightarrow (z' \Leftrightarrow z)) \wedge (h \Leftrightarrow x).$$

The conjuncts here are dictated by the following identities.

$$TXT^\dagger = \tfrac{1}{\sqrt{2}}(Y + X) \qquad TYT^\dagger = \tfrac{1}{\sqrt{2}}(Y - X) \qquad TZT^\dagger = Z$$

– Only X or Y are mapped to a linear combination of $\{X, Y\} \equiv x$, therefore $x' \Leftrightarrow x$ and z' is undetermined iff $x = 1$, and $h \Leftrightarrow x$ with $W(h) = 1/\sqrt{2}$ and $W(\bar{h}) = 1$.

– The coefficient is negative only when Y is mapped to X, hence $r \Leftrightarrow xz\bar{z}'$ with $W(r) = -1$ and $W(\bar{r}) = 1$.

In the computational basis, we had no need for $W(\bar{h})$ as the Hadamard gate always introduced this factor. In the Pauli basis, this factor is introduced conditioned on $x = 1$.

Table 2. Overview of the encoding aspects in both bases. Without loss of generality, we may assume that one sign and factor variable r_j, h_j exists for j-th gate (of m gates) in the circuit.

	Computational basis	Pauli basis
Unitary for 1 qubit ($U1$)	$F_{U1}(q, q')$	$F_{U1}(x, z, x', z')$
Unitary for n qubits (Un)	$F_{Un}(q_1, \ldots, q_n)$	$F_{Un}(x_1, z_1, \ldots, x_n, z_n)$
$H = 1/\sqrt{2}\left[\begin{smallmatrix} 1 & 1 \\ 1 & -1 \end{smallmatrix}\right]$	$h \wedge (r \Leftrightarrow qq')$	$(r \Leftrightarrow xz) \wedge (z' \Leftrightarrow x) \wedge (x' \Leftrightarrow z)$
$S = \left[\begin{smallmatrix} 1 & 0 \\ 0 & i \end{smallmatrix}\right]$	*add variable u s.t.* $w(u) = i$	*explained in* [46]
$T = \left[\begin{smallmatrix} 1 & 0 \\ 0 & \omega \end{smallmatrix}\right]$	*use u, h to represent* $\omega = \frac{i+1}{\sqrt{2}}$	*explained above and in* [46]
$CX = \left[\begin{smallmatrix} 1&0&0&0 \\ 0&1&0&0 \\ 0&0&0&1 \\ 0&0&1&0 \end{smallmatrix}\right]$	$(q_1' \Leftrightarrow q_1) \wedge (q_2' \Leftrightarrow (q_2 \oplus q_1))$	*explained in* [46]
Toffoli	$(q_1' \Leftrightarrow q_1) \wedge (q_2' \Leftrightarrow q_2) \wedge (q_3' \Leftrightarrow (q_1 \oplus q_2 \oplus q_3))$	*explained in* [47]

For both bases, we define function evaluation, which computes the weight of an assignment for a Boolean formula F_U and weight function W that represents a simple gate U. That is, given the variables $\vec{q}, \vec{q}'$ which encode the quantum state before and after the gate, then for two concrete states $\vec{b} \in \mathbb{B}^{\vec{q}}$ and $\vec{b}' \in \mathbb{B}^{\vec{q}'}$, we define the function $FVP_{\mathbb{C}}(\langle F_U, W, \vec{b}, \vec{b}' \rangle) \triangleq [\![F_U(\vec{b}, \vec{b}')]\!]_W$. Since all auxiliary variables are always determined by the Boolean variables in $\vec{b}, \vec{b}'$, we know this problem $FVP_{\mathbb{C}} \in \mathsf{FP}_{\mathbb{C}}$ (or, more specifically, $\mathsf{FP}_{\mathbb{R}}$ for the Pauli basis) for all n-qubit simple gates. By construction we know that $FVP_{\mathbb{C}}(\langle F_U, W, \vec{b}, \vec{b}' \rangle) = \langle \vec{b} | U | \vec{b}' \rangle$. We later see that instead of formula evaluation, we could also allow for model counting to define simple gates. But, it is not clear when this would be useful, nor does it fit the purpose of individual gates, which by purpose should allow "easy" descriptions (circuits, on the other hand, are hard to analyze). Since formula evaluation is complete for FP, this definition should also suffice in terms of expressiveness.

3.3   Encoding Quantum Circuits

An n-qubit quantum circuit C is a sequence of *simple* gates $(U_1, \ldots, U_m)$ (all on n qubits). With the variables as defined in Sect. 3.1, this leads to the following overview circuit of the encoding.

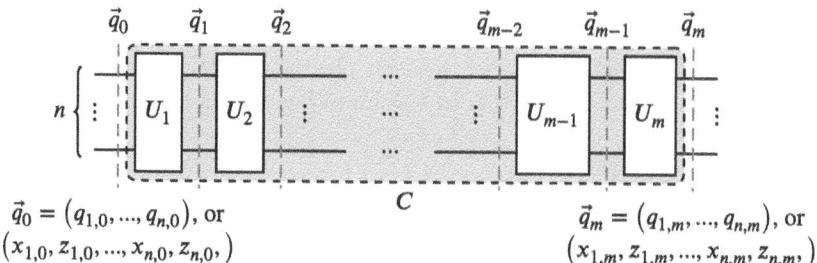

$$\vec{q}_0 = (q_{1,0}, \ldots, q_{n,0}), \text{ or}$$
$$\left(x_{1,0}, z_{1,0}, \ldots, x_{n,0}, z_{n,0}, \right)$$

$$\vec{q}_m = (q_{1,m}, \ldots, q_{n,m}), \text{ or}$$
$$\left(x_{1,m}, z_{1,m}, \ldots, x_{n,m}, z_{n,m}, \right)$$

Like a gate, a circuit is also a unitary matrix, i.e., $C = U_m \cdots U_1$, with a slight abuse of notation. To compute the entry $(\vec{b}, \vec{b}')$ of a circuit (unitary) C, i.e., $\langle \vec{b}'|C|\vec{b}\rangle$, we can use Feynman's algorithm [49], also known as the path sum approach, as follows.

$$\langle \vec{b}_m|C|\vec{b}_0\rangle = \sum_{\vec{b}_{m-1},\ldots,\vec{b}_1 \in \mathbb{B}^n} \prod_{j \in \{1,\ldots,m\}} \langle \vec{b}_j|U_j|\vec{b}_{j-1}\rangle \qquad (2)$$

Recall that we have the conjugation $P_m = CP_0C^\dagger \Leftrightarrow |P_m\rangle = \tilde{C}|P_0\rangle$ and the inner product $\langle P_0|P_m\rangle = \mathrm{tr}(P_0 \cdot P_m)$. Thus we can express path-sum in Pauli basis as follows.

$$\langle P_m|\hat{C}|P_0\rangle = P_mCP_0C^\dagger$$
$$= \sum_{P_{m-1},\ldots,P_1 \in \{X,Y,Z,I\}^{\otimes n}} \prod_{j \in \{1,\ldots,m\}} \langle P_j|\tilde{U}_j|P_{j-1}\rangle \qquad (3)$$

Combining the path integral with the encoding of local gates, we obtain the following definition for the WMC instance for a single path over the computational basis states identified by $\vec{b}_0, \ldots, \vec{b}_m \in \mathbb{B}^n$ (or $\mathbb{B}^{2n}$ for the Pauli basis encoding).

In the previous section, we saw that each component in Feynman's path sum approach $\langle \vec{b}_j|U_j|\vec{b}_{j-1}\rangle$ can be encoded as $F_U^W(\vec{b}_j, \vec{b}_{j-1})$ the evaluation of a Boolean formula F_U with weight function W, and assignment that encodes $\vec{b}_j$ and $\vec{b}_{j-1}$. Filling in this circuit, we obtain the following equation.

$$\langle \vec{b}_m|C|\vec{b}_0\rangle = \sum_{\vec{b}_{m-1},\ldots,\vec{b}_1 \in \mathbb{B}^n} \prod_{j \in \{1,\ldots,m\}} [\![F_U(\vec{b}_j, \vec{b}_{j-1})]\!]$$

Since we have that $FVP_\mathbb{C} \in \mathsf{FP}_\mathbb{C} \subseteq \#\mathsf{P}_\mathbb{C}$. From the $\#P$ closure properties Property 1 and Property 2, we derive that computing the amplitude $\langle \vec{b}_0|C|\vec{b}_m\rangle$ of circuit C is in $\#\mathsf{P}_\mathbb{C}$.

Indeed, the encoding of a path of the circuit in $\#\mathsf{SAT}_\mathbb{C}$ is similar to bounded model checking instances [7,46]:

$$F_C(\vec{q}_0, \vec{q}_1, \ldots, \vec{q}_m) \triangleq F_{U_0}(\vec{q}_0, \vec{q}_1) \wedge \cdots \wedge F_{U_m}(\vec{q}_{m-1}, \vec{q}_m).$$

Therefore, a model counter can compute $\langle \vec{q}_0 | C | \vec{q}_m \rangle$ by assigning $\vec{q}_0, \vec{q}_m :=$ $\vec{b}_0, \vec{b}_m$ and freely quantifying the intermediate states $\vec{q}_1, \ldots, \vec{q}_{m-1}$,

$$F_C(\vec{b}_0, \vec{b}_m) \triangleq \bigvee_{\vec{b}_1, \ldots, \vec{b}_{m-1} \in \mathbb{B}^{\vec{b}_0}} F_C(\vec{b}_0, \vec{b}_1, \ldots, \vec{b}_m),$$

such that,

$$[\![F_C(\vec{b}_0, \vec{b}_m)]\!] \equiv \sum_{\vec{b}_1, \ldots, \vec{b}_{m-1} \in \mathbb{B}^{\vec{b}_0}} [\![F_C(\vec{b}_0, \ldots, \vec{b}_m)]\!] \equiv \langle \vec{b}_0 | C | \vec{b}_m \rangle.$$

Again, we can do this for both the computational basis, where $\vec{q}_i = (q_{i,1}, \ldots, q_{i,n})$, and the Pauli basis, where $\vec{q}_i = (x_{i,1}, z_{i,1}, \ldots, x_{i,n}, z_{i,n})$ (omitting the auxiliary dependent weighted variables like h and r introduced earlier).

4   Reducing Quantum Circuits to Algebraic Model Counting

We use the complexity-theoretic framework from Sect. 2.2 for reducing quantum circuits to #SAT instances from first principles.

We propose an exact reduction of the semantics of quantum circuits to model counting (#SAT) and discuss its applications and tradeoffs. In contrast to earlier encodings [46,47], we eventually avoid using floating-point computations, which could potentially cause numerical instability [50], by gradually reducing the problem from $\#P_{\mathbb{C}}$ to $\#P_{\mathbb{Z}[\sqrt{2}]}$ to $\#P_{\mathbb{B}} = \#P$ via metric reductions. For the sake of readability, we will not always make the reduction formal as in Definition 3. Instead, we can rely on the basic insight that it constitutes a usual many-one reduction with polynomial time postprocessing, as explained above the definition, and implicitly assume that such postprocessing is allowed.

An alternative to metric reductions from $\#P_{\mathbb{A}}$ to $\#P_{\mathbb{B}}$ is to allow multiple calls to the model counter, i.e., using $\mathsf{FP}_{\mathbb{B}}^{\#P_{\mathbb{A}}}$ instead of $\mathsf{FP}_{\mathbb{B}}^{\#P_{\mathbb{A}}[1]}$. As we shall see, the weaker reduction is always a first step in the stronger (metric) reduction, so both approaches can be distilled from this section. This is relevant [51] when considering also approximation-preserving reductions [22] (outside of the scope of this work).

4.1   Getting Rid of Complex Numbers

There are three ways to obviate the need for complex numbers in our encoding, thereby reducing the problem from $\#P_{\mathbb{C}}$ to $\#P_{\mathbb{R}}$ and possibly simplifying the solver implementation (or at least extend the portfolio of solvers [16,19,26,28, 42–44,55,57,61] that can be used to solve the problem).

The first approach is to convert the circuit C to a circuit using the Toffoli + H. Given that this gate set is (computationally) universal [2], any quantum circuit C consisting of gates from some universal gate set can be efficiently transformed into a circuit C' the Toffoli $+ H$ gate as a consequence of the Solovay-Kitaev theorem [49]. However, the circuit C' only approximates the probability distribution for any observable on C [2]. Therefore, unless the circuit C already uses the Toffoli $+ H$ gate set or, by pure accident, happens to be exactly expressible in it, this method is not suitable for the exact analysis applications we study here (see Sect. 5 for a discussion on approximate versus exact analysis methods).

The second approach is to use the Pauli basis, which immediately obviates the need for complex numbers as explained in Sect. 2.1. This approach was taken in [46,47]. The tradeoff here is that it duplicates the number of Boolean variables required in the encoding, because a Pauli gate requires two bits to encode, but in the computational bases, we need one bit as illustrated in Sect. 3.2. As we shall see in Sect. 5, however, the encoding of circuit simulation in the computation basis will double the formula length.

The third and final approach is use the trick due to Bernstein and Vazarani [5]. They split the real and imaginary parts of quantum gates and states by introducing a separate qubit. Define $\Re(A)/\Im(A)$ be the real/imaginary part of a gate unitary A, or a state vector or density matrix A. As usual, let $|i\rangle = 1/\sqrt{2} \begin{bmatrix} 1 \\ i \end{bmatrix}$ and $|-i\rangle = 1/\sqrt{2} \begin{bmatrix} 1 \\ -i \end{bmatrix}$. For each state $|\varphi\rangle$, we define $|\hat{\varphi}\rangle \triangleq |i\rangle \otimes \Re(|\varphi\rangle) + |-i\rangle \otimes \Im(|\varphi\rangle)$. For a unitary U (or a density matrix ρ), we define $\hat{U} \triangleq |i\rangle\langle i| \otimes \Re(U) + |-i\rangle\langle -i| \otimes \Im(U)$ (or analogously $\hat{\rho}$). It is easy to check that $|\hat{\varphi}\rangle, \hat{U}$ and $\hat{\rho}$ are real matrices. Moreover, due to orthogonality of $|i\rangle$ and $|-i\rangle$, we can see that $U|\varphi\rangle = \psi$ iff $\hat{U}|\hat{\varphi}\rangle = |\hat{\psi}\rangle$ and that $U\rho U^\dagger = \rho'$ iff $\hat{U}\hat{\rho}\hat{U}^\dagger = \hat{\rho}'$. The downside of this last approach is that it introduces an extra qubit that interacts with all gate applications. How w this performs in practice is hard to predict and should probably be investigated empirically.

4.2   Getting Rid of Negative Numbers

To go from $\#P_\mathbb{R}$ to $\#P_{\mathbb{R}_{\geq 0}}$, we can borrow insights from the gap-definable complexity classes. GapPwas introduced in [4] (and independently as Z#P in [32]) to achieve closure under subtractions for counting classes, while preserving the other #Pclosure properties. Instead of the number of accepting paths, the semantics of GapPis the difference between the number of accepting paths and rejecting paths. Just like $\#P_{\{0,1\}} = \#P$, it is easy to see that $\#P_{\{-1,0,1\}} = \mathsf{GapP}$ (just assign the negative weight to the rejecting paths). Since gaps can also be negative values, this class is now closed under subtraction. More importantly, Fenner, Fortnow and Kurtz [25] show that computing the gap of a function is not much harder than counting the number of accepting paths as $\mathsf{GapP} = \#P - FP$, i.e., $\mathsf{GapP} = \{g - f \mid g \in \#P, f \in FP\}$. Since this constitutes a metric reduction to $\#P$, where the computation of f and the subtraction is done as postprocessing, we use a similar reduction here.

A few gates have negative amplitudes for both the Toffoli $+ H$ and the Clifford $+ T$ gate sets. In the computational basis, only the Hadamard gate has a negative amplitude $-1/\sqrt{2}$. In the Pauli basis, all gates of both gates sets can introduce a negative coefficient, which is consistently encoded with an r variable in [46] (one per gate in the circuit), just like the computational basis encoding of the Hadamard gate as given in Sect. 3.2. For a circuit $C = (U_1, \ldots, U_m)$, we will label these variables r_j, so we have that r_j is assigned to true iff $F_{U_j}(\vec{b}, \vec{b}')$ is negative for $\vec{b}, \vec{b}' \in \mathbb{B}^n$ (or $\mathbb{B}^{2n}$ in the Pauli basis). Now, we can decompose the encoding F_C into a positive and a negative component as follows.

$$F_C^+(\vec{q}_0, \ldots, \vec{q}_m) \triangleq F_C(\vec{q}_0, \ldots, \vec{q}_m, r_1, \ldots, r_m) \wedge \neg \bigoplus_{i \in [m]} r_i,$$

$$F_C^-(\vec{q}_0, \ldots, \vec{q}_m) \triangleq F_C(\vec{q}_0, \ldots, \vec{q}_m, r_1, \ldots, r_m) \wedge \bigoplus_{i \in [m]} r_i.$$

Finally, we can obtain a metric reduction from $\#P_\mathbb{R}$ to $\#P_{\mathbb{R} \geq 0}$ by computing the value $v := \#\mathrm{SAT}_{\mathbb{R} \geq 0}(F_C^+, W) - \#\mathrm{SAT}_{\mathbb{R} \geq 0}(F_C^-, W)$ with only one call to the model counter. Here, we use the approach from [25] (which has been lifted to the algebraic classes in [17]) by computing $v = \#\mathrm{SAT}_{\mathbb{R} \geq 0}(F_C^+, W) + \#\mathrm{SAT}_{\mathbb{R} \geq 0}(\overline{F_C^-}, W) - c$, where c is the total sum of all weighted assignments in F_C^-. The addition is realized in one #SAT call by branching over a fresh variable u, i.e.: $u F_C^+ \vee \overline{u} \neg F_C^-$.

4.3 Getting Rid of Continuous Domains

Continued from Sect. 4.2, here, we remove the positive real numbers in the weight function, thus reducing the problem from $\#P_{\mathbb{R} \geq 0}$ to $\#P_{\mathbb{Q}[\sqrt{2}]}$. Since the following reduction works for both F_C^+ and F_C^-, from Sect. 4.2, we will focus on F_C^+ for the rest of this section. Moreover, since we got rid of complex and negative weights, the only weight encountered in both bases is the weight $1/\sqrt{2}$; from T in the Pauli basis and H in the computational basis.[3]

Without loss of generality, we assume that each simple gate U_j in the circuit introduces an h_j variable that conditionally introduces the algebraic weight $W(h_j) = 1/\sqrt{2}$ (but $W(\overline{h}_j) = 1$). For any particular path over basis states identified by $\vec{b}_0, \vec{b}_1, \ldots, \vec{b}_m \in \mathbb{B}^{\vec{q}}$, we have that

$$[\![F_C^+(\vec{b}_0, \vec{b}_1, \ldots, \vec{b}_m, h_1, \ldots, h_m)]\!] = \begin{cases} \frac{1}{2^{c/2}} & \text{if } c \text{ is even} \\ \frac{1}{2^{(c-1)/2}} \cdot \frac{1}{\sqrt{2}} & \text{if } c \text{ is odd} \end{cases} \quad \text{where } c = \sum_{j \in [m]} h_j.$$

Now we can split the formula again into two parts:

$$F_C^{+,\square}(\vec{q}_0, \ldots, \vec{q}_m) \triangleq F_C(\vec{q}_0, \ldots, \vec{q}_m, h_1, \ldots, h_m) \wedge \neg \bigoplus_{j \in [m]} h_j \wedge \overline{d_0}, \text{ and}$$

$$F_C^{+,\triangle}(\vec{q}_0, \ldots, \vec{q}_m) \triangleq F_C(\vec{q}_0, \ldots, \vec{q}_m, h_1, \ldots, h_m) \wedge \bigoplus_{j \in [m]} h_j \wedge d_0.$$

---

[3] Toffoli gate encodings [47] use $1/2$, but we can duplicate the $1/\sqrt{2}$-weighted variable.

To change weights from real to rational numbers, we count modulo 2 by adding additional variables d_j for every gate U_j. For $F_C^{+,\square}$, they track when $h_j \mod 2$ becomes false (compared to $h_{j-1} \mod 2$) and the opposite for $F_C^{+,\triangle}$. This way, the number of d_j assigned true along every path equals $c/2$ for $F_C^{+,\triangle}$ and $(c-1)/2$ for $F_C^{+,\square}$. We can now count in $\mathbb{Q}$ by letting $W(h_j) = W(\neg h_j) = 1$ and $W(d_j) = \frac{1}{2}$ and $W(\overline{d}_j) = 1$, obtaining the following identity.

$$\#\text{SAT}_{\mathbb{R}_{\geq 0}}(F_C^+, W) = \#\text{SAT}_{\mathbb{Q}_{\geq 0}}(F_C^{+,\square}, W) + \tfrac{1}{\sqrt{2}} \cdot \#\text{SAT}_{\mathbb{Q}_{\geq 0}}(F_C^{+,\triangle}, W)$$

This encoding can be further reduced to unweighted model counting based on the method in [9], which reduces both encodings from $\#P_{\mathbb{Q}}$ to $\#P_{\{0,1\}}$. More precisely, we scale the weights $W'(d_j) = 2$ and $W'(\overline{d}_j) = 1$ to natural numbers, and $W'(h_j) = 1$, but $W'(\overline{h}_j) = 2$ as normalization factor. Let $c = \sum_{j \in [m]} h_j$, then $\#\text{SAT}_{\mathbb{N}}(F_C^{+,\triangle}, W') = 2^{m-c} * 2^{\frac{c}{2}} = 2^{m-\frac{c}{2}}$, and $\#\text{SAT}_{\mathbb{N}}(F_C^{+,\square}, W') = 2^{m-c} * 2^{\frac{c}{2}-1} = 2^{m-\frac{c}{2}-1}$. By scaling with the normalization constant 2^{-n} we derive the following equation.

$$\#SAT_{\mathbb{R}_{\geq 0}}(F_C, W) = \tfrac{1}{2^m} \cdot (\#\text{SAT}_{\mathbb{N}}(F_C^{+,\square}, W') + \tfrac{1}{\sqrt{2}} \cdot \#\text{SAT}_{\mathbb{N}}(F_C^{+,\triangle}, W'))$$

The final step towards $\#P_{0,1}$, consists of adding fresh variables u_i for each d_i (and u_{m+i} for h_i) to encode the weight $W'(d_i) = 1$ (resp. $W'(h_i) = 1$) by adding the conjunct $d_i \wedge u_i$ (resp. $h_i \wedge u_{m+i}$) to the Boolean formulas.

5   Applications

In this section, we show how the #SAT encodings presented in Sect. 3 and Sect. 4 can be used for quantum circuit simulation and equivalence checking.

Weak simulation is the problem of sampling the measurement outcomes according to the probability distribution induced by the circuit's semantics. This is most similar to an actual run of the quantum circuit on a quantum computer, which executes the circuit and probabilistically returns one of the possible measurement outcomes. Strong simulation, on the other hand, computes the probability of obtaining a specific measurement outcome up to a certain accuracy, as defined in Definition 4. Here, we assume that a circuit is initialized to the all-zero state $|0\rangle^{\otimes n}$, which does not lose expressive power and is common practice in circuit evaluation.

A (projective) measurement is given by a set of *projectors* $\{\mathbb{P}_1, \ldots, \mathbb{P}_k\}$ —one for each measurement outcome $[k]$— satisfying $\sum_{j \in [k]} \mathbb{P}_j = I$. A linear operator $\mathbb{P}$ is a projector if and only if $\mathbb{P}\mathbb{P} = \mathbb{P}^\dagger = \mathbb{P}$.

Definition 4 (Strong Simulation). *Given an n-qubit quantum circuit C, the strong simulation of circuit C, with measurement $\{\mathbb{P}_1, \ldots, \mathbb{P}_k\}$, computes the probability of getting any outcome $l \in [k]$, i.e., the value $\langle 0|^{\otimes n} C^\dagger \mathbb{P}_l C |0\rangle^{\otimes n} \in [0,1]$, up to a number of desired bits of precision.*

The measurement can be specified in a certain basis. A commonly used one is *computational basis measurement* defined as $\{\mathbb{P}_l = \otimes_{j\in[n]}\mathbb{P}_{l,j} \mid \mathbb{P}_{l,j} \in \{|0\rangle\langle0|, |1\rangle\langle1|, I\}\}$ satisfying $\sum_l \mathbb{P}_l = I$. For example, given a three-qubit system, measuring the first two qubits under computational basis is given by the measurement $\{|b_1\rangle\langle b_1| \otimes |b_2\rangle\langle b_2| \otimes I \mid b_1, b_2 \in \mathbb{B}\}$.

The following proposition shows that the encoding from Sect. 4 can be used to obtain a metric reduction from strong simulation to #P.

Proposition 1. *There is a metric reduction from strong simulation with computational basis measurements to #P.*

Proof. We seek a metric reduction from computing $\langle 0|^{\otimes n} C^\dagger \mathbb{P}_l C |0\rangle^{\otimes n}$ to #P, for a quantum circuit C and projector $\mathbb{P}_l \in \{\mathbb{P}_1, \ldots, \mathbb{P}_k\}$. We show the metric reduction can be done in both computational basis and Pauli basis.

First, we introduce a metric reduction for the computational basis, which means to perform the projective measurement with $\mathbb{P}_l = \otimes_{i\in[n]}\mathbb{P}_{l,i}$ for $\mathbb{P}_{l,i} \in \{|0\rangle\langle0|, |1\rangle\langle1|, I\}$. Denote the encoding of $\mathbb{P}_l$ as $F_{\mathbb{P}_l}$. In computational basis encoding, we have

$$F_{|0\rangle\langle0|}(q, q') = (q' \Leftrightarrow q) \wedge \bar{q}' \quad F_{|1\rangle\langle1|}(q, q') = (q' \Leftrightarrow q) \wedge q'.$$

Thus $F_{\mathbb{P}_l} = \bigwedge_{i\in[n]} F_{\mathbb{P}_{l,i}}$ for $\mathbb{P}_{l,i} \in \{|0\rangle\langle0|, |1\rangle\langle1|, I\}$. The value $\langle 0|^{\otimes n} C^\dagger \mathbb{P}_l C |0\rangle^{\otimes n}$ can be computed as $\#SAT(F_{\langle0|^{\otimes n}} \wedge F_{C^\dagger} \wedge F_{\mathbb{P}_l} \wedge F_C \wedge F_{|0\rangle^{\otimes n}}, W)$, where $F_{\langle0|^{\otimes n}}$ and $F_{|0\rangle^{\otimes n}}$ are given in Sect. 3.1 and F_C is given in Sect. 3.2 and Sect. 3.3. As for $F_{C^\dagger}$, since the circuit $C^\dagger$ consists of simple gates $U_1^\dagger, \ldots U_m^\dagger$, which can easily be constructed using the available gate encodings: $F_{U_j^\dagger}(\vec{q}, \vec{q}') = F_{U_j}(\vec{q}', \vec{q})$ with a conjugated weight function.

While in Pauli basis encoding, since $|0\rangle\langle0| = \frac{I+Z}{2}$ and $|1\rangle\langle1| = \frac{I-Z}{2}$, we have $\mathbb{P}_l = \sum_j P_{l,j}$, where $P_{l,j} \in \{Z, I, -Z\}^{\otimes n}$ and $(|0\rangle\langle0|)^{\otimes n} = \sum_k \frac{1}{2^n} P_k'$ where $P_k' \in \{Z, I\}^{\otimes n}$. We have that:

$$\langle 0|^{\otimes n} C^\dagger \mathbb{P}_l C |0\rangle^{\otimes n} = \mathrm{tr}(\mathbb{P}_l C(|0\rangle\langle0|)^{\otimes n} C^\dagger)$$

$$= \mathrm{tr}\left(\left(\sum_j P_{l,j}\right) C \left(\sum_k \frac{1}{2^n} P_k'\right) C^\dagger\right) \quad \text{(by Pauli decomposition)}$$

$$= \sum_j \langle P_{l,j}|\tilde{C} \sum_k \frac{1}{2^n}|P_k'\rangle \quad (U A U^\dagger \Leftrightarrow \tilde{U}|A\rangle)$$

$$= \sum_{j,k} \langle P_{l,j}'|\tilde{C}|P_k\rangle/2^n \quad \text{(by linearity of trace)}$$

The idea of encoding $\langle P_{l,j}'|\tilde{C}|P_k\rangle$ is given in Sect. 3.3. We can now apply Property 1 to see that this is in #P. In the post-processing phase of the metric reduction, we can perform the division by 2^n. A concrete encoding for strong simulation in the Pauli basis is also given in [46]. $\square$

The problem of equivalence checking involves determining whether two quantum circuits are equivalent up to a complex factor $c \in \mathbb{C}$, known as the *global phase* [49].

Definition 5 (Quantum Circuit Equivalence Checking). *Given two n-qubit circuits U and V, U is equivalent to V, written $U \equiv V$, if there is a complex number $c \in \mathbb{C}$ such that for all input states $|\psi\rangle$, we have $U|\psi\rangle = cV|\psi\rangle$.*

Proposition 2. *There is a metric reduction from equivalence checking of circuits to #P.*

Proof. First, we observe that equivalence checking of two quantum circuits U, V reduces to identity checking $UV^\dagger = cI^{\otimes n}$, where $|c|^2 = 1$. We thus consider identity checking of circuit $C = UV^\dagger$.

In the case of computational basis encoding, in order to check $C = cI^{\otimes n}$, it suffices to check for all $\vec{b} \in \mathbb{B}^n$, we have $\langle \vec{b}|C|\vec{b}\rangle = c$ [49]. We thus compute $c_{\vec{b}} := \langle \vec{b}|C|\vec{b}\rangle$. We can now use Property 1 to see that $\sum_{\vec{b} \in \mathbb{B}^n} c_{\vec{b}}$ is in #P. The encoding would be

$$F_C(\vec{q}_0, \vec{q}_m) \wedge \vec{q}_0 \Leftrightarrow \vec{q}_m \quad \equiv \quad F_C(\vec{q}_0, \vec{q}_0).$$

By the triangle inequality, we have that $\sum_{\vec{b} \in \mathbb{B}^n} c_{\vec{b}}$ only equals $2^n \cdot c$ when all terms equal the same complex number c with $|c|^2 = 1$, which we can check in post-processing.

In the case of Pauli basis encoding, the idea is to check $\langle P|\tilde{C}|P\rangle = 1$ for all Pauli strings P, where we can also use Property 1 to see that $\sum_{P \in \{X,Y,Z,I\}^{\otimes n}} \langle P|\tilde{C}|P\rangle$ is in #P. As above, this can also be encoded cyclically as $F_C(\vec{q}_0, \vec{q}_0)$, but in the Pauli basis, where the summation only equals 4^n if and only if all terms equal 1. In [47], it is shown that only $2n$ Pauli strings need to be checked, so we could add initial and final constraints to limit the check to $2n$ Pauli strings. For a concrete encoding please refer to [47].   □

For simulation, the computational basis requires doubling the length of the encoding because it needs to compose the paths of $\langle \vec{b}|C^\dagger$ and $C|\vec{b}\rangle$. In the Pauli basis with density matrices, on the other hand, we need double as many variables, i.e., $\vec{q} = (x_1, z_1, \ldots, x_n, z_n)$ versus $\vec{q} = (q_1, \ldots, q_n)$. For equivalence checking, this overhead is not needed, but the Pauli basis still uses more variables.

6   Related Work

More generic counting problems are studied as algebraic model counting in [17]. Eiter and Kiesel study the sum of products on arbitrary semirings very generically [23]. Yamakami presents an analysis of the power of quantum functions, relating them to counting classes [69].

Various model counting tools support real weights [16,18,19,26,28,42–44,55]. Some even support negative real weights [57,61]. The model counting competition [27] contains quantum computing problems since 2024. The tradeoffs and insights about different encodings for these problems presented here could inform the further development of these tools.

In [9], a reduction from ℓ^1-weighted to unweighted model counting is given that assumes the ℓ^1 norm. Drawing inspiration from that work, this paper generalizes the reduction for the case of quantum circuits with several universal gate sets encoded in different bases.

Alternative approaches for discretization is by using abstract interpretation [6,70]

Exact reasoning is used extensively in the ZX-calculus [14,15], which is a graphical calculus for quantum circuits equipped with powerful rewrite rules, for simulation [8,39–41], equivalence checking [37,38,52,53], synthesis [21] and circuit optimization [20]. It can also be used in the tree automata [13], where it can compactly represent quantum states and gates algebraically. Then the verification problem can be framed as a Hoare triple. A method of reducing a quantum circuit modulo a notion of bisimulation is studied in [34], with the goal to simplify the exact simulation problem.

7 Conclusion

We discussed various ways to reduce both quantum circuit simulation and equivalence checking to #SAT, comparing the structure of the encodings in various counting domains and two different bases. We found that the Pauli basis halves encoding length compared to the computational basis, but doubles the number of variables. We also found that we need two solver calls, or double the encoding length, to discretize the encoding fully, and that the same penalty is paid for getting rid of negative weights. These results could facilitate the quest for better model counting algorithms for quantum computing tasks.

This work also contributes a new weighted to unweighted reduction that liberates an earlier counterpart [9] from the constraints of the probability domain.

A limitation of our work is that we do not show that these tradeoffs are the best possible. Since we only provide a specific encoding, this should be considered merely an upper bound on, e.g., the number of extra variables needed or the length of the formula required. While better encodings would be of interest, lower bounds are probably not worthwhile, considering that all discussed variations merely increase the length or number of variables by a constant factor.

Moreover, we focus on the exact versions of the problems discussed in Sect. 5, i.e., strong instead of weak simulation and exact instead of approximate equivalence checking. The exact version is harder than their approximate counterparts, e.g., strong simulation is already #P-complete [12,35,65]. Nonetheless, exact reasoning can be appealing because it allows discretization using an extended semiring as in Sect. 4.3. Surprisingly, exact reasoning methods can sometimes be used to compute the approximate versions of these compilation tasks more efficiently. The advantage of using exact methods is that the computation can benefit from powerful heuristics for symbolic computations, such as decision diagrams and satisfiability [62]. For example, [33,68] even successfully solve approximate circuit equivalence using exact methods by computing the fidelity between circuits (a distance metric).

Finally, this paper can be viewed as a framework for various encodings of tasks in quantum computing. This could serve future studies of approximation-preserving reductions [22,51], which could, in turn, further enable the use of approximate counters and samplers [30,45,58] for quantum circuit analysis [10,11,59]. Another issue not yet considered in this work is direct support for exclusive-or (XOR) constraints, which seem to be abundant in both the Pauli basis encoding and our methods to eliminate negative and real weights. This motivates the development of model counting algorithms supporting XOR constraints directly, as has been done for satisfiability [54,60].

Acknowledgements. This work is supported by the Dutch National Growth Fund, as part of the Quantum Delta NL program.

References

1. Aaronson, S., Gottesman, D.: Improved simulation of stabilizer circuits. Phys. Rev. A **70**(5) (2004). https://doi.org/10.1103/physreva.70.052328
2. Aharonov, D.: A simple proof that Toffoli and Hadamard are quantum universal. arXiv preprint quant-ph/0301040 (2003)
3. Baßler, P., et al.: Synthesis of and compilation with time-optimal multi-qubit gates. Quantum **7**, 984 (2023). https://doi.org/10.22331/q-2023-04-20-984
4. Beigel, R., Reingold, N., Spielman, D.: Pp is closed under intersection. In: Proceedings of the Twenty-Third Annual ACM Symposium on Theory of Computing, pp. 1–9 (1991)
5. Bernstein, E., Vazirani, U.: Quantum complexity theory. In: Proceedings of the Twenty-Fifth Annual ACM symposium on Theory of Computing, pp. 11–20 (1993)
6. Bichsel, B., Paradis, A., Baader, M., Vechev, M.: Abstraqt: analysis of quantum circuits via abstract stabilizer simulation. Quantum **7**, 1185 (2023). https://doi.org/10.22331/q-2023-11-20-1185
7. Biere, A.: Bounded model checking. In: Handbook of Satisfiability, pp. 739–764. IOS Press (2021)
8. Cam, T., Martiel, S.: Speeding up quantum circuits simulation using ZX-calculus (2023). arXiv:2305.02669
9. Chakraborty, S., Fried, D., Meel, K.S., Vardi, M.Y.: From weighted to unweighted model counting. In: Proceedings of IJCAI, pp. 689–695 (2015)
10. Chakraborty, S., Meel, K.S., Vardi, M.Y.: A scalable approximate model counter. In: Schulte, C. (ed.) CP 2013. LNCS, vol. 8124, pp. 200–216. Springer, Heidelberg (2013). https://doi.org/10.1007/978-3-642-40627-0_18
11. Chakraborty, S., Meel, K.S., Vardi, M.Y.: Algorithmic improvements in approximate counting for probabilistic inference: from linear to logarithmic sat calls. In: IJCAI, pp. 3569–3576 (2016)
12. Chen, Y., Chen, Y., Kumar, R., Patro, S., Speelman, F.: QSETH strikes again: finer quantum lower bounds for lattice problem, strong simulation, hitting set problem, and more. arXiv preprint arXiv:2309.16431 (2023)
13. Chen, Y.-F., Chung, K.-M., Lengál, O., Lin, J.-A., Tsai, W.-L., Yen, D.-D.:. An automata-based framework for verification and bug hunting in quantum circuits. Proc. ACM Program. Lang. **7**(PLDI) (2023). https://doi.org/10.1145/3591270
14. Coecke, B., Duncan, R.: Interacting quantum observables: categorical algebra and diagrammatics. New J. Phys. **13**(4), 043016 (2011)

15. Coecke, B., Kissinger, A.: Picturing Quantum Processes: A First Course in Quantum Theory and Diagrammatic Reasoning. Cambridge University Press, Cambridge (2017)
16. Darwiche, A., et al.: New advances in compiling CNF to decomposable negation normal form. In: Proceedings of ECAI, pp. 328–332. Citeseer (2004)
17. de Campos, C.P., Stamoulis, G., Weyland, D.: A structured view on weighted counting with relations to counting, quantum computation and applications. Inf. Comput. **275**, 104627 (2020). https://doi.org/10.1016/j.ic.2020.104627
18. Dubray, A., Schaus, P., Nijssen, S.: Probabilistic inference by projected weighted model counting on horn clauses. In: 29th International Conference on Principles and Practice of Constraint Programming (CP 2023), vol. 280, p. 15. Schloss Dagstuhl–Leibniz-Zentrum für Informatik (2023)
19. Dudek, J.M., Vardi, M.Y.: Parallel weighted model counting with tensor networks. arXiv preprint arXiv:2006.15512 (2020)
20. Duncan, R., Kissinger, A., Perdrix, S., van de Wetering, J.: Graph-theoretic simplification of quantum circuits with the ZX-calculus. Quantum **4**, 279 (2020). https://doi.org/10.22331/q-2020-06-04-279
21. Duncan, R., Perdrix, S.: Rewriting measurement-based quantum computations with generalised flow. In: Abramsky, S., Gavoille, C., Kirchner, C., Meyer auf der Heide, F., Spirakis, P.G. (eds.) ICALP 2010. LNCS, vol. 6199, pp. 285–296. Springer, Heidelberg (2010). https://doi.org/10.1007/978-3-642-14162-1_24
22. Dyer, M., Goldberg, L.A., Greenhill, C., Jerrum, M.: The relative complexity of approximate counting problems. Algorithmica **38**, 471–500 (2004)
23. Eiter, T., Kiesel, R.: On the complexity of sum-of-products problems over semirings. In: Proceedings of the AAAI Conference on Artificial Intelligence, vol. 35, pp. 6304–6311 (2021). https://doi.org/10.1609/aaai.v35i7.16783
24. Faliszewski, P., Hemaspaandra, L.: The complexity of power-index comparison. Theoret. Comput. Sci. **410**(1), 101–107 (2009)
25. Fenner, S.A., Fortnow, L.J., Kurtz, S.A.: Gap-definable counting classes. J. Comput. Syst. Sci. **48**(1), 116–148 (1994). https://www.sciencedirect.com/science/article/pii/S0022000005800248, https://doi.org/10.1016/S0022-0000(05)80024-8
26. Fichte, J.K., Hecher, M., Hamiti, F.: The model counting competition 2020. ACM J. Exp. Algorithmics **26** (2021). 10.1145/3459080
27. Fichte, J.K., Hecher, M., Hamiti, F.: The model counting competition 2020. J. Exp. Algorithmics (JEA) **26**, 1–26 (2021)
28. Fichte, J.K., Hecher, M., Woltran, S., Zisser, M.: Weighted model counting on the gpu by exploiting small treewidth. In: Azar, Y., Bast, H., Herman, G. (eds.) 26th Annual European Symposium on Algorithms (ESA 2018). Leibniz International Proceedings in Informatics (LIPIcs), Dagstuhl, Germany, vol. 112, pp. 28:1–28:16. Schloss Dagstuhl – Leibniz-Zentrum für Informatik (2018)
29. Giles, B., Selinger, P.: Exact synthesis of multiqubit clifford+ T circuits. Phys. Rev. A **87**(3), 032332 (2013)
30. Golia, P., Soos, M., Chakraborty, S., Meel, K.S.: Designing samplers is easy: the boon of testers. In: 2021 Formal Methods in Computer Aided Design (FMCAD), pp. 222–230. IEEE (2021)
31. Gomes, C.P., Sabharwal, A., Selman, B.: Model counting. In: Biere, A., Heule, M., van Maaren, H., Walsch, T. (eds.) Handbook of Satisfiability, pp. 993–1014. IOS Press (2008)
32. Gupta, S.: The power of witness reduction. In: 1991 Proceedings of the Sixth Annual Structure in Complexity Theory Conference, pp. 43–44. IEEE Computer Society (1991)

33. Hong, X., Ying, M., Feng, Y., Zhou, X., Li, S.: Approximate equivalence checking of noisy quantum circuits. In: 2021 58th ACM/IEEE Design Automation Conference (DAC), pp. 637–642 (2021). https://doi.org/10.1109/DAC18074.2021.9586214
34. Jiménez-Pastor, A., Larsen, K.G., Tribastone, M., Tschaikowski, M.: Forward and backward constrained bisimulations for quantum circuits. In: Finkbeiner, B., Kovács, L. (eds.) TACAS 2024. LNCS, vol. 14571, pp. 343–362. Springer, Cham (2024). https://doi.org/10.1007/978-3-031-57249-4_17
35. Jozsa, R., van den Nest, M.: Classical simulation complexity of extended Clifford circuits. Quantum Inf. Comput. **14**(7–8), 633–648 (2014). https://doi.org/10.26421/QIC14.7-8-7
36. Kimmig, A., van den Broeck, G., De Raedt, L.: Algebraic model counting. J. Appl. Log. **22**, 46–62 (2017). https://doi.org/10.1016/j.jal.2016.11.031
37. Kissinger, A., van de Wetering, J.: PyZX: large scale automated diagrammatic reasoning. In: QPL (2019). https://api.semanticscholar.org/CorpusID:104292461
38. Kissinger, A., van de Wetering, J.: Reducing the number of non-Clifford gates in quantum circuits. Phys. Rev. A **102**, 022406 (2020). https://doi.org/10.1103/PhysRevA.102.022406
39. Kissinger, A., van de Wetering, J.: Simulating quantum circuits with ZX-calculus reduced stabiliser decompositions. Quantum Sci. Technol. **7**(4), 044001 (2022). https://doi.org/10.1088/2058-9565/ac5d20
40. Kissinger, A., van de Wetering, J., Vilmart, R.: Classical simulation of quantum circuits with partial and graphical stabiliser decompositions. Schloss Dagstuhl - Leibniz-Zentrum für Informatik (2022). https://drops.dagstuhl.de/opus/volltexte/2022/16512/, https://doi.org/10.4230/LIPICS.TQC.2022.5
41. Koch, M., Yeung, R., Wang, Q.: Speedy contraction of ZX diagrams with triangles via stabiliser decompositions (2023). arXiv:2307.01803
42. Korhonen, T., Jarvisalo, M.: SharpSAT-TD in model counting competitions 2021–2023 (2023). arXiv:2308.15819
43. Lagniez, J.-M., Marquis, P.: An improved decision-DNNF compiler. IJCAI **17**, 667–673 (2017)
44. Lai, Y., Meel, K.S., Yap, R.H.C.: Fast converging anytime model counting. In: Proceedings of the AAAI Conference on Artificial Intelligence, vol. 37, pp. 4025–4034 (2023)
45. Meel, K.S., Yang, S., Liang, V.: A scalable incremental weighted sampler. In: FMCAD 2022, vol. 3, p. 205. TU Wien Academic Press (2022)
46. Mei, J., Bonsangue, M., Laarman, A.: Simulating quantum circuits by model counting. In: Gurfinkel, A., Ganesh, V. (eds.) CAV 2024. LNCS, vol. 14683, pp. 555–578. Springer, Cham (2024). https://doi.org/10.1007/978-3-031-65633-0_25. Preprint arXiv:2403.07197
47. Mei, J., Coopmans, T., Bonsangue, M., Laarman, A.: Equivalence checking of quantum circuits by model counting. In: Benzmüller, C., Heule, M.J., Schmidt, R.A. (eds.) IJCAR 2024. LNCS, vol. 14740, pp. 401–421. Springer, Cham (2024). https://doi.org/10.1007/978-3-031-63501-4_21
48. Nagy, S., Paredes, R., Dudek, J.M., Dueñas-Osorio, L., Vardi, M.Y.: Ising model partition-function computation as a weighted counting problem. Phys. Rev. E **109**(5), 055301 (2024)
49. Nielsen, M.A., Chuang, I.L.: Quantum Information and Quantum Computation, vol. 2, no. 8, p. 23. Cambridge University Press, Cambridge (2000)
50. Niemann, P., Zulehner, A., Drechsler, R., Wille, R.: Overcoming the tradeoff between accuracy and compactness in decision diagrams for quantum computa-

tion. IEEE Trans. Comput. Aided Des. Integr. Circuits Syst. **39**(12), 4657–4668 (2020)

51. O'Donnell, R., Say, A.C.C.: The weakness of CTC qubits and the power of approximate counting. ACM Trans. Comput. Theory (TOCT) **10**(2), 1–22 (2018)

52. Peham, T., Burgholzer, L., Wille, R.: Equivalence checking of quantum circuits with the ZX-calculus. IEEE J. Emerg. Sel. Top. Circuits Syst. **12**(3), 662–675 (2022). https://doi.org/10.1109/JETCAS.2022.3202204

53. Peham, T., Burgholzer, L., Wille, R.: Equivalence checking of parameterized quantum circuits: Verifying the compilation of variational quantum algorithms. In: 2023 28th Asia and South Pacific Design Automation Conference (ASP-DAC), pp. 702–708 (2023)

54. Reeves, J.E., Heule, M.J.H., Bryant, R.E.: From clauses to klauses. In: Gurfinkel, A., Ganesh, V. (eds.) CAV 2024. LNCS, vol. 14681, pp. 110–132. Springer, Cham (2024). https://doi.org/10.1007/978-3-031-65627-9_6

55. Sang, T., Bacchus, F., Beame, P., Kautz, H.A., Pitassi, T.: Combining component caching and clause learning for effective model counting. SAT **4**, 7th (2004)

56. Sang, T., Beame, P., Kautz, H.A.: Performing Bayesian inference by weighted model counting. In: AAAI, vol. 5, pp. 475–481 (2005)

57. Sharma, S., Roy, S., Soos, M., Meel, K.S.: GANAK: a scalable probabilistic exact model counter. In: IJCAI, vol. 19, pp. 1169–1176 (2019)

58. Soos, M., Aggarwal, D., Chakraborty, S., Meel, K.S., Obremski, M.: Engineering an efficient approximate DNF-counter. In: Elkind, E. (ed.) IJCAI-23, pp. 2031–2038. International Joint Conferences on Artificial Intelligence Organization (2023). https://doi.org/10.24963/ijcai.2023/226

59. Soos, M., Meel, K.S.: BIRD: engineering an efficient CNF-XOR sat solver and its applications to approximate model counting. In: Proceedings of the AAAI Conference on Artificial Intelligence, vol. 33, pp. 1592–1599 (2019)

60. Soos, M., Nohl, K., Castelluccia, C.: Extending SAT solvers to cryptographic problems. In: Kullmann, O. (ed.) SAT 2009. LNCS, vol. 5584, pp. 244–257. Springer, Heidelberg (2009). https://doi.org/10.1007/978-3-642-02777-2_24

61. Suzuki, R., Hashimoto, K., Sakai, M.: Improvement of projected model-counting solver with component decomposition using SAT solving in components. Technical report, JSAI Technical Report, SIG-FPAI-103-B506 (2017). (in Japanese)

62. Thanos,D., et al.: Automated reasoning in quantum circuit compilation. In: SPIN 2024 (2024). https://spin-web.github.io/SPIN2024/assets/preproceedings/SPIN2024-paper6.pdf

63. Valiant, L.G.: The complexity of computing the permanent. Theor. Comput. Sci. **8**(2), 189–201 (1979). https://doi.org/10.1016/0304-3975(79)90044-6

64. Van de Wetering, J.: Constructing quantum circuits with global gates. New J. Phys. **23**(4), 043015 (2021)

65. van den Nest, M.: Classical simulation of quantum computation, the Gottesman-Knill theorem, and slightly beyond. Quantum Inf. Comput. **10**(3), 258–271 (2010)

66. Vardi, M.Y., Zhang, Z.: Quantum-inspired perfect matching under vertex-color constraints. arXiv preprint arXiv:2209.13063 (2022)

67. Watrous, J.: The Theory of Quantum Information. Cambridge University Press, Cambridge (2018)

68. Wei, C.-Y., Tsai, Y.-H., Jhang, C.-S., Jiang, J.-H.R.: Accurate BDD-based unitary operator manipulation for scalable and robust quantum circuit verification. In: Proceedings of the 59th ACM/IEEE Design Automation Conference, pp. 523–528 (2022)

69. Yamakami, T.: Analysis of quantum functions. Int. J. Found. Comput. Sci. **14**(05), 815–852 (2003)
70. Yu, N., Palsberg, J.: Quantum abstract interpretation. In: Proceedings of the 42nd ACM SIGPLAN International Conference on Programming Language Design and Implementation, pp. 542–558 (2021)

Automata, Languages, and Learning

Well-Behaved (Co)algebraic Semantics
of Regular Expressions in Dafny

Stefan Zetzsche[1(✉)] and Wojciech Różowski[2]

[1] Amazon Web Services, London, UK
stefanze@amazon.co.uk
[2] University College London, London, UK
w.rozowski@cs.ucl.ac.uk

Abstract. Regular expressions are commonly understood in terms of
their denotational semantics, that is, through formal languages – the
regular languages. This view is inductive in nature: two primitives are
equivalent if they are constructed in the same way. Alternatively, regular
expressions can be understood in terms of their operational semantics,
that is, through deterministic finite automata. This view is coinductive in nature: two primitives are equivalent if they are deconstructed
in the same way. It is implied by Kleene's famous theorem that both
views are equivalent: regular languages are precisely the formal languages
accepted by deterministic finite automata. In this paper, we use Dafny,
a verification-aware programming language, to formally verify, for the
first time, what has been previously established only through proofs-by-
hand: the two semantics of regular expressions are well-behaved, in the
sense that they are in fact one and the same, up to pointwise bisimilarity.
At each step of our formalisation, we propose an interpretation in the
language of Coalgebra. We found that Dafny is particularly well suited
for the task due to its inductive and coinductive features and hope our
approach serves as a blueprint for future generalisations to other theories.

Keywords: Coalgebra · Dafny · Regular Expressions · Semantics

1 Introduction

Regular expressions stand as one of the most ubiquitous formalisms in all of
theoretical computer science. Their inception can be traced back all the way
to Kleene's seminal paper in 1951 [25]. Today, they play a pivotal role as a
foundational element for a wide spectrum of applications [7,18,40], encompassing
text searching, pattern matching, lexical analysis, and more.

Typically, regular expressions are understood denotationally, through the
formal languages, that is, sets of finite words over a fixed alphabet, that they
denote. This view is inductive in nature, in the sense that the denotational
semantics of regular expressions is constructed from the bottom-up by following
the finite inductive structure of an expression.

ⓒ The Author(s), under exclusive license to Springer Nature Switzerland AG 2025
C. Anutariya and M. M. Bonsangue (Eds.): ICTAC 2024, LNCS 15373, pp. 43–61, 2025.
https://doi.org/10.1007/978-3-031-77019-7_3

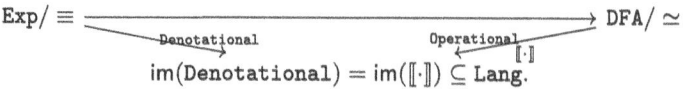

$$\text{im}(\texttt{Denotational}) = \text{im}(\llbracket\cdot\rrbracket) \subseteq \texttt{Lang}.$$

Fig. 1. The triptych of regular expressions, deterministic finite automata, and regular languages.

Alternatively, regular expressions can be understood operationally, through the lenses of deterministic finite automata. This view is coinductive in nature, in the sense that the operational semantics of regular expressions is assigned from the top-down, by deconstructing an expression, following the coinductive nature of a potentially infinite language initially observed by Brzozowski [13].

One of Kleene's many contributions was to show that the denotational and operational semantics of regular expressions are two sides of the same coin – they are *well-behaved*. That is, the denotational interpretation of a regular expression matches exactly the observable behaviour of its operational interpretation. Kleene's theorem is of great practical significance, too: for any given regular expression that represents a text pattern, one can derive, in a canonical way, an automaton that gives rise to a deterministic algorithm that decides, in finite time, whether some given string matches the text pattern specified by the expression [21,22]. The full triptych of regular expressions, deterministic finite automata, and regular languages is depicted in Fig. 1: the set of regular expressions modulo the axioms of *Kleene Algebra* [26] ($\equiv$), the set of deterministic finite automata modulo behavioural equivalence ($\simeq$), and the set of regular languages are in bijection. The composition on the right-hand side of the diagram can be seen as a function that assigns the operational semantics to an expression.

In more recent years, a more general approach to automata through the lenses of category theory has become popular: state-based systems are generalised as *coalgebras* over an endofunctor [19,24,44]. There are many advantages to using the coalgebraic abstraction of state-based systems. Among others, it allows one to set aside irrelevant specifics of concrete instantiations, and instead work with elegant, universal properties. Of particular interest for us are systems that have both an algebraic (inductive) and a coalgebraic (coinductive) component.

In this paper, we use the built-in inductive and coinductive reasoning capabilities of *Dafny* [3], a programming language and static verifier, to formalise the denotational and operational semantics of regular expressions and formally prove that they are well-behaved, that is, coincide pointwise, up to bisimilarity[1]. Dafny is a statically typed programming language with native support for writing and verifying specifications about programs that was first developed by Leino at Microsoft Research [4,32]. Dafny combines various paradigms such as imperative, functional, and object-oriented programming and supports common programming concepts such as inductive datatypes, immutable and mutable data structures, lambda functions, and subset types. Dafny can be integrated with common software development IDEs such as VSCode and emacs. It has been

---

[1] The full Dafny source code is available at [51].

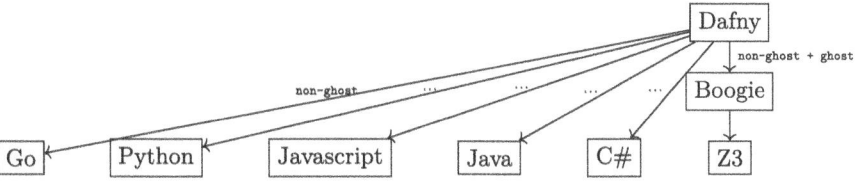

Fig. 2. The compilation pipeline of Dafny.

used in academia for research and the teaching of program verification [39], as well as in industry by e.g. Amazon [1], ConsenSys [14], and Intel [50]. Teaching material is available online [31,48] and in print [36]. A blog covers various aspects of the Dafny ecosystem [2].

One of the features of Dafny is that it allows the clear distinction between an idealised mathematical specification and an efficient implementation thereof. As a first example, consider the following purely functional specification of the Fibonacci sequence:

```
function Fib(n: nat): nat {
  if n <= 1 then n else Fib(n - 1) + Fib(n - 2)
}
```

While elegant in its recursive definition, Fib is not particularly efficient. A more realistic implementation is given by the imperative method ComputeFib below:

```
method ComputeFib(n: nat) returns (b: nat)
  ensures b == Fib(n)
{
  var c := 1;
  b := 0;
  for i := 0 to n
    invariant b == Fib(i) && c == Fib(i + 1)
  {
    b, c := c, b + c;
  }
}
```

Dafny allows us to extend the method signature with an **ensures** clause, which in this case indicates that the outputs of Fib and ComputeFib coincide on all possible inputs. To aid Dafny with proving the correctness of the **ensures** clause, we have to identify an appropriate **invariant** of the for loop in the body of ComputeFib. While not displayed, **ensures** admits a dual, the **requires** clause, which is used to restrict the domain of functions and methods to a subset. The two clauses are best thought of in terms of pre- and postconditions in the spirit of Hoare triples [20].

As illustrated above, Dafny programs contain both so-called *ghost* and *non-ghost* parts. Ghost code is meant for the specification of the behaviour of functions and the proof thereof only, not for compilation. Functions, methods, and variables can be marked ghost with a designated keyword. A method that is ghost and doesn't modify the heap is called a lemma. Pre- and postconditions, assertions, and loop invariants are always considered ghost. The Dafny verifier translates the ghost and non-ghost parts of a Dafny program into a program in the intermediate verification language Boogie [8], such that the correctness of the output program implies the correctness of the input program. To verify the correctness of a Boogie program, a verification condition is generated from it and passed to the SMT solver Z3 [16] (Fig. 2). Besides Dafny, there are other verification-aware languages built on top of Boogie and Z3 (e.g. VCC [15] and Spec# [9]). The non-ghost part of a verified Dafny program can be compiled to C#, Java, Javascript, Python, and Go, making possible the integration of verified code with an existing code base (Fig. 2).

We found that Dafny is particularly well suited for the task and would like our approach to serve as a blueprint for future generalisations to other theories. At each step of our formalisation, we propose an interpretation in the language of Coalgebra. We hope that the presentation is accessible both for readers that are familiar with Coalgebra but not so much with Dafny, and for readers unexposed to Coalgebra, but experienced in Dafny.

In detail, the paper makes the following contributions:

- We formalise regular expressions as an inductive datatype (Sect. 2.1) and formal languages as a coinductive codatatype (Sect. 2.2). We introduce the concept of bisimilarity of languages (Sect. 2.5). We equip languages with an algebraic structure (Sect. 2.3) and in consequence define the denotational semantics of regular expressions as an induced function from regular expressions to formal languages (Sect. 2.4). Finally, we prove that the latter preserves algebraic structures up to pointwise bisimilarity (Sect. 2.6). At each step, we propose an interpretation in the language of Coalgebra.
- We equip the set of regular expressions with a coalgebraic structure of the type of unpointed deterministic automata (Sect. 3.1). We then formalise the operational semantics of regular expressions as an induced function from regular expressions to formal languages (Sect. 3.2). Finally, we prove that the latter preserves coalgebraic structures (Sect. 3.3).
- We show that the function that formalises the denotational semantics is also a coalgebra homomorphism (Sect. 4.1), and that coalgebra homomorphisms are unique up to pointwise bisimilarity (Sect. 4.2). We deduce that the denotational and operational semantics coincide, up to pointwise bisimilarity (Sect. 4.3). Finally, we show that the function that formalises the operational semantics is also an algebra homomorphism (Sect. 4.4).

2   Denotational Semantics

In this section, we define, in Dafny, regular expressions and formal languages, introduce the concept of bisimilarity, formalise the *denotational* semantics of regular expressions as a function from regular expressions to formal languages, and prove that the latter is an algebra homomorphism.

2.1 Regular Expressions as Datatype

We define the set of regular expressions parametric in an alphabet A as an inductive datatype:

```
datatype Exp<A> = | Zero | One | Char(A) | Plus(Exp, Exp) | Comp(Exp, Exp) | Star(Exp)
```

Note that above, and later, we make use of Dafny's type parameter completion [33], which allows us to write Exp instead of Exp<A>.

The definition above captures that a regular expression is either a primitive character Char(a), a non-deterministic choice between two regular expressions Plus(e1, e2), a sequential composition of two regular expressions Comp(e1, e2), a finite number of self-iterations Star(e), or one of the constants Zero (the unit of Plus) and One (the unit of Comp). At a higher level, the above defines Exp<A> as the smallest algebraic structure that is equipped with two constants, contains all elements of type A, and is closed under two binary operations and one unary operation. Even more abstractly, Exp<A> can be viewed as the initial algebra for the set endofunctor Σ defined on objects by $\Sigma X = 1 + 1 + A + X^2 + X^2 + X$.

2.2 Formal Languages as Codatatype

We define the set of formal languages parametric in an alphabet A as a coinductive codatatype:

```
codatatype Lang<!A> = Alpha(eps: bool, delta: A -> Lang<A>)
```

Note that we used Dafny's type-parameter mode !, which indicates that there could be strictly more values of type Lang<A> than values of type A, for any type A, and that there is no subtype relation between Lang<A> and Lang<B>, for any two types A, B. A more detailed explanation of the topic is available at [35].

To some, our way of modelling formal languages might seem odd at first sight. Typically, a formal language is defined intrinsically, as a set of finite sequences, that is, an element of type $\mathcal{P}(A^*)$ or iset<seq<A>> in Dafny. In our approach, we instead treat languages extrinsically, in terms of their universal property: it is well known that iset<seq<A>> forms the greatest abstract coalgebraic structure S that is equipped with functions eps: S -> bool and delta: S -> (A -> S). Indeed, for any set U of finite sequences, we can verify whether U contains the empty sequence, U.eps == ([] in U), and for any a: A we can transition to derivative U.delta(a) == (iset s | [a] + s in U). In the language of Coalgebra, Lang<!A> can be modelled as the final coalgebra for the set endofunctor B defined on objects by $BX = 2 \times X^A$ [44]. Coalgebras for the functor B correspond precisely to unpointed deterministic automata, and the final object among them provides a universal semantic domain for their behaviour.

We choose the more abstract perspective on formal languages as it hides irrelevant specifics and thus allows us to write more elegant proofs. With this decision, we follow a coalgebraic characterisation of formal languages in Isabelle [47], but depart from e.g. previous formalisations in Coq [38].

2.3 An Algebra of Formal Languages

If one thinks of a formal language as a set of finite sequences, one will soon realise that languages admit quite a bit of algebraic structure. In fact, it becomes clear that formal languages can be equipped with the same type of algebraic structure as regular expressions.

First, there exists the empty language `Zero()` that contains no words at all. Under the view above, we find `Zero().eps == false` since the empty set does not contain the empty sequence, and `Zero().delta(a) == Zero()`, since the derivative `iset s | [a] + s in iset{}` with respect to any `a: A` yields again the empty set. We thus define:

```
function Zero<A>(): Lang {
  Alpha(false, (a: A) => Zero())
}
```

Using similar reasoning, we additionally formalise i) the language `One()` that contains only the empty sequence; ii) for any `a: A` the language `Singleton(a)` that consists of only the word `[a]`; iii) the language `Plus(L1, L2)` which consists of the union of the languages `L1` and `L2`; iv) the language `Comp(L1, L2)` that consists of all possible concatenation of words in `L1` and `L2`; and v) the language `Star(L)` that consists of all finite compositions of `L` with itself. Our definitions match what is well-known as *Brzozowski derivatives* [13]:

```
function One<A>(): Lang {
  Alpha(true, (a: A) => Zero())
}

function Singleton<A(==)>(a: A): Lang {
  Alpha(false, (b: A) => if a == b then One() else Zero())
}

function {:abstemious} Plus<A>(L1: Lang, L2: Lang): Lang {
  Alpha(L1.eps || L2.eps, (a: A) => Plus(L1.delta(a), L2.delta(a)))
}

function {:abstemious} Comp<A>(L1: Lang, L2: Lang): Lang {
  Alpha(L1.eps && L2.eps,
      (a: A) => Plus(Comp(L1.delta(a), L2),
                     Comp(if L1.eps then One() else Zero(), L2.delta(a))))
}

function Star<A>(L: Lang): Lang {
  Alpha(true, (a: A) => Comp(L.delta(a), Star(L)))
}
```

Note the use of the equality-supporting type parameter `==` in the definition of `Singleton`, which restricts the use of the function to types `A` that are known to support run-time equality comparisons (all types support equality in static contexts). In this case, the restriction is needed to ensure the well-definedness of the expression `a == b` in the definition of `Singleton`.

Also note that the `{:abstemious}` attribute above signals that a function does not need to unfold a codatatype instance very far (perhaps just one destructor call) to prove a relevant property. Knowing this is the case can aid in proofs of

$$\Sigma(\text{Exp}) \xdashrightarrow{\Sigma(\text{Denotational})} \Sigma(\text{Lang})$$
$$\downarrow \qquad\qquad \downarrow [\text{Zero,One,Singleton,Plus,Comp,Star}]$$
$$\text{Exp} \xdashrightarrow{\text{Denotational}} \text{Lang}$$

$$\text{Exp} \xdashrightarrow{\text{Operational}} \text{Lang}$$
$$\downarrow \langle \text{Eps,Delta} \rangle \qquad\qquad \downarrow$$
$$B(\text{Exp}) \xdashrightarrow{B(\text{Operational})} B(\text{Lang})$$

Fig. 3. Denotational and Operational as induced unique Σ-algebra and B-coalgebra homomorphisms, respectively.

the properties of the function. In this case, it is needed to convince Dafny that the corecursive calls in Comp and Star are logically consistent.

In the language of Coalgebra, the above is best described by us equipping Lang with an algebra structure for the functor Σ. To derive a function such as e.g. Comp above, one gives the product (Lang, Lang) an appropriate B-coalgebra structure and deduces a unique morphism (Lang, Lang) -> Lang from the finality of Lang as B-coalgebra [44].

2.4 Denotational Semantics as Induced Morphism

The denotational semantics of regular expressions can now be defined through induction, as a function Denotational: Exp -> Lang, by making use of the operations on languages we have just defined in Sect. 2.3. For the sake of clarity, we encapsulate those in a module named Languages:

```
function Denotational<A(==)>(e: Exp): Lang {
  match e
  case Zero => Languages.Zero()
  case One => Languages.One()
  case Char(a) => Languages.Singleton(a)
  case Plus(e1, e2) => Languages.Plus(Denotational(e1), Denotational(e2))
  case Comp(e1, e2) => Languages.Comp(Denotational(e1), Denotational(e2))
  case Star(e1) => Languages.Star(Denotational(e1))
}
```

The high-level view through the lenses of Coalgebra is depicted in Fig. 3. By the initiality of Exp as algebra for Σ, there exists a unique morphism Denotational: Exp -> Lang that commutes with the algebraic structures (we formally prove the latter in Dafny in Sect. 2.6).

2.5 Bisimilarity and Coinduction

Let us briefly recall the notion of bisimilarity of formal languages. A binary relation R between languages is called *bisimulation*, if for any two languages L1, L2 related by R the following holds: i) L1 contains the empty word iff L2 does; and ii) for any a: A, the derivatives L1.delta(a) and L2.delta(a) are again related by R. As it turns out, the union of two bisimulations is again a bisimulation. In consequence, one can combine all possible bisimulations into a single relation: the *greatest* bisimulation. Two languages are called bisimilar if they are related by this greatest bisimulation. In Dafny, we can formalise the latter as follows:

```
greatest predicate Bisimilar<A(!new)>[nat](L1: Lang, L2: Lang) {
  && (L1.eps == L2.eps)
  && (forall a :: Bisimilar(L1.delta(a), L2.delta(a)))
}
```

Note that we used Dafny's type-parameter mode !new, which restricts the use of Bisimilar to values of type A that are not heap-based. This is necessary since a forall expression involved in a greatest predicate definition is not allowed to depend on the set of allocated references.

Two languages that are equal are also bisimilar, but the reverse is not necessarily true, since there is no extensional equality for functions in Dafny.

It is instructive to think of a greatest predicate as pure syntactic sugar. Indeed, under the hood, Dafny's compiler uses the body above to implicitly generate i) for any k: nat, a *prefix predicate* Bisimilar#[k](L1, L2) that signifies that the languages L1 and L2 concur on the first k-unrollings of the definition above; and ii) a predicate Bisimilar(L1, L2) that is true iff Bisimilar#[k](L1, L2) is true for all k: nat:

```
/* Pseudo code for illustration purposes */

predicate Bisimilar#<A(!new)>[k: nat](L1: Lang, L2: Lang)
  decreases k
{
  if k == 0 then
    true
  else
    && (L1.eps == L2.eps)
    && (forall a :: Bisimilar#[k-1](L1.delta(a), L2.delta(a)))
}

predicate Bisimilar<A(!new)>(L1: Lang, L2: Lang) {
  forall k: nat :: Bisimilar#[k](L1, L2)
}
```

Note the use of the decreases clause in the definition of Bisimilar#[k](L1, L2). Dafny requires us to convince it that all functions terminate. A decreases clause is used to support the proof of termination of a function in the presence of recursion. At each recursive call to a function, Dafny checks that the decreases clause is strictly smaller than the one of its caller with respect to a built-in well-founded order. In this case, Dafny verifies the inequality k-1 < k with respect to the natural well-founded order < of nat.

Now that we have its definition in place, let us establish a property about bisimilarity, say, that it is a reflexive relation. With the greatest lemma construct, Dafny is able to derive a proof completely on its own:

```
greatest lemma BisimilarityIsReflexive<A(!new)>[nat](L: Lang)
  ensures Bisimilar(L, L)
{}
```

Once again, it is instructive to think of a greatest lemma as pure syntactic sugar. Under the hood, Dafny's compiler uses the body of BisimilarityIsReflexive above to generate i) for any k: nat, a *prefix lemma* BisimilarityIsReflexive#[k](L) that ensures that the prefix predicate Bisimilar#[k](L, L) is satisfied; and ii) a lemma

`BisimilarityIsReflexive(L)` that ensures that `Bisimilar(L, L)` is true by calling `BisimilarityIsReflexive#[k](L, L)` for all `k: nat`:

```
/* Pseudo code for illustration purposes */

lemma BisimilarityIsReflexive#<A(!new)>[k: nat](L: Lang)
  ensures Bisimilar#[k](L, L)
  decreases k
{
  if k == 0 {
  } else {
    forall a ensures Bisimilar#[k-1](L.delta(a), L.delta(a)) {
      BisimilarityIsReflexive#[k-1](L.delta(a));
    }
  }
}

lemma BisimilarityIsReflexive<A(!new)>(L: Lang)
  ensures Bisimilar(L, L)
{
  forall k: nat ensures Bisimilar#[k](L, L) {
    BisimilarityIsReflexive#[k](L);
  }
}
```

We refer the reader interested in further details about Dafny's take on coinduction, predicates, and ordinals to [37].

2.6   Denotational Semantics as Algebra Homomorphism

In this section, we are interested in homomorphisms of type `f: Exp -> Lang` (more precisely, in `Denotational`), that is, functions which commute, up to bisimilarity, with the algebra structures we encountered in Sect. 2.1 and Sect. 2.3, respectively. In Dafny, we call such functions simply algebra homomorphisms. We define pointwise commutativity by comparing languages for bisimilarity:

```
ghost predicate IsAlgebraHomomorphism<A(!new)>(f: Exp -> Lang) {
  forall e :: IsAlgebraHomomorphismPointwise(f, e)
}

ghost predicate IsAlgebraHomomorphismPointwise<A(!new)>
  (f: Exp -> Lang, e: Exp) {
  Bisimilar<A>(
    f(e),
    match e
    case Zero => Languages.Zero()
    case One => Languages.One()
    case Char(a) => Languages.Singleton(a)
    case Plus(e1, e2) => Languages.Plus(f(e1), f(e2))
    case Comp(e1, e2) => Languages.Comp(f(e1), f(e2))
    case Star(e1) => Languages.Star(f(e1))
  )
}
```

Note that we used the `ghost` modifier (which signals that an entity is meant for specification only, not for compilation). A `greatest predicate` is always implicitly `ghost`, so `IsAlgebraHomomorphismPointwise` must be declared `ghost` to call `Bisimilar`, and `IsAlgebraHomomorphism` must be declared `ghost` to call `IsAlgebraHomomorphismPointwise`.

The proof that `Denotational` is an algebra homomorphism is straightforward; it essentially follows from bisimilarity being reflexive:

```
lemma DenotationalIsAlgebraHomomorphism<A(!new)>()
  ensures IsAlgebraHomomorphism<A>(Denotational)
{
  forall e ensures IsAlgebraHomomorphismPointwise<A>(Denotational, e) {
    BisimilarityIsReflexive<A>(Denotational(e));
  }
}
```

3 Operational Semantics

In this section, we provide an alternative perspective on the semantics of regular expressions. In Dafny, we equip the set of regular expressions with a coalgebraic structure of the type of unpointed deterministic automata, formalise its *operational* semantics as a function from regular expressions to formal languages, and prove that the latter is a coalgebra homomorphism.

3.1 A Coalgebra of Regular Expressions

In Sect. 2.3 we equipped the set of formal languages with an algebraic structure that resembled the one of regular expressions. Now, we are aiming for the dual: we would like to equip the set of regular expressions with a coalgebraic structure that resembles the one of formal languages. More concretely, we would like to turn the set of regular expressions into a B-coalgebra, that is, a deterministic automaton (without initial state) in which a state `e` is i) accepting iff `Eps(e) == true` and ii) transitions to a state `Delta(e)(a)` if given the input `a: A`. Note how our definitions resemble the Brzozowski derivatives:

```
function Eps<A>(e: Exp): bool {
  match e
  case Zero => false
  case One => true
  case Char(a) => false
  case Plus(e1, e2) => Eps(e1) || Eps(e2)
  case Comp(e1, e2) => Eps(e1) && Eps(e2)
  case Star(e1) => true
}

function Delta<A(==)>(e: Exp): A -> Exp {
  (a: A) =>
    match e
    case Zero => Zero
    case One => Zero
    case Char(b) => if a == b then One else Zero
    case Plus(e1, e2) => Plus(Delta(e1)(a), Delta(e2)(a))
    case Comp(e1, e2) =>
      Plus(Comp(Delta(e1)(a), e2), Comp(if Eps(e1) then One else Zero, Delta(e2)(a)))
    case Star(e1) => Comp(Delta(e1)(a), Star(e1))
}
```

3.2   Operational Semantics as Induced Morphism

The operational semantics of regular expressions can now in Dafny be defined via coinduction, as a function `Operational: Exp -> Lang`, by making use of the coalgebraic structure on expressions for the functor B we have just defined in Sect. 3.1:

```
function Operational<A(==)>(e: Exp): Lang {
  Alpha(Eps(e), (a: A) => Operational(Delta(e)(a)))
}
```

The high-level view through the lenses of Coalgebra is depicted in Fig. 3. By the finality of `Lang` as B-coalgebra, there exists a unique morphism `Operational: Exp -> Lang` that commutes with the B-coalgebra structures (the latter is formally proven in Dafny in Sect. 3.3).

3.3   Operational Semantics as Coalgebra Homomorphism

In Sect. 2.6 we defined in Dafny algebra homomorphisms as functions of type `Exp -> Lang` that commute, up to bisimilarity, with the Σ-algebra structures of regular expressions and formal languages, respectively. Analogously, we now define a function of the same type as coalgebra homomorphism, if it commutes, up to pointwise bisimilarity, with the B-coalgebra structures of regular expressions and formal languages, respectively:

```
ghost predicate IsCoalgebraHomomorphism<A(!new)>(f: Exp -> Lang) {
  && (forall e :: f(e).eps == Eps(e))
  && (forall e, a :: Bisimilar(f(e).delta(a), f(Delta(e)(a))))
}
```

It is straightforward to formally prove that `Operational` is a coalgebra homomorphism in the above sense: once again, the central argument is that bisimilarity is a reflexive relation.

```
lemma OperationalIsCoalgebraHomomorphism<A(!new)>()
  ensures IsCoalgebraHomomorphism<A>(Operational)
{
  forall e, a ensures Bisimilar<A>(Operational(e).delta(a), Operational(Delta(e)(a))) {
    BisimilarityIsReflexive(Operational(e).delta(a));
  }
}
```

4   Well-Behaved Semantics

So far, we have seen two dual approaches for assigning formal language semantics to regular expressions:

- `Denotational`: an algebra homomorphism obtained via induction
- `Operational`: a coalgebra homomorphism obtained via coinduction

Next, we show in Dafny that the denotational and operational semantics of regular expressions are *well-behaved* (a term we adapt from [49]): they constitute two sides of the same coin. First, we show that `Denotational` is also a coalgebra homomorphism, and that coalgebra homomorphisms are unique up to bisimilarity. We then deduce from the former that `Denotational` and `Operational` coincide pointwise, up to bisimilarity. Finally, we show that `Operational` is also an algebra homomorphism.

4.1   Denotational Semantics as Coalgebra Homomorphism

In this section, we establish that `Denotational` not only commutes with the algebraic structures of regular expressions and formal languages but also with their coalgebraic structures:

```
lemma DenotationalIsCoalgebraHomomorphism<A(!new)>()
  ensures IsCoalgebraHomomorphism<A>(Denotational)
```

The proof of the lemma is a bit more elaborate than the ones we have encountered so far. It can be divided into two subproofs, both of which make use of induction. One of the subproofs is straightforward, the other, more difficult one, again uses the reflexivity of bisimilarity, but also that the latter is a congruence relation with respect to `Plus` and `Comp`:

```
greatest lemma PlusCongruence<A(!new)>[nat]
  (L1a: Lang, L1b: Lang, L2a: Lang, L2b: Lang)
  requires Bisimilar(L1a, L1b)
  requires Bisimilar(L2a, L2b)
  ensures Bisimilar(Plus(L1a, L2a), Plus(L1b, L2b))
{}

lemma CompCongruence<A(!new)>(L1a: Lang, L1b: Lang, L2a: Lang, L2b: Lang)
  requires Bisimilar(L1a, L1b)
  requires Bisimilar(L2a, L2b)
  ensures Bisimilar(Comp(L1a, L2a), Comp(L1b, L2b))
```

Dafny is able to prove `PlusCongruence` on its own, as it can take advantage of the syntactic sugaring of the **greatest lemma** construct. For `CompCongruence` we have to put in a bit of manual work ourselves.

4.2   Coalgebra Homomorphisms Are Unique

The aim of this section is to show in Dafny that, up to pointwise bisimilarity, there only exists one coalgebra homomorphism of type `Exp -> Lang`:

```
lemma UniqueCoalgebraHomomorphism<A(!new)>(f: Exp -> Lang, g: Exp -> Lang, e: Exp)
  requires IsCoalgebraHomomorphism(f)
  requires IsCoalgebraHomomorphism(g)
  ensures Bisimilar(f(e), g(e))
```

Of course, the perspective of Coalgebra suggests that the statement may in fact be strengthened to: for *any* coalgebra C there exists exactly one coalgebra homomorphism of type `C -> Lang`, up to pointwise bisimilarity. For our purposes, the weaker statement above will be sufficient. At the heart of the proof lies the observation that bisimilarity is transitive:

```
greatest lemma BisimilarityIsTransitive<A(!new)>[nat](L1: Lang, L2: Lang, L3: Lang)
  requires Bisimilar(L1, L2) && Bisimilar(L2, L3)
  ensures Bisimilar(L1, L3)
{}
```

In fact, in practice, we actually use a slightly more fine-grained formalisation, as is illustrated below by the call to `BisimilarityIsTransitivePointwise` in the proof of `UniqueCoalgebraHomomorphismHelperPointwise`, which in turn is used to prove `UniqueCoalgebraHomomorphism`:

```
lemma UniqueCoalgebraHomomorphismHelperPointwise<A(!new)>
  (k: nat, f: Exp -> Lang, g: Exp -> Lang, L1: Lang, L2: Lang)
  requires IsCoalgebraHomomorphism(f)
  requires IsCoalgebraHomomorphism(g)
  requires exists e :: Bisimilar#[k](L1, f(e)) && Bisimilar#[k](L2, g(e))
  ensures Bisimilar#[k](L1, L2)
{
  var e :| Bisimilar#[k](L1, f(e)) && Bisimilar#[k](L2, g(e));
  if k != 0 {
    forall a ensures Bisimilar#[k-1](L1.delta(a), L2.delta(a)) {
      BisimilarityIsTransitivePointwise(
        k-1, L1.delta(a),  f(e).delta(a), f(Delta(e)(a))
      );
      BisimilarityIsTransitivePointwise(
        k-1, L2.delta(a),  g(e).delta(a), g(Delta(e)(a))
      );
      UniqueCoalgebraHomomorphismHelperPointwise(
        k-1, f, g, L1.delta(a), L2.delta(a)
      );
    }
}}
```

```
lemma BisimilarityIsTransitivePointwise<A(!new)>(k: nat, L1: Lang, L2: Lang, L3: Lang)
  ensures Bisimilar#[k](L1, L2) && Bisimilar#[k](L2, L3) ==> Bisimilar#[k](L1, L3)
{
  if k != 0 {
    if Bisimilar#[k](L1, L2) && Bisimilar#[k](L2, L3) {
      assert Bisimilar#[k](L1, L3) by {
        forall a ensures Bisimilar#[k-1](L1.delta(a), L3.delta(a)) {
          BisimilarityIsTransitivePointwise(k-1, L1.delta(a), L2.delta(a), L3.delta(a));
        }
}}}}
```

Note the use of Dafny's let-such-that assignment `:|` in the body of the lemma `UniqueCoalgebraHomomorphismHelperPointwise`. For any predicate `P`, the expression `x :| P(x)` assigns a value to `x` such that `P(x)` is true. The predicate `P` needs to be non-empty, but in a ghost context doesn't have to constrain `x` uniquely: the choice of the latter is non-deterministic. To be compilable, the value of a let-such-that expression must be uniquely determined, however. In this case, the precondition of the lemma guarantees that the predicate is non-empty. For further background, we refer the reader to the Dafny Power User note [34].

4.3 Denotational and Operational Semantics Are Bisimilar

From the previous results, we can immediately deduce our main claim that denotational and operational semantics coincide, up to pointwise bisimilarity:

$$\begin{array}{ccc}
\Sigma(\mathbf{Exp}) & \xrightarrow{\ \ \Sigma(\text{Denotational}\cong\text{Denotational})\ \ } & \Sigma(\mathbf{Lang}) \\
\downarrow & & \downarrow{\scriptstyle[\text{Zero,One,Singleton,Star,Plus,Comp}]} \\
\mathbf{Exp} & \xrightarrow{\ \ \text{Denotational}\cong\text{Operational}\ \ } & \mathbf{Lang} \\
{\scriptstyle\langle\text{Eps,Delta}\rangle}\downarrow & & \downarrow \\
B(\mathbf{Exp}) & \xrightarrow{\ \ B(\text{Denotational}\cong\text{Operational})\ \ } & B(\mathbf{Lang})
\end{array}$$

Fig. 4. The `Denotational` and `Operational` semantics of regular expressions are well-behaved.

```
lemma OperationalAndDenotationalAreBisimilar<A(!new)>(e: Exp)
  ensures Bisimilar<A>(Operational(e), Denotational(e))
{
  OperationalIsCoalgebraHomomorphism<A>();
  DenotationalIsCoalgebraHomomorphism<A>();
  UniqueCoalgebraHomomorphism<A>(Operational, Denotational, e);
}
```

4.4   Operational Semantics as Algebra Homomorphism

As a bonus, for the sake of symmetry, let us also prove that `Operational` is an algebra homomorphism. (We already know that it is a coalgebra homomorphism, and that `Denotational` is both an algebra and coalgebra homomorphism.)

```
lemma OperationalIsAlgebraHomomorphism<A(!new)>()
  ensures IsAlgebraHomomorphism<A>(Operational)
```

The idea of the proof is to take advantage of `Denotational` being an algebra homomorphism, by translating its properties to `Operational` via the lemma in Sect. 4.3. The relevant new statements capture that bisimilarity is symmetric and a congruence with respect to the `Star` operation:

```
greatest lemma BisimilarityIsSymmetric<A(!new)>[nat](L1: Lang, L2: Lang)
  ensures Bisimilar(L1, L2) ==> Bisimilar(L2, L1)
  ensures Bisimilar(L1, L2) <== Bisimilar(L2, L1)
{}

lemma StarCongruence<A(!new)>(L1: Lang, L2: Lang)
  requires Bisimilar(L1, L2)
  ensures Bisimilar(Star(L1), Star(L2))
```

The full picture is depicted in Fig. 4: `Denotational` is induced by the initiality of `Exp` and `Operational` is induced by the finality of `Lang`. By uniqueness, the two homomorphisms coincide, up to pointwise bisimilarity – the semantics of regular expressions are well-behaved.

5   Discussion and Related Work

We have used Dafny's built-in inductive and coinductive reasoning capabilities to define the denotational and operational semantics of regular expressions and to prove that they are well-behaved. The concept of well-behaved semantics, in the context of bialgebras (which consist of an algebra and a coalgebra over the same carrier that interact with each other in a suitable way), goes back to Turi and Plotkin [49] and was adapted by Jacobs to the case of regular expressions [23]. The bialgebraic perspective on regular expressions can be thought of as a generalisation of the classical automata-theoretic construction from Brzozowski in the 1960s [13]. A more modern presentation can be found in e.g. [45]. The coalgebraic aspects build on results by Rutten [44], Gumm [19], and others [24]. As our presentation focused on the most important and high-level aspects of the proofs in Dafny, we invite the interested reader to take a look at the full Dafny source code [51].

The work closest to ours in spirit is [47], in which the authors use Isabelle [41], an LCF-style interactive theorem prover, to prove that formal languages represented as a coinductively defined trie satisfy the axioms of *Kleene Algebra* (KA) [26]. As for the differences, the authors of [47] don't touch on the aspect of well-behaved semantics, and we leave a formal proof of the axioms of KA in Dafny as future work. For the latter, because of the interplay between algebraic and coalgebraic structures, we plan to employ so-called up-to-techniques [43], which allow for compact coinductive proofs by making use of the underlying algebraic structure. Further related to this paper and [47] are [11,12], in which the implementation of corecursion in Isabelle is discussed.

We depart from other work [30,38,42], which models formal languages intrinsically, as sets of words, and consequently begins by equipping the set of languages with an appropriate coalgebraic structure, whereas our extrinsic treatment in Dafny essentially axiomatises the latter.

6   Future Work

Besides proving in Dafny the soundness of Kleene Algebra axioms for coalgebraically defined languages, we are mainly interested in adapting our formalisation of the semantics of regular expressions and the proof of their well-behavedness to other theories.

An immediate target is *Kleene Algebra with Tests* (KAT) [27], which extends the theory of regular expressions, Kleene Algebra, with so-called *tests* (elements of a finitely generated Boolean Algebra). KAT can be used to reason about the equivalence of uninterpreted imperative programs, with tests used to model program guards. The theory has been successfully applied to program schematology [6] and has been used to reason about compiler optimizations [29] and cache control [10]. KAT admits both denotational semantics, through so-called guarded string languages, and operational semantics, through so-called automata on guarded strings [28].

There are more natural targets since KAT has been further extended in multiple directions. One such example is *Guarded Kleene Algebra with Tests* (GKAT) [46], an efficiently decidable fragment of KAT that admits operational semantics through strictly deterministic automata on guarded strings [46]. Another example is *NetKAT* [5], which extends KAT with primitives that allow the reasoning about Software Defined Networks. The verification of properties of such networks can be reduced to deciding the equivalence of NetKAT expressions, which in turn relies on their operational semantics [17].

Overall, we hope that the present formalisation both illustrates Dafny's potential for coalgebraic reasoning and serves as a blueprint for further adaption.

Acknowledgments. The authors are thankful to Aaron Tomb and Rustan Leino for their comments on an earlier version of this paper.

Disclosure of Interests. The authors have no competing interests to declare that are relevant to the content of this article.

References

1. AWS encryption SDK for Dafny. https://github.com/aws/aws-encryption-sdk-dafny
2. Dafny blog. https://dafny.org/blog/
3. The dafny programming and verification language. https://dafny.org/
4. Microsoft research. https://www.microsoft.com/en-us/research/
5. Anderson, C.J., et al.: NetKAT: semantic foundations for networks. In: The 41st Annual ACM SIGPLAN-SIGACT Symposium on Principles of Programming Languages, POPL 2014, San Diego, CA, USA, 20–21 January 2014, pp. 113–126. ACM (2014). https://doi.org/10.1145/2535838.2535862
6. Angus, A., Kozen, D.: Kleene algebra with tests and program schematology. Technical report, Cornell University (2002)
7. Ausaf, F., Dyckhoff, R., Urban, C.: POSIX lexing with derivatives of regular expressions (proof pearl). In: Blanchette, J.C., Merz, S. (eds.) ITP 2016. LNCS, vol. 9807, pp. 69–86. Springer, Cham (2016). https://doi.org/10.1007/978-3-319-43144-4_5
8. Barnett, M., Chang, B.-Y.E., DeLine, R., Jacobs, B., Leino, K.R.M.: Boogie: a modular reusable verifier for object-oriented programs. In: de Boer, F.S., Bonsangue, M.M., Graf, S., de Roever, W.-P. (eds.) FMCO 2005. LNCS, vol. 4111, pp. 364–387. Springer, Heidelberg (2006). https://doi.org/10.1007/11804192_17
9. Barnett, M., Fähndrich, M., Leino, K.R.M., Müller, P., Schulte, W., Venter, H.: Specification and verification: the spec# experience. Commun. ACM **54**(6), 81–91 (2011)
10. Barth, A., Kozen, D.: Equational verification of cache blocking in LU decomposition using kleene algebra with tests. Technical report, Cornell University (2002)
11. Blanchette, J.C., Bouzy, A., Lochbihler, A., Popescu, A., Traytel, D.: Friends with benefits: implementing corecursion in foundational proof assistants. In: Yang, H. (ed.) ESOP 2017. LNCS, vol. 10201, pp. 111–140. Springer, Heidelberg (2017). https://doi.org/10.1007/978-3-662-54434-1_5
12. Blanchette, J.C., Popescu, A., Traytel, D.: Foundational extensible corecursion: a proof assistant perspective. In: Proceedings of the 20th ACM SIGPLAN International Conference on Functional Programming, pp. 192–204 (2015)
13. Brzozowski, J.A.: Derivatives of regular expressions. J. ACM (JACM) **11**(4), 481–494 (1964)

14. Cassez, F., Fuller, J., Ghale, M.K., Pearce, D.J., Quiles, H.M.: Formal and executable semantics of the ethereum virtual machine in dafny. In: Chechik, M., Katoen, J.P., Leucker, M. (eds.) FM 2023. LNCS, vol. 14000, pp. 571–583. Springer, Cham (2023). https://doi.org/10.1007/978-3-031-27481-7_32
15. Cohen, E., Dahlweid, M., Hillebrand, M., Leinenbach, D., Moskal, M., Santen, T., Schulte, W., Tobies, S.: VCC: a practical system for verifying concurrent C. In: Berghofer, S., Nipkow, T., Urban, C., Wenzel, M. (eds.) TPHOLs 2009. LNCS, vol. 5674, pp. 23–42. Springer, Heidelberg (2009). https://doi.org/10.1007/978-3-642-03359-9_2
16. de Moura, L., Bjørner, N.: Z3: an efficient SMT solver. In: Ramakrishnan, C.R., Rehof, J. (eds.) TACAS 2008. LNCS, vol. 4963, pp. 337–340. Springer, Heidelberg (2008). https://doi.org/10.1007/978-3-540-78800-3_24
17. Foster, N., Kozen, D., Milano, M., Silva, A., Thompson, L.: A coalgebraic decision procedure for NetKAT. In: Proceedings of the 42nd Annual ACM SIGPLAN-SIGACT Symposium on Principles of Programming Languages, POPL 2015, Mumbai, India, 15–17 January 2015, pp. 343–355. ACM (2015). https://doi.org/10.1145/2676726.2677011
18. Friedl, J.E.F.: Mastering Regular Expressions, 3rd edn. O'Reilly Media, Sebastopol (2006)
19. Gumm, H.P.: Elements of the general theory of coalgebras (2000)
20. Hoare, C.A.R.: An axiomatic basis for computer programming. Commun. ACM 12(10), 576–580 (1969). https://doi.org/10.1145/363235.363259
21. Holzer, M., Kutrib, M.: The complexity of regular(-like) expressions. Int. J. Found. Comput. Sci. 22(7), 1533–1548 (2011). https://doi.org/10.1142/S0129054111008866
22. Hopcroft, J.E., Karp, R.M.: A linear algorithm for testing equivalence of finite automata (1971). https://api.semanticscholar.org/CorpusID:120207847
23. Jacobs, B.: A bialgebraic review of deterministic automata, regular expressions and languages. In: Futatsugi, K., Jouannaud, J.-P., Meseguer, J. (eds.) Algebra, Meaning, and Computation. LNCS, vol. 4060, pp. 375–404. Springer, Heidelberg (2006). https://doi.org/10.1007/11780274_20
24. Jacobs, B., Silva, A., Sokolova, A.: Trace semantics via determinization. In: Pattinson, D., Schröder, L. (eds.) CMCS 2012. LNCS, vol. 7399, pp. 109–129. Springer, Heidelberg (2012). https://doi.org/10.1007/978-3-642-32784-1_7
25. Kleene, S.: Representation of events in nerve nets and finite automata. Autom. Stud. 3 (1951)
26. Kozen, D.: A completeness theorem for Kleene algebras and the algebra of regular events. Inf. Comput. 110(2), 366–390 (1994). https://doi.org/10.1006/INCO.1994.1037
27. Kozen, D.: Kleene algebra with tests. ACM Trans. Program. Lang. Syst. 19(3), 427–443 (1997). https://doi.org/10.1145/256167.256195
28. Kozen, D.: Automata on guarded strings and applications. Technical report, Cornell University (2001)
29. Kozen, D., Patron, M.-C.: Certification of compiler optimizations using Kleene algebra with tests. In: Lloyd, J., et al. (eds.) CL 2000. LNCS (LNAI), vol. 1861, pp. 568–582. Springer, Heidelberg (2000). https://doi.org/10.1007/3-540-44957-4_38
30. Krauss, A., Nipkow, T.: Proof pearl: regular expression equivalence and relation algebra. J. Autom. Reason. 49(1), 95–106 (2012). https://doi.org/10.1007/S10817-011-9223-4

31. Leino, K.R.M.: Dafny power user. https://leino.science/dafny-power-user/
32. Leino, K.R.M.: Dafny: an automatic program verifier for functional correctness. In: Clarke, E.M., Voronkov, A. (eds.) LPAR 2010. LNCS, vol. 6355, pp. 348–370. Springer, Cham (2010). https://doi.org/10.1007/978-3-642-17511-4_20
33. Leino, K.R.M.: Type-parameter completion (2019). https://leino.science/papers/krml270.html
34. Leino, K.R.M.: Iterating over a collection (2020). https://leino.science/papers/krml275.html
35. Leino, K.R.M.: Type-parameter modes: variance and cardinality preservation (2021). https://leino.science/papers/krml280.html
36. Leino, K.R.M.: Program Proofs. MIT Press, Cambridge (2023)
37. Leino, K.R.M., Tristan, J.B.: Working with coinduction, extreme predicates, and ordinals (2023). https://leino.science/papers/krml285.html
38. Moreira, N., Pereira, D., de Sousa, S.M.: Deciding Kleene algebra terms equivalence in coq. J. Log. Algebraic Methods Program. **84**(3), 377–401 (2015)
39. Noble, J., Streader, D., Gariano, I.O., Samarakoon, M.: More programming than programming: teaching formal methods in a software engineering programme. In: Deshmukh, J.V., Havelund, K., Perez, I. (eds.) NFM 2022. LNCS, vol. 13260, pp. 431–450. Springer, Cham (2022). https://doi.org/10.1007/978-3-031-06773-0_23
40. Owens, S., Reppy, J.H., Turon, A.: Regular-expression derivatives re-examined. J. Funct. Program. **19**(2), 173–190 (2009). https://doi.org/10.1017/S0956796808007090
41. Paulson, L.C.: Isabelle: The next seven hundred theorem provers. In: Lusk, E., Overbeek, R. (eds.) CADE 1988. LNCS, vol. 310, pp. 772–773. Springer, Heidelberg (1988). https://doi.org/10.1007/BFB0012891
42. Paulson, L.C.: A formalisation of finite automata using hereditarily finite sets. In: Felty, A.P., Middeldorp, A. (eds.) CADE 2015. LNCS (LNAI), vol. 9195, pp. 231–245. Springer, Cham (2015). https://doi.org/10.1007/978-3-319-21401-6_15
43. Rot, J., Bonsangue, M., Rutten, J.: Coinductive proof techniques for language equivalence. In: Dediu, A.-H., Martín-Vide, C., Truthe, B. (eds.) LATA 2013. LNCS, vol. 7810, pp. 480–492. Springer, Heidelberg (2013). https://doi.org/10.1007/978-3-642-37064-9_42
44. Rutten, J.J.M.M.: Universal coalgebra: a theory of systems. Theoret. Comput. Sci. **249**(1), 3–80 (2000). https://doi.org/10.1016/S0304-3975(00)00056-6
45. Silva, A.: Kleene coalgebra. Ph.D. thesis, University of Nijmegen (2010)
46. Smolka, S., Foster, N., Hsu, J., Kappé, T., Kozen, D., Silva, A.: Guarded Kleene algebra with tests: verification of uninterpreted programs in nearly linear time. Proc. ACM Program. Lang. **4**(POPL), 61:1–61:28 (2020). https://doi.org/10.1145/3371129
47. Traytel, D.: Formal languages, formally and coinductively. Log. Methods Comput. Sci. **13** (2017)
48. Tristan, J.B., Leino, K.R.M.: AWS dafny training. https://dafny.org/teaching-material/
49. Turi, D., Plotkin, G.D.: Towards a mathematical operational semantics. In: Proceedings, 12th Annual IEEE Symposium on Logic in Computer Science, Warsaw, Poland, 29 June–2 July 1997. pp. 280–291. IEEE Computer Society (1997). https://doi.org/10.1109/LICS.1997.614955

50. Yang, Z., Wang, W., Casas, J., Cocchini, P., Yang, J.: Towards a correct-by-construction FHE model. Cryptology ePrint Archive (2023)
51. Zetzsche, S., Różowski, W.: Well-behaved (co)algebraic semantics of regular expressions in dafny (2024). https://dafny.org/blog/assets/src/semantics-of-regular-expressions/Archive.zip

Jump Complexity of Deterministic Finite Automata with Translucent Letters

Szilárd Zsolt Fazekas[1]([✉]), Victor Mitrana[2], Andrei Păun[3,4],
and Mihaela Păun[3,4]

[1] Akita University, Akita, Japan
szilard.fazekas@ie.akita-u.ac.jp
[2] Universidad Politecnica de Madrid, Madrid, Spain
victor.mitrana@upm.es
[3] National Institute of Research and Development for Biological Sciences,
Bucharest, Romania
{andrei.paun,mihaela.paun}@incdsb.ro
[4] University of Bucharest, Bucharest, Romania

Abstract. We investigate a dynamical complexity measure defined for finite automata with translucent letters (FAwtl). Roughly, this measure counts the minimal number of necessary jumps for such an automaton in order to accept an input. The model considered here is the deterministic finite automaton with translucent letters (DFAwtl). Unlike in the case of the nondeterministic variant, the function describing the jump complexity of any DFAwtl is either bounded by a constant or it is linear. We give a polynomial-time algorithm for deciding whether the jump complexity of a DFAwtl is constant-bounded or linear and we prove that the equivalence problem for DFAwtl of $\mathcal{O}(1)$ jump complexity is decidable. We also consider another fundamental problem for extensions of finite automata models, deciding whether the language accepted by a FAwtl is regular. We give a positive partial answer for DFAwtl over the binary alphabet, in contrast with the case of NFAwtl, where the problem is undecidable.

1 Introduction

The finite automaton is a cornerstone of theoretical computer science, providing a fundamental model for understanding regular languages. Over the years, various extensions of finite automata have been proposed to increase their expressive power and applicability in various areas. Some of those extensions attempted to introduce a non-sequential processing of the inputs, where read letters are consumed from the tape, and the automaton is allowed to jump over certain parts of

This study was supported by PNRR/2022/C9/MCID/I8 project 760096. It was also performed through the Core Program within the National Research, Development and Innovation Plan 2022-2027, carried out with the support of MRID, project no. 23020101(SIA-PRO), contract no 7N/2022, and project no. 23020301(SAFE-MAPS), contract no 7N/2022. The first author was supported by JSPS KAKENHI Grant Number 23K10976.

the input or shift the remaining input word. These latter types of models include the input-revolving automaton [2], the jumping automaton [9] or the one-way [4] and two-way jumping automaton [7].

The Finite Automaton with Translucent Letters (FAwtl) [11] is such an extension of classical finite automata (FA). The FAwtl introduces the concept of translucency, allowing certain input symbols to be skipped over in particular states. Translucent letters in FAwtl enable the automaton to "ignore" certain symbols in specified states, effectively jumping to the next non-translucent symbol. This feature extends the classical finite automata model by introducing a controlled form of non-sequential input reading and it enhances the computational power of FAwtl, enabling them to recognize patterns that are beyond the reach of traditional FA, while inheriting many good algorithmic properties from them. A recent survey by Otto [12] provides a detailed picture of variants of the model and their computational power and closure properties.

The jump complexity of a FAwtl refers to the number of jumps required during the processing of an input string in the worst case, for each length. Understanding this complexity seems crucial for evaluating the computational efficiency and language recognition power of FAwtl, as well as related models, like the one-way jumping FA [4]. This paper explores the jump complexity of deterministic FAwtl and its implications for the decidability of language equivalence.

In the broader context of automata theory, the study of jump complexity aligns with ongoing research into non-regular complexity measures for models such as extended automata over groups [1] (group memory operations), one-way jumping automata [5,6] (jump and sweep complexity), and even context-free grammars (number of applications of non-regular rules), or push-down automata [3] (number of push operations). The study of the complexity classes defined through those models sharpens the picture of how complicated languages are at the lower end of the computational complexity hierarchies and, in particular, seeks to understand the threshold in the amount of non-regular resources to cross the boundary between regular and non-regular language classes.

The notion of jump complexity for nondeterministic FAwtl (NFAwtl) has been recently investigated [10], establishing a detailed hierarchy of separable complexity classes $\mathcal{O}(1)$, $\mathcal{O}(\log n)$, $\mathcal{O}(\sqrt{n})$ and $\mathcal{O}(n)$. It was shown that NFAwtl with $\mathcal{O}(1)$ jump complexity accept regular languages, directly implying the same conclusion for deterministic FAwtl (DFAwtl). This provides a sufficient condition for regularity, though it is not a necessary one. Some FAwtl with $\omega(1)$ jump complexity can still recognize regular languages, also opening the possibility to study descriptional complexity tradeoffs versus classical DFA/NFA.

The objective of this paper is to provide a detailed analysis of the jump complexity of DFAwtl. We settle the topic by showing that the complexity hierarchy collapses to the two extremes $\Theta(1)$ and $\Theta(n)$, and we give a polynomial time algorithm that decides for a given DFAwtl which extreme its jump complexity falls into. We also demonstrate the applications of our approach to achieve positive results regarding two of the most fundamental problems in the study of extensions of finite automata: decidability of language equivalence and decidability of regularity.

2   Definitions and Notations

The basic concepts and notations that are to be used throughout the paper are defined in the sequel; the reader may consult [13] for basic concepts that are not defined here.

We will denote by $\mathbb{N}$ the set of natural numbers starting from 1 and $\mathbb{N}_0 = \mathbb{N} \cup \{0\}$. For all $i, j \in \mathbb{N}_0$ with $i \leq j$, we denote the closed interval between i and j by $[i, j] = \{i, \ldots, j\}$. For succinctness we also use $[n] = [0, n]$.

In addition, we use the following concepts and notations:

- $\#(X)$ is the cardinality (number of elements) of the finite set X;
- V^* is the set of all finite words formed by symbols in the alphabet V;
- $|x|$ is the length of word x;
- $|x|_U$ is the length of the word obtained from x by erasing all letters that are not in U; when U is a singleton $\{a\}$, we sometimes write $|x|_a$;
- $\varepsilon \in V^*$ is the empty word, $|\varepsilon| = 0$;
- for $x \in V^*$, $alph(x)$ is the minimal alphabet $U \subseteq V$ such that $x \in U^*$.

A *nondeterministic finite automaton* (NFA) is a quintuple $M = (Q, V, \delta, q_0, F)$, where Q is a finite set of states, V is an alphabet disjoint from Q, δ is a mapping from $Q \times V$ into 2^Q, called the transition mapping, $q_0 \in Q$ is the initial state, and $F \subseteq Q$ is the set of final states.

A configuration of M is a pair in $Q \times V^*$. A transition relation is defined on the set of configurations of M as follows: $(s, ay) \rightarrow (p, y)$ if $p \in \delta(s, a)$, $s, p \in Q$, $a \in V$, $y \in V^*$. The reflexive and transitive closure of the relation $\rightarrow$ is denoted by $\rightarrow^*$. The language accepted by M is $L(M) = \{w \in V^* \mid (q_0, w) \rightarrow^* (s, \varepsilon), s \in F\}$.

M is a *deterministic finite automaton* (DFA) if for each $s \in Q$ and each $a \in V$, there is at most one state in $\delta(s, a)$.

A *nondeterministic finite automaton with translucent letters* (NFAwtl) is an NFA M as above, such that the transition relation is defined in the following way. First, we define the partial relation $\circlearrowleft$ on the set of all configurations of M: $(s, xay) \circlearrowleft (p, xy)$ iff $p \in \delta(s, a)$, and $\delta(s, b)$ is not defined for any $b \in alph(x)$, $s, p \in Q$, $a, b \in V$, $x \in V^+$, $y \in V^*$. We now write

$$(p, x) \models_M (q, y), \text{ if either } (p, x) \rightarrow (q, y) \text{ or } (p, x) \circlearrowleft (q, y).$$

The subscript M is omitted when it is understood from the context.

The language accepted by M is defined by

$$L(M) = \{x \in V^* \mid (q_0, x) \models^* (f, \varepsilon), f \in F\}.$$

It is worth mentioning that the NFAwtl was introduced in [11], with a slightly different definition. Our definition is a variant of an NFAwtl in the normal form

in [11] without a marker for the end of the input word, following the definition
used in the study of jump complexity of NFAwtl [10]. Actually, a more in-depth
discussion is necessary here. The original model allows multiple initial states.
This feature is dropped in our version, and it is not particularly relevant for
us, as our results only tangentially mention the nondeterministic machines. The
translucent function is missing but this can be replaced as follows: (i) no transition is defined for a state and its translucent letters, and (ii) a deadlock state
is defined for any state q and any symbol a that is not in the set of translucent
letters of q and there is no transition for the pair (q, a) in the original automaton.
Furthermore, the original automaton could accept the input without reading all
of it, but this is not possible in our model. In spite of all these differences, we
preferred to keep the original name of the model. An alternative name could be
one-way returning jumping finite automaton, as it resembles features from the
one-way jumping automata model as well. As the model considered here is not
exactly the original NFAwtl, we will make use of results known for the original
NFAwtl only if the result remains valid for our model.

This automaton is also related to the *one way jumping automaton* introduced
in [4] with the difference that after each jump it returns to its previous position
and does not shift the jumped part to the end of the word.

The condition for a finite automaton with translucent letters to be deterministic (DFAwtl) is exactly the same to that for a finite automaton.

To simplify referencing states that jump over certain letters, we introduce
the following terminology. For a DFAwtl $A = (Q, \Sigma, q_0, \delta, F)$ and a non-empty
set of letters $\Gamma \subset \Sigma$, we say that a state $q \in Q$ is Γ-deficient if for each letter
$a \in \Gamma$, the transition $\delta(q, a)$ is undefined. A state is *deficient* if it is Γ-deficient
for some non-empty $\Gamma \subset \Sigma$.

We continue by introducing the complexity measure that is the main focus
of this paper. Let M be an NFAwtl; we consider $w \in L(M)$, and the accepting
computation in M on the input w:

$$C_M(w) : (q_0, w) \models (q_1, w_1) \models (q_2, w_2) \models \ldots \models (q_m, \varepsilon),$$

with $q_i \in Q$, $1 \leq i \leq m$, and $q_m \in F$. We define

$$\varphi(C_M(w)) = \{i \mid (i \geq 1)\&((q_{i-1}, w_{i-1}) \circlearrowright (q_i, w_i))\}.$$

In words, $\varphi(C_M(w))$ contains all the jumping steps in the computation $C_M(w)$.

We now define the *jump complexity* of the computation of M on the word
w by

$$jc_M(w) = \begin{cases} \min\{\#(\varphi(C_M(w))) \mid C_M(w) \text{ is an accepting computation}\} \\ \underline{\text{undefined}}, \text{ if } w \notin L(M). \end{cases}$$

In other words, the jump complexity of an accepted word with respect to M
is computed by taking into consideration the "least non-regular computation",
if there is one. Equivalently, the jump complexity of a word $w \in L(M)$ with
respect to M is the number of jumping steps of an accepting computation of M

on w with the minimal number of jumping steps. If the word is not accepted by the automaton, then its jump complexity is undefined.

The jump complexity of an automaton M as above is a partial mapping from $\mathbb{N}$ to $\mathbb{N}$ defined by

$$JC_M(n) = \max\{jc_M(w)\,|\,|w| = n, w \in L(M)\}.$$

As one can see, the most "non-regular" word of each length in the accepted language is considered. If $L(M)$ does not contain any word of some length n, then $JC_M(n)$ is undefined. It is clear that $JC_M(n) \leq n$, for every NFAwtl M, as one letter is consumed in every step of a computation.

Let f be a function from $\mathbb{N}$ to $\mathbb{N}$; we define the family of languages

$$JCL(f(n)) = \{L \mid \exists \text{ NFAwtl } M \text{ such that } L = L(M) \text{ and}$$
$$JC_M(n) \in \mathcal{O}(f(n))\}.$$

The above definitions naturally apply to DFAwtl, where the least non-regular computation for any input is the only computation performed by the machine on that input.

We start with an example which will be used later. Consider the non-regular language $L = \{w \in \{a, b\}^* \mid |w|_a = |w|_b = n \geq 0\}$. The very simple DFAwtl M, depicted in Fig. 1, accepts this language.

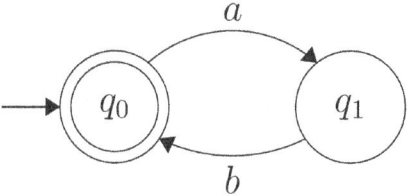

Fig. 1. A DFAwtl accepting L.

Indeed, the automaton accepts the language $L = \{w \in \{a, b\}^* \mid |w|_a = |w|_b = n \geq 0\}$ by the following simple observation. Whenever the automaton is in the initial state, it has to consume an a (no matter if that a is the current symbol or the automaton must do a jump) in order to reach q_1. As q_1 is not a final state, the automaton must consume a b for returning to the initial state, which is also final. Therefore, the number of occurrences of a's and b's must be the same.

On the other hand, it is easy to check that $0 \leq jc_M(w) \leq n$ for any $w \in L$ of length $2n$. As explained above, for going out from and returning to q_0, the automaton consumes an a and a b, with at most one jump. For $jc_M(b^n a^n) = n$, it follows that $JC_M(n)$ is either $n/2$, if n is even, or undefined, otherwise. From here, $L \in JCL(n/2)$ holds.

As the algorithms presented later reference the graph, or digraph of the automata considered, we briefly define that notion. An (unlabeled) digraph is a pair $G = (V, E)$ where V is a finite set of *vertices* and $E \subseteq V \times V$ is a set of ordered pairs of vertices, called *edges* or *arcs*.

3   Results

Theorem 1. *Given a DFAwtl M it is algorithmically decidable whether or not the jump complexity of M is bounded by a constant.*

Proof. Let $M = (Q, V, \delta, q_0, F)$ be a DFAwtl. Without loss of generality we may assume that all the states of M are useful, namely for each state $q \in Q$ there exist $x, y \in V^*$ such that $(q_0, x) \to^* (q, \varepsilon)$ and $(q, y) \to^* (f, \varepsilon)$, with $f \in F$. It is an easy exercise to remove all the useless states exactly as it is done for a finite automaton.

We start with an important remark. Let us consider the following computation in M:

$$(q_0, w_1 w_2) \to^* (q, w_2) \circlearrowright (s, w_2') \models^* (f, \varepsilon),$$

with $f \in F$, and $jc_M(w_1 w_2) = n$, for some n. We deduce that the next computation is also valid in M:

$$(q_0, w_1 a w_2') \to^* (q, a w_{21} w_{22}) \to (s, w_{21} w_{22}) \models^* (f, \varepsilon),$$

where $\delta(q, b) = \emptyset$ for all $b \in alph(w_{21})$, $\delta(q, a) = s$, $w_2' = w_{21} w_{22}$, and $w_2 = w_{21} a w_{22}$. Informally, we moved the letter consumed by M when jumping from q in the former computation as the current symbol in the latter computation. Clearly, $jc_M(w_1 a w_2') = n - 1$ holds. Actually, this fact may be extended such that starting from a given a partial valid computation with n jumps, one can construct a partial valid computation with $n - 1$ jumps.

For each pair $q \in Q, a \in V$ such that $\delta(q, a) = \emptyset$, we construct the set

$$\langle q, a \rangle = \{ s \in Q \mid \text{ there exist } x \in V^+, y \in V^* \text{ such that } (q, x) \to^* (s, \varepsilon) \text{ and}$$
$$(s, ax) \models^* (q, \varepsilon) \}.$$

Claim 1. If there exists a pair (q, a) such that $\delta(q, a) = \emptyset$ and $\langle q, a \rangle \neq \emptyset$, then $JC_M(n)$ is not a constant-bounded function.

Proof of Claim 1. Let $\delta(q, a) = \emptyset$, $\delta(q, b) = s$, and $(s, ax) \to^* (q, \varepsilon)$. Furthermore, let $y, z \in V^*$ such that $(q_0, y) \to^* (q, \varepsilon)$ and $(q, z) \to^* (f, \varepsilon)$, with $f \in F$. We now consider the words

$$w_n = y(abx)^n z,$$

for all $n \geq 1$. Obviously, all these words are accepted by M, and $jc_M(w_n) \geq n$, for all $n \geq 1$. As the automaton is deterministic, these computations are unique for each w_n, which concludes the proof of Claim 1.

Claim 2. If we have a state q and letter a such that the following conditions hold, then $JC(M)$ is not constant-bounded:

- $\delta(q, a) = \emptyset$;
- there is some word x such that $(q, x) \to^* (q, \varepsilon)$;
- for each prefix x' of x, the state $\delta(q, x')$ is a-deficient;

– there are some words y and z (with y not containing a and z possibly empty) such that $(q, yaz) \to^* (f, \varepsilon)$, for some final state f, and for each prefix y' of y, the state $\delta(q, y')$ is a-deficient.

Proof of Claim 2. If those conditions hold, then words of the form uax^nyz are accepted with at least n jumps, so the jump complexity is linear (where u is a word such that $(q_0, u) \to^* (q, \varepsilon)$).

Claim 3. If all the sets $\langle q, a \rangle$ computed above are empty, and the conditions in Claim 2 are not satisfied, then $JC_M(n)$ is a constant-bounded function.

Proof of Claim 3. Assume by contradiction that for any constant c, there exists a word w_c in $L(M)$ such that $jc_M(w_c) > c$, and take c to be the cardinality of Q. By the pigeonhole principle, this means that at least two of the jumps happen in the same state q and that in the transition graph of M there is a cycle starting and ending in q. More formally, if the jump complexity of M is not bounded by any constant, then there must be deficient states q for which there exists some word x with $(q, x) \to^* (q, \varepsilon)$, and any computation with more than $|Q|$ jumps must go through such a state q at least twice. For each such $q \in Q$, $a \in V$ and $x \in V^*$ such that $\delta(q, a) = \emptyset$ and $(q, x) \to^* (q, \varepsilon)$:

– if x contains a, then $\langle q, a \rangle \neq \emptyset$, so the condition of Claim 1 is met;
– if all prefixes x' of x are such that $\delta(q, x')$ is a-deficient, then the conditions of Claim 2 are met.

Now let us assume that the conditions of Claims 1 and 2 do not hold. Furthermore, let q be a state in which at least two jumps are performed during the computation with more than $|Q|$ jumps. When the first jump in state q happens, let us assume that the letter jumped over was a, that is, a was the first letter of the remaining input and q is a-deficient. Depending on when the a that was jumped over was read, we distinguish the following cases:

1. the a was read between the two jumps from q: this means that there is some cycle in q labeled by a word containing a, satisfying the conditions of Claim 1, a contradiction.
2. the a was read after the second jump from q: this means all states visited between the two jumps from q are a-deficient, but that implies the existence of a cycle in q with only a-deficient states in it, satisfying the conditions of Claim 2, again a contradiction.

From the contradictions above we can deduce that the conditions of Claims 1 or 2 are necessary for M to have jump complexity not bounded by any constant, and earlier we have seen that they are sufficient, too, concluding the proof.

By these claims it follows that the algorithm for deciding the stated problem consists in computing all the sets $\langle q, a \rangle$, $q \in Q$, $a \in V$, and checking the existence of reachable cycles that consist of a-deficient states for some a, and from which there is a path to a final state containing at least one a transition. It is straightforward that the checks above are effective, e.g., by a brute force search of the transition graph of M, but as we will see later, one can do them efficiently. □

It is worth mentioning that the conditions for M to have jump complexity not included in $\mathcal{O}(1)$ can be easily checked by using algorithms for searching paths in a directed graph, see, e.g., [8]. More precisely,

Theorem 2. *The complexity of the algorithm in the proof of Theorem 1 is* $\mathcal{O}(\#(Q^3) \cdot \#(V))$, *where Q and V is the set of states and the alphabet of M, respectively.*

Proof. For each pair $q \in Q, a \in V$ such that $\delta(q, a) = \emptyset$, besides the definition of the set $\langle q, a \rangle$, we construct the set

$$[q, a] = \{s \in Q \mid \text{ there exist } x \in V^+, y \in V^* \text{ such that } (q, x) \rightarrow^* (s, \varepsilon) \text{ and}$$
$$(s, ax) \rightarrow^* (q, \varepsilon)\}.$$

Clearly, $[q, a] \subseteq \langle q, a \rangle$, for all pairs (q, a) such that $\delta(q, a) =$. For simplicity, we set $[q, a] = \langle q, a \rangle = \emptyset$, for all pairs (q, a) such that $\delta(q, a) \neq \emptyset$.

Claim 1. All the sets $[q, a]$ are empty if and only if all the sets $\langle q, a \rangle$ are empty.

Proof of Claim 1. It suffices to prove that all the sets $\langle q, a \rangle$ are empty by assuming that all the sets $[q, a]$ are empty. Let us assume that $\delta(q, a) = \emptyset$ and the set $\langle q, a \rangle$ is not empty for some state q and letter a. Let $s \in \langle q, a \rangle$, which means that $\delta(q, b) = s$ and $(s, ax) \models^* (q, \varepsilon)$, for some letter b and string x. We argue about the states in this cycle beginning and ending in q. If $\delta(s, a) \neq \emptyset$, then $s \in [q, a]$, which contradicts $[s, a]$ being empty. If $\delta(s, a) = \emptyset$, then $\langle s, a \rangle \neq \emptyset$ and we try to show that $[s, a] \neq \emptyset$, shifting the argument to the next state in the cycle. If we keep shifting the state in the cycle, eventually we reach the state r from which the last jump is performed before reading a sequentially, that is, $\langle r, a \rangle \neq \emptyset$ and $[r, a] \neq \emptyset$. Such a state r must exist, because the a is read in the cycle, by the definition of $\langle q, a \rangle$, contradicting the assumption that $[r, a]$ is empty (see Fig. 2).

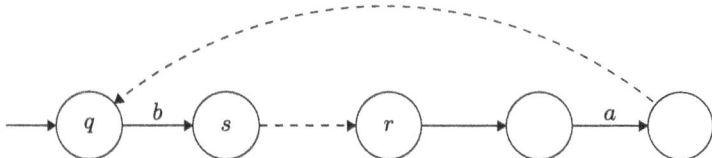

Fig. 2. If $\langle q, a \rangle$ is not empty, then there exists r such that $[r, a]$ is not empty.

We now check the conditions of the Claims 1 and 2 from the previous proof. For checking the condition of Claim 1 in that proof, we actually check the equivalent condition proved in Claim 1 above.

Formally, we consider the unlabeled digraph of the automaton M and construct the transitive closure of this graph. As it is known, see, for instance, the Floyd-Warshall algorithm, this can be done in $\mathcal{O}(\#(Q^3))$. Now, for each pair $(q, a) \in Q \times V$, we construct the following sets:

- $X = \{q_1, q_2, \ldots, q_p\} \subseteq Q$, where each q_i, $1 \le i \le p$, is reachable from q in M in one step. This step requires $\mathcal{O}(\#(Q))$ time.
- $Y = \{r_1, r_2, \ldots, r_m\} \subseteq Q$, where each element of Y is reached from some element of X by reading a. If $q \in Y$, then $\lfloor q, a \rfloor \ne \emptyset$, and the algorithm halts. This step can be accomplished in $\mathcal{O}(\#(Q^2))$ time.

By using the transitive closure computed above, we deduce that $[s, a]$ is empty if and only if s is not reachable from any state in Y. By these explanations regarding each pair $(s, a) \in Q \times V$, the complexity of checking the condition of Claim 1 in the proof of Theorem 1 follows.

If all $\lfloor q, a \rfloor$ sets are empty, we go on to check the conditions of Claim 2 from the previous proof, i.e., for each $a \in V$, whether there exists an a-deficient cycle in a state q reachable from q_0 and from which a final state can be reached while first reading some word y visiting only a-deficient states and then reading at least one a. To check this, for each a, we first restrict the graph to a-deficient vertices and construct its transitive closure. Then, for each state q having a cycle in the restriction, we check whether there is a path from q to an accepting state, such that the path first visits only a-deficient states and then reads an a from a state r. The number of possible candidates for q is $\#(Q)$, the same holds for r, and for each candidate pair q, r we need to check whether q is reachable from q_0 (using the transitive closure), whether r is reachable from q visiting only a-deficient states (using the transitive closure of the restriction), and whether some final state f is reachable from r (one can remove states from which no final state is reachable after the construction of the transitive closure, making this step $O(1)$ at this stage). Altogether, checking the conditions of Claim 2 takes $\mathcal{O}(\#(V)\#(Q)^3)$ time, dominated by constructing the transitive closures for the restrictions. □

Next we show that the previous decision algorithm is, in fact, enough to compute the asymptotic jump complexity of a given DFAwtl, due to the collapsing hierarchy.

Theorem 3. *Let $f : \mathbb{N} \to \mathbb{N}$ be a non-constant-bounded function such that* $\lim_{n \to \infty} \dfrac{f(n)}{n} = 0$. *There is no DFAwtl M such that $JC_M(n) = f(n)$.*

Proof. Assume the contrary, namely let $M = (Q, V, \delta, q_0, F)$ be a DFAwtl such that $JC_M(n) \notin \mathcal{O}(1)$ and $\lim_{n \to \infty} \frac{JC_M(n)}{n} = 0$. We consider a sufficiently large n and let w be a word in $L(M)$ of length n such that $jc_M(w) = JC_M(n)$. For simplicity, we denote $JC_M(n) = m$. The word w can be decomposed into $2m + 1$ subwords, not necessarily nonempty, $x_1, x_2, \ldots, x_{2m+1}$, such that w can be recomposed by

$$w = x_1 \diamond x_2 \diamond x_3 \ldots x_{2m} \diamond x_{2m+1},$$

where each diamond represents either a position in w when a jumping step is to be made or a letter which is consumed in a jumping step, therefore each diamond has to be replaced by either ε or a letter, satisfying the following conditions:

(i) m diamonds are to be replaced by ε and the other m by letters;

(ii) for any prefix, the number of diamonds replaced by letters is at most the number of diamonds replaced by ε.

Assume that the number of states of Q is k. We construct another word w', derived from w, as follows:

(i) Each segment x_i is left unchanged, provided its length is smaller than k, or it is replaced by a word x'_i, of length at most $k-1$ with the property that if $q \in Q$ is the current state when x_i is to be read, $\delta(q, x_i) = \delta(q, x'_i)$, without any jump. Clearly, this can be done by removing all the cycles of the path $\delta(q, x_i)$.
(ii) The letters inserted for reconstructing w as above are inserted at the same positions for the construction of w'.

It follows that $w' \in L(M)$ and $|w'| \leq (2m+1)(k-1)+m = m(2k-1)+k-1$. Obviously, $jc_M(w') \leq JC_M(m(2k-1)+k-1)$ must hold. On the other hand, from our construction $jc_M(w') = m = JC_M(n)$. However, we can argue like that about any word w with $jc_M(w) = JC_M(n) = m$, which means that for any n we have words w' with length $\mathcal{O}(m)$ accepted with m jumps, contradicting $\lim_{n \to \infty} \frac{JC_M(n)}{n} = 0$. □

This is in stark contrast with the nondeterministic case:

Theorem 4. ([10]). *There exists an NFAwtl M such that $L(M)$ is a non-regular language, and $JC_M(n) \in \mathcal{O}(\sqrt{n})$.*

Corollary 1. ([10]). $JCL(\log n) \setminus JCL(1) \neq \emptyset$.

Now let us prove an upper bound on the number of jumps made by DFAwtl with $\mathcal{O}(1)$ complexity, that will allow us to deduce an algorithm for deciding the language equivalence of those machines.

Lemma 1. *If DFAwtl $M = (Q, \Sigma, q_0, \delta, F)$ makes at least $\#(Q)$ jumps on some input, then $JC(M) \in \Omega(n)$.*

Proof. Suppose that there exists a word w that is accepted by M with at least $\#(Q)$ jumps, and consider the computation leading to its acceptance. The computation can be described by a sequence of position triples $(s_1, e_1, p_1), (s_2, e_2, p_2), \ldots$, where each triple (s_i, e_i, p_i) means the machine reads $w[s_i..e_i]$ sequentially after which it jumps and reads $w[p_i]$, the letter at position p_i. For simplicity we assume that the positions refer to the original input w, not to the remaining input.

Since the machine makes at least $\#(Q)$ jumps, we get that there exist $i < j$ such that reading $w[s_1..e_1]w[p_1]w[s_2..e_2]w[p_2] \cdots w[s_i..e_i]$ from the initial state leads to the same state r as reading $w[s_1..e_1]w[p_1] \cdots w[s_j..e_j]$. Let i and j be the smallest such values.

We separate out the jumping positions that are between the first and second time we reach the repeated state r, but are read before the state is reached for the first time:
$$S_r = \{p_1, \ldots, p_{i-1}\} \cap \{p \mid e_i < p < e_j\}.$$

For instance, if the input $abcde$ is read in the order $adbce$ such that

$$(q_0, abcde) \to (q_1, bcde) \to (q_2, bce) \to (r, ce) \to (q_3, e) \to (r, \varepsilon),$$

then d is between the letters read the first and second time r is reached, but is actually consumed before r is reached for the first time, so $S_r = \{4\}$.

Furthermore, for a factor $w[i..j]$ of w and a set of positions S in w, let us denote by $w[i..j]_{-S}$ the word we obtain from $w[i..j]$ by deleting the positions S:

$$w[i..j]_{-S} = \prod_{k \in [i..j] \setminus S} w[k].$$

Now we are ready to construct a sequence of words v_n of length $O(n)$ that are accepted by M with $\Omega(n)$ jumps. If $\prod_{k=i_1}^{j} w[s_k..e_k] \neq \varepsilon$, then let x be the word we get if we insert $w[p_i]$ into the second position of $\prod_{k=i+1}^{j}(w[s_k..e_k]_{-S_r} \cdot w[p_k])$. We define

$$v_n = w[1..e_j]x^n w[e_j + 1..|w|].$$

If $\prod_{k=i_1}^{j} w[s_k..e_k] = \varepsilon$, then $w[s_{j+1}]$ is translucent for each state on the path from r when reading $\prod_{k=i+1}^{j} w[p_k]$, because those letters are read in jumps. In this case, let $x = \prod_{k=i+1}^{j} w[p_k]$ and we define

$$v_n = w[1..s_{j+1}]x^n w[s_{j+1} + 1..|w|].$$

The length of the word is $|w| + n|x|$ and in the accepting computation for v_n, the machine makes a jump each time it reads x, giving n jumps.   □

Using the upper bound from the previous theorem, and the jump complexity reducing simulation for NFAwtl from [10], we can design an algorithm for testing the language equivalence of DFAwtl with jump complexity $\mathcal{O}(1)$.

Theorem 5. *The equivalence problem for DFAwtl of constant jump complexity is decidable.*

Proof. First we recall that for each NFAwtl A such that $JC_A(n) = k$, it is possible to construct NFAwtl A' with $JC_{A'}(n) = k - 1$, such that $L(A) = L(A')$ [10]. As DFAwtl are implicitly also NFAwtl, we can construct NFAwtl for them, too, decreasing the jump complexity by one. Now suppose that for two given DFAwtl A and B having m and n states, respectively, we want to decide whether $L(A) = L(B)$. We iterate the above mentioned NFAwtl construction m and n times, respectively, to obtain NFAwtl A' and B' such that $L(A) = L(A')$ and $L(B) = L(B')$. By Lemma 1 this is enough to obtain NFAwtl with jump complexity 0 accepting the same language as the input machines. Note that the resulting NFAwtl accept each word in their respective languages on at least one path without any jumps. Now consider the machines A' and B' as classical NFA: each accepting path without jumps is still an accepting path when treated as classical NFA, and each word in the language having one, we get that $L(A') \subseteq$

$L_{NFA}(A')$, where $L_{NFA}(A')$ is the language accepted by A' when treated as an NFA. It is also immediate that any accepting path in the NFA A' is an accepting path in the NFAwtl A', so $L(A') = L_{NFA}(A')$. Therefore, after constructing the NFAs A' and B', we can check $L(A') = L(B')$ by classical methods and answer the decision problem accordingly. $\square$

Note that, due to the need of determinizing the resulting NFA before we can check equivalence, the resulting algorithm has exponential time complexity in the size of the input DFAwtl. We have no hardness results to present at the moment, and we propose to further investigate the open problem whether the equivalence of constant jump complexity DFAwtl is decidable in polynomial time.

4   Deciding Regularity for DFAwtl over Binary Alphabets

In this section we look at deciding regularity of the language of a given DFAwtl. We do not have a characterization of regular languages accepted by DFAwtl in terms of jumping complexity, since there are DFAwtl accepting regular languages with linear jumping complexity (asymptotically maximal), as illustrated in Fig. 3.

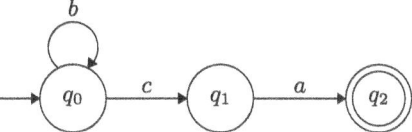

Fig. 3. DFAwtl accepting the regular language $ab^*c+b^*ac+b^*ca$ with jump complexity $\Theta(n)$, witnessed by inputs ab^*c.

However, not unexpectedly, analyzing the jumping behavior of DFAwtl is crucial in determining regularity. In what follows, we present a solution for DFAwtl over binary alphabets. The method may not generalize to larger alphabets, although we conjecture that in those cases regularity is still decidable, and the characterization on which a decision algorithm could be based, is similar in spirit to the binary case.

Problem 1. Given a DFAwtl A with a binary input alphabet, is $L(M)$ regular?

Definition 1. *A circuit* $p_0, \ldots, p_n = p_0 \in Q$ *is* a-**jumping** *for some* $a \in \Sigma$, *if for each* $i \in [n-1]$ *such that* $\delta(p_i, a) = p_{i+1}$, *the state* p_i *is* b-*deficient for some* $b \in \Sigma$, *and there is at least one* i *such that* $\delta(p_i, b) = p_{i+1}$ *for* $b \neq a$.

As we will argue in the decision algorithm later, it is enough to consider circuits that are cycles, too, that is, do not visit states repeatedly, but for now we do not require it.

Lemma 2. *A DFAwtl* $M = (Q, \{a, b\}, q_0, \delta, F)$ *accepts a non-regular language if and only if it has a reachable x-jumping circuit for some* $x \in \{a, b\}$.

Proof. For the if direction, w.l.o.g. suppose that a reachable a-jumping circuit $p_0, \ldots, p_n$ in the automaton, such that $\delta(p_i, a_i) = p_{i+1}$ for letters $a_0, \ldots, a_{n-1} \in \{a, b\}$. As the circuit can be shifted circularly, w.l.o.g. we may assume that $a_0 = a$. This means that we can write $a_0 \cdots a_{n-1} = ab^{k_1}ab^{k_2}\cdots ab^{k_\ell}$, for some $k_1, \ldots, k_\ell$.such that $\ell + k_1 + \cdots + k_\ell = n$. The circuit being a-jumping, we know that all states reading a in this circuit, i.e., $p_0, p_{k_1+1}, \ldots$ are b-deficient. This means that $p_0 b^{n-\ell} a^\ell \vdash^* p_0$, because the a's can be read with jumps. Further, we get $p_0(b^{n-\ell})^i(a^\ell)^i \vdash^* p_0$ for all $i \geq 0$. Now consider the language $L' = L(M) \cap u(b^{n-\ell})^+ a^+ v$, where u, v are some words such that $\delta(q_0, u) = p_0$, $\delta(p_0, v) \in F$ without jumps. Suppose that $L(M)$ is regular, implying that L' must be as well, and by the previous argument we know that $u(b^{n-\ell})^i a^i v \in L'$, for any $i \geq 0$. Taking an i large enough that the length of $(b^{n-\ell})^i$ is larger than the number of states accepting L', we get that there is some $r > 0$ such that $u(b^{n-\ell})^i(b^r)^+ a^i v \subset L'$. Now taking the word $u(b^{n-\ell})^i(b^r)^{(n-\ell)|v|} a^i v$ which should be in L', we notice that after reading u and looping in the circuit for i times, then looping some more until all the a's from v are also read from the tape, M ends up in one of the b-deficient states $p_0, p_{k_1+1}, \ldots$ with only b's left on the tape, rejecting the input and contradicting the assumption that L' is regular. From here, $L(M)$ cannot be regular.

For the only if direction, we assume that M has no x-jumping circuit for any $x \in \{a, b\}$, and we will construct an ε-NFA M' that simulates M, defined as follows:

- $M' = (Q', \{a, b\}, \delta', (q_0, 0, 0), F')$.
- $Q' = \{(q, m, n) \mid q \in Q \text{ and } m, n \in \{0, \ldots, |Q| - 1\}\}$; the second and third component of states will remember the number of jumps performed while reading a's and b's, respectively.
- $F' = \{(f, 0, 0) \mid f \in F\}$;
- the transitions of M' will be of three types, recording jumps (1), amortizing jumps (2), sequential transitions inherited from M (3). In detail:
  1. for each a-deficient state q, such that $\delta(q, b) = p$ we define $\delta'((q, m, n), \varepsilon) = (p, m, n + 1)$; we define the transitions jumping over b's analogously.
  2. for each state q and $n \geq 1$, we define $\delta'((q, m, n), b) = (q, m, n - 1)$; for each state q and $m \geq 1$, we define $\delta'((q, m, n), a) = (q, m - 1, n)$.
  3. for each state q, and each n, we define $\delta'((q, 0, n), a) = (p, 0, n)$ if $\delta(q, a) = p$, and $\delta'((q, n, 0), b) = (p, n, 0)$ if $\delta(q, b) = p$.

The constructed ε-NFA simulates M's computations. Whenever a jump occurs reading x during a computation of M, the NFA M' will perform the state change of M recording it in the first component and increment the respective counter. The next time it encounters x on the tape, it will decrement it without changing the first component tracking the state of M. The final states have counters set to 0, meaning all jumps have been accounted for. The key for the finite state simulation is that the automaton will never need to remember more than $\#(Q) - 1$ jumps that have not been accounted for yet. This is ensured by the fact that in any circuit of M having y-deficient states, since the circuit is not x-jumping, after at most $\#(Q) - 1$ transitions we encounter an x-transition from a state p for which $\delta(p, y)$ is also defined. Continuing with that x-transition means reading an x sequentially, i.e., x must be the leftmost symbol left on the tape. This implies that any x that has been read earlier while jumping, must occur before this position. The simulating machine, therefore, can keep recording jumps on reading x and accounting for all of them no later than $\#(Q) - 1$ steps after the first one was recorded.   □

Theorem 6. *Problem 1 is decidable in $\mathcal{O}(n^4)$ time, where n is the number of states in the input DFAwtl.*

Proof. Let the input DFAwtl be $A = (Q, \{a, b\}, \delta, q_0, F)$ with $\#(Q) = n$. Removing unreachable states and states from which no final state is reachable (except, possibly, a sink state) can be done in time $\mathcal{O}(n^3)$ by, e.g., the Floyd-Warshall algorithm [8], so from here on we may assume that A has only useful states.

From the characterization of DFAwtl accepting binary regular languages in Lemma 2, we get that it is enough to check whether x-jumping circuits exist in A. First we note that, in fact, it is enough to check whether x-jumping cycles exist. Suppose that there is some x-jumping circuit $p_0, \ldots, p_n \in Q$ for $x \in \{a, b\}$, so for each i such that $\delta(p_i, x) = p_{i+1}$, the state p_i is y-deficient for $y \neq x$, and there is at least one i such that $\delta(p_i, y) = p_{i+1}$. Let us also assume that there are $i, j \in [n]$ such that $i \neq j$ but $p_i = p_j$. We get two circuits $C_1 = p_0, \ldots, p_i, p_{j+1}, \ldots, p_n$ and $C_2 = p_i, \ldots, p_j$. If $C_1 = C_2$, then removing C_2 still leaves an x-jumping circuit, and we repeat the argument with the reduced circuit. Otherwise, C_1 and C_2 share some states (at least p_i), but not all states. As A is deterministic, there is a shared state p_k for some $k \in [n]$, from which x follows C_1 and y follows C_2 (or the other way around). This means that the original circuit cannot be x-jumping, because y is not translucent for p_k and $\delta(p_k, x) = p_{k+1}$. From this contradiction we conclude that if A has an x-jumping circuit, it must have an x-jumping cycle.

Detecting x-jumping cycles can be done by dynamic programming. First, we note that since x-transitions from not y-deficient states p are never parts of such cycles, we may remove those $\delta(p, x)$ transitions from the transition graph. Let the transition function having only the remaining transitions be δ'. From there, the question reduces to checking whether there exists a cycle having at least one transition for each of the letters. We construct a 4-dimensional matrix M indexed by step count, pairs of states and the alphabet. For any $i \in [n]$, $p, q \in Q$ and $a \in \Sigma$ we want $M[i, p, q, a] = 1$ if and only if there exists a path of length at most i from state p to q such that there is at least one transition on the path labeled by a. We initialize the whole matrix with 0's. In the inductive step, suppose that the matrix is computed up to step i, that is, all entries $M[j, p, q, a]$ with $j \leq i$. There are three possibilities to set $M[i + 1, p, q, a]$ to 1:

(1) if $M[i, p, q, a] = 1$, or

(2) if $\delta'(p, a) = q$, or
(3) if there exists some $r \in Q$ such that $M[i, p, r, b] = 1$ and $\delta'(r, a) = q$.

We stop computing M when $i > \#(Q)$. From the construction it is clear that indeed $M[i, p, q, a] = 1$ if and only from p to q there is some path of length at most i, having at least one a transition. The last step is to check whether there exist some $p, q, r \in Q$ such that $M[n, p, r, a] = 1$ and $M[n, r, q, b] = 1$.

The size of the matrix is $\mathcal{O}(n^3)$ (since the alphabet is fixed with $\#(V) = 2$), and to compute each entry we need to check conditions (1)-(3) from above. The first two can be checked in $\mathcal{O}(1)$ time and (3) can be checked in $\mathcal{O}(n)$ time, iterating over r. Constructing M, hence, takes $\mathcal{O}(n^4)$ time. To perform the last step, we need to iterate over triples $p, q, r \in Q$ and check in each iteration the corresponding matrix entry (in $\mathcal{O}(1)$ time), which yields complexity $\mathcal{O}(n^3)$ for the last step. Altogether, the time complexity of the algorithm is dominated by constructing M, so it is $\mathcal{O}(n^4)$.   □

5   Conclusion

The jump complexity landscape of DFAwtl is in stark contrast both with NFAwtl and with deterministic one-way jumping automata. As we have proved here, DFAwtl only has two separable asymptotic jump complexity classes, $\mathcal{O}(1)$ and $\mathcal{O}(n)$, whereas for NFAwtl we also have separable classes $\mathcal{O}(\log n)$ and $\mathcal{O}(\sqrt{n})$, and deterministic one-way automata, too, have a separable $\mathcal{O}(\log n)$ sweep complexity class (a measure similar to jump complexity). Due to the collapsing jump complexity hierarchy for DFAwtl, we were able to obtain a polynomial time algorithm for computing the asymptotic jump complexity of a given input machine, a problem which is still open for the other two aforementioned models. Upper bounding the number of jumps possible in DFAwtl with $\mathcal{O}(1)$ jump complexity made it possible to decide equivalence for two such machines. This suggests that it is possible that the minimal DFAwtl is computable for constant complexity inputs. We think that is also a very interesting problem, which could lead to other directions of inquiry regarding, for instance, descriptional complexity. A related research objective worth considering is to find a better way to decide equivalence, as the current algorithm runs in exponential time in the worst case due to the built-in NFA determinization step.

Finally, deciding regularity is one of the most fundamental problem considered for all such non-sequentially processing automata models. The problem is undecidable for NFAwtl [11] and nothing is known about the case of one-way jumping automata. Here we showed that at least over binary alphabets, the problem is decidable for DFAwtl. We conjecture that this is still the case for larger alphabets, perhaps provable by adapting the characterization obtained in Lemma 2.

References

1. Arroyo, F., Mitrana, V., Păun, A., Păun, M., Sánchez-Couso, J.: On the group memory complexity of extended finite automata over groups. J. Log. Alge-

braic Methods Program. **117**, 100605 (2020). https://doi.org/10.1016/j.jlamp.2020.100605

2. Bensch, S., Bordihn, H., Holzer, M., Kutrib, M.: On input-revolving deterministic and nondeterministic finite automata. Inf. Comput. **207**(11), 1140–1155 (2009). https://doi.org/10.1016/j.ic.2009.03.002

3. Bordihn, H., Mitrana, V.: On the degrees of non-regularity and non-context-freeness. J. Comput. Syst. Sci. **108**, 104–117 (2020). https://doi.org/10.1016/j.jcss.2019.08.001

4. Chigahara, H., Fazekas, S., Yamamura, A.: One-way jumping finite automata. Int. J. Found. Comput. Sci. **27**(3), 391–405 (2016). https://doi.org/10.1142/S0129054116500211

5. Fazekas, S., Mercas, R.: Sweep complexity revisited. In: Implementation and Application of Automata - 27th International Conference, CIAA 2023. Lecture Notes in Computer Science, vol. 14151, pp. 116–127. Springer (2023). https://doi.org/10.1007/978-3-031-26501-1_11

6. Fazekas, S., Mercas, R., Wu, O.: Complexities for jumps and sweeps. J. Autom. Lang. Comb. **27**(1–3), 131–149 (2022)

7. Fazekas, S.Z., Hoshi, K., Yamamura, A.: Two-way deterministic automata with jumping mode. Theor. Comput. Sci. **864**, 92–102 (2021). https://doi.org/10.1016/j.tcs.2021.02.030

8. Floyd, R.W.: Algorithm 97: shortest path. Commun. ACM **5**(6), 345 (1962). https://doi.org/10.1145/367766.368168

9. Meduna, A., Zemek, P.: Jumping finite automata. Int. J. Found. Comput. Sci. **23**(7), 1555–1578 (2012). https://doi.org/10.1142/S012905411250039X

10. Mitrana, V., Păun, A., Păun, M., Sánchez-Couso, J.: Jump complexity of finite automata with translucent letters. Theor. Comput. Sci. **992**, 114450 (2024). https://doi.org/10.1016/j.tcs.2024.114450

11. Nagy, B., Otto, F.: Finite state acceptors with translucent letters. In: Proceedings of of the First International Workshop on AI Methods for Interdisciplinary Research in Language and Biology (BILC-2011), pp. 3–13. SCITEPRESS (2011)

12. Otto, F.: A survey on automata with translucent letters. In: Nagy, B. (ed.) Implementation and Application of Automata, pp. 21–50. Springer Nature Switzerland, Cham (2023)

13. Rozenberg, G., Salomaa, A. (eds.): Handbook of Formal Languages. Springer-Verlag, Berlin (1997)

Learning Closed Signal Flow Graphs

Ekaterina Piotrovskaya[1]([✉])[ID], Leo Lobski[1][ID], and Fabio Zanasi[1,2][ID]

[1] University College London, London, UK
{kate.piotrovskaya.21,leo.lobski.21,f.zanasi}@ucl.ac.uk
[2] University of Bologna, Bologna, Italy

Abstract. *Signal flow graphs* are a graphical model of signal transducers, which play a foundational role in control theory and engineering. In this work, we develop a learning algorithm for closed (i.e. with no inputs) signal flow graphs, which are behaviourally equivalent to *weighted finite automata* on a singleton alphabet. Analogously to the case of automata learning, our algorithm constructs a signal flow graph from a given set of output behaviours. We demonstrate that this procedure results in a genuine reduction of complexity: our algorithm fares better than existing learning algorithms for weighted automata restricted to the case of a singleton alphabet.

Keywords: Signal flow graph · Automata learning · Weighted automaton

1 Introduction

Signal flow graphs (SFG) are a graphical formalism for signal transducers, which play a foundational role in control theory and engineering [35]. A signal flow graph is typically specified as a circuit, with gates corresponding to basic signal operations: addition, copying, amplification by a scalar, and delay. Moreover, signal flow graphs allow for the formation of feedback loops. From an expressiveness viewpoint, these models capture precisely rational functions: the Taylor expansion of the function may be regarded as the sequence of signals processed by the signal flow graph, as in Fig. 1 below.

In the last decade, there has been a renewed interest in the theory of signal flow graphs, which has been studied through the lenses of (co)algebra [32,33], logic [26], and category theory [2,8–10]. The overall aim of these approaches is providing an abstract and expressive mathematical framework to reason about the behaviour of signal flow graphs, with emphasis on *compositional* methods of analysis. In particular, these works have established a formal correspondence (in terms of functors) between the syntax of signal flow graphs—variously represented as a stream calculus, string diagrams, or a graph formalism, and their semantics—linear subspaces over a field of streams.

In this work, we focus on one aspect that such approaches leave mostly to guesswork and intuition, which is how to *learn* the structure of a signal flow

© The Author(s), under exclusive license to Springer Nature Switzerland AG 2025
C. Anutariya and M. M. Bonsangue (Eds.): ICTAC 2024, LNCS 15373, pp. 78–95, 2025.
https://doi.org/10.1007/978-3-031-77019-7_5

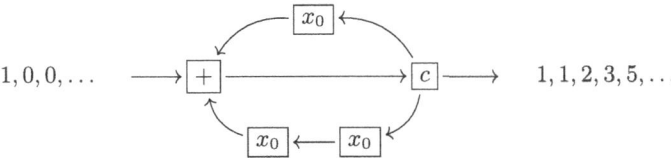

Fig. 1. The signal flow graph for the Fibonacci sequence. That means, received as input the sequence $1, 0, 0, \ldots$ of signals, it outputs the Fibonacci numbers $1, 1, 2, 3, 5, \ldots$. Note these are the coefficients of the formal power series expanding the rational function $\frac{1}{1-x-x^2}$. The semantics of SFG is further explained in Subsect. 2.2.

graph from the observed behaviour of the system it represents. More precisely, we are interested in the following scenario: given a "black box" signal flow graph, of which we may just observe the output behaviour, can we compute its graph structure in an algorithmic manner?[1]

To tackle this question, our starting point is the observation, elaborated in [33], of a formal correspondence between signal flow graphs and *weighted finite automata* (WFA), a generalisation of finite state automata where transitions are weighted over a field. More precisely, *closed* signal flow graphs (cSFG), where no inputs are provided to the system, are equivalent to WFAs with a singleton alphabet, in the sense that both compute the same subclass of streams (namely, *rational streams*).

This correspondence allows us to study learning of cSFGs by considering formal learning techniques [1] for weighted automata. A learning algorithm for WFA, which infers the automaton structure from a given language, has been first introduced by Bergadano and Varricchio [6]. There also exist learning algorithms for weighted tree automata—a generalisation of WFA—by Maletti [25] and Habrard and Oncina [18], where the latter works for nondeterministic automata; as well as for a special case of stochastic free automata—weighted tree automata where weights are drawn from the interval [0, 1] [14]. However, our approach is closer to the more recent work [19], whose algorithm may be viewed as a weighted adaptation of Angluin's L* [1] parametric on an arbitrary semiring.

Taking inspiration from the above approaches, we propose an algorithm to learn a closed signal flow graph from output behaviour of a given system. Compared to [19], our algorithm comes with an explicit calculation of the complexity bound. This allows us to observe that it is more efficient than learning arbitrary weighted finite automata with a singleton alphabet. The improvement is largely due to exploiting the linear algebraic structure of rational streams. Even though it focusses on cSFGs, we believe our approach paves the way to a study of learning for signal flow graphs with arbitrary inputs and outputs: we return to this point in the conclusion (Sect. 6).

---

[1] Of course, one can only hope to learn the signal flow graph structure up to semantic equivalence. There is a purely equational theory axiomatising this equivalence, as studied in [2, 10].

2   Preliminaries

We recall the notions of rational streams, signal flow graphs and weighted automata. Some of the results stated have references to [33] as the paper nicely condenses them in one place; however, most of them have already been established in the literature prior to it. The proof of rational series having finite representations appears in [7]. It is further elaborated on with respect to rational streams in [30], together with their property of having a finite number of linearly independent derivatives.

2.1   Rational Streams

A *stream* over a field k is an infinite sequence of elements of k.

Definition 1 (Stream). *Let k be a field. Define the set of k-valued streams as the function set k^ω. We denote a stream $\sigma \in k^\omega$ by $\sigma = (\sigma_0, \sigma_1, \sigma_2, \dots)$, where σ_0 is the initial value of σ.*

Definition 2 (Stream derivative [32]). *The stream derivative is a function $()' : k^\omega \to k^\omega$ defined by $\sigma' = (\sigma_1, \sigma_2, \sigma_3, \dots)$. Higher-order stream derivatives, for all $n \in \mathbb{N}$, are defined as $\sigma^{(0)} = \sigma$, $\sigma^{(n+1)} = (\sigma^{(n)})'$.*

We refer to a stream σ as *polynomial* if it has a finite number of non-zero elements, i.e. if it is of the form $\sigma = (c_0, c_1, c_2, \dots , c_n, 0, 0, 0, ..)$, where $c_i \in k$ for all i. In this work, we will need *rational streams* obtained as ratios of polynomial streams, as these are precisely the class of streams computed by cSFGs. A stream is rational if it is a so-called convolution product of a polynomial stream with an inverse of another polynomial stream. We refer the reader to [32] for the details of these definitions. As an example, take two polynomial streams $p = (1, 0, 0, ..)$ and $q = (1, 0, -1, 0, 0, ..)$; then $\sigma = p/q = (1, 0, 1, 0, 1, 0, ..)$ is rational.

Rational streams are "periodic", in the sense that they only have a finite number of linearly independent stream derivatives:

Lemma 1 ([33]). *For a rational stream σ, there exists an $n \geq 1$ such that $\{\sigma^{(0)}, \sigma^{(1)}, \sigma^{(2)}, \dots , \sigma^{(n-1)}\}$ are linearly independent in the vector space k^n, and $\sigma^{(n)} = \sum_{i=0}^{n-1} c_i \times \sigma^{(i)}$, for some unique $c_0, \dots , c_{n-1} \in k$.*

Rational streams have long been used as a means to characterise finite circuits in the field of signal processing [24, p. 694], and can be defined via linear recurrent sequences or difference equations [30].

2.2   Signal Flow Graphs

Given a field k, we think of its elements as basic units of signals. A *signal flow* can then be modelled as an infinite stream of elements from k. The transducers that can add, copy, multiply and delay signals are represented as *signal flow graphs* first introduced by Shannon [35]. For a mathematically more succinct definition of signal flow graphs as morphisms in a prop, see [9].

Definition 3 (Signal flow graph (SFG)). *Let k be a field. Define the set of gate labels as*

$$L := k \sqcup \{x_a : a \in k\} \sqcup \{+, c, i, o\}.$$

A signal flow graph with signals from k is a tuple (G, E, l), where (G, E) is a finite directed graph and $l : G \to L$ is a function such that for all $s \in G$ we have (we write $Es := \{t \in G : tEs\}$ and $sE := \{t \in G : sEt\}$):

- *if $l(s) = i$, then $|Es| = 0$ and $|sE| = 1$,*
- *if $l(s) = o$, then $|Es| = 1$ and $|sE| = 0$,*
- *if $l(s) = +$, then $|Es| \geq 2$ and $|sE| = 1$,*
- *if $l(s) = c$, then $|Es| = 1$ and $|sE| \geq 2$,*
- *if $l(s) = a$ (a $\in k$), then $|Es| = 1$ and $|sE| = 1$,*
- *if $l(s) = x_a$ (a $\in k$), then $|Es| = 1$ and $|sE| = 1$,*

and such that each cycle contains at least one x_a-labelled vertex. The vertices G are called gates, *and we refer to l as the* gate labelling function.

The intuition behind the gate labels of a SFG is as follows. The gates labelled i are the inputs, o stands for outputs, a $+$-gate is an *adder* which adds all the incoming signals (of which there are at least two) and produces the sum as the output, a c-gate is a *copier* that takes in a signal and produces a copy of it in each outgoing edge, a gate labelled with a field element a is a *multiplier* which amplifies the signal by multiplying it by a, finally, an x_a-gate is a *register* that stores the signal a passing it along the outgoing edge and taking a new value to be stored from the incoming edge.

We draw the four basic *generators* (the adder, the copier, the multiplier and the register) of SFGs below; note that the input/output labels are not part of the data of a SFG, but define how it computes a stream function, as discussed below.

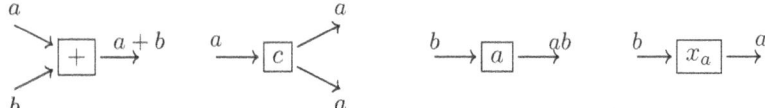

All SFGs can be built built by composing such vertices [9]. Writing $i, o \in \mathbb{N}$ for the number of inputs and outputs of a signal flow graph, the graph implements a function $(k^\omega)^i \to (k^\omega)^o$ as follows: at step n, the input vertices are assigned the nth element of the corresponding stream, the labelled vertices pass on the incoming values to the outgoing values as indicated in the above picture, with the additional requirement that the register value is updated to x_b [9].

Crucially, two SFGs can be composed by plugging (some of) the outputs of one into (some of) the inputs of the other. We have already given an example of a composite SFG computing the Fibonacci sequence (Fig. 1).

The class of stream functions computed by SFGs is characterised by multiplication by rational streams [10,32]. The simplest case of no inputs and one output can be used to characterise rational streams.

Definition 4 (Closed signal flow graph (cSFG)). *A* closed signal flow graph (cSFG) *is a SFG* (G, E, l) *with no inputs* $(l^{-1}(i) = \varnothing)$ *and exactly one output* $(|l^{-1}(o)| = 1)$.

Example 1. We give an example of a cSFG below, which computes the stream $\sigma_n = a + n + 1$:

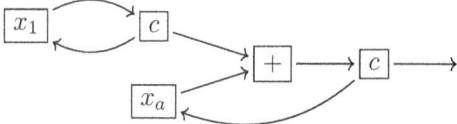

The following result shows that cSFGs precisely capture the rational streams.

Theorem 1 ([33]). *A stream* $\sigma \in k^\omega$ *is rational if and only is there exists a cSFG that implements it.*

Example 2. Let σ be the rational stream defined by $\sigma_0 := 1$, $\sigma_1 := 2$, $\sigma_2 := 3$ and $\sigma_n := -\sigma_{n-3} + \sigma_{n-2} + 2 \times \sigma_{n-1}$, i.e. the first few elements are $(1, 2, 3, 7, 15, 34, \dots)$. Then σ has three linearly independent derivatives, and a cSFG that computes it is as follows:

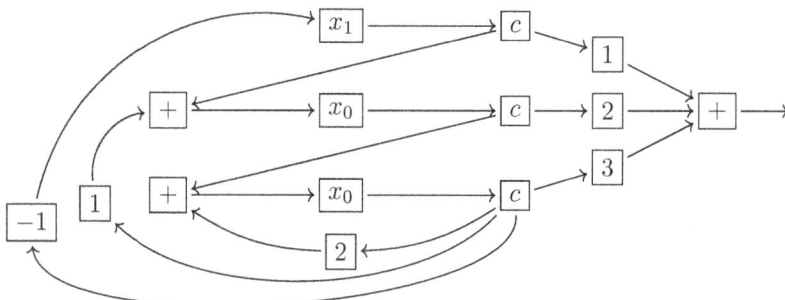

where the coefficients $c_0 = -1$, $c_1 = 1$, $c_2 = 2$ are those from Lemma 1, and the initial register values are obtained by solving a certain system of linear equations (see proof of Theorem 3).

2.3   Weighted Automata

Weighted finite automata (WFA), first introduced in [34], can be seen as a generalisation of non-deterministic automata, with each transition having a weight (or a 'cost') associated to it. WFAs have found applications in multiple areas ranging from speech recognition [27] and image processing [13] to control theory [21] and financial modelling [3]. We formally define a WFA over a field k.

Definition 5 (Weighted finite automaton (WFA) [34]). *Let* k *be a field and let* A *be a finite set. A* weighted finite automaton *over* k *with an* alphabet A *is a tuple* $(Q, \langle o, t \rangle)$, *where* Q *is a finite set of* states, $o : Q \to k$ *is an* output function *and* $t : Q \to (k^Q)^A$ *is a* transition function.

Remark 1. WFA are usually defined as a tuple (Q, i, o, t), where Q, o, t are as above and $i : Q \to k$ is the initial weights function. We omit the latter from our definition, as the notion of a stream represented by a state is equivalent to assigning input 1 to it, and 0 to all other states.

In the singleton alphabet case, it is equivalent to work with *weighted stream automata (WSA)* [31]. The data of a WSA is that of a WFA, except that the transition function has the type $t : Q \times Q \to k$. When drawing a WSA, we may either see it as a special case of a WFA and include (Example 4) or omit (Example 3) the unique transition letter.

Example 3. We give an example of a WSA below, where we do not draw the transitions labelled with 0:

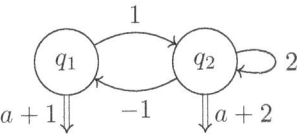

Definition 6 (Reachable state). *A state q_R of a WFA $(Q, \langle o, t \rangle)$ is reachable within R steps from state q_0 at cost $C_R = \prod_{i=0}^{R} c_i$ if, starting from state q_0, there exist $q_1, q_2, \ldots, q_{R-1}$ such that $t(q_i)(q_{i+1}) = c_i$ for $i = 0, \ldots, R-1$, and $c_R = o(q_R)$.*

Let C_j^q be the multiset containing the costs of all states reachable from q in j steps with multiplicity, i.e.

$$C_j^q := \{C_j : \text{ there exists a state } p \text{ reachable from } q \text{ in } j \text{ steps at cost } C_j\}$$

We next define what it means for a state q of a WSA to represent a stream.

Definition 7 (Stream represented by a state [33]). *A state q of a WSA $(Q, \langle o, t \rangle)$ represents the stream $S(q) = (s_0, s_1, s_2, \ldots)$ where $s_j = \sum C_j^q$.*

In other words, we say that a state q of a WSA *represents* the stream $S(q) = (s_0, s_1, s_2, \ldots)$, where s_n is the sum of all weights of paths of length n starting at q, where the weight of a path is obtained by multiplying the weights of the individual transitions in the path and the output weight of the last state. For instance, the state q_1 of the WSA in Example 3 represents the stream $\sigma_n = a + n + 1$, which we recognise as the same stream as in the cSFG in Example 1. In fact, we have the following result:

Theorem 2 ([33]). *A stream $\sigma \in k^\omega$ is rational if and only if there is a k-valued WSA $(Q, \langle o, t \rangle)$ and a state $q \in Q$ representing σ.*

To construct a WSA from a rational stream σ, we first find the number of linearly independent derivatives of σ, call it n; then assign σ_i to the output of each state q_i (for $i = 0, \ldots, n-1$) and use the coefficients $c_0, \ldots, c_{n-1}$ (Lemma 1) to define the transition function. This induces a specific shape of a WSA described in Sect. 3.

Example 4. A WFA over a singleton alphabet $A = \{a\}$, whose state q_0 represents the stream from Example 2 is as follows:

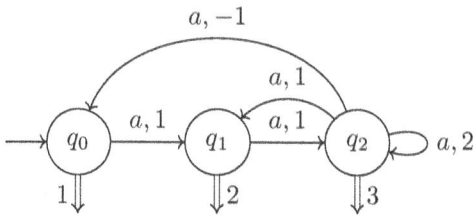

2.4 Automata Learning

Automata learning is a process whose aim is to algorithmically infer an automaton from observed behaviour of an underlying system. There exist two approaches to it—*passive* [17,20,28] and *active* [1,22] learning. In the former, the learner does not interact with the system directly and instead attempts to infer the structure of the automaton based on a pre-determined dataset of observations of the system's behaviour. In the latter, the learner is equipped with an *oracle* in order to interact with the system by making queries. An active learner can adapt based on feedback during the learning process and hence infer the desired automaton more efficiently. The original algorithm that introduced the idea of active learning is Angluin's L* [1], allowing to infer deterministic finite automata.

We give an overview of L* and begin by fixing the following notation and definitions. Let A be a finite set of labels, referred to as an *alphabet*. A *language* $\mathcal{L}$ over A is a subset of words in A^*, that is, $\mathcal{L} \subseteq A^*$.

Definition 8 (Observation table [1]). *An observation table is a tuple (S, E) where $S, E \subseteq A^*$ are finite sets; we refer to elements of S as* prefixes *and to those of E as* suffixes.

Definition 9 (DFA). *A deterministic finite automaton (DFA) is a 5-tuple (Q, q_0, A, δ, F), where Q is a finite set of states, $q_0 \in Q$ is the initial state, A is an alphabet, $\delta : Q \times A \to Q$ is the transition function and $F \subseteq Q$ is a finite set of final states.*

The algorithm seeks to learn a minimal DFA accepting the language $\mathcal{L}$. It incrementally constructs the observation table, where rows range over S (the top part of the table) and $S \cdot A$ (the bottom part of the table) and columns range over E. For each $u \in S \cup S \cdot A$ and $v \in E$, the resulting cell corresponds to $\mathcal{L}(uv)$. An example of a table over $A = \{a, b\}$ is presented below:

$$
\begin{array}{c}
\overbrace{}^{E} \\[-2pt]
\begin{array}{cc|ccc}
 & & \varepsilon & a & aa \\
\hline
S \,[& \varepsilon & 1 & 0 & 0 \\
\cline{2-5}
 & a & 0 & 0 & 1 \\
S \cdot A & b & 0 & 1 & 0
\end{array}
\end{array}
$$

Note that S and $S \cdot A$ may intersect. For convenience, rows lying in the intersection are only depicted in the top part of the table. The following functions are used to describe the top and bottom parts of the table, respectively:

Definition 10 (Row functions [1]). *Let (S, E) be an observation table and $\mathcal{L}$ be a language. Then define the following* row *functions:*

- $\mathrm{row} : S \to 2^E$ *as* $\mathrm{row}(u)(v) = \mathcal{L}(uv)$,
- $\mathrm{srow} : S \cdot A \to 2^E$ *as* $\mathrm{srow}(ua)(v) = \mathcal{L}(uav)$.

An observation table has important properties allowing for constructing and guessing the desired DFA: *closedness* and *consistency*.

Definition 11 (Closedness [1]). *Let (S, E) be an observation table and $\mathcal{L}$ be a language. The table is* closed *if for all $s \in S$ and $a \in A$ there exists $t \in S$ such that $\mathrm{srow}(sa) = \mathrm{row}(t)$.*

Hence an observation table is closed if every row in the bottom part $(S \cdot A)$ already appears in the top part (S).

Definition 12 (Consistency [1]). *Let (S, E) be an observation table and $\mathcal{L}$ be a language. The table is* consistent *if for all $s_1, s_2 \in S$ such that $\mathrm{row}(s_1) = \mathrm{row}(s_2)$, we have $\mathrm{srow}(s_1 a) = \mathrm{srow}(s_2 a)$ for all $a \in A$.*

Hence an observation table is consistent if for any two rows in the top part (S) that have identical entries, their extensions by a single letter likewise have identical entries.

The key step of the algorithm is constructing a conjecture DFA from the rows of the observation table. It is defined as follows:

Definition 13 (Conjecture automaton [1]). *Let (S, E) be a closed and consistent observation table. Then a conjecture DFA $M(S, E) = (Q, q_0, A, \delta, F)$ can be constructed from the observation table in the following way:*

$$
\begin{aligned}
Q &= \{\mathrm{row}(s) \mid s \in S\} & \delta(\mathrm{row}(s), a) &= \mathrm{srow}(sa) \\
q_0 &= \mathrm{row}(\varepsilon) & F &= \{\mathrm{row}(s) \mid s \in S,\ \mathrm{row}(s)(\varepsilon) = 1\}.
\end{aligned}
$$

The algorithm assumes access to an oracle that answers the following types of queries:

- *Membership query*: given a word $w \in A^*$, an oracle replies with $\mathcal{L}(w)$; and

– *Equivalence query*: given a conjecture DFA $M(S, E)$, an oracle replies with "yes" if the DFA accepts the language $\mathcal{L}$ we seek to learn, and with a *counterexample*—a word $w \in A^*$ incorrectly classified by the conjecture, otherwise.

L* works as follows: initially, an empty observation table is constructed ($S = E = \{\varepsilon\}$). Then it is filled up and made closed (by expanding S) and consistent (by expanding E) via membership queries. Then the algorithm constructs a DFA and guesses it by making an equivalence query. If the guess is incorrect, the oracle returns a counterexample whose prefixes are added to S and the algorithm jumps back to updating the observation table, otherwise the conjecture is returned and the algorithm terminates.

3   The Learning Algorithm

Here we introduce a learning algorithm for closed signal flow graphs (Algorithm 1). As in L*, we construct a conjecture cSFG (Definition 18) from an observation table, which, in turn, is filled by repeated membership queries to the teacher/oracle. This amounts to observing a finite number of stream elements. We note that our version of the algorithm does not rely on counterexamples provided by the oracle: rather, the oracle simply replies "yes" or "no" to equivalence queries.

We begin by fixing the definitions needed by the algorithm. Throughout this section, let k be a fixed field and $\sigma \in k^\omega$ a stream. We think of σ as the (unknown) stream computed by the cSFG we want to learn. By an *observation table* we mean a pair (S, E) of finite subsets of ω.

Definition 14 (Row function). *Let* (S, E) *be an observation table. Then define the* row function $\mathtt{row} : S \to k^E$ *by* $\mathtt{row}(v)(e) = \sigma_{v+e}$ *for* $v \in S$, $e \in E$.

Definition 15 (Last row function). *Let* (S, E) *be an observation table and* w *be the largest element of* S. *Define the* last row function $\mathtt{srow} : E \to k$ *by* $\mathtt{srow}(e) = \sigma_{w+e+1}$ *for* $e \in E$.

Definition 16 (Closedness). *We say that an observation table* (S, E) *is* closed *if there exist constants* $c_s \in k$ *such that* $\mathtt{srow} = \sum_{s \in S} c_s \cdot \mathtt{row}(s)$.

Unlike in [1], the $\mathtt{row}$ and $\mathtt{srow}$ functions map to values in k, i.e. stream elements whose indices are determined via adding elements of S and E. Furthermore, we leave only E in the domain of the $\mathtt{srow}$ function, as in our case there is always a unique row in the bottom part of the observation table.

We next introduce the notion of the *coefficient function* that outputs the solution to a system of linear equations if it exists, or returns $\bot$ otherwise. Note that it can be computed efficiently by Lemma 1.

Definition 17 (Coefficient function). *Let* (S, E) *be an observation table. Define the* coefficient function $\mathtt{cs} \in \{\bot\} \cup k^S$ *as the function* $\mathtt{cs} : S \to k$ *such that* $\mathtt{srow} = \sum_{s \in S} \mathtt{cs}(s) \cdot \mathtt{row}(s)$ *if the table is closed, and as the symbol* $\bot$ *otherwise.*

The algorithm assumes access to an oracle that answers the following types of queries:

- *Membership query*: given an index $n \in \omega$, an oracle replies with the nth element of the corresponding stream; and
- *Equivalence query*: given a cSFG, an oracle replies with "yes" if the cSFG constructed is correct, and with "no" otherwise.

We now have all the ingredients to define the learning algorithm, aslo referred to as the *learner* (Algorithm 1). An observation table is created, with S and E initially only containing 0. The learner also keeps a counter i, initially assigned 1, to keep track of the smallest index not in S, which will improve the overall complexity of the algorithm. The inner while loop repeatedly checks whether the table is closed (lines 4-8) and if not, the index i is added to S and E (i.e. expanding the table proportionally) and the counter is incremented.

The learner can now construct the conjecture cSFG (lines 9-14). Thus suppose that the observation table is closed, so that a coefficient function $\mathtt{cs} : S \to k$ exists. Note that the set $S = \{0, \ldots, i-1\}$ has i elements.

Definition 18 (Conjecture cSFG). *We define the conjecture cSFG (G, E, l) as follows:*

- *it has i registers $r_0, \ldots, r_{i-1}$, whose labels are the solutions to the linear equations in Theorem 3,*
- *it has i copiers $q_0, \ldots, q_{i-1}$,*
- *it has i adders $a_0, \ldots, a_{i-2}$ and a_{final},*
- *it has $2i$ multipliers $m_0, \ldots, m_{i-1}$ and $n_0, \ldots, n_{i-1}$ with labels $l(m_j) := \mathtt{row}(j)(0) = \sigma_j$ and $l(n_j) := \mathtt{cs}(j)$,*
- *for each $j \in \{0, \ldots, i-1\}$, there are edges (r_j, q_j), (q_j, m_j) and (m_j, a_{final}),*
- *for each $j \in \{0, \ldots, i-2\}$, there are edges (q_j, a_j) and (a_j, r_{j+1}),*
- *there are edges (q_{i-1}, n_0) and (n_0, r_0), and for each $j \in \{1, \ldots, i-1\}$, edges (q_{i-1}, n_j) and (n_j, a_j),*
- *there is an edge (a_{final}, o), where o is the unique output.*

Below, we give a cSFG graph obtained from the construction in Definition 18 for $i = 3$. We denote the label of the vertex inside a box, while its name is put next to it.

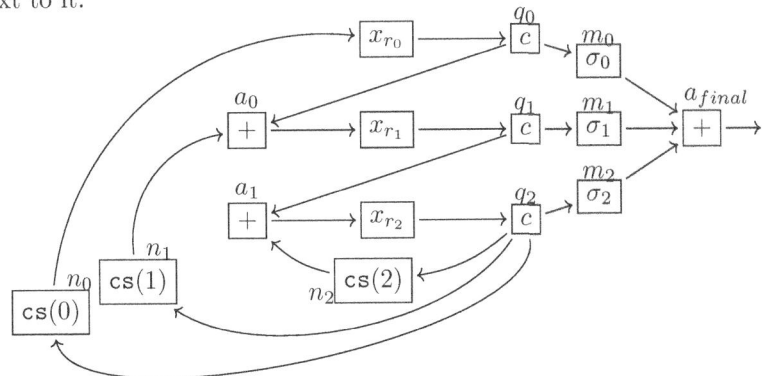

Remark 2. We note that, when constructing a conjecture cSFG, we essentially get a WSA equivalent to it "for free" (recall Theorem 2 and that membership queries return stream elements): the values from the first column are assigned to the output of each state $s \in S$; each transition from state s to $s + 1$ is assigned value 1, and the coefficients returned by the coefficient function are assigned to transitions from the state $i - 1$ to each $s \in S$. We represent the resulting WSA below:

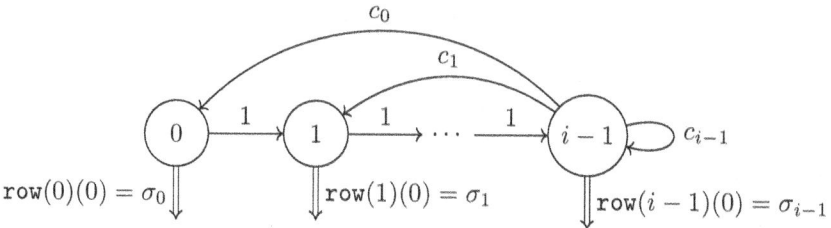

Finally, the conjecture cSFG is given to the oracle as an equivalence query, which results in oracle either rejecting it, which indicates that the corresponding stream has more linearly independent derivatives than the learner has guessed, thence i is added to S and E and the counter is incremented and the outer while loop is executed again; or accepting it and hence the algorithm outputs the cSFG and terminates.

We note that, since E gets expanded together with S during the closedness check and after receiving "no" from the equivalence query, a separate check for consistency is no longer required.

Example 5. We give an example run of the algorithm. We first fix the cSFG from Example 2 as the one we wish to learn. Recall that it computes the stream $\sigma = (1, 2, 3, 7, 15, 34, \dots)$. We run our algorithm: initially, $S = E = \{0\}$, $i = 1$. As the first step, we build the following observation table:

$$\begin{array}{c|c} & 0 \\ \hline 0 & 1 \\ 1 & 2 \end{array}$$

It is closed, hence we can construct the conjecture cSFG:

$$\boxed{2} \longleftarrow \atop \downarrow \qquad \boxed{c} \longrightarrow \boxed{1} \longrightarrow \atop \boxed{x_1} \nearrow$$

The oracle replies with "no". We thus add $i = 1$ to E and S, and increment the counter to $i = 2$:

$$\begin{array}{c|cc} & 0 & 1 \\ \hline 0 & 1 & 2 \\ 1 & 2 & 3 \\ 2 & 3 & 7 \end{array}$$

Algorithm 1: Abstract learning algorithm for a cSFG over k

---

1 $S, E \leftarrow \{0\}$
2 $i \leftarrow 1$
3 **while** *true* **do**
4 $\quad$ **while** cs $= \perp$ **do**
5 $\quad\quad$ $S \leftarrow S \cup \{i\}$
6 $\quad\quad$ $E \leftarrow E \cup \{i\}$
7 $\quad\quad$ $i \leftarrow i + 1$
8 $\quad$ **end**
9 $\quad$ **for** $s \in S$ **do**
10 $\quad\quad$ $o(s) \leftarrow$ **row**$(s)(0)$
11 $\quad\quad$ $t(i - 1)(s) \leftarrow$ cs(s)
12 $\quad\quad$ $t(s)(s + 1) \leftarrow 1$
13 $\quad$ **end**
14 $\quad$ Construct $cSFG$
15 $\quad$ **if** $EQ(cSFG) =$ *no* **then**
16 $\quad\quad$ $S \leftarrow S \cup \{i\}$
17 $\quad\quad$ $E \leftarrow E \cup \{i\}$
18 $\quad\quad$ $i \leftarrow i + 1$
19 $\quad$ **else**
20 $\quad\quad$ **return** $cSFG$
21 $\quad$ **end**
22 **end**

This table is not closed, as there are no $c_0, c_1 \in k$ such that

$$\texttt{srow} = c_0 \cdot \texttt{row}(0) + c_1 \cdot \texttt{row}(1).$$

Hence we add $i = 2$ to E and S, increment the counter to $i = 3$ and build the following table:

	0	1	2
0	1	2	3
1	2	3	7
2	3	7	15
3	7	15	34

This table is closed: $\texttt{srow} = -1 \cdot \texttt{row}(0) + 1 \cdot \texttt{row}(1) + 2 \cdot \texttt{row}(2)$, hence we can construct the conjecture cSFG, which is precisely our target; the algorithm thus terminates.

4   Correctness

We proceed to give a proof of the correctness of our algorithm. This amounts to showing that the constructed WFA and cSFG indeed compute the stream we expect them to.

Theorem 3. *Let σ be the hidden stream fixed at the beginning of Sect. 3. The output cSFG returned by Algorithm 1 (and hence the corresponding WFA) compute σ.*

Proof. We first prove the statement for the WFA. Recall the definition of the stream $S(q_0)$ computed by the WFA (Definition 7) that we know the values $\sigma_0, \ldots, \sigma_{n-1}$ from the membership queries. Hence, for the first n elements of the resulting stream we have:

$$\begin{cases} s_0 = C_0 = o(q_0) = \sigma_0 \\ s_1 = C_1 = t(q_0)(q_1) \times o(q_1) = 1 \times \sigma_0^{(1)} = \sigma_1 \\ \vdots \\ s_{n-1} = C_{n-1} = t(q_0)(q_1) \times \cdots \times t(q_{n-2})(q_{n-1}) \times o(q_{n-1}) \\ \qquad\quad = 1 \times \cdots \times 1 \times \sigma_0^{(n-1)} = \sigma_{n-1} \end{cases}$$

as expected. Until now, there existed a unique path of length j from q_0 to q_j, $0 \le j \le n-1$. Let us then show how an element of the stream, namely s_n, is calculated when this isn't the case anymore, i.e. for $j \ge n$:

$$s_n = \sum_{i=0}^{n-1} C_n = \sum_{i=0}^{n-1} t(q_0)(q_1) \times t(q_1)(q_2) \times \cdots \times t(q_{n-1})(q_i) \times o(q_i) = \sum_{i=0}^{n-1} c_i \times \sigma_0^{(i)}$$

which is precisely the definition of our rational stream σ. This concludes the proof for WFA.

Now, recall that our cSFG has n registers. We can think of each register r^i, where $i = 0, \ldots, n-1$, as having a certain stream v^i feeding into it, and a certain stream τ^i coming out of it. We then have n linear equations in the form $\tau^i = r^i + X \times v^i$. We obtain the following set of equations:

$$\begin{cases} \tau^0 = r^0 + X \times (c_0 \times \tau^{n-1}) \\ \tau^1 = r^1 + X \times (\tau^0 + c_1 \times \tau^{n-1}) \\ \vdots \\ \tau^{n-1} = r^{n-1} + X \times (\tau^{n-2} + c_{n-1} \times \tau^{n-1}) \end{cases}$$

Notice that we can rewrite each τ^i in terms of τ^{n-1} and substitute τ^{n-2} in the last equation. We then get

$$\tau^{n-1} = (r^{n-1}, r^{n-2} + c_{n-1} \times \tau_0^{n-1}, r^{n-3} + c_{n-2} \times \tau_0^{n-1} + c_{n-1} \times \tau_1^{n-1}, \ldots)$$

We can see that the definition of the stream is recursive and depends on the values of r^i. We can calculate each of τ^i in the exact same manner. Recall that the constructed cSFG, based on its structure in the algorithm, computes σ if $\sigma_0 \times \tau^0 + \sigma_1 \times \tau^1 + \cdots + \sigma_{n-1} \times \tau^{n-1} = \sigma$. Hence, by adding up the corresponding elements τ_j^i of n streams and equating the result to the known σ_j, $j = 0, \ldots, n-1$, we obtain n equations in n unknowns $r^0, \ldots, r^{n-1}$. This way, we have $\sigma_0 \times r^0 + \cdots + \sigma_{n-1} \times r^{n-1} = \sigma_0$, and so on. Having obtained the solution, we now know the initial register values of our cSFG, and hence, by definition, the resulting cSFG computes the expected stream σ.

5   Complexity

We first note that the algorithm always terminates. Computing the coefficient function consists of checking for linear independence of stream derivatives, of which there are finitely many (Lemma 1). Hence, linear dependence is guaranteed to be reached within a finite number of the main loop executions.

Theorem 4. *Algorithm 1 has a computational complexity of $O(n^4)$.*

Proof. Let n be the number of linearly independent derivatives of the stream that the cSFG computes (which is also the number of registers in the cSFG we will learn). Then we have that (1) $|S| \leq n$, (2) $|E| \leq n$, and (3) the main loop in the algorithm is repeated at most n times. All of these hold by Lemma 1.

Now, let us evaluate complexity bounds of parts of the algorithm inside the main loop. We begin by determining the complexity of the coefficient function (line 4). Since it checks whether the row i is a linear combination of rows corresponding to elements of S, each call amounts to solving a system of at most n linear equations in at most n unknowns, as S and E expand evenly. This can be done using Gauss's method with complexity $O(n^3)$ [11, 15, p. 12]. Since we make at most n calls to the coefficient function throughout the algorithm (as there are n linearly independent derivatives), we need to solve at most n such systems of equations. So the overall complexity of closing the table is $O(n^4)$. As a side note, the counter on line 7 of the algorithm is introduced precisely to enable calling the coefficient function as infrequently as possible, as it is a task of, as we will deduce later, highest computational complexity.

Next, we consider the complexity of filling the table. In the worst case, the table is of size $|S||E| = n^2$. However, since repeated table entries do not need to be re-queried and each membership query for filling one entry of the table corresponds to a stream index which is at most $n + n = 2n$, the number of membership queries and hence the complexity of filling the table is $O(n)$. As the main loop in the algorithm is executed at most n times, the number of equivalence queries is $O(n)$.

Finally, let us evaluate the complexity of constructing a cSFG (line 14). The multiplier values come from the first n elements of the stream and from the coefficients $c_0, \ldots, c_{n-1}$ from Lemma 1; all we have to do now is find the initial register values. There are n registers, so we have to solve n linear equations in n unknowns (this appears in the proof of Theorem 3). It can be done via Gauss's method of complexity $O(n^3)$.

We conclude that the task of highest complexity is closing the table, $O(n^4)$, which is hence also the overall complexity of our algorithm; i.e. it runs in polynomial time.

Remark 3. We note that this bound can still be improved—instead of expanding S and E linearly, we could do so exponentially, i.e. by doubling their sizes whenever the table is not closed and after each unsuccessful equivalence query. This way, we would make at most $O(log\ n)$ equivalence queries and would only make $O(log\ n)$ calls to the coefficient function. The overall complexity of the algorithm would then be $O(n^3 log\ n)$.

5.1   Comparison

Our algorithm has a strictly lower complexity bound (from Remark 3) than those of learning algorithms for WFAs restricted to the singleton alphabet case. Denote by m the size of the longest counterexample provided by oracles in such algorithms. In [6], the bound is $O(n^5 m^2)$ and in [5] the bound is $O(n^{3.376} + mn^3)$ (it can be checked by, e.g. L'Hôpital's rule, that our bound $O(n^3 log\ n)$ is indeed lower). In the case of the learning algorithms for *weighted tree automata* (WTA)—a generalisation of WFA, the algorithm by Maletti [25] for deterministic WTA simplifies in our case to having the complexity of $O(n^3(n + m))$. We note that the lack of the need for counterexamples in our algorithm allows for the improvement in complexity, as counterexamples are provided non-deterministically and can be arbitrarily large. This, as well as the procedure outlined in Remark 3, is the case precisely due to the rational streams' property of having a finite number of linearly independent derivatives.

We also calculated the computational complexity of the algorithm in [19]. The algorithm is for general WFA and relies on the existence of the so-called closedness strategy (cs) that checks whether an observation table is closed; the algorithm only checks for closedness and not for consistency, as the counterexamples are handled in a way that the constructed observation table is always consistent. Said closedness strategy is a rather generic function, and in order to be able to compare the algorithms, we assume that in the case of a singleton alphabet it would mirror the behaviour of our coefficient function; it is, just like in our algorithm, the task of highest complexity. Hence, as $|E|$ is bounded by $m + 1$ (it only expands from suffixes of counterexamples) and $|S|$ is bounded by n, we have that the complexity of solving at most $m + 1$ equations in at most n variables is $O(n(m + 1) \min(n, m + 1)) = O(nm \min(n, m))$. Since cs is called when assigning values to the transition function for each state whenever a conjecture is constructed, and $|S| \leq n$ and the outer loop is repeated at most n times, the overall complexity of the algorithm is $O(n^3 m \min(n, m))$. However, if we assume that cs is never recomputed for rows in S during the conjecture construction even after adding counterexamples to E, the complexity bound is $O(n^2 m \min(n, m))$. In both cases, our algorithm has a better bound—as noted earlier, m can be arbitrarily large. We thus conclude that our algorithm genuinely uses the structure of cSFGs, rather than just restricting a generic algorithm for WFAs.

6   Concluding Remarks

The main contribution of this work is establishing a learning algorithm for closed signal flow graphs and calculating its computational complexity, considering both the time complexity and the number of queries made. To the best of our knowledge, this work is the first to study signal flow graphs in the light of automata learning. Our results show that the proposed algorithm has a better complexity than that for arbitrary weighted automata in [19], even if the latter one is restricted to WFA over a singleton alphabet. It also has a better computational complexity than learning algorithms for WFA introduced in [6] and in [5].

An obvious direction for future work is to find a learning algorithm for all SFGs. This would either require proving their equivalence to some family of automata first, or building on the algorithm for closed signal flow graphs. Since a signal flow graph with one input and one output is determined by its action on the zero stream and on the stream $(1, 0, 0, \dots)$, the latter approach is especially promising. In their work, Basold et al. [4] show the equivalence between open SFGs and Mealy Machines; the authors of this paper would also wish to explore whether such equivalence exists between SFGs and (some subset of) WFAs. An interesting related question is whether learning respects the compositional structure of SFGs: is learning a composite SFG equivalent to learning its parts and composing back? A way to approach this question could be to rely on a more fine-grained algebraic analysis of signal flow graphs, as in the framework of Bonchi et al. [9].

Automata learning has extensive applications in areas such as software verification [29], network protocol analysis [12], and natural language processing [23]. Learning signal flow graphs opens the door to exploring similar techniques in control theory as well as in the design and analysis of related families of systems, such as digital circuits [16].

Acknowledgments. The authors would like to thank Wojciech Różowski for reading and providing helpful feedback on this paper. The authors would also like to thank the anonymous reviewers for their detailed comments and suggestions. Fabio Zanasi acknowledges support from EPSRC EP/V002376/1.

Disclosure of Interests. The authors have no competing interests to declare that are relevant to the content of this article.

References

1. Angluin, D.: Learning regular sets from queries and counterexamples. Inf. Comput. **75**(2), 87–106 (1987). https://doi.org/10.1016/0890-5401(87)90052-6
2. Baez, J.C., Erbele, J.: Categories in control. Theory Appl. Categ. **30** (2008), http://www.tac.mta.ca/tac/volumes/30/24/30-24abs.html
3. Baier, C., Größer, M., Ciesinski, F.: Model checking linear-time properties of probabilistic systems. In: Handbook of Weighted Automata, pp. 519–570. Springer (2009). https://doi.org/10.1007/978-3-642-01492-5_13

4. Basold, H., Bonsangue, M., Hansen, H.H., Rutten, J.: (co) algebraic characterizations of signal flow graphs. Horizons of the Mind. A Tribute to Prakash Panangaden: Essays Dedicated to Prakash Panangaden on the Occasion of His 60th Birthday, pp. 124–145 (2014). https://doi.org/10.1007/978-3-319-06880-0_6

5. Beimel, A., Bergadano, F., Bshouty, N.H., Kushilevitz, E., Varricchio, S.: Learning functions represented as multiplicity automata. J. ACM (JACM) **47**(3), 506–530 (2000). https://doi.org/10.1145/337244.337257

6. Bergadano, F., Varricchio, S.: Learning behaviors of automata from multiplicity and equivalence queries. SIAM J. Comput. **25**(6), 1268–1280 (1996). https://doi.org/10.1137/S009753979326091X

7. Berstel, J., Reutenauer, C.: Rational Series and Their Languages, vol. 12. Springer-Verlag (1988)

8. Bonchi, F., Sobociński, P., Zanasi, F.: A categorical semantics of signal flow graphs. In: Baldan, P., Gorla, D. (eds.) CONCUR 2014 - Concurrency Theory, pp. 435–450. Springer Berlin Heidelberg, Berlin, Heidelberg (2014). https://doi.org/10.1007/978-3-662-44584-6_30

9. Bonchi, F., Sobociński, P., Zanasi, F.: A Survey of Compositional Signal Flow Theory, pp. 29–56. Springer International Publishing, Cham (2021). https://doi.org/10.1007/978-3-030-81701-5_2

10. Bonchi, F., Sobociński, P., Zanasi, F.: The calculus of signal flow diagrams i: Linear relations on streams. Inf. Comput. **252**, 2–29 (2017). https://doi.org/10.1016/j.ic.2016.03.002

11. Boyd, S., Vandenberghe, L.: Introduction to Applied Linear Algebra: Vectors, Matrices, and Least Squares. Cambridge University Press (2018). https://doi.org/10.1017/9781108583664

12. Comparetti, P.M., Wondracek, G., Kruegel, C., Kirda, E.: Prospex: protocol specification extraction. In: 2009 30th IEEE Symposium on Security and Privacy, pp. 110–125. IEEE (2009). https://doi.org/10.1109/SP.2009.14

13. Culik, K., II., Kari, J.: Image compression using weighted finite automata. Comput. Graph. **17**(3), 305–313 (1993). https://doi.org/10.1016/0097-8493(93)90079-O

14. Denis, F., Habrard, A.: Learning rational stochastic tree languages. In: International Conference on Algorithmic Learning Theory, pp. 242–256. Springer (2007). https://doi.org/10.1007/978-3-540-75225-7_21

15. Farebrother, R.W.: Linear Least Squares Computations. Statistics, Textbooks and Monographs, vol. 91. Marcel Dekker, New York (1988). https://doi.org/10.1201/9780203748923

16. Ghica, D.R., Kaye, G., Sprunger, D.: A Fully Compositional Theory of Sequential Digital Circuits: Denotational, Operational and Algebraic Semantics (2024). https://doi.org/10.48550/arXiv.2201.10456

17. Gold, E.M.: Complexity of automaton identification from given data. Inf. Control **37**(3), 302–320 (1978). https://doi.org/10.1016/S0019-9958(78)90562-4

18. Habrard, A., Oncina, J.: Learning multiplicity tree automata. In: Grammatical Inference: Algorithms and Applications: 8th International Colloquium, ICGI 2006, Tokyo, Japan, September 20-22, 2006. Proceedings 8, pp. 268–280. Springer (2006). https://doi.org/10.1007/11872436_22

19. van Heerdt, G.: CALF: Categorical Automata Learning Framework. Doctoral Dissertation, University College London (2020). http://www.gerco.me/files/thesis_final_ucl.pdf

20. De la Higuera, C.: Grammatical Inference: Learning Automata and Grammars. Cambridge University Press (2010)

21. Isidori, A.: Nonlinear Control Systems: an Introduction. Springer (1985). https://doi.org/10.1007/BFb0006368
22. Kearns, M.J., Vazirani, U.: An Introduction to Computational Learning Theory. MIT Press (1994). https://doi.org/10.7551/mitpress/3897.001.0001
23. Knight, K., May, J.: Applications of weighted automata in natural language processing. In: Handbook of Weighted Automata, pp. 571–596. Springer (2009). https://doi.org/10.1007/978-3-642-01492-5_14
24. Lathi, B.P.: Signal Processing and Linear Systems. Oxford University Press, Oxford (1998)
25. Maletti, A.: Learning deterministically recognizable tree series—revisited. In: International Conference on Algebraic Informatics, pp. 218–235. Springer (2007). https://doi.org/10.1007/978-3-540-75414-5_14
26. Milius, S.: A sound and complete calculus for finite stream circuits. In: Proceedings of 25th Annual Symposium on Logic in Computer Science (LICS'10), pp. 449–458 (2010).https://doi.org/10.1109/LICS.2010.11
27. Mohri, M., Pereira, F., Riley, M.: Weighted Automata in Text and Speech Processing (2005). arXiv preprint: https://doi.org/10.48550/arXiv.cs/0503077
28. Oncina, J., Garcia, P.: Identifying regular languages in polynomial time. In: Advances in structural and syntactic pattern recognition, pp. 99–108. World Scientific (1992). https://doi.org/10.1142/9789812797919_0007
29. Peled, D., Vardi, M.Y., Yannakakis, M.: Black box checking. In: International Conference on Protocol Specification, Testing and Verification, pp. 225–240. Springer (1999). https://doi.org/10.1007/978-0-387-35578-8_13
30. Rutten, J.J.: Elements of stream calculus: (an extensive exercise in coinduction). Electron. Notes Theor. Comput. Sci. **45**, 358–423 (2001). https://doi.org/10.1016/S1571-0661(04)80972-1
31. Rutten, J.J.: Behavioural differential equations: a coinductive calculus of streams, automata, and power series. Theor. Comput. Sci. **308**(1–3), 1–53 (2003). https://doi.org/10.1016/S0304-3975(02)00895-2
32. Rutten, J.J.: A tutorial on coinductive stream calculus and signal flow graphs. Theor. Comput. Sci. **343**(3), 443–481 (2005). https://doi.org/10.1016/j.tcs.2005.06.019
33. Rutten, J.J.: Rational streams coalgebraically. In: Logical Methods in Computer Science, vol. 4, no. 3 (2008). https://doi.org/10.2168/lmcs-4(3:9)2008
34. Schützenberger, M.P.: On the definition of a family of automata. Inf. Control **4**(2–3), 245–270 (1961). https://doi.org/10.1016/S0019-9958(61)80020-X
35. Shannon, C.E.: The Theory and Design of Linear Differential Equation Machines. Report to National Defense Research Council, January, 1942., pp. 514–559. Wiley-IEEE Press (1942). https://doi.org/10.1109/9780470544242.ch33

Dual Adjunction Between Ω-Automata and Wilke Algebra Quotients

Anton Chernev[1]($\boxtimes$) , Helle Hvid Hansen[1] , and Clemens Kupke[2]

[1] University of Groningen, Groningen, The Netherlands
{a.chernev,h.h.hansen}@rug.nl
[2] University of Strathclyde, Glasgow, UK
clemens.kupke@strath.ac.uk

Abstract. Ω-automata and Wilke algebras are formalisms for characterising ω-regular languages via their ultimately periodic words. Ω-automata read finite representations of ultimately periodic words, called lassos, and they are a subclass of lasso automata. We introduce lasso semigroups as a generalisation of Wilke algebras that mirrors how lasso automata generalise Ω-automata, and we show that finite lasso semigroups characterise regular lasso languages. We then show a dual adjunction between lasso automata and quotients of the free lasso semigroup with a recognising set, and as our main result we show that this dual adjunction restricts to one between Ω-automata and quotients of the free Wilke algebra with a recognising set.

Keywords: Infinite words · ω-regular languages · Ultimately periodic words · Ω-automata · Wilke algebra · Coalgebra

1 Introduction

Ω-automata [8,9] were introduced as a way of capturing ω-regular languages coalgebraically [20]. This is based on two main observations. First, every ω-regular language L is determined by its set of *ultimately periodic words* $\{uv^\omega \mid uv^\omega \in L\}$ (e.g., [6, Fact 1]). Second, for every ω-regular language L, the language $\{u\$v \mid uv^\omega \in L\}$ is regular [6, Prop. 4]. Ω-automata run on *lassos*, which are pairs of finite words (u, v) representing uv^ω. Thus every ω-regular language L is identified by an Ω-automaton accepting the *lasso language* $\{(u, v) \mid uv^\omega \in L\}$. The fact that Ω-automaton bisimilarity corresponds to lasso language equivalence [8] enables algorithms for deciding language equivalence of Ω-automata, as well as minimisation algorithms using partition refinement [9] or Brzozowski-style via dual adjunctions [10, Ch. 8].

Ω-automata are defined as the subclass of *lasso automata* [8] that satisfy two conditions (circularity and coherence) which ensure that Ω-automata accept lasso languages that are *saturated*, meaning that $u_1v_1^\omega = u_2v_2^\omega$ implies (u_1, v_1) and (u_2, v_2) are both accepted or both rejected. This is required in order for Ω-automata languages to correspond to ω-regular languages. Lasso automata

C. Anutariya and M. M. Bonsangue (Eds.): ICTAC 2024, LNCS 15373, pp. 96–113, 2025.
https://doi.org/10.1007/978-3-031-77019-7_6

(accepting non-saturated languages) are of independent interest. They are studied in [1] (under the name FDFAs) in the context of learning ω-regular languages. There it is shown that certain lasso automaton representations of ω-regular languages can be factorially smaller than their Ω-automaton representations[1].

Our motivation for the present work is to better understand the mathematical connections between the coalgebraic theory of ω-regular languages, given by Ω-automata, and the algebraic theory of ω-regular languages, given by *algebraic recognition* via *Wilke algebras* [16, Sect. 2.5]. In the setting of finite words, [12,18] show an adjunction between deterministic finite automata, on the coalgebra side, and monoid congruences [17], on the algebra side. We are interested in establishing a similar result for Ω-automata and Wilke algebras. In [10, Ch. 5], a construction is given from Ω-automata to Wilke algebra homomorphisms that recognise the same language. However, the construction is only defined on objects, and the converse direction is not treated.

In this paper, we exhibit a dual adjunction between Ω-automata and *extended Wilke algebras*. We define the latter as surjective homomorphisms with the freely generated Wilke algebra as their domain, together with a recognising set. We obtain this adjunction as the restriction of another adjunction, between lasso automata and a new type of algebraic structures that we call *extended lasso semigroups*. We define lasso semigroups by omitting the *circularity* and *coherence* axioms of Wilke algebras. The lasso automaton adjunction looks as follows:

$$\text{(1)}$$

On the right, $Rev \dashv Rev^{\mathrm{op}}$ is the transition-reversal adjunction described in [10, Sect. 8.1]. On the left, Aut and Alg are new constructions between extended lasso semigroups and lasso automata that *reverse* the accepted language. In particular, Alg is different from the construction in [10, Ch. 5]. By taking suitable restrictions of the functors in Diagram (1), we obtain the adjunction:

$$\text{(2)}$$

Here Ω^{rv}-automata (in words, *reverse-Ω-automata*) are a new type of lasso automata that correspond to the reverse of Ω-automata.

Furthermore, we show that lasso semigroups provide an algebraic characterisation of lasso languages beyond saturated languages. That is, homomorphisms into finite lasso semigroups recognise precisely the regular lasso languages.

We note that dual adjunctions between coalgebras and algebras have been shown in [3,5,19] to give rise to abstract minimisation algorithms for a wide range

---

[1] In the terminology of [1], *syntactic* and *recurrent FDFAs* can be smaller than $L_\$$.

of automata that operate on finite words. Similar results have been shown for Ω-automata in [10, Ch. 8]. These dual adjunctions are of a different nature from the ones studied here, but they have also served as motivation and inspiration.

The paper is organised as follows. In Sect. 2 we collect basic definitions and notation on lasso automata, Ω-automata and Wilke algebras. In Sect. 3 we introduce lasso semigroups, define the maps *Aut*, *Alg* and *Rev* and use them to show that finite lasso semigroups recognise ω-regular languages (Theorem 2). In Sect. 4 we extend these maps to functors and prove the adjunction from Diagram (1) (Theorem 2). We use it to derive the adjunction from Diagram (2) (Theorem 3) in Sect. 5. At the end of Sects. 4 and 5, we briefly discuss how our functors relate minimal automata and maximal Wilke algebra quotients, and applications of the adjunction. We conclude with a summary and a discussion of related and future work in Sect. 6.

2   Preliminaries

We assume familiarity with basic concepts from category theory, such as categories, functors and adjunctions (see, e.g., [2,15]), and from the theory of ω-regular languages (e.g., [13]).

2.1   Languages of Infinite Words

Throughout this paper, we fix a set of symbols $\Sigma = \{a, b, \dots\}$, called an *alphabet*. Let Σ^* denote the set of *finite words* over Σ and Σ^+ denote the set of *non-empty words*. We have $\Sigma^+ = \Sigma^* \setminus \{\epsilon\}$, where ϵ stands for the empty word. We often use the notation au or ua, where $a \in \Sigma$ and $u \in \Sigma^*$, for an arbitrary non-empty word. An *infinite word* over Σ is a sequence of elements of Σ of length ω. An *ultimately periodic word* is an infinite word of the form $uv^\omega := uvv\dots$, and the set of all ultimately periodic words is written as Σ^{up}. A *lasso* is a pair $(u, v) \in \Sigma^* \times \Sigma^+$, with the set of all lassos written as Σ^{*+}. Intuitively, the lasso (u, v) represents the ultimately periodic word uv^ω. A *lasso language* is a subset of Σ^{*+}. Similarly, a *language of infinitely periodic words* is a subset of Σ^{up}. A lasso language L is *saturated* if $u_1 v_1^\omega = u_2 v_2^\omega$ implies $(u_1, v_1) \in L \iff (u_2, v_2) \in L$.

Given some $u = a_1 \dots a_n \in \Sigma^*$, we write $u^{rv} := a_n \dots a_1$ for the *reverse word of u*. While infinite words cannot be reversed, lassos can, because they are finite objects. Thus define the *reverse of a lasso* (u, av) as the lasso $(u, av)^{rv} := (v^{rv}, au^{rv})$. On the level of languages, given a lasso language L, we write $L^{rv} := \{(u, av)^{rv} \mid (u, av) \in \Sigma^{*+}\}$ for the *reverse lasso language of L*.

2.2   Lasso Automata and Ω-Automata

Lasso automata were introduced in [8,9] as acceptors of lasso languages.

Definition 1 (Lasso automaton [8]). *A lasso automaton is a tuple $A = (X, Y, q, \rho, \sigma, \xi, F)$ where:*

- X and Y are disjoint finite sets whose elements are called states;
- q is a state in X called the initial state;
- the functions $\rho : X \times \Sigma \to X$, $\sigma : X \times \Sigma \to Y$ and $\xi : Y \times \Sigma \to Y$ are called transition functions;
- F is a subset of Y whose elements are called final states.

The transition function ρ will often be tacitly used as a function from $X \times \Sigma^*$ to X in the standard way. That is, $\rho(x, \epsilon) := x$ and $\rho(x, ua) := \rho(\rho(x, u), a)$. This applies analogously to ξ.

The lasso automaton structure allows for a natural definition of lasso acceptance. A lasso (u, av) is read as follows: ρ transitions read u, σ reads a, and ξ reads v. Formally, given a lasso automaton $A = (X, Y, q, \rho, \sigma, \xi, F)$, define *the lasso language accepted by A* as $Lasso(A) := \{(u, av) \in \Sigma^{*+} \mid \xi(\sigma(\rho(q, u), a), v) \in F\}$. A lasso language is called *regular* if it is accepted by some *finite* lasso automaton.

Example 1. In Fig. 1 we see two examples of lasso automata for $\Sigma = \{a, b\}$. It can easily be verified that $Lasso(A_1) = \{(u, bv) \mid u, v \in \Sigma^*\}$ and $Lasso(A_2) = \{(ub, a^n) \mid u \in \Sigma^*, n \in \omega\}$. Note that $Lasso(A_1)$ is not saturated, since it contains (ϵ, ba), but not (b, ab).

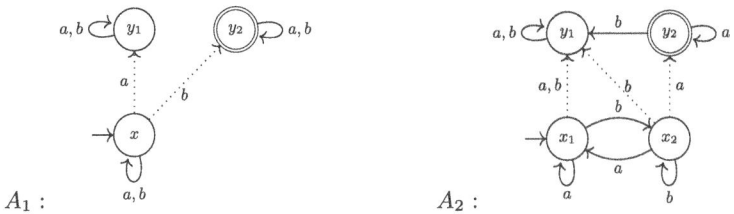

$A_1 :$ $A_2 :$

Fig. 1. Examples of lasso automata. The dotted arrows are σ-transitions.

A state z in a lasso automaton is called *reachable* if there exists a path along ρ, σ and ξ from the initial state to z. If all states in an automaton are reachable, we call it a *reachable automaton*.

A *lasso automaton morphism* is a structure-preserving map between lasso automata. More precisely, given two lasso automata $A_i = (X_i, Y_i, q_i, \rho_i, \sigma_i, \xi_i, F_i)$, for $i \in \{1, 2\}$, a lasso automaton morphism is a pair of maps $h = (h^X, h^Y)$ such that $h^X : X_1 \to X_2$ and $h^Y : Y_1 \to Y_2$ satisfy:

- $h^X(q_1) = q_2$;
- for all $x \in X_1, y \in Y_1, a \in \Sigma$: $h^X(\rho_1(x, a)) = \rho_2(h^X(x), a)$ and
  $$h^Y(\sigma_1(x, a)) = \sigma_2(h^X(x), a) \text{ and } h^Y(\xi_1(y, a)) = \xi_2(h^Y(y), a);$$
- for all $y \in Y_1$: $y \in F_1 \iff h^Y(y) \in F_2$.

Remark 1. Consider the endofunctor G on $\mathsf{Set} \times \mathsf{Set}$ defined by $G(X, Y) := \langle X^\Sigma \times Y^\Sigma, Y^\Sigma \times 2 \rangle$ on objects [8]. Lasso automata are G-coalgebras, together with an initial state. Lasso automaton morphisms coincide with initial-state-preserving G-coalgebra morphisms.

In order to capture lasso languages of the form $\{(u, v) \mid uv^\omega \in L\}$ for an ω-regular language L, [8] introduces a subclass of lasso automata called Ω-automata.

Definition 2 (Ω-automaton [8]). *An Ω-automaton is a lasso automaton $A = (X, Y, q, \rho, \sigma, \xi, F)$ that satisfies the following two conditions.*

Circularity *For all $x \in X, av \in \Sigma^+, k > 0$:*
$$\xi(\sigma(x, a), v) \in F \iff \xi(\sigma(x, a), v(av)^k) \in F.$$
Coherence *For all $x \in X, abv \in \Sigma^+$:*
$$\xi(\sigma(x, a), bv) \in F \iff \xi(\sigma(\rho(x, a), b), va) \in F.$$

It is shown in [8] that for any Ω-automaton A, the language $Lasso(A)$ is *saturated*. Furthermore, Ω-automata accept precisely the languages of the form $\{(u, v) \mid uv^\omega \in L\}$ for an ω-regular language L.

Example 2. In Fig. 1, the automaton A_2 is an Ω-automaton, and its corresponding ω-regular language is $(a + b)^* ba^\omega$. The automaton A_1 is circular, but not coherent, because $\xi(\sigma(x, b), a) = y_2 \in F$, $\xi(\sigma(\rho(x, b), a), b) = y_1 \notin F$.

2.3   Wilke Algebras

Another approach to characterising the ultimately periodic fragments of ω-regular languages is via recognition by Wilke algebra homomorphisms [22] (see also [16, Sect. 2.5]).

Definition 3 (Wilke algebra [22]). *A Wilke algebra is a two-sorted algebra of the form $W = (W^{\mathrm{fin}}, W^{\mathrm{inf}}, \cdot, \times, (-)^\omega)$, where $W^{\mathrm{fin}}, W^{\mathrm{inf}}$ are sets equipped with the operations:*

$$\cdot : W^{\mathrm{fin}} \times W^{\mathrm{fin}} \to W^{\mathrm{fin}}, \qquad \times : W^{\mathrm{fin}} \times W^{\mathrm{inf}} \to W^{\mathrm{inf}}, \qquad (-)^\omega : W^{\mathrm{fin}} \to W^{\mathrm{inf}},$$

satisfying the axioms:

$$(s \cdot t) \cdot u = s \cdot (t \cdot u), \qquad\qquad s \times (t \times \alpha) = (s \cdot t) \times \alpha,$$
$$(s^n)^\omega = s^\omega, \qquad\qquad s \times (t \cdot s)^\omega = (s \cdot t)^\omega.$$

for all $s, t \in W^{\mathrm{fin}}, \alpha \in W^{\mathrm{inf}}$. The axioms in the second line are called circularity *and* coherence, *respectively.*

If no confusion arises, we write $W = (W^{\mathrm{fin}}, W^{\mathrm{inf}})$, i.e., we omit the operations. A *Wilke algebra homomorphism* between W_1 and W_2 is a pair $f = (f^{\mathrm{fin}}, f^{\mathrm{inf}})$ of maps $f^{\mathrm{fin}} : W_1^{\mathrm{fin}} \to W_2^{\mathrm{fin}}$ and $f^{\mathrm{inf}} : W_1^{\mathrm{inf}} \to W_2^{\mathrm{inf}}$ that preserves the operations $\cdot$, $\times$ and $(-)^\omega$. That is:

$$f^{\mathrm{fin}}(s \cdot t) = f^{\mathrm{fin}}(s) \cdot f^{\mathrm{fin}}(t), \qquad\qquad f^{\mathrm{inf}}(s \times \alpha) = f^{\mathrm{fin}}(s) \times f^{\mathrm{inf}}(\alpha),$$
$$f^{\mathrm{inf}}(s^\omega) = (f^{\mathrm{fin}}(s))^\omega.$$

The freely generated Wilke algebra with generators $(\Sigma, \emptyset)$ is $(\Sigma^+, \Sigma^{\text{up}})$, where $\cdot$ is finite-word concatenation, $\times$ is finite-infinite-word concatenation, and $(-)^\omega$ is infinite power. Given a Wilke algebra W and a homomorphism $f : (\Sigma^+, \Sigma^{\text{up}}) \to W$, we say f *recognises* a language L of ultimately periodic words if $L = (f^{\text{inf}})^{-1}(P)$ for some *recognising subset* $P \subseteq W^{\text{inf}}$, and we write $L = UP(W, f, P)$. The languages recognised by homomorphisms into *finite* Wilke algebras are precisely the languages of the form $\{uv^\omega \mid uv^\omega \in L\}$ for an ω-regular L.

3   Algebraic Recognition of Lasso Languages

In this section, we introduce *lasso semigroups* as generalisations of Wilke algebras, and show that homomorphisms into *finite* lasso semigroups recognise precisely the regular lasso languages. We do this by defining mappings transforming a lasso automaton into a surjective lasso semigroup homomorphism with a recognising set, and vice versa.

3.1   Lasso Semigroups

Lasso semigroups are obtained by omitting the circularity and coherence axioms of Wilke algebras. We show that the freely generated lasso semigroup over an alphabet Σ consists of Σ^+ as its first sort and Σ^{*+} as its second sort. This allows us to define recognition of lasso languages via lasso semigroups, analogously to language recognition by Wilke algebras.

Definition 4 (Lasso semigroup). *A lasso semigroup has the same type as a Wilke algebra $W = (W^{\text{fin}}, W^{\text{inf}}, \cdot, \times, (-)^\omega)$, but the circularity and coherence axioms need not be satisfied (cf. Definition 3). A lasso semigroup homomorphism preserves operations in the same way as Wilke algebra homomorphisms.*

From the above definition it follows that Wilke algebras are a full subcategory of lasso semigroups, with their homomorphisms.

Remark 2. A lasso semigroup is, equivalently, a semigroup W^{fin} acting on a set W^{inf} by $\times$, together with a function $(-)^\omega : W^{\text{fin}} \to W^{\text{inf}}$.

Proposition 1. *The free lasso semigroup generated by $(\Sigma, \emptyset)$ is (isomorphic to) (Σ^+, Σ^{*+}), where for every $u, v \in \Sigma^+$ and $w \in \Sigma^*$:*

$$u \cdot v := uv, \qquad u \times (w, v) := (uw, v), \qquad u^\omega := (\epsilon, u).$$

Proof (sketch). Suppose $(W^{\text{fin}}, W^{\text{inf}})$ is a lasso semigroup and $f_0 : \Sigma \to W^{\text{fin}}$ is a function. Then f_0 can be uniquely extended to a homomorphism $f : (\Sigma^+, \Sigma^{*+}) \to (W^{\text{fin}}, W^{\text{inf}})$ as follows: $f^{\text{fin}}(a_1 \ldots a_n) := f_0(a_1) \cdot \ldots \cdot f_0(a_n)$ and $f^{\text{inf}}(u, v) := f^{\text{fin}}(u) \times \left(f^{\text{fin}}(v)\right)^\omega$. $\qquad \square$

Now, analogously to Wilke algebras, given a lasso semigroup homomorphism $(f^{\text{fin}}, f^{\text{inf}}) : (\Sigma^+, \Sigma^{*+}) \to (W^{\text{fin}}, W^{\text{inf}})$ and a set $P \subseteq W^{\text{inf}}$, we have that $(f^{\text{inf}})^{-1}(P)$ is a lasso language. We say that $(f^{\text{fin}}, f^{\text{inf}})$ *recognises* $(f^{\text{inf}})^{-1}(P)$ via P. Note that for every homomorphism $(f^{\text{fin}}, f^{\text{inf}})$, there exists a surjective homomorphism that recognises the same languages. Indeed, the codomain restriction $(f^{\text{fin}}, f^{\text{inf}}) : (\Sigma^+, \Sigma^{*+}) \twoheadrightarrow (\text{Im}(f^{\text{fin}}), \text{Im}(f^{\text{inf}}))$ recognises the same languages. Hence in the next definition we only consider surjective homomorphisms.

Definition 5 (Extended lasso semigroup). *An* extended lasso semigroup *is a triple* (W, f, P) *where* W *is a lasso semigroup,* $f : (\Sigma^+, \Sigma^{*+}) \twoheadrightarrow W$ *is a surjective homomorphism and* $P \subseteq W^{\text{inf}}$. *We call* (W, f, P) finite *if* W *is finite. The* lasso language recognised by (W, f, P) *is the set* $Lasso(W, f, P) := (f^{\text{inf}})^{-1}(P)$.

Remark 3. Surjective homomorphisms $f : (\Sigma^+, \Sigma^{*+}) \twoheadrightarrow W$ are in 1-1 correspondence with congruences on (Σ^+, Σ^{*+}) by taking kernels and quotient maps, respectively.

In the remainder of this section, we show that the languages recognised by *finite* extended lasso semigroups coincide with the regular lasso languages. Our strategy is to show that: (1) any finite extended lasso semigroup can be transformed into a finite lasso automaton that accepts the *reverse language*; (2) any finite lasso automaton can be transformed into a finite extended lasso semigroup that recognises the *reverse language*. The result then follows from the fact that a language is regular precisely when its reverse is regular (see [10, Sect. 8.1]).

3.2   From Lasso Semigroups to Lasso Automata

We define a mapping Aut that sends an extended lasso semigroup (W, f, P) to a lasso automaton $Aut(W, f, P)$ accepting $L(W, f, P)^{\text{rv}}$.

Recall from Remark 2 that a lasso semigroup $(W^{\text{fin}}, W^{\text{inf}})$ can be seen as a left-action of the semigroup W^{fin} on the set W^{inf} via the operation $\times$. The lasso semigroup operations provide a natural way of defining a lasso automaton structure on its two-sorted carrier. This construction is similar to the classic construction of a transition structure from a semigroup S with a semigroup morphism $f : \Sigma^+ \to S$ where the transitions are defined by $s \xrightarrow{a} s \cdot f(a)$ [17]. However, since $\times$ is a left-action, we define transitions by multiplying on the left rather than on the right as in the classic construction.

Definition 6 (Aut). *For an extended lasso semigroup* (W, f, P), *we define* $Aut(W, f, P)$ *as* $(W^{\text{fin}} \sqcup \{*\}, W^{\text{inf}}, *, \rho, \sigma, \xi, P)$ *where for all* $t \in W^{\text{fin}}, \alpha \in W^{\text{inf}}$:

- $\rho(*, a) := f^{\text{fin}}(a)$ *and* $\rho(t, a) := f^{\text{fin}}(a) \cdot t$;
- $\sigma(*, a) := f^{\text{fin}}(a)^\omega$ *and* $\sigma(t, a) := (f^{\text{fin}}(a) \cdot t)^\omega$;
- $\xi(\alpha, a) := f^{\text{fin}}(a) \times \alpha$.

Remark 4. It is clear that if (W, f, P) is finite, then $Aut(W, f, P)$ is finite.

Due to defining transitions by multiplying on the left, we have (by an easy induction argument) that for all $w \in \Sigma^+$, $\rho(*, w) = f^{\mathsf{fin}}(w^{\mathsf{rv}})$. Similar identities hold for σ and ξ, and this is essentially the reason why $Aut(W, f, P)$ accepts the reverse of $Lasso(W, f, P)$ rather than $Lasso(W, f, P)$ itself.

Proposition 2. *For every extended lasso semigroup* (W, f, P):

$$Lasso(Aut(W, f, P)) = Lasso(W, f, P)^{\mathsf{rv}}.$$

Proof (sketch). Let $Aut(W, f, P) = (W^{\mathsf{fin}} \sqcup \{*\}, W^{\mathsf{inf}}, *, \rho, \sigma, \xi, P)$. By definition, for all $(u, av) \in \Sigma^{*+}$:

$$(u, av) \in Lasso(Aut(W, f, P)) \iff \xi(\sigma(\rho(*, u), a), v) \in P, \text{ and}$$
$$(u, av)^{\mathsf{rv}} \in Lasso(W, f, P) \iff f^{\mathsf{inf}}((u, av)^{\mathsf{rv}}) \in P$$

The proof is completed by showing that:

$$\text{for all } (u, av) \in \Sigma^{*+} : \xi(\sigma(\rho(*, u), a), v) = f^{\mathsf{inf}}((u, av)^{\mathsf{rv}}). \qquad (3) \qquad \square$$

3.3 From Lasso Automata to Lasso Semigroups

We now describe a converse transformation, i.e., a mapping *Alg* sending a lasso automaton $A = (X, Y, q, \rho, \sigma, \xi, F)$ to an extended lasso semigroup. Cruchten [10, Ch. 5] gives a construction of a Wilke algebra from an Ω-automaton which can be seen as a generalisation of the classic construction of a transition semigroup from a finite automaton. In the construction in ibid., an element of the algebra represents paths in the automaton corresponding to a word. Our construction *Alg* is a variation of Cruchten's idea, with the crucial difference that here paths are reversed. The choice of *Alg* is justified in Sect. 4, where we show that *Alg* is the (unique) right adjoint of *Aut* (Proposition 8).

As the carrier of the algebra we take $U_A := (X^X \times Y^X \times Y^Y, Y)$. That is, elements of U_A^{fin} are triples (α, β, γ), where α encodes (the endpoints of) ρ-paths, β encodes ρ-paths with a single σ-transition at the end, and γ encodes ξ-paths. Elements $y \in U^{\mathsf{inf}}$ represent the state reached after reading some lasso *in reverse*, starting from q. Before defining the operations on U_A, it is insightful to see what the desired homomorphism $f_A : (\Sigma^+, \Sigma^{*+}) \to U_A$ is:

$$f_A^{\mathsf{fin}}(av) = (\lambda x.\rho(x, v^{\mathsf{rv}} a), \lambda x.\sigma(\rho(x, v^{\mathsf{rv}}), a), \lambda y.\xi(y, v^{\mathsf{rv}} a)), \qquad (4)$$
$$f_A^{\mathsf{inf}}(u, av) = \xi(\sigma(\rho(q, v^{\mathsf{rv}}), a), u^{\mathsf{rv}}). \qquad (5)$$

In fact, in defining the operations on U_A, we are guided by the goal of ensuring f_A becomes a homomorphism. The fact that our construction reverses the language will follow from the form of f_A.

Definition 7. *Let* $A = (X, Y, q, \rho, \sigma, \xi, F)$ *be a lasso automaton. Define the algebraic structure* $U_A := (X^X \times Y^X \times Y^Y, Y)$ *with the following operations:*

$$(\alpha_1, \beta_1, \gamma_1) \cdot (\alpha_2, \beta_2, \gamma_2) := (\alpha_1 \alpha_2, \beta_1 \alpha_2, \gamma_1 \gamma_2),$$
$$(\alpha, \beta, \gamma)^\omega := \beta(q),$$
$$(\alpha, \beta, \gamma) \times y := \gamma(y),$$

for each $\alpha_i \in X^X$, $\beta_i \in Y^X$, $\gamma_i \in Y^Y$, $y \in Y$ *(here* $\alpha_1 \alpha_2$ *denotes* $\alpha_1 \circ \alpha_2$).

Proposition 3. *The structure defined in Definition 7 is a lasso semigroup.*

Proposition 4. *Let* $A = (X, Y, q, \rho, \sigma, \xi, F)$ *be a lasso automaton and* $f_A : (\Sigma^+, \Sigma^{*+}) \rightarrow U_A$ *be defined by Eqs. (4) and (5). Then* f_A *is a lasso semigroup homomorphism.*

Note that f_A is not surjective, but we can define the desired extended lasso semigroup by taking the image of f_A.

Definition 8 (Alg). *Given a lasso automaton* $A = (X, Y, q, \rho, \sigma, \xi, F)$, *we define* $Alg(A) := (W_A, f_A, F)$, *where* W_A *is the image of* f_A *in* U_A.

Remark 5. It follows immediately that if A is finite, then $Alg(A)$ is finite.

Proposition 5. *For every lasso automaton* $A = (X, Y, q, \rho, \sigma, \xi, F)$:

$$Lasso(Alg(A)) = Lasso(A)^{rv}.$$

Proof. Suppose $Alg(A) = (W, f, P)$. We have that $Lasso(W, f, P)$ consists of all lassos (u, av) such that $f^{inf}(u, av) \in P$. By Eq. (5), this is equivalent to $\xi(\sigma(\rho(s, v^{rv}), a), u^{rv}) \in P = F$, i.e., $(v^{rv}, au^{rv}) \in Lasso(A)$. Hence $Lasso(W, f, P) = Lasso(A)^{rv}$. □

3.4   Finite Lasso Semigroups Recognise Regular Lasso Languages

From Propositions 2 and 5 it follows that the languages recognised by finite extended lasso semigroups are the reverse of regular lasso languages. In order to conclude that finite extended lasso semigroups recognise regular lasso languages, it remains to show that L is regular if and only if L^{rv} is regular. This follows from the fact that, analogously to DFAs, every lasso automaton can be reversed. The construction is described in [10, Sect. 8.1]. States in the reversed automaton are sets of states of the original automaton, while transitions correspond to taking preimages of the original transition functions. We include the definition here, since it will be used in Sects. 4 and 5.

Definition 9 (Reverse lasso automaton [10, Def. 8.17]). *Let* $A = (X, Y, q, \rho, \sigma, \xi, F)$ *be a lasso automaton. Define the reverse automaton* $Rev(A) := (2^Y, 2^X, F, \hat{\xi}, \hat{\sigma}, \hat{\rho}, \{S \mid q \in S\})$, *where, for* $\delta \in \{\rho, \sigma, \xi\}$, $\hat{\delta}$ *is defined as:*

$$\hat{\delta}(S, a) := \{z \mid \delta(z, a) \in S\}.$$

Proposition 6 ([10, Prop. 8.22]). *Let* A *be a lasso automaton. Then* $Lasso(Rev\ (A)) = Lasso(A)^{rv}$.

We can now state our algebraic characterisation of regular lasso languages.

Theorem 1. *A lasso language* L *is recognised by a finite extended lasso semigroup if and only if* L *is regular.*

Proof. Suppose $L = Lasso(W, f, P)$ for some finite extended lasso semigroup (W, f, P). Then $L = Lasso(Rev(Aut(W, f, P)))$, where $Rev(Aut(W, f, P))$ is a finite lasso automaton, thus L is regular. Conversely, if $L = Lasso(A)$ for some finite lasso automaton, then $L = Lasso(Alg(Rev(A)))$, where $Alg(Rev(A))$ is a finite extended lasso semigroup. □

Noting that (W, f, P) recognises L iff $(W, f, W^{\text{inf}} \setminus P)$ recognises the complement of L, Theorem 1 implies that regular lasso languages are closed under complementation. This was already proved using automata in [8], but the algebraic argument is immediate.[2]

Corollary 1. *Regular lasso languages are closed under complementation.*

4 Dual Adjunction Between Lasso Automata and Lasso Semigroups

In the last section we introduced the mappings *Aut* and *Alg* as tools for characterising language recognition by finite extended lasso semigroups. In this section, we show that *Aut* and *Alg* also reveal the categorical relationship between the *category of lasso automata* and the *category of extended lasso semigroups*. More precisely, we show that *Aut* and *Alg* can be extended to a pair of adjoint functors. By composing this adjunction with the adjunction $Rev \dashv Rev^{\text{op}}$ proven in [10, Sect. 8.1], we arrive at a language-preserving dual adjunction between extended lasso semigroups and lasso automata. See Diagram (1).

4.1 Categories of Lasso Automata and Lasso Semigroups

A natural notion of a morphism between extended lasso semigroups is a homomorphism that preserves the quotient structure and the recognising subset.

Definition 10 (Category of extended lasso semigroups). *Given two extended lasso semigroups (W_i, f_i, P_i), an extended lasso semigroup morphism $g : (W_1, f_1, P_1) \to (W_2, f_2, P_2)$ is a homomorphism $g : W_1 \to W_2$ such that $g \circ f_1 = f_2$ and $\alpha \in P_1 \iff g^{\text{inf}}(\alpha) \in P_2$, for all $\alpha \in W_1^{\text{inf}}$. We write ELSgp for the category of extended lasso semigroups and their morphisms.*

On the automaton side, we use the standard notion of automaton morphism (see Sect. 2). Apart from the category of all lasso automata, we define its full subcategory of reachable lasso automata. A restriction to reachable automata is necessary in Proposition 7 for ensuring *Alg* is functorial.

Definition 11 (Categories of lasso automata). *Let LAut denote the category of lasso automata and lasso automata morphisms. Let RLAut denote the full subcategory of LAut of all reachable lasso automata.*

---

[2] To prove closure under union and intersection, we would additionally need to consider limits of lasso semigroups.

It follows from surjectivity of f_1 that there is at most one extended lasso semigroup morphism $g : (W_1, f_1, P_1) \to (W_2, f_2, P_2)$. Moreover, observe that if A is a reachable lasso automaton, then there exists at most one morphism with domain A. That is:

Lemma 1. RLAut *and* ELSgp *are posetal categories.*

4.2   Functoriality of *Aut* and *Alg*

We begin with an example showing that *Alg cannot be extended* to a functor LAut → ELSgp.

Example 3. Consider the lasso automata $A := (\{x\}, \{y\}, x, \rho, \sigma, \xi, \emptyset)$ (where ρ, σ and ξ are uniquely determined by their types) and $A' = (\{x'_1, x'_2\}, \{y'\}, x'_1, \rho', \sigma',$ $\xi', \emptyset)$ with $\rho'(x'_1, a) = \rho'(x'_1, b) = \rho(x'_2, a) = x'_1$, $\rho'(x'_2, b) = x'_2$. The map $h = (h^X, h^Y)$ with $h^X(x) = x'_1$ and $h^Y(y) = y'$ is a lasso automaton morphism. However, there is no map from $Alg(A) := (W, f, P)$ to $Alg(A') := (W', f', P')$, because $f^{\mathsf{fin}}(a) = \langle \{x \mapsto x\}, \{x \mapsto y\}, \{y \mapsto y\} \rangle = f^{\mathsf{fin}}(b)$, but $(f')^{\mathsf{fin}}(a) = \langle \{x'_1 \mapsto x'_1, x'_2 \mapsto x'_1\}, \cdots, \cdots \rangle \neq \langle \{x'_1 \mapsto x'_1, x'_2 \mapsto x'_2\}, \cdots, \cdots \} \rangle = (f')^{\mathsf{fin}}(b)$.

Hence in order to obtain a functor *Alg*, we need to restrict the domain LAut. In the example above, the automaton A' was not reachable, which gives us the idea to restrict the domain to RLAut. Moreover, the next lemma shows that the codomain of *Aut* can also be restricted to RLAut.

Lemma 2. *Let* (W, f, P) *be an extended lasso semigroup. Then* $Aut(W, f, P)$ *is reachable.*

Since ELSgp is a posetal category (Lemma 1), for any lasso automaton morphism $h : A_1 \to A_2$, there exists at most one candidate for $Alg(h)$. Thus, in order to show functoriality of *Alg*, it suffices to prove that such a candidate exists. Likewise for functoriality of *Aut*.

We reduce existence of morphisms in ELSgp and RLAut to comparing certain equivalence relations on Σ^+ and Σ^{*+}.

Definition 12. *Let* $A = (X, Y, q, \rho, \sigma, \xi, F)$ *be a lasso automaton. We write:*

$$\chi_A(ua) := (\lambda x.\rho(x, ua), \lambda x.\sigma(\rho(x, u), a), \lambda y.\xi(y, ua)).$$

Define the pair $\approx_A = (\approx_A^{\mathsf{fin}}, \approx_A^{\mathsf{inf}})$ *of equivalence relations* $\approx_A^{\mathsf{fin}}$ *on* Σ^+ *and* $\approx_A^{\mathsf{inf}}$ *on* Σ^{*+} *by:*

$$u_1 \approx_A^{\mathsf{fin}} u_2 \iff \chi_A(u_1) = \chi_A(u_2)$$
$$(v_1, a_1 u_1) \approx_A^{\mathsf{inf}} (v_2, a_2 u_2) \iff \xi(\sigma(\rho(q, v_1), a_1), u_1) = \xi(\sigma(\rho(q, v_2), a_2), u_2).$$

We say that $\approx_{A_1}$ *refines* $\approx_{A_2}$ *if* $\approx_{A_1}^{\mathsf{fin}} \subseteq \approx_{A_2}^{\mathsf{fin}}$ *and* $\approx_{A_1}^{\mathsf{inf}} \subseteq \approx_{A_2}^{\mathsf{inf}}$. *Define* $\approx_A^{\mathsf{rv}}$ *by:*

$$u_1 \approx_A^{\mathsf{rv}} u_2 \iff u_1^{\mathsf{rv}} \approx_A u_2^{\mathsf{rv}},$$
$$(v_1, a_1 u_1) \approx_A^{\mathsf{rv}} (v_2, a_2 u_2) \iff (v_1, a_1 u_1)^{\mathsf{rv}} \approx_A (v_2, a_2 u_2)^{\mathsf{rv}}.$$

Compare the definition of $\approx_A$ to Eqs. (4) and (5). We have $u_1 \approx_A u_2 \iff f_A^{\text{fin}}(u_1^{\text{rv}}) = f_A^{\text{fin}}(u_2^{\text{rv}})$, and $(v_1, u_1) \approx_A (v_2, u_2) \iff f_A^{\text{inf}}((v_1, u_1)^{\text{rv}}) = f_A^{\text{inf}}((v_2, u_2)^{\text{rv}})$. Furthermore, note that $\approx_A$ resembles the relation from [10, Def. 6.3] used for deriving a Myhill-Nerode theorem [10, Th. 6.13] for Ω-automata. There u_1 and u_2 are identified if $\rho(q, u_1) = \rho(q, u_2)$. Our $\approx_A^{\text{fin}}$ is more restrictive, since it considers all types of transitions ρ, σ, ξ, and all starting states.

Definition 13. *Let (W, f, P) be an extended lasso semigroup. Define the pair $\sim_W = (\sim_W^{\text{fin}}, \sim_W^{\text{inf}})$ of equivalence relations $\sim_W^{\text{fin}}$ on Σ^+ and $\sim_A^{\text{inf}}$ on Σ^{*+} where $\sim_W^{\text{fin}}$ is the kernel of f^{fin} and $\sim_W^{\text{inf}}$ is the kernel of f^{inf}. Refinement and $\sim_W^{\text{rv}}$ are defined analogously to Definition 12.*

Lemma 3. *1. Let A_1 and A_2 be reachable lasso automata. There exists an automaton morphism $h : A_1 \to A_2$ if and only if $\approx_{A_1}$ refines $\approx_{A_2}$ and $Lasso(A_1) = Lasso(A_2)$.*
2. Let (W_1, f_1, P_1) and (W_2, f_2, P_2) be extended lasso semigroups. There exists an extended lasso semigroup morphism $g : (W_1, f_1, P_1) \to (W_2, f_2, P_2)$ if and only if $\sim_{W_1}$ refines $\sim_{W_2}$ and $Lasso(W_1, f_1, P_1) = Lasso(W_2, f_2, P_2)$.

Lemma 4. *Let A be a lasso automaton and (W, f, P) be an extended lasso semigroup. Then $\sim_{Alg(A)} = \approx_A^{\text{rv}}$ and $\approx_{Aut(W,f,P)} = \sim_W^{\text{rv}}$.*

Proposition 7. *The mappings Alg and Aut can be extended uniquely to functors $Alg : \mathsf{RLAut} \to \mathsf{ELSgp}$ and $Aut : \mathsf{ELSgp} \to \mathsf{RLAut}$.*

Proof. First, we prove functoriality of Alg. Let $h = (h^X, h^Y) : A_1 \to A_2$ be a lasso automaton morphism. Because of Lemma 1, it suffices to show that there exists a morphism $g : Alg(A_1) \to Alg(A_2)$. By Lemma 3, $\approx_{A_1}$ refines $\approx_{A_2}$ and $Lasso(A_1) = Lasso(A_2)$. By Lemma 4, $\sim_{Alg(A_1)}^{\text{rv}}$ refines $\sim_{Alg(A_2)}^{\text{rv}}$, so $\sim_{Alg(A_1)}$ refines $\sim_{Alg(A_2)}$. By Proposition 5, $Lasso(Alg(A_1)) = Lasso(A_1)^{\text{rv}} = Lasso(A_2)^{\text{rv}} = Lasso(Alg(A_2))$. By Lemma 3 again, there exists a morphism $g : Alg(A_1) \to Alg(A_2)$. Functoriality of Aut follows analogously.

4.3   Lasso Adjunction

Below we prove the dual adjunction between lasso automata and extended lasso semigroups. It is obtained as the composition of three simpler adjunctions (cf. Diagram (6)). We start with the adjunction between reachable lasso automata and extended lasso semigroups $Aut \dashv Alg$. It is the key technical result of this paper. In the proof, we work with the definition of adjunctions in terms of hom-sets, cf. [2, Sect. 9.2].

Proposition 8. *There exists an adjunction $Aut \dashv Alg : \mathsf{ELSgp} \to \mathsf{RLAut}$.*

Proof. Let $A = (X, Y, q, \rho, \sigma, \xi, F)$ be an arbitrary reachable lasso automaton, (W, f, P) an arbitrary extended lasso semigroup. Since RLAut and ELSgp are posetal categories, it suffices to show that there exists a morphism $g :$

$(W, f, P) \to Alg(A)$ if and only if there exists a morphism $h : Aut(W, f, P) \to A$. Suppose there exists $g : (W, f, P) \to Alg(A)$. By Lemma 3, $\sim_W$ refines $\sim_{Alg(A)}$ and $Lasso(Alg(A)) = Lasso(W, f, P)$. By Lemma 4, $\sim_W$ refines $\approx_A^{\mathrm{rv}}$. By Lemma 4 again, $\approx_{Aut(W,f,P)}^{\mathrm{rv}}$ refines $\approx_A^{\mathrm{rv}}$, so $\approx_{Aut(W,f,P)}$ refines $\approx_A$. By Propositions 2 and 5, $Lasso(A) = Lasso(Alg(A))^{\mathrm{rv}} = Lasso(W, f, P)^{\mathrm{rv}} = Lasso(Aut(W, f, P))$. By Lemma 3 again, there exists $h : Aut(W, f, P) \to A$. The other direction is analogous. □

Although $Aut \dashv Alg$ reveals a relationship between lasso automata and extended lasso semigroups, it leaves more to be desired. Concretely, we look for an adjunction: (1) that is also defined for non-reachable automata, and (2) whose constituent functors preserve the accepted language. Language-preservation enables specialising the adjunction to Ω-automata and Wilke algebras in Sect. 5.

In order to handle the first requirement, we give an adjunction between RLAut and LAut. It is analogous to a similar adjunction between reachable DFAs and all DFAs [5, Sect. 9.4]. In one direction, we have an inclusion functor $Inc : \mathsf{RLAut} \to \mathsf{LAut}$. For the the other direction, there exists a functor $Rch : \mathsf{LAut} \to \mathsf{RLAut}$ mapping an automaton A to its reachable part $Rch(A)$. Moreover, Rch maps an automaton morphism to its restriction to reachable states.

Proposition 9. *There exists an adjunction* $Inc \dashv Rch : \mathsf{RLAut} \to \mathsf{LAut}$.

Proof (sketch). Every morphism in $\mathrm{Hom}(A, Rch(B))$ can be mapped bijectively to a morphism in $\mathrm{Hom}(Inc(A), B)$ by expanding its codomain.

In order to handle the second requirement, we recall from [10, Sect. 8.1] that Rev from Definition 9 can be extended to a functor which is its own dual adjoint. That is, [10, Def. 8.23] extends Rev to a functor by defining it on morphisms as $Rev(h^X, h^Y) = ((h^X)^{-1}, (h^Y)^{-1})$. Then [10, Cor. 8.24] states that there is an adjunction $Rev \dashv Rev^{\mathrm{op}} : \mathsf{LAut} \to \mathsf{LAut}^{\mathrm{op}}$.

Now we are ready to collect all adjunctions into the main result of this section.

Theorem 2. *The functors* $Rev \circ Inc \circ Aut$ *and* $Aut \circ Rch \circ Rev^{\mathrm{op}}$ *are language-preserving adjoints, with* $Rev \circ Inc \circ Aut \dashv Alg \circ Rch \circ Rev^{\mathrm{op}} : \mathsf{ELSgp} \to \mathsf{LAut}^{\mathrm{op}}$.

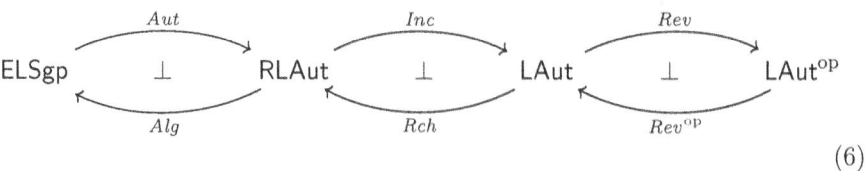

$$(6)$$

We make some observations about the adjunction. The functor Rev maps a reachable lasso automaton to an observable lasso automaton [10, Chap.8]. Informally, a lasso automaton is observable if distinct states accept distinct lasso languages. A lasso automaton is minimal if it is both reachable and observable. It follows that for all $(W, f, P) \in \mathsf{ELSgp}$, the automaton $(Rev \circ Inc \circ Aut)(W, f, P)$ is observable. Hence by taking its reachable part, we obtain a minimal automaton accepting $Lasso(W, f, P)$.

Going in the other direction, if we start with a reachable lasso automaton A accepting L, then $(Rch \circ Rev^{\mathrm{op}})(A)$ is a minimal automaton accepting L^{rv}, and $(Alg \circ Rch \circ Rev^{\mathrm{op}})(A)$ is the maximal quotient of (Σ^+, Σ^{*+}) that recognises L. This comes about as follows, cf. [5, Sect. 9.2]. The categories ELSgp and RLAut do not have initial or final objects, since morphisms preserve the language, but if we fix a lasso language L and denote by ELSgp(L) and RLAut(L) the full subcategories of structures that recognise, resp. accept, L then we do obtain initial and final objects in ELSgp(L) and RLAut(L). Since Aut and Alg reverse the language, they restrict to an adjunction between ELSgp(L) and RLAut(L^{rv}). The final object in RLAut(L^{rv}) is the minimal lasso automaton for L^{rv}, and the final object in ELSgp(L) is the maximal quotient of (Σ^+, Σ^{*+}) that recognises L. Since Alg is a right adjoint, it preserves final objects, hence Alg maps the minimal lasso automaton for L^{rv} to the maximal quotient of (Σ^+, Σ^{*+}) that recognises L.

This, in particular, shows that $Alg \circ Rch \circ Rev^{\mathrm{op}}$ differs from Cruchten's construction [10, Ch. 5], because the latter does not map all reachable Ω-automata accepting L to the maximal Wilke algebra quotient for L. For instance, one can observe that Cruchten's construction maps the initial Ω-automaton for $L = \Sigma^{*+}$, with states $X = \Sigma^*, Y = \Sigma^{*+}$, to the minimal Wilke algebra quotient $(\Sigma^+, \Sigma^{\mathrm{up}})$.

5 Restricting the Adjunction to Ω-Automata and Wilke Algebras

In this section, we show that the adjunction from Theorem 2 restricts to Ω-automata and Wilke algebras. First, we note that we can define a notion of extended Wilke algebra by adding a recognising subset to a Wilke algebra homomorphisms $f : (\Sigma^+, \Sigma^{\mathrm{up}}) \to W$. The main observation is that Ω-automata are a full subcategory of LAut, and extended Wilke algebras can be identified with a full subcategory of ELSgp. In general, restricting an adjunction to full subcategories yields another adjunction, as long as the restricted functors are well-defined on objects. This is because hom-sets in a full subcategory are inherited from the ambient category. Therefore our task is to show that restricting the functors from Theorem 2 to Ω-automata and Wilke algebras is well-defined.

We begin with specialising extended lasso semigroups to Wilke algebras.

Definition 14 (Extended Wilke Algebra). *An* extended Wilke algebra *is an extended lasso semigroup (W, f, P) such that W is a Wilke algebra, i.e., W satisfies the circularity and coherence axioms. We write* EWAlg *for the full subcategory of* ELSgp *of all extended Wilke algebras.*

Note that in the above definition $f : (\Sigma^+, \Sigma^{*+}) \twoheadrightarrow W$ has the free lasso semigroup as its domain, instead of the free Wilke algebra. But, given a Wilke algebra W, there exists a bijective correspondence between maps of type $(\Sigma^+, \Sigma^{\mathrm{up}}) \twoheadrightarrow W$ and maps of type $(\Sigma^+, \Sigma^{*+}) \twoheadrightarrow W$. This correspondence is given by precomposition with the map $\phi : (\Sigma^+, \Sigma^{*+}) \twoheadrightarrow (\Sigma^+, \Sigma^{\mathrm{up}})$ defined by $\phi^{\mathrm{fin}}(s) = s$ and

$\phi^{\mathrm{inf}}(u,v) = uv^\omega$. We prefer the type $(\Sigma^+, \Sigma^{\mathrm{up}}) \twoheadrightarrow W$, as it allows us to view EWAlg as a subcategory of ELSgp.

Next, we turn to the automaton categories. As we remarked, Ω-automata form a full subcategory of LAut, which we write as ΩAut. However, the functor $Rev : \mathsf{LAut} \to \mathsf{LAut}^{\mathrm{op}}$ does not restrict to $Rev : \Omega\mathsf{Aut} \to \Omega\mathsf{Aut}^{\mathrm{op}}$. In order to see why the reverse of an Ω-automaton is not an Ω-automaton, recall that for any Ω-automaton A, the language $Lasso(A)$ is saturated. But we cannot expect that $Lasso(A^{\mathrm{rv}}) = Lasso(A)^{\mathrm{rv}}$ is also saturated. Hence we introduce a new type of lasso automata which turn out to be exactly the reverse of some Ω-automaton.

Definition 15 (Ω^{rv}-automata). *A Ω^{rv}-automaton (in words, reverse-Ω-automaton) is a lasso automaton $A = (X,Y,q,\rho,\sigma,\xi,F)$ satisfying, for all $va, vba \in \Sigma^+$ and $k > 0$:*

$$\sigma(\rho(q,v),a) = \sigma(\rho(q,(va)^k v),a) \quad and \quad \sigma(\rho(q,vb),a) = \xi(\sigma(\rho(q,av),b),a).$$

We call these identities reverse-circularity *and* reverse-coherence, *respectively.*

Proposition 10. *Let A be a lasso automaton. If A is circular, then $Rev(A)$ is reverse-circular, and if A is reverse-circular, then $Rev(A)$ is circular. Likewise for coherence and reverse coherence.*

Proof (sketch). Let $A = (X,Y,q,\rho,\sigma,\xi,F)$ and $Rev(A) = (X^{\mathrm{rv}},Y^{\mathrm{rv}},q^{\mathrm{rv}},\rho^{\mathrm{rv}},\sigma^{\mathrm{rv}}, \xi^{\mathrm{rv}},F^{\mathrm{rv}})$. If A is circular, $va \in \Sigma^+$ and $k > 0$:

$$\sigma^{\mathrm{rv}}(\rho^{\mathrm{rv}}(q^{\mathrm{rv}},v),a) = \{x \in X \mid \xi(\sigma(x,a),v^{\mathrm{rv}}) \in F\} =$$
$$= \{x \in X \mid \xi(\sigma(x,a),v^{\mathrm{rv}}(av^{\mathrm{rv}})^k) \in F\} = \sigma^{\mathrm{rv}}(\rho^{\mathrm{rv}}(F,(va)^k v),a),$$

where the second equality uses circularity, and the first and third equalities use the identity $\xi^{\mathrm{rv}}(\sigma^{\mathrm{rv}}(\rho^{\mathrm{rv}}(q^{\mathrm{rv}},v),a),w) = \{x \in X \mid \xi(\sigma(\rho(x,w^{\mathrm{rv}}),a),v^{\mathrm{rv}}) \in F\}$. Hence $Rev(A)$ is reverse-circular. The other parts of the proposition follow by similar reasoning. □

Proposition 11. *Let $A \in \mathsf{LAut}$ and $(W,f,P) \in \mathsf{ELSgp}$. If A is reverse-circular, then $Alg(A)$ satisfies the circularity axiom, and if (W,f,P) satisfies the circularity axiom, then $Aut(W,f,P)$ is reverse-circular. Likewise for reverse-coherence and the coherence axiom.*

Proof (sketch). We show that applying Alg to a reverse-coherent automaton yields a coherent algebra. The other parts of the proposition follows by similar reasoning. Let $A = (X,Y,q,\rho,\sigma,\xi,F)$ and $Alg(A) = (W_A,f_A,P_A)$. Suppose that A is reverse-coherent and let $(\alpha_i,\beta_i,\gamma_i) \in W_A^{\mathrm{fin}}$, for $i \in \{1,2\}$. We have $(\alpha_1,\beta_1,\gamma_1) = f^{\mathrm{fin}}(a_1 \ldots a_n)$ and $(\alpha_2,\beta_2,\gamma_2) = f^{\mathrm{fin}}(bv)$, for some $a_1,\ldots,a_n,b \in \Sigma$, $v \in \Sigma^*$. Hence:

$$(\alpha_1,\beta_1,\gamma_1) \times \big((\alpha_2,\beta_2,\gamma_2) \cdot (\alpha_1,\beta_1,\gamma_1)\big)^\omega = (\alpha_1,\beta_1,\gamma_1) \times (\alpha_1\alpha_2,\beta_1\alpha_2,\gamma_1\gamma_2)^\omega$$
$$= (\alpha_1,\beta_1,\gamma_1) \times \beta_1\alpha_2(q) = \gamma_1\beta_2\alpha_1(q) = \xi(\sigma(\rho(q,a_n \ldots a_1 v^r),b),a_n \ldots a_1)$$
$$= \xi(\sigma(\rho(q,a_{n-1} \ldots a_1 v^{\mathrm{rv}} b),a_n),a_{n-1} \ldots a_1) = \ldots = \sigma(\rho(q,v^{\mathrm{rv}} b a_n \ldots a_2),a_1)$$
$$= \beta_1(\alpha_2(q)) = (\alpha_1\alpha_2,\beta_1\alpha_2,\gamma_1\gamma_2)^\omega = \big((\alpha_1,\beta_1,\gamma_1) \cdot (\alpha_2,\beta_2,\gamma_2)\big)^\omega,$$

where we use reverse-coherence n-many times in the third line. □

Now we are ready to present the adjunction from Theorem 2, restricted to Ω-automata and Wilke algebras.

Definition 16. *Write* ΩAut *for the full subcategory of* LAut *of all* Ω*-automata. Write* Ω^{rv}Aut *for the full subcategory of* LAut *of all* Ω^{rv}*-automata. Finally, write* RΩ^{rv}Aut *for the full subcategory of* Ω^{rv}Aut *of all reachable* Ω^{rv}*-automata.*

Theorem 3. *The adjunction from Theorem 2 restricts to:*

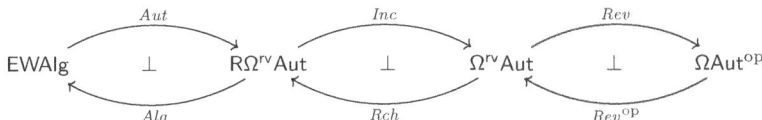

Proof. It follows from Proposition 11 that the restrictions Aut : EWAlg $\to$ RΩ^{rv}Aut and Alg : RΩ^{rv}Aut $\to$ EWAlg are well-defined. It is straightforward to see that reverse-circularity and reverse-coherence are preserved by Rch, so the restrictions Inc : RΩ^{rv}Aut $\to$ Ω^{rv}Aut and Rch : Ω^{rv}Aut $\to$ RΩ^{rv}Aut are well-defined. Finally, from Proposition 10, we have that the restrictions Rev : Ω^{rv}Aut $\to$ ΩAut^{op} and Rev^{op} : ΩAut^{op} $\to$ Ω^{rv}Aut are well-defined. Therefore $Rev \circ Inc \circ Aut \dashv Alg \circ Rch \circ Rev^{op}$: EWAlg $\to$ ΩAut^{op}. □

The observations made below Theorem 2 apply also in the setting of Theorem 3, including the relationships between minimal automata and maximal quotients. In [9], a decision procedure was given for checking whether a lasso automaton is an Ω-automaton. Theorems 2 and 3 provide an alternative algebraic procedure via the following proposition.

Proposition 12. *A lasso automaton A is circular and coherent iff the extended lasso semigroup* $(Alg \circ Rch \circ Rev)(A)$ *is circular and coherent. Checking whether a finite lasso semigroup* (W^{fin}, W^{inf}) *is circular and coherent can be done in time* $O(n^2)$ *where* $n = |W^{fin}|$.

The size of $(Alg \circ Rch \circ Rev)(A)$ is in the worst case doubly-exponential in the number of states of A. However, the exponential blow-up in the reverse-determinise construction is known to often not turn up in practice [7], so it could be interesting to evaluate the algebraic decision procedure on some real-life examples.

6   Conclusion

In this paper, we introduced and studied lasso semigroups as generalisations of Wilke algebras. We proved that homomorphisms into finite lasso semigroups characterise regular lasso languages by giving language-preserving transformations between lasso automata and extended lasso semigroups. We extended these transformations to dually adjoint functors between the categories of lasso automata and of lasso semigroups extended with a recognising set, and showed that this adjunction restricts to a dual adjunction between Ω-automata and extended Wilke algebras.

Since lasso semigroups characterise regular lasso languages, we believe that they are also of interest in their own right. This is motivated by the relevance of non-saturated lasso languages (which cannot be described by a Wilke algebra) in automata learning [1]. A categorical approach to learning ω-regular languages [21] is also based on lasso languages and algebraic recognition. Ideas from [21] relating language acceptance via Wilke algebras with automata acceptance provided useful inspiration for our own constructions. A different algebraic approach to lasso languages is found in [11] where so-called lasso algebras are introduced as counterparts of Kleene algebra for reasoning about language equivalence of lasso expressions.

Closely related to our work is a very recent and independently developed dual adjunction [12] between lasso/Ω-automata and certain *bisimulation congruences*. Bisimulation congruences correspond to lasso semigroup quotients satisfying an extra bisimulation condition. Another difference with the present work is that the adjunction in [12], which is based on constructions from [10], is language-preserving whereas the adjunction $Aut \dashv Alg$ is language-reversing. We leave a detailed comparison between the two approaches as future work.

The adjunctions we have established are instrumental for clarifying the relationship between coalgebraic and algebraic approaches to languages of infinite words (although we deliberately kept the coalgebraic perspective implicit). This could aid the discovery of new coalgebraic or algebraic approaches to language theory beyond infinite words. In particular, there are extensions of Wilke algebras for *infinite trees* [4,14], but no notions of lasso or Ω-automata on infinite trees. We see this as a fruitful direction for future work.

References

1. Angluin, D., Fisman, D.: Learning regular omega languages. Theor. Comput. Sci. **650**, 57–72 (2016). https://doi.org/10.1016/j.tcs.2016.07.031
2. Awodey, S.: Category Theory, 2nd edn. Oxford University Press, Inc. (2010). https://dl.acm.org/doi/10.5555/2060081
3. Bezhanishvili, N., et al.: Minimisation in logical form. In: Palmigiano, A., Sadrzadeh, M. (eds.) Samson Abramsky on Logic and Structure in Computer Science and Beyond, pp. 89–127. Springer, Cham (2023). https://doi.org/10.1007/978-3-031-24117-8_3
4. Bojańczyk, M., Idziaszek, T.: Algebra for Infinite Forests with an Application to the Temporal Logic EF. In: Bravetti, M., Zavattaro, G. (eds.) CONCUR 2009. LNCS, vol. 5710, pp. 131–145. Springer, Heidelberg (2009). https://doi.org/10.1007/978-3-642-04081-8_10
5. Bonchi, F., Bonsangue, M.M., Hansen, H.H., Panangaden, P., Rutten, J.J.M.M., Silva, A.: Algebra-coalgebra duality in Brzozowski's minimization algorithm. ACM Trans. Comput. Log. **15**(1), 1–29 (2014). https://doi.org/10.1145/2490818
6. Calbrix, H., Nivat, M., Podelski, A.: Ultimately periodic words of rational ω-languages. In: Brookes, S., Main, M., Melton, A., Mislove, M., Schmidt, D. (eds.)

MFPS 1993. LNCS, vol. 802, pp. 554–566. Springer, Heidelberg (1994). https://doi.org/10.1007/3-540-58027-1_27

7. Champarnaud, J.M., Khorsi, A., Paranthoën, T.: Split and join for minimizing: Brzozowski's algorithm. In: Proceedings of the Prague Stringology Conference, pp. 96–104 (2002). https://www.stringology.org/event/2002/p11.html

8. Ciancia, V., Venema, Y.: Stream Automata Are Coalgebras. In: Pattinson, D., Schröder, L. (eds.) CMCS 2012. LNCS, vol. 7399, pp. 90–108. Springer, Heidelberg (2012). https://doi.org/10.1007/978-3-642-32784-1_6

9. Ciancia, V., Venema, Y.: Ω-automata: A coalgebraic perspective on regular ω-languages. In: 8th Conference on Algebra and Coalgebra in Computer Science (CALCO 2019). Leibniz International Proceedings in Informatics (LIPIcs), vol. 139, pp. 5:1–5:18 (2019). https://doi.org/10.4230/LIPIcs.CALCO.2019.5

10. Cruchten, M.: Topics in Ω-Automata: a Journey Through Lassos, Algebra, Coalgebra and Expressions. Master's thesis, University of Amsterdam (2022). https://eprints.illc.uva.nl/id/eprint/2209

11. Cruchten, M.: Kleene theorems for lasso languages and ω-languages. In: Chen, X., Li, B. (eds.) Theory and Applications of Models of Computation, pp. 111–123. Springer Nature Singapore (2024). https://doi.org/10.1007/978-981-97-2340-9_10

12. Cruchten, M.: On transition constructions for automata: A categorical perspective. Tech. rep. (2024). http://arxiv.org/abs/2406.19312

13. Grädel, E., Thomas, W., Wilke, T. (eds.): Automata Logics, and Infinite Games: a Guide to Current Research. Springer-Verlag (2002). https://doi.org/10.1007/3-540-36387-4

14. Idziaszek, T., Skrzypczak, M., Bojanczyk, M.: Regular languages of thin trees. Theory Comput. Syst. **58**(4), 614–663 (2016). https://doi.org/10.1007/S00224-014-9595-Z

15. MacLane, S.: Categories for the Working Mathematician, Graduate Texts in Mathematics, vol. 5. Springer-Verlag (1971). https://doi.org/10.1007/978-1-4757-4721-8

16. Perrin, D., Pin, J.E.: Infinite Words: Automata, Semigroups, Logic and Games, Pure and Applied Mathematics, vol. 141. Elsevier (2004). https://doi.org/10.1017/S107989860000336X

17. Pin, J.E.: Mathematical Foundations of Automata Theory (2022). https://www.irif.fr/~jep/PDF/MPRI/MPRI.pdf

18. Planting, A.: From Automata to Monoids and Back Again. Master's thesis, Radboud University (2013)

19. Rot, J.: Coalgebraic minimization of automata by initiality and finality. In: Birkedal, L. (ed.) Mathematical Foundations of Programming Semantics, MFPS 2016. Electronic Notes in Theoretical Computer Science, vol. 325, pp. 253–276. Elsevier (2016). https://doi.org/10.1016/J.ENTCS.2016.09.042

20. Rutten, J.J.M.M.: Universal coalgebra: a theory of systems. Theor. Comput. Sci. **249**(1), 3–80 (2000). https://doi.org/10.1016/S0304-3975(00)00056-6

21. Urbat, H., Schröder, L.: Automata learning: an algebraic approach. In: Proceedings of the 35th Annual ACM/IEEE Symposium on Logic in Computer Science. LICS '20, pp. 900–914 (2020). https://doi.org/10.1145/3373718.3394775

22. Wilke, T.: An algebraic theory for regular languages of finite and infinite words. Int. J. Algebra Comput. **3**(4), 447–490 (1993). https://doi.org/10.1142/S0218196793000287

On Concurrent Program Algebra and Demonic Automata

Emil Sekerinski[(⊠)]

McMaster University, Hamilton, ON, Canada
emil@mcmaster.ca

Abstract. Regular expressions describe languages accepted by finite state automata with angelic nondeterminism. Regular expressions obey the axioms of Kleene algebra. We consider automata with demonic nondeterminism, using a different criterion for acceptance. The demonic nondeterminism corresponds to that of predicate transformers; it allows nondeterministic sequential and concurrent programs to be modelled. The corresponding regular expressions obey the axioms of the left (lazy) Kleene algebra. The algebra is extended with operators for parallel composition, intersection (to express that a program must satisfy multiple properties), complement (to express that a program must not have a certain property), and difference (to express that certain properties must be excluded). The "naive" algorithm for the equivalence of two automata is adapted to automata with demonic nondeterminism. The theory is implemented in an interactive notebook.

Keywords: Concurrent Kleene Algebra · Regular Expressions · Finite State Automata · Automated Verification

1 Introduction

There is a well-known connection between regular expressions and program statements. Writing $\perp$ for the "zero" regular expression, ε for the "unit" regular expressions, $x\,y$ for the concatenation of two regular expressions, $x \mid y$ for their choice, x^* for repetition (Kleene star), and taking an alphabet consisting of $b, \neg b, \ldots, s, t, \ldots$, the connection is:

$$stop = \perp \qquad s\,;t = s\,t \qquad \textbf{if } b \textbf{ then } s \textbf{ else } t = b\,s \mid \neg b\,t$$

$$skip = \varepsilon \qquad \textbf{if } b \textbf{ then } s = b\,s \mid \neg\, b \qquad \textbf{while } b \textbf{ do } s = (b\,s)^*\,\neg b$$

Regular expressions satisfy the axioms of the Kleene algebra [11]; these allow completely equational reasoning of uninterpreted program statements. This is even true in the Kleene algebra with tests (KAT), where a Boolean structure for guards of if- and while-statements is added [13,16].

Concurrent regular expressions, which extend regular expressions with an operator for parallel composition, have a long history for the specification of

© The Author(s), under exclusive license to Springer Nature Switzerland AG 2025
C. Anutariya and M. M. Bonsangue (Eds.): ICTAC 2024, LNCS 15373, pp. 114–131, 2025.
https://doi.org/10.1007/978-3-031-77019-7_7

concurrent executions [4,7]. The concurrent Kleene algebra (CKA) provides a complete set of axioms [10]. The appeal of the CKA is its elegance, the familiarity through regular expressions, and the ability to state properties of sets of executions without quantification.

This paper is on reasoning about *interactive programs*. In Kleene algebra, *stop* is a left and right zero of sequential composition:

$$stop \, ; s = stop = s \, ; stop$$

However, in interactive programs, s may have an effect before stopping: (1) $print(5)\, ; stop$ has a visible effect before stopping, hence is different from *stop*. (2) If $v := 3\, ; stop$ is a process (program statement) that is composed in parallel with process s, then s can be influenced by $v := 3\, ; stop$ but would not be influenced by *stop*. (3) If in message passing system $c?x\, ; stop$ is a process that receives from channel c and s is a process that sends over c, then s is affected differently if the first process is just *stop*. Hence, we consider $stop = s \, ; stop$ not to hold generally. The second observation is that in Kleene algebra, choice distributes over sequential composition to the left:

$$s \, ; (t \mid u) = s \, ; t \mid s \, ; u$$

As $\mid$ chooses whichever operand is enabled, there is a difference between the points when the choice is made: on the left-hand side, the *enabledness* of t and u determines the choice; on the right-hand side, the choice is arbitrary. For example, $s \, ; (t \mid stop) = s \, ; t$ as $t \mid stop = t$, which is different from $s \, ; t \mid s \, ; stop$, as $s \, ; stop \neq stop$ in general. Generally, $s \, ; (t \mid u) = s \, ; t \mid s \, ; u$ does not hold. The third observation is that in CKA, *stop* is a zero of parallel composition:

$$stop \parallel s = stop$$

While $stop \parallel s$ will not terminate, s can have an observable effect by, say, printing or communicating with a third process. If the parallel composition is defined through interleaving and a is an atomic program statement, $stop \parallel a = stop \, ; a \mid a \, ; stop = stop \mid a \, ; stop = a \, ; stop \neq stop$. Hence, in general, $stop \parallel s \neq stop$. The fourth observation is that in CKA, $\parallel$ distributes over $\mid$:

$$s \parallel (t \mid u) = (s \parallel t) \mid (s \parallel u)$$

On the right hand, the choice between $s \parallel t$ and $s \parallel u$ is made at the beginning; on the left hand, the choice between t and u possibly after s has run. Hence, in general, $s \parallel (t \mid u) = (s \parallel t) \mid (s \parallel u)$ does not hold.

The left (lazy) Kleene algebra relaxes the Kleene algebra by not requiring that ; distributes over | to the right and $\bot$ being a right zero of ; [14]. Predicate transformers and infinite strings are models of the left Kleene algebra. The left Kleene algebra is also in line with OCCAM: in the algebraic laws resulting from its semantics, SEQ (";" here) also distributes over ALT (nondeterministic choice with guards) to the left but not to the right [15](law 4.4).

In this paper, we extend the left Kleene algebra with concurrency. To this end, we propose *finite state automata with demonic nondeterminism* as a model. These are automata that accept a string if all possible sequences of states accept the string rather than on some possible sequence of states. Our treatment is inspired by the duality of demonic and angelic nondeterminism in predicate transformers [2]. The automata are constructed similarly to classical automata; only the acceptance criterion changes. The parallel composition is expressed as the *interleaving product* of two automata. In the proposed algebraic laws, the *exchange axiom* of CKA that relates sequential composition with parallel composition is replaced with the *interleaving axiom*.

The resulting "concurrent left Kleene algebra" is extended with further operators. The *intersection* $s \& t$ specifies executions that behave as both s and t. The *complement* $\sim\!s$ specifies executions that don't behave as s. Together with $\bot$ (*stop*) and $\top$ (*chaos*), program statements form a Boolean algebra. By comparison, in KAT, only the guards form a Boolean algebra. Besides intersection and complement being of potential usefulness, their inclusion is also motivated by a result about regular expressions: when eliminating intersection and complement, an exponential and double exponential increase in size, respectively, may not be avoidable [8]. The added operators bring automata closer to the lattice structure of predicate transformers [2]. The *meet* operator has also been studied in action algebras [12].

A contribution of this paper is to provide automata with demonic nondeterminism as a model of the proposed algebra. We modify the well-known "naive" algorithm for checking the equivalence of two (angelically) nondeterministic automata to the proposed demonically nondeterministic automata. In addition to the above operators, we introduce *difference* $s - t$, which specifies executions that behave as s but not t; while it does not add a theoretical novelty, for practical purposes, it avoids the need to implement $\sim\!s$, which can cause a blowup of the size of the automaton if the alphabet is large and requires a symbolic representation if the alphabet is unbounded.

Section 2 proposes the algebraic structure. Section 3 gives the construction of finite state automata and defines their angelic and demonic acceptance and reach equivalences. Section 4 defines the operators on automata that correspond to the operators of the proposed algebraic structure. Section 5 presents algorithms for deciding the equivalence and inclusion of automata. Section 6 is on the implementation and some examples. Section 7 concludes with an outlook.

2   Algebra of Concurrent Program Statements

Preliminaries. A *semigroup* is an algebraic structure $(S, \cdot)$ where S is a set and $\cdot$ is an *associative* binary operation on S, meaning $x \cdot (y \cdot z) = (x \cdot y) \cdot z$ for all $x, y, z \in S$. This allows us to write $x \cdot y \cdot z$ without ambiguity.

A *monoid* is an algebraic structure $(S, \cdot, 1)$ where $(S, \cdot)$ is a semigroup and 1 is a distinguished element of S that is both a left and right identity for $\cdot$, meaning $1 \cdot x = x \cdot 1 = x$ for all $x \in S$. A monoid is *commutative* if $x + y = y + x$ for all $x, y \in S$. A monoid is *idempotent* if $x + x = x$ for all $x \in S$.

A *left semiring* is an algebraic structure $(S, +, \cdot, 0, 1)$ such that

- $(S, +, 0)$ is a commutative monoid,
- $(S, \cdot, 1)$ is a monoid,
- $\cdot$ distributes over $+$ to the left, $(x + y) \cdot z = x \cdot z + y \cdot z$ for all $x, y, z \in S$,
- 0 is a left zero for '$\cdot$', meaning $0 \cdot x = 0$ for all $x \in S$.

A *semiring* is an algebraic structure $(S, +, \cdot, 0, 1)$ such that

- $(S, +, \cdot, 0, 1)$ is a left semiring,
- $\cdot$ distributes over $+$ to the right, $x \cdot (y + z) = x \cdot y + x \cdot z$ for all $x, y, z \in S$,
- 0 is a right zero for $\cdot$, meaning $x \cdot 0 = 0$ for all $x \in S$.

To avoid writing parenthesis, we let $\cdot$ bind tighter than $+$. A *partial order* is a binary relation $\leq$ on a set S that is *reflexive*, $x \leq x$ for all $x \in S$, *antisymmetric*, $x \leq y \land y \leq x \Rightarrow x = y$ for all $x, y \in S$, and *transitive*, $x \leq y \land y \leq z \Rightarrow x \leq z$ for all $x, y, z \in S$. Any idempotent monoid has a naturally-defined partial order $\leq$ associated with it, $x \leq y \equiv x + y = y$.

A *(left) semiring is idempotent* if the monoid $(S, +, 0)$ is idempotent and $\cdot$ is right-monotone, $y \leq z \Rightarrow x \cdot y \leq x \cdot z$ for all $x, y, z \in S$. The left-monotony of $\cdot$ follows from its left-distributivity.

A *left (or lazy) Kleene algebra* is a structure $(S, +, \cdot, ^*, 0, 1)$ such that the substructure $(S, +, \cdot, 0, 1)$ is an idempotent left semiring and

- * unfolds to the left, $1 + x \cdot x^* \leq x^*$ for all $x \in S$,
- * unfolds to the right, $1 + x^* \cdot x \leq x^*$ for all $x \in S$,
- * allows left induction, $x + y \cdot z \leq z \Rightarrow y^* \cdot x \leq z$ for all $x, y, z \in S$,
- * allows right induction, $x + y \cdot z \leq y \Rightarrow x \cdot z^* \leq y$ for all $x, y, z \in S$.

This corresponds to the *strong* left Kleene algebra of [14]. A *Kleene algebra* is a structure $(S, +, \cdot, ^*, 0, 1)$ that is a left Kleene algebra and $(S, +, \cdot, 0, 1)$ is a semiring. A concurrent Kleene algebra (CKA) is an algebraic structure $(S, +, \cdot, \|, 0, 1)$ such that $(S, +, \cdot, ^*, 0, 1)$ is a Kleene algebra, $(S, +, \|, 0, 1)$ is a commutative semiring ($\|$ is commutative), and the exchange axiom holds,

$$(x \parallel y) ; (x' \parallel y') \leq x ; x' \parallel y ; y'$$

for all $x, x', y, y' \in S$. Note that an unary operator $!$ for repeated parallel composition (analogous to *) can be added [9].

Syntax. The *program statements* $\mathcal{S}$ over a set Σ of *atomic programs* or *actions* consist of

- *stop* (blocking program),
- *chaos* (chaotic program),
- *skip* (identity program),
- any $a \in \Sigma$ (action, atomic program),
- $s ; t$, if s, t are program statements (sequential composition, first s then t),
- $s \mid t$, if s, t are program statements (union, choice between s and t),

- $s \& t$, if s, t are program statements (intersection, requiring both s and t),
- $s \parallel t$, if s, t are program statements (parallel composition, actions of s and t interleaved),
- $\sim s$, if s is a program statement (complement, the opposite of s),
- s^*, if s is a program statement (repetition, s zero or more times).

The sequential composition $s \, ; t$ is also written as $s \, t$. When writing program statements, we let the unary operators $\sim$ and $*$ bind tighter than concatenation, which itself binds tighter than the binary operators $|$, $\&$, and $\parallel$.

Algebraic Structure. Let s, t, u be program statements and let a, b be actions, *stop*, *chaos*, or *skip*:

$$s \mid (t \mid u) = (s \mid t) \mid u \qquad \text{| associative} \qquad (1)$$

$$s \mid t = t \mid s \qquad \text{| commutative} \qquad (2)$$

$$s \mid s = s \qquad \text{| idempotent} \qquad (3)$$

$$s \mid stop = s \qquad \text{| identity} \qquad (4)$$

$$s \& (t \& u) = (s \& t) \& u \qquad \text{\& associative} \qquad (5)$$

$$s \& t = t \& s \qquad \text{\& commutative} \qquad (6)$$

$$s \& s = s \qquad \text{\& idempotent} \qquad (7)$$

$$s \& chaos = s \qquad \text{\& identity} \qquad (8)$$

$$s \mid (t \& u) = (s \mid t) \& (s \mid u) \qquad \text{\&-| distributivity} \qquad (9)$$

$$s \& (t \mid u) = (s \& t) \mid (s \& t) \qquad \text{|-\& distributivity} \qquad (10)$$

$$s \mid \sim s = chaos \qquad \text{| complement} \qquad (11)$$

$$s \& \sim s = stop \qquad \text{\& complement} \qquad (12)$$

$$s \, ; (t \, ; u) = (s \, ; t) \, ; u \qquad \text{; associative} \qquad (13)$$

$$skip \, ; s = s \qquad \text{; left identity} \qquad (14)$$

$$s \, ; skip = s \qquad \text{; right identity} \qquad (15)$$

$$stop \, ; s = stop \qquad \text{; left zero} \qquad (16)$$

$$(s \mid t) \, ; u = s \, ; u \mid t \, ; u \qquad \text{|-; left distributivity} \qquad (17)$$

$$skip \mid s \, ; s^* \leq s^* \qquad \text{* left unfold} \qquad (18)$$

$$skip \mid s^* \, ; s \leq s^* \qquad \text{* right unfold} \qquad (19)$$

$$s \mid t \, ; u \leq u \;\Rightarrow\; t^* \, ; s \leq u \qquad \text{* left induction} \qquad (20)$$

$$s \mid t \, ; u \leq t \;\Rightarrow\; s \, ; u^* \leq t \qquad \text{* right induction} \qquad (21)$$

$$s \parallel (t \parallel u) = (s \parallel t) \parallel u \qquad\qquad \parallel \text{ associative} \quad (22)$$
$$s \parallel t = t \parallel s \qquad\qquad \parallel \text{ commutative} \quad (23)$$
$$s \parallel skip = s \qquad\qquad \parallel \text{ identity} \quad\;\; (24)$$

$$a\,;\,s \parallel b\,;\,t = a\,;\,(s \parallel b\,;\,t) \mid b\,;\,(a\,;\,s \parallel t) \qquad\qquad \text{interleaving} \quad (25)$$

Above, $s \leq t$ stands for the naturally defined order, $s \mid t = t$, which can be shown to be equivalent to $s \& t = s$. There are several algebraic structures underlying program statements.

- $(\mathcal{S}, \mid, \&, \sim, stop, chaos)$ is a Boolean algebra, axioms (1)–(12);
- $(\mathcal{S}, \mid, ;, {}^*, stop, skip)$ is a left Kleene algebra, axioms (1)–(4) and (13)–(21);
- $(\mathcal{S}, \parallel, skip)$ is a commutative monoid, axioms (22)–(24);
- $\parallel$ and $;$ are connected by axiom (25).

The resulting algebra could be called the *concurrent Boolean left Kleene algebra*, which we abbreviate as *concurrent program algebra (CPA)*. In contrast to CKA, $(\mathcal{S}, \mid, \parallel, stop, skip)$ is not an idempotent semiring: *stop* is not a zero for $\parallel$, i.e. $stop \parallel s \neq stop$ in general; also, $\parallel$ does not distribute over $\mid$, i.e. $s \parallel (t \mid u) \neq (s \parallel t) \mid (s \parallel u)$ does not hold in general. In CKA, parallel and sequential composition are related to by the exchange axiom:

$$(s \parallel t)\,;\,(s' \parallel t') \leq s\,;\,s' \parallel t\,;\,t'$$

In general, equality does not hold if s or t are composed program statements. In case they are atomic actions, according to [10], equality should not hold either. Here we define parallel composition by interleaving, and hence, we have for actions a, b:

$$a \parallel b = a\,;\,skip \parallel b\,;\,skip \qquad\qquad\qquad\quad \text{by (15)}$$
$$= a\,;\,(skip \parallel b\,;\,skip) \mid b\,;\,(a\,;\,skip \parallel skip) \qquad \text{by (25)}$$
$$= a\,;\,b \mid b\,;\,a \qquad\qquad\qquad\qquad \text{by (15), (23), (24)}$$

The *difference* $s - t$ between program statements s and t is defined as:

$$s - t = s \& \sim t$$

3   Automata and Their Equivalence

Automata Representation. Assume Σ is a set of actions; Σ can be finite or infinite. Let $\mathcal{Q}$ be the set of all possible states; $\mathcal{Q}$ can be finite or infinite. A *(finite state) automaton* A over Σ and $\mathcal{Q}$ is a triple (I, δ, F) where

- $I \subseteq \mathcal{Q}$ are the *initial states*,
- $\delta : \mathcal{Q} \to \Sigma \to \mathcal{P}\,\mathcal{Q}$ is the *transition function*,
- $F \subseteq \mathcal{Q}$ are the *final states*.

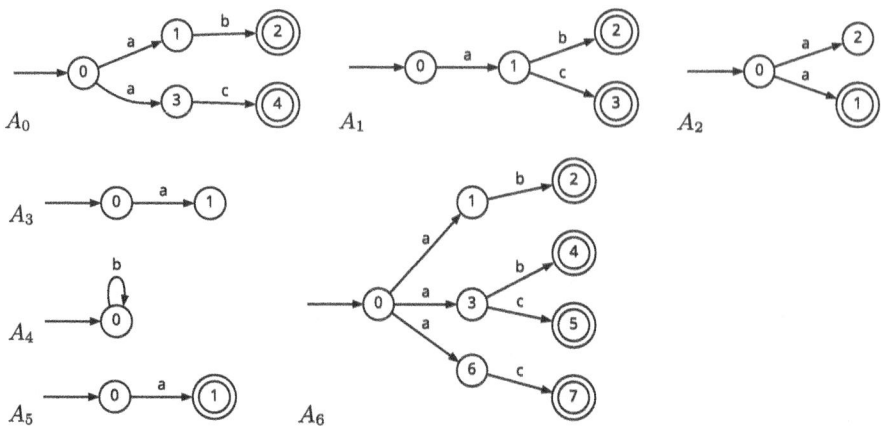

Fig. 1. Automata illustrating the difference between angelic and demonic interpretations.

The *domain* of δ is the set of all *source states* which map to some *target state*, $dom\,\delta = \{p \mid \exists a : \Sigma \bullet \delta\,p\,a \neq \emptyset\}$. The domain of δ has to be finite. The sets I and F can be empty.

If $|\delta\,p\,a| \leq 1$ for all p and a, the automaton is *deterministic*, otherwise *nondeterministic*. The automata considered here do not have ε-transitions. For automaton $A = (I, \delta, F)$, its components are referred to by $A.I$, $A.\delta$, and $A.F$.

Automata Equivalence. Consider A_0 and A_1 in Fig. 1. In classical automata theory, the two automata are equivalent: in A_0, the choice to move to 1 or 3 in state 0 on a is *angelic*. With angelic choice, A_0 and A_1 accept ab and ac. If the choice is *demonic*, A_1 still accepts both ab and ac, but A_0 is neither guaranteed to accept ab nor ac.

Given transition function δ, its *angelic extension* $\delta^a\,P\,\alpha$ and its *demonic extensions* $\delta^d\,P\,\alpha$ to a set P of states and a sequence α of actions are defined as:

$$\delta^a\,P\,\varepsilon = P \qquad \delta^a\,P\,(\alpha a) = (\cup\,p \in \delta^a\,P\,\alpha \bullet \delta\,p\,a)$$
$$\delta^d\,P\,\varepsilon = P \qquad \delta^d\,P\,(\alpha a) = (\cap\,p \in \delta^d\,P\,\alpha \bullet \delta\,p\,a) \text{ if } \delta^d\,P\,\alpha \neq \emptyset \text{ else } \emptyset$$

The angelic successors of P on input α are the union of all the states to which α leads; the demonic successors are the intersection. Since the intersection of the empty set of sets is formally the universal set, the else-part of the definition of $\delta^d\,P\,(\alpha a)$ makes the empty intersection empty.

The targets of automaton A for input α is the set of states that are either *angelically reached* or *demonically reached* from its initial states:

$$A.reach^a\,\alpha = A.\delta^a\,A.I\,\alpha$$
$$A.reach^d\,\alpha = A.\delta^d\,A.I\,\alpha$$

For example, in A_0, input a angelically reaches $\{1, 3\}$ and ab angelically reaches $\{2\}$. Input a demonically reaches $\{1, 3\}$ but ab demonically reaches $\emptyset$:

$$
\begin{aligned}
& A_0.reach^a\, ab && \text{def } A.reach^a \\
&= A_0.\delta^a\, \{0\}\, ab && \text{def } \delta^a \\
&= (\cup\, p \in A_0.\delta^a\, \{0\}\, a \bullet A_0.\delta\, p\, b) && \text{def } \delta^a \text{twice} \\
&= (\cup\, p \in \{1, 3\} \bullet A_0.\delta\, p\, b) && \text{simplification} \\
&= \{2\}
\end{aligned}
$$

$$
\begin{aligned}
& A_0.reach^d\, ab && \text{def } A.reach^d \\
&= A_0.\delta^d\, \{0\}\, ab && \text{def } \delta^d \\
&= (\cap\, p \in A_0.\delta^d\, \{0\}\, a \bullet A_0.\delta\, p\, b) \text{ if } A_0.\delta^d\, \{0\}\, a \neq \emptyset \text{ else } \emptyset && \text{def } \delta^d \text{twice} \\
&= (\cap\, p \in \{1, 3\} \bullet A_0.\delta\, p\, b) && \text{simplification} \\
&= \emptyset
\end{aligned}
$$

Automaton A *angelically accepts* sequence α if α angelically targets at least one state in $A.F$ and *demonically accepts* α if all demonic targets of α are in $A.F$ and at least one such target exists:

$$A.accepts^a\, \alpha \equiv A.reach\, \alpha \cap A.F \neq \emptyset$$
$$A.accepts^d\, \alpha \equiv \emptyset \neq A.reach\, \alpha \subseteq A.F$$

For example, automaton A_0 angelically accepts ab but does not demonically accept ab. Automaton A_2 angelically accepts a, as $A_2.\delta^a\, A_2.I\, a = \{1, 2\}$, which contains a final state, but does not demonically accept a, as $A_2.\delta^d\, A_2.I\, a = \{1, 2\}$, which is not a subset of the final states.

Automata A and B are *angelically (demonically) acceptance equivalent* if they angelically (demonically) accept the same inputs:

$$A \simeq^a_{acc} B \equiv (\forall \alpha \bullet A.accepts^a\, \alpha \equiv B.accepts^a\, \alpha)$$
$$A \simeq^d_{acc} B \equiv (\forall \alpha \bullet A.accepts^d\, \alpha \equiv B.accepts^d\, \alpha)$$

For example, A_0 and A_1 are angelically equivalent but not demonically equivalent. Angelic acceptance and equivalence are as in classic automata. Both angelic and demonic acceptance equivalence are reflexive, symmetric, and transitive. Consider now A_3 and A_4. Acceptance equivalence makes all non-terminating automata equivalent to the empty automaton. Hence, A_3 and A_4 are angelically and demonically acceptance equivalent. We consider now automata that may interact with their environment without reaching a final state, which would make A_3 and A_4 not equivalent.

Automata A and B are *angelically (demonically) reach equivalent* if for all possible inputs α, if one automaton has an angelically (demonically) reachable state, so has the other:

$$A \simeq^a_{reach} B \equiv (\forall \alpha \bullet A.reach^a\,\alpha = \emptyset \equiv B.reach^a\,\alpha = \emptyset)$$
$$A \simeq^d_{reach} B \equiv (\forall \alpha \bullet A.reach^d\,\alpha = \emptyset \equiv B.reach^d\,\alpha = \emptyset)$$

Reach equivalence does not depend on the final states. For example, A_2, A_3, and A_5 are angelically and demonically reach equivalent: on a, a state can be angelically and demonically reached, and on no other input, a state is reached.

Both angelic and demonic reach equivalence are reflexive, symmetric, and transitive. Acceptance equivalence does not imply reach equivalence: A_3 and A_4 are acceptance equivalent but not reach equivalent, both angelically and demonically. Neither does reach equivalence imply acceptance equivalence: A_2 and A_3 are angelically reach equivalent but not acceptance equivalent; A_3 and A_5 are demonically reach equivalent but not demonically acceptance equivalent. As a final example, consider A_6: it is both angelically and demonically acceptance and reach equivalent to A_0.

Henceforth, we consider only demonic equivalence. Automata A and B are (demonically) *equivalent* if they are both acceptance and reach equivalent:

$$A \simeq B \equiv A \simeq^d_{acc} B \wedge A \simeq^d_{reach} B$$

Naturally, $\simeq$ is reflexive, symmetric, and transitive. The inclusion of automata can be defined in an algebraic manner:

$$A \precsim^a_{acc} B \equiv A \mid B \simeq^a_{acc} B \qquad\qquad A \precsim^d_{acc} B \equiv A \mid B \simeq^d_{acc} B$$
$$A \precsim^a_{reach} B \equiv A \mid B \simeq^a_{reach} B \qquad\qquad A \precsim^d_{reach} B \equiv A \mid B \simeq^d_{reach} B$$

Since the underlying structures are idempotent monoids, they are all partial orders. Finally, we define:

$$A \precsim B \equiv A \mid B \simeq B$$

4   Constructing Automata

On transition functions $\gamma, \delta : Q \to \Sigma \to \mathcal{P}\,Q$, we define the following constants and operations, where S is a subset of Σ:

$$\emptyset\,p\,a = \emptyset$$
$$\{P \xrightarrow{S} Q\}\,p\,a = Q \text{ if } p \in P \wedge a \in S \text{ else } \emptyset$$
$$(\gamma \cup \delta)\,p\,a = \gamma\,p\,a \cup \delta\,p\,a$$
$$(\gamma \times \delta)\,(p,q)\,a = \gamma\,p\,a \times \delta\,q\,a$$
$$(\gamma \parallel \delta)\,(p,q)\,a = (\gamma\,p\,a \times \{q\}) \cup (\{p\} \times \delta\,q\,a)$$
$$(\sim\delta)\,p\,a = Q \setminus \delta\,p\,a$$

In $\{P \xrightarrow{S} Q\}$, if P, Q, or S consist of single elements, we identify that set with its element and write, for example, $\{p \xrightarrow{a} q\}$ for a function that "moves" from p on a to q.

Both $\times$ and $\parallel$ construct transition functions that take pairs of states as arguments, which we assume to be elements of Q as well: $\times$ moves to a new pair of states by simultaneous moves according to γ and δ and $\parallel$ moves to a new pair of states according to either γ or δ and leaving the other state unchanged.

For $a \in \Sigma$, we define the construction of automata in a way that avoids the introduction of ε-transitions. This includes the *stop* automaton, which for classical automata is less useful:

$$stop = (\emptyset, \emptyset, \emptyset)$$
$$chaos = (\{p\}, \{p \xrightarrow{\Sigma} p\}, \{p\}) \text{ for fresh } p$$
$$skip = (\{p\}, \emptyset, \{p\}) \text{ for fresh } p$$
$$a = (\{p\}, \{p \xrightarrow{a} q\}, \{q\}) \text{ for fresh } p, q$$
$$A \,;B = (A.I, A.\delta \cup B.\delta \cup \{A.F \xrightarrow{a} q \mid B.I \xrightarrow{a} q\},$$
$$B.F \cup (A.F \text{ if } B.I \cap B.F \neq \emptyset \text{ else } \emptyset))$$
$$A \mid B = (A.I \cup B.I, A.\delta \cup B.\delta, A.F \cup B.F)$$
$$A \,\&\, B = (A.I \times B.I, A.\delta \times B.\delta, A.F \times B.F)$$
$$A \parallel B = (A.I \times B.I, A.\delta \parallel B.\delta, A.F \times B.F)$$
$$A^* = (A.I, A.\delta \cup \{A.F \xrightarrow{a} q \mid A.I \xrightarrow{a} q\}, A.I \cup A.F)$$
$$\sim A = (A.I, \sim A.\delta, A.F)$$

Above, we identify a with the automaton accepting a. When composing two automata, we assume that the set of states of the automata is disjoint. This is achieved by requiring using a "fresh" state for each of the basic automata, *chaos*, *skip*, and a.

We now turn the attention to showing that two automata are equivalent, $A \simeq B$. For this, we consider homomorphic functions from the states of one automaton to the other.

Lemma 1. *Let $h : Q \to Q$ be a function from states to states. For set P of states, define $h\,P = \{h\,p \mid p \in P\}$. Then for any $\gamma, \delta : Q \to \Sigma \to \mathcal{P}\,Q$:*

$$(\forall p, a \bullet h(\gamma\,p\,a) = \delta\,h(p)\,a) \Rightarrow (\forall P, \alpha \bullet h(\gamma^d\,P\,\alpha) = \delta^d\,h(P)\,\alpha)$$

Proof. Assuming the left-hand side, the right-hand side follows by induction over the length of α:

Base $\alpha = \varepsilon$:

$$
\begin{array}{ll}
h(\gamma^d\,P\,\alpha) & \text{as } \alpha = \varepsilon, \text{def } \gamma^d\,P\,\varepsilon \\
= h\,P & \text{def } \delta^d\,P\,\varepsilon, \text{as } \alpha = \varepsilon \\
= \delta^d\,h(P)\,\alpha
\end{array}
$$

Step $\alpha = \beta a$: The induction assumption is $h(\gamma^d P \beta) = \delta^d h(P) \beta$:

$$h(\gamma^d P \beta a) \hfill \text{def} \gamma^d P (\beta \, a)$$

$$= h((\cap p \in \gamma^d P \beta \bullet \gamma p \, a) \text{ if } \gamma^d P \beta \neq \emptyset \text{ else } \emptyset)$$

$$\text{as } h(\cap q \in Q \bullet x) = (\cap q \in Q \bullet h \, x)$$

$$= (\cap p \in \gamma^d P \beta \bullet h(\gamma p \, a)) \text{ if } \gamma^d P \beta \neq \emptyset \text{ else } \emptyset \hfill \text{as } Q = \emptyset \equiv h \, Q = \emptyset$$

$$= (\cap p \in \gamma^d P \beta \bullet h(\gamma p \, a)) \text{ if } h(\gamma^d P \beta) \neq \emptyset \text{ else } \emptyset \hfill \text{assumption}$$

$$= (\cap p \in \gamma^d P \beta \bullet \gamma \, h(p) \, a) \text{ if } h(\gamma^d P \beta) \neq \emptyset \text{ else } \emptyset \hfill \text{bound variable}$$

$$= (\cap p \in h(\gamma^d P \beta) \bullet \gamma p \, a) \text{ if } h(\gamma^d P \beta) \neq \emptyset \text{ else } \emptyset \hfill \text{induction assumption}$$

$$= (\cap p \in \delta^d h(P) \beta \bullet \delta p \, a) \text{ if } \delta^d h(P) \beta \neq \emptyset \text{ else } \emptyset \hfill \text{def } \delta^d P (\beta \, a)$$

$$= \delta^d h(P) (\beta a)$$

This completes the proof.

Theorem 1. *Let $h : Q \to Q$ be a function from states to states. For set P of states, define $h \, P = \{h \, p \mid p \in P\}$. Assume automata A and B have states Q and actions Σ. If*

1. $\forall p, a \bullet h(A.\delta \, p \, a) = B.\delta \, h(p) \, a$
2. $h(A.I) = B.I$
3. $h(A.F) = B.F$

then $A \simeq B$.

Proof. By the definition of $\simeq$, the conclusion is equivalent to $A \simeq^d_{acc} B$ and $A \simeq^d_{reach} B$. The latter amounts to:

$$\forall \alpha \bullet A.\delta^d \, A.I \, \alpha = \emptyset \equiv B.\delta^d \, B.I \, \alpha = \emptyset \hfill (*)$$

For arbitrary α:

$$\emptyset = A.\delta^d \, A.I \, \alpha \hfill \text{as } h \, P = \emptyset \equiv P = \emptyset \text{ for any } P$$

$$\equiv \emptyset = h(A.\delta^d \, A.I \, \alpha) \hfill \text{by assumption 1, Lemma 1}$$

$$\equiv \emptyset = B.\delta^d \, h(A.I) \, \alpha \hfill \text{by assumption 2}$$

$$\equiv \emptyset = B.\delta^d \, B.I \, \alpha$$

By definitions, $A \simeq^d_{acc} B$ is equivalent to

$$\forall \alpha \bullet \emptyset \neq A.\delta^d \, A.I \, \alpha \subseteq A.F \equiv \emptyset \neq B.\delta^d \, B.I \, \alpha \subseteq B.F$$

The proof of this is split into two parts. For arbitrary α,

$$A.\delta^d \, A.I \, \alpha \subseteq A.F \hfill \text{from def } h \, P$$

$$\equiv h(A.\delta^d \, A.I \, \alpha) \subseteq h(A.F) \hfill \text{by assumption 1, Lemma 1}$$

$$\equiv B.\delta^d \, h(A.I) \, \alpha \subseteq h(A.F) \hfill \text{by assumptions 2 and 3}$$

$$\equiv B.\delta^d \, B.I \, \alpha \subseteq B.F$$

The second part, $\forall \alpha \bullet \emptyset \neq A.\delta^d A.I \alpha \equiv \emptyset \neq B.\delta^d B.I \alpha$, follows from (*). Conjoining the two logical equivalences completes the proof.

Theorem 2. *Automata with $\simeq$ satisfy the axioms of CPA, (1) to (25).*

Proof. As the proofs of the axioms are similar, for space, only those of axioms (1) to (8) are given.

For axiom (1), $A \mid (B \mid C) \simeq (A \mid B) \mid C$, we show equality, as it implies equivalence:

$$
\begin{aligned}
& A \mid (B \mid C) & \text{def } \mid \\
&= (A.I \cup (B.I \cup C.I), A.\delta \cup (B.\delta \cup C.\delta), A.F \cup (B.F \cup C.F)) & (*) \\
&= ((A.I \cup B.I) \cup C.I), (A.\delta \cup B.\delta) \cup C.\delta, (A.F \cup B.F) \cup C.F) & \text{def } \mid \\
&= (A \mid B) \mid C
\end{aligned}
$$

The step (*) relies on $\cup$ on sets being associative and $\cup$ on transition functions being associative.

Axiom (2), $A \mid B \simeq B \mid A$ follows from both sides being equal, as $\cup$ on sets and transition functions is commutative.

For axiom (3), $A \mid A \simeq A$, recall that only automata with disjoint states can be composed. Let A_0, A_1 be isomorphic copies of A with disjoint states such that h_0, h_1 maps the states of A_0, A_1 to the states of A, respectively. Define $h\,p = h_0\,p$ if p is a state of A_0 and $h\,p = h_1\,p$ if p is a state of A_1. According to Theorem 1, the axiom follows, after simplifications, from

1. $\forall p, a \bullet h((A_0.\delta \cup A_1.\delta)\,p\,a) = A.\delta\,h(p)\,a$
2. $h(A_0.I \cup A_1.I) = A.I$
3. $h(A_0.F \cup A_1.F) = A.F$

These hold by the definitions of h and $\cup$ on transition functions.

Axiom (4), $A \mid stop \simeq A$ follows from both sides being equal, as $\emptyset$ is an identity for $\cup$ on sets and transition functions.

For axiom (5), $A \& (B \& C) \simeq (A \& B) \& C$, let $h((q, r), s) = h(q, (r, s))$. According to Theorem 1, the axiom follows, after simplifications, from

1. $\forall p, a \bullet h((A.\delta \times (B.\delta \times C.\delta))\,p\,a) = ((A.\delta \times B.\delta) \times C.\delta)\,h(p)\,a$
2. $h(A.I \times (B.I \times C.I)) = (A.I \times B.I) \times C.I$
3. $h(A.F \times (B.F \times C.F)) = (A.F \times B.F) \times C.F$

By taking p in the quantification above to be the tuple $(q, (r, s))$, all three follow from the definitions of h and $\times$ on transition functions.

For axiom (6), $A \& B \simeq B \& A$, let $h(q, r) = (r, q)$. The axiom follows similarly by Theorem 1.

Axiom (7), $A \& A \simeq A$ is equivalent to $A \simeq A \& A$ as $\simeq$ is symmetric. Let A_0 and A_1 be isomorphic copies of A such that h_0, h_1 maps the states of A to the states of A_0, A_1, respectively. Define $h\,p = (h_0\,p, h_1\,p)$. According to Theorem 1, $A \simeq A \& A$ follows, after simplifications, from

1. $\forall p, a \bullet h(A.\delta\, p\, a) = (A_0.\delta \times A_1.\delta)\, h(p)\, a$
2. $h(A.I) = A_0.I \times A_1.I$
3. $h(A.F) = A_0.F \times A_1.F$

These hold by the definitions of h and $\times$ on transition functions.

For axiom (8), $A\,\&\,chaos \simeq A$ let $h(q, r) = q$. According to Theorem 1, the axiom follows, after simplifications, from

1. $\forall p, a \bullet h((A.\delta \times chaos.\delta)\, p\, a) = A.\delta\, h(p)\, a$
2. $h(A.I \times chaos.I) = A.I$
3. $h(A.F \times chaos.F) = A.F$

These hold by the definitions of h and $\times$ on transition functions.

5   Algorithms for Equivalence and Inclusion

We start with the well-known algorithm for the (angelic acceptance) equivalence of two finite state automata, $A \simeq^a_{acc} B$, called the "naive" algorithm in [3, 6], adapted to an infinite set of actions (input symbols). Since any automaton uses only finitely many, we define $act(\delta, P)$ to be the set of actions for which a transition from a state of P by δ is possible:

$$act(\delta, P) = \{a \mid \exists p \in P \bullet \delta\, p\, a \neq \emptyset\}$$

The algorithm uses two variables, W (work) and V (visited); both contain a set of pairs of states. These sets contain all possible successor states under angelic nondeterminism. The algorithm performs the subset construction on the fly.

```
1    procedure equivalent^a_acc(A, B: FSA) → bool
2        W, V := {(A.I, B.I)}, ∅
3        while W ≠ ∅ do
4            P, Q :∈ W ; W := W \ {(P, Q)}
5            if (P, Q) ∉ V then
6                if  P ∩ A.F = ∅ ≢ Q ∩ B.F = ∅ then return false
7                for  a ∈ act(A.δ, P) ∪ act(B.δ, Q) do
8                    W := W ∪ {(A.δ^a P a, B.δ^a Q a)}
9                V := V ∪ {(P, Q)}
10       return true
```

Initially, W contains only the initial states. As long as W is not empty, a pair is nondeterministically selected $(P, Q :\in W)$ and removed from W. If a state of one of the two automata is final and no state of the other automata is final, line 6, the automata cannot be equivalent and *false* is returned. Otherwise, for all actions on which a transition from any of the states of P or Q is possible, the sets with the successor states are added to W. If W is exhausted and no counterexample is found, the automata must be equivalent and *true* is returned, line 10. The successors of P are $A.\delta^a\, P\, a$, line 8. From the definition of δ^a we have:

$$\delta^a\, P\, a = (\cup p \in \delta^a\, P\, \epsilon \bullet \delta\, p\, a) = (\cup p \in P \bullet \delta\, p\, a)$$

Hence, all angelic successor states on a of all states of P are considered.

The algorithm for angelic reach equivalence, $A \simeq^a_{reach} B$, is derived from the above algorithm by replacing the condition on line 6 with checking if one of P or Q is empty and the other is not, i.e. one automaton reaches a next state and the other not:

```
1   procedure equivalentᵃreach(A, B: FSA) → bool
        ...
6                  if P = ∅ ≢ Q = ∅ then return false
        ...
```

The argument for its correctness is analogous: if one automaton accepts and the other does not, they cannot be equivalent; if no counterexample is found, they must be equivalent.

The algorithm for demonic acceptance equivalence, $A \simeq^d_{acc} B$, uses δ^d instead of δ^a, line 8; if one of P or Q is not empty and in the accepting states but the other not, the two automata are not demonically equivalent, line 6. The algorithm also performs the subset construction on the fly, but now using the demonic successors instead of the angelic successors:

```
1    procedure equivalentᵈacc(A, B: FSA) → bool
2        W, V := {(A.I, B.I)}, ∅
3        while W ≠ ∅ do
4            P, Q :∈ W ; W := W \ {(P,Q)}
5            if (P, Q) ∉ V then
6                if (∅ ≠ P ⊆ A.F) ≢ (∅ ≠ Q ⊆ B.F) then return false
7                for a ∈ act(A.δ, P) ∪ act(B.δ, Q) do
8                    W := W ∪ {(A.δᵈ P a, B.δᵈ Q a)}
9                V := V ∪ {(P,Q)}
10       return true
```

Again, if no counterexample is found, the automata must be equivalent and $true$ is returned, line 10. The successors of P are $\delta^d P a$, line 8. From the definition of δ^d we have:

$$\delta^d P a = (\cap p \in \delta^a P \epsilon \bullet \delta p a) \text{ if } \delta^d P \epsilon \neq \emptyset \text{ else } \emptyset$$
$$= (\cap p \in P \bullet \delta p a) \text{ if } P \neq \emptyset \text{ else } \emptyset$$

Hence, all successor states on a of all states of P are considered.

The algorithm for demonic reach equivalence, $A \simeq^d_{reach} B$ is derived from the above algorithm by replacing the condition on line 6 with checking if one of P or Q is empty and the other is not, i.e. one automaton reaches a next state and the other not:

1   **procedure** $equivalent^d_{reach}(A,\ B\colon FSA) \rightarrow bool$
 ...

6   **if** $P = \emptyset \not\equiv Q = \emptyset$ **then return** $false$
 ...

The argument for its correctness is analogous: if one automaton accepts and the other does not, they cannot be equivalent; if no counterexample is found, they must be equivalent.

The procedure for the (demonic) equivalence of two automata, $A \simeq B$, combines the conditions on line 6 for demonic acceptance and reach equivalence:

1   **procedure** $equivalent(A,\ B\colon FSA) \rightarrow bool$
 ...

6   **if** $(P = \emptyset \not\equiv Q = \emptyset) \vee (P \subseteq A.F \not\equiv Q \subseteq B.F)$ **then return** $false$
 ...

The algorithms for inclusion are similar to those for equivalence. This paper contains only some; the accompanying implementation contains all. The algorithm for the angelic acceptance inclusion of two automata, $A \lesssim^a_{acc} B$, is derived from $equivalent^a_{acc}$ by modifying line 6. If a final state of A is found and the corresponding states of B are not final, A cannot be included in B:

1   **procedure** $incl^a_{acc}(A,\ B\colon FSA) \rightarrow bool$
 ...

6   **if** $(P \cap A.F \neq \emptyset) \wedge (Q \cap B.F = \emptyset)$ **then return** $false$
 ...

It is easy to see from line 6 that mutual inclusion implies equivalence as in line 6 of $equivalent^a_{acc}$. This also holds for all subsequent inclusion algorithms. The algorithm for angelic reach inclusion, $A \lesssim^a_{reach} B$, is derived from that for $equivalent^a_{reach}$ by changing line 6:

1   **procedure** $incl^a_{reach}(A, B\colon FSA) \rightarrow bool$
 ...

6   **if** $P \neq \emptyset \wedge Q = \emptyset$ **then return** $false$
 ...

We leave out the algorithms for demonic acceptance inclusion and reach inclusion and jump to, the algorithm for (demonic) inclusion, $A \lesssim B$, as combines the conditions for demonic acceptance and reach inclusion. It is derived from $equivalent$ by changing line 6:

1   **procedure** $incl(A,\ B\colon FSA) \rightarrow bool$
 ...

6   **if** $(P \neq \emptyset \wedge Q = \emptyset) \vee (\emptyset \neq P \subseteq A.F \wedge \neg(\emptyset \neq Q \subseteq B.F))$ **then return** $false$
 ...

6   Implementation and Examples

A prototypical implementation as an interactive Jupyter notebook is available online from the author's website[1]. That notebook also contains the concrete grammar and the attribute rules for constructing the abstract syntax tree. The parser allows the use of $s?$, defined as $s \mid skip$ and s^+, defined as $s ; s^*$. The implementation focuses on clarity and correctness rather than efficiency. The notebook also illustrates the intermediate steps in constructing the automata.

The following two examples involve implementation relations that are expressed in terms of actions that abstract program states.

Fair Scheduling. A scheduler is supposed to execute a, b, and c repeatedly but may stop at any time. When it stops, it must have executed all of a, b, and c at least once. This is expressed as:

$$FS = (a \mid b \mid c)^* - (a \mid b)^* - (a \mid c)^* - (b \mid c)^*$$

A cyclic scheduler is a valid implementation:

$$CS = (a ; b ; c)^*$$

Then we have $CS \lesssim FS$.

Barrier Synchronization. Suppose three processes repeatedly execute a task, t_i, and then have to synchronize at their barrier, b_i, before repeating their task:

$$PT = (t_0 ; b_0)^* \parallel (t_1 ; b_1)^* \parallel (t_1 ; b_1)^*$$

For PT to be correctly executed, all processes must "pause" at their barrier, which is expressed by:

$$BS = ((t_0 \parallel t_1 \parallel t_2) ; (b_0 \parallel b_1 \parallel b_2))^*$$

Then we have $BS \lesssim PT$.

7   Conclusion

This work proposes a concurrent left Kleene algebra to reason about programs that interact with their environment without reaching a final state. To this end, we propose automata with demonic acceptance and reachability as a model.

The completeness and independence of the proposed axioms is an open question. In fact, in the (strong) left Kleene algebra, * right unfold, axiom (19) follows from the others [14].

The algorithms for deciding the equivalence of automata are variations of the "naive" algorithm. Improved algorithms for angelic acceptance based on a generalization of the Hopcroft-Karp algorithm were proposed [1]. Bisimulation up-to congruence and antichain algorithms are more recent developments that can be studied in this setting [3,5,6].

---

[1] https://www.cas.mcmaster.ca/~emil/.

Acknowledgements. The author is grateful to the reviewers for their thoughtful and constructive comments.

References

1. Almeida, M., Moreira, N., Reis, R.: Testing the equivalence of regular languages. Electron. Proc. Theor. Comput. Sci. **3**, 47–57 (2009). https://doi.org/10.4204/eptcs.3.4
2. Back, R.J., Wright, J.V.: Refinement Calculus: a Systematic Introduction. Springer-Verlag (1998). https://doi.org/10.1007/978-1-4612-1674-2
3. Bonchi, F., Pous, D.: Checking NFA equivalence with bisimulations up to congruence. In: Proceedings of 40th Annual ACM SIGPLAN-SIGACT Symposium on Principles of Programming Languages, pp. 457–468. POPL '13, Association for Computing Machinery, New York, NY, USA (2013). https://doi.org/10.1145/2429069.2429124
4. Campbell, R.H., Habermann, A.N.: The specification of process synchronization by path expressions. In: Gelenbe, E., Kaiser, C. (eds.) Operating Systems, pp. 89–102. Springer, Berlin, Heidelberg (1974). https://doi.org/10.1007/BFb0029355
5. De Wulf, M., Doyen, L., Henzinger, T.A., Raskin, J.F.: Antichains: a new algorithm for checking universality of finite automata. In: Ball, T., Jones, R.B. (eds.) Computer Aided Verification. CAV 2006, pp. 17–30. Springer, Berlin, Heidelberg (2006). https://doi.org/10.1007/11817963_5
6. Fu, C., Deng, Y., Jansen, D.N., Zhang, L.: On equivalence checking of nondeterministic finite automata. In: Larsen, K.G., Sokolsky, O., Wang, J. (eds.) Dependable Software Engineering. Theories, Tools, and Applications. SETTA 2017, pp. 216–231. Springer, Cham (2017). https://doi.org/10.1007/978-3-319-69483-2_13
7. Garg, V.K.: Modeling of distributed systems by concurrent regular expressions. In: Proceedings of the IFIP TC/WG6.1 Second International Conference on Formal Description Techniques for Distributed Systems and Communication Protocols, pp. 313–327. FORTE '89, North-Holland Publishing Co. (1989)
8. Gelade, W., Neven, F.: Succinctness of the complement and intersection of regular expressions. ACM Trans. Comput. Logic **13**(1), 1 (2012). https://doi.org/10.1145/2071368.2071372
9. Hoare, T., Möller, B., Struth, G., Wehrman, I.: Concurrent Kleene algebra and its foundations. J. Logic Algebraic Program. **80**(6), 266–296 (2011). https://doi.org/10.1016/j.jlap.2011.04.005
10. Hoare, T., van Staden, S., Möller, B., Struth, G., Zhu, H.: Developments in concurrent Kleene algebra. J. Log. Algebr. Methods Programm. **85**(4), 617–636 (2016). https://doi.org/10.1016/j.jlamp.2015.09.012
11. Kozen, D.: A completeness theorem for Kleene algebras and the algebra of regular events. Inf. Comput. **110**(2), 366–390 (1994). https://doi.org/10.1006/inco.1994.1037
12. Kozen, D.: On action algebras. In: van Eijck, J., Visser, A. (eds.) Logic and Information Flow, pp. 78–88. MIT Press (1994). https://doi.org/10.7551/mitpress/4286.001.00
13. Kozen, D.: Kleene algebra with tests. ACM Trans. Program. Lang. Syst. **19**(3), 427–443 (1997). https://doi.org/10.1145/256167.256195
14. Möller, B.: Kleene getting lazy. Sci. Comput. Program. **65**(2), 195–214 (2007). https://doi.org/10.1016/j.scico.2006.01.010

15. Roscoe, A.W., Hoare, C.A.R.: The laws of OCCAM programming. Theor. Comput. Sci. **60**(2), 177–229 (1988). https://doi.org/10.1016/0304-3975(88)90049-7
16. Smolka, S., Foster, N., Hsu, J., Kappé, T., Kozen, D., Silva, A.: Guarded Kleene algebra with tests: verification of uninterpreted programs in nearly linear time. Proc. ACM Program. Lang. **4**, 1 (2020). https://doi.org/10.1145/3371129

Bisimulations and Logics
for Higher-Dimensional Automata

Safa Zouari[1]([⊠]), Krzysztof Ziemiański[2], and Uli Fahrenberg[3]

[1] Norwegian University of Science and Technology, Gjøvik, Norway
safa.zouari@ntnu.no
[2] University of Warsaw, Warsaw, Poland
ziemians@mimuw.edu.pl
[3] EPITA Research Lab, Rennes, France
uli@lrde.epita.fr

Abstract. Higher-dimensional automata (HDAs) are models of non-interleaving concurrency for analyzing concurrent systems. There is a rich literature that deals with bisimulations for concurrent systems, and some of them have been extended to HDAs. However, no logical characterizations of these relations are currently available for HDAs.

In this work, we address this gap by introducing Ipomset modal logic, a Hennessy-Milner type logic over HDAs, and show that it characterizes Path-bisimulation, a variant of the standard ST-bisimulation. We also define a notion of Cell-bisimulation, using the open-maps framework of Joyal, Nielsen, and Winskel, and establish the relationship between these bisimulations (and also their "strong" variants, which take restrictions into account). In our work, we rely on the new categorical definition of HDAs as presheaves over concurrency lists and on track objects.

Keywords: Higher Dimensional Automaton · Ipomset Modal Logic · Hennessy-Milner logic · Bisimulation · Open map · Pomset

1 Introduction

Higher-Dimensional Automata (HDAs), introduced by Vaughan Pratt [25] and Rob van Glabbeek [14], are a powerful model for non-interleaving concurrency. Van Glabbeek [14] places HDAs at the top of a hierarchy of concurrency models, demonstrating how other concurrency models, such as Petri nets [22], configuration structures [29], asynchronous systems [7,28], and event structures [31,32], can be incorporated into HDAs.

As its name implies, a Higher-Dimensional Automaton consists of a collection of n-dimensional hypercubes or n-cells connected via source and target maps. The well-known automata or labeled transition systems are 1-dimensional HDAs. However, HDAs allow for more expressive modeling of concurrent and distributed systems. For example, the concurrent execution of two events a and b can be modeled by a square labeled as in Fig. 2, while an empty square represents mutual

© The Author(s), under exclusive license to Springer Nature Switzerland AG 2025
C. Anutariya and M. M. Bonsangue (Eds.): ICTAC 2024, LNCS 15373, pp. 132–150, 2025.
https://doi.org/10.1007/978-3-031-77019-7_8

exclusion. Analogously, a filled-in 3-dimensional cube in an HDA can represent three events a_1, a_2, and a_3 that execute concurrently, while when considering a hollow cube, each 2-dimensional face models $a_i \parallel a_j$ for $1 \leq i \neq j \leq 3$. See Fig. 1.

A *higher-dimensional automaton* is a *precubical set* together with an *initial cell* and a set of *final cells*. Like a simplicial set, a *precubical set* is constructed by systematically gluing hypercubes. Formally, it is a graded set $X = \bigcup_{n \in \mathbf{N}} X_n$, where X_n represents the set of *n-cells*, with face maps δ^0 resp δ^1 defining the mapping of an *n*-cell to its lower resp. upper face. Each *n*-cell is associated with a linearly ordered and labeled set V of length n. From a concurrency point of view, such a cell models a list V of n active events. A lower face of a cell $x_n \in X_n$ is a cell $\delta^0_{V \setminus U}(x)$ that has $U \subseteq V$ as active events. For example, in Fig. 3, the square has active *events* $[ab]$. Its faces have active events $[a]$ and $[b]$, respectively. In Sect. 2, we make this precise by defining *precubical sets* as presheaves over a category of linearly ordered sets with appropriate morphisms [9, 10].

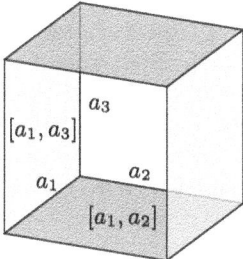

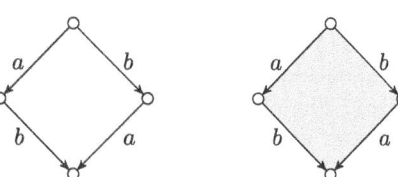

Fig. 1. How HDA models concurrency: The filled-in cube models the events $[a_1, a_2, a_3]$. The 2-dimensional faces with the same color model the same 2 events. The uncolored faces model the events $[a_2, a_3]$. (Color figure online)

Fig. 2. HDA models distinguishing interleaving $a.b + b.a$ (left) from non-interleaving concurrency $a \parallel b$ (right).

In addition to concurrency models, equivalence relations should also be considered when describing concurrent systems. Various notions of equivalence have been suggested in studies [13, 15–17, 20, 26], guided by considerations of the critical aspects of system behavior within a specific context and the elements from which to abstract. Parallel to behavioral equivalences, modal logic is a useful formalism for specifying and verifying properties of concurrent systems [1, 3, 6, 24].

Characterization of bisimulation in terms of Hennessy-Milner logic (HML) provides additional confidence in both approaches. Two finitely branching systems are bisimilar iff they satisfy the same logical assertions. The literature focusing on logical characterization includes the Van Glabbeek spectrum [13] for sequential processes and [4, 5, 8, 21, 23, 27] for concurrent systems. Some of these behavioral equivalences have been extended to HDAs. Among them are hereditary history-preserving bisimulations (hh-bisimulation) and ST-bisimulations

[14]. However, to the best of our knowledge, their logical counterparts have not been investigated for HDA.

This paper presents a variant of HML interpreted over HDAs, namely *Ipomset Modal Logic* (IPML). The original HML in the interleaving setting [17] contains negation ($\neg$), conjunction ($\wedge$), a formula $\top$ that always holds, and a diamond modality $\langle a \rangle F$, which says that it is possible to perform an action labeled by a and reach a state that satisfies F. Unlike the standard HML, IPML considers both sequential and concurrent computations. Thus, it differs from the standard HML within the diamond modality, so it becomes $\langle P \rangle F$ where P is an *interval pomset with interfaces* (interval ipomset). It is interpreted over a *path* α, and says that there is a path β that recognizes P and extends α to a path (concatenation of α and β) that satisfies F. For example, in Fig. 2, the formula $\langle (a \longrightarrow b) \rangle \top \vee \langle (b \longrightarrow a) \rangle \top$, which stands for mutual exclusion, holds at the top edge of both squares. However, formula $\langle [\begin{smallmatrix} a \\ b \end{smallmatrix}] \rangle \top$ holds only in the upper corner of the filled-in square (on the right). The latter formula shows that our logic is powerful enough to distinguish interleaving from true concurrency.

Pomsets were first introduced by Winkowski [30]. *Interval orders*, a subclass of *pomsets*, have been introduced by Fishburn [12]. Then, they have been equipped with *interfaces* [9], facilitating the definition of the *gluing composition* of HDA languages. A computational run in an HDA is modeled by a *path*, a sequence of *cells*. Each two consecutive *cells* are related by a *source* or a *target map*. The observable contents of a path α are described by $\mathsf{ev}(\alpha)$, an *interval pomset with interfaces*.

Fig. 3. Two-dimensional cell with its faces. The labels of each cell are shown on the left.

To define *cell-bisimulation* and IPML over HDAs, we employ the notion of open map bisimulation [19]. This approach requires a category of models $\mathbf{M}$ (the category of HDAs in our case) and a path category $\mathbf{T}$ (the category of *track objects* in our case), a subcategory of $\mathbf{M}$ that we call the HDA-path category. Track objects have originally been introduced in [9] to define languages of HDAs. They form a subcategory of $\mathbf{M}$. A *track object* is a particular HDA that can be constructed from a given interval ipomset P, denoted $\square^P$. Intuitively, for a given path π labeled with an interval ipomset P, the track object $\square^P$ is the smallest HDA containing π. We show that the resulting logic characterizes path-bisimulation [9], a variant of ST-bisimulation [14]. However, its extension, equipped with backward modality characterizes the strong path-bisimulation.

Finally, we finish this paper with a hierarchy of the equivalence relations encountered in the paper. This is summarized in Fig. 4. Other contributions, that deepen the understanding of mathematical structures and may be of independent interest, include establishing a relation between track objects and interval ipomsets in Theorem 19, a relation between the notion of paths of van Glabbeek [14] and tracks of [9] in Theorem 35, and a generalization of the Yoneda lemma to interval ipomsets in Proposition 33.

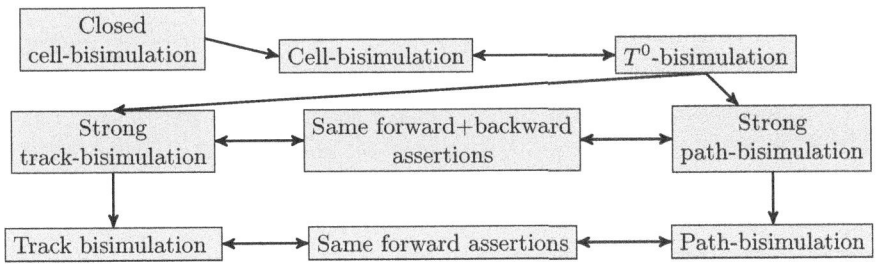

Fig. 4. Hierarchy of notions of equivalence.

2   Higher Dimensional Automata

We review the definition of Higher Dimensional Automata. We rely on a categorical approach proposed and studied in [9,10], where an HDA is defined as a specific precubical set. To define precubical sets as presheaves over the labeled precube category $\Box$, we introduce conclists and conclist maps, which are the objects and the morphisms of $\Box$. We restrict our study to finitely branching HDAs.

Definition 1. *A concurrency list or* conclist *is a tuple* $(U, \dashrightarrow, \lambda)$*, where* U *is a finite set totally ordered by the strict order* $\dashrightarrow$ *and* $\lambda : U \to \Sigma$ *is a labeling map. Elements of* U *will be called* events*.*

Definition 2. *A conclist-map from a conclist* U *to* T *is a pair* (f, ε) *such that:*

- $f : U \to T$ *is a label and order-preserving function;*
- $\varepsilon : T \to \{0, \ulcorner, 1\}$ *is a function such that* $\varepsilon^{-1}(\ulcorner) = f(U)$*.*

The composition of morphisms $(f, \varepsilon) : U \to T$ *and* $(g, \zeta) : T \to V$ *is* $(g, \zeta) \circ (f, \varepsilon) = (g \circ f, \eta)$*, where*

$$\eta(u) = \begin{cases} \varepsilon(g^{-1}(u)) & \text{for } u \in g(T), \\ \zeta(u) & \text{otherwise.} \end{cases}$$

Let $\Box$ *be the category of conclists and conclist maps. We write* $U \simeq V$ *for isomorphic conclists; if two conclists are isomorphic, then the isomorphism between them is unique.*

For a conclist map $(f, \varepsilon) : U \to V$, since the order $\dashrightarrow$ is total, f is an injective function, which is determined by $V \setminus f(U) = V \setminus \varepsilon^{-1}(\lrcorner)$, and hence by ε. For instance, the identity morphism $\mathrm{id}_V^{\square} : V \to V$ is uniquely determined by ε_V where $\varepsilon_V(v) = \lrcorner$ for all $v \in V$. Intuitively the map f injects the list of events of U into the list of events of V, while the map ε guarantees that the events of U are active in V by giving them the value $\lrcorner$, and specifies the state of the remaining events by giving them the value 0 if they are not yet started and 1 if they are terminated.

Notation. A morphism $(f, \varepsilon) : U \to V$ might be denoted $d_{A,B} : U \to V$ where $A = \varepsilon^{-1}(0)$ and $B = \varepsilon^{-1}(1)$. Such a morphism is usually called a coface map [10]. We write d_A^0 for $d_{A,\emptyset}$ and d_B^1 for $d_{\emptyset,B}$.

Definition 3. *A precubical set X is a presheaf over $\square$, that is, a functor $X : \square^{op} \to \mathbf{Set}$. A precubical map between precubical sets is a natural transformation of functors.*

The value of X on the object U of $\square$ is denoted $X[U]$. For the face map associated to coface map $d_{A,B} : U \setminus (A \cup B) \to U$, we write $\delta_{A,B} = X[d_{A,B}] : X[U] \to X[U \setminus (A \cup B)]$. Elements of $X[U]$ are cells of X. For any $x \in X[U]$, elements of U are called events of x. We write $\mathsf{ev}(x) = U$. A precubical set is said to be finitely branching if every cell is the face of a finite number of cells.

Definition 4. *A higher-dimensional automaton (HDA) $\mathcal{X}$ is a triple (X, i_X, F_X) where X is a precubical set, i_X is a cell called the initial cell, and F_X is the set of final cells. An HDA map $f : \mathcal{X} \to \mathcal{Y}$ is a precubical map $X \to Y$ that preserves the initial cell[1], that is, $f(i_X) = i_Y$. We denote $\mathbf{HDA}$ the category formed by HDAs as objects and HDA maps as morphisms.*

We assume that all HDAs are finitely branching.

Definition 5. *Let S be a conclist. The standard S-cube is the presheaf $\square^S$ represented by S, that is,*

- *for any conclists T, $\square^S[T] = \mathbf{hom}_{\square}(T, S)$;*
- *$\square^S[(f, \varepsilon)](g, \eta) = (g, \eta) \circ (f, \varepsilon)$ for $(f, \varepsilon) \in \mathbf{hom}_{\square}(U, T)$, $(g, \eta) \in \square^S[T]$.*

Example 6. Figure 1 and Fig. 3 show examples of standard S-cubes, where $S = [a_1 \dashrightarrow a_2 \dashrightarrow a_3]$ in Fig. 1 and $S = [a \dashrightarrow b]$ in Fig. 3.

Denote $\mathbf{y}_S \in \square^S[S]$ the cell that corresponds to the identity morphism. The following is a crucial result for this work and is implied by the Yoneda lemma.

Lemma 7. *Let X be a precubical set, S be a conclist, and $x \in X$. If $\mathsf{ev}(x) = S$, then there exists a unique precubical map $\iota_x : \square^S \to X$ such that $\iota_x(\mathbf{y}_S) = x$.*

---

[1] In our study, final cells are ignored because they are not relevant for bisimulation.

3 Interval Pomsets with Interfaces vs Track Objects

Pomsets are concurrent counterparts of words [25,30]. Interval pomsets [12] equipped with interfaces have been used to develop the language theory of HDAs [2,9–11]. They generalize the notion of conclist. Like standard cubes are presheaf representations of conclists, track objects are presheaf representations of interval pomsets with interfaces. As we proceed in this section, we revisit these concepts, then we present important new results for constructing the HDA-path category.

Background. A *partially ordered multiset (pomset)* is a tuple $(P, <_P, \dashrightarrow_P, \lambda_P)$ where P is a finite set, $\lambda_P : P \to \Sigma$ is a labeling function over an alphabet Σ, $<_P$ is a strict partial order on P called *precedence order*, and $\dashrightarrow_P$ is a strict partial order on P called *event order* such that the relation $<_P \cup \dashrightarrow_P$ is total. Elements of P are called *events*. Intuitively, the latter condition means that any two events in P either are concurrent, thus can happen in parallel and ordered by $\dashrightarrow_P$, or occur sequentially, thus ordered by $<_P$. For $x, y \in P$, write $x \parallel y$ if x and y are *incomparable*, i.e., $x \neq y$, $x \not< y$, and $y \not< x$. We say that an element $x \in P$ is *minimal* if there is no element $y \in P$ such that $y < x$. Similarly, we say that x is *maximal* if there is no element $y \in P$ such that $x < y$. For $Q \subseteq P$, we say that Q is an *antichain* if $x \parallel y$ for all $x, y \in Q$. An antichain is maximal if it is not contained in another antichain. As the relation $<_P \cup \dashrightarrow_P$ is total, an antichain is a conclist.

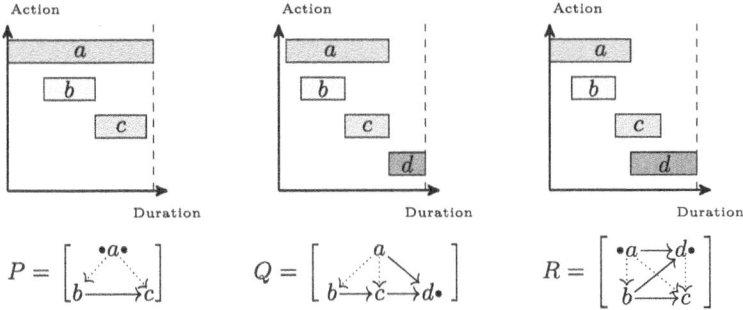

Fig. 5. Interval ipomsets (below) with their corresponding interval representations (above). An event with a dot on the left (resp. on the right) is an element of a source (resp. target) interface. Full arrows indicate precedence order, while dashed arrows indicates event order.

A *partially ordered multiset with interfaces* or *ipomset* is a tuple $(P, <_P, \dashrightarrow_P, \lambda_P, S_P, T_P)$, where $(P, <_P, \dashrightarrow_P, \lambda_P)$ is a pomset, S_P is a subset of the $<$-minimal elements of P called *source interface*, and T_P is a subset of the $<$-maximal elements of P called *target interface*. The source and target interfaces are antichains, and thus, conclists. An ipomset P with empty precedence order, i.e. $P = (U, \emptyset, \dashrightarrow_U, \lambda_U, S, T)$, is referred to as a *discrete ipomset* and will be denoted $_S U_T$. Pomsets may be regarded as ipomsets with empty interfaces. An

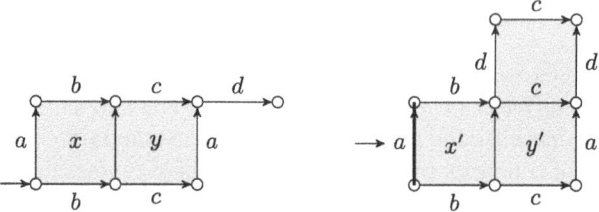

Fig. 6. Example of track objects: $\square^Q$ on the left and $\square^R$ on the right, where Q and R are the interval ipomsets of Fig. 5. The initial cell on the right is highlighted with a thick arrow.

interval ipomset is an ipomset P in which, for $x, y, z, w \in P$, if $x < z$ and $y < w$ then we have either $x < w$ or $y < z$.

Definition 8. *Let P and Q be ipomsets with $T_P \simeq S_Q$. The gluing composition of P and Q is $P * Q = ((P \sqcup Q)_{x \simeq f(x)}, <, \dashrightarrow, \lambda, S_P, T_Q)$, where $(P \sqcup Q)_{x \simeq f(x)}$ is the disjoint union of P and Q quotiented by the unique isomorphism $f : T_P \to S_Q$, and $\lambda(x) = \begin{cases} \lambda_P(x) \text{ if } x \in P, \\ \lambda_Q(x) \text{ if } x \in Q, \end{cases}$ $\quad < = <_P \cup <_Q \cup (P \setminus T_P) \times (Q \setminus S_Q),$ $\quad \dashrightarrow = (\dashrightarrow_P \cup \dashrightarrow_Q)^+$*

Definition 9. *Let P an ipomset. We define the order $\prec$ on maximal antichains of P as follows: $U \prec T$ iff $U \neq T$ and for all $u \in U$, $t \in T$, $t \not<_P u$.*

Proposition 10 *([9,18]). Let P be an ipomset. The following assertions are equivalent:*

1. *P is an interval order;*
2. *P is a finite gluing of discrete ipomsets;*
3. *The order $\prec$ defined on the maximal antichains of P is linear.*

In this work, we focus solely on interval ipomsets: **all ipomsets are assumed to be interval even if not stated explicitly.**

Another instrumental tool for this work is track objects. They generalize the standard cubes of Definition 5, replacing a conclist with an interval ipomset.

Definition 11 . *For a given interval ipomset P, the track object is an HDA $(\square^P, i_{\square^P}, f_{\square^P})$ where $\square^P[U] = \hom_{\mathbf{IP}}(U, P)$, $\square^P[(f, \varepsilon)](g, \zeta) = (f, \varepsilon) \circ (g, \zeta)$, and $i_{\square^P} = (S_P \xrightarrow{\subseteq} P, \varepsilon)$ and $f_{\square^P} = (T_P \xrightarrow{\subseteq} P, \zeta)$ where*

$$\varepsilon = \begin{cases} \text{\Lsh} & \text{if } p \in S_P, \\ 0 & \text{if } p \notin S_P, \end{cases} \qquad \zeta = \begin{cases} \text{\Lsh} & \text{if } p \in T_P, \\ 1 & \text{if } p \notin T_P. \end{cases}$$

Example 12. Fig. 6 shows examples of track objects. For instance, the cell x resp. y is modeled by $(f, x) \in \square^Q[U]$ resp. $(g, y) \in \square^Q[T]$, where $U = [b \dashrightarrow a]$, $T = [c \dashrightarrow a]$, and

$$x = \begin{bmatrix} \end{bmatrix} \qquad\qquad y = \begin{bmatrix} \end{bmatrix}$$

It is easy to determine f and g as they are label preserving.

3.1 The Category of Interval Ipomsets

The decomposition of an interval ipomset P into discrete ipomsets is not unique. However, there is a special decomposition that is unique with respect to specific properties, which we call the minimal discrete decomposition, defined as follows.

Definition 13. *The* minimal discrete decomposition *of an interval ipomset P into discrete ipomsets is $P = P_1 * \cdots * P_m$ where $P_i = (Q_i, \emptyset, \dashrightarrow_{|P_i}, \lambda_{|P_i}, S_i, T_i)$, Q_i are the maximal antichains[2], $S_1 = S_P$, $T_m = T_P$, and $T_i = S_{i+1} = P_i \cap P_{i+1}$.*

The minimal discrete decomposition plays a central role in our work. We rely heavily on it throughout the forthcoming proofs. Notably, such decomposition is unique.

Example 14. The minimal discrete decompositions of interval ipomsets of Fig. 5 are as follows:

$$P = \begin{bmatrix} \bullet a \bullet \\ b \end{bmatrix} * \begin{bmatrix} \bullet a \bullet \\ c \end{bmatrix}; \qquad Q = \begin{bmatrix} a \bullet \\ b \end{bmatrix} * \begin{bmatrix} \bullet a \\ c \end{bmatrix} * d \bullet; \qquad R = \begin{bmatrix} \bullet a \bullet \\ b \end{bmatrix} * \begin{bmatrix} \bullet a \\ c \bullet \end{bmatrix} * \begin{bmatrix} d \bullet \\ \bullet c \end{bmatrix}.$$

Since the notion of interval ipomset generalizes the concept of conclist, it is convenient to think about a category with interval ipomsets as objects that extends the $\square$ category.

Definition 15. *The category* **IP** *consists of the following.*

- *Objects are interval ipomsets;*
- *A morphism[3] between two interval ipomsets P and Q is a pair (f, ε) such that $f : P \to Q$ is an injective map that reflects the precedence order, that is, for $x, y \in P$, if $f(x) <_Q f(y)$ then $x <_P y$ and preserves the essential event order, i.e., for $x \parallel y \in P$ if $x \dashrightarrow_P y$ then $f(x) \dashrightarrow_Q f(y)$; and $\varepsilon : Q \to \{0, \lrcorner, 1\}$ such that $f(P) = \varepsilon^{-1}(\lrcorner)$ and if $q <_Q q'$ then $(\varepsilon(q), \varepsilon(q')) \in \preceq_{ipom}$,*

  where $\preceq_{ipom} = \{(1, 1), (0, 0), (\lrcorner, \lrcorner), (1, \lrcorner), (1, 0), (\lrcorner, 0)\}$

- *The composition of morphisms $(f, \varepsilon) : P \to Q$ and $(g, \zeta) : Q \to R$ is*

  $$((g, \zeta) \circ (f, \varepsilon)) = (g \circ f, \eta), \text{ where } \eta(u) = \begin{cases} \varepsilon(g^{-1}(u)) & \text{for } u \in g(Q), \\ \zeta(u) & \text{otherwise.} \end{cases}$$

---

[2] In this case, we have $Q_1 \prec \cdots \prec Q_m$.
[3] For morphisms of **IP**, we do not care about interfaces.

We write $P \simeq Q$ if there exists a bijective map $f : P \to Q$ such that f is also an order isomorphism. If such an isomorphism exists, then it is unique [9].

The definition of the morphisms of the category **IP** will serve later to define the track objects (Definition 11). The intuition for the values of $\varepsilon(q)$ is to be 1 if the event q happens before the events of $f(P)$, $\lrcorner$ if the event q is in $f(P)$, and 0 if the event q happens after the events of $f(P)$. That is why we allow all possible cases for $(\varepsilon(q), \varepsilon(q'))$, in $\preceq_{ipom}$, except the cases where q' terminate while $q \in f(P)$ so we eliminate pairs $(\lrcorner, 1)$ and the case where q has not started yet while $q' \in f(P)$ so we eliminate $(0, \lrcorner)$.

Definition 16. *Let P and R be composable ipomsets. There are two morphisms related to the gluing[4] $P * R$:*

- *initial inclusions $i_P^{P*R} = (P \subseteq P * R, \varepsilon)$, and*
- *final inclusions $f_R^{P*R} = (R \subseteq P * R, \zeta)$, where*

$$\varepsilon(x) = \begin{cases} \lrcorner & \text{for } x \in P, \\ 0 & \text{otherwise,} \end{cases} \qquad \zeta(x) = \begin{cases} \lrcorner & \text{for } x \in R, \\ 1 & \text{otherwise.} \end{cases}$$

Definition 17. *For a conclist S, let $\mathbf{IP}_S^0 \subseteq \mathbf{IP}$ be a subcategory with ipomsets P with $S_P = S$ as objects and morphisms[5] $\hom_{\mathbf{IP}_S^0}(P, Q) = \{i_P^{P*R} \mid R$ is an ipomset such that $P * R \cong Q\}$. We define the category $\mathbf{IP}^0 = \bigcup_{S \in \square} \mathbf{IP}_S^0$.*

Example 18. The following are initial inclusions.

1. $R_1 : \begin{bmatrix} \bullet a \bullet \\ b \end{bmatrix} \to \begin{bmatrix} \bullet a \bullet \\ b \longrightarrow c \end{bmatrix}$ where $R_1 = \begin{bmatrix} \bullet a \bullet \\ c \end{bmatrix}$;

2. $R_2 : \begin{bmatrix} \bullet a \\ b \longrightarrow c \end{bmatrix} \to \begin{bmatrix} \bullet a \longrightarrow d \bullet \\ b \longrightarrow c \end{bmatrix}$, where $R_2 = \begin{bmatrix} d \bullet \\ \bullet c \end{bmatrix}$.

We use categories $\mathbf{IP}_S^0$ to construct the bisimulation and the modal logic later in Sect. 5. In the next section, we show how we may regard $\mathbf{IP}^0$ as a subcategory of **HDA**, as required to apply the open map technique.

3.2   Defining the HDA-Path Category

Theorem 19. *The functor $\mathsf{Tr} : \mathbf{IP} \to \mathbf{HDA}$, given by formulas $\mathsf{Tr}(P) = \square^P$ and $\mathsf{Tr}(f, \varepsilon)(g, \zeta) = (f, \varepsilon) \circ (g, \zeta)$ for $(f, \varepsilon) \in \hom_{\mathbf{IP}}(P, Q)$, is faithful.*

Definition 20. *The category $\mathbf{T}^0$ is the subcategory of **HDA** given by $\mathbf{T}^0 = \mathsf{Tr}(\mathbf{IP}^0)$. Thus, it is defined by track objects as objects and morphisms are $\mathbf{i}_P^{P*R} = \mathsf{Tr}(i_P^{P*R})$, for $\mathbf{i}_P^{P*R}$ defined in Definition 16, and called* initial inclusions.

---

[4] We regard both P and Q as sub-pomsets of $P * Q$.
[5] Since i_P^{P*R} is uniquely determined by R, we might identify i_P^{P*R} and R.

Similarly, we call $\text{Tr}(f_P^{P*R})$, for f_P^{P*R} defined in Definition 16, a *final inclusion*, and we write $\mathbf{f}_P^{P*R}$.

Definition 21. *Let $\square^Q$ and $\square^R$ be track objects such that $T_Q \simeq S_R \simeq U$. The gluing composition of $\square^Q$ and $\square^R$ is the pushout HDA $(\square^Q * \square^R, I_{\square^Q}, F_{\square^R})$ where $\square^Q * \square^R = \text{colim}(\square^R \xleftarrow{i_U^R} \square^U \xrightarrow{f_U^Q} \square^Q)$*

Lemma 22 ([9]). *If Q and R are composable ipomsets, then $\square^{Q*R} = \square^Q * \square^R$. In addition, $i_Q^{Q*R}(g, \zeta) = (g, i_Q^{Q*R}(\zeta))$ and $\mathbf{f}_R^{Q*R}(g, \zeta) = (g, \mathbf{f}_R^{Q*R}(\zeta))$ are given by*

$$i_Q^{Q*R}(\zeta)(p) = \begin{cases} \zeta(p) & \text{for } p \in Q, \\ 0 & \text{otherwise}, \end{cases} \qquad \mathbf{f}_R^{Q*R}(\zeta)(p) = \begin{cases} \zeta(p) & \text{for } p \in R, \\ 1 & \text{otherwise}. \end{cases}$$

Proposition 23. *Let $\square^P$ be a track object. If $P = P_1 * P_2 * \cdots * P_m$ is the minimal discrete decomposition of P, then $\square^P = \square^{P_1} * \cdots * \square^{P_m}$.*

Note that $\hom_{\mathbf{T}^\circ}(\square^P, \square^Q) \cong \{\square^R \mid \square^Q = \square^P * \square^R\}$ by Lemma 22 and Proposition 23.

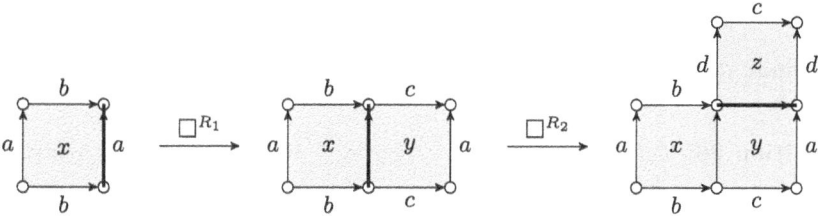

Fig. 7. Examples of morphisms of $\mathbf{T}^\circ$. R_1 and R_2 are initial inclusions of Example 18

4   Paths and Tracks

The computations or runs of HDAs, which track traversed cells and face maps, have been modeled by paths in [14] and by tracks in the categorical framework [9]. In the following subsection, we revisit these concepts and then in Subsect. 4.2 establish a relation between them. This link is crucial for expressing the satisfaction relation of IPML on paths, similarly to temporal logic.

4.1   Background: Paths and Their Labels

Definition 24. *A path in a precubical set X is a sequence $\alpha = (x_0, \varphi_1, x_1, \varphi_2, \ldots, \varphi_n, x_n)$, where $x_k \in X[U_k]$ are cells, and for all k, either*

- *$\varphi_k = d_A^0 \in \square(U_{k-1}, U_k), A \subseteq U_k$ and $x_{k-1} = \delta_A^0(x_k)$ (up-step), or*

$$- \varphi_k = d_B^1 \in \square\,(U_k, U_{k-1})\,, B \subseteq U_{k-1}, \delta_B^1\,(x_{k-1}) = x_k \ \textit{(down-step)}.$$

We write $x_{k-1} \nearrow^A x_k$ for the up-steps and $x_{k-1} \searrow_A x_k$ for the down-steps in α. Intuitively, moving by an up step $x_{k-1} \nearrow^A x_k$ means that the list of events A started and became active in the next cell x_k. Similarly, moving by a down step $x_{k-1} \searrow_A x_k$ means that the list of events A terminated and became inactive in the cell x_k. For a path written as above, we write $\mathsf{start}(\alpha)$ and $\mathsf{end}(\alpha)$ for the first cell x_0 and the final cell x_m, respectively. We write Path_X for the set of all paths on a precubical set X.

A precubical map $f : X \to Y$ induces a map $f : \mathrm{Path}_X \to \mathrm{Path}_Y$. For α denoted as above, $f(\alpha)$ is the path $(f(x_0), \varphi_1, f(x_1), \varphi_2, \ldots, \varphi_n, f(x_n))$. We say that a path is *sparse* if its steps are alternating between up-steps and down-steps. The *concatenation* of α denoted as above and $\beta = (y_0, \psi_1, y_1, \psi_2, \ldots, \psi_m, y_m)$, defined if $x_n = y_0$, is the path $\alpha * \beta$ given by $\alpha * \beta = (x_0, \varphi_1, x_1, \varphi_2, \ldots, \varphi_n, x_n, \psi_1, y_1, \psi_2, \ldots, \psi_m, y_m)$.

Definition 25. *The label of a path α is the ipomset $\mathsf{ev}(\alpha)$, computed recursively:*

1. *If $\alpha = (x)$ has length 0, then $\mathsf{ev}(\alpha) = {}_{\mathsf{ev}(x)}\mathsf{ev}(x)_{\mathsf{ev}(x)}$.*
2. *If $\alpha = (y \nearrow^A x)$, where $A \subseteq \mathsf{ev}(x)$, then $\mathsf{ev}(\alpha) = {}_{\mathsf{ev}(x) \setminus A}\mathsf{ev}(x)_{\mathsf{ev}(x)}$.*
3. *If $\alpha = (x \searrow_B y)$, where $B \subseteq \mathsf{ev}(x)$, then $\mathsf{ev}(\alpha) = {}_{\mathsf{ev}(x)}\mathsf{ev}(x)_{\mathsf{ev}(x) \setminus B}$.*
4. *If $\alpha = \beta_1 * \cdots * \beta_n$, where β_i are steps, then $\mathsf{ev}(\alpha) = \mathsf{ev}(\beta_1) * \cdots * \mathsf{ev}(\beta_n)$.*

As a finite gluing of discrete ipomsets, by Proposition 10, $\mathsf{ev}(\alpha)$ is an interval ipomset.

Definition 26. *Let $\alpha = (x_0, \varphi_1, x_1, \ldots, \varphi_n, x_n)$. We say that β is a restriction of α and write $\beta \xrightarrow{0} \alpha$, if $\beta = (x_0, \varphi_1, x_1, \varphi_2, \ldots, x_{j-1}, \varphi_j', x_j')$, where $j \leq n$ and*

- *if $\varphi_j = d_B^1$ then $\varphi_j' = d_A^1$ for $A \subseteq B$;*
- *if $\varphi_j = d_B^0$ then $\varphi_j' = d_A^0$ for $A \subseteq B$ and $x_j' = \delta_{B \setminus A}^0(x_j)$.*

Example 27. On the left, the path $(\delta_a^0 x \nearrow^a x)$ in blue is a restriction of the path $(\delta_a^0 x \nearrow^a x \searrow_b \delta_b^1 x)$ in orange. On the right, the paths $(\delta_a^0 \delta_b^0 x \nearrow^a \delta_b^0 x)$ and $(\delta_a^0 \delta_b^0 x \nearrow^b \delta_b^0 x)$ in orange are restrictions of $\alpha_2 = (\delta_a^0 x \nearrow^a x)$ in blue.

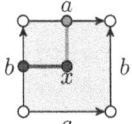 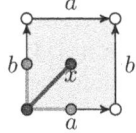

Definition 28. *Congruence of paths is the equivalence relation generated by $(x \nearrow^A y \nearrow^B z) \simeq x \nearrow^{A \cup B} z$, $(x \searrow_A y \searrow_B z) \simeq x \searrow_{A \cup B} z$, and if $\alpha \simeq \alpha'$ then $\gamma * \alpha * \beta \simeq \gamma * \alpha' * \beta$. If $\alpha \simeq \beta$, then $\mathsf{start}(\alpha) = \mathsf{start}(\beta)$ and $\mathsf{end}(\alpha) = \mathsf{end}(\beta)$. Furthermore, every path α is congruent to a unique sparse path, which is denoted $\mathsf{sp}(\alpha)$.*

Definition 29. *A track in a precubical set X is a precubical map $g : \Box^P \to X$ where P is an ipomset.*

In the case of a track in an HDA (X, i_X, I_F), we say that g is an initial track if P is a discrete ipomset and $g(\mathbf{y}_P) = i_X$.

4.2   The Categories of Tracks and Paths

The relation $\simeq$ is an equivalence relation, which allows the following definition.

Definition 30. *Let X be a precubical set. We define the category $\mathbb{P}_X$ as follows.*

– *Objects are equivalence classes of paths with respect to $\simeq$.*
– *Morphisms are $\hom_{\mathbb{P}_X}(P[\alpha], [\beta]) = \{[\gamma] \mid \alpha * \gamma \simeq \beta\})$, called* path extensions *and denoted $e_\alpha^{\alpha*\gamma} = [\alpha] \to [\alpha * \gamma]$.*
– *The composition of $e_\alpha^{\alpha*\beta}$ and $e_{\alpha*\beta}^{\alpha*\beta*\gamma}$ is $e_\alpha^{\alpha*\beta*\gamma}$.*

Let $p : \Box^P \to X$ and $q : \Box^Q \to X$ be two tracks such that $p(F_P) = q(I_Q)$. By Lemma 22, p and q glue to a track $p * q : \Box^{P*Q} \to X$, called the *the gluing of tracks p and q, that satisfies $(p * q) \circ \mathbf{i}_P^{P*Q} = p$ and $(p * q) \circ \mathbf{f}_Q^{P*Q} = q$.*

Definition 31. *Let X be a precubical set. We define the category of tracks $\mathbb{T}_X$ as follows.*

– *Objects are tracks $p : \Box^P \to X$;*
– *Morphisms are $\hom_{\mathbb{T}_X}(p, q) = \{r \mid q = p * r\})$, called* track extensions *and denoted $\mathbf{e}_P^{P*R}$, where $p : \Box^P \to X$, $r : \Box^R \to X$ and thus $q : \Box^{P*R} \to X$. In other words, there is a morphism $\mathbf{e}_P^{P*R}$ between tracks $p : \Box^P \to X$ and $p' : \Box^Q \to X$ iff $Q = P * R$ and they are related by the left triangle in the*

following diagram:

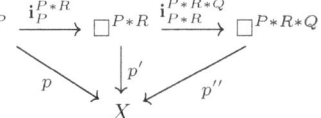

– *Composition of $\mathbf{e}_P^{P*R} : p \to p'$ and $\mathbf{e}_{P*R}^{P*R*Q} : p' \to p''$ is $\mathbf{e}_P^{P*R*Q} : p \to p''$, as shown in the diagram above.*

The Yoneda Lemma 7 is based on the unique cell $\mathbf{y}_S$ of a conclist S. For an ipomset P, we introduce the characteristic path ρ_P that allows a generalization of the Yoneda lemma by substituting ρ_P for $\mathbf{y}_S$. It is a key contribution of this work that will be used to bridges tracks and paths.

Definition 32. *Consider an interval ipomset P and $P = P_1 * P_2 * \cdots * P_m$ its minimal discrete decomposition with $P_i = {}_{U \backslash A}U_{U \backslash B}$. The characteristic path of P is $\rho_P = \beta_1 * \beta_2 \cdots * \beta_m$ the concatenation of steps $\beta_i = (\delta_A^0(\mathbf{y}_U), \mathbf{y}_U, \delta_B^1(\mathbf{y}_U))$.*
Note that the characteristic path is the sparse path $\rho_P \in P_{\Box^P}$ such that $\mathsf{ev}(\rho) = P$, $\mathsf{start}(\rho) = I_{\Box^P}$, and $\mathsf{end}(\rho) = F_{\Box^P}$, calculated by induction as follows.

– *If $P = {}_{U \backslash A}U_{U \backslash B}$ is discrete, then $\rho_P = (\delta_A^0(\mathbf{y}_U), \mathbf{y}_U, \delta_B^1(\mathbf{y}_U))$.*

– If $P = R*Q$, then $\rho_P = \mathbf{i}_R^{R*Q}(\rho_R)*\mathbf{f}_Q^{R*Q}(\rho_Q)^6$, where $\rho_R \in P_{\square^R}$ and $\rho_Q \in P_{\square^Q}$ the characteristic paths of R and Q respectively.

The following Prop. generalizes Yoneda Lemma 7. Instead of cells, here we have paths, and instead of conclist, we have ipomsets.

Proposition 33. *Let X be a precubical set, P an ipomset, $\alpha \in \mathrm{Path}_X$. If $\mathsf{ev}(\alpha) = P$, then there exist a unique $\rho'_P \simeq \rho_P$ and a unique track $g_\alpha : \square^P \to X$ such that $g_\alpha(\rho'_P) = \alpha$.*

The track g_α depends on the class of α up to $\simeq$ rather than α:

Lemma 34. *If $\alpha \simeq \beta$, then $g_\alpha = g_\beta$.*

Theorem 35. *For any precubical set X, the categories $\mathbb{P}_X$ and $\mathbb{T}_X$ are isomorphic.*

5 Bisimulation and Modal Logic

Fix a conclist S and denote by $\mathbf{HDA}_S$ the full subcategory of $\mathbf{HDA}$ with HDAs (X, i_X, F_X) such that $\mathsf{ev}(i_X) = S$. So that we have $\mathbf{HDA} = \bigcup_{S \in \square} \mathbf{HDA}_S$. Similarly, $\mathbf{T}_S^0$ is the category that has track objects $\square^P$, with $S_P \simeq S$, as objects and initial inclusions as morphisms. In this section, we apply the open map bisimulation technique [19] with $\mathbf{T}_S^0$ as the HDA-path category to define the $\mathbf{T}^0$-*bisimulation* and then to define the IPML.

Overview. A morphism $\varphi : \mathcal{X} \to \mathcal{Y}$ in $\mathbf{HDA}_S$ has the *path lifting-property* with respect to $\mathbf{T}_S^0$ if whenever for $\mathbf{i}_P^Q \in \mathrm{hom}_{\mathbf{T}_S^0}$ (thus $Q \cong P * R$ for some ipomset R), $p : \square^P \to X$ and $q : \square^Q \to Y$, $q \circ \mathbf{i}_P^{P*R} = \varphi \circ p$ i.e. the following diagram commutes,

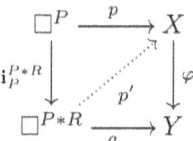

then there exists a track p' such that $p' \circ \mathbf{i}_P^{P*R} = p$ and $\varphi \circ p' = q$ i.e. the two triangles in the previous diagram commute. In this case, we say that φ is $\mathbf{T}_S^0$-*open* or that φ is *open with respect to* $\mathbf{T}_S^0$. This gives rise to a notion of bisimulation with respect to $\mathbf{T}_S^0$.

---

[6] We can check that $\mathbf{i}_R^{R*Q}(\rho_R)$ and $\mathbf{f}_Q^{R*Q}(\rho_Q)$ can be concatenated by elementary calculations, using the expression of initial and final inclusion of Lemma 22 and of the initial and final cells in Definition 11.

5.1   Bisimulation from Open Maps for HDA

Definition 36. *Let $\mathcal{Y}$, $\mathcal{Z}$ be HDAs. We say that $\mathcal{Y}$ and $\mathcal{Z}$ are $\mathbf{T}_S^0$-bisimilar if there is a span of $\mathbf{T}_S^0$-open HDA maps $\mathcal{Y} \xleftarrow{\varphi} \mathcal{X} \xrightarrow{\psi} \mathcal{Z}$ with a common HDA $\mathcal{X}$.*

A path α in an HDA $\mathcal{X}$ is a path in the precubical set X such that $\mathsf{start}(\alpha) = i_X$. We denote $\mathrm{Path}_\mathcal{X}$ the set of paths in $\mathcal{X}$. Similarly, we denote $\mathbb{P}_\mathcal{X}$ the category of classes of paths in an HDA. A morphism $\varphi : \mathcal{X} \to \mathcal{Y}$ in **HDA** has the *future path lifting property* if for $\alpha \in \mathrm{Path}_\mathcal{X}$ and $\beta \in \mathrm{Path}_\mathcal{Y}$, if $\varphi(\alpha)$ and β can be concatenated, then there exists α' in X such that α and α' can be concatenated and $\varphi(\alpha * \alpha') = \varphi(\alpha) * \beta$.

Lemma 37. *For any HDA map $\varphi : \mathcal{X} \to \mathcal{Y}$, φ is $\mathbf{T}_S^0$-open iff φ has the future path lifting.*

Definition 38. *A closed cell-bisimulation between HDAs $\mathcal{Y}$ and $\mathcal{Z}$ is a relation $\overline{R}$ between cells in Y and Z such that*

1. *initial cells i_Y and i_Z are related;*
2. *$\overline{R}$ respects labels: for all $(y, z) \in \overline{R}$, $\mathsf{ev}_Y(y) = \mathsf{ev}_Z(z)$;*
3. *if $(y, z) \in \overline{R}$, then $(\delta_A^\nu(y), \delta_A^\nu(z)) \in \overline{R}$ for $A \subseteq \mathsf{ev}_Y(y) = \mathsf{ev}_Z(z)$, $\nu \in \{0, 1\}$;*
4. *for all $(y, z) \in \overline{R}$, if there exists y' such that $\delta_A^0(y') = y$ for some $A \subseteq \mathsf{ev}(y')$, then there exists z' such that $\delta_A^0(z') = z$ and $(y', z') \in \overline{R}$;*
5. *for all $(y, z) \in \overline{R}$, if there exists z' such that $\delta_A^0(z') = z$ for some $A \subseteq \mathsf{ev}(z')$, then there exists y' such that $\delta_A^0(y') = y$ and $(y', z') \in \overline{R}$;*

A cell x in an HDA $\mathcal{X}$ is said to be accessible if there exists $\alpha_x \in \mathrm{Path}_\mathcal{X}$ such that $\mathsf{end}(\alpha_x) = x$, we denote $\mathcal{X}_{acc}$ the set of accessible cells in $\mathcal{X}$.

Definition 39. *A cell-bisimulation between $\mathcal{Y}$ and $\mathcal{Z}$ is a relation R between $\mathcal{Y}_{acc}$ and $\mathcal{Z}_{acc}$ that satisfies the same properties as Definition 38, replacing @refen:Ubarbisim.e4. by*

3. *for all $(y, z) \in R$, for all $A \subseteq \mathsf{ev}_Y(y) = \mathsf{ev}_Z(z)$,*
   (a) *$(\delta_A^1(y), \delta_A^1(z)) \in R$*
   (b) *$\delta_A^0(y) \in \mathcal{Y}_{acc}$ iff $\delta_A^0(z) \in \mathcal{Z}_{acc}$. In this case, $(\delta_A^0(y), \delta_A^0(z)) \in R$*

Theorem 40. *Two HDAs $\mathcal{Y}$ and $\mathcal{Z}$ are $\mathbf{T}_S^0$-bisimilar iff they are cell-bisimilar.*

5.2   Modal Characterization

In this section, we delve into the core contributions of our work. Initially, we introduce the concept of track bisimulation, followed by a formal presentation of the Ipomset modal logic. Notably, the notion of track bisimulation serves as a crucial link connecting our logic's modalities with the existing concept of ST-bisimulation found in the literature. More specifically, it will demonstrate that our logic characterizes the notion of ST-bisimulation.

Definition 41. *A* track-bisimulation, *with respect to* $\mathbf{T}_S^0$, *between HDAs* $\mathcal{Y}$ *and* $\mathcal{Z}$ *is a symmetric relation* R *of pairs of tracks* (p_1, p_2) *with common domain* $\square^P$, *so* $p_1 : \square^P \to Y$ *is a track in* Y *and* $p_2 : \square^P \to Z$ *is a track in* Z, *such that*

1. *initial tracks* $\iota_{\mathcal{X}} : \square^S \to X$ *and* $\iota_{\mathcal{Y}} : \square^S \to Y$ *are related;*
2. *For* $(p_1, p_2) \in \mathsf{R}$, *if* $p_1' \circ \mathbf{i}_P^{P*R} = p_1$, *in the diagram*

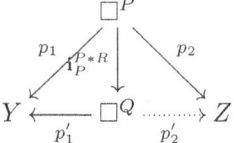

then there is p_2' *such that* $(p_1', p_2') \in \mathsf{R}$ *and* $p_2' \circ \mathbf{i}_P^{P*R} = p_2$.

We say that a track-bisimulation is strong *if, in addition, it satisfies:*

3. *If* $(p_1, p_2) \in \mathsf{R}$ *for* $p_1 : \square^Q \to Y$, $p_2 : \square^Q \to Z$, *then for every* $\mathbf{i}_P^{P*R} : \square^P \to \square^Q \in \mathbf{T}_S^0$ *we have* $(p_1 \circ \mathbf{i}_P^{P*R}, p_2 \circ \mathbf{i}_P^{P*R}) \in \mathsf{R}$.

We say that two HDAs are (strong) track-bisimilar *iff there is a (strong) track-bisimulation* between them.

We introduce the novel modal logic IPML with HDAs as models, following the approach of Nielsen and Winskel [19].

Definition 42 (Ipomset Modal Logic). *The set of formulae in Ipomset Modal Logic (IPML) is given by the following syntax:*

$$F, G ::= \top \mid \bot \mid F \wedge G \mid F \vee G \mid \langle \mathbf{i}_P^{P*R} \rangle F \mid \overline{\langle \mathbf{i}_P^{P*R} \rangle} F,$$

where $\mathbf{i}_P^{P*R}$ *is a morphism in* $\mathbf{T}_S^0$. *The modality* $\overline{\langle \mathbf{i}_P^{P*R} \rangle}$ *is a backward modality, while* $\langle \mathbf{i}_P^{P*R} \rangle$ *is a forward modality.*

Like Nielsen and Winskel's original approach, IPML should also have infinitary conjunctions. In contrast, we only consider HDAs with finitely branching, for which no infinitary conjunction is required.

The satisfaction relation between a track $p : \square^P \to X$ and a formula F is given by structural induction on assertions as follows:

- $p \models \top$ for all p, $p \models \bot$ for no p, $p \models F \wedge G$ iff $p \models F$ and $p \models G$, and $p \models F \vee G$ iff $p \models F$ or $p \models G$;
- $p \models \langle \mathbf{i}_P^{P*R} \rangle F$ where $\mathbf{i}_P^{P*R} : \square^P \to \square^{P*R}$, iff there exists is a track $q : \square^{P*R} \to X$ for which $q \models F$ and $p = q \circ \mathbf{i}_P^{P*R}$;
- $p \models \overline{\langle \mathbf{i}_Q^P \rangle} F$ where $\mathbf{i}_Q^P : \square^Q \to \square^P$, with $P = Q * S$, iff there exists a track $q : \square^Q \to X$ for which $q \models F$ and $q = p \circ \mathbf{i}_Q^{Q*S}$.

By Theorem 35, the previous modal logic, given with satisfaction relation on tracks, induces a modal logic interpreted over paths, where congruent paths satisfy the same formulas. The induced satisfaction relation is thus a binary relation $\models$ that relates $\alpha \in \mathbb{P}_{\mathcal{X}}$, with $\mathrm{ev}(\alpha) = P$, to formulae.

For a given track, the forward modality is uniquely determined by the choice of the extending ipomset R. While the backward modality is uniquely determined by the decomposition of P into two ipomsets. Thus, our modalities could be reformulated, as follows.

- $\alpha \models \langle R \rangle F$ with R an ipomset iff there is $\beta \in \mathbb{P}_X$ for which $\alpha * \beta \models F$ and $\mathsf{ev}(\beta) = R$;
- $\alpha \models \overline{\langle Q * S \rangle} F$ with $P = Q * S$ iff there is $\alpha' \xrightarrow{0} \alpha$ in $\mathbb{P}_X$ for which $\mathsf{ev}(\alpha') = Q$ and $\alpha' \models F$.

Example 43. Consider the paths in the HDAs of Fig. 8. We have the following:

- $(i_{X_2}) \models \langle [\begin{smallmatrix} c\bullet \\ \bullet a\bullet \end{smallmatrix}] \rangle \langle [\bullet a \to d\bullet] \rangle \top$, meaning that there is a path α_2 labeled by $[\begin{smallmatrix} c\bullet \\ \bullet a\bullet \end{smallmatrix}]$ from which it is possible to terminate an event labeled by a and start an event labeled by d, by executing the path β_2.
- $\alpha_1 \models \overline{\langle c * [\begin{smallmatrix} d \\ a \end{smallmatrix}] \rangle} \langle [\begin{smallmatrix} b \\ d \end{smallmatrix}] \rangle \top$, meaning that there exists a restriction α_1' of α_1 such that $\mathsf{ev}(\alpha_1') = c$ and $\alpha_1' \models \langle [\begin{smallmatrix} b \\ d \end{smallmatrix}] \rangle \top$, that is, α_1' can be concatenated with a path β_1 labeled by $[\begin{smallmatrix} b \\ d \end{smallmatrix}]$.

[19, Thm. 15] now immediately implies the following.

Theorem 44. *HDAs are (strong) track-bisimilar iff initial tracks satisfy the same forward (and backward) assertions.*

Theorem 45. *If HDAs are $\mathbf{T}_S^0$-bisimilar, then they are strong track-bisimilar.*

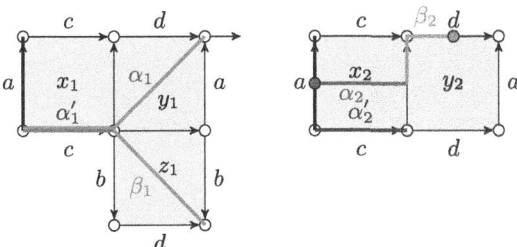

Fig. 8. Two HDAs $\mathcal{X}_1$ and $\mathcal{X}_2$ in $\mathbf{HDA}_a$ that are strong track-bisimilar, cell-bisimilar, but not closed cell-bisimilar HDAs. Each HDA has the edge labeled by a with a thick line as the unique initial cell.

It is clear that closed cell-bisimilarity implies cell-bisimilarity. The following example shows that the opposite direction is false. It also shows that track-bisimilarity does not imply closed cell bisimilarity. The opposite direction of the later remains an open question that we would like to answer in an extended version of this work.

Example 46. Figure 8 shows two HDAs $(X_1, \delta_c^0(x_1))$ (on the left) and $(X_2, \delta_c^0(x_2))$ (on the right) that are track-bisimilar but not closed cell-bisimular. Let $P_1 = [\,{}^{\bullet a \bullet}_c\,]$, $P_2 = [\,{}^{\bullet a}_{d \bullet}\,]$, $P_3 = [\,{}^{\bullet d}_b\,]$. It is not difficult to check that $K = \{(g, g') \mid g : \square^P \to X_1, g' : \square^P \to X_2 \mid \text{there exists } i_P^{P_1 * P_2}\}$ is a strong track-bisimulation. However, they cannot be closed cell-bisimilar, because if there is a closed cell-bisimulation between them, then $\delta_a^0(y_1)$ and $\delta_a^0(y_2)$ are related. However, $\delta_b^0(z_1) = \delta_a^0(y_1)$ while there exists no cell $z_2 \in X_2$ such that $\delta_b^0(z_2) = \delta_a^0(y_2)$.

Remark 47. To check the track bisimilarity of the HDAs of the previous example, one may check that initial *paths* satisfy the same forward assertions. Note that if we allow i_{X_1} and i_{X_2} to be the nodes $\delta_{ac}^0(x_1)$ and $\delta_{ac}^0(x_2)$ respectively, $\mathcal{X}_1$ and $\mathcal{X}_2$ will no longer be track bisimilar. Due to the distinguishing formulae $\langle (c) \rangle \langle [\,{}^b_d\,] \rangle \top$ that holds in (i_{X_1}) but not in (i_{X_2}). In fact, in this case, we will have equivalence between the notions of strong track bisimilarity and cell-bisimilarity.

We say that paths $\alpha = (x_0, \varphi_1, x_1, \varphi_2, \ldots, \varphi_n, x_n)$ and $\beta = (y_0, \psi_1, y_1, \psi_2, \ldots, \psi_m, y_m)$ have the same shape if $n = m$ and $\varphi_i = \psi_i$ for all i. The following notion of behavioral equivalence was originally introduced by van Glabbeek [14] as ST-bisimulation. In our setting it has been formulated in [9] as follows.

Definition 48. *A* path-bisimulation *between HDAs $\mathcal{Y}$ and $\mathcal{Z}$ is a symmetric relation R between paths in Y and Z such that*

1. *initial paths (i_Y) and (i_Z) are related;*
2. *R respects the shape: for all $(\rho, \sigma) \in \mathsf{R}$, ρ and σ have the same shape;*
3. *for all $(\rho, \sigma) \in \mathsf{R}$ and path ρ' in Y where ρ and ρ' may be concatenated, there exists a path σ' in Z such that $(\rho * \rho', \sigma * \sigma') \in \mathsf{R}$;*

A path-bisimulation is called strong *if, in addition, it satisfies:*

4. *for all $(\rho, \sigma) \in \mathsf{R}$ and ρ' a restriction of ρ, there exists σ' a restriction of σ such that $(\rho', \sigma') \in \mathsf{R}$.*

Finally, $\mathcal{X}$ and $\mathcal{Y}$ are (strong) path-bisimilar *if there exists a (strong) path-bisimulation R between them; this is an equivalence relation.*

Theorem 49. *Two HDAs $\mathcal{X}_1$ and $\mathcal{X}_2$ are (strong) track-bisimilar iff they are (strong) path-bisimilar.*

Conclusion. We have investigated open maps for the category $\mathbf{T}^0 \subseteq \mathbf{T}$. The general approach yields the abstract notion of $\mathbf{T}^0$-bisimulation and a path logic, IPML (with past modality) for which the logical equivalence is equivalent to the (strong) Track-bisimulation. We showed that our logic is powerful enough to capture true concurrency and characterize (strong) Path-bisimulation, known in the literature as ST-bisimulation. We summarize the hierarchy of the different notions in Fig. 4. In future work, we aim to look at the extension of IPML that captures the finest bisimulation equivalence, hereditary history preserving bisimulation. We would thus have a complete spectrum for concurrency bisimulation notions that might be interpreted over other models of concurrency such as Petri nets, event structures, and configuration structures, due to the expressiveness of HDA.

References

1. Aceto, L., Ingolfsdottir, A., Larsen, K., Srba, J.: Reactive Systems: Modelling, Specification and Verification. Cambridge University Press, Cambridge (2007)
2. Amrane, A., Bazille, H., Fahrenberg, U., Ziemiański, K.: Closure and decision properties for higher-dimensional automata. In: Ábrahám, E., Dubslaff, C., Tarifa, S.L.T. (eds.) ICTAC 2023. LNCS, vol. 14446, pp. 295–312. Springer, Cham (2023). https://doi.org/10.1007/978-3-031-47963-2_18
3. Baier, C., Katoen, J.P.: Principles of Model Checking. MIT Press, Cambridge (2008)
4. Baldan, P., Crafa, S.: A logic for true concurrency. In: Gastin, P., Laroussinie, F. (eds.) CONCUR 2010. LNCS, vol. 6269, pp. 147–161. Springer, Heidelberg (2010). https://doi.org/10.1007/978-3-642-15375-4_11
5. Baldan, P., Crafa, S.: Hereditary history-preserving bisimilarity: logics and automata. In: Garrigue, J. (ed.) APLAS 2014. LNCS, vol. 8858, pp. 469–488. Springer, Cham (2014). https://doi.org/10.1007/978-3-319-12736-1_25
6. Baldan, P., Padoan, T.: Model checking a logic for true concurrency. ACM Trans. Comput. Log. (TOCL) **21**(4), 1–49 (2020)
7. Bednarczyk, M.A.: Categories of asynchronous systems. Ph.D. thesis, University of Sussex (1987)
8. De Nicola, R., Vaandrager, F.: Three logics for branching bisimulation. J. ACM (JACM) **42**(2), 458–487 (1995)
9. Fahrenberg, U., Johansen, C., Struth, G., Ziemiański, K.: Languages of higher-dimensional automata. Math. Struct. Comput. Sci. **31**(5), 575–613 (2021). https://doi.org/10.1017/S0960129521000293
10. Fahrenberg, U., Johansen, C., Struth, G., Ziemiański, K.: A kleene theorem for higher-dimensional automata. In: Klin, B., Lasota, S., Muscholl, A. (eds.) 33rd International Conference on Concurrency Theory (CONCUR 2022). Leibniz International Proceedings in Informatics (LIPIcs), vol. 243, pp. 29:1–29:18. Schloss Dagstuhl – Leibniz-Zentrum für Informatik, Dagstuhl (2022). https://doi.org/10.4230/LIPIcs.CONCUR.2022.29
11. Fahrenberg, U., Ziemiański, K.: A Myhill-Nerode theorem for higher-dimensional automata. In: Gomes, L., Lorenz, R. (eds.) PETRI NETS 2023. LNCS, vol. 13929, pp. 167–188. Springer, Cham (2023). https://doi.org/10.1007/978-3-031-33620-1_9
12. Fishburn, P.C.: Intransitive indifference with unequal indifference intervals. J. Math. Psychol. **7**(1), 144–149 (1970)
13. Glabbeek, R.J.: The linear time - branching time spectrum. In: Baeten, J.C.M., Klop, J.W. (eds.) CONCUR 1990. LNCS, vol. 458, pp. 278–297. Springer, Heidelberg (1990). https://doi.org/10.1007/BFb0039066
14. van Glabbeek, R.J.: On the expressiveness of higher dimensional automata. Theoret. Comput. Sci. **356**(3), 265–290 (2006)
15. van Glabbeek, R.J., Goltz, U.: Refinement of actions and equivalence notions for concurrent systems. Acta Inform. **37**(4), 229–327 (2001)
16. van Glabbeek, R.J., Vaandrager, F.: The difference between splitting in n and n+1. Inf. Comput. **136**(2), 109–142 (1997)
17. Hennessy, M., Milner, R.: Algebraic laws for nondeterminism and concurrency. J. ACM (JACM) **32**(1), 137–161 (1985)
18. Janicki, R., Koutny, M.: Structure of concurrency. Theoret. Comput. Sci. **112**(1), 5–52 (1993)

19. Joyal, A., Nielsen, M., Winskel, G.: Bisimulation from open maps. Inf. Comput. **127**(2), 164–185 (1996). https://doi.org/10.1006/inco.1996.0057

20. Leifer, J.J., Milner, R.: Deriving bisimulation congruences for reactive systems. In: Palamidessi, C. (ed.) CONCUR 2000. LNCS, vol. 1877, pp. 243–258. Springer, Heidelberg (2000). https://doi.org/10.1007/3-540-44618-4_19

21. Nielsen, M., Clausen, C.: Bisimulation for models in concurrency. In: Jonsson, B., Parrow, J. (eds.) CONCUR 1994. LNCS, vol. 836, pp. 385–400. Springer, Heidelberg (1994). https://doi.org/10.1007/978-3-540-48654-1_29

22. Nielsen, M., Plotkin, G., Winskel, G.: Petri nets, event structures and domains, part I. Theoret. Comput. Sci. **13**(1), 85–108 (1981)

23. Phillips, I., Ulidowski, I.: Event identifier logic. Math. Struct. Comput. Sci. **24**(2) (2014)

24. Pnueli, A., Manna, Z.: The temporal logic of reactive and concurrent systems. Springer **16**, 12 (1992)

25. Pratt, V.: Modeling concurrency with geometry. In: Proceedings of the 18th Symposium on Principles of Programming Languages, POPL 1991, pp. 311-322. Association for Computing Machinery (1991). https://doi.org/10.1145/99583.99625

26. Sangiorgi, D.: On the bisimulation proof method. Math. Struct. Comput. Sci. **8**(5), 447–479 (1998)

27. Shehtman, V.B.: Bisimulation games and locally tabular logics. Russ. Math. Surv. **71**(5), 979 (2016). https://doi.org/10.1070/RM9731

28. Shields, M.W.: Concurrent machines. Comput. J. **28**(5), 449–465 (1985)

29. Van Glabbeek, R., Plotkin, G.: Configuration structures. In: 10th Annual IEEE Symposium on Logic in Computer Science, LICS 1995, pp. 199–209. IEEE (1995). https://doi.org/10.1109/LICS.1995.523257

30. Winkowski, J.: An algebraic characterization of the behaviour of non-sequential systems. Inf. Process. Lett. **6**(4), 105–109 (1977)

31. Winskel, G.: Event structures. In: Brauer, W., Reisig, W., Rozenberg, G. (eds.) ACPN 1986. LNCS, vol. 255, pp. 325–392. Springer, Heidelberg (1987). https://doi.org/10.1007/3-540-17906-2_31

32. Winskel, G.: An introduction to event structures. In: de Bakker, J.W., de Roever, W.-P., Rozenberg, G. (eds.) REX 1988. LNCS, vol. 354, pp. 364–397. Springer, Heidelberg (1989). https://doi.org/10.1007/BFb0013026

Algorithms and Complexity

Maximizing Weighted Dominance in the Plane

Waseem Akram[✉] and Sanjeev Saxena

Department of Computer Science and Engineering, Indian Institute of Technology, Kanpur, Kanpur 208016, India
{akram,ssax}@iitk.ac.in

Abstract. Let P be a set of n weighted points, Q be a set of m unweighted points in the plane, and k a non-negative integer. We study the k-*maxDominance* problem, where the objective is to find a subset $Q' \subseteq Q$ with size at most k such that the sum of the weights of the points in P dominated by at least one point in Q' is maximized. A point q in the plane dominates another point p if and only if $x(q) \geq x(p)$ and $y(q) \geq y(p)$, and at least one inequality is strict. An algorithm for the k-maxDominance problem can be used to solve problems previously examined in scheduling, graph optimization, and database systems.

We present a simple algorithm solving the problem in $O(km^2 + n \log m)$ time and $O(n + m)$ space. The algorithm is faster than the existing one when $m = o(\sqrt{n})$. Additionally, we provide another solution to the problem with $O(k \min\{n + m, \frac{n}{k} + m^2\} \log m)$ time and $O(n+m)$ space. These bounds are the same or better than those of the existing solution (the bounds are better when $m = o(\sqrt{n})$). The expected number of skyline points is $\theta(\log n)$, a term much less than $\sqrt{n}$.

To obtain the second solution, we design a general technique that can be used to reduce the number of points n in P to $\min\{n, m^2\}$ in any algorithm for the k-maxDominance problem.

Keywords: Dominance · Optimization · Representative Skyline · Algorithms · Data Structures

1 Introduction

Let S be a set of points in the d-dimensional Euclidean space. A point $q \in S$ dominates another point $p \in S$ if and only if the coordinates of q are greater than or equal to that of p in all dimensions and strictly greater in at least one dimension [10]. A point $p \in S$ is called a *skyline point* if no other point in S dominates the point p. The *skyline* of the set S consists of all skyline points. Computation of the skyline of a given set is an important and well-studied problem in computational geometry [1,3,4,18]. The problem finds applications in numerous domains, including database management, multi-criteria decision-making, and Machine Learning [1–3,6,7,9,11–13].

This research work was partially supported by Research-I Foundation of the Department of CSE at IIT Kanpur.

C. Anutariya and M. M. Bonsangue (Eds.): ICTAC 2024, LNCS 15373, pp. 153–163, 2025.
https://doi.org/10.1007/978-3-031-77019-7_9

In scenarios with many skyline points, reporting the entire skyline maybe less helpful; a user may find it challenging to understand the possible trade-offs the complete skyline offers. This leads to the concept of *representative skyline* [8,10]: instead of computing and reporting the entire skyline, find a subset of the skyline points that "best" represent them in some sense. In this paper, we study the following optimization problem (a generalisation of a representative skyline problem studied in [8]) introduced by Choi, Cabello, and Ahn [2]:

> Given a set P of n (possibly negative) weighted points, a set Q of m unweighted points in the plane, and a non-negative integer k, find a subset $Q' \subseteq Q$ of size at most k such that the sum of weights of the points of P that are dominated by at least one point of Q' is maximized.

We will refer to this problem as *k-maxDominance* problem. Choi et al. [2] solved it using $O(m + n)$-space and $O(k(m + n) \log m)$-time. The problem has applications in numerous domains including databases, multiobjective optimization, decision analysis, statistics, economics, operations research, and Machine Learning [2,5,7–11,13]. Moreover, the k-maxDominance problem can also be used to solve other optimization problems like the *disjoint union of cliques* problem for interval graphs, the *hitting intervals* problem [2]. The k-maxDominance problem can be viewed as a generalisation of the *top-k representative skyline points* problem, introduced by Lin, Yuan, Zhang, and Zhang [8]. For a random data set of n points in the d-dimensional space, the expected number of skyline points is $\theta(\log^{d-1} n/(d-1)!)$ [6,11,13,16]. In particular, the expected size of the skyline of a (random) set in 2-d is $\theta(\log n)$. Moreover, Morse et al. [17] conducted extensive experimentations on both real and synthetic data sets, demonstrating that the number of skyline points are very few.

In this paper, we present two results for the k-maxDominance problem. Our first algorithm is simple and takes $O(km^2 + n \log m)$-time and $O(n + m)$-space. The time bound is interesting only when $m = o(\sqrt{n})$. The algorithm uses no advanced data structures (not even a segment tree as used in [2]). A similar technique was used earlier by Lin et al. [8] for the unweighted case. By applying the proposed k-maxDominance algorithm for the top-k representative skyline points problem, we can solve the later problem in $O(kh^2 + n \log h)$ time and $O(n)$ space, where h is the number of the skyline points. The algorithm of Lin et al. [8] takes $O(n + h^2)$ space. Choi et al. [2] observed that the space can be reduced to $O(n + kh)$ using some additional data structures. The space used by us is $O(n)$ as we are storing only non-zero values (ρ-values in Section 2).

In the second solution, we employ a preprocessing step, which (possibly) reduces the number of weighted points. Consequently, we solve the k-maxDominance problem in $O(m + n)$ space and $O(k \min\{n + m, \frac{n}{k} + m^2\} \log m)$ time. The bounds are better than existing ones [2] when $m = o(\sqrt{n})$, and for the other cases, the bounds become the same as that of Choi et al.'s [2] up to a constant multiplicative factor. The proposed technique of reducing the number of weighted points can be used in any algorithm for the k-maxDominance problem.

For a random data set of n points in the 2-dimensional space, the expected number of skyline points is $\theta(\log n)$ [6,11,13,16], and as by the experiments of Morse et al. [17] the number of skyline points are very few. Thus, for the top-k representative skyline points problem and the k-maxDominance problem (positive weights version), our proposed algorithms will do better than the earlier algorithm of Choi et al. as the number of skyline points is expected to be much less than $\sqrt{n}$.

Moreover, our proposed algorithms can also be used to solve the maximum piercing problem. Our second algorithm has either same or better bounds compared to the result of Choi et al. [2]. Both our algorithms have better bounds when $m = o(\sqrt{n})$.

1.1 Previous and Related Works

The k-maxDominance problem was first studied by Choi et al. [2], who solved it in $O(k(m+n)\log m)$ time and $O(m+n)$ space. For the case when the points in P are allowed to have positive weights only, their simplified algorithm takes $O(m\log h + k(n+h)\log h)$ time and $O(n+m)$ space, where h is the number of skyline points in Q.

Lin et al. [8] studied the problem of computing k skyline points so that the number of points dominated by at least one of the k points is maximized. This is known as the *top-k representative skyline points* problem. They present a dynamic-programming algorithm that solves the problem in $O(kh^2 + n\log h)$ time and $O(n + kh^2)$ space in the plane. Here, n and h are the numbers of input and skyline points, respectively. Note that it is a particular case of the k-maxDominance problem: assign unit weight to every point in P and set Q as the set of skyline points.

In the *maximum piercing* problem, we are given a set $\mathcal{I}$ of n weighted intervals on the real line, a set S of m points, and a integer $k > 0$, and we have to find k points from the set S such that the combined weight of the intervals in $\mathcal{I}$ pierced by the points is maximised. Choi et al. [2] showed that the k-maxDominance problem can be used to solve the problem in $O(k(m+n)\log m)$ time and $O(m+n)$ space.

The *maximum volume subset selection* [14] is also a related problem. Given a set of axis-parallel boxes in $\mathbb{R}^d$ with a corner at the origin, the goal is to select k boxes such that the volume of their union is maximum. For $d = 2$, it can be solved in time $O((n-k)k + n\log n)$ [14,15]. However, for $d = 3$, the problem is NP-hard.

See [1,10] for other related works in the context of representative skylines problem.

1.2 Definitions and Notations

We use the notations from [2]. Let P be a set of n weighted points, Q be a set of m unweighted points in the plane, and k a positive integer. The weight of a point p, denoted by $w(p)$, can be negative. We denote by $x(p)$ and $y(p)$ the x-coordinate and y-coordinate of a point p in the plane, respectively. Let x_{min} and x_{max} be the minimum and the maximum x-coordinates in the set $P \cup Q$, respectively. Similarly, y_{min} and y_{max} are defined. The set of the points $p \in P$ (strictly) lying above the horizontal line through the point $q_i \in Q$ is denoted by P_i. Formally, $P_i = \{p \in P : y(p) > y(q_i)\}$.

For a given region $R \in \mathbb{R}^2$, the weight of region $R \in \mathbb{R}^2$ is defined as the sum of the weights of all points of P contained in the region R. It is denoted by $w(R)$. If no point from the set P lies in R, then $w(R)$ is defined as zero. For any point q in the plane, $dom(q)$ represents the region $(-\infty, x(q)] \times (-\infty, y(q)]$. For a set Q of points, $dom(Q)$ is defined as the union of the regions $dom(q), q \in Q$. Let $[t]$ denotes the set of natural numbers $\{1, 2, \ldots, t\}$.

In the k-maxDominance problem, we are to find a subset $Q' \subseteq Q$ with size at most k such that $w(dom(Q'))$ is maximized. Formally, we want to compute $\text{maxDominance}(P, Q, k) = \max\{w(dom(Q')) : Q' \subseteq Q, |Q'| \leq k\}$ and to obtain a subset $Q' \subseteq Q$ with size at most k and $w(Q') = \text{maxDominance}(P, Q, k)$.

A simple algorithm to solve the k-maxDominance problem is presented in Sect. 2. In Sect. 3, we describe a transformation which (possibly) reduces the number of weighted points, using which we get a solution to the problem. Some conclusions are offered in Sect. 4.

2   An $O(km^2 + n \log m)$-Time Algorithm

In this section, we present an algorithm for the k-maxDominance problem, which does not employ any sophisticated data structures. The algorithm uses $O(km^2 + n \log m)$ time and $O(n + m)$ space. Our approach is similar to that of Choi et al. [2]. We use the plane sweep technique to solve the problem: a horizontal line is swept over the plane k times. In the $l^{th} (1 \leq l \leq k)$ iteration, we compute the value of an optimal solution to the problem with size at most l using (some) values computed in the $(l-1)^{th}$ iteration. Thus, at the end of the kth iteration, we will have the value of an optimal solution to our main problem. A similar technique was used earlier by Lin et al. [8] for the unweighted case.

We assume that no two points of Q have the same x- or y-coordinate: the points in the set Q can be transformed so that no two (transformed) points have the same x- or y-coordinate and $dom(q) \cap P = dom(q') \cap P$, where q' is the transformed point of $q \in Q$. This step can be done in $O((n+m) \log m)$ time [2]. We add a point $q_{m+1} = (x_{max} + 1, y_{min} - 1)$ to the set Q. Note that no point in $P \cup Q$ dominates the point q_{m+1}.

Let $Q = \{q_1, q_2, \ldots, q_{m+1}\}$ be sorted in decreasing order of y-coordinates. We denote by $T_l(i)$ the value of an optimal solution with size at most l to the k-maxDominance problem when restricted to P_i, and $Q = \{q_1, q_2, \ldots, q_i\}$. Recall that P_i is the set of points of P with y-coordinates greater than $y(q_i)$. Note that $T_k(m+1)$ corresponds to the value of an optimal solution to the $\text{maxDominance}(P, Q, k)$ problem, and $T_0(i) = 0$ for all $i \in [m+1]$. For all $i, j \in [m+1]$ with $j < i$, let $\rho(i, j)$ be the sum of the weights of the points in P_i

dominated by point q_j. If no such point exists, $\rho(i, j)$ is taken as 0. We will later describe an algorithm to efficiently compute all $\rho(i, j)$ values. Here, we assume that all $\rho(i, j)$ values are known and can be accessed in $O(1)$ time.

We now describe our algorithm to compute the value of an optimal solution to the k-maxDominance problem. We know that $T_0(i) = 0$ for every $i \in [m+1]$. For each $l = 1, 2, \ldots, k$, we compute $T_l(i)$ values using the values $T_{l-1}(i)$ computed in the previous iteration as follows. We process the points $q_1, q_2, \ldots q_{m+1}$ one by one in order. Let q_i be the current point being processed. We find a point q_j among the points $q_1, q_2, \ldots, q_{i-1}$ with $x(q_j) \leq x(q_i)$ such that the sum $T_{l-1}(j) + \rho(i, j)$ is maximized. At the end of the kth iteration, we report the obtained maximum value as the value of an optimal solution. A pseudo-code of the algorithm is described in Algorithm 1 (with the assumption that $\rho(i, j)$ values are available).

Algorithm 1. An $O(km^2 + n \log m)$-time algorithm for k-$maxDominance$ problem

1: $x_{max} \leftarrow$ the maximum x-coordinate among the points of $P \cup Q$.
2: $y_{min} \leftarrow$ the minimum y-coordinate among the points of $P \cup Q$.
3: $q_{m+1} \leftarrow (1 + x_{max}, -1 + y_{min})$
4: $Q' \leftarrow Q \cup \{q_{m+1}\}$
5: Let the set $Q' = \{q_1, q_2, q_3, \ldots, q_{m+1}\}$ be sorted in decreasing order of the y-coordinates.
6: $T_0(i) \leftarrow 0$ for each $i \in [m + 1]$ ▷ Initialization (T_l is 0 for $l = 0$)
7: **for** $l \leftarrow 1$ to k **do**   ▷ Solution set is of size at most l
8:     **for** $i \leftarrow 2$ to $m + 1$ **do**
9:         $max \leftarrow -\infty$
10:         **for** $j \leftarrow 1$ to i **do**
11:             **if** $x(q_j) \leq x(q_i)$ and $T_{l-1}(j) + \rho(i, j) > max$ **then**
12:                 $max \leftarrow T_{l-1}(j) + \rho(i, j)$
13:             **end if**
14:         **end for**
15:     **end for**
16:     $T_l(i) \leftarrow max$
17: **end for**
18: report $T_k(m + 1)$

Remark 1. The term $\rho(i, j)$ is similar to $\Delta(s_i, s_j)$ used by Lin et al. [8].

'ithm 1 directly follows from Lemma 2 of [2]. The Lemma is stated below for the sake of completeness.

Lemma 1 (Lemma 2 of [2]). *Let $Q_i^{\lrcorner}$ denotes the set of the points of Q contained in the region $(-\infty, x(q_i)] \times [y(q_i), +\infty)$, and $w_i(dom(q_j))$ denotes the sum of the weights of the points of P_i present in the region $(-\infty, x(q_j)] \times (-\infty, y(q_j)]$. For each $l \in \{1, 2, \ldots, k\}, i \in \{1, \ldots, m + 1\}$ and $j = \{1, 2, \ldots, i\}$, we have*

$$T_l(i) = \max\{S_l(i, j) : q_j \in Q_i^{\lrcorner}\},$$

$$S_l(i,j) = T_{l-1}(j) + w_i(dom(q_j)).$$

$\square$

Steps 1–5 takes $O(m + n + m \log m)$ time. The time taken by steps 6–18 is $O(km^2)$, provided the $\rho(i,j)$ values are accessible in $O(1)$ time (In Sect. 2.1, we describe a method that, for any given pair (i,j), implicitly computes $\rho(i,j)$ value in constant time with $O(m^2 + n \log m)$ preprocessing time and $O(\min\{n, m^2\})$ space). Thus, Algorithm 1 uses $O(km^2 + n \log m)$ time and $O(n + m)$ space in total.

Theorem 1. *Given a set of P of n weighted points, a set Q of m unweighted points, and a positive integer k, the k-maxDominance problem can be solved using $O(km^2 + n \log m)$-time and $O(n + m)$-space.*

$\square$

The algorithm is simple and does not use any complicated data structures. However, only for the case when $m = o(\sqrt{n})$, the algorithm is faster than the existing algorithm Choi et al. [2]. In other case, it is slower. The case $m = o(\sqrt{n})$ is particularly interesting in the context of the top-k representative skyline points problem, as the number of skyline points is $\theta(\log n)$ (for random input), a term much smaller than $\sqrt{n}$.

2.1   Computation of $\rho(i,j)$ Values

Let the set $Q = \{q_1, q_2, \ldots, q_{m+1}\}$ be sorted in decreasing order of the y-coordinates. Recall that no two points in Q have the same x or y-coordinates. Consider a partition of the plane induced by horizontal and (half) vertical lines through the points of Q. The plane will be divided into a collection of $(m + 1)^2$ non-overlapping rectangles, which we will call cells. The cells between the horizontal lines through q_i and q_{i+1}, for any $i \in [m]$, are characterized as follows: Let π be a permutation of $[i]$ such that $q_{\pi(1)}, q_{\pi(2)}, \ldots, q_{\pi(i)}$ is sorted in increasing order of x-coordinates. For every $j \leq i$, we denote the cell with lower-left corner $(x(q_{\pi(j-1)}), y(q_{i+1}))$ and upper-right corner $(x(q_{\pi(j)}), y(q_i))$ by C_{ij}. Here, $q_0 = (x_{min} - 1, y_{max} + 1)$ and $q_{m+1} = (x_{max} + 1, y_{min} - 1)$ with $q_0 = q_{\pi(0)}$ and $q_{m+1} = q_{\pi(m+1)}$. See Fig. 1. We call a cell empty if it contains no point from the set P. The points in non-empty cells form a partition of the set P, i.e., no two cells have a point in common, and the union of points of all the non-empty cells gives the set P. One can compute the points contained in each cell using sorting and binary searches. The total time needed to perform this task is $O((n + m) \log m)$.

Remark 2. As the total number of cells is $(m + 1)^2$. Thus, the number of non-empty cells in the partition can not be more than $(m + 1)^2$.

The following fact is used to compute ρ-values. For any pair (i,j) with $1 \leq i, j \leq m + 1$ and $j < i$, the value $\rho(i,j)$ can be expressed as follows.

$$\rho(i,j) = \rho(i-1,j) + \sum_{t=1}^{\pi(j)} w(C_{(i-1)t}) \tag{1}$$

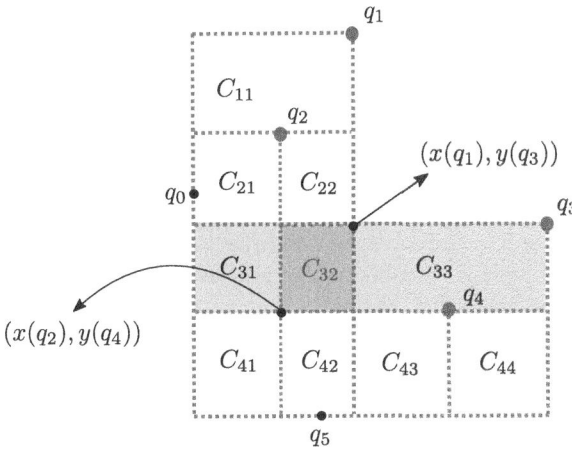

Fig. 1. Cells between lines through q_3 and q_4 are shaded with grey. The cell C_{32} has been shown in green shade along with corner points.

We use the above recurrence relation as follows. For each $i \in [m]$, we compute prefix sums $psum(i, l) = \sum_{t=1}^{l} w(C_{it})$, for all $l \leq i$; the total time used for computing all the prefix sums is $O(m^2)$. Using the prefix sums and the recurrence relation (1), we then compute $\rho(i, j)$ for all $j < i$ in $O(m^2 + n \log m)$ time. The space used is $O(n + m^2)$; the factor $O(m^2)$ is for storing all ρ values.

Further Improvements. Instead of explicitly storing $\rho(i, j)$ for all $j < i$, we can implicitly compute them using prefix sums. For each $i \in [m]$, we compute prefix sums $psum(i, l) = \sum_{t=1}^{l} w(C_{it})$, for all $l \leq i$; the total time used for computing all the prefix sums is $O(m^2)$. We store the prefix sum $psum(i, j)$ if the corresponding cell has non-zero weight, i.e., $w(C_{ij}) \neq 0$. Hence, the space used to store the prefix sums is $O(\min\{n, m^2\})$. Having known these prefix sums, we can retrieve $\rho(i, j)$ value, for any $j < i$, in constant time when algorithm needs it.

The algorithm sweeps the plane k times. In each iteration, the algorithm needs $\rho(i, j)$ values in increasing order of i, that is, i takes values $1, 2, 3, \ldots, m+1$ in order. From the recurrence relation (1), observe that in order to compute $\rho(i, j)$ value, we need only $\rho(i-1, j)$ value and prefix sum $psum(i, \pi(j))$. Therefore, it is sufficient to keep only the ρ-values of the previous row (in subdivision), allowing us to discard the ρ-values from earlier rows. In any given row, the number of cells (and thus ρ-values) is $O(m)$. Thus, the space-bound reduces to $O(n + m)$.

Lemma 2. *We can preprocess the sets P and Q so that, given any pair (i, j) of integers with $1 \leq j < i \leq m + 1$, the value $\rho(i, j)$ can be retrieved in $O(1)$ time. The preprocessing takes $O(m^2 + n \log m)$ time and $O(n + m)$ space.* $\square$

3   Transformation of Input Points

In this section, we show that the set P of weighted points can be transformed into a new set P' with $|P'| = \min\{n, m^2\}$ such that maxDominance$(P, Q, k) = $ maxDominance(P', Q, k). As a consequence of this preprocessing step, we solve the k-maxDominance problem using $O(k \min\{n + m, \frac{n}{k} + m^2\} \log m)$ time and $O(m+n)$ space. The time is less than that of Choi et al.'s algorithm for the case when $m = o(\sqrt{n})$ and is the same for the other case.

In Sect. 2.1, we defined a collection of non-overlapping cells C_{ij} partitioning the plane. We have Lemma 3 related to the points in a cell.

Lemma 3. *All points of P contained in a given cell C_{ij} have the same dominating points from the set Q.*

Proof. For the sake of contradiction, let us assume that two points p_r and p_s contained in the cell C_{ij} do not have the same set of dominating points from the set Q. Without loss of generality, let us assume that $y(p_r) > y(p_s)$. Since points p_r and p_s are in the cell C_{ij}, so their x- coordinates would lie in the range $[x(q_{\pi(j-1)}), x(q_{\pi(j)})]$ and y-coordinates in the range $[y(q_i), y(q_{i+1})]$.

Since the points p_r and p_s do not have the same set of dominating points, at least one point, say q, of Q, would dominate one point but not the other. Let point q dominates p_r, but not p_s. The other scenario, where q dominates p_s, but not p_r, can be dealt with analogously. Note that $x(q)$ must be less than $x(p_s)$, otherwise, q would dominate p_s as well. So $x(q)$ is in the range $[x(p_r), x(p_s)] \subseteq [x(q_{\pi(j-1)}), x(q_{\pi(j)})]$. However, by the construction of cells, there can not be a point of Q having x-coordinate (or y- coordinate) in any cell's x-range (resp. y-range). This contradiction shows that all the points of set P in C_{ij} have the set of dominating points from the set Q.   □

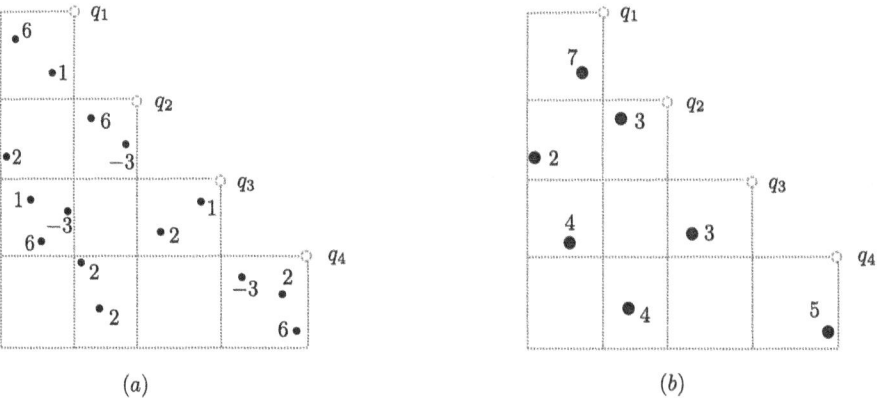

(a)   (b)

Fig. 2. (a) represents the non-empty cells of the partition, and (b) the cells containing their representatives.

We create a weighted point p for each non-empty cell C_{ij} with $w(C_{ij}) \neq 0$ such that p lies in C_{ij} and its weight is $w(C_{ij})$. We call the point p the representative of the points in the cell C_{ij}. The set P' consists of the representatives of the non-empty cells C_{ij} with $w(C_{ij}) \neq 0$. See Fig. 2.

Note that the number of points in P' is at most $\min\{n, m^2\}$. From Lemma 3 and the construction of P', we get

Corollary 1. $maxDominance(P, Q, k) = maxDominance(P', Q, k)$.

We now describe an algorithm that efficiently computes the representative of each non-empty cell. We store the set Q into two sorted lists L_x and L_y. The list L_x is sorted in increasing order of x-coordinates, and L_y is sorted in decreasing order of y-coordinates. We create a tuple (i, j) for each point $p \in P$, where i is the index of the next smaller x-coordinate in L_x and j is the index of the next larger y-coordinate in L_y. Let S be the set of all tuples, one for each point in P. Thus, $|S| = |P| = n$. Note that a tuple in the set may correspond to more than one point of P. All points having the same tuple (i, j) belong to the cell C_{ij}. We now sort the set S using the radix sort. In the sorted set, all copies of a tuple would be contiguous. Thus, we can compute the representative of each non-empty cell C_{ij} using a single scan of the sorted set S. The algorithm uses $O((n + m) \log m)$-time and $O(n + m)$-space. Thus, we have the following lemma.

Lemma 4. *We can compute the representative of every non-empty cell in $((n + m) \log m)$-time and $O(n + m)$-space.*   □

Choi et al. [2] gave an efficient dynamic programming-based algorithm for the k-maxDominance problem. Their main result is as follows.

Theorem 2 (Theorem 4 of [2]). *The k-maxDominance problem in the plane for n weighted points in P and m points in Q using at most k points of Q can be solved in $O(k(n + m) \log m)$ time using $O(n + m)$ space. The result also holds when weights may be negative.*   □

We now employ Choi et al.'s algorithm [2] to solve the new instance (P', Q, k) of the k-maxDominance problem. As $|P'| = \min\{n, m^2\}$, we get the following result.

Theorem 3. *Given a set of P of n weighted points, a set Q of m unweighted points, and a positive integer k, we can solve the k-maxDominance problem in $O(k \min\{n + m, \frac{n}{k} + m^2\} \log m)$ time and $O(n + m)$ space.*   □

For the case when $m = o(\sqrt{n})$, our algorithm is asymptotically faster than the Choi et al.'s algorithm. For the other case when $m = \Omega(\sqrt{n})$, the time taken by the proposed algorithm is asymptotically the same as that of the Choi et al's algorithm. Recall that as for a random data set of n points in the 2-dimensional space, the expected number of skyline points is $\theta(\log n)$ [6,11,13,16], and as by the experiments of Morse et al. [17] the number of skyline points are very few.

4 Conclusion

We proposed two algorithms for the $k\text{-}maxDominance$ problem. The first algorithm is simple and easy to explain. It uses simple and classical data structures, and its bounds are better than the existing ones only when $m = o(\sqrt{n})$. The other proposed algorithm is (asymptotically) faster as compared to the existing algorithm [2] when $m = o(\sqrt{n})$. For the other case, the bounds of our algorithm are the same as Choi et al.'s algorithm (up to a constant multiplicative factor).

Acknowledgement. We wish to thank anonymous referees for careful reading of the manuscript, their comments, queries and suggestions. We believe the suggestions have helped in improving the manuscript.

References

1. Cabello, S.: Faster distance-based representative skyline and k-center along Pareto front in the plane. J. Glob. Optim. **86**(2), 441–466 (2023)
2. Choi, J., Cabello, S., Ahn, H.K.: Maximizing dominance in the plane and its applications. Algorithmica **83**(11), 3491–3513 (2021)
3. Chan, T.M.: Optimal output-sensitive convex hull algorithms in two and three-dimensions. Discrete Comput. Geom. **16**(4), 361–368 (1996)
4. Cormen, T.H., Leiserson, C.E., Rivest, R.L., Stein, C.: Introduction to Algorithms, 3rd edn. MIT Press, C. (2009)
5. Emmerich, M.T.M., Deutz, A.: A tutorial on multiobjective optimization: fundamentals and evolutionary methods. Nat. Comput. **17**(3), 585–609 (2018)
6. Godfrey, P., Shipley, R., Gryz, J.: Maximal vector computation in large data sets. VLDB **5**, 229–240 (2005)
7. Li, M., Yao, X.: Quality evaluation of solution sets in multiobjective optimisation: a survey. ACM Comput. Surv. **52**(2), 1–38 (2019)
8. Lin, Y., Yuan, Y., Zhang, Q., Zhang, Y.: Selecting stars: the k most representative skyline operator. In: 2007 IEEE 23rd International Conference on Data Engineering, pp. 86–95 (2006)
9. Mukhopadhyay, A., Maulik, U., Bandyopadhyay, S., Coello, C.A.C.: A survey of multiobjective evolutionary algorithms for data mining: part i. IEEE Trans. Evolut. Comput. **18**(1), 4–19 (2014)
10. Tao, Y., Ding, L., Lin, X., Pei, J.: Distance-based representative skyline. In: IEEE 25th International Conference on Data Engineering, pp. 892–903 (2009)
11. Preparata, F.P., Shamos, M.I.: Convex hulls: extensions and applications. In: Computational Geometry: an Introduction, pp. 150–184. Springer (1985)
12. Kalyvas, C., Maragoudakis, M.: A skyline-based decision boundary estimation method for binominal classification in big data. Computation **8**(3), 80 (2020)
13. Buchta, C.: On the average number of maxima in a set of vectors. Inf. Process. Lett. **33**(2), 63–65 (1989)
14. Bringmann, K., Friedrich, T., Klitzke, P.: Two-dimensional subset selection for hypervolume and epsilon-indicator. In: Proceedings of the 2014 Annual Conference on Genetic and Evolutionary Computation, pp. 589–596 (2014)
15. Kuhn, T., Fonseca, C.M., Paquete, L., Ruzika, S., Duarte, M.M., Figueira, J.: Hypervolume subset selection in two dimensions: formulations and algorithms. Evol. Comput. **24**(3), 411–425 (2016)

16. Bentley, J.L., Kung, H.T., Schkolnick, M., Thompson, C.D.: On the average number of maxima in a set of vectors and applications. J. ACM **25**(4), 536–543 (1978)
17. Morse, M., Patel, J.M., Jagadish, H.V.: Efficient skyline computation over low-cardinality domains. In: Proceedings of the 33rd International Conference on Very Large Data Bases, pp. 267–278 (2007)
18. Kirkpatrick, D.G., Seidel, R.: Output-size sensitive algorithms for finding maximal vectors. In: Proceedings of the First Annual Symposium on Computational Geometry, pp. 89–96 (1985)

Generalized Parikh Matrices for Tracking Subsequence Occurrences

Szilárd Zsolt Fazekas$^{(\boxtimes)}$ and Xinhao Huang$^{(\boxtimes)}$

Akita University, Akita, Japan
szilard.fazekas@ie.akita-u.ac.jp, d8523004@s.akita-u.ac.jp

Abstract. We introduce and study a generalized Parikh matrix mapping based on tracking the occurrence counts of special types of subsequences. These matrices retain more information about a word than the original Parikh matrix mapping while preserving the homomorphic property. We build the generalization by first introducing the Parikh factor matrix mapping and extend it to the Parikh sequence matrix mapping. We establish an interesting connection between the generalized Parikh matrices and the original ones and use it to prove that certain important submatrices of a Parikh sequence matrix have nonnegative minors. Finally, we generalize the concept of subword histories and show that each generalized subword history is equivalent to a linear one.

Keywords: Combinatorics on Words · Parikh Matrix · Scattered Subsequences · Subword History

1 Introduction

The study of scattered subwords in combinatorics on words has been a topic of interest for nearly a century. Scattered subwords, also known as scattered factors, subsequences, or simply subwords, are defined as follows: for words u and v, u is a scattered subword of v if there exist words $u_1, \ldots, u_n$ and $y_0, \ldots, y_n$, some of which may be empty, such that $u = u_1 \cdots u_n$ and $v = y_0 u_1 y_1 \cdots u_n y_n$. For instance, if $u = aab$ and $v = acbab$, then u is a scattered subword of v.

A fundamental result in this area is Higman's lemma (1952) [13], which states that any subset of words over a finite alphabet that are pairwise incomparable for the subword ordering is finite, thus establishing that subword ordering is a well partial ordering. Higman's lemma has been rediscovered multiple times, often also credited to Haines (1969). Since then, the concept of subwords has garnered increasing attention from researchers.

One notable recent application of the theory of subwords is in the study of downward closures. The downward closure of a language is the set of all scattered subwords of its members. Abstracting languages by their downward closure as proxy can make equivalence and inclusion decidable/efficient when direct comparisons are undecidable or computationally hard [30,31].

© The Author(s), under exclusive license to Springer Nature Switzerland AG 2025
C. Anutariya and M. M. Bonsangue (Eds.): ICTAC 2024, LNCS 15373, pp. 164–181, 2025.
https://doi.org/10.1007/978-3-031-77019-7_10

Another topic that garnered a lot of interest in the last few years is the algorithmics of the so called Simon congruence, that compares the set of all subwords of given words. A recent breakthrough result is that this congruence is efficiently decidable [10], which was a starting point to investigating the question in the context of pattern matching [8,16], and subword analysis problems [15].

Our research focuses on the direction that began with the Parikh vector mapping, introduced by R. J. Parikh [20], which has become a significant concept in the theory of formal languages. The Parikh vector of a word records the number of occurrences of each letter in the word. Although mapping a word to a vector in this way loses much information, there have been several refinements of the mapping to address that, perhaps most notably, by Mateescu et al., who introduced the so called Parikh matrices [18]. Parikh matrices count the occurrences of scattered subwords instead of letters, with the Parikh vector appearing on the second diagonal of the matrix. Attempts to generalize these matrices and their related problems generated a vast literature.

Since the Parikh matrix mapping is not injective, reducing its ambiguity and studying its extent has been one of the core research directions. Fossé and Richomme explored the equivalence of binary words through their Parikh matrices [9]. Atanasiu examined properties of binary words with the same Parikh matrix, referring to these words as amiable [2]. He characterized conditions under which equivalence classes of amiable words contain multiple elements and extended some of the results to larger alphabets [4]. For ternary alphabets the first characterization was provided by Salomaa [26], and Atanasiu [3] expanded the work to a wider class of M-equivalence preserving rewriting rules for the ternary alphabet. Teh introduced Parikh rewriting systems [28] to generalize the Thue system proposed by Salomaa. Teh also investigated the relationship between core words and Parikh matrices [29] with Kwa. A long awaited recent development [12] gave an effective characterization over ternary alphabets of unambiguous words, using a finite set of rewriting rules to obtain equivalence classes. Salomaa investigated conditions for uniquely determining a word from its Parikh matrix [24].

Extensive work has also been done on sharpening these mappings. The q-Parikh matrices, introduced in [21,22], extend the definition of binomial coefficients to q-deformations, recording occurrences and positions of each letter for richer information. Şerbănuţă considered the original Parikh matrices, which only track letters following an ordered alphabet, and proposed an extended Parikh matrix mapping where the matrix rank is determined by the word length rather than the alphabet size [27]. Dick et al. introduced paired mappings by so called $\mathbb{P}$-Parikh matrices and $\mathbb{L}$-Parikh matrices [6].

In this paper, we extend Parikh matrices to be able track subsequences in which we can require that some of the letters are matched to consecutive positions. This is a significantly stronger formalism than simple subwords, although not quite as flexible as others, such as subsequences with gap constraints. Recent papers have also studied gaps in sequences and combinatorial problems related to reconstructing sequences from gapped decks [11,23]. Based on our results it seems that expanding further in that direction may be possible by significantly increasing the size of the matrices used in the mapping. In Sect. 3, we first develop simple matrices that count the number of occurrences of factors, which are similar to the mappings introduced by Karhumäki and Whiteland [14], but arranged differently to allow our later generalization. Building on that, in Sect. 4 we introduce Parikh sequence matrices. Their entries are counts of certain types of subsequences of interest in matching DNA strings in bioinformatics. We show that both mappings are homomorphisms and examine the minors of certain submatrices of special interest that immediately yield generalized analogues of the subword inequalities introduced by Mateescu et al. [19]. We then define generalized subword histories and we show how to reduce them to linear forms, laying the foundations of generalizing a vast collection of results about Parikh matrices to these new, sharper mappings.

2   Preliminaries

We will denote by $\mathbb{N}$ the set of natural numbers starting from 1 and $\mathbb{N}_0 = \mathbb{N} \cup \{0\}$. For all $i, j \in \mathbb{N}_0$ with $i \leq j$, we denote the closed interval between i and j by $[i, j] = \{i, \ldots, j\}$. For succinctness we also use $[n] = [0, n]$. An ordered alphabet is an alphabet $\Sigma = \{a_1, a_2, \ldots, a_k\}$ with a linear order $<$ on it. If we have $a_1 < a_2 < \cdots < a_k$, then we use the notation $\Sigma = \{a_1 < a_2 < \cdots < a_k\}$.

For a word $u = a_1 \cdots a_n$, where $a_i \in \Sigma$ for all $i \in \{1, \ldots, n\}$, the length of u is denoted by $|u|$ and it is equal to n. The word of length 0, having no letters, is called the *empty word* and is denoted by ε. Let u, v be words over an alphabet Σ. The word u is a *factor* of v if there exists words $s, t \in \Sigma^*$ such that $v = sut$. The word u is a *(scattered) subword* of v if there exists letters $a_1, \ldots, a_n$ and words $t_0, \ldots, t_n \in \Sigma^*$ such that $u = a_1 \cdots a_n$ and $v = t_0 a_1 t_1 \cdots a_n t_n$. Now let $u = a_1 \cdots a_n$. For some $i \in [1, n]$, the ith letter of u is denoted by $u[i]$, that is $u[i] = a_i$. For all $i, j \in [1, n]$ with $i \leq j$, the factor of u between positions i and j is denoted by $u[i, j] = a_i \cdots a_j$. An *occurrence as a factor* of u in v is a position $i \in [1, |v|]$ such that $v[i, i + |u| - 1] = u$. The number of different occurrences of u in v as a subword is denoted by $|v|_u$. An *occurrence as a subword* of u in v is a tuple $(i_1, \ldots, i_n)$ of increasing elements of $[1, |v|]$ such that $v[i_j] = a_j$ for all $j \in [1, |u|]$. We denote the number of distinct occurrences of a nonempty word u as a scattered subword in v by writing $\binom{v}{u}$. For example, $\binom{aab}{a} = 2$, $\binom{aaabb}{ab} = 6$.

The starting point of our study are the so called Parikh matrices, introduced by Mateescu et al., which are square matrices where the entries track subword occurrences, and are named after Parikh, because they represent a sharpening of the well-known Parikh vector mapping from words over Σ to $\mathbb{N}_0^{|\Sigma|}$. In what follows, $\mathcal{M}_n$ denotes the monoid of $n \times n$ integer matrices with multiplication.

The Parikh matrix mappings introduced by Mateescu et al. [18] are homomorphisms $\Psi_{M_k} : \Sigma^* \to \mathcal{M}_{k+1}$ that track the number of certain subword occurrences, where $\Sigma = \{a_1 < a_2 < \cdots < a_k\}$, $k \geq 1$. For an alphabet Σ, the Parikh matrix $\Psi(w) = (a_{ij})$ is an upper triangular matrix with 1's on the main diagonal and with entry $a_{i,j} = \binom{w}{a_i \cdots a_{j-1}}$.

Example 1. Consider the word $w = abcb$ over alphabet $\Sigma = \{a < b < c\}$. Since the Parikh matrix mapping is a homomorphism, we can write

$$\Psi_{M_k}(w) = \Psi_{M_k}(a)\Psi_{M_k}(b)\Psi_{M_k}(c)\Psi_{M_k}(b)$$

$$= \begin{bmatrix} 1 & 1 & 0 & 0 \\ 0 & 1 & 0 & 0 \\ 0 & 0 & 1 & 0 \\ 0 & 0 & 0 & 1 \end{bmatrix} \begin{bmatrix} 1 & 0 & 0 & 0 \\ 0 & 1 & 1 & 0 \\ 0 & 0 & 1 & 0 \\ 0 & 0 & 0 & 1 \end{bmatrix} \begin{bmatrix} 1 & 0 & 0 & 0 \\ 0 & 1 & 0 & 0 \\ 0 & 0 & 1 & 1 \\ 0 & 0 & 0 & 1 \end{bmatrix} \begin{bmatrix} 1 & 0 & 0 & 0 \\ 0 & 1 & 1 & 0 \\ 0 & 0 & 1 & 0 \\ 0 & 0 & 0 & 1 \end{bmatrix} = \begin{bmatrix} 1 & 1 & 2 & 1 \\ 0 & 1 & 2 & 1 \\ 0 & 0 & 1 & 1 \\ 0 & 0 & 0 & 1 \end{bmatrix}$$

The first extension of the Parikh matrix mapping relaxed the condition on the kind of subwords that can be tracked in these matrices [27]. The formalism is almost identical, but for the extended Parikh matrix mapping induced by *any* word $v = b_1 \cdots b_k$, the entries above the main diagonal become $m_{i,j+1} = \binom{w}{b_i \cdots b_j}$ for all $1 \leq i \leq j \leq k$. The original Parikh matrix is the special case when v is just the concatenation of the letters of the alphabet.

3   Parikh Factor Matrices

Parikh matrices only count the occurrences of *scattered subwords*. In order to generalize this mapping for tracking more complex subsequences, as a first step we introduce Parikh-style matrices capable of counting occurrences of *factors*. A similar study has been conducted by Karhumäki and Whiteland [14]. They constructed a kind of matrices that could track the occurrence of one factor, and for any word w, using matrices tracking all factors in $\Sigma^{\leq |w|} \setminus (a\Sigma^* \cup \Sigma^* a), a \in \Sigma$ as building blocks of a diagonal matrix. It is evident that a key question is this matrix can not track all sub-factors of a word. Our purpose is to construct matrices that are similar to Parikh matrices and can track all sub-factors' occurrences.

In general, to be able to construct a homomorphic mapping that computes the number of occurrences as factors of some word u in a word $v_1 v_2$, trivially the mapping must preserve information about $|v_1|_u$, $|v_2|_u$, but also about suffixes of v_1 that are prefixes of u and prefixes of v_2 that are suffixes of u, since $|v_1 v_2|_u = |v_1|_u + |v_2|_u + D$, where D is the number of decompositions $u = u'u''$ such that u' is a nonempty suffix of v_1 and u'' is a nonempty prefix of v_2. To illustrate the idea on a simple case, we begin by constructing the matrices to track the number of occurrences of ab as a factor. In this case the necessary information about each word is the number of ab factors in it, whether they finish with a and whether they start with b. We introduce the following mappings, where $u, v, w \in \Sigma^*$:

$$s_u^w = \begin{cases} 1 & \text{if } w \text{ starts with } u \ (w = uv) \\ 0 & \text{otherwise} \end{cases} \qquad \delta_v^w = \begin{cases} 1 & \text{if } w = v \\ 0 & \text{otherwise} \end{cases}$$

$$e_v^w = \begin{cases} 1 & \text{if } w \text{ ends with } v \ (w = uv) \\ 0 & \text{otherwise} \end{cases}$$

and for a more uniform (and more compact) notation use f_u^w to indicate the number of factors u in word w, instead of the previously introduced and more usual $|w|_u$. To be able to track the necessary values through matrix multiplication, the simplest way to arrange them in a matrix is

$$\Phi(w) = \begin{bmatrix} 1 & e_a^w & f_{ab}^w \\ 0 & \delta_\varepsilon^w & s_b^w \\ 0 & 0 & 1 \end{bmatrix}$$

and for any two binary words w_1, w_2, it is straightforward that

$$\Phi(w_1)\Phi(w_2) = \begin{bmatrix} 1 & e_a^{w_1} & f_{ab}^{w_1} \\ 0 & \delta_\varepsilon^{w_1} & s_b^{w_1} \\ 0 & 0 & 1 \end{bmatrix} \begin{bmatrix} 1 & e_a^{w_2} & f_{ab}^{w_2} \\ 0 & \delta_\varepsilon^{w_2} & s_b^{w_2} \\ 0 & 0 & 1 \end{bmatrix}$$

$$= \begin{bmatrix} 1 & e_a^{w_2} + e_a^{w_1} \cdot \delta_\varepsilon^{w_2} & f_{ab}^{w_1} + f_{ab}^{w_2} + e_a^{w_1} \cdot s_b^{w_2} \\ 0 & \delta_\varepsilon^{w_1} \cdot \delta_\varepsilon^{w_2} & s_b^{w_1} + \delta_\varepsilon^{w_1} \cdot s_b^{w_2} \\ 0 & 0 & 1 \end{bmatrix} = \Phi(w_1 w_2).$$

Following the idea above we can generalize the matrix so that it could record the number of longer factors in a word, as follows.

Definition 1 (Parikh factor matrix mapping). *Let $\Sigma = \{a_1 < \cdots < a_k\}$ be an alphabet and consider the concatenation of all the letters $\sigma = a_1 a_2 \cdots a_k$, where $k \geq 1$. The Parikh factor matrix mapping, denoted*

$$\Phi_\sigma : \Sigma^* \to \mathcal{M}_{3(k-1)},$$

is defined for any $w \in \Sigma^*$ as

$$\Phi_\sigma(w) = \begin{bmatrix} I & E^w & F^w \\ O & C^w & S^w \\ O & O & I \end{bmatrix},$$

where I and O are the identity and the zero matrix of size $k - 1$, and

$$F^w = \begin{bmatrix} f_{a_1 a_2}^w & f_{a_1 a_2 a_3}^w & \cdots & f_{a_1 \cdots a_k}^w \\ 0 & f_{a_2 a_3}^w & \cdots & f_{a_2 \cdots a_k}^w \\ \vdots & \vdots & \ddots & \vdots \\ 0 & 0 & \cdots & f_{a_{k-1} a_k}^w \end{bmatrix},$$

is a matrix tracking occurrences of factor of $a_1 \cdots a_k$ as factors of w. Finally, S^w and E^w include the necessary information about starting factors (prefixes) and end factors (suffixes):

$$S^w = \begin{bmatrix} s_{a_2}^w & s_{a_2 a_3}^w & \cdots & s_{a_2 \cdots a_k}^w \\ 0 & s_{a_3}^w & \cdots & s_{a_3 \cdots a_k}^w \\ \vdots & \vdots & \ddots & \vdots \\ 0 & 0 & \cdots & s_{a_k}^w \end{bmatrix}, \quad E^w = \begin{bmatrix} e_{a_1}^w & e_{a_1 a_2}^w & \cdots & e_{a_1 \cdots a_{k-1}}^w \\ 0 & e_{a_2}^w & \cdots & e_{a_2 \cdots a_{k-1}}^w \\ \vdots & \vdots & \ddots & \vdots \\ 0 & 0 & \cdots & e_{a_{k-1}}^w \end{bmatrix},$$

while matrix C makes sure that the mapping works correctly for short words (shorter than k), too,

$$
C^w = \begin{bmatrix} \delta_\varepsilon^w & \delta_{a_2}^w & \cdots & \delta_{a_2\cdots a_{k-1}}^w \\ 0 & \delta_\varepsilon^w & \cdots & \delta_{a_3\cdots a_{k-1}}^w \\ \vdots & \vdots & \ddots & \vdots \\ 0 & 0 & \cdots & \delta_\varepsilon^w \end{bmatrix}.
$$

Next we argue that the mapping indeed works for tracking the occurrences when concatenating the containing words, that is, the mapping is homomorphic.

Theorem 1. *The Parikh factor matrix mapping $\Phi_\sigma : \Sigma^* \to \mathcal{M}_{3(k-1)}$ is a homomorphism.*

Proof. For all words $w_1, w_2 \in \Sigma^*$, $\sigma = a_1 a_2 \cdots a_k$, where $k \geq 1$ and $a_1, a_2, \ldots, a_k \in \Sigma$, the following holds.

$$
\Phi_\sigma(w_1)\Phi_\sigma(w_2) = \begin{bmatrix} I & E^{w_1} & F^{w_1} \\ O & C^{w_1} & S^{w_1} \\ O & O & I \end{bmatrix} \begin{bmatrix} I & E^{w_2} & F^{w_2} \\ O & C^{w_2} & S^{w_2} \\ O & O & I \end{bmatrix}
$$

$$
= \begin{bmatrix} I & E^{w_2} + E^{w_1} \cdot C^{w_2} & F^{w_1} + F^{w_2} + E^{w_1} \cdot S^{w_2} \\ O & C^{w_1} \cdot C^{w_2} & S^{w_1} + C^{w_1} \cdot S^{w_2} \\ O & O & I \end{bmatrix}
$$

$$
\Phi_\sigma(w_1 w_2) = \begin{bmatrix} I & E^{w_1 w_2} & F^{w_1 w_2} \\ O & C^{w_1 w_2} & S^{w_1 w_2} \\ O & O & I \end{bmatrix}
$$

As $\Phi_\sigma(\epsilon) = I$ follows directly from the definition, and $\Phi_\sigma(w_1)\Phi_\sigma(w_2) = \Phi_\sigma(w_1 w_2)$, for all words $w_1, w_2 \in \Sigma^*$, we get that the Parikh factor matrix mapping is a morphism. □

Example 2. Let $\Sigma = \{a, b, c\}$, $w_1, w_2 \in \Sigma^*$, $w_1 = b$, $w_2 = cabc$, $\sigma = abc$,

$$
\Phi_\sigma(w_1)\Phi_\sigma(w_2) = \begin{bmatrix} I & E^{w_1} & F^{w_1} \\ O & C^{w_1} & S^{w_1} \\ O & O & I \end{bmatrix} \begin{bmatrix} I & E^{w_2} & F^{w_2} \\ O & C^{w_2} & S^{w_2} \\ O & O & I \end{bmatrix}
$$

$$
= \begin{bmatrix} I & \begin{bmatrix} e_a^{w_1} & e_{ab}^{w_1} \\ 0 & e_b^{w_1} \end{bmatrix} & \begin{bmatrix} f_{ab}^{w_1} & f_{abc}^{w_1} \\ 0 & f_{bc}^{w_1} \end{bmatrix} \\ O & \begin{bmatrix} \delta_\varepsilon^{w_1} & \delta_b^{w_1} \\ 0 & \delta_\varepsilon^{w_1} \end{bmatrix} & \begin{bmatrix} s_b^{w_1} & s_{bc}^{w_1} \\ 0 & s_c^{w_1} \end{bmatrix} \\ O & O & I \end{bmatrix} \begin{bmatrix} I & \begin{bmatrix} e_a^{w_2} & e_{ab}^{w_2} \\ 0 & e_b^{w_2} \end{bmatrix} & \begin{bmatrix} f_{ab}^{w_2} & f_{abc}^{w_2} \\ 0 & f_{bc}^{w_2} \end{bmatrix} \\ O & \begin{bmatrix} \delta_\varepsilon^{w_2} & \delta_b^{w_2} \\ 0 & \delta_\varepsilon^{w_2} \end{bmatrix} & \begin{bmatrix} s_b^{w_2} & s_{bc}^{w_2} \\ 0 & s_c^{w_2} \end{bmatrix} \\ O & O & I \end{bmatrix}
$$

$$
= \begin{bmatrix} I & \begin{bmatrix} 0 & 0 \\ 0 & 1 \end{bmatrix} & \begin{bmatrix} 0 & 0 \\ 0 & 0 \end{bmatrix} \\ O & \begin{bmatrix} 0 & 1 \\ 0 & 0 \end{bmatrix} & \begin{bmatrix} 1 & 0 \\ 0 & 0 \end{bmatrix} \\ O & O & I \end{bmatrix} \begin{bmatrix} I & \begin{bmatrix} 0 & 0 \\ 0 & 0 \end{bmatrix} & \begin{bmatrix} 1 & 1 \\ 0 & 1 \end{bmatrix} \\ O & \begin{bmatrix} 0 & 0 \\ 0 & 0 \end{bmatrix} & \begin{bmatrix} 0 & 0 \\ 0 & 1 \end{bmatrix} \\ O & O & I \end{bmatrix} = \begin{bmatrix} I & \begin{bmatrix} 0 & 0 \\ 0 & 0 \end{bmatrix} & \begin{bmatrix} 1 & 1 \\ 0 & 2 \end{bmatrix} \\ O & \begin{bmatrix} 0 & 0 \\ 0 & 0 \end{bmatrix} & \begin{bmatrix} 1 & 1 \\ 0 & 0 \end{bmatrix} \\ O & O & I \end{bmatrix} = \Phi_\sigma(w_1 w_2)
$$

4   Parikh Sequence Matrices

Now that we have already constructed the Parikh factor matrices and showed that the mapping is a homomorphism, we are ready to generalize the classical Parikh matrix mapping and Parikh factor matrix mapping to track subsequences more flexibly defined. We will use the operation $\bullet$ for combining factors q_1, q_2 over Σ to generalize the notion of subwords to *generalized subsequences*. These are still subwords, but with conditions attached to them on certain letters having to occur right next to each other in the containing word.

Definition 2 (Generalized subsequences). *Let $q_1, q_2, \ldots, q_n, v$ be nonempty words over Σ. The sequence $Q = q_1 \bullet q_2 \bullet \cdots \bullet q_n$ is a* generalized subsequence *of v if there exists words $t_0, t_1, \ldots, t_n \in \Sigma^*$ such that $v = t_0 q_1 t_1 \cdots q_n t_n$. An occurrence of Q in v is a tuple $(i_1, \ldots, i_n)$ of increasing positions of v such that for each $j \in [1, n-1]$ we have $i_{j+1} - i_j \geq |q_j|$ and $v[i_j, i_j + |q_j| - 1] = q_j$. The number of distinct occurrences of Q in v will be denoted as $|v|_Q$.*

Example 3. The $\bullet$ notation intuitively represents a gap (possibly of length 0), when matching a generalized subsequence in the word containing it. For instance $|aabb|_{ab \bullet b} = 1$, but $|aabb|_{a \bullet bb} = 2$.

Note that when $q_1, \ldots, q_n$ are all single letters, then $q_1 \bullet \cdots \bullet q_n$ being a generalized subsequence of v is equivalent to saying that $q_1 \cdots q_n$ is a subword of v, and $|w|_{q_1 \bullet \cdots \bullet q_n} = \binom{w}{q_1 \cdots q_n}$. For convenience we set $q \bullet \varepsilon = \varepsilon \bullet q = q$ for any $q \in \Sigma^*$ and we adopt the convention that $|w|_\varepsilon = 1$ for any $w \in \Sigma^*$. When $n = 1$, then the generalized subsequence becomes a single factor, therefore the notion generalizes both subwords and factors.

Such subsequences have been considered in many contexts and under various names, such as gapped sequences [1,7] in bioinformatics or subsequences with gap constraints [5], a notion that is even more general than what we suggest here. The gapped binomials introduced by Golm et al. [11] and further investigated by Rigo et al. [23] are very similar to our sequences involving $\bullet$. In gapped binomials a minimum gap length is imposed between matched occurrences of consecutive symbols, and the $\bullet$ operator can be seen as a minimum gap length 0. The difference between gapped binomials and our generalized subsequences is that the latter also imposes no-gap constraints (inside the factors). The number of occurrences of those various types of subsequences can be thought of as lossy representations of the containing word and are natural mathematical models for situations where one has to deal with input strings with missing or erroneous symbols in DNA sequences or digital signals.

Similarly to the case of Parikh factor matrices, we use the following mappings for words $u, v, w \in \Sigma^*$:

$$s_{u \bullet v}^w = \begin{cases} f_v^w & \text{if } w \text{ starts with } u \ (u \text{ can be the empty word.}) \\ 0 & \text{otherwise} \end{cases}$$

$$e_{u \bullet v}^w = \begin{cases} f_u^w & \text{if } w \text{ ends with } v \text{ (v can be the empty word.)} \\ 0 & \text{otherwise} \end{cases}$$

$$\delta_{u \bullet v}^w = \begin{cases} 1 & \text{if } w = uxv \text{ for some } x \in \Sigma^* \\ 0 & \text{otherwise} \end{cases} \tag{1}$$

and write $f_{u \bullet v}^w$ to indicate the number of the occurrences of all factors of the form uxv in w. For a sequence $Q = q_1 \bullet q_2 \bullet \cdots \bullet q_n$, we define $|Q| = \sum_{i=1}^n |q_i|$. In what follows, $Q[i : j]$ denotes the subsequence from ith letter to jth in Q, where the $\bullet$ operations do not count as taking up positions, so $ab \bullet cd[2 : 3] = b \bullet c$. So, f_Q^w indicates the number of occurrences of all factors of the form $q_1 x_1 q_2 x_2 ... q_{n-1} x_{n-1} q_n$, where $x_i \in \Sigma^*$.

Definition 3 (Parikh sequence matrix mapping). *Let Σ be any alphabet and $Q = q_1 \bullet q_2 \bullet \cdots \bullet q_x$ a generalized subsequence, where $x \geq 1$. We use l_i to indicate the position where factor q_i ends in the sequence, that is, $l_i = \sum_{j=1}^i |q_j|$. The Parikh sequence matrix mapping, denoted X_Q, is the morphism:*

$$X_Q : \Sigma^* \to \mathcal{M}_{3(|Q|-1)},$$

defined by

$$X_Q(w) = \begin{bmatrix} I & E^w & F^w \\ O & C^w & S^w \\ O & O & I \end{bmatrix}$$

where

$$E^w = \begin{bmatrix} e_{Q[1]}^w & \cdots & e_{Q[1:l_1]\bullet}^w & \cdots & e_{Q[1:l_2]\bullet}^w & \cdots & e_{Q[1:l_x-1]}^w \\ \vdots & & \vdots & & \vdots & & \vdots \\ 0 & \cdots & e_{Q[l_1]\bullet}^w & \cdots & e_{Q[l_1:l_2]\bullet}^w & \cdots & e_{Q[l_1:l_x-1]}^w \\ \vdots & & \vdots & & \vdots & & \vdots \\ 0 & \cdots & 0 & \cdots & 0 & \cdots & e_{Q[l_x-2:l_x-1]}^w \end{bmatrix}$$

$$F^w = \begin{bmatrix} f_{Q[1:2]}^w & \cdots & f_{Q[1:l_1+1]}^w & \cdots & f_{Q[1:l_2+1]}^w & \cdots & f_{Q[1:l_x]}^w \\ \vdots & & \vdots & & \vdots & & \vdots \\ 0 & \cdots & f_{Q[l_1:l_1+1]}^w & \cdots & f_{Q[l_1:l_2+1]}^w & \cdots & f_{Q[l_1:l_x]}^w \\ \vdots & & \vdots & & \vdots & & \vdots \\ 0 & \cdots & 0 & \cdots & 0 & \cdots & f_{Q[l_x-1:l_x]}^w \end{bmatrix}$$

$$C^w = \begin{bmatrix} \delta_\varepsilon^w & \cdots & s_{Q[2:l_1]}^w & \cdots & s_{Q[2:l_2]}^w & \cdots & \delta_{Q[2:l_x-1]}^w \\ \vdots & & \vdots & & \vdots & & \vdots \\ 0 & \cdots & 1 & \cdots & e_{Q[l_1+1:l_2]}^w & \cdots & e_{Q[l_1+1:l_x-1]}^w \\ \vdots & & \vdots & & \vdots & & \vdots \\ 0 & \cdots & 0 & \cdots & 0 & \cdots & \delta_\varepsilon^w \end{bmatrix}$$

$$S^w = \begin{bmatrix} s^w_{Q[2]} & \cdots & s^w_{Q[2:l_1+1]} & \cdots & s^w_{Q[2:l_2+1]} & \cdots & s^w_{Q[2:l_x]} \\ \vdots & & \vdots & & \vdots & & \vdots \\ 0 & \cdots & s^w_{\bullet Q[l_1+1]} & \cdots & s^w_{\bullet Q[l_1+1:l_2+1]} & \cdots & s^w_{\bullet Q[l_1+1:l_x]} \\ \vdots & & \vdots & & \vdots & & \vdots \\ 0 & \cdots & 0 & \cdots & 0 & \cdots & s^w_{Q[l_x]} \end{bmatrix}$$

Theorem 2. *For any generalized subsequence Q, the Parikh sequence matrix mapping $X_Q : \Sigma^* \to \mathcal{M}_{3(|Q|-1)}$ is a homomorphism.*

Proof. The argument is very similar to the case of Parikh matrices or Parikh factor matrices presented earlier, and we omit the formal description due to space constraints. $\qquad\square$

Example 4. Let $\Sigma = \{a, b, c\}$, $w_1, w_2 \in \Sigma^*$, $w_1 = babcab, w_2 = cbcba, Q = ab \bullet c$.

$$X_{M_{ab\bullet c}}(w_1) X_{M_{ab\bullet c}}(w_2) = \begin{bmatrix} I & E^{w_1} & F^{w_1} \\ O & C^{w_1} & S^{w_1} \\ O & O & I \end{bmatrix} \begin{bmatrix} I & E^{w_2} & F^{w_2} \\ O & C^{w_2} & S^{w_2} \\ O & O & I \end{bmatrix}$$

$$= \begin{bmatrix} I & \begin{bmatrix} e^{w_1}_a & e^{w_1}_{ab\bullet} \\ 0 & e^{w_1}_{b\bullet} \end{bmatrix} & \begin{bmatrix} f^{w_1}_{ab} & f^{w_1}_{ab\bullet c} \\ 0 & f^{w_1}_{b\bullet c} \end{bmatrix} \\ O & \begin{bmatrix} \delta^{w_1}_{\varepsilon} & s^{w_1}_b \\ 0 & 1 \end{bmatrix} & \begin{bmatrix} s^{w_1}_b & s^{w_1}_{b\bullet c} \\ 0 & s^{w_1}_{\bullet c} \end{bmatrix} \\ O & O & I \end{bmatrix} \begin{bmatrix} I & \begin{bmatrix} e^{w_2}_a & e^{w_2}_{ab\bullet} \\ 0 & e^{w_2}_{b\bullet} \end{bmatrix} & \begin{bmatrix} f^{w_2}_{ab} & f^{w_2}_{ab\bullet c} \\ 0 & f^{w_2}_{b\bullet c} \end{bmatrix} \\ O & \begin{bmatrix} \delta^{w_2}_{\varepsilon} & s^{w_2}_b \\ 0 & 1 \end{bmatrix} & \begin{bmatrix} s^{w_2}_b & s^{w_2}_{b\bullet c} \\ 0 & s^{w_2}_{\bullet c} \end{bmatrix} \\ O & O & I \end{bmatrix}$$

$$= \begin{bmatrix} I & \begin{bmatrix} 0 & 2 \\ 0 & 3 \end{bmatrix} & \begin{bmatrix} 2 & 1 \\ 0 & 2 \end{bmatrix} \\ O & \begin{bmatrix} 0 & 1 \\ 0 & 1 \end{bmatrix} & \begin{bmatrix} 1 & 1 \\ 0 & 1 \end{bmatrix} \\ O & O & I \end{bmatrix} \begin{bmatrix} I & \begin{bmatrix} 1 & 0 \\ 0 & 2 \end{bmatrix} & \begin{bmatrix} 0 & 0 \\ 0 & 1 \end{bmatrix} \\ O & \begin{bmatrix} 0 & 0 \\ 0 & 1 \end{bmatrix} & \begin{bmatrix} 0 & 0 \\ 0 & 2 \end{bmatrix} \\ O & O & I \end{bmatrix} = \begin{bmatrix} I & \begin{bmatrix} 1 & 2 \\ 0 & 5 \end{bmatrix} & \begin{bmatrix} 2 & 5 \\ 0 & 9 \end{bmatrix} \\ O & \begin{bmatrix} 0 & 1 \\ 0 & 1 \end{bmatrix} & \begin{bmatrix} 1 & 3 \\ 0 & 3 \end{bmatrix} \\ O & O & I \end{bmatrix} = X_{M_{ab\bullet c}}(w_1 w_2)$$

5   Minors of Submatrices

In this section we look at the minors of certain submatrices of the newly defined Parikh sequence matrices. We aim to obtain the generalization of the result that states that each submatrix of Parikh matrices has nonnegative determinants [18,19]. By looking at the minor $\begin{vmatrix} f^w_{abc} & f^w_{abcd} \\ f^w_{bc} & f^w_{bcd} \end{vmatrix} = \begin{vmatrix} 1 & 1 \\ 2 & 1 \end{vmatrix}$ in $\Phi_{abcd}(bcabcd)$ it is immediate that this is no longer the case for Parikh factor matrices, and hence for Parikh sequence matrices, either, so only certain minors are guaranteed to be nonnegative. Our matrices contain two kinds of occurrence tracking entries, those followed by a letter in the sequence (auxiliary entries necessary for the mapping to be homomorphic) and those followed by a bullet or the end of the word (the actual entries we are interested in tracking). The submatrices we consider here consist only of the latter type of entries. We will call those *special submatrices*. Formally, for a word w and a generalized subsequence $Q = q_1 \bullet \cdots \bullet q_n$, a special submatrix of $X_Q(w)$ is the one consisting of columns indexed i_j and rows indexed $3(|Q| - 1) + 1 - i_j$, for $j \in [1, n+1]$, where $i_1 = 1$, $i_j = |Q| - 1 + |q_1 \cdots q_{j-1}|$, for each $j \in [2, n]$ and $i_{n+1} = 3(|Q| - 1)$, that is, the matrix

$$M = \begin{bmatrix} 1 & e^w_{q_1\bullet} & \cdots & f^w_{q_1\bullet\cdots\bullet q_n} \\ 0 & 1 & \cdots & s^w_{\bullet q_2\bullet\cdots\bullet q_n} \\ \vdots & \vdots & \ddots & \vdots \\ 0 & 0 & \cdots & s^w_{\bullet q_n} \\ 0 & 0 & \cdots & 1 \end{bmatrix} = \begin{bmatrix} 1 & f^w_{q_1} & \cdots & f^w_{q_1\bullet\cdots\bullet q_n} \\ 0 & 1 & \cdots & f^w_{q_2\bullet\cdots\bullet q_n} \\ \vdots & \vdots & \ddots & \vdots \\ 0 & 0 & \cdots & f^w_{q_n} \\ 0 & 0 & \cdots & 1 \end{bmatrix}$$

where the second equality follows from the definition of s, e and f. The special submatrices of the Parikh sequence matrices induced by $q_1 \bullet \cdots \bullet q_n$ correspond exactly to the original Parikh matrices induced by $q_1 \cdots q_n$, whenever each factor q_i is a single letter. We start by recalling the aforementioned result about Parikh matrices.

Theorem 3 ([19], **Theorem 6**). *The determinant of each submatrix of any Parikh matrix is a nonnegative integer.*

The proof of the theorem above relies on inverses of Parikh matrices and is not easily reproducible for our more general matrices, so we choose a different argument, which maps those special submatrices of a Parikh sequence matrix induced by $q_1 \bullet \cdots \bullet q_n$ to Parikh matrices defined over an alphabet with n letters. Our argument uses a construction very similar to the one used by Şerbănuţă for showing that their extended Parikh matrices mentioned earlier can be reduced to the original ones [27]. Note that the reduction here is not trivially possible by replacing each q_i with a letter a_i, as the following example demonstrates.

Example 5. Consider the generalized subsequence $q_1 \bullet q_2 \bullet q_1$ with $q_1 = a$, $q_2 = aba$ and the matrix tracking its occurrences in the word aba:

$$X_{a\bullet aba\bullet a}(aba) = \begin{bmatrix} I & \begin{bmatrix} 2&1&0&0 \\ 0&1&0&1 \\ 0&0&0&1 \\ 0&0&0&2 \end{bmatrix} & \begin{bmatrix} 1&0&0&0 \\ 0&1&1&0 \\ 0&0&1&0 \\ 0&0&0&1 \end{bmatrix} \\ O & \begin{bmatrix} 1&2&0&1 \\ 0&0&0&0 \\ 0&0&0&2 \\ 0&0&0&1 \end{bmatrix} & \begin{bmatrix} 2&1&1&0 \\ 0&0&0&0 \\ 0&0&2&1 \\ 0&0&0&2 \end{bmatrix} \\ O & O & I \end{bmatrix}$$

where the special submatrix is

$$\begin{bmatrix} 1 & e^w_{a\bullet} & e^w_{a\bullet aba\bullet} & f^w_{a\bullet aba\bullet a} \\ 0 & 1 & f^w_{aba} & s^w_{\bullet aba\bullet a} \\ 0 & 0 & 1 & s^w_{\bullet a} \\ 0 & 0 & 0 & 1 \end{bmatrix} = \begin{bmatrix} 1 & f^w_a & f^w_{a\bullet aba} & f^w_{a\bullet aba\bullet a} \\ 0 & 1 & f^w_{aba} & f^w_{aba\bullet a} \\ 0 & 0 & 1 & f^w_a \\ 0 & 0 & 0 & 1 \end{bmatrix} = \begin{bmatrix} 1&2&0&0 \\ 0&1&1&0 \\ 0&0&1&2 \\ 0&0&0&1 \end{bmatrix}.$$

If we simply mapped q_1 to a letter c and q_2 to a letter d, then we get cdc as the word inducing the extended Parikh matrix mapping, but the matrix above is not equal to the extended Parikh matrix induced by the word cdc of any word $w \in \{c, d\}^*$, because any word w such that $\binom{w}{c} = 2$ and $\binom{w}{d} = 1$ will have either cd or dc occurring in it as a subword, that is $\binom{w}{cd} > 0$ or $\binom{w}{dc} > 0$, which is in contradiction with entries $(1, 3)$ and $(2, 4)$.

Theorem 4. *Let M be the special submatrix of $X_Q(w)$ for a generalized subsequence $Q = q_1 \bullet q_2 \bullet \cdots \bullet q_n$, and a word w. Then, every minor of M is a nonnegative integer.*

Proof. The proof proceeds by constructing a word $w' \in \{a_1, \ldots, a_n\}^*$ such that $\Psi_{a_1 \cdots a_n}(w') = M$. From there, we can apply Theorem 3 and get that each minor of M is nonnegative.

First we define the order $\{q_1 < q_2 < \cdots < q_n\}$ on the factors of Q, such that if q_i is a proper prefix of q_j, then $q_i < q_j$. For factors q_i, q_j incomparable by the prefix ordering, the relation between them can be set arbitrarily. In the word w, of length $k = |w|$, we find all occurrences of the factors $q_1, \ldots, q_n$. Suppose that starting at some position i in w, we have occurrences of factors $q_{i_1} < q_{i_2} < \cdots < q_{i_s}$. We define the word $u_i = a_{i_s} \cdots a_{i_2} a_{i_1}$. Now we concatenate all the u_i to get the word $w' = \prod_{i=1}^{k} u_k$.

For each ℓ running from n to 2, for each i running from $|w|_{q_\ell}$ to 1 and for each j running from $|w|_{q_{\ell-1}}$ to 1, if all of the following conditions apply

1. the ith occurrence of q_ℓ in w overlaps with the jth occurrence of $q_{\ell-1}$
2. the ith occurrence of a_ℓ is at position i' in w', the jth occurrence of $a_{\ell-1}$ is at position j' in w', and $j' < i'$

then we exchange the positions of the two letters in the word w', that is, we set $w'[i'] = a_{\ell-1}$ and $w'[j'] = a_\ell$. We run this process iteratively, as long as in the previous iteration there were any changes made, similarly to the bubble-sort algorithm. The position of the largest letters swapped cannot increase throughout the algorithm. Once they are in their final position, the positions of the second largest letters cannot increase, and so on, ensuring the termination of the algorithm.

The definition of u_i, moving a_p in front of a_r when they represent $q_r < q_p$ starting at the same position is done because the $\Psi_{a_1 \cdots a_n}$ mapping counts subwords of the form $a_i a_{i+1}$, but does not count $a_{i+1} a_i$, which is in line with a pair q_i and q_{i+1} starting at the same position not contributing towards $f^w_{q_i \bullet q_{i+1}}$. The other rearrangements were necessary, so that if a pair of occurrences of q_i and q_{i+1} are overlapping, the corresponding occurrences of a_i and a_{i+1} will not be counted as an occurrence of subword $a_i a_{i+1}$. These two rules make sure that we do not introduce 'extra' tracked occurrences during the construction of w'.

The word w' obtained through this process satisfies the conditions

C1 For any i with $1 \leq i \leq n$, we have $|w'|_{a_i} = f^w_{q_i}$.
C2 For any i, k, with $1 \leq i < n$ and $k \in [1, |w|_{q_{i+1}}]$, the number of occurrences of a_i before the kth occurrence of a_{i+1} in w' is equal to the number of occurrences of q_i that end before the start of the kth occurrence of q_{i+1} in w.

Condition C1 holds, because we map each occurrence of the factor q_i in the word w to an occurrence of a_i in v, one by one.

As for condition C2, each individual swap of a_i and a_{i+1} only happens if the corresponding occurrences of q_i and q_{i+1} overlapped, not reducing the number of $a_i a_{i+1}$ occurrences in w' below the number of occurrences of $q_i \bullet q_{i+1}$ in w. Such swaps also do not affect the number of occurrences $a_{i-1} a_i$ or $a_{i+1} a_{i+2}$ except in the cases when they would have to be swapped later anyway.

Finally, each occurrence of $q_i \bullet \cdots \bullet q_j$ in w can be uniquely identified by indices $l_i, ..., l_j$ where l_k denotes that this occurrence of $q_i \bullet \cdots \bullet q_j$ uses the $l_k - th$ occurrence of q_k, for each $k \in [i, j]$, and we know that the l_k-th occurrence of q_k does not overlap with the l_{k+1}-th occurrence of q_{k+1}, for any $k \in [i, j-1]$. This means that there exists an occurrence of the subword $a_i \cdots a_j$ in w' using the l_k-th occurrence of a_k in w', for each $k \in [i, j]$, and vice versa. This means that for each i, j with $1 \leq i \leq j \leq n$ we have $\binom{w'}{a_i \cdots a_j} = |w|_{q_i \bullet \cdots \bullet q_j}$, so $\Psi_{a_1 \cdots a_n}(w') = M$. From here, by Theorem 3 we can conclude our statement, that each minor of M is nonnegative.   □

Example 6. Let $Q = ab \bullet aba \bullet ba, w = abababa$. First, we have $q_1 = ab, q_2 = aba, q_3 = ba$, and define the order $\{q_1 < q_2 < q_3\}$. Then map all factors q_1, q_2, q_3 in w to letters c, d, e, $w' = cdecdecde$. Next, exchange the position following the algorithm, $cdecdecde \to dcecdecde \to edccdecde \to \cdots \to edcedcedc$. Finally, the classical Parikh matrix of $w' = edcedcedc$ and the special submatrix of $X_Q(w)$ are equal.

6   Generalized Subword Histories

In this section we generalize the concept of subword histories and the main tool used in their analysis, that each subword history is equivalent to a linear one, by a method of eliminating products. The definitions and the relatively simple arguments are mainly reformulations of the ones for the original subword histories [19,25], as they generalize very naturally for our case with small adaptations to account for the $\bullet$ operator. First let us recall the notion of subword history defined by Mateescu et al.

Definition 4 ([19])**.** *Consider an alphabet Σ and a word $w \in \Sigma^*$. A subword history over Σ and its value in w are defined recursively as follows.*

– *Every $u \in \Sigma^*$ is a subword history over Σ, referred to as a monomial, and its value in w equals $\binom{w}{u}$.*

– *Assume SH_1 and SH_2 are subword histories with values α_1 and α_2, respectively. Then $-(SH_1)$, $(SH_1) + (SH_2)$ and $(SH_1) \times (SH_2)$ are subword histories and their values are $-\alpha_1$, $\alpha_1 + \alpha_2$ and $\alpha_1 \alpha_2$, respectively.*

In [19] it is proved that every subword history is equivalent to a linear subword history, i.e., one that does not use $\times$, only $+$, $-$ and monomials. Moreover, given a polynomial $p(u_1, ..., u_n)$, a linear polynomial representing an equivalent subword history can be effectively constructed. We will show that subword histories defined through generalized subsequences hold the same properties.

Definition 5. *Consider an alphabet Σ and a word $w \in \Sigma^*$. A monomial generalized subword history over Σ and its value in w is defined as a generalized subsequence $Q = q_1 \bullet q_2 \bullet \cdots \bullet q_n$, with $q_i \in \Sigma^*$, for all $i \in [1, n]$, and its value in w equals f_Q^w. Assume Q_1 and Q_2 are generalized subword histories with values α_1 and α_2, respectively. Then $-(Q_1)$, $(Q_1) + (Q_2)$ and $(Q_1) \times (Q_2)$ are also generalized subword histories, with values $-\alpha_1$, $\alpha_1 + \alpha_2$ and $\alpha_1 \alpha_2$, respectively.*

GSH are functions mapping words to integers, e.g., the GSH $ab \bullet b \times cd + a \bullet c$ maps a word w to $f_{ab \bullet b}^w f_{cd}^w + f_{a \bullet c}^w$. Equivalence of two GSH means the functions are equal for their whole domain. For the sake of more succinct expression of the definitions below, we let $\bullet$ be distributive over $+$, allowing the shorthand $Q_1 \bullet (Q_2 + Q_3)$ for $Q_1 \bullet Q_2 + Q_1 \bullet Q_3$ by composing linear GSH using $\bullet$. For convenience, we also define the GSH $\emptyset$, whose value is 0 in any w, the GSH ε whose value is 1 in any w and define the following identities for all generalized subword histories Q in any word w:

$$\emptyset \bullet Q = Q \bullet \emptyset = \emptyset$$
$$\varepsilon \bullet Q = Q \bullet \varepsilon = Q$$
$$\emptyset + Q = Q + \emptyset = Q.$$

Furthermore, $\times$ and $+$ are associative, $+$ is commutative, and $\times$ is left and right distributive over $+$.

Two generalized subword histories (GSH) are called *equivalent* if their values are the same in any word w. A generalized subword history is *linear* if it is obtained from monomials without using the operation $\times$.

For two monomial GSH $Q = q_1 \bullet q_2 \bullet \cdots \bullet q_x$ and $P = p_1 \bullet p_2 \bullet \cdots \bullet p_y$, we define the ground shuffle of P and Q, denoted $P \sqcup Q$ as the set of all sequences $u_0 \bullet q_1 \bullet u_1 \cdots u_{x-1} \bullet q_x \bullet u_x$, where $u_0 \bullet \cdots \bullet u_x = p_1 \bullet \cdots \bullet p_y$ and any u_i may contain several terms p_j or be empty.

Example 7. For $Q_1 = ab \bullet c$, $Q_2 = d$, their ground shuffle is $\sum_{x \in Q_1 \sqcup Q_2} x = \{ab \bullet c \bullet d, ab \bullet d \bullet c, d \bullet ab \bullet c\}$

Two GSH Q_1 and Q_2 are disjoint if they can be defined over disjoint alphabets.

Proposition 1. *Assume that Q_1 and Q_2 are disjoint GSH. Then, $Q_1 \times Q_2$ and the ground shuffle $\sum_{x \in Q_1 \sqcup Q_2} x$ are equivalent.*

Proof. The argument is straightforward: each pair of occurrences of Q_1 and Q_2 defines an occurrence of a term in their ground shuffle, since factors of Q_1 cannot overlap with factors of Q_2, and the other direction is immediate.   □

We speak of the generalized subword history Q in the word w, defined by the $GSH(w, Q)$. If GSH Q_1 and Q_2 are not disjoint then we get

$$GSH(w, Q_1 \times Q_2) \geq GSH(w, \sum_{x \in Q_1 \sqcup\!\sqcup Q_2} x)$$

because each occurrence of a term in $Q_1 \sqcup\!\sqcup Q_2$ trivially defines a pair of occurrences of Q_1 and Q_2, but some occurrence of Q_1 might overlap with an occurrence of Q_2, so that pair would not correspond to any ground shuffle term occurrence.

6.1   Reduction to Linear Generalized Subword Histories

Now we move on to show how to construct a linear GSH equivalent to a given GSH that uses the $\times$ operation. Let us denote by GSH_Σ the set of all GSH over Σ. For Σ, we consider the primed version $\Sigma' = \{a' | a \in \Sigma\}$. Let $h : (\Sigma \cup \Sigma')^* \to \Sigma^*$ be the morphism defined by $h(a) = h(a') = a$. By a slight abuse of the notation we extend it to the domain of monomial GSH as $h(Q) = h(q_1) \bullet \cdots \bullet h(q_n)$ for any $Q = q_1 \bullet \cdots \bullet q_n$, where $q_i \in (\Sigma \cup \Sigma')^*$, and then further as $h(Q_1 + Q_2) = h(Q_1) + h(Q_2)$, where $Q_1, Q_2 \in GSH_{(\Sigma \cup \Sigma')}$. Let the morphism $g : \Sigma^* \to \Sigma'^*$ be defined as $g(a) = a'$ for all $a \in \Sigma$ and extended to GSH similarly to h.

For the generalized subsequences $Q_1 = p_1 \bullet \cdots \bullet p_m$ and $Q_2 = q_1 \bullet \cdots \bullet q_n$, both occurring in w, a pair of occurrences of Q_1 and Q_2 is *interleaved* if for each $i \in [1, m-1]$ there is a $j \in [1, n]$ such that q_j overlaps with both p_i and p_{i+1} and for each $i \in [1, n-1]$ there is a $j \in [1, m]$ such that p_j overlaps with both q_i and q_{i+1}.

Now we introduce a function to reduce the $\bullet$ of two monomial GSH defined over Σ and Σ', respectively. Suppose that the GSH given by the generalized subsequence $Q_1 = p_1 \bullet \cdots \bullet p_i$ is over Σ and $Q_2 = q_1 \bullet \cdots \bullet q_j$ is over Σ'. We define the function red, such that $red(p_1 \bullet \cdots \bullet p_i \bullet q_1 \bullet \cdots \bullet q_j) = a_1 v_1 + a_2 v_2 + \cdots + a_k v_k$, where for all $d \in [1, k]$, we have $a_d \in \mathbb{N}$ and $v_d \in \Sigma^+$ are factors satisfying the conditions:

1. v_d contains interleaved occurrences of Q_1 and $h(Q_2)$ starting at the first position of v_d and ending at the last position of v_d
2. a_d is the number of distinct interleaved occurrences of Q_1 and $h(Q_2)$ in v_d starting at the first position of v_d and ending at the last position of v_d.

If such v_d exist, then we say that $Q_1 \bullet Q_2$ is reducible. If v_d does not exist, then $red(Q_1 \bullet Q_2) = \emptyset$. Note that $|v_d| < |p_1| + \cdots + |p_i| + |q_1| + \cdots + |q_j|$, due to the conditions on interleaved occurrences stretching across v_d, therefore $|v_d|_{p_1 \bullet \cdots \bullet p_i \bullet h(q_1 \bullet \cdots \bullet q_j)} = 0$.

Example 8. Assume that $Q_1 = abc \bullet c$ and $Q_2 = c' \bullet d'$. Then $red(Q_1 \bullet Q_2) = \emptyset$. However, if $Q_3 = abc \bullet de$, $Q_4 = a' \bullet c'd'$, then $red(Q_3 \bullet Q_4) = a_1 v_1$ with $a_1 = 1$ and $v_1 = abcde$.

Now we can construct for the general case of GSH over $\Sigma \cup \Sigma'$ the reduction function $R : GSH_{(\Sigma \cup \Sigma')} \to GSH_\Sigma$ inductively as follows.

1. For GSH P over Σ and Q over Σ', let $R(P) = P$ and $R(Q) = h(Q)$.
2. For monomial GSH P over Σ and Q over Σ' let $R(P \bullet Q) = P \bullet h(Q) + red(P \bullet Q)$.
3. For monomial GSH $P_1, \ldots, P_m$ over Σ and $Q_1, \ldots, Q_m$ over Σ', with $m > 1$:

$$R(P_1 \bullet Q_1 \bullet P_2 \bullet Q_2 \bullet \cdots \bullet P_m \bullet Q_m) = R(P_1 \bullet Q_1) \bullet R(P_2 \bullet Q_2 \bullet \cdots \bullet P_m \bullet Q_m).$$

4. For GSH Q over $\Sigma \cup \Sigma'$ and $z \in \mathbb{Z}$, let $R(zQ) = zR(Q)$.

Theorem 5. *For all monomials GSH Q_1 and Q_2, the GSH $Q_1 \times Q_2$ is equivalent to the linear GSH*

$$\sum_{Q \in Q_1 \sqcup g(Q_2)} R(Q).$$

Proof. There is a one-to-one correspondence between pairs of occurrences of Q_1, Q_2 and the set of occurrences of (1) terms of the ground shuffle of Q_1 and Q_2 and (2) reduced terms of the ground shuffle, where the red function applied to some factor. The former is the case when the pair of occurrences of Q_1 and Q_2 has no interleaved parts, and the latter otherwise. The correspondence is straightforward from the construction of the reduction functions. The value of $\sum_{Q \in Q_1 \sqcup g(Q_2)} R(Q)$ is clearly greater or equal to the value of $Q_1 \times Q_2$, due to rule 2. in the definition of R. Conversely, each term in $\sum_{Q \in Q_1 \sqcup g(Q_2)} R(Q)$ that does not occur in the ground shuffle, is obtained as $P_1 \bullet red(Q_1' \bullet Q_2') \bullet P_2$ for some ground shuffle term containing the subsequence $Q_1' \bullet Q_2'$ and corresponds to counting occurrences of pairs of Q_1 and Q_2 where the Q_1' part of Q_1 is interleaved with the Q_2' part of Q_2. $\square$

By applying the laws of distributivity of $\times$ over $+$ and the reduction above, we can obtain an equivalent linear GSH from any starting GSH. An important consequence of the ability to linearize GSH is that, by a simple proof just like in the case of the original subword histories [19], two linear GSH are equivalent if and only if they are identical up to a reordering of their terms. This means that equivalence of GSH is decidable by a simple algorithm, but with high time complexity induced by the need to compute $\Omega(k!)$ many ground shuffle terms from a GSH with k terms as is the case, e.g., for the $k!$ term linear GSH equivalent to $a_1 \times \cdots \times a_k$, where $a_1, \ldots, a_k$ are all distinct letters.

7   Conclusion

We proposed a generalization of Parikh matrices that are able to track factors and subsequences with gaps. For these new mappings, We also obtained the generalized versions of the most fundamental properties applied in the study of Parikh matrices: that they are homomorphisms and that significant submatrices of the matrices have nonnegative minors. The latter property gave rise to a well-investigated direction of research into equations and inequalities involving subword histories. To be able to continue the study of subsequences with gaps in that direction, we also showed that subword histories defined with those generalized subsequences can also be linearized, just as was the case with the subword histories based on scattered subword occurrences. One open road ahead that we think is worth investigating, is to describe the class of languages that can be defined through generalized subword history conditions.

Another meaningful way to expand on this research is to consider the 'ultimate' generalizations of subwords: subsequences with gap constraints provided as length (the maximum allowed distance individually defined between each consecutive pair of letters of the subsequence when matched in the containing word) or even more generally subsequences with regular gap constraints (for exciting recent results, see [17]), that is, when matching the subsequence, the gap between two consecutive letters has to be a word in a given regular language. The formalism we developed seems flexible enough to handle length constraints by minor modification, but we do not yet know whether the regular constraints are implementable through such matrix mappings.

Acknowledgements. We would like to express our warm thanks to the anonymous reviewers for their constructive technical comments and for pointing out several very relevant earlier works that we originally missed and that needed to be discussed in our study.

References

1. Andreatta, M., Nielsen, M.: Gapped sequence alignment using artificial neural networks: application to the MHC class I system. Bioinform. **32**(4), 511–517 (2016). https://doi.org/10.1093/BIOINFORMATICS/BTV639
2. Atanasiu, A.: Binary Amiable Words. Int. J. Found. Comput. Sci. **18**(02), 387–400 (2007). https://doi.org/10.1142/S0129054107004735
3. Atanasiu, A.: Parikh matrix mapping and amiability over a ternary alphabet. In: Discrete Mathematics and Computer Science in Memoriam Alexandru Mateescu (1952–2005) (2014)
4. Atanasiu, A., Atanasiu, R., Petre, I.: Parikh matrices and amiable words. Theor. Comput. Sci. **390**(1), 102–109 (2008). https://doi.org/10.1016/j.tcs.2007.09.017
5. Day, J.D., Kosche, M., Manea, F., Schmid, M.L.: Subsequences with gap constraints: complexity bounds for matching and analysis problems. In: 33rd International Symposium on Algorithms and Computation (ISAAC). Leibniz International Proceedings in Informatics (LIPIcs), vol. 248, pp. 64:1–64:18. Schloss Dagstuhl – Leibniz-Zentrum für Informatik (2022). https://doi.org/10.4230/LIPIcs.ISAAC.2022.64
6. Dick, J., Hutchinson, L.K., Mercaş, R., Reidenbach, D.: Reducing the Ambiguity of Parikh Matrices. In: Language and Automata Theory and Applications (LATA). Lecture Notes in Computer Science, vol. 12038, pp. 96–109. Springer, Cham (2020). https://doi.org/10.1007/978-3-030-40608-0_8

7. Edwards, R.J., Shields, D.C.: GASP: gapped ancestral sequence prediction for proteins. BMC Bioinform. **5**, 123 (2004). https://doi.org/10.1186/1471-2105-5-123

8. Fleischmann, P., Kim, S., Koß, T., Manea, F., Nowotka, D., Siemer, S., Wiedenhöft, M.: Matching patterns with variables under simon's congruence. In: Bournez, O., Formenti, E., Potapov, I. (eds.) Reachability Problems, pp. 155–170. Springer, Cham (2023). https://doi.org/10.1007/978-3-031-45286-4_12

9. Fossé, S., Richomme, G.: Some characterizations of Parikh matrix equivalent binary words. Inf. Process. Lett. **92**(2), 77–82 (2004). https://doi.org/10.1016/J.IPL.2004.06.011

10. Gawrychowski, P., Kosche, M., Koß, T., Manea, F., Siemer, S.: Efficiently testing Simon's congruence. In: Bläser, M., Monmege, B. (eds.) 38th International Symposium on Theoretical Aspects of Computer Science (STACS 2021). Leibniz International Proceedings in Informatics (LIPIcs), vol. 187, pp. 34:1–34:18. Schloss Dagstuhl – Leibniz-Zentrum für Informatik, Dagstuhl, Germany (2021). https://doi.org/10.4230/LIPIcs.STACS.2021.34

11. Golm, R., Nahvi, M., Gabrys, R., Milenkovic, O.: The gapped k-deck problem. In: IEEE International Symposium on Information Theory, ISIT 2022, Espoo, Finland, 26 June–1 July 2022, pp. 49–54. IEEE (2022). https://doi.org/10.1109/ISIT50566.2022.9834537

12. Hahn, J., Cheon, H., Han, Y.: M-equivalence of parikh matrix over a ternary alphabet. In: Nagy, B. (ed.) CIAA 2023. LNCS, vol. 14151, pp. 141–152. Springer, Heidelberg (2023). https://doi.org/10.1007/978-3-031-40247-0_10

13. Higman, G.: Ordering by divisibility in abstract algebras. Proc. Lond. Math. Soc. **s3-2**(1), 326–336 (1952). https://doi.org/10.1112/plms/s3-2.1.326

14. Karhumäki, J., Whiteland, M.A.: A compactness property of the k-abelian monoids. Theor. Comput. Sci. **834**, 3–13 (2020). https://doi.org/10.1016/J.TCS.2020.01.023

15. Kim, S., Han, Y.S., Ko, S.K., Salomaa, K.: On the Simon's congruence neighborhood of languages. In: Developments in Language Theory: 27th International Conference, DLT 2023, Umeå, Sweden, 12–16 June 2023, Proceedings, pp. 168–181. Springer-Verlag, Heidelberg (2023). https://doi.org/10.1007/978-3-031-33264-7_14

16. Kim, S., Ko, S.K., Han, Y.S.: Simon's congruence pattern matching. Theor. Comput. Sci. **994**, 114478 (2024). https://doi.org/10.1016/j.tcs.2024.114478

17. Manea, F., Richardsen, J., Schmid, M.L.: Subsequences with generalised gap constraints: upper and lower complexity bounds. In: Inenaga, S., Puglisi, S.J. (eds.) 35th Annual Symposium on Combinatorial Pattern Matching, CPM 2024, 25–27 June 2024, Fukuoka, Japan. LIPIcs, vol. 296, pp. 22:1–22:17. Schloss Dagstuhl - Leibniz-Zentrum für Informatik (2024). https://doi.org/10.4230/LIPICS.CPM.2024.22

18. Mateescu, A., Salomaa, A., Salomaa, K., Yu, S.: A sharpening of the Parikh mapping. RAIRO - Theor. Inf. Appl. **35**(6), 551–564 (2001). https://doi.org/10.1051/ita:2001131

19. Mateescu, A., Salomaa, A., Yu, S.: Subword histories and Parikh matrices. J. Comput. Syst. Sci. **68**(1), 1–21 (2004). https://doi.org/10.1016/j.jcss.2003.07.001

20. Parikh, R.J.: On context-free languages. J. ACM **13**(4), 570–581 (1966). https://doi.org/10.1145/321356.321364

21. Renard, A., Rigo, M., Whiteland, M.A.: Introducing q-deformed binomial coefficients of words. CoRR arxiv:2402.05838 (2024). https://doi.org/10.48550/ARXIV.2402.05838

22. Renard, A., Rigo, M., Whiteland, M.A.: q-parikh matrices and q-deformed binomial coefficients of words. CoRR arxiv:2402.05657 (2024). https://doi.org/10.48550/ARXIV.2402.05657
23. Rigo, M., Stipulanti, M., Whiteland, M.A.: Gapped binomial complexities in sequences. In: IEEE International Symposium on Information Theory, ISIT 2023, Taipei, Taiwan, 25–30 June 2023, pp. 1294–1299. IEEE (2023). https://doi.org/10.1109/ISIT54713.2023.10206676
24. Salomaa, A.: Connections between subwords and certain matrix mappings. Theor. Comput. Sci. **340**(2), 188–203 (2005). https://doi.org/10.1016/j.tcs.2005.03.032
25. Salomaa, A.: Subword histories and associated matrices. Theor. Comput. Sci. **407**(1), 250–257 (2008). https://doi.org/10.1016/j.tcs.2008.05.023
26. Salomaa, A.: Criteria for the matrix equivalence of words. Theor. Comput. Sci. **411**(16), 1818–1827 (2010). https://doi.org/10.1016/j.tcs.2010.01.036. https://www.sciencedirect.com/science/article/pii/S0304397510000733
27. Serbanuta, T.: Extending Parikh matrices. Theor. Comput. Sci. **310**(1–3), 233–246 (2004). https://doi.org/10.1016/S0304-3975(03)00396-7
28. Teh, W.C.: Parikh matrices and parikh rewriting systems. Fundam. Informaticae **146**(3), 305–320 (2016). https://doi.org/10.3233/FI-2016-1388
29. Teh, W.C., Kwa, K.H.: Core words and Parikh matrices. Theor. Comput. Sci. **582**, 60–69 (2015). https://doi.org/10.1016/J.TCS.2015.03.037
30. Zetzsche, G.: The Complexity of Downward Closure Comparisons. In: Chatzigiannakis, I., Mitzenmacher, M., Rabani, Y., Sangiorgi, D. (eds.) 43rd International Colloquium on Automata, Languages, and Programming, ICALP 2016, Rome, Italy, 11–15 July 2016. LIPIcs, vol. 55, pp. 123:1–123:14. Schloss Dagstuhl - Leibniz-Zentrum für Informatik (2016). https://doi.org/10.4230/LIPICS.ICALP.2016.123
31. Zetzsche, G.: Separability by piecewise testable languages and downward closures beyond subwords. In: Dawar, A., Grädel, E. (eds.) Proceedings of the 33rd Annual ACM/IEEE Symposium on Logic in Computer Science, LICS 2018, Oxford, UK, 09-12 July 2018, pp. 929–938. ACM (2018). https://doi.org/10.1145/3209108.3209201

Card-Based Protocols with Single-Card Encoding

Kazumasa Shinagawa[1,2][✉]

[1] Ibaraki University, Hitachi, Japan
`kazumasa.shinagawa.np92@vc.ibaraki.ac.jp`
[2] National Institute of Advanced Industrial Science and Technology, Tokyo, Japan

Abstract. Card-based cryptography allows multiple players to compute a function of their inputs without revealing any information on the inputs beyond the output value. In card-based protocols, although a bit value is usually encoded as a pair of cards (which we call a *two-card encoding*), a *single-card encoding* that encodes a bit value to a single card can be naturally considered. In 1998, Niemi and Renvall designed a COPY protocol that takes a single-card encoding of $x \in \{0, 1\}$ and outputs k copies of the encoding of x without revealing the input value x. However, as the authors claim in the paper, the security of the COPY protocol is not perfect: There is some "failure" probability of revealing the input value x. In 2014, Mizuki and Shizuya showed that there exists no perfectly-secure COPY protocol with single-card encoding, i.e., the failure of the Niemi–Renvall's COPY protocol is unavoidable. In this paper, we design single-card encoding protocols with a failure probability. First, we show that every Boolean function can be computed based on the Niemi–Renvall's COPY protocol and existing protocols with two-card encoding. Second, we propose AND and XOR protocols, both of which have a lower failure probability compared to the general protocol.

Keywords: Card-based cryptography · Secure Computation · Single-card encoding

1 Introduction

1.1 Background

Secure computation allows multiple parties $P_1, P_2, \ldots, P_n$, each P_i with a secret input x_i, to compute an output value $y := f(x_1, x_2, \ldots, x_n)$ of a function f of their inputs without revealing any information on the inputs beyond the output value y. Although secure computation is usually implemented on electronic devices, there is a line of research to implement secure computation using a deck of physical cards, which is known as *card-based cryptography*. Since card-based protocols can be actually performed in front of an audience, it tends to be easier for people to understand the correctness and security of protocols than those executed on electronic devices.

C. Anutariya and M. M. Bonsangue (Eds.): ICTAC 2024, LNCS 15373, pp. 182–194, 2025.
https://doi.org/10.1007/978-3-031-77019-7_11

In card-based protocols, a bit value $x \in \{0,1\}$ is usually encoded as an ordered pair of cards $\clubsuit$ and $\heartsuit$ with the following encoding rule:

$$\boxed{\clubsuit}\,\boxed{\heartsuit} = 0, \quad \boxed{\heartsuit}\,\boxed{\clubsuit} = 1.$$

We call it a *two-card encoding*. A *two-card commitment* to $x \in \{0,1\}$ is defined by a pair of face-down cards holding x with two-card encoding. In this setting, Crépeau and Kilian [1] first designed a Las Vegas protocol for any function f, and later Mizuki and Sone [5] improved it to a finite-runtime protocol.

It is also natural to consider the following encoding rule:

$$\boxed{\clubsuit} = 0, \quad \boxed{\heartsuit} = 1.$$

We call it a *single-card encoding*. A *single-card commitment* to $x \in \{0,1\}$ is defined by a face-down card holding x with single-card encoding.

Niemi and Renvall [6] first introduced single-card encoding and proposed a COPY protocol that takes a single-card commitment to x and outputs k copies of the single-card commitment to x as follows:

$$\underbrace{\boxed{?}}_{x}\underbrace{\boxed{\heartsuit}\,\boxed{\clubsuit}\,\boxed{\heartsuit}\,\boxed{\clubsuit}\cdots\boxed{\heartsuit}\,\boxed{\clubsuit}}_{\text{helping cards}} \rightarrow \underbrace{\underbrace{\boxed{?}}_{x}\,\underbrace{\boxed{?}}_{x}\cdots\underbrace{\boxed{?}}_{x}}_{k \text{ copies}}.$$

As the authors claimed in the paper, the security of the Niemi–Renvall's COPY protocol is not perfect: There is some "failure" probability to reveal the input value x although the failure probability can be reduced to sufficiently small by increasing the number of cards. In particular, if we use $2k + 2^{s+2} - 1$ cards, then the failure probability will be $1/2^{s+1}$.

In 2014, Mizuki and Shizuya [4] introduced a mathematical model of card-based protocols the so-called *Mizuki–Shizuya model*. They showed that there exists no COPY protocol for single-card encoding with perfect security, i.e., the failure of the Niemi–Renvall's COPY protocol is unavoidable. After this impossibility result, protocols with single-card encoding have been no longer studied. Except for the tentative use of single-card encoding within protocols for two-card encoding (e.g., an AND protocol by Mizuki [3]), single-card encoding seems to have been largely forgotten in the research area of card-based cryptography.

1.2 Our Contribution

In this paper, we study card-based protocols with single-card encoding. In particular, we construct three protocols: a protocol for any function $f : \{0,1\}^n \to \{0,1\}$, an AND protocol, and an XOR protocol. The latter two protocols, AND and XOR protocols, have lower failure probabilities than directly applying the protocol for any function. Thus, if you want to compute AND or XOR functions, the latter two protocols are more efficient than the protocol for any function.

Our protocol for any function $f : \{0,1\}^n \to \{0,1\}$ takes n single-card commitments to $x_1, x_2, \ldots, x_n \in \{0,1\}$ and outputs a two-card commitment to

Table 1. Summary of Our Results

Function	# of Cards	Failure Probability
$f : \{0,1\}^n \rightarrow \{0,1\}$ (Sect. 3)	$n \cdot (2^{s+2} + 1)$	$n/2^{s+1}$
$x_1 \wedge x_2$ (Sect. 4)	$2k + 2^{s+2} + 1$	$1/2^{s+1}$
$x_1 \oplus x_2$ (Sect. 5)	$2k + 2^{s+2} - 2$	$(s+2)/2^{s+1}$

$f(x_1, \ldots, x_n)$, whose left card is a single-card commitment. The protocol with failure probability $n/2^{s+1}$ is given as follows:

Our AND protocol takes two single-card commitments to $x, y \in \{0,1\}$ and outputs a single-card commitment to $x \wedge y$ and k copies of the input commitment to x. The protocol with failure probability $1/2^{s+1}$ is given as follows:

When $k = 0$, the protocol does not output copies of the input commitment, i.e., the standard AND protocol. When $k \geq 1$, the protocol is called an input-preserving AND protocol [7,10].

Our XOR protocol takes two single-card commitments to $x, y \in \{0,1\}$ and outputs k copies of the single-card commitment to $x \oplus y$. The protocol with failure probability $(s+2)/2^{s+1}$ is given as follows:

This protocol can be generalized to the n-input XOR function $x_1 \oplus x_2 \oplus \cdots \oplus x_n$ while the failure probability increases to $p_n/2^{s+1}$ for $p_n := \sum_{i=0}^{n-1} {}_{s+1}C_i$. (Note that $p_2 = {}_{s+1}C_0 + {}_{s+1}C_1 = s + 2$.) In Sect. 5, we describe our XOR protocol for the n-input XOR function.

Table 1 shows a summary of our results.

2 Preliminaries

2.1 Cards

We use a *two-colored deck*, which consists of two types of cards ♣ and ♡. Their backs are all identical and written as ?.

For a symbol $a \in \{♣, ♡\}$, a face-up card is written by $a/?$ and a face-down card is written by $?/a$. For example, a sequence of cards ♣♡?, where the face-down card has a symbol ♣, is written by $(♣/?, ♡/?, ?/♣)$.

2.2   Single-Card Commitment

Consider the following encoding rule:

$$\boxed{\clubsuit} = 0, \quad \boxed{\heartsuit} = 1.$$

We call it a *single-card encoding*. For a bit $x \in \{0, 1\}$, a face-down card holding the value with the single-card encoding is called a *sigle-card commitment* to x.

Consider another encoding rule as follows:

$$\boxed{\clubsuit}\boxed{\heartsuit} = 0, \quad \boxed{\heartsuit}\boxed{\clubsuit} = 1.$$

We call it a *two-card encoding*. In this paper, we call a pair of face-down cards holding $x \in \{0, 1\}$ with the two-card encoding a *two-card commitment* to x.

Although most of existing protocols mainly use the two-card commitment, we focus on the single-card commitment. Hereafter, a single-card commitment will be referred to as a *commitment*.

2.3   Shuffles

In this paper, we use three types of shuffle operations: complete shuffle, random cut, and random bisection cut.

Complete Shuffle. A *complete shuffle*, introduced by Niemi and Renvall [6] and named by Nuida [8], is a shuffle that applies a uniformly random permutation to a sequence of cards. Here, the chosen permutation is completely hidden from all players. Applying a complete shuffle to a sequence Γ of cards is denoted by $[\Gamma]$. For example, a complete shuffle for three cards rearranges it as:

Random Cut. A *random cut* introduced by den Boer [2] is a shuffle that cyclically shifts a sequence of cards uniformly at random. Here, the number of shifts is completely hidden from all players. Applying a random cut to a sequence

Γ of cards is denoted by $\langle \Gamma \rangle$. For example, a random cut for a sequence of three cards rearranges it as follows:

$$\left\langle \begin{array}{ccc} 1 & 2 & 3 \\ ? & ? & ? \end{array} \right\rangle \rightarrow \begin{cases} \begin{array}{ccc} 1 & 2 & 3 \\ ? & ? & ? \end{array} \\ \begin{array}{ccc} 2 & 3 & 1 \\ ? & ? & ? \end{array} \\ \begin{array}{ccc} 3 & 1 & 2 \\ ? & ? & ? \end{array} \end{cases} .$$

Random Bisection Cut. A *random bisection cut* introduced by Mizuki and Sone [5] is a shuffle that randomly swaps two piles of cards, each having the same number of cards. Here, whether it is swapped or not is completely hidden from all players. Applying a random bisection cut to a sequence $\Gamma = (\Gamma_0, \Gamma_1)$, where Γ_0 and Γ_1 are of the equal length, is denoted by $[\Gamma_0 | \Gamma_1]$. For example, a random bisection cut for a sequence of two piles each having three cards rearranges it as:

$$\left[\begin{array}{ccc|ccc} 1 & 2 & 3 & 4 & 5 & 6 \\ ? & ? & ? & ? & ? & ? \end{array} \right] \rightarrow \begin{cases} \begin{array}{cccccc} 1 & 2 & 3 & 4 & 5 & 6 \\ ? & ? & ? & ? & ? & ? \end{array} \\ \begin{array}{cccccc} 4 & 5 & 6 & 1 & 2 & 3 \\ ? & ? & ? & ? & ? & ? \end{array} \end{cases} .$$

2.4 Niemi–Renvall's COPY Protocol

Niemi and Renvall [6] designed a COPY protocol with single-card encoding. It takes a commitment to $x \in \{0,1\}$ and outputs k copies of the commitment to x. The protocol with failure probability $1/2^{s+1}$ proceeds as follows.

1. Arrange $k + 1$ pairs of ♣♡ as follows:

$$\underbrace{♣ ♡ ♣ ♡ \cdots ♣ ♡}_{(k+1) \text{ pairs}} .$$

2. Turn these cards as follows:

$$♣ ♡ ♣ ♡ \cdots ♣ ♡ \rightarrow ? ? ? ? \cdots ? ? .$$

3. Apply a random cut:

$$\left\langle ? ? ? ? \cdots ? ? \right\rangle \rightarrow \underset{r\ \bar{r}\ r\ \bar{r}}{? ? ? ?} \cdots \underset{r\ \bar{r}}{? ?} ,$$

where $r \in \{0,1\}$ is a uniformly random bit and $\bar{r} = 1 - r$.

4. For each $i = 1, \ldots, s$, do the following:

(a) Arrange 2^i pairs of ♣♡ as follows:

$$\underbrace{♣\,♡\,♣\,♡\,\cdots\,♣\,♡}_{2^i \text{ pairs}}.$$

(b) Turn these helping cards as follows:

$$♣\,♡\,♣\,♡\,\cdots\,♣\,♡ \;\rightarrow\; \boxed{?}\,\boxed{?}\,\boxed{?}\,\boxed{?}\,\cdots\,\boxed{?}\,\boxed{?}.$$

(c) Apply a random cut:

$$\left\langle\, \boxed{?}\,\boxed{?}\,\boxed{?}\,\boxed{?}\,\cdots\,\boxed{?}\,\boxed{?}\, \right\rangle \;\rightarrow\; \underset{r_i\ \overline{r_i}\ \ r_i\ \overline{r_i}\qquad\ \ r_i\ \overline{r_i}}{\boxed{?}\,\boxed{?}\,\boxed{?}\,\boxed{?}\,\cdots\,\boxed{?}\,\boxed{?}}.$$

5. Arrange the cards as follows next to the input commitment to x:

$$\underset{x\ \ r}{\boxed{?}\,\boxed{?}}\ \ \underset{\underbrace{r_1\ r_1}_{2\text{ cards}}}{\boxed{?}\,\boxed{?}}\ \ \underset{\underbrace{r_2\ r_2\ r_2\ r_2}_{2^2\text{ cards}}}{\boxed{?}\,\boxed{?}\,\boxed{?}\,\boxed{?}}\ \cdots\ \underset{\underbrace{r_s\ r_s\qquad\ \ r_s}_{2^s\text{ cards}}}{\boxed{?}\,\boxed{?}\,\cdots\,\boxed{?}},$$

where r and r_i are the cards generated in Step 4 and the number of r_i is 2^i. (Note that the number of cards in this sequence is 2^{s+1} in total.)

6. Apply a complete shuffle to the sequence:

$$\left[\,\boxed{?}\,\boxed{?}\,\cdots\,\boxed{?}\,\right] \;\rightarrow\; \boxed{?}\,\boxed{?}\,\cdots\,\boxed{?}.$$

7. Open the cards that appear in Step 6. Let h be the number of $♡$ in the sequence. If h is even, the protocol outputs k commitments to r. Otherwise, the protocol outputs k commitments to $\overline{r}$.

$$♣\,♡\,♡\,\cdots\,♣ \;\rightarrow\; \begin{cases} (?/r, ?/r, \ldots, ?/r) & \text{if } h \text{ is even;} \\ (?/\overline{r}, ?/\overline{r}, \ldots, ?/\overline{r}) & \text{otherwise.} \end{cases}$$

If h is 0 or 2^{s+1}, the input value x is leaked. Otherwise, the protocol does not leak any information about the input.

The number of cards in the above protocol is $2k + 2^{s+2} - 1$. The number of shuffles in the above protocol is $s + 2$ consisting of $s + 1$ random cuts and one complete shuffle.

Note that the cards that are face down at the end of the protocol should never be opened, even if a complete shuffle is applied. This is because if the number of $♡$ on these cards is revealed, some information about the input value x will be leaked. Unlike two-card encoding protocols, single-card encoding protocols require the number of $♡$ to be kept secret, so it is basically difficult to reuse the remaining cards in many cases.

3 Protocol for Any Function

In this section, we construct a protocol for any function $f : \{0,1\}^n \rightarrow \{0,1\}$ with single-card encoding based on Niemi–Renvall's COPY protocol.

3.1   Another Look at Niemi–Renvall's COPY Protocol

Niemi–Renvall's COPY protocol takes a commitment to x and outputs k copies of the commitment to x. In Step 7, it outputs $(?/r, ?/r, \ldots, ?/r)$ if the number of $\heartsuit$ is even and $(?/\overline{r}, ?/\overline{r}, \ldots, ?/\overline{r})$ otherwise. We can observe that the pair of $(?/r, ?/\overline{r})$ is a two-card commitment to x if the number of $\heartsuit$ is even and $(?/\overline{r}, ?/r)$ is a two-card commitment to x otherwise. Thus, the Niemi–Renvall's protoocol can output k copies of the two-card commitment to x:

When $k = 1$, it can be viewed as a *commitment conversion protocol* that takes a single-card commitment and outputs a two-card commitment.

3.2   Protocol for Any Function

Based on the commitment conversion protocol, we can compute any function $f : \{0,1\}^n \to \{0,1\}$ as follows:

1. For each $1 \le i \le n$, apply the commitment conversion protocol for a single-card commitment to x_i and obtain a two-card commitment to x_i:

2. Apply the Nishida–Mizuki–Sone's protocol [7] computing f as follows:

We estimate the number of cards required in the above protocol. Suppose that the commitment conversion protocol successes for all $1 \le i \le n$. Then for each commitment conversion protocol, the number of $\heartsuit$ (resp. $\clubsuit$) in the opened cards at the last step is at least 1. Thus, after Step 1 of the above protocol, we have at least n $\boxed{\heartsuit}$s and n $\boxed{\clubsuit}$s. Therefore, if $n \ge 3$, Step 2 does not require additional helping cards, and thus the number of required cards is $n \cdot (2^{s+2} + 1)$. If $n = 2$, we need to prepare two cards $\boxed{\clubsuit}\boxed{\heartsuit}$ additionally, thus the number of required cards is $2 \cdot (2^{s+2} + 1) + 2 = 2^{s+3} + 4$.

Note that although we use the Nishida–Mizuki–Sone's protocol in Step 2, we can choose any other protocol with two-card encoding. The reason we chose this protocol is that, as far as is known, it achieves the smallest number of cards of any existing protocol for any function. If we want to reduce the number of shuffles, we can use Ono et al.'s protocol [9], which is a protocol with a single shuffle based on the card-based garbled circuit technique [11].

4   Our AND Protocol

In this section, we construct an AND protocol with single-card encoding. Our AND protocol takes two commitments to $x, y \in \{0, 1\}$ and outputs a commitment to $x \wedge y$ and k copies of the input commitment to x. The protocol with failure probability $1/2^{s+1}$ is given as follows:

$$\underbrace{\boxed{?}\,\boxed{?}}_{x \quad y}\underbrace{\boxed{\clubsuit}\,\boxed{\clubsuit}\,\boxed{\clubsuit}\,\cdots\,\boxed{\clubsuit}}_{(k+2^{s+1})\text{ cards}}\underbrace{\boxed{\heartsuit}\,\boxed{\heartsuit}\,\boxed{\heartsuit}\,\cdots\,\boxed{\heartsuit}}_{(k+2^{s+1}-1)\text{ cards}} \rightarrow \underbrace{\boxed{?}}_{x \wedge y}\underbrace{\boxed{?}\,\boxed{?}\,\cdots\,\boxed{?}}_{\substack{x \quad x \qquad\quad x \\ k \text{ copies}}}.$$

When $k = 0$, the protocol does not output copies of the input commitment, i.e., the standard AND protocol. When $k \geq 1$, the protocol is called an input-preserving AND protocol [7,10].

4.1   Protocol Description

1. Arrange $2k + 3$ helping cards and a commitment to y as follows:

$$\underbrace{\boxed{\clubsuit}\,\boxed{\clubsuit}\,\boxed{\clubsuit}\,\cdots\,\boxed{\clubsuit}}_{k+1 \text{ cards}}\boxed{\underset{y}{?}}\underbrace{\boxed{\heartsuit}\,\boxed{\heartsuit}\,\cdots\,\boxed{\heartsuit}}_{k+1 \text{ cards}}.$$

2. Turn these helping cards as follows:

$$\underbrace{\boxed{\clubsuit}\,\boxed{\clubsuit}\,\cdots\,\boxed{\clubsuit}}_{k+1 \text{ cards}}\boxed{\underset{y}{?}}\underbrace{\boxed{\heartsuit}\,\cdots\,\boxed{\heartsuit}}_{k+1 \text{ cards}} \rightarrow \underbrace{\boxed{?}\,\boxed{?}\,\cdots\,\boxed{?}}_{k+1 \text{ cards}}\boxed{\underset{y}{?}}\underbrace{\boxed{?}\,\boxed{?}\,\cdots\,\boxed{?}}_{k+1 \text{ cards}}.$$

3. Apply a random bisection cut:

$$\left[\underbrace{\boxed{?}\,\boxed{?}\,\cdots\,\boxed{?}}_{k+2 \text{ cards}}\;\Bigg|\;\underbrace{\boxed{?}\,\boxed{?}\,\cdots\,\boxed{?}}_{k+2 \text{ cards}}\right] \rightarrow \underset{a_0}{\boxed{?}}\underbrace{\underset{r}{\boxed{?}}\underset{r}{\boxed{?}}\,\cdots\,\underset{r}{\boxed{?}}}_{k+1 \text{ cards}}\underset{a_1}{\boxed{?}}\underbrace{\underset{\bar{r}}{\boxed{?}}\underset{\bar{r}}{\boxed{?}}\,\cdots\,\underset{\bar{r}}{\boxed{?}}}_{k+1 \text{ cards}},$$

    where $r \in \{0, 1\}$ is a uniformly random bit, and $(a_0, a_1) = (0, y)$ if $r = 0$ and $(a_0, a_1) = (y, 0)$ otherwise.
4. For each $i = 1, \ldots, s$, do the following:
   (a) Arrange 2^i pairs of $\boxed{\clubsuit}\,\boxed{\heartsuit}$ as follows:

$$\underbrace{\boxed{\clubsuit}\,\boxed{\heartsuit}\,\boxed{\clubsuit}\,\boxed{\heartsuit}\,\cdots\,\boxed{\clubsuit}\,\boxed{\heartsuit}}_{2^i \text{ pairs}}.$$

   (b) Turn these helping cards as follows:

$$\boxed{\clubsuit}\,\boxed{\heartsuit}\,\boxed{\clubsuit}\,\boxed{\heartsuit}\,\cdots\,\boxed{\clubsuit}\,\boxed{\heartsuit} \rightarrow \boxed{?}\,\boxed{?}\,\boxed{?}\,\boxed{?}\,\cdots\,\boxed{?}\,\boxed{?}.$$

   (c) Apply a random cut:

$$\left\langle \boxed{?}\,\boxed{?}\,\boxed{?}\,\boxed{?}\,\cdots\,\boxed{?}\,\boxed{?} \right\rangle \rightarrow \underset{r_i}{\boxed{?}}\underset{\bar{r}_i}{\boxed{?}}\underset{r_i}{\boxed{?}}\underset{\bar{r}_i}{\boxed{?}}\,\cdots\,\underset{r_i}{\boxed{?}}\underset{\bar{r}_i}{\boxed{?}}.$$

Table 2. Correctness of Our AND Protocol

x	r	(a_0, a_1)	h	output
0	0	$(0, y)$	even	$(?/a_0, ?/r, \ldots, ?/r) - (?/0, ?/0, \ldots, ?/0)$
0	1	$(y, 0)$	odd	$(?/a_1, ?/\overline{r}, \ldots, ?/\overline{r}) = (?/0, ?/0, \ldots, ?/0)$
1	0	$(0, y)$	odd	$(?/a_1, ?/\overline{r}, \ldots, ?/\overline{r}) = (?/y, ?/1, \ldots, ?/1)$
1	1	$(y, 0)$	even	$(?/a_0, ?/r, \ldots, ?/r) = (?/y, ?/1, \ldots, ?/1)$

5. Arrange the cards as follows:

$$\boxed{?}\boxed{?}\ \boxed{?}\boxed{?}\ \boxed{?}\boxed{?}\boxed{?}\boxed{?}\ \cdots\ \boxed{?}\boxed{?}\ \cdots\ \boxed{?},$$

$\underset{x}{}\ \underset{r}{}\ \underset{r_1\ r_1}{\underbrace{}}\ \underset{r_2\ r_2\ r_2\ r_2}{\underbrace{}}\quad \underset{r_s\ r_s}{}\quad \underset{r_s}{}$

$\underset{2\ \text{cards}}{\underbrace{}}\quad \underset{2^2\ \text{cards}}{\underbrace{}}\quad \underset{2^s\ \text{cards}}{\underbrace{}}$

where the number of r_i is 2^i.

6. Apply a complete shuffle to the sequence:

$$\left[\boxed{?}\boxed{?}\cdots\boxed{?}\right]\ \rightarrow\ \boxed{?}\boxed{?}\cdots\boxed{?}.$$

7. Open the cards that appear in Step 6. Let h be the number of $\heartsuit$ in the sequence. If h is even, the protocol outputs a commitment to a_0 and k commitments to r. Otherwise, it outputs a commitment to a_1 and k commitments to $\overline{r}$.

$$\boxed{\clubsuit}\boxed{\heartsuit}\boxed{\heartsuit}\cdots\boxed{\clubsuit}\ \rightarrow\ \begin{cases} (?/a_0, ?/r, ?/r, \ldots, ?/r) & \text{if } h \text{ is even;} \\ (?/a_1, ?/\overline{r}, ?/\overline{r}, \ldots, ?/\overline{r}) & \text{otherwise.} \end{cases}$$

If $h = 0$ (resp. 2^s), the input bit x is leaked and determined to be 0 (resp. 1). Otherwise, the protocol does not leak any information about the inputs. The failure probability of the protocol is 2^{s+1}, which is the probability that all of $(r, r_1, \ldots, r_s)$ coincide with x.

4.2 Correctness

Table 2 shows the correctness of our AND protocol. In Step 3, we have $(a_0, a_1) = (0, y)$ if $r = 0$ and $(y, 0)$ if $r = 1$. Since the number of r_i is even for each i in Step 5, h is even if $x = r$ and odd otherwise. Thus, the protocol outputs $(?/0, ?/0, \ldots, ?/0)$ if $x = 0$ and $(?/y, ?/1, \ldots, ?/1)$ otherwise, both of which are $(?/(x \wedge y), ?/x, \ldots, ?/x)$. This shows the correctness of the protocol.

4.3 Security

We can observe that r and r_i $(1 \le i \le s)$ are chosen uniformly and independently at random since each bit is generated by a random cut independently. If $x = 0$, h ranges from 0 to $2^{s+1} - 1$ each with probability $1/2^{s+1}$. Similarly, if $x = 1$, h ranges from 1 to 2^{s+1} each with probability $1/2^{s+1}$. Thus, in the range $1 \le h \le 2^s - 1$, the probability distribution of h is independent of the probability distribution of the input x. This shows the security of the protocol.

4.4 Efficiency

The total number of cards used in the protocol is $2k+5+2\sum_{i=1}^{s} 2^i = 2k+2^{s+2}+1$. The number of shuffles in the protocol is $s+2$ consisting of one random bisection cut, s random cuts, and one complete shuffle.

5 Our XOR Protocol

In this section, we construct an XOR protocol with single-card encoding. Our XOR protocol takes n commitments to $x_1, x_2, \ldots, x_n \in \{0,1\}$ and outputs k copies of the commitment to $x_1 \oplus x_2 \oplus \cdots \oplus x_n$. The protocol with failure probability $p_n/2^{s+1}$ for $p_n := \sum_{i=0}^{n-1} {}_{s+1}C_i$ is given as follows:

where $z = x_1 \oplus x_2 \oplus \cdots \oplus x_n$. When $k = 1$, the protocol outputs a commitment to z, i.e., the standard XOR protocol.

5.1 Protocol Description

1. Arrange k pairs of ♣♡ as follows:

   k pairs

2. Turn these cards as follows:

3. Apply a random cut:

4. For each $i = 1, \ldots, s$, do the following:
   (a) Arrange 2^i pairs of ♣♡ as follows:

   2^i pairs

   (b) Turn these helping cards as follows:

(c) Apply a random cut:

$$\left\langle \boxed{?}\boxed{?}\boxed{?}\boxed{?} \cdots \boxed{?}\boxed{?} \right\rangle \;\to\; \underset{r_i\ \ \overline{r_i}\ \ r_i\ \ \overline{r_i}}{\boxed{?}\boxed{?}\boxed{?}\boxed{?}} \cdots \underset{r_i\ \ \overline{r_i}}{\boxed{?}\boxed{?}}.$$

5. Arrange the cards as follows:

$$\underset{x_1\ x_2}{\boxed{?}\boxed{?}} \cdots \underset{x_n\quad r}{\boxed{?}\boxed{?}} \underset{r_1\ r_1}{\boxed{?}\boxed{?}} \underset{r_2\ r_2\ r_2\ r_2}{\boxed{?}\boxed{?}\boxed{?}\boxed{?}} \cdots \underset{r_s\ r_s}{\boxed{?}\boxed{?}} \cdots \underset{r_s}{\boxed{?}},$$

$$\underbrace{}_{2\ \text{cards}} \quad \underbrace{}_{2^2\ \text{cards}} \quad \underbrace{}_{2^s\ \text{cards}}$$

where the number of r_i is 2^i.

6. Apply a complete shuffle to the sequence:

$$\left[\boxed{?}\boxed{?} \cdots \boxed{?} \right] \;\to\; \boxed{?}\boxed{?} \cdots \boxed{?}.$$

7. Open the cards that appear in Step 6. Let h be the number of $\heartsuit$ in the sequence. The protocol outputs $(?/r, ?/r, \ldots, ?/r)$ if h is even and $(?/\overline{r}, ?/\overline{r}, \ldots, ?/\overline{r})$ otherwise.

$$\boxed{\clubsuit}\boxed{\heartsuit} \cdots \boxed{\clubsuit} \;\to\; \begin{cases} (?/r, ?/r, \ldots, ?/r) & \text{if } h \text{ is even};\\ (?/\overline{r}, ?/\overline{r}, \ldots, ?/\overline{r}) & \text{otherwise}. \end{cases}$$

If $h \le n - 1$ (resp. $h \ge 2^{s+1}$), the number of $x_i = 0$ (resp. $x_i = 1$) for $1 \le i \le n$ is at most $n - 1$, which leaks some nontrivial information about the inputs. Otherwise, the protocol does not leak any information about the inputs. Thus, the failure probability of the protocol is at most $p_n/2^{s+1}$ for $p_n = \sum_{i=0}^{n-1} {}_{s+1}C_i$, which is the probability that $r + r_1 + \cdots + r_s \le n - 1$ when $x_1 = x_2 = \cdots = x_n = 0$. For example, we have $p_2/2^{s+1} = (s+2)/2^{s+1}$ since the probability that $r + r_1 + \cdots + r_s = 0$ is $1/2^{s+1}$ and the probability that $r + r_1 + \cdots + r_s = 1$ is $(s+1)/2^{s+1}$.

5.2   Correctness

Since the number of r_i is 2^i in Step 5, they do not affect the parity of h in Step 7. Thus, we have $x_1 \oplus x_2 \oplus \cdots \oplus x_n = r$ if h is even and $x_1 \oplus x_2 \oplus \cdots \oplus x_n \ne r$ otherwise. This shows the correctness of the protocol.

5.3   Security

We can observe that r and r_i $(1 \le i \le s)$ are chosen uniformly and independently at random since each bit is generated by a random cut independently. For $\ell :=$ $x_1 + x_2 + \cdots + x_n \in \{0, 1, \ldots, n\}$, the value h ranges from ℓ to $\ell + 2^{s+1} - 1$ each with probability $1/2^{s+1}$. Thus, in the range $n \le h \le 2^s - 1$, the probability distribution of h is independent of the probability distribution of the input x. This shows the security of the protocol.

5.4   Efficiency

The total number of cards used in the protocol is $n + 2k + 2\sum_{i=1}^{s} 2^i = n + 2k + 2^{s+2} - 4$. The number of shuffles in the protocol is $s + 2$ consisting of $s + 1$ random cuts and one complete shuffle.

6   Conclusion

In this paper, we design card-based protocols with single-card encoding. First, we show that any function can be computed based on the Niemi–Renvall's COPY protocol. Second, we propose AND and XOR protocols, both of which have a lower failure probability compared to the general protocol.

Research on single-card encoding has just begun, and there are many unsolved problems. Is it possible to improve the efficiency (i.e., the number of cards and shuffles) of Niemi–Renvall's COPY protocol? Is there any way to compute any function $f : \{0,1\}^n \rightarrow \{0,1\}$ more efficiently than the general protocol in Sect. 3 based on Niemi–Renvall's COPY protocol? Is it possible to improve the efficiency of our AND and XOR protocols? Are there other functions that can be efficiently computable? Is it possible to construct a protocol for a function on k-valued inputs using a single-card encoding of a k-colored deck? Here, a k-colored deck is a deck having k types of cards and a single-card encoding of the deck maps a value $i \in \{1, 2, \ldots, k\}$ to the i-th type of card.

Acknowledgment. This work was supported in part by JSPS KAKENHI Grant Numbers 21K17702 and 23H00479, and JST CREST Grant Number MJCR22M1.

References

1. Crépeau, C., Kilian, J.: Discreet solitary games. In: Stinson, D.R. (ed.) CRYPTO 1993. LNCS, vol. 773, pp. 319–330. Springer, Berlin, Heidelberg (1994). https://doi.org/10.1007/3-540-48329-2_27
2. den Boer, B.: More efficient match-making and satisfiability the five card trick. In: Quisquater, J.-J., Vandewalle, J. (eds.) EUROCRYPT 1989. LNCS, vol. 434, pp. 208–217. Springer, Heidelberg (1990). https://doi.org/10.1007/3-540-46885-4_23
3. Mizuki, T.: Card-based protocols for securely computing the conjunction of multiple variables. Theor. Comput. Sci. **622**(C), 34–44 (2016)
4. Mizuki, T., Shizuya, H.: A formalization of card-based cryptographic protocols via abstract machine. Int. J. Inf. Secur. **13**(1), 15–23 (2014)
5. Mizuki, T., Sone, H.: Six-card secure AND and four-card secure XOR. In: Deng, X., Hopcroft, J.E., Xue, J. (eds.) FAW 2009. LNCS, vol. 5598, pp. 358–369. Springer, Heidelberg (2009). https://doi.org/10.1007/978-3-642-02270-8_36
6. Niemi, V., Renvall, A.: Secure multiparty computations without computers. Theor. Comput. Sci. **191**(1–2), 173–183 (1998)
7. Nishida, T., Hayashi, Y., Mizuki, T., Sone, H.: Card-based protocols for any Boolean function. In: Jain, R., Jain, S., Stephan, F. (eds.) TAMC 2015. LNCS, vol. 9076, pp. 110–121. Springer, Cham (2015). https://doi.org/10.1007/978-3-319-17142-5_11

8. Nuida, K.: Efficient card-based Millionaires' protocols via non-binary input encoding. In: Shikata, J., Kuzuno, H. (eds.) IWSEC 2023. LNCS, vol. 14128, pp. 237–254. Springer, Cham (2023). https://doi.org/10.1007/978-3-031-41326-1_13

9. Ono, T., Shinagawa, K., Nakai, T., Watanabe, Y., Iwamoto, M.: Single-shuffle card-based protocols with six cards per gate. In: Seo, H., Kim, S. (eds.) ICISC 2023. LNCS, vol. 14562, pp. 157–169. Springer, Singapore (2024). https://doi.org/10.1007/978-981-97-1238-0_9

10. Shinagawa, K., Mizuki, T.: Secure computation of any Boolean function based on any deck of cards. In: Chen, Y., Deng, X., Lu, M. (eds.) FAW 2019. LNCS, vol. 11458, pp. 63–75. Springer, Cham (2019). https://doi.org/10.1007/978-3-030-18126-0_6

11. Shinagawa, K., Nuida, K.: A single shuffle is enough for secure card-based computation of any Boolean circuit. Discret. Appl. Math. **289**, 248–261 (2021)

Graphs and Games

Winning Strategy Templates for Stochastic Parity Games Towards Permissive and Resilient Control

Kittiphon Phalakarn[1]([⊠]), Sasinee Pruekprasert[2], and Ichiro Hasuo[1,3]

[1] National Institute of Informatics, Tokyo, Japan
{kphalakarn,hasuo}@nii.ac.jp
[2] National Institute of Advanced Industrial Science and Technology, Tokyo, Japan
s.pruekprasert@aist.go.jp
[3] The Graduate University for Advanced Studies (SOKENDAI), Kanagawa, Japan

Abstract. *Stochastic games* play an important role for many purposes such as the control of cyber-physical systems (CPS), where the controller and the environment are modeled as players. Conventional algorithms typically solve the game for a single *winning strategy* in order to develop a controller. However, in applications such as CPS control, permissive controllers are crucial as they allow the controlled system to adapt if additional constraints need to be imposed and also remain resilient to system changes at runtime. In this work, we generalize the concept of *permissive winning strategy templates*, introduced by Anand et al. at TACAS and CAV 2023 for deterministic games, to encompass stochastic games. These templates represent an infinite number of winning strategies and can adapt strategies to system changes efficiently. We focus on five key winning objectives—safety, reachability, Büchi, co-Büchi, and parity—and present algorithms to construct templates for each objective. In addition, we propose a novel method to extract a winning strategy from a template and provide discussions on template comparison.

Keywords: stochastic game · parity game · strategy template · game-based control · permissive controller · resiliency

1 Introduction

Games on graphs play a crucial role in the control fields and cyber-physical system (CPS) design [22], offering a powerful framework for analyzing and designing systems that interact with their environments dynamically. Within this framework, game-based controllers leverage principles from game theory to effectively manage interactions between systems and their environments. Particularly, control problems are modeled as two-player games between the controller and the environment. While the controller player aims to influence the system's behavior to achieve desired objectives, the environment player introduces uncertainties and external influences that challenge the controller's decisions.

© The Author(s), under exclusive license to Springer Nature Switzerland AG 2025
C. Anutariya and M. M. Bonsangue (Eds.): ICTAC 2024, LNCS 15373, pp. 197–214, 2025.
https://doi.org/10.1007/978-3-031-77019-7_12

Stochastic games expand upon the traditional two-player game model by incorporating probabilistic transitions to represent uncertainty about system process evolution. Conceptually termed as "2.5"-player games, stochastic games feature two main players and an additional player, often referred to as the "0.5" player, which represents the stochastic or random nature of the environment. In these games, players must design strategies that account for both the strategies of their opponents and the probabilistic transitions. Stochastic games find applications across various fields including theoretical computer science, especially in the analysis of probabilistic systems and programs.

1.1   Related Works

Conventional algorithms for solving games traditionally focus on finding a single winning strategy for each player without explicitly considering the strategy's *permissiveness*. However, permissive controllers are crucial for practical applications. The concept of permissiveness in control theory, particularly in supervisory control, was formally introduced in 1987 by Ramadge and Wonham in their influential work [18], and is often referred to as the classical notion of permissiveness. In their work, a controller is considered more permissive (or less restrictive) than the other if it allows all behaviors permitted by the latter without disabling any additional system behaviors. This notion of permissiveness offers flexibility by allowing the system to adapt its behavior if additional constraints are needed or operational conditions change unpredictably during runtime.

Consequently, the classical notion of permissiveness has inspired the development of several related concepts of permissive controllers, e.g., penalizing the controller based on the disable costs of each control action [14,20], and maximally permissive controllers that are limited by the number of allowable losing loops for the controller player [17]. Moreover, the concept of permissiveness is fundamental in resilient control and is crucial for addressing the uncertainties encountered in applications across various domains, including flexible manufacturing systems [10,19], warehouse automation [21], and resilient control against potential attacks in CPS [15].

In the context of games, the classical notion of permissiveness was studied in parity games in [5]. They showed that a maximally permissive strategy exists if we consider only memoryless strategies and provide an algorithm to find such a strategy. Another notion of permissive strategies was considered for Muller games in [16], wherein a maximally permissive strategy is restricted to winning strategies that permit visiting losing loops at most twice. In [6,7], quantitative measures for permissiveness are defined based on weight of transitions disabled by the strategies. In [13], a related concept called *weakest* strategies are studied for safety games with imperfect information. Using this concept, the authors also developed a compositional control synthesis method for the weakest safety controllers under partial observation in [12]. Another related concept called a *most general* strategy is proposed for the compositional construction of controllers in [11]. The work introduced *decision function templates*, which specifies all the legal control choices for a given observable history. Then, a most general

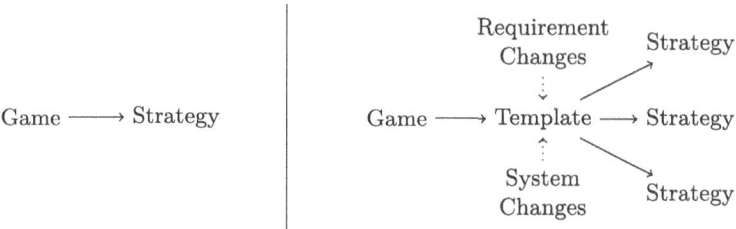

Fig. 1. Left: A conventional winning strategy construction, giving one strategy. Right: An overview of a winning strategy construction utilizing a strategy template, allowing strategy adaptation for requirement and system changes.

controller is constructed using the templates and a suitable fairness condition, choosing the legal choices in a fair way.

Recently, Anand et al. introduced a new concept of strategy templates in [1] and [2], which is more compositional than that of previous works. The former work [1] introduced the concept of *adequately permissive assumptions* on the other player, representing other distributed components. An assumption, given by a set of linear temporal logic (LTL) formulae defined on vertices and edges, is *adequately permissive* if it permits all feasible cooperative system behaviors to achieve the desired objective. These formulae were later developed into *permissive winning strategy templates* for deterministic zero-sum games in [2]. Their experimental results showcase two applications of the proposed strategy templates. Firstly, when additional objectives arrive after a winning strategy has been computed, strategy templates can construct an adapted winning strategy faster than reconstructing from scratch. Furthermore, their templates support fault-tolerance control as a new strategy can be produced when some actions are disabled by system faults at run-time. To summarize, templates take into account both requirement changes and system changes.

1.2   Contributions

To our best knowledge, no permissive winning strategy templates have been proposed for stochastic games. In this work, we expand the concept of strategy templates from previous works, illustrated in Fig. 1, to encompass stochastic games. Our contributions are listed as follows.

1. We present algorithms to construct winning strategy templates for five key winning objectives of stochastic games by incorporating set operations of [4] and gadgets of [9]. The correctness proofs are provided. (Sect. 4)
2. We propose a novel procedure to extract strategies from templates which balances between the winning objective and the permissiveness. (Sect. 5)
3. We discuss on *sizes* of templates and some potential applications of small templates. (Sect. 6)

In addition, we redefine the concept of strategy templates and their permissiveness using sets of edges, LTL formulae, and formal languages. (Sect. 3)

2   Preliminaries

2.1   Linear Temporal Logic

We briefly review *linear temporal logic (LTL)*, which is later used to define winning objectives. We invite interested readers to see [3] for a formal definition.

Definition 1 (Linear Temporal Logic Formula). *LTL formulae over the set AP of atomic propositions are formed by the following grammar, where $a \in AP$.*

$$\varphi ::= \text{true} \mid a \mid \varphi_1 \wedge \varphi_2 \mid \neg\varphi \mid X\varphi \mid \varphi_1 \cup \varphi_2$$

For simplicity, we define the semantics of an LTL formula over an infinite sequence $\bar{v} = v_0 v_1 \ldots \in AP^\omega$ of atomic propositions inductively as follows.

$\bar{v} \vDash \text{true}.$

$\bar{v} \vDash a$ if $v_0 = a$, for $a \in AP$.

$\bar{v} \vDash \varphi_1 \wedge \varphi_2$ if $\bar{v} \vDash \varphi_1$ and $\bar{v} \vDash \varphi_2$.

$\bar{v} \vDash \neg\varphi$ if $\bar{v} \vDash \varphi$ does not hold.

$\bar{v} \vDash X\varphi$ if $v_1 v_2 \ldots \vDash \varphi$.

$\bar{v} \vDash \varphi_1 \cup \varphi_2$ if $\exists i \geq 0, v_i v_{i+1} \ldots \vDash \varphi_2 \wedge (\forall j < i, v_j v_{j+1} \ldots \vDash \varphi_1)$.

We say that $\bar{v}$ *satisfies* an LTL formula φ if $\bar{v} \vDash \varphi$. Given $X \subseteq AP$, we write $\bar{v} \vDash X$ to denote $\bar{v} \vDash \bigvee_{x \in X} x$ for notational convenience. Also, the temporal modalities *eventually* and *always* are defined by $F\varphi := \text{true}\cup\varphi$ and $G\varphi := \neg F(\neg\varphi)$.

2.2   Stochastic Games

The following definition is adapted from [9].

Definition 2 (Stochastic Game). *A stochastic game (SG) is denoted by $G = (V, E, (V_\square, V_\bigcirc, V_\triangle))$ where (V, E) is a finite directed graph and $(V_\square, V_\bigcirc, V_\triangle)$ is a partition of V.*

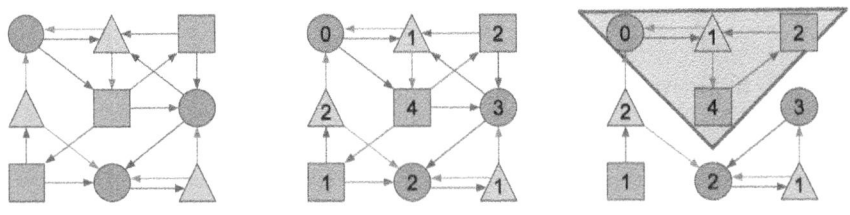

Fig. 2. Left: An example of a stochastic game. Middle: The same stochastic game with a priority function. Right: An example of strategies for players Even and Odd, and the winning set of player Even for the parity objective (shown as the bold border region).

The game consists of three players: Even ($\square$), Odd ($\bigcirc$), and Random ($\triangle$). They take turns moving a token from vertex to vertex, forming a path. At a vertex in $V_\square$ (resp. $V_\bigcirc$), player Even (resp. Odd) moves the token to one of its successors. When the token is at a vertex in $V_\triangle$, player Random moves the token to one of its successors uniformly at random. We assume that there always exists at least one out-going edge at each vertex, implying that any path in the game can always be extended to an infinite path. An example of a stochastic game is illustrated in Fig. 2. Let $\mathcal{D}(V)$ denote the set of probability distributions on V. *Strategies* for players Even and Odd are defined as follows.

Definition 3 (Strategy). *A strategy for player Even is* $\sigma_\square : V^* \times V_\square \to \mathcal{D}(V)$ *describing its next move. A strategy for player Odd is* $\sigma_\bigcirc : V^* \times V_\bigcirc \to \mathcal{D}(V)$.

Intuitively, a strategy assigns the probability for a player to move to a successor vertex based on the path of previously visited vertices. Given a measurable set of infinite paths $P \subseteq V^\omega$, an initial vertex v_0, and a pair $(\sigma_\square, \sigma_\bigcirc)$ of strategies, the probability that an infinite path generated under $(\sigma_\square, \sigma_\bigcirc)$ belongs to P is uniquely defined. We write $\Pr_{v_0}^{\sigma_\square, \sigma_\bigcirc}[P]$ for the probability that a path belongs to P if the game starts at v_0 and the players' strategies are $\sigma_\square$ and $\sigma_\bigcirc$.

We specify *winning objectives* of the game using LTL formulae where atomic propositions are vertices (i.e., the set AP in Definition 1 is V). For notational convenience, we write $\Pr_{v_0}^{\sigma_\square, \sigma_\bigcirc}[\varphi]$ for $\Pr_{v_0}^{\sigma_\square, \sigma_\bigcirc}[P_\varphi]$ where $P_\varphi = \{\bar{v} \in V^\omega : \bar{v} \models \varphi\}$. Given $X \subseteq V$, we focus on five key winning objectives: *safety* $\mathsf{G}\, X$ means a path always stays in X, *reachability* $\mathsf{F}\, X$ means a path eventually reaches X, *Büchi* $\mathsf{GF}\, X$ means a path visits X infinitely often, *co-Büchi* $\mathsf{FG}\, X$ means a path eventually stays in X, and *parity*. For a parity objective, we are given a *priority function* $p : V \to \{0, \dots, d\}$ for some $d \in \mathbb{N}$. Let $V_i := \{v \in V : p(v) = i\}$. Then, the parity objective is $\bigwedge_{i \in \{1,3,\dots,2\cdot\lceil d/2 \rceil - 1\}} \left(\mathsf{GF}\, V_i \implies \bigvee_{j \in \{0,2,\dots,i-1\}} \mathsf{GF}\, V_j \right)$. In other words, an infinite path satisfies a parity objective if the minimum priority seen infinitely often along the path is even. Figure 2(middle) shows an instance of a stochastic game with a parity objective, where the priority of each vertex is written inside that vertex.

Consider a winning objective φ, we say that a strategy $\sigma_\square$ of player Even is *almost-sure winning* from v_0 if for all strategies $\sigma_\bigcirc$ of player Odd, we have $\Pr_{v_0}^{\sigma_\square, \sigma_\bigcirc}[\varphi] = 1$. Let $W_\square \subseteq V$, called the *winning set*, be the set of vertices from which there exists an almost-sure winning strategy for player Even. Then, we are interested in the following problem.

Definition 4 (Winning Strategy Computation). *Given an SG G and a winning objective φ, the* winning strategy computation problem *is to compute a strategy $\sigma_\square$ of player Even such that it is almost-sure winning from all $v \in W_\square$.*

Figure 2(right) provides an example of the set $W_\square$ for the parity objective and an almost-sure winning strategy $\sigma_\square$ of player Even. We note that, under the strategy $\sigma_\square$, an infinite path starting from any $v \in W_\square$ visits the vertex with priority 0 infinitely often with probability 1.

2.3   Set Operators

Using μ-calculus, $\mu Y.f(Y)$ and $\nu Y.f(Y)$ denote the least and greatest fixed points of a function $f : 2^V \rightarrow 2^V$. They can be computed via Kleene's fixed point theorem. For $X \subseteq V$, we define the following set operators.

- $\text{PRE}(X) := \{u \in V : \forall v \in V, (u,v) \in E \implies v \in X\}$
- $\text{PRE}_\square(X) := \{u \in V_\square : \exists v \in V, (u,v) \in E \wedge v \in X\}$
- $\text{PRE}_\bigcirc(X) := \{u \in V_\bigcirc : \exists v \in V, (u,v) \in E \wedge v \in X\}$
- $\text{ATTR}(X) := \mu Y.(X \cup \text{PRE}(Y))$
- $\text{ATTR}_\square(X) := \mu Y.(X \cup \text{PRE}(Y) \cup \text{PRE}_\square(Y))$
- $\text{ATTR}_\bigcirc(X) := \mu Y.(X \cup \text{PRE}(Y) \cup \text{PRE}_\bigcirc(Y))$

In brief, $\text{PRE}(X)$ contains vertices that must reach X in one step, and $\text{PRE}_\square(X)$ (resp. $\text{PRE}_\bigcirc(X)$) contains player Even's (resp. player Odd's) vertices that can reach X in one step. The ATTR operators are defined similarly but for reaching X in finitely many steps. Additionally, we define more set operators inspired by Banerjee et al. [4], where $X, X' \subseteq V$.

- $\text{PRE}_\triangle(X', X) := \{u \in V_\triangle : (\forall v \in V, (u,v) \in E \implies v \in X') \wedge (\exists v \in V, (u,v) \in E \wedge v \in X)\}$
- $\text{ATTR}'(X) := \nu Z.\mu Y(X \cup \text{PRE}(Y) \cup \text{PRE}_\triangle(Z,Y))$
- $\text{ATTR}'_\square(X) := \nu Z.\mu Y(X \cup \text{PRE}_\square(Y) \cup \text{PRE}(Y) \cup \text{PRE}_\triangle(Z,Y))$

The set $\text{PRE}_\triangle(X', X)$ consists of player Random's vertices whose all edges lead to X' and some edges lead to X. The operators ATTR' and $\text{ATTR}'_\square$ are defined analogously to ATTR and $\text{ATTR}_\square$, respectively, accounting for player Random's vertices. With these set operators, we state below the result from [4].

Theorem 1 ([4, Thm. 3–4]). *Given an SG $G = (V, E, (V_\square, V_\bigcirc, V_\triangle))$ and $X \subseteq V$. The set $\text{ATTR}'_\square(X)$ is the winning set of player Even for* F X. *Furthermore, the set $\nu Z.\mu Y((X \cap \text{PRE}_\square(Z) \cap \text{PRE}(Z)) \cup \text{PRE}_\square(Y) \cup \text{PRE}(Y) \cup \text{PRE}_\triangle(Z,Y))$ is the winning set of player Even for* GF X.

2.4   Solving Stochastic Parity Games

Stochastic parity games can be solved by first reducing them into deterministic parity games (i.e., no player Random) and then using existing techniques for deterministic parity games to solve them.

   The reduction from stochastic parity games to deterministic parity games was proposed by Chatterjee et al. [9]. Briefly, the reduction, described in Algorithm 1, replaces vertices of player Random by *gadgets*, which are vertices arranged in three layers (Fig. 3). It was proved that if player Even wins at a vertex in the (reduced) deterministic parity game, then player Even almost-sure wins at the corresponding vertex in the stochastic parity game.

Lemma 1 ([9, Lem. 3]). *Let $G' = \text{REDUCE}(G, p)$. For every vertex v in G, if player Even has a winning strategy from v' in G', then player Even has an almost-sure winning strategy from v.*

Algorithm 1: Reducing stochastic to deterministic parity games [9].

1 REDUCE($G = (V, E, (V_\square, V_\bigcirc, V_\triangle)), p : V \rightarrow \{0, \ldots, d\}$)
2    $V'_\square \leftarrow \emptyset; V'_\bigcirc \leftarrow \emptyset; E' \leftarrow \emptyset$
3   **foreach** $v \in V_\square$ **do** $V'_\square \leftarrow V'_\square \cup \{v'\}; p'(v') \leftarrow p(v)$
4   **foreach** $v \in V_\bigcirc$ **do** $V'_\bigcirc \leftarrow V'_\bigcirc \cup \{v'\}; p'(v') \leftarrow p(v)$
5   **foreach** $v \in V_\triangle$ **do**
6      $V'_\bigcirc \leftarrow V'_\bigcirc \cup \{v'\}; p'(v') \leftarrow p(v)$
7   **for** $i \in \{0, \ldots, \lceil p(v)/2 \rceil\}$ **do**
8        $V'_\square \leftarrow V'_\square \cup \{v'_i\}; p'(v'_i) \leftarrow p(v); E' \leftarrow E' \cup \{(v', v'_i)\}$
9   **for** $j \in \{0, \ldots, p(v)\}$ **do**
10   **if** j is even **then** $V'_\bigcirc \leftarrow V'_\bigcirc \cup \{v'_{\lceil j/2 \rceil, j}\}$ **else** $V'_\square \leftarrow V'_\square \cup \{v'_{\lceil j/2 \rceil, j}\}$
11       $p'(v'_{\lceil j/2 \rceil, j}) \leftarrow j; E' \leftarrow E' \cup \{(v'_{\lceil j/2 \rceil}, v'_{\lceil j/2 \rceil, j})\}$
12   **foreach** $(u, v) \in E$ **do**
13   **if** $u \in V_\triangle$ **then** **for** $j \in \{0, \ldots, p(u)\}$ **do** $E' \leftarrow E' \cup \{(u'_{\lceil j/2 \rceil, j}, v')\}$
14   **else** $E' \leftarrow E' \cup \{(u', v')\}$
15   **return** $(G' = (V' = V'_\square \cup V'_\bigcirc, E', (V'_\square, V'_\bigcirc, \emptyset)), p')$

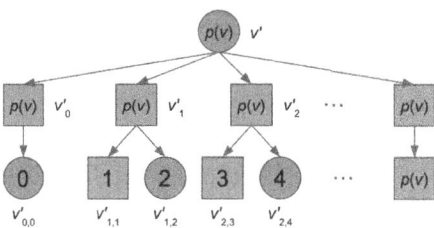

Fig. 3. Gadget of [9] for reducing stochastic parity games to deterministic parity games.

To solve deterministic parity games, various algorithms can be used [8,23]. In this work, we mainly consider the recursive algorithm by Zielonka [23] shown in Algorithm 2. The algorithm returns $(W_\square, W_\bigcirc)$ where $W_\square$ (resp. $W_\bigcirc$) is the set of vertices from which there exists a winning strategy for player Even (resp. Odd). For $G = (V, E, (V_\square, V_\bigcirc, V_\triangle))$ and $X \subseteq V$, we use $G \setminus X$ as a shorthand for a game $(V \setminus X, E \setminus (X \times V \cup V \times X), (V_\square \setminus X, V_\bigcirc \setminus X, V_\triangle \setminus X))$.

3   Winning Strategy Templates and Permissiveness

The concept of *strategy templates* considered in this work was introduced in [1,2]. In this section, we redefine *strategy templates* and their *permissiveness* for our setting of stochastic games.

Definition 5 (Strategy Template). *Given an SG* $G = (V, E, (V_\square, V_\bigcirc, V_\triangle))$ *and let* $E_\square := E \cap (V_\square \times V)$, *a strategy template is* $T = (P, \boldsymbol{L}, C)$ *where* $P \subseteq E_\square$ *is a set of prohibited edges,* $\boldsymbol{L} \subseteq 2^{E_\square}$ *is a set of live-groups, and* $C \subseteq E_\square$ *is a set of co-live edges.*

Algorithm 2: Solving deterministic parity games [23].

1 $\text{SOLVE}(G = (V, E, (V_\square, V_\bigcirc, \emptyset)), p : V \to \{0, \dots, d\})$
2   **if** $V = \emptyset$ **then return** $(W_\square, W_\bigcirc) = (\emptyset, \emptyset)$
3     $x \leftarrow \min\{p(v) : v \in V\}; X \leftarrow \arg\min\{p(v) : v \in V\}$
4   **if** x is even **then**
5        $A \leftarrow \text{ATTR}_\square(X)$
6        $(W_\square', W_\bigcirc') \leftarrow \text{SOLVE}(G \setminus A, p)$
7   **if** $W_\bigcirc' = \emptyset$ **then return** $(W_\square, W_\bigcirc) = (V, \emptyset)$
8        $B \leftarrow \text{ATTR}_\bigcirc(W_\bigcirc')$
9        $(W_\square'', W_\bigcirc'') \leftarrow \text{SOLVE}(G \setminus B, p)$
10   **return** $(W_\square, W_\bigcirc) = (W_\square'', W_\bigcirc'' \cup B)$
11   **else**
12       $A \leftarrow \text{ATTR}_\bigcirc(X)$
13       $(W_\square', W_\bigcirc') \leftarrow \text{SOLVE}(G \setminus A, p)$
14   **if** $W_\square' = \emptyset$ **then return** $(W_\square, W_\bigcirc) = (\emptyset, V)$
15       $B \leftarrow \text{ATTR}_\square(W_\square')$
16       $(W_\square'', W_\bigcirc'') \leftarrow \text{SOLVE}(G \setminus B, p)$
17   **return** $(W_\square, W_\bigcirc) = (W_\square'' \cup B, W_\bigcirc'')$

Definition 6 (LTL Formula induced from Template). *Given a strategy template $T = (P, \boldsymbol{L}, C)$, we define four LTL formulae induced from T as follows.*

- $\psi_P := \bigwedge_{(u,v) \in P} \mathsf{G}(u \implies \neg\mathsf{X}\, v)$,
- $\psi_L := \bigwedge_{L \in \boldsymbol{L}} \left(\left(\bigvee_{(u,v) \in L} \mathsf{GF}\, u \right) \implies \left(\bigvee_{(u,v) \in L} \mathsf{GF}(u \wedge \mathsf{X}\, v) \right) \right)$,
- $\psi_C := \bigwedge_{(u,v) \in C} \mathsf{FG}(u \implies \neg\mathsf{X}\, v)$,
- $\psi_T := \psi_P \wedge \psi_L \wedge \psi_C$.

In brief, a strategy template $T = (P, \boldsymbol{L}, C)$ describes a set of infinite paths with certain properties. Namely, infinite paths satisfying ψ_P do not use edges in P; those satisfying ψ_L have a property that: for each $L \in \boldsymbol{L}$, if there is a vertex u such that $(u, v) \in L$ and u is visited infinitely often, then an edge in L is used infinitely often; and those satisfying ψ_C use edges in C only finitely often.

To define *winning strategy templates* and the *permissiveness* of strategy templates, we first introduce the definition of the *language generated by an LTL formula* as follows.

Definition 7 (Language generated by LTL Formula). *Given an SG G, $X \subseteq V$, and an LTL formula ψ, the* language generated from X by ψ *is $\mathcal{L}_X(\psi) = \{\bar{v} \in X \times V^\omega : \bar{v} \models \psi\}$.*

Given a winning objective φ, we now state the definitions of *winning strategy templates* and *permissiveness*. Recall that $W_\square \subseteq V$ denotes the winning set of player Even for the winning objective φ.

Definition 8 (Winning Strategy Template). *Given an SG G and a winning objective φ, a strategy template $T = (P, \boldsymbol{L}, C)$ is* winning *for φ if $\mathcal{L}_{W_\square}(\psi_T) \subseteq \mathcal{L}_{W_\square}(\varphi)$.*

Definition 9 (Permissiveness of Strategy Template). *Given an SG G, a winning objective φ, and two strategy templates $T = (P, \boldsymbol{L}, C)$, $T' = (P', \boldsymbol{L}', C')$, we say that T is no more permissive than T' if $\mathcal{L}_{W_\square}(\psi_T) \subseteq \mathcal{L}_{W_\square}(\psi_{T'})$.*

From definitions above, we prove two propositions shown below.

Proposition 1. *Given an SG G, a winning objective φ, and two LTL formulae ψ and ψ', if $\mathcal{L}_{W_\square}(\psi) \subseteq \mathcal{L}_{W_\square}(\psi')$, then $\Pr_{v_0}^{\sigma_\square, \sigma_\bigcirc}[\psi] = 1 \implies \Pr_{v_0}^{\sigma_\square, \sigma_\bigcirc}[\psi'] = 1$, for any $v_0 \in W_\square$ and any pair of strategies $(\sigma_\square, \sigma_\bigcirc)$.*

Proof. We suppose $\mathcal{L}_{W_\square}(\psi) \subseteq \mathcal{L}_{W_\square}(\psi')$. Consider $v_0 \in W_\square$ and $(\sigma_\square, \sigma_\bigcirc)$ such that $\Pr_{v_0}^{\sigma_\square, \sigma_\bigcirc}[\psi] = 1$. Then, an infinite path under $(\sigma_\square, \sigma_\bigcirc)$ that starts from v_0 satisfies ψ with probability 1. Since $\mathcal{L}_{W_\square}(\psi) \subseteq \mathcal{L}_{W_\square}(\psi')$, that infinite path must also satisfy ψ' with probability 1. Therefore, $\Pr_{v_0}^{\sigma_\square, \sigma_\bigcirc}[\psi'] = 1$. □

Proposition 2. *Given an SG G, a winning objective φ, and two strategy templates $T = (P, \boldsymbol{L}, C)$ and $T' = (P', \boldsymbol{L}', C')$, T is no more permissive than T' if $P \supseteq P'$, $\boldsymbol{L} \supseteq \boldsymbol{L}'$, and $C \supseteq C'$.*

Proof. If $P \supseteq P'$, then $\mathcal{L}_{W_\square}(\psi_P) \subseteq \mathcal{L}_{W_\square}(\psi_{P'})$. Similarly, $\boldsymbol{L} \supseteq \boldsymbol{L}'$ and $C \supseteq C'$ imply $\mathcal{L}_{W_\square}(\psi_{\boldsymbol{L}}) \subseteq \mathcal{L}_{W_\square}(\psi_{\boldsymbol{L}'})$ and $\mathcal{L}_{W_\square}(\psi_C) \subseteq \mathcal{L}_{W_\square}(\psi_{C'})$. As a result, we obtain $\mathcal{L}_{W_\square}(\psi_T = \psi_P \wedge \psi_{\boldsymbol{L}} \wedge \psi_C) = \mathcal{L}_{W_\square}(\psi_P) \cap \mathcal{L}_{W_\square}(\psi_{\boldsymbol{L}}) \cap \mathcal{L}_{W_\square}(\psi_C) \subseteq \mathcal{L}_{W_\square}(\psi_{P'}) \cap \mathcal{L}_{W_\square}(\psi_{\boldsymbol{L}'}) \cap \mathcal{L}_{W_\square}(\psi_{C'}) = \mathcal{L}_{W_\square}(\psi_{T'} = \psi_{P'} \wedge \psi_{\boldsymbol{L}'} \wedge \psi_{C'})$. □

Proposition 1 implies that any winning strategy template T for a winning objective φ satisfies $\Pr_{v_0}^{\sigma_\square, \sigma_\bigcirc}[\psi_T] = 1 \implies \Pr_{v_0}^{\sigma_\square, \sigma_\bigcirc}[\varphi] = 1$, for any $v_0 \in W_\square$ and any pair of strategies $(\sigma_\square, \sigma_\bigcirc)$.

We end this section with a remark on combining templates, discussed in [2]. In short, we can combine two templates $T = (P, \boldsymbol{L}, C)$ and $T' = (P', \boldsymbol{L}', C')$ into $T'' = (P \cup P', \boldsymbol{L} \cup \boldsymbol{L}', C \cup C')$, unless T and T' *conflict* (e.g., $P \cap L' \neq \emptyset$ for some $L' \in \boldsymbol{L}'$). Otherwise, the conflict requires us to recompute a new template from scratch. We refer interested readers to [2] for further details.

4   Constructing Winning Strategy Templates for Stochastic Games

We now present algorithms to construct winning strategy templates for five key winning objectives—safety, reachability, Büchi, co-Büchi, and parity—and prove their correctness. We let $\text{EDGES}_\square(X, Y) := \{(u, v) \in E : u \in X \cap V_\square \wedge v \in Y\}$.

4.1   Templates for Safety Objectives

A safety objective is of the form $\mathsf{G}\, X$ where $X \subseteq V$. Algorithm 3 first computes $W_\square$ and then returns $T = (P, \emptyset, \emptyset)$. Since player Even must not leave $W_\square$, the set P contains all player Even's edges that leave $W_\square$.

Algorithm 3: Constructing templates for G X.

1   SAFETYTEMPLATE($G = (V, E, (V_\Box, V_\bigcirc, V_\triangle)), X \subseteq V$)
2     $W_\Box \leftarrow \nu Y.(X \cap (\mathrm{PRE}_\Box(Y) \cup \mathrm{PRE}(Y)))$
3     $P \leftarrow \mathrm{EDGES}_\Box(W_\Box, V \setminus W_\Box)$
4   **return** $(P, \boldsymbol{L} = \emptyset, C = \emptyset)$

Algorithm 4: Constructing templates for F X.

1   REACHABILITYTEMPLATE($G = (V, E, (V_\Box, V_\bigcirc, V_\triangle)), X \subseteq V$)
2     $A \leftarrow \mathrm{ATTR}'(X)$
3     $W_\Box \leftarrow \mathrm{ATTR}'_\Box(A)$
4     $P \leftarrow \mathrm{EDGES}_\Box(W_\Box, V \setminus W_\Box)$
5     $C \leftarrow \mathrm{EDGES}_\Box(W_\Box \setminus A, W_\Box \setminus A)$
6   **return** $(P, \boldsymbol{L} = \emptyset, C)$

Theorem 2. SAFETYTEMPLATE(G, X) *is winning for* G X.

Proof. The greatest fixed point in Line 2 provides the winning set $W_\Box$ for G X. Then, the template is constructed as $T = (P, \emptyset, \emptyset)$ where $P = \mathrm{EDGES}_\Box(W_\Box, V \setminus W_\Box)$. Consider any infinite path $v_0 v_1 \ldots \in \mathcal{L}_{W_\Box}(\psi_T)$. We have $v_0 \in W_\Box$ by definition. Next, for any $i \in \mathbb{N}$, if $v_i \in W_\Box$ then $v_{i+1} \in W_\Box$, as P does not allow a path to use an edge (v_i, v_{i+1}) where $v_{i+1} \in V \setminus W_\Box$. Therefore, by induction, $v_i \in W_\Box$ for all $i \in \mathbb{N}$ and $\mathcal{L}_{W_\Box}(\psi_T) \subseteq \mathcal{L}_{W_\Box}(G\ X)$. $\qquad\square$

4.2 Templates for Reachability Objectives

A reachability objective is of the form F X where $X \subseteq V$. Firstly, Algorithm 4 computes $A \leftarrow \mathrm{ATTR}'(X)$, meaning that all infinite paths starting in A eventually reach X. Then, it computes $W_\Box \leftarrow \mathrm{ATTR}'_\Box(A)$. By definition, player Even can eventually reach A from a vertex in $W_\Box$ regardless of player Odd's strategy. Since player Even must neither leave $W_\Box$ nor stay in $W_\Box \setminus A$ infinitely often (before reaching X), the sets P and C are computed correspondingly.

Theorem 3. REACHABILITYTEMPLATE(G, X) *is winning for* F X.

Proof. By definition, A is the largest possible set of vertices from which any infinite path reaches X almost-surely, regardless of players' strategy. From Line 3 and Theorem 1 ([4, Thm. 4]), $W_\Box$ is the winning set for F X. Then, T is $(P, \emptyset, C)$ where $P = \mathrm{EDGES}_\Box(W_\Box, V \setminus W_\Box)$ and $C = \mathrm{EDGES}_\Box(W_\Box \setminus A, W_\Box \setminus A)$. Consider any infinite path $v_0 v_1 \ldots \in \mathcal{L}_{W_\Box}(\psi_T)$. If $v_0 \in A$, then it almost-surely reaches X. Otherwise, $v_0 \in W_\Box \setminus A$. By constraints of P and C, the path can neither leave $W_\Box$ nor stay in $W_\Box \setminus A$ infinitely often. Thus, the path must almost-surely reach A and therefore X. $\qquad\square$

Algorithm 5: Constructing templates for GF X.

---

1   BÜCHITEMPLATE($G = (V, E, (V_\square, V_\bigcirc, V_\triangle)), X \subseteq V$)

2     $W_\square \leftarrow \nu Z.\mu Y((X \cap \text{PRE}_\square(Z) \cap \text{PRE}(Z)) \cup \text{PRE}_\square(Y) \cup \text{PRE}(Y) \cup \text{PRE}_\triangle(Z, Y))$

3     $P \leftarrow \text{EDGES}_\square(W_\square, V \setminus W_\square)$

4   **return** $(P, \boldsymbol{L} = \text{LIVEGROUPS}(G, X \cap W_\square), C = \emptyset)$

5

6   LIVEGROUPS($G = (V, E, (V_\square, V_\bigcirc, V_\triangle)), X \subseteq V$)

7     $\boldsymbol{L} \leftarrow \emptyset$

8   **while true do**

9        $A \leftarrow \text{ATTR}'(X)$

10      $X \leftarrow A \cup \text{PRE}_\square(A)$

11   **if** $X = A$ **then break**

12      $\boldsymbol{L} \leftarrow \boldsymbol{L} \cup \{\text{EDGES}_\square(X \setminus A, A)\}$

13   **return** $\boldsymbol{L}$

4.3   Templates for Büchi Objectives

A Büchi objective is of the form GF X where $X \subseteq V$. The set $W_\square$ can be described as a fixed point in Line 2 of Algorithm 5. The set P is again the set of all edges leaving $W_\square$. The function LIVEGROUPS(G, X) iteratively constructs $A \leftarrow \text{ATTR}'(X)$ and $X \leftarrow A \cup \text{PRE}_\square(A)$. For each of player Even's vertices in $X \setminus A$, there must be an edge going to A. When a path arrives in $X \setminus A$, one of such edges must be used in order to go to A. And eventually, the path arrives in X. This results in the construction of the set $\boldsymbol{L}$.

Theorem 4. BÜCHITEMPLATE(G, X) *is winning for* GF X.

Proof. Let $T = (P, \boldsymbol{L}, \emptyset) \leftarrow$ BÜCHITEMPLATE(G, X). The set $W_\square$ in Line 2 is the winning set of GF X by Theorem 1 ([4, Thm. 3]). The set P is the set of edges leaving $W_\square$. Hence, it is sufficient to show that all paths in $\mathcal{L}_{W_\square}(\psi_T)$ visit $X \cap W_\square$ infinitely often. Consider LIVEGROUPS($G, X \cap W_\square$). Let A_i and X_i be the sets A and X computed in the i-th iteration with $X_0 = X \cap W_\square$. By Lines 9–10, any path from A_i reaches X_{i-1} almost-surely, and player Even can move from $X_i \setminus A_i$ to A_i. Notice that LIVEGROUPS always terminates when $X_i = A_i = W_\square$, as $W_\square$ is the winning set. Since $\boldsymbol{L}$ contains $\text{EDGES}_\square(X_i \setminus A_i, A_i)$, when a path in $\mathcal{L}_{W_\square}(\psi_T)$ reaches $X_i \setminus A_i$, it cannot stay there forever due to the restriction of $\boldsymbol{L}$. Thus, the path eventually reaches A_i and then X_{i-1}, and by induction, reaches X_0. The path then either stays in X_0 or continues to any X_i or A_i, in which case returns to X_0. Hence, the path visits $X_0 = X \cap W_\square$ infinitely often.   □

4.4   Templates for Co-Büchi Objectives

A co-Büchi objective is of the form FG X where $X \subseteq V$. Algorithm 6 constructs a winning strategy template with two main steps. First, the algorithm finds the set of vertices that can almost-surely satisfy G X. Then, the algorithm computes the set of vertices that can almost-surely reach that set.

Algorithm 6: Constructing templates for FG X.

---

1 CO-BÜCHITEMPLATE($G = (V, E, (V_\square, V_\bigcirc, V_\triangle)), X \subseteq V$)
2      $X \leftarrow \nu Y.(X \cap (\text{PRE}_\square(Y) \cup \text{PRE}(Y)))$
3      $A \leftarrow \text{ATTR}'(X)$
4      $W_\square \leftarrow \text{ATTR}'_\square(A)$
5      $P \leftarrow \text{EDGES}_\square(W_\square, V \setminus W_\square)$
6      $C \leftarrow \text{EDGES}_\square(X, W_\square \setminus X) \cup \text{EDGES}_\square(W_\square \setminus A, W_\square \setminus A)$
7   **return** $(P, \boldsymbol{L} = \emptyset, C)$

Theorem 5. CO-BÜCHITEMPLATE(G, X) *is winning for* FG X.

Proof. We can show, in the same manner as Theorem 3, that X in Line 2 becomes the winning set of G X. For Lines 3–6, Algorithm 6 follows Algorithm 4. Hence, by Theorem 3, $T = (P, \emptyset, C)$ is winning for F(G X) = FG X. □

4.5 Templates for Parity Objectives

A parity objective comes with a priority function $p : V \to \{0, \ldots, d\}$ for some $d \in \mathbb{N}$. We construct a winning strategy template for a parity objective by (i) reducing a stochastic game to a deterministic game (i.e., with REDUCE in Algorithm 1), (ii) constructing a winning strategy template for the reduced deterministic game, and (iii) converting the template for the deterministic game into a template for the stochastic game.

The construction of a winning strategy template for a deterministic parity game was presented in [2], detailed in Algorithm 7. It extends Algorithm 2 by Zielonka which solves deterministic parity games. Instead of returning the set P, the algorithm returns $W_\square$ and $W_\bigcirc$, which can then be used to construct P. The algorithm also utilizes the function LIVEGROUPS from Algorithm 5.

Regarding the process of converting the template, we give the algorithm in Algorithm 8. Essentially, we remove from $\boldsymbol{L}'$ and C' all edges (u', v') such that u' is part of a gadget (i.e., there is no corresponding vertex u in G). The result of this procedure is then a winning strategy template for the parity objective.

Theorem 6. PARITYTEMPLATE(G, p) *is winning for a parity objective on* p.

Proof. Let $(G', p') \leftarrow$ REDUCE(G, p). Algorithm 7 returns $(W'_\square, W'_\bigcirc, \boldsymbol{L}', C')$. The template $T' = (P' = \text{EDGES}_\square(W'_\square, W'_\bigcirc), \boldsymbol{L}', C')$ is winning for the parity objective of (G', p') due to [2, Thm. 4]. Moreover, it is shown in the proof of Lem. 1 ([9, Lem. 3]) that $W'_\square$ and any winning strategy $\sigma'_\square$ for the parity objective of (G', p') can be converted to $W_\square$ and a winning strategy $\sigma_\square$ for the parity objective of (G, p) by removing all vertices and edges introduced by gadgets. In a similar manner, a winning template T' for the parity objective of (G', p') can be converted to a winning template T for the parity objective of (G, p) by removing all edges introduced by gadgets. This is exactly Algorithm 8. Therefore, PARITYTEMPLATE(G, p) is winning for the parity objective on p. □

Algorithm 7: Constructing templates for deterministic parity games [2].

1 DETPARITYTEMPLATE$(G = (V, E, (V_\Box, V_\bigcirc, \emptyset)), p : V \to \{0, \ldots, d\})$
2     $x \leftarrow \min\{p(v) : v \in V\}; X \leftarrow \arg\min\{p(v) : v \in V\}$
3   **if** x is even **then**
4        $A \leftarrow \text{ATTR}_\Box(X)$
5   **if** $A = V$ **then**
6   **return** $(W_\Box, W_\bigcirc, \boldsymbol{L}, C) = (V, \emptyset, \text{LIVEGROUPS}(G, X), \emptyset)$
7        $(W_\Box', W_\bigcirc', \boldsymbol{L}', C') \leftarrow \text{DETPARITYTEMPLATE}(G \setminus A, p)$
8   **if** $W_\bigcirc' = \emptyset$ **then**
9   **return** $(W_\Box, W_\bigcirc, \boldsymbol{L}, C) = (V, \emptyset, \boldsymbol{L}' \cup \text{LIVEGROUPS}(G, X), C')$
10       $B \leftarrow \text{ATTR}_\bigcirc(W_\bigcirc')$
11       $(W_\Box'', W_\bigcirc'', \boldsymbol{L}'', C'') \leftarrow \text{DETPARITYTEMPLATE}(G \setminus B, p)$
12   **return** $(W_\Box, W_\bigcirc, \boldsymbol{L}, C) = (W_\Box'', W_\bigcirc'' \cup B, \boldsymbol{L}'', C'')$
13   **else**
14       $A \leftarrow \text{ATTR}_\bigcirc(X)$
15   **if** $A = V$ **then**
16   **return** $(W_\Box, W_\bigcirc, \boldsymbol{L}, C) = (\emptyset, V, \emptyset, \emptyset)$
17       $(W_\Box', W_\bigcirc', \boldsymbol{L}', C') \leftarrow \text{DETPARITYTEMPLATE}(G \setminus A, p)$
18   **if** $W_\Box' = \emptyset$ **then**
19   **return** $(W_\Box, W_\bigcirc, \boldsymbol{L}, C) = (\emptyset, V, \emptyset, \emptyset)$
20       $\boldsymbol{L}' \leftarrow \boldsymbol{L}' \cup \text{LIVEGROUPS}(G, W_\Box')$
21       $C' \leftarrow C' \cup \text{EDGES}_\Box(W_\Box', V \setminus W_\Box')$
22       $B \leftarrow \text{ATTR}_\Box(W_\Box')$
23       $(W_\Box'', W_\bigcirc'', \boldsymbol{L}'', C'') \leftarrow \text{DETPARITYTEMPLATE}(G \setminus B, p)$
24   **return** $(W_\Box, W_\bigcirc, \boldsymbol{L}, C) = (W_\Box'' \cup B, W_\bigcirc'', \boldsymbol{L}' \cup \boldsymbol{L}'', C' \cup C'')$

---

5 Extracting Strategies from Templates

Strategy templates constructed in the previous section provide useful information about restrictions on edges of the game. From these templates, our goal is to extract a winning strategy for player Even that satisfies the winning objective.

As a consequence of Proposition 1, given a winning strategy template T for a winning objective φ, it holds that $\text{Pr}_{v_0}^{\sigma_\Box, \sigma_\bigcirc}[\psi_T] = 1 \implies \text{Pr}_{v_0}^{\sigma_\Box, \sigma_\bigcirc}[\varphi] = 1$ for any $v_0 \in W_\Box$ and any pair of strategies $(\sigma_\Box, \sigma_\bigcirc)$. Hence, it suffices to construct a strategy $\sigma_\Box$ of player Even such that $\text{Pr}_{v_0}^{\sigma_\Box, \sigma_\bigcirc}[\psi_T] = 1$ for any $v_0 \in W_\Box$ and $\sigma_\bigcirc$. The work [2] proposed the procedure EXTRACT, shown below, to construct player Even's winning strategy $\tilde{\sigma}_\Box : V^* \times V_\Box \to V$ (i.e., a *pure* strategy). By construction, $\tilde{\sigma}_\Box$ is almost-sure winning from all $v \in W_\Box$.

EXTRACT$(G = (V, E, (V_\Box, V_\bigcirc, V_\triangle)), T = (P, \boldsymbol{L}, C))$
1. Remove all edges in P and C from G
2. $\tilde{\sigma}_\Box(v)$ alternates between all edges available at v

---

The procedure EXTRACT is simple yet restrictive on the constraint of co-live edges. More precisely, a strategy template $T = (P, \boldsymbol{L}, C)$ requires all edges in C

Algorithm 8: Constructing templates for stochastic parity games.

1 PARITYTEMPLATE($G = (V, E, (V_\square, V_\bigcirc, V_\triangle)), p : V \to \{0, \dots, d\}$)
2 $(G', p') \leftarrow$ REDUCE(G, p)   // Algorithm 1
3 $(W'_\square, W'_\bigcirc, L', C') \leftarrow$ DETPARITYTEMPLATE(G', p')
4 $P \leftarrow \{(u, v) \in E : (u', v') \in$ EDGES$_\square(W'_\square, W'_\bigcirc)\}$
                                                    // u' in G' corresponds to u in G
5 $L \leftarrow \emptyset; C \leftarrow \emptyset$
6 **foreach** $L' \in \mathbf{L}'$ **do**
7      $L \leftarrow \emptyset$
8   **foreach** $(u, v) \in E \cap (V_\square \times V)$ **do**
9   **if** $(u', v') \in L'$ **then** $L \leftarrow L \cup \{(u, v)\}$
10      $\mathbf{L} \leftarrow \mathbf{L} \cup \{L\}$
11 **foreach** $(u, v) \in E \cap (V_\square \times V)$ **do**
12   **if** $(u', v') \in C'$ **then** $C \leftarrow C \cup \{(u, v)\}$
13 **return** $(P, \mathbf{L}, C)$

---

to be used only finitely often in a path. However, $\tilde{\sigma}_\square$ does not allow any usage of those edges in a path at all. Although this restriction does not affect the correctness of $\tilde{\sigma}_\square$, we prefer a winning strategy constructed to be permissive, defined in term of formal language as follows.

Definition 10 (Language generated by Strategy). *Given an SG G, $X \subseteq V$, and a strategy $\sigma_\square$ of player Even, the* language generated from X by $\sigma_\square$ *is $\mathcal{L}_X(\sigma_\square) \subseteq X \times V^\omega$ containing all infinite paths $v_0 v_1 \dots$ in G such that $v_0 \in X$ and, for all $i \in \mathbb{N}$, if $v_i \in V_\square$, then $\sigma_\square(v_0 \dots v_i)(v_{i+1}) > 0$.*

Definition 10 defines generated languages for *mixed* strategies (i.e., $\sigma_\square$ is a function $\sigma_\square : V^* \times V_\square \to \mathcal{D}(v)$). For pure strategies, we simply replace the last condition with "$\sigma_\square(v_0 \dots v_i) = v_{i+1}$".

Definition 11 (Permissiveness of Strategy). *Given an SG G, a winning objective φ, and two player Even's strategies $\sigma_\square$ and $\sigma'_\square$, we say that $\sigma_\square$ is* no more permissive than $\sigma'_\square$ *if $\mathcal{L}_{W_\square}(\sigma_\square) \subseteq \mathcal{L}_{W_\square}(\sigma'_\square)$. Also, we say that $\sigma'_\square$ is* more permissive than $\sigma_\square$ *if $\mathcal{L}_{W_\square}(\sigma_\square) \subsetneq \mathcal{L}_{W_\square}(\sigma'_\square)$.*

Notice that Definition 11 does not require that a path in $\mathcal{L}_{W_\square}(\sigma_\square)$ satisfies a winning objective. Thereby, the maximally permissive strategy is the one that allows all paths, corresponding to the template $(\emptyset, \emptyset, \emptyset)$. However, we focus only on winning strategies and aim for the winning strategy to be as permissive as possible. Below, we present a procedure to construct a winning strategy $\hat{\sigma}_\square$ from a winning strategy template using parameters $\alpha < 1$ and $\beta \geq 1$. These parameters balance between the permissiveness and the speed of reaching key target vertices needed to satisfy the winning objective.

Our proposed procedure PARAMETERIZEDEXTRACT constructs a winning strategy $\hat{\sigma}_\square$ from a winning strategy template. An infinite path generated by $\hat{\sigma}_\square$ can use edges in C. Nevertheless, every time $\hat{\sigma}_\square$ uses an edge in C, the probability that it is used again becomes smaller. Hence, the probability that an edge in C is used infinitely often is zero, complying with the requirement of $T = (P, \boldsymbol{L}, C)$. We also modify the extraction procedure further by increasing the probability that an edge in live-groups in $\boldsymbol{L}$ is used again once it is used. In this way, a path targets edges in live-groups more often.

PARAMETERIZEDEXTRACT($G = (V, E, (V_\Box, V_\bigcirc, V_\triangle)), T = (P, \boldsymbol{L}, C)$)
1. Remove all edges in P from G
2. For $v \in V_\Box$ and $v' \in V$, set $d(v)(v') \leftarrow 1$ if $(v, v') \in E$ and 0 otherwise
3. Define $\hat{\sigma}_\Box(v_0 \ldots v)(v') = d(v)(v') / \sum_{v'' \in V} d(v)(v'') \in [0, 1]$
4. When $(v, v') \in C$ is used, update $d(v)(v') \leftarrow \alpha \cdot d(v)(v')$ where $\alpha < 1$
5. When $(v, v') \in L$ for some $L \in \boldsymbol{L}$ is used, update $d(v)(v') \leftarrow \beta \cdot d(v)(v')$
   where $\beta \geq 1$

We prove the permissiveness of our winning strategy in the following theorem. We emphasize that the original procedure EXTRACT of [2] considers pure strategies. However, our definition of strategies is mixed. Thus, it is not surprising that PARAMETERIZEDEXTRACT can be more permissive than EXTRACT. Notice also that one could generalize EXTRACT to construct mixed strategies by changing Line 2 to "$\tilde{\sigma}_\Box(v)$ chooses an edge available at v uniformly at random". Nonetheless, this generalization still completely prohibits the usage of co-live edges in C, which is allowed to be used finitely often by our proposed procedure.

Theorem 7. *Given an SG G and a strategy template $T = (P, \boldsymbol{L}, C)$. Let $\tilde{\sigma}_\Box$ and $\hat{\sigma}_\Box$ follow EXTRACT(G, T) and PARAMETERIZEDEXTRACT(G, T), respectively. Then, $\tilde{\sigma}_\Box$ is no more permissive than $\hat{\sigma}_\Box$. Moreover, if there is an infinite path $\bar{v} = v_0 v_1 \ldots \in \mathcal{L}_{W_\Box}(\hat{\sigma}_\Box)$ such that $(v_i, v_{i+1}) \in C$ for some $i \in \mathbb{N}$, then $\hat{\sigma}_\Box$ is more permissive than $\tilde{\sigma}_\Box$.*

Proof. It is not hard to see that $\mathcal{L}_{W_\Box}(\tilde{\sigma}_\Box) \subseteq \mathcal{L}_{W_\Box}(\hat{\sigma}_\Box)$ by construction, which makes $\tilde{\sigma}_\Box$ no more permissive than $\hat{\sigma}_\Box$. In addition, assuming the existence of an infinite path $\bar{v} = v_0 v_1 \ldots \in \mathcal{L}_{W_\Box}(\hat{\sigma}_\Box)$ with $(v_i, v_{i+1}) \in C$ for some $i \in \mathbb{N}$. Then, $\bar{v} \notin \mathcal{L}_{W_\Box}(\tilde{\sigma}_\Box)$ since EXTRACT removes all edges in C from G. Under this assumption, $\mathcal{L}_{W_\Box}(\tilde{\sigma}_\Box) \subsetneq \mathcal{L}_{W_\Box}(\hat{\sigma}_\Box)$ and thus the theorem holds.   □

6   Sizes of Strategy Templates

A property of templates we can compare is their *sizes*, formally defined as follows.

Definition 12 (Size of Template). *Given two templates $T = (P, \boldsymbol{L}, C)$ and $T' = (P', \boldsymbol{L}', C')$. The overall size of T is $|T| = |P| + \sum_{L \in \boldsymbol{L}} |L| + |C|$ and the element-wise size of T is the tuple $\|T\| = (|P|, \sum_{L \in \boldsymbol{L}} |L|, |C|)$. We say that T is no overall larger than T' if $|T| \leq |T'|$. Also, we say that T is no element-wise larger than T' if $|P| \leq |P'|$, $|\boldsymbol{L}| \leq |\boldsymbol{L}'|$, and $|C| \leq |C'|$.*

Proposition 2 implies that a template of smaller size can possibly be more permissive. However, the following example shows templates that are of different sizes but are equally permissive.

Example. Figure 4 provides three winning strategy templates for F w: $T_i = (\emptyset, \emptyset, C_i)$ for $i \in \{1, 2, 3\}$ with $C_1 = \{(u, v), (v, u)\}$, $C_2 = \{(u, v)\}$, and $C_3 = \{(v, u)\}$. We have that $\mathcal{L}_{W_\square}(\psi_{T_1}) = \mathcal{L}_{W_\square}(\psi_{T_2}) = \mathcal{L}_{W_\square}(\psi_{T_3})$, but $C_2 \subsetneq C_1$ and $C_3 \subsetneq C_1$.

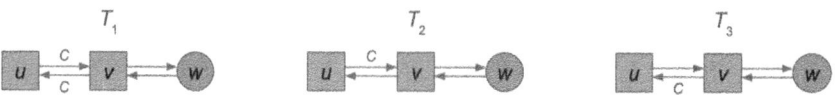

Fig. 4. Three winning strategy templates for F w. Their permissiveness are equal but T_1 is larger than T_2, T_3.

Nevertheless, equally permissive templates may induce different strategies that are not equally permissive, depending on the strategy extraction procedure. For example, let $\sigma_{\square, T_1}$ and $\sigma_{\square, T_3}$ be the strategies constructed from the procedure EXTRACT in Sect. 5 using T_1 and T_3 as inputs. Since the procedure removes all co-live edges in C from the game, the path $u(vw)^\omega$ is allowed by $\sigma_{\square, T_3}$ but prohibited by $\sigma_{\square, T_1}$. As a result, although T_1 and T_3 are equally permissive, $\sigma_{\square, T_3}$ is more permissive than $\sigma_{\square, T_1}$.

Given a template T, the problem of constructing a smallest template $\widehat{T}$, in term of either overall or element-wise size, such that $\mathcal{L}_{W_\square}(\psi_{\widehat{T}}) = \mathcal{L}_{W_\square}(\psi_T)$ can be of interest when the memory of a controller is constrained, such as in a case of embedded devices. Also, templates that are small may yield less conflict when combining with other templates (see [2] for details). We yet to explore this problem in depth and leave it as a future work.

7   Conclusion

This work has illustrated how winning strategy templates can be further generalized to encompass 2.5-player stochastic games. We firstly redefined strategy templates and their permissiveness. Next, several algorithms for constructing winning strategy templates for objectives of stochastic games were presented. The key idea is that we incorporated additional set operators accounting for player Random, motivated by the work of Banerjee et al., and the gadgets of Chatterjee et al. in order to tackle the problem. We then proposed the procedure to extract winning strategies from templates which balances between the permissiveness and the speed of reaching key target vertices needed to satisfy the winning objective. Finally, we provided discussions on the sizes of templates.

In our future works, we intend to look at the problem of constructing a smaller template that is equally permissive to a given template. This would improve the practicality of using templates in various settings. Also, we are interested in constructing templates for a wider range of winning objectives, such as those specified using metric temporal logic (MTL) formulae whose operations are time-constrained. This would enable the usage of templates in real-time systems.

Acknowledgments. The authors would like to thank the reviewers for their comments on improving the manuscript. K. Phalakarn and I. Hasuo are supported by ERATO HASUO Metamathematics for Systems Design Project (No. JPMJER1603) and the ASPIRE grant No. JPMJAP2301, JST. S. Pruekprasert is supported by JSPS KAKENHI Grant Number JP22KK0155.

References

1. Anand, A., Mallik, K., Nayak, S.P., Schmuck, A.K.: Computing adequately permissive assumptions for synthesis. In: Sankaranarayanan, S., Sharygina, N. (eds.) TACS 2023, vol. 13994, pp. 211–228. Springer, Heidelberg (2023). https://doi.org/10.1007/978-3-031-30820-8_15
2. Anand, A., Nayak, S.P., Schmuck, A.K.: Synthesizing permissive winning strategy templates for parity games. In: Enea, C., Lal, A. (eds.) CAV 2023, pp. 436–458. Springer, Heidelberg (2023). https://doi.org/10.1007/978-3-031-37706-8_22
3. Baier, C., Katoen, J.: Principles of Model Checking. MIT Press, Cambridge (2008)
4. Banerjee, T., Majumdar, R., Mallik, K., Schmuck, A.-K., Soudjani, S.: A direct symbolic algorithm for solving stochastic Rabin games. In: TACAS 2022. LNCS, vol. 13244, pp. 81–98. Springer, Cham (2022). https://doi.org/10.1007/978-3-030-99527-0_5
5. Bernet, J., Janin, D., Walukiewicz, I.: Permissive strategies: from parity games to safety games. RAIRO-Theor. Inf. Appl.-Informatique Théorique et Applications **36**(3), 261–275 (2002)
6. Bouyer, P., Duflot, M., Markey, N., Renault, G.: Measuring permissivity in finite games. In: Bravetti, M., Zavattaro, G. (eds.) CONCUR 2009. LNCS, vol. 5710, pp. 196–210. Springer, Heidelberg (2009). https://doi.org/10.1007/978-3-642-04081-8_14
7. Bouyer, P., Markey, N., Olschewski, J., Ummels, M.: Measuring permissiveness in parity games: mean-payoff parity games revisited. In: Bultan, T., Hsiung, P.-A. (eds.) ATVA 2011. LNCS, vol. 6996, pp. 135–149. Springer, Heidelberg (2011). https://doi.org/10.1007/978-3-642-24372-1_11
8. Calude, C.S., Jain, S., Khoussainov, B., Li, W., Stephan, F.: Deciding parity games in quasipolynomial time. In: Proceedings of the 49th Annual ACM SIGACT Symposium on Theory of Computing, pp. 252–263 (2017)
9. Chatterjee, K., Jurdziński, M., Henzinger, T.A.: Simple stochastic parity games. In: Baaz, M., Makowsky, J.A. (eds.) CSL 2003. LNCS, vol. 2803, pp. 100–113. Springer, Heidelberg (2003). https://doi.org/10.1007/978-3-540-45220-1_11
10. Chen, Y., Li, Z.: Design of a maximally permissive liveness-enforcing supervisor with a compressed supervisory structure for flexible manufacturing systems. Automatica **47**(5), 1028–1034 (2011)
11. Klein, J., Baier, C., Klüppelholz, S.: Compositional construction of most general controllers. Acta Informatica **52**(4), 443–482 (2015)
12. Kuijper, W., van de Pol, J.: Compositional control synthesis for partially observable systems. In: Bravetti, M., Zavattaro, G. (eds.) CONCUR 2009. LNCS, vol. 5710, pp. 431–447. Springer, Heidelberg (2009). https://doi.org/10.1007/978-3-642-04081-8_29

13. Kuijper, W., van de Pol, J.: Computing weakest strategies for safety games of imperfect information. In: Kowalewski, S., Philippou, A. (eds.) TACAS 2009. LNCS, vol. 5505, pp. 92–106. Springer, Heidelberg (2009). https://doi.org/10.1007/978-3-642-00768-2_10

14. Lv, P., Xu, Z., Ji, Y., Li, S., Yin, X.: Optimal supervisory control of discrete event systems for cyclic tasks. Automatica **164**, 111634 (2024)

15. Ma, Z., Cai, K.: On resilient supervisory control against indefinite actuator attacks in discrete-event systems. IEEE Control Syst. Lett. **6**, 2942–2947 (2022)

16. Neider, D., Rabinovich, R., Zimmermann, M.: Down the Borel hierarchy: solving Muller games via safety games. Theor. Comput. Sci. **560**, 219–234 (2014)

17. Pruekprasert, S., Ushio, T., Kanazawa, T.: Quantitative supervisory control game for discrete event systems. IEEE Trans. Autom. Control **61**(10), 2987–3000 (2015)

18. Ramadge, P.J., Wonham, W.M.: Supervisory control of a class of discrete event processes. SIAM J. Control. Optim. **25**(1), 206–230 (1987)

19. Rezig, S., Ghorbel, C., Achour, Z., Rezg, N.: PLC-based implementation of supervisory control for flexible manufacturing systems using theory of regions. Int. J. Autom. Control **13**(5), 619–640 (2019)

20. Sengupta, R., Lafortune, S.: An optimal control theory for discrete event systems. SIAM J. Control. Optim. **36**(2), 488–541 (1998)

21. Tatsumoto, Y., Shiraishi, M., Cai, K.: Application of supervisory control theory with warehouse automation case study. Syst. Control Lett. **62**(6), 203–208 (2018)

22. Tushar, W., et al.: A survey of cyber-physical systems from a game-theoretic perspective. IEEE Access **11**, 9799–9834 (2023)

23. Zielonka, W.: Infinite games on finitely coloured graphs with applications to automata on infinite trees. Theor. Comput. Sci. **200**(1–2), 135–183 (1998)

Disconnection Rules are Complete for Chemical Reactions

Ella Gale[1] , Leo Lobski[2(✉)] , and Fabio Zanasi[2,3]

[1] University of Bristol, Bristol, UK
ella.gale@bristol.ac.uk
[2] University College London, London, UK
{leo.lobski.21,f.zanasi}@ucl.ac.uk
[3] University of Bologna, Bologna, Italy

Abstract. We provide a category theoretical framework capturing two approaches to graph-based models of chemistry: formal *reactions* and *disconnection rules*. We model a translation from the latter to the former as a functor, which is faithful, and full up to isomorphism. This allows us to state, as our main result, that the disconnection rules are sound, complete and universal with respect to the reactions. Concretely, this means that every reaction can be decomposed into a sequence of disconnection rules in an essentially unique way. This provides a uniform way to store reaction data, and gives an algorithmic interface between (forward) reaction prediction and (backward) reaction search or retrosynthesis.

Keywords: Chemical reactions · Disconnection rules · Completeness

1 Introduction

Graph-based models of chemical processes typically come at two different levels of abstraction: formal *reactions* and *disconnection rules*. Formal reactions are combinatorial rearrangements of atoms and charge, and are used for reaction prediction and storage of reaction data (see e.g. the rightmost part of Fig. 1 below). Disconnection rules constitute hypothetical bond breaking in the direction opposite to a reaction, and are used for designing synthetic pathways and reaction search, known as *retrosynthesis* [5,6,15,16,18] (see e.g. Fig. 2 below). Retrosynthetic analysis starts with a target molecule we wish to produce but do not know how. The aim is to "reduce" the target molecule to known starting molecules in such a way that when the starting molecules react, the target molecule is obtained as a product. This is done by (formally) partitioning the target molecule into functional parts referred to as *synthons*, which are replaced by actual molecules acting as the new targets [5–7,16]. We refer the reader to our previous work on formalising retrosynthesis [9] for the details. In the current work, we are merely interested in the first step of this process: our key observation is that the bond breaking disconnection rules (together with their converse rules), as found in the theory and practise of retrosynthesis (see Fig. 2), are, in fact, enough to capture all reactions.

ⓒ The Author(s), under exclusive license to Springer Nature Switzerland AG 2025
C. Anutariya and M. M. Bonsangue (Eds.): ICTAC 2024, LNCS 15373, pp. 215–231, 2025.
https://doi.org/10.1007/978-3-031-77019-7_13

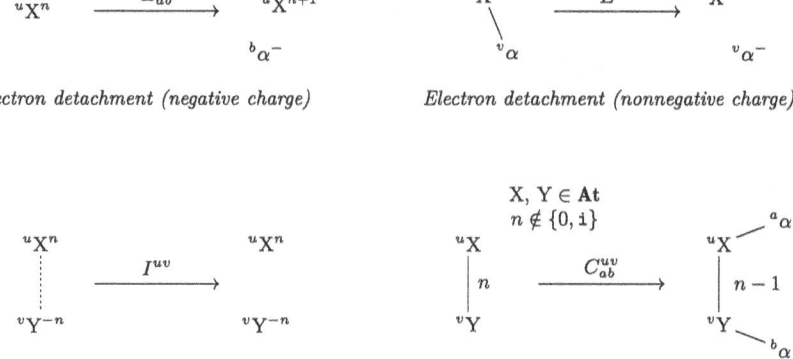

Fig. 1. A simple retrosynthetic sequence. A molecule (far left) is disconnected at the O-COPh bond giving rise to two synthons (left) which can be mapped to precursor molecules (right) which can react to give the product (far right).

$$X \in \mathbf{At}$$
$$n < 0$$
$$^u X^n \xrightarrow{\quad E^u_{ab} \quad} \begin{array}{c} {}^a\alpha \\ | \\ {}^u X^{n+1} \\ \diagdown \\ {}^b\alpha^- \end{array}$$

Electron detachment (negative charge)

$$X \in \mathbf{At}$$
$$n \geq 0$$
$$\begin{array}{c} {}^u X^n \\ \diagdown \\ {}^v\alpha \end{array} \xrightarrow{\quad E^{uv} \quad} \begin{array}{c} {}^u X^{n+1} \\ \\ {}^v\alpha^- \end{array}$$

Electron detachment (nonnegative charge)

$$\begin{array}{c} {}^u X^n \\ \vdots \\ {}^v Y^{-n} \end{array} \xrightarrow{\quad I^{uv} \quad} \begin{array}{c} {}^u X^n \\ \\ {}^v Y^{-n} \end{array}$$

Ionic bond breaking

$$X, Y \in \mathbf{At}$$
$$n \notin \{0, 1\}$$
$$\begin{array}{c} {}^u X \\ | \\ n \\ | \\ {}^v Y \end{array} \xrightarrow{\quad C^{uv}_{ab} \quad} \begin{array}{c} {}^u X \diagup {}^a\alpha \\ | \\ n-1 \\ | \\ {}^v Y \diagdown {}^b\alpha \end{array}$$

Covalent bond breaking

Fig. 2. The four disconnection rules

Whereas chemical reactions have been studied formally before, a mathematical description of disconnection rules has received far less attention [4,9]. Our approach takes a novel perspective on the basic units of retrosynthetic analysis – the disconnection rules – by making them first-class citizens of reaction representation. The mathematical and conceptual justification for doing so is the fact that, as we show, both disconnection rules and reactions can be arranged into (monoidal) categories [9], such that there is a functor taking each sequence of disconnection rules to a reaction. More broadly, our contribution incorporates disconnection rules within the framework of applied category theory [8], which emphasises compositional modelling as a means to uniformly study systems across various disciplines of science.

The reactions are formalised as certain partial bijections between labelled graphs representing molecules (Definition 4). The disconnection rules are defined as partial functions on the labelled graphs, corresponding to the four basic rules in Fig. 2 (Definition 5). The sequences of disconnection rules together with equations between them form the *disconnection category* (Definition 9), which we think of as syntax for the reactions. This is made precise by constructing a functor from the disconnection category to the category of reactions (Sect. 4). Our main results state that the functor is faithful (Theorem 1) and full up to isomorphism (Theorem 2). Such a categorical perspective provides a precise mathematical meaning to the claim that disconnection rules are sound, complete and universal with respect to the reactions. This implies that every reaction can be decomposed into a sequence of disconnection rules (universality) in an essentially unique way (completeness).

The rest of the paper is structured as follows. Section 2 defines the chemical graphs and the category of reactions. Section 3 defines the disconnection rules and their category. It is moreover shown that any sequence of well-typed disconnection rules has a normal form. Section 4 defines a functor from the disconnection category to the category of reactions, and proves completeness and universality. Section 5 concludes.

2   Chemical Graphs and Reactions

We first define the chemical graphs in Subsect. 2.1, which form the objects both in the category of reactions (Definition 4) and the disconnection category (Definition 9). Chemical reactions are modelled as certain combinatorial rearrangements of chemical graphs that preserve matter and charge in the appropriate sense. The core of the section is the category of reactions (Definition 4), the semantic domain for our interpretation of disconnection rules in Sect. 4.

2.1   Chemical Graphs

Let us fix a finite set of *vertex labels* **At**, containing the special symbol α. Formally, the only assumptions we make about **At** are (1) it is finite, (2) it contains the special symbol α, and (3) **At** $\setminus \{\alpha\}$ has at least two elements. However, in all the examples we shall assume that **At** contains a symbol for each main-group element of the periodic table: $\{H, C, O, P, \dots\} \subseteq$ **At**. For this reason we will also refer to **At** as the *atom labels*. The special symbol α may be thought of as representing an unpaired electron. Similarly, we fix a *valence function* $\mathbf{v} : \mathbf{At} \to \mathbb{N}$ with the only formal assumption that $\mathbf{v}(\alpha) = 1$, but shall assume in the examples that the valence of an element symbol is the number of (unpaired) electrons in its outer electron shell.

Remark 1. The reason for choosing such level of generality for the atom labels and their valencies is the ability to model elements which exhibit different valence depending on the context. For instance, one could have separate atom labels for nitrogen whose valence is 5 (all outer shell electrons are shared or take part in a reaction) or 3 (two of the outer shell electrons pair with each other).

Let **Lab** := $\{0, 1, 2, 3, 4, \mathtt{i}\}$ denote the set of *edge labels*, where the integers stand for a covalent bond, and $\mathtt{i}$ for an ionic bond. We further define maps $\mathtt{cov}, \mathtt{ion} : \mathbf{Lab} \to \mathbb{N}$: for $\mathtt{cov}$, assign to each edge label 0, 1, 2, 3, and 4 the corresponding natural number and let $\mathtt{i} \mapsto 0$, while for $\mathtt{ion}$, let $0, 1, 2, 3, 4 \mapsto 0$

and $\mathbf{i} \mapsto 1$. Finally, let us fix a countable set **VN** of *vertex names*; we usually denote the elements of **VN** by lowercase Latin letters $u, v, w, \ldots$.

Definition 1 (Chemically labelled graph). *A chemically labelled graph is a triple (V, τ, m), where $V \subseteq \mathbf{VN}$ is a finite set of vertices, $\tau : V \to \mathbf{At} \times \mathbb{Z}$ is a vertex labelling function, and $m : V \times V \to \mathbf{Lab}$ is an edge labelling function satisfying $m(v, v) = 0$ and $m(v, w) = m(w, v)$ for all $v, w \in V$.*

Thus, a chemically labelled graph is irreflexive (we interpet the edge label 0 as no edge) and symmetric, and each of its vertices is labelled with an element of **At**, together with an integer indicating the charge. Given a chemically labelled graph A, we write (V_A, τ_A, m_A) for its vertex set and the labelling functions. We abbreviate the vertex labelling function followed by the first projection as τ_A^{At}, and similarly we write τ_A^{Crg} for composition with the second projection.

Given a chemically labelled graph A and vertex names $u, v \in \mathbf{VN}$ such that $u \in V_A$ but $v \notin V_A \setminus \{u\}$, we denote by $A(u \mapsto v)$ the chemically labelled graph whose vertex set is $(V_A \setminus \{u\}) \cup \{v\}$, and whose vertex and edge labelling functions agree with those of A, treating v as if it were u. Further, we define the following special subsets of vertices:

- *α-vertices*, whose label is the special symbol: $\alpha(A) := \tau_A^{-1}(\alpha, \mathbb{Z})$,
- *chemical vertices*, whose label is not α: $\mathrm{Chem}(A) := V_A \setminus \alpha(A)$,
- *neutral vertices*, whose charge is zero: $\mathrm{Neu}(A) := \tau_A^{-1}(\mathbf{At}, 0)$,
- *charged vertices*, which have a non-zero charge: $\mathrm{Crg}(A) := V_A \setminus \mathrm{Neu}(A)$,
- *negative vertices*, which have a negative charge:

$$\mathrm{Crg}^-(A) := \{v \in V_A : \tau_A^{\mathrm{Crg}}(v) < 0\},$$

- *positive vertices*, which have a positive charge:

$$\mathrm{Crg}^+(A) := \{v \in V_A : \tau_A^{\mathrm{Crg}}(v) > 0\}.$$

The *net charge* of a subset $U \subseteq V_A$ is the integer $\mathrm{Net}(U) := \sum_{v \in U} \tau_A^{\mathrm{Crg}}(v)$.

Example 1. We give three examples of chemically labelled graphs: **A**, **B** (carbonate anion) and **C** (sodium cloride). We adopt the following conventions: (1) the vertex label from **At** is drawn at the centre of a vertex, (2) the vertex name is drawn as a superscript on the left (so within a single graph, no left superscript appears twice), (3) a non-zero charge is drawn as a superscript on the right, (4) n-ary covalent bonds are drawn as n parallel lines, and (5) ionic bonds are drawn as dashed lines.

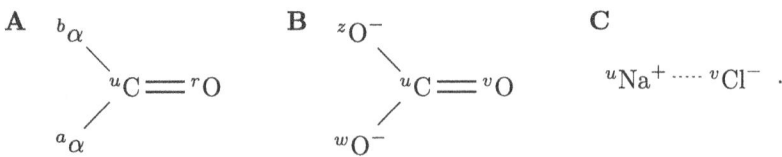

	A	B	C
α-vertices	$\{a, b\}$	$\varnothing$	$\varnothing$
chemical vertices	$\{r, u\}$	V_B	V_C
neutral vertices	V_A	$\{u, v\}$	$\varnothing$
charged vertices	$\varnothing$	$\{w, z\}$	V_C
negative vertices	$\varnothing$	$\{w, z\}$	$\{v\}$
positive vertices	$\varnothing$	$\varnothing$	$\{u\}$
net charge	0	-2	0

Below we give a table with different kinds of vertex subsets for the graphs:

Definition 2 (Neighbours). *Given a chemically labelled graph A and a vertex $u \in V_A$, we define the sets of neighbours $N_A(u)$, covalent neighbours $CN_A(u)$ and ionic neighbours $IN_A(u)$ of u as follows:*

$$N_A(u) := \{v \in V_A : m_A(u, v) \neq 0\},$$
$$CN_A(u) := \{v \in V_A : \mathtt{cov}(m_A(u, v)) \neq 0\},$$
$$IN_A(u) := \{v \in V_A : \mathtt{ion}(m_A(u, v)) \neq 0\}.$$

Definition 3 (Chemical graph). *A chemical graph $A = (V_A, \tau_A, m_A)$ is a chemically labelled graph satisfying the following additional conditions:*

1. for all $v \in V_A$, we have

$$\left| \tau_A^{\mathrm{Crg}}(v) \right| + \sum_{u \in V_A} \mathtt{cov}\left(m_A(u, v)\right) = v\tau_A^{\mathrm{At}}(v),$$

2. for all $v \in \alpha(A)$ and $w \in V_A$ we have
   (a) $\tau_A^{\mathrm{Crg}}(v) \in \{-1, 0\}$,
   (b) $m_A(v, w) \in \{0, 1\}$,
   (c) $N_A(u)$ has at most one element, and if $w \in N_A(u)$, then $w \in \mathrm{Chem}\,(A)$,
3. for all $v \in \mathrm{Chem}\,(A)$, the set $IN_A(v)$ has at most one element, and if $u \in IN_A(v)$, then $\tau_A^{\mathrm{Crg}}(v) = -\tau_A^{\mathrm{Crg}}(u)$.

Condition 1 states that the sum of incident covalent bonds together with the absolute value of the charge must equal the valence of the vertex. Conditions 2a–2c say that a vertex labelled by α is either neutral or has charge -1, has at most one neighbour, which is chemical and to which it is connected via a single covalent bond. Condition 3 says that an edge with label i only connects charged chemical vertices with equal net charges of opposite signs.

A *synthon* is a chemical graph whose set of α-vertices is nonempty.

Example 2. The chemically labelled graphs in Example 1 are, in fact, chemical graphs with the standard valences of the atoms (i.e. $\mathbf{v}(C) = 4$, $\mathbf{v}(O) = 2$ and $\mathbf{v}(H) = \mathbf{v}(Cl) = \mathbf{v}(Na) = 1$). Moreover, $\mathbf{A}$ is a synthon.

2.2   Category of Reactions

We define reactions between chemically labelled graphs as partial bijections preserving the atom labels of chemical vertices whose domain and image have the same net charge, with the additional condition that the complements of the domain and image are isomorphic. The intuition is that electrons and atoms' charge may appear and disappear in the course of a reaction in such a way that the overall charge is preserved. We emphasise that these are indeed *formal* reactions, in the sense that the only constraints we impose are preservation of matter and charge: in order to capture the chemically feasible reactions, further constraints are needed either in the form of empirical data, or introduction of kinematics or dynamics into the model.

This way of representing reactions is motivated by and formally connected to *double pushout graph rewriting* [1–3]: in fact, every reaction can be represented as a double pushout diagram in the category of chemical graphs.

Definition 4 (Category of reactions). *We denote by* **React** *the category of reactions, whose*

- *objects are chemical graphs,*
- *morphisms $A \to B$ are tuples (U_A, U_B, b, i), where*
  - *$U_A \subseteq V_A$ and $U_B \subseteq V_B$ are subsets with $\text{Net}(U_A) = \text{Net}(U_B)$,*
  - *$b : \text{Chem}(U_A) \to \text{Chem}(U_B)$ is a bijection preserving the atom labels,*
  - *$i : V_A \setminus U_A \to V_B \setminus U_B$ is an isomorphism of labelled graphs,*
  such that for all $u \in \text{Chem}(U_A)$ and $a \in V_A \setminus U_A$ we have

$$m_A(u, a) = m_B(bu, ia),$$

- *the composition of $(U_A, U_B, b, i) : A \to B$ and $(W_B, W_C, c, j) : B \to C$ is*

$$(Z_A, Z_C, (c + j)(b + i), ji) : A \to C,$$

  where $Z_A := U_A \cup i^{-1}(W_B \cap (V_B \setminus U_B))$ and $Z_C := W_C \cup j(U_B \cap (V_B \setminus W_B))$,
- *for a chemical graph A, the identity is given by $(\varnothing, \varnothing, !, \text{id}_A)$, where $!$ is the unique endomorphism on the empty set.*

Note that the composition in **React** is *not* the composition in the usual category of partial bijections: instead, it crucially relies on the fact that there is an isomorphism between the unchanged parts of the graph. The category **React** has a dagger structure [10,12]: the dagger of $(U_A, U_B, b, i) : A \to B$ is given by $(U_B, U_A, b^{-1}, i^{-1}) : B \to A$. The dagger of $r \in$ **React** is denoted by $\bar{r}$.

Example 3. We give an example of a reaction (formation of benzyl benzoate from benzoyl chloride and benzyl alcohol) below, where both b and i are identity maps. Here Ph stands for the phenyl group, and we use the convention from chemistry where an unlabelled vertex is a carbon atom with an appropriate number of hydrogen atoms attached.

3 Disconnection Rules

A *disconnection rule* is a partial endofunction on the set of chemical graphs. We define four classes of disconnection rules, all of which have a clear chemical significance: two versions of *electron detachment*, *ionic bond breaking* and *covalent bond breaking*. The reader may want to return to Fig. 2 in Sect. 1 before Definition 5 below, as it gives an intuitive explanation of our approach.

For the purposes of mathematical precision, our set of four disconnection rules is more fine-grained than what one would see in a typical textbook on retrosynthesis, where movement of electrons is usually implicitly modelled in the same step as disconnecting a bond, rather than including electron detachment as a separate step (see e.g. the discussion on the choice of polarity in [16, p. 9]).

We treat the disconnection rules as syntax, which generate the *terms* (Definition 6), whose equivalence classes under the equations of Fig. 4 form the morphisms in the *disconnection category* (Definition 9). The payoff such a syntactic presentation is an axiomatic view of chemical reactions: in Sect. 4, we construct a functor from the disconnection category to the category of reactions, and show that every reaction can be represented as a sequence of disconnection rules in an essentially unique way.

Definition 5 (Disconnection rules). *Let $u, v, a, b \in \mathbf{VN}$ be pairwise distinct vertex names. Let $U \in \{u, uv\}$ and $D \in \{\varnothing, ab\}$ range over the specified lists of vertex names. The four disconnection rules are defined by the tables in Fig. 3 as follows: a chemical graph A is in the domain of d_D^U if $U \subseteq V_A$ but $D \cap V_A = \varnothing$, and the additional conditions of the first column (top table) hold; the output chemical graph $d(A)$ has the vertex set $V_A \cup D$, and the labelling functions on $U \cup D$ are defined by the remaining columns (vertex labelling in the top table, edge labelling in the bottom table), while the labelling functions agree with those of A on $V_A \setminus U$.*

Note that the disconnection rules look a lot like (a subset of) morphisms in **React**, except that we keep track of the precise vertex names, and a rule applies to a whole set of chemical graphs. We make this connection precise in Sect. 4. We further observe that each disconnection rule is injective (as a partial function), and hence has an inverse partial function.

We use the disconnection rules to define the *terms*, which will be used to define the morphisms in the disconnection category.

Definition 6 (Terms). *The set of terms with types is generated by the following recursive procedure:*

d_D^U	$A \in \mathbf{dom}(d)$	$\tau_{d(A)}^{\mathrm{Crg}}(u)$	$\tau_{d(A)}^{\mathrm{Crg}}(v)$	$\tau_{d(A)}(a)$	$\tau_{d(A)}(b)$
E_{ab}^u	$u \in \mathbf{Chem}(A)$ $u \in \mathbf{Crg}^-(A)$	$\tau_A^{\mathrm{Crg}}(u)+1$	N/A	$(\alpha,0)$	$(\alpha,-1)$
E^{uv}	$u \in \mathbf{Chem}(A)$ $u \notin \mathbf{Crg}^-(A)$ $v \in \alpha(A)$ $m_A(u,v)=1$	$\tau_A^{\mathrm{Crg}}(u)+1$	-1	N/A	N/A
I^{uv}	$m_A(u,v)=\mathtt{i}$ $u \in \mathbf{Crg}^+(A)$ $v \in \mathbf{Crg}^-(A)$	$\tau_A^{\mathrm{Crg}}(u)$	$\tau_A^{\mathrm{Crg}}(v)$	N/A	N/A
C_{ab}^{uv}	$u,v \in \mathbf{Chem}(A)$ $m_A(u,v) \notin \{0,\mathtt{i}\}$	$\tau_A^{\mathrm{Crg}}(u)$	$\tau_A^{\mathrm{Crg}}(v)$	$(\alpha,0)$	$(\alpha,0)$

d_D^U	$m_{d(A)}(u,v)$	$m_{d(A)}(u,a)$	$m_{d(A)}(v,b)$
E_{ab}^u	N/A	1	N/A
E^{uv}	0	N/A	N/A
I^{uv}	0	N/A	N/A
C_{ab}^{uv}	$m_A(u,v)-1$	1	1

Fig. 3. The disconnection rules defined as partial functions

- for every chemical graph A, let $\mathrm{id}: A \to A$ be a term,
- for every chemical graph A and every $u \in V_A$, let $S^u : A \to A$ be a term,
- for every chemical graph A, every $u \in \alpha(A)$ and every $v \in \mathbf{VN}$ such that $v \notin V_A \setminus \{u\}$, let $R^{u \mapsto v} : A \to A(u \mapsto v)$ be a term,
- for every disconnection rule d and every chemical graph A in the domain of d, both $d : A \to d(A)$ and $\bar{d} : d(A) \to A$ are terms,
- if $\mathtt{t} : A \to B$ and $\mathtt{s} : B \to C$ are terms, then $\mathtt{t}; \mathtt{s} : A \to C$ is a term.

The first and the fifth items take care of the usual categorical structure, while the terms S^u generated by the second item correspond to "touching" the vertex u without changing the structure of the graph, and the terms $R^{u \mapsto v}$ rename an existing vertex u into a fresh vertex v.

We refer to the terms of the form $d : A \to B$ and $\bar{d} : B \to A$ generated by the fourth item as *disconnections* and *connections*, respectively. More specifically, we use the symbols $E^{<0}$, $E^{\geq 0}$, I and C to denote the disconnections corresponding to the specific disconnection rules, and similarly the symbols $\bar{E}^{<0}$, $\bar{E}^{\geq 0}$, $\bar{I}$ and $\bar{C}$ refer to the corresponding connections. Similarly, S and R refer to the terms generated by the second and third items. The same letters in the typewriter type font ($\mathtt{E}^{<0}$, $\mathtt{E}^{\geq 0}$, $\mathtt{I}$, $\mathtt{C}$, $\bar{\mathtt{E}}^{<0}$, $\bar{\mathtt{E}}^{\geq 0}$, $\bar{\mathtt{I}}$, $\mathtt{S}$ and $\mathtt{R}$) are used to denote a sequence of terms of the corresponding kind.

Let us define the endofunction $\overline{()}$ on terms by the following recursion:

- $(\mathrm{id} : A \to A) \mapsto (\mathrm{id} : A \to A)$,
- $(S^u : A \to A) \mapsto (S^u : A \to A)$,
- $(R^{u \mapsto v} : A \to A(u \mapsto v)) \mapsto (R^{v \mapsto u} : A(u \mapsto v) \to A)$,
- $(d : A \to B) \mapsto (\bar{d} : B \to A)$,

– $(\bar{d} : A \to B) \mapsto (d : B \to A)$,
– $\overline{t; s} := \bar{s}; \bar{t}$.

For defining equations, it will be useful to allow untyped terms: the equations (Fig. 4) capture interactions between local graph transformations (i.e. the disconnection rules), so that the same equation should hold for a whole class of chemical graphs.

Definition 7 (Untyped terms, well-typedness). *An untyped term is an element of the free monoid on the set*

$$\{\mathrm{id}, S^u, R^{a \mapsto b}, E^{ua}, E^u_{ab}, C^{uv}_{ab}, I^{uv}, \bar{E}^{ua}, \bar{E}^u_{ab}, \bar{C}^{uv}_{ab}, \bar{I}^{uv} : u, v, a, b \in \mathbf{VN}\},$$

where we use the symbol ; *to indicate the multiplication of the monoid.*

Given an untyped term t *and chemical graphs A and B, we say that the expression* t : A → B *is* well-typed *if it is in fact a term, that is, if it can be constructed using the recursive procedure of Definition 6.*

We define the binary relation $\leq$ on the set of untyped terms by letting $t \leq s$ if whenever $t : A \to B$ is well-typed, then so is $s : A \to B$.

The endofunction $\bar{()}$ on the untyped terms is defined in exactly the same way as for the terms with types, simply ignoring the types. Note that $t : A \to B$ is well-typed if and only if $\bar{t} : B \to A$ is. Moreover, observe that $\leq$ defines a preorder on the untyped terms. Consequently, we have $t \leq s$ if and only if $\bar{t} \leq \bar{s}$.

Given an untyped term t, there are either no chemical graphs such that $t : A \to B$ is well-typed, or there are infinitely many such graphs. The latter case is the reason for introducing the untyped terms: we want certain equalities to hold *whenever* both sides are well-typed.

Definition 8 (Term equality). *Let* $\approx$ *be an equivalence relation on the set of untyped terms. This induces the equivalence relation* $\equiv$ *on the set of terms as follows: for two terms* t, s : A → B *with the same type, we let* t ≡ s *if either* t ≈ s *or* $\bar{t} \approx \bar{s}$ *as untyped terms.*

Given an equivalence relation $\approx$ on the untyped terms, let us introduce the following shorthand binary relations on the untyped terms: (1) $t \lesssim s$ if $t \approx s$ and $t \leq s$, and (2) $t \simeq s$ if $t \lesssim s$ and $s \lesssim t$.

Definition 9 (Disconnection category). *The* disconnection category **Disc** *has as objects the chemical graphs. The set of morphisms* **Disc**(A, B) *is given by the terms of type A → B, subject to the usual associativity and unitality equations of a category, together with the identities* $\equiv$ *induced (in the sense of Definition 8) by the equivalence relation defined in Fig. 4.*

Note that the assignment $\bar{()} :$ **Disc** → **Disc** is functorial, thus making **Disc** a dagger category [10,12].

$$R^{u \mapsto z}; R^{z \mapsto w} \lesssim R^{u \mapsto w} \tag{1}$$

$$R^{u \mapsto z}; R^{v \mapsto w} \approx R^{v \mapsto w}; R^{u \mapsto z} \tag{2}$$

$$R^{u \mapsto u} \lesssim S^u \tag{3}$$

$$R^{b \mapsto z}; R^{a \mapsto b} \approx S^b; R^{a \mapsto z} \tag{4}$$

$$R^{u \mapsto v}; S^w \approx S^w; R^{u \mapsto v} \tag{5}$$

$$R^{u \mapsto v}; S^v \simeq S^u; R^{u \mapsto v} \simeq R^{u \mapsto v} \tag{6}$$

$$S^u; S^v \simeq S^v; S^u \tag{18}$$

$$S^u; S^u \simeq S^u \tag{19}$$

$$S^u; d_D^U \lesssim d_D^U; S^u \tag{20}$$

$$d_D^{U[v]}; S^v \simeq d_D^{U[v]} \tag{21}$$

$$C_{ab}^{uv} \simeq C_{ba}^{vu} \tag{22}$$

$$R^{u \mapsto v}; d_D^U \approx d_D^U; R^{u \mapsto v} \tag{7}$$

$$R^{u \mapsto v}; E^{wv} \simeq E^{wu}; R^{u \mapsto v} \tag{8}$$

$$d_{D[u]}^U; R^{u \mapsto v} \simeq d_{D[v/u]}^U \tag{9}$$

$$d_{ij}^{U'}; \bar{h}_{ab}^U; R^{i \mapsto c}; R^{j \mapsto d} \lesssim \bar{h}_{ab}^U; d_{cd}^{U'} \tag{10}$$

$$d_D^U; d_{D'}^{U'} \simeq d_{D'}^{U'}; d_D^U \tag{23}$$

$$C_{ab}^{uv}; I^{wz} \simeq I^{wz}; C_{ab}^{uv} \tag{24}$$

$$E_{ab}^u; I^{wz} \lesssim I^{wz}; E_{ab}^u \tag{25}$$

$$E^{uv}; I^{wz} \lesssim I^{wz}; E^{uv} \tag{26}$$

$$\bar{E}^{uv}; I^{wz} \lesssim I^{wz}; \bar{E}^{uv} \tag{27}$$

$$\bar{E}_{ab}^u; I^{wz} \lesssim I^{wz}; \bar{E}_{ab}^u \tag{28}$$

$$\bar{C}_{ab}^{uv}; I^{wz} \lesssim I^{wz}; \bar{C}_{ab}^{uv} \tag{29}$$

$$E_{ab}^u; C_{cd}^{wz} \simeq C_{cd}^{wz}; E_{ab}^u \tag{30}$$

$$E^{uv}; C_{cd}^{wz} \lesssim C_{cd}^{wz}; E^{uv} \tag{31}$$

$$\bar{E}^{uv}; C_{cd}^{wz} \simeq C_{cd}^{wz}; \bar{E}^{uv} \tag{32}$$

$$E^{uv}; E_{cd}^w \lesssim E_{cd}^w; E^{uv} \tag{33}$$

$$\bar{E}^{uv}; E_{cd}^w \simeq E_{cd}^w; \bar{E}^{uv} \tag{34}$$

$$d_{ab}^U; \bar{d}_{cd}^U \approx S^U; R^{c \mapsto a}; R^{d \mapsto b} \tag{11}$$

$$d_{ab}^U; \bar{d}_{cb}^U \approx S^U; R^{c \mapsto a} \tag{12}$$

$$d_{ab}^U; \bar{d}_{ad}^U \approx S^U; R^{d \mapsto b} \tag{13}$$

$$d_D^U; \bar{d}_D^U \lesssim S^U \tag{14}$$

$$\bar{d}_D^U; d_D^U \lesssim S^U; S^D \tag{15}$$

$$E^{ua}; \bar{E}^{ub} \approx S^u; R^{a \mapsto z}; R^{b \mapsto a}; R^{z \mapsto b} \tag{16}$$

$$\bar{d}^{uv}; d^{wz} \approx d^{wz}; \bar{d}^{uv} \tag{17}$$

Fig. 4. The equivalence relation $\approx$ inducing the identities in the disconnection category. Here d and h range over $\{E, C, I\}$, while S^U stands for the sequence $S^u; S^w$ if $U = uw$. Given vertex names $a, b \in \mathbf{VN}$, the notation $D[a]$ means a occurs in D, and $D[b/a]$ means the occurrence of a in D is replaced with b. Note that we use the shorthand relations $\lesssim$ and $\simeq$: these are strictly speaking not part of the definition, but we use them to provide the extra information of when well-typedness of one side of an identity implies well-typedness of the other.

Proposition 1. *The following identities are derivable in* **Disc***:*

$$d_{D[a]}^U; S^a \simeq d_{D[a]}^U, \tag{35}$$

$$\bar{d}_{ab}^U; d_{cd}^U \lesssim S^U; R^{a \mapsto c}; R^{b \mapsto d}, \tag{36}$$

$$R^{z \mapsto c}; R^{w \mapsto d}; d_{ab}^U \approx R^{z \mapsto a}; R^{w \mapsto b}; d_{cd}^U, \tag{37}$$

$$R^{z \mapsto c}; d_{ab}^U \approx R^{z \mapsto a}; d_{cb}^U, \tag{38}$$

$$R^{w \mapsto d}; d_{ab}^U \approx R^{w \mapsto b}; d_{ad}^U, \tag{39}$$

$$d_{ab}^U; d_{cd}^U \simeq d_{ad}^U; d_{cb}^U. \tag{40}$$

3.1   Normal Form

In this subsection, we define a normal form (Definition 12), and show that every term is equal to a term in a normal form under the equalities of **Disc** (Proposition 3). We also identify a class of syntactic manipulations of terms in a normal form (Definition 13) that both keep the normal form and preserve equality (Lemma 2). These results are used in the next section to prove completeness.

Definition 10 (*ICE*-form). *We say that a term is in an ICE-form if it is either an identity term, or if it has the following structure:*

$$\mathsf{I};\mathsf{C};\mathsf{E}^{<0};\mathsf{E}^{\geq 0};\bar{\mathsf{E}}^{\geq 0};\bar{\mathsf{E}}^{<0};\bar{\mathsf{C}};\bar{\mathsf{I}};\mathsf{R};\mathsf{S},$$

where every letter is a sequence of generating terms of the corresponding kind.

Proposition 2. *Any term is equal to a term in an ICE-form.*

Proof (sketch). The proof proceeds by repeated inductions: one first shows that all I-terms can always be commuted to the left, then that all C-terms can be commuted to the left of anything that is not an I-term, and so on.

Definition 11 (Renaming form). *A well-typed sequence of renaming terms* $\mathsf{R} : H \to G$ *is in a* renaming form *if there are sets of vertex names* $A = \{a_1,\ldots,a_n\}$, $B = \{b_1,\ldots,b_n\}$, $C = \{c_1,\ldots,c_m\}$ *and* $D = \{d_1,\ldots,d_m\}$ *such that (1)* R *can be split into two sequences* $\mathsf{R} = \mathsf{A};\mathsf{B}$ *with*

$$\mathsf{A} = R^{a_1 \mapsto b_1};\ldots;R^{a_n \mapsto b_n} \quad and \quad \mathsf{B} = R^{c_1 \mapsto d_1};\ldots;R^{c_m \mapsto d_m},$$

where B *can be possibly empty, (2)* $A \cap B = \varnothing$, *(3)* $C \subseteq B$, *(4)* $D \subseteq A$, *and (5) if* $c_i \in C$ *and* $b_j \in B$ *is the unique element such that* $b_j = c_i$, *then* $\mathsf{N}_H(a_j) \neq \mathsf{N}_H(d_i)$.

Lemma 1. *Any well-typed sequence of renaming terms is equal to a term* $\mathsf{R};\mathsf{S}$, *where* $\mathsf{R} = \mathsf{A};\mathsf{B}$ *is in a renaming form and* S *is a sequence of S-terms.*

Proof (sketch). The idea is that if a vertex a is to be renamed to b, then $a \in A$, and we have two cases: (1) b does not already occur in the original chemical graph, and (2) b does occur in the original graph. If (1), then $R^{a \mapsto b} \in \mathsf{A}$ and $b \in B \setminus C$. If (2), then we first rename a using some "dummy" name c, so that $R^{a \mapsto c} \in \mathsf{A}$, $R^{c \mapsto b} \in \mathsf{B}$, $c \in C$ and $b \in D$. Note that condition (4) of the renaming form is satisfied, as b must itself be renamed in order for the vertex name become free. Any term of the form $R^{a \mapsto a}$ is replaced by S^a. The formal proof proceeds by induction on the length of the original sequence.

A term is said to be in an *ICER*-form if it is in an *ICE*-form whose sequence of renaming terms is in a renaming form (or is empty).

Definition 12 (Normal form). *Let*

$$\mathsf{t} = \mathsf{I};\mathsf{C};\mathsf{E}^{<0};\mathsf{E}^{\geq 0};\bar{\mathsf{E}}^{\geq 0};\bar{\mathsf{E}}^{<0};\bar{\mathsf{C}};\bar{\mathsf{I}};\mathsf{A};\mathsf{B};\mathsf{S}$$

be a term in an ICER-form. Let us denote the sets of vertex names in the renaming form by A_t, B_t, C_t *and* D_t. *Let us additionally define the following sets of vertex names occurring in* t:

- $D_t^{add} := \left\{ a \in \mathbf{VN} : d_{D[a]}^U \in \mathsf{t} \right\}$ – the vertex names appearing as subscripts in the disconnections,
- $D_t^{remove} := \left\{ a \in \mathbf{VN} : \bar{d}_{D[a]}^U \in \mathsf{t} \right\}$ – the vertex names appearing as subscripts in the connections,
- $U_t := \left\{ v \in \mathbf{VN} : d_D^{U[v]} \in \mathsf{t} \text{ or } \bar{d}_D^{U[v]} \in \mathsf{t} \right\}$ – the vertex names appearing as superscripts of the (dis)connections,
- $S_t := \{ u \in \mathbf{VN} : S^u \in \mathsf{t} \}$ – the vertex names appearing in the S-terms.

We say that a term t is in a normal form if it is in an $ICER$-form as above, and additionally the following conditions hold:

(1) for every $u \in S_t$, the term S^u occurs in t exactly once,
(2) $(U_t \cup A_t \cup B_t) \cap S_t = \varnothing$,
(3) $D_t^{add} \setminus D_t^{remove} \subseteq A_t \setminus D_t$,
(4) $D_t^{add} \cap B_t = \varnothing$,
(5) if a connection $\bar{d}_{D[a]}^U : A \to B$ and a renaming term $R^{z \mapsto a}$ both occur, then A is not in the domain of $\bar{d}_{D[z/a]}^U$,
(6) if $d \neq I$ and a disconnection d_D^U occurs in t, then the connections $\bar{d}_F^U$ and $\bar{d}_F^{U^r}$ do not occur in t for any F,
(7) if the disconnection E^{uv} occurs in t, then for any vertex name $w \in \mathbf{VN}$, the connection $\bar{E}^{uw}$ does not occur in t,
(8) if the disconnection I^{uv} and the connection $\bar{I}^{uv}$ both occur in t, then one of the terms E_D^v, $\bar{E}_D^v$, E^{va} or $\bar{E}^{va}$ occurs in t.

Proposition 3. *Any term is equivalent to a term in normal form.*

Proof. (sketch). By Proposition 2 and Lemma 1, every terms is equal to a term in an $ICER$-form. Conditions (1) and (2) for S-terms are obtained by absorbing the "excess" terms using Eqs. (6), (19) and (21). Conditions (3) and (4) are obtained by treating all the vertex names in D_t^{add} as "dummy" names, which are removed either by a connection or a renaming term. Condition (5) is obtained by Eqs. (38) and (39). Conditions (6) and (7) are minimal change conditions: if the number of bonds (or electrons) is decreased, then it should not be increased again. These are obtained by cancelling the redundant disconnection-connection pairs. Finally, condition (8) says that an ionic bond is first removed and then reintroduced between the same pair of vertices just in case the charge of the vertices has to be changed.

Definition 13 (Normal form equivalence). *Let*

$$\mathsf{t} = \mathsf{I}; \mathsf{C}; \mathsf{E}^{<0}; \mathsf{E}^{\geq 0}; \bar{\mathsf{E}}^{\geq 0}; \bar{\mathsf{E}}^{<0}; \bar{\mathsf{C}}; \bar{\mathsf{I}}; \mathsf{A}; \mathsf{B}; \mathsf{S}$$

be a term in a normal form. Define the following syntactic manipulations of t:

1. *commuting the terms inside each of the named sequences in the normal form,*
2. *permuting vertex names in C-terms: if the term C_{ab}^{uv} occurs, we may substitute it with C_{ba}^{vu},*

3. *if $d \in \{C, E, \bar{C}, \bar{E}\}$ such that $d^U_{ab}; d^U_{cd}$ occurs, we may substitute $d^U_{ab}; d^U_{cd} \mapsto$*
   $d^U_{ad}; d^U_{cb}$,
4. *renaming of vertices that are introduced and removed: if $a \in D^{add}_{\mathsf{t}} \cup C_{\mathsf{t}}$ and*
   $z \in \mathbf{VN}$ does not occur in t or its domain, then we may substitute $\mathsf{t} \mapsto \mathsf{t}[z/a]$,
5. *exchanging vertex names between $\bar{E}^{<0}$-, $\bar{C}$- and R-terms: if $d \in \{E, C\}$, and*
   $\bar{d}^U_{D[a]} : A \to B$ and $R^{z \mapsto b}$ both occur such that A is in the domain of $\bar{d}^U_{D[z/a]}$,
   then we may substitute $\bar{d}^U_{D[a]} \mapsto \bar{d}^U_{D[z/a]}$ and $R^{z \mapsto b} \mapsto R^{a \mapsto b}$.

We say that two terms t and s in a normal form are equivalent, *written $\mathsf{t} \sim \mathsf{s}$, if one can be obtained from the other by a sequence of the syntactic manipulations defined above.*

Observing that each syntactic manipulation in Definition 13 is reversible, we see that $\sim$ is an equivalence relation on the set of terms in normal form.

Lemma 2. *Let t and s be terms in normal forms such that $\mathsf{t} \sim \mathsf{s}$. Then $\mathsf{t} \equiv \mathsf{s}$.*

Proof. This follows by noticing that every syntactic manipulation of Definition 13 keeps the term in a normal form, and moreover preserves equality:

1. the terms may be commuted by Eqs. (23), (2) and (18),
2. vertex names in C-terms may be permuted by (22),
3. the indices in repeated (dis)connections may be exchanged by (40),
4. if $a \in D^{add}_{\mathsf{t}}$, so that there is a disconnection $d^U_{D[a]}$, we use Eq. (9) to obtain
   $d^U_{D[a]} \simeq d^U_{D[b/a]}; R^{b \mapsto a}$ to introduce the desired fresh variable b; the renaming
   term can then be absorbed into the second occurrence of a, hence replacing
   a with b (the case when $a \in C_{\mathsf{t}}$ is similar),
5. the last syntactic manipulation is obtained by Eqs. (38) and (39).

4   From Disconnections to Reactions, Functorially

We are finally ready to tie together the constructions in the previous sections: here we construct a functor $R : \mathbf{Disc} \to \mathbf{React}$ and prove that it is faithful and full up to an isomorphism, hence establishing the claimed soundness, completeness and universality results. Proving faithfulness (completeness) relies crucially on the normal form results (Subsect. 3.1). In combination, the results of this section allow for algebraic reasoning about the reactions using the equations for disconnection rules (Fig. 4).

We define a function R from terms to morphisms in **React** as follows. Given a term $\mathsf{t} : A \to B$, the morphism $R(\mathsf{t}) : A \to B$ has the form $R(R_1(\mathsf{t}), R_2(\mathsf{t}), \mathrm{id}, \mathrm{id})$, where $\mathrm{id} : \mathrm{Chem}(R_1(\mathsf{t})) \to \mathrm{Chem}(R_2(\mathsf{t}))$ and $\mathrm{id} : V_A \setminus R_1(\mathsf{t}) \to V_B \setminus R_2(\mathsf{t})$ are both identity maps. Since all the terms are mapped to morphisms whose bijection and isomorphism parts are the identities, we omit these, and write $R(\mathsf{t}) = (R_1(\mathsf{t}), R_2(\mathsf{t}))$. The recursive definition of this mapping is given below:

$$R(\mathrm{id}_A) := (\varnothing, \varnothing) \qquad\qquad R(E^{uv}) := (\{u, v\}, \{u, v\})$$
$$R(S^u) := (\{u\}, \{u\}) \qquad\qquad R(I^{uv}) := (\{u, v\}, \{u, v\})$$
$$R(R^{u \mapsto v}) := (\{u\}, \{v\}) \qquad\qquad R(C_{ab}^{uv}) := (\{u, v\}, \{u, v, a, b\})$$
$$R(E_{ab}^{u}) := (\{u\}, \{u, a, b\}) \qquad\qquad R\left(\bar{d}_{ab}^{uv}\right) := \overline{R\left(d_{ab}^{uv}\right)}$$
$$R(\mathsf{t}; \mathsf{s}) := R(\mathsf{t}); R(\mathsf{s}).$$

Observe that for all the disconnections we have $R(d_D^U) = (U, U \cup D)$.

Soundness of disconnection rules with respect to reactions is expressed as functoriality:

Proposition 4. *The assignment* $R : \mathbf{Disc} \to \mathbf{React}$ *is a dagger functor.*

Proof (sketch). Functoriality and preservation of dagger structure follow immediately by construction. We have to show that R preserves the equations of Fig. 4. Most of these follow immediately by applying R to expressions on both sides of the equality. We give an example derivation of Eq. (10) below. To further simplify the notation, we omit the curly brackets of set-builder notation as well as the commas separating vertex names from each other: so e.g. $(uv, uvab)$ stands for $(\{u, v\}, \{u, v, a, b\})$.

Denote $R(d_{ij}^{U'}) = (u'v', u'v'ij)$, $R(d_{cd}^{U'}) = (u'v', u'v'cd)$ and $R(\bar{h}_{ab}^{U}) = (uvab, uv)$. Note that d and h are not $E^{\geq 0}$-terms, whence it follows that $i, j \notin U$ and $a, b \notin U'$. From the fact that the left-hand side is defined, we obtain that $\{i, j\}$ and $\{a, b\}$ are disjoint. The left-hand side is thus translated to

$$(u'v', u'v'ij); (uvab, uv); (i, c); (j, d) = (u'v'uvab, uvu'v'ij); (i, c); (j, d)$$
$$= (u'v'uvab, cuvu'v'j); (j, d)$$
$$= (u'v'uvab, dcuvu'v')$$
$$= (uvu'v'ab, uvu'v'cd)$$
$$= (uvab, uv); (u'v', u'v'cd),$$

which we recognise as the translation of the right-hand side.

Recall the syntactic manipulations of terms in normal form of Definition 13. We have seen that these manipulations preserve equality (Lemma 2). The following lemma is the core of the completeness argument.

Lemma 3. *Let* t *and* s *be terms in a normal form such that* $R(\mathsf{t}) = R(\mathsf{s})$. *Then* $\mathsf{t} \sim \mathsf{s}$.

Proof (sketch). The minimal change conditions of a normal form ((6), (7) and (8)) imply that the terms have the same (dis)connections up to renaming the α-vertices. The case analysis of the renaming terms then shows that t and s have the same renaming forms, up to renaming and exchange allowed by the normal form equivalence.

Combining the above lemma with the results from the previous section, we conclude that the functor $R : \mathbf{Disc} \to \mathbf{React}$ is faithful. We spell this out in detail in the following:

Theorem 1 (Completeness). *For all terms* $\mathtt{t}$ *and* $\mathtt{s}$, *we have* $\mathtt{t} \equiv \mathtt{s}$ *in* **Disc** *if and only if* $R(\mathtt{t}) = R(\mathtt{s})$ *in* **React**.

Proof. The 'only if' direction is functoriality (Proposition 4). The 'if' direction follows from the fact that every term is equal to a term in normal form (Proposition 3) and from Lemmas 3 and 2.

The argument for universality turns out to be much simpler than that for completeness. However, in combination with Theorem 1, it gives a rather strong representation result for reactions: not only can every reaction be decomposed into a sequence of disconnection rules, but this sequence is also unique, up to changing the vertex names and up to the equations in **Disc**. In abstract terms, the statement of universality is that the functor $R : \textbf{Disc} \to \textbf{React}$ is full up to isomorphism in **React**. As for completeness, we spell out the details:

Theorem 2 (Universality). *Given a reaction* $r : A \to C$, *there is a term* $\mathtt{t} : A \to B$ *and an isomorphism* $\iota : B \xrightarrow{\sim} C$ *such that* $R(\mathtt{t}); \iota = r$.

Proof (sketch). Observe that every reaction $r : A \to C$ factorises as

$$(U_A, U_B, \mathrm{id}, \mathrm{id}); (\varnothing, \varnothing, !, \iota),$$

where $(U_A, U_B) : A \to B$ is some reaction and $\iota : B \to C$ is an isomorphism of labelled graphs. Now, we may disconnect all possible bonds inside U_A, and then connect all possible bonds to obtain U_B. The fact that U_A and U_B have the same atom labels and net charge guarantees that this can always be done.

Example 4. Following the procedure of Theorem 2, the reaction in Example 3 decomposes into the following sequence of (dis)connection rules:

$$C_{ab}^{zu}; C_{cd}^{vw}; C_{ij}^{ru}; C_{nm}^{ru}; E^{vc}; E^{wd}; E^{za}; E^{ub}; E^{ri}; E^{uj}; E^{rn}; E^{um};$$
$$\bar{E}^{vc}; \bar{E}^{wd}; \bar{E}^{za}; \bar{E}^{ub}; \bar{E}^{ri}; \bar{E}^{uj}; \bar{E}^{rn}; \bar{E}^{um}; \bar{C}_{ij}^{ru}; \bar{C}_{nm}^{ru}; \bar{C}_{da}^{wz}; \bar{C}_{bc}^{uv}.$$

The normal form of the above sequence is given by: $C_{ab}^{zu}; C_{cd}^{vw}; \bar{C}_{da}^{wz}; \bar{C}_{bc}^{uv}; S^r$.

5   Conclusion

We have formalised and axiomatised the retrosynthetic rules as a category, showing that there is a sound, complete and universal translation into the category of reactions – a more familiar object to study in computational chemistry.

Universality can be thought of as a consistency result for reactions: their definition captures exactly those rearrangements of chemical graphs which result from local, chemically motivated rewrite rules. Completeness says that there is no redundancy in the representation: treating the (dis)connection rules as terms, the terms can be endowed with equations such that the terms describing the same reaction are identified. As the decomposition of a reaction into a sequence of (dis)connection rules is algorithmic, these results can be used to automatically break a reaction (or its part) into smaller components: the purpose can be, *inter alia*, retrosynthetic analysis or storing reaction data in a systematic way.

5.1 Future Work

Chemical Questions. An important part of chemical data is stereochemistry, that is, spatial orientation of the molecule: many molecules of interest (like pharmaceuticals) possess chiral enantiomers (i.e. molecules that have the same atoms and connectivity, but are mirror images of each other due to spatial orientation) which have different properties. We therefore wish to incorporate spatial data into our categorical representation. While stereochemistry is relatively straightforward to account for on the level of chemical graphs and reactions [9], it is unclear how to do this for the disconnection rules, as they only operate at one or two vertices at a time. A more straightforward extension of the formalism presented here would introduce energy and dynamics into the disconnection rules by quantifying how much energy each (dis)connection (in a particular context) requires to occur.

Computational Questions. Given the algorithmic nature of both completeness and universality proofs, the next step is to implement both. The first algorithm would take an arbitrary reaction as an input, and output a sequence of disconnection rules representing it. The second algorithm would decide whether two terms are equal or not, implementing the normalisation procedure. Another direction for connecting this work with more standard approaches to computational chemistry would be translating our formalism to a widely used notation such as SMILES [14,17].

Mathematical Questions. An important mathematical development is to introduce monoidal terms in the disconnection category, so as to allow parallel reactions, as well as usage of graphical calculi for monoidal categories [11,13]. Another mathematical question is whether the categories **Disc** and **React** have any interesting categorical structure, apart from being dagger categories. Finally, we would like to make precise the connection between the category of reactions and double pushout rewriting [1–3].

Acknowledgments. Fabio Zanasi acknowledges support from EPSRC EP/V002376/1 and MIUR P2022HXNSC (PRIN 2022 PNRR - Next Generation EU).

References

1. Andersen, J.L., Flamm, C., Merkle, D., Stadler, P.F.: Inferring chemical reaction patterns using rule composition in graph grammars. J. Syst. Chem. **4**(1), 1–4 (2013). https://doi.org/10.1186/1759-2208-4-4
2. Andersen, J.L., Flamm, C., Merkle, D., Stadler, P.F.: An intermediate level of abstraction for computational systems chemistry. Philos. Trans. R. Soc. A Math. Phys. Eng. Sci. **375**(2109), 20160354 (2017). https://doi.org/10.1098/rsta.2016.0354

3. Behr, N., Krivine, J., Andersen, J.L., Merkle, D.: Rewriting theory for the life sciences: a unifying theory of CTMC semantics. Theor. Comput. Sci. **884**, 68–115 (2021). https://doi.org/10.1016/j.tcs.2021.07.026

4. Bournez, O., Ibănescu, L., Kirchner, H.: From chemical rules to term rewriting. Electron. Notes Theor. Comput. Sci. **147**(1), 113–134 (2006). https://doi.org/10.1016/j.entcs.2005.06.040. Proceedings of the 6th International Workshop on Rule-Based Programming (RULE 2005)

5. Clayden, J., Greeves, N., Warren, S.: Organic Chemistry, 2nd edn. Oxford University Press, Oxford (2012)

6. Corey, E.J., Cheng, X.: The Logic of Chemical Synthesis. Wiley, New York (1989)

7. Corey, E.J.: General methods for the construction of complex molecules. Pure Appl. Chem. **14**(1), 19–38 (1967). https://doi.org/10.1351/pac196714010019

8. Fong, B., Spivak, D.I.: An Invitation to Applied Category Theory: Seven Sketches in Compositionality. Cambridge University Press, Cambridge (2019)

9. Gale, E., Lobski, L., Zanasi, F.: A categorical approach to synthetic chemistry. In: Ábrahám, E., Dubslaff, C., Tarifa, S.L.T. (eds.) Theoretical Aspects of Computing – ICTAC 2023, pp. 276–294. Springer, Cham (2023). https://doi.org/10.1007/978-3-031-47963-2_17

10. Heunen, C., Vicary, J.: Categories for Quantum Theory: An Introduction. Oxford University Press, Oxford (2019). https://doi.org/10.1093/oso/9780198739623.001.0001

11. Piedeleu, R., Zanasi, F.: An Introduction to String Diagrams for Computer Scientists. Cambridge University Press, Cambridge (2024, to appear). https://arxiv.org/abs/2305.08768

12. Selinger, P.: Dagger compact closed categories and completely positive maps: (extended abstract). Electron. Notes Theor. Comput. Sci. **170**, 139–163 (2007). https://doi.org/10.1016/j.entcs.2006.12.018. Proceedings of the 3rd International Workshop on Quantum Programming Languages (QPL 2005)

13. Selinger, P.: A survey of graphical languages for monoidal categories. Lect. Notes Phys. (2010). https://doi.org/10.1007/978-3-642-12821-9_4

14. SMILES tutorial. https://daylight.com/dayhtml_tutorials/languages/smiles/index.html. https://daylight.com/dayhtml_tutorials/languages/smiles/index.html. Accessed 13 Aug 2024

15. Sun, Y., Sahinidis, N.V.: Computer-aided retrosynthetic design: fundamentals, tools, and outlook. Curr. Opin. Chem. Eng. **35**, 100721 (2022). https://doi.org/10.1016/j.coche.2021.100721

16. Warren, S., Wyatt, P.: Organic Synthesis: The Disconnection Approach, 2nd edn. Wiley, Hoboken (2008)

17. Weininger, D.: SMILES, a chemical language and information system. 1. introduction to methodology and encoding rules. J. Chem. Inf. Comput. Sci. **28**(1), 31–36 (1988). https://doi.org/10.1021/ci00057a005

18. Zhong, Z., et al.: Recent advances in deep learning for retrosynthesis. Wiley Interdisc. Rev. Comput. Mol. Sci. **14**(1), e1694 (2024). https://doi.org/10.1002/wcms.1694

Verification with Common Knowledge
of Rationality for Graph Games

Rindo Nakanishi[1]([✉]), Yoshiaki Takata[2], and Hiroyuki Seki[1]

[1] Graduate School of Informatics, Nagoya University, Furo-cho, Chikusa, Nagoya
464-8601, Japan
{rindo,seki}@sqlab.jp
[2] School of Informatics, Kochi University of Technology, Tosayamada, Kami City,
Kochi 782-8502, Japan
takata.yoshiaki@kochi-tech.ac.jp

Abstract. Realizability asks whether there exists a program satisfying
its specification. In this problem, we assume that each agent has her own
objective and behaves rationally to satisfy her objective. Traditionally,
the rationality of agents is modeled by a Nash equilibrium (NE), where
each agent has no incentive to change her strategy because she cannot
satisfy her objective by changing her strategy alone. However, an NE is
not always an appropriate notion for the rationality of agents because the
condition of an NE is too strong; each agent is assumed to know strategies
of the other agents completely. In this paper, we use an epistemic model
to define common knowledge of rationality of all agents (CKR). We define
the verification problem as a variant of the realizability problem, based on
CKR, instead of NE. We then analyze the complexity of the verification
problems for the class of positional strategies.

Keywords: graph game · epistemic model · common knowledge of
rationality

1 Introduction

A graph game is a formal model for analyzing or controlling a system consisting
of multiple agents (or processes) that behave independently according to their
own preferences or objectives. One of the useful applications of graph game is
reactive synthesis, which is the problem of synthesizing a reactive system that
satisfies a given specification. The standard approach to the problem is as follows
[1]. When a specification is given by a linear temporal logic (LTL) formula (or
nondeterministic ω-automaton) φ, we translate φ to an equivalent deterministic
ω-automaton $\mathcal{A}$. Next, we convert $\mathcal{A}$ to a tree automaton (or equivalently, a
parity game) $\mathcal{B}$. Then, we test whether the language recognized by $\mathcal{B}$ is empty,
i.e., $L(\mathcal{B}) = \varnothing$ (or equivalently, there is a winning strategy for player 0, which is
the system player in $\mathcal{B}$). The answer to the problem is affirmative if and only if
$L(\mathcal{B}) \neq \varnothing$, and any $t \in L(\mathcal{B})$ (or any winning strategy for the system player in
$\mathcal{B}$) is an implementation of the specification.

© The Author(s), under exclusive license to Springer Nature Switzerland AG 2025
C. Anutariya and M. M. Bonsangue (Eds.): ICTAC 2024, LNCS 15373, pp. 232–248, 2025.
https://doi.org/10.1007/978-3-031-77019-7_14

As described above, reactive synthesis can be viewed as a two-player zero-sum game, in which the system player aims at satisfying the specification as her goal (or winning objective) whereas the objective of the environment player is the negation of the specification. If there is a winning strategy for the system player, then any one of them is an implementation satisfying the specification. However, the assumption that the objective of the environment is antagonistic to the system's objective is too conservative; usually, the environment behaves based on its own preference or interest. Also, the environment often consists of multiple agents, and hence a multi-player non-zero-sum game is a more appropriate model than a two-player zero-sum game. Furthermore, it is natural to require that the system should satisfy the specification under the assumption that all players behave *rationally*, i.e., they behave aiming to satisfy their own objectives.

Rational synthesis (abbreviated as RS) asks whether a given specification is satisfied whenever all the players behave rationally. *Rational verification* (abbreviated as RV) is the problem asking whether every rational strategy profile satisfies a specification. RV is defined by adding the rationality assumption on the usual model checking, which asks whether every execution of a given model satisfies a specification [2]. Note that RV and RS are closely related. The answer of RV for a specification ψ is *no* if and only if the answer of RS for $\neg\psi$ is *yes*. Namely, RV fails for ψ iff there is a counter-example to ψ (a rational behavior that satisfies $\neg\psi$). As described in the related work section below, rationality is traditionally captured by Nash equilibrium, which is one of the most important concepts in game theory. We say that a tuple of strategies of all players (called a strategy profile) is a *Nash equilibrium* (abbreviated as NE) when no one can improve her own payoff, which is the reward she receives from the game, by changing her strategy alone. An NE locally maximizes each player's payoff and hence each player has no incentive to change her strategy. From the viewpoint of epistemic game theory, however, NE is not always suitable for the concept of rationality because each player is assumed to know the strategies of the other players. (Also see the related work below.)

Epistemic game theory [3] uses a Kripke frame that consists of a set of worlds (or states) W and a subset $R_p(w) \subseteq W$ for each player p and a world w. For a world w and a player p, $R_p(w)$ represents the set of possible worlds from the viewpoint of p in the actual world w of p. For instance, if $R_p(w) = \{w, w', w''\}$, it means that the information given to p in w is incomplete and p cannot distinguish w from w' or w''. Possible world is useful for modelling a situation such that each player (or process) cannot know the internal states of the other players (e.g., the contents of local variables of the other processes). An *epistemic model* is a pair of a Kripke frame and a mapping that associates a strategy profile with each world. We say that a player p is rational in a world w, if for every possible world w' of p in w, there is no better strategy of p than the one associated with w. Then, a strategy profile is said to be *epistemically rational* if there exist an epistemic model M and a world w in M such that every player is rational in w and this property is a common knowledge among all players. (The formal definition of common knowledge is postponed to the next section.)

In this paper, we propose a new framework for reactive synthesis and verification, by augmenting graph game with epistemic models. We then define the rational verification problem based on the proposed model and present some results on the complexity of the problem.

Related Work

Studies on reactive synthesis has its origin in 1960s and has been one of central topics in formal methods as well as model checking. The problem is EXPTIME-complete when a specification is given by an ω-automaton [4] and 2EXPTIME-complete when a specification is given by an LTL formula [5]. Rational synthesis (RS) is in 2EXPTIME [6] when a specification and objectives (in what follows, we refer to as objectives only) are given as LTL formulas. It is PSPACE-complete when objectives of players are restricted to GR(1) [7]. The complexity of RS is also studied for ω-regular objectives. RS is PTIME-complete with Büchi objectives, NP-complete with coBüchi, parity, Streett objectives [8] and PSPACE-complete with Muller objectives [9]. RS has been applied to the synthesis of non-repudiation and fair exchange protocols [10,11]. RS is optimistic in the sense that the system first proposes a strategy profile and all environment players will follow it as far as they do not have profitable deviations. For this reason, another type of RS was proposed, called non-cooperative rational synthesis (NCRS) in [12]. NCRS asks whether there is a strategy s_0 of the system such that every 0-fixed NE (a strategy profile where no environment player has a profitable deviation) including s_0 satisfies the specification. Decidability and complexity of NCRS have also been studied [9,12,13].

Bruyère, et al. [14] investigated the complexity of rational verification (RV) taking Pareto-optimality as the notion of rationality, and show that RV is coNP-complete, Π_2^P-complete and PSPACE-complete with parity, Boolean Büchi and LTL objectives, respectively. Brice, et al. [15] considered weighted (or duration) games, adopted NE and subgame-perfect equilibrium as the notions of rationality and showed that RV is coNP-complete with mean payoff objectives and undecidable with energy objectives.

Epistemic rationality does not always imply NE. In [16], Aumann and Brandenburger show an epistemic sufficient condition for NE in terms of strategic form game (not graph game). (Also see [17].)

As described above, there are already many studies on the decidability and complexity of RS and RV. However, all of them take NE or its refinement as criteria of rationality. This paper is the first step for defining and analyzing RV where the rationality is defined in an epistemic way. Also, we think that combining an epistemic model with a usual graph game enables us to express incomplete information of a player in a natural way.

Outline

In Sects. 2 and 3, we review graph game and epistemic model. In Sect. 4, we define rational verification problems $VPCKR_S$, $VPCKR_{P,S}$ and $VPNash_S$. The problem $VPCKR_S$ asks whether all strategy profiles over the class S of strategies satisfy a given specification when CKR holds. The problem $VPCKR_{P,S}$ is a variant of $VPCKR_S$, where the size of an epistemic model is not greater than a polynomial size of a game arena. The problem $VPNash_S$ asks whether all NE over the class S of strategies satisfy a given specification. Table 1 shows the complexities of these problems. Str is the class of all strategies and Pos is the class of all positional strategies. In Sect. 5, we summarize the paper and give future work.

Table 1. The complexities of verification problems

	$VPCKR_{\mathsf{Pos}}$	$VPCKR_{\mathsf{P,Pos}}$	$VPNash_{\mathsf{Pos}}$	$VPNash_{\mathsf{Str}}$
Upper bound	coNEXP^{NP}	Π_2^{P}	Π_2^{P}-complete	PSPACE-complete [9]
Lower bound	Σ_2^{P}-hard	coNP-hard		

2 Graph Game

In this section, we provide basic definitions and notions on graph games, which are needed to present our new framework. We start with the definition of game arena, winning objective and strategy and so on, followed by the definition of Nash equilibrium (NE).

A graph game is a directed graph with an initial vertex. Each vertex is controlled by a player who chooses next vertex. A game is started from the initial vertex. Then, players repeatedly choose the next vertex according to their strategies. An infinite sequence of vertices generated by such a process is called a play. If the play satisfies the winning objective of a player, then she wins. Otherwise, she loses. Note that our setting is non-zero-sum, hence it is possible that there are multiple winners. An NE is a tuple of strategies of all players where each loser cannot become a winner by changing her strategy alone.

For a binary relation $R \subseteq X \times X$ over a set X and a subset $A \subseteq X$, we define $R(A) = \{x \in X \mid (a, x) \in R \land a \in A\} \subseteq X$.

Game Arena

Definition 1. *A game arena is a tuple $G = (P, V, (V_p)_{p \in P}, v_0, \Delta)$, where*

- *P is a finite set of players,*
- *V is a finite set of vertices,*
- *$(V_p)_{p \in P}$ is a partition of V, namely, $V_i \cap V_j = \varnothing$ for all $i \neq j$ $(i, j \in P)$ and $\bigcup_{p \in P} V_p = V$,*
- *$v_0 \in V$ is the initial vertex, and*
- *$\Delta \subseteq V \times V$ is a set of edges where $\Delta(v) \neq \varnothing$ for all $v \in V$.*

Play and History. An infinite sequence of vertices $v_0 v_1 v_2 \cdots$ ($v_i \in V, i \geq 0$) starting from the initial vertex v_0 is a *play* if $(v_i, v_{i+1}) \in \Delta$ for all $i \geq 0$. A *history* is a non-empty (finite) prefix of a play. The set of all plays is denoted by $Play_G$ and the set of all histories is denoted by $Hist_G$. We often write a history as hv where $h \in Hist \cup \{\varepsilon\}$ and $v \in V$. For a player $p \in P$, let $Hist_{G,p} = \{hv \in Hist \mid v \in V_p\}$. That is, $Hist_{G,p}$ is the set of histories ending with a vertex controlled by player p. We abbreviate $Play_G$, $Hist_{G,p}$ and $Hist_G$ as $Play$, $Hist_p$ and $Hist$ respectively, if G is clear from the context. For a play $\rho = v_0 v_1 v_2 \cdots \in Play$, we define $Inf(\rho) = \{v \in V \mid \forall i \geq 0.\ \exists j \geq i.\ v_j = v\}$.

Strategy. For a player $p \in P$, a *strategy* of p is a function $s_p : Hist_p \to V$ such that $(v, s_p(hv)) \in \Delta$ for all $hv \in Hist_p$. At a vertex $v \in V_p$, player p chooses $s_p(hv)$ as the next vertex according to her strategy s_p. Note that because the domain of s_p is $Hist_p$, the next vertex may depend on the whole history in general. Let $\mathsf{Str}_{G,p}$ denote the set of all strategies of p.

When a p's strategy $s_p \in \mathsf{Str}_{G,p}$ satisfies $s_p(hv) = s_p(h'v)$ for all $hv, h'v \in Hist_p$, we say that s_p is *positional* because the next vertex depends only on the current vertex v. We regard a function $s_p : V_p \to \Delta(V)$ as a p's positional strategy where $s_p(hv) = s_p(v)$ for all $hv \in Hist_p$. Let $\mathsf{Pos}_{G,p} \subseteq \mathsf{Str}_{G,p}$ denote the set of all positional strategies of p.

We abbreviate $\mathsf{Str}_{G,p}$ and $\mathsf{Pos}_{G,p}$ as Str_p and Pos_p respectively, if G is clear from the context.

Strategy Profile. A *strategy profile* is a tuple $s = (s_p)_{p \in P}$ of strategies of all players, namely $s_p \in \mathsf{Str}_p$ for all $p \in P$. Let Str_G (resp. Pos_G) be the set of all strategy profiles (resp. the set of all strategy profiles ranging over positional strategies). We define the function $out_G : \mathsf{Str}_G \to Play$ as $out_G((s_p)_{p \in P}) = v_0 v_1 v_2 \cdots$ where $v_{i+1} = s_p(v_0 \cdots v_i)$ for all $i \geq 0$ and for $p \in P$ with $v_i \in V_p$. We call the play $out_G(s)$ the *outcome* of s. We abbreviate Str_G, Pos_G and out_G as Str, Pos and out respectively, if G is clear from the context. For a strategy profile $s \in \mathsf{Str}_G$ and a strategy $s'_p \in \mathsf{Str}_p$ of a player $p \in P$, let $s[p \mapsto s'_p] \in \mathsf{Str}_G$ denote the strategy profile obtained from s by replacing the strategy of p in s with s'_p.

Objective. We assume that the result a player obtains from a play is either a winning or a losing. Each player has her own winning condition over plays, and we represent a winning condition by a subset $O \subseteq Play$ of plays; i.e., the player wins if and only if the play belongs to the subset O. We call the subset O the *objective* of that player. In this paper, we focus on the following important classes of objectives.

Definition 2. *Let $U \subseteq V$ be a subset of vertices and φ be a Boolean formula whose variables are the vertices of V. We will use U and φ as finite representations for specifying an objective as follows.*

- *Büchi objective:*
  Büchi$(U) = \{\rho \in Play \mid Inf(\rho) \cap U \neq \varnothing\}$.

– *Muller objective:*
   Muller(φ) = $\{\rho \in Play \mid \varphi$ *is true under* $\theta_\rho\}$ *where* θ_ρ *is the truth assignment defined as* $\theta_\rho(v) = true$ *iff* $v \in Inf(\rho)$.

Note that a Büchi objective is also a Muller objective: For any $U \subseteq V$, it holds that Büchi(U) = Muller($\bigvee_{u \in U} u$).

Objective Profile. An *objective profile* is a tuple $\boldsymbol{\alpha} = (O_p)_{p \in P}$ of objectives of all players, namely $O_p \subseteq Play$ for all $p \in P$. For a strategy profile $\boldsymbol{s} \in \mathsf{Str}$ and an objective profile $\boldsymbol{\alpha} = (O_p)_{p \in P}$, we define the set $\mathrm{Win}_G(\boldsymbol{\alpha}, \boldsymbol{s}) \subseteq P$ of winners as $\mathrm{Win}_G(\boldsymbol{\alpha}, \boldsymbol{s}) = \{p \in P \mid \mathrm{out}_G(\boldsymbol{s}) \in O_p\}$. That is, a player p is a winner if and only if $\mathrm{out}_G(\boldsymbol{s})$ belongs to the objective O_p of p. If $p \in \mathrm{Win}_G(\boldsymbol{\alpha}, \boldsymbol{s})$, we also say that p wins for G and $\boldsymbol{\alpha}$ (by the strategy profile $\boldsymbol{s}$). Note that it is possible that no player wins the game or all the players win the game. In this sense, a game is *non-zero-sum*. If an objective profile $\boldsymbol{\alpha} = (O_p)_{p \in P}$ is a partition of *Play*, i.e., $O_i \cap O_j = \varnothing$ for all $i \neq j$ $(i, j \in P)$ and $\bigcup_{p \in P} O_p = Play$, then the game is called *zero-sum*. When a game is zero-sum, there is one and only one winner and the other players are all losers. We abbreviate Win_G as Win if G is clear from the context.

Winning Strategy. Let $S \in \{\mathsf{Pos}, \mathsf{Str}\}$ be a class of strategy profiles. When the objective of player p is O_p, a strategy $s \in S_p$ is called a *winning strategy* of p if it holds that $\mathrm{out}(\boldsymbol{s}[p \mapsto s]) \in O_p$ for every strategy profile $\boldsymbol{s} \in S$. That is, s is a winning strategy of p if p always wins by taking s regardless of the strategies of the other players.

Nash Equilibrium. Let $\boldsymbol{\alpha} = (O_p)_{p \in P}$ be an objective profile and $S \in \{\mathsf{Pos}, \mathsf{Str}\}$ be a class of strategy profiles. A strategy profile $\boldsymbol{s} \in S$ is called a *Nash equilibrium* (NE) for $\boldsymbol{\alpha}$ and S if it holds that $\forall p \in P. \forall s_p \in S_p. p \in \mathrm{Win}(\boldsymbol{\alpha}, \boldsymbol{s}[p \mapsto s_p]) \implies p \in \mathrm{Win}(\boldsymbol{\alpha}, \boldsymbol{s})$. Intuitively, $\boldsymbol{s}$ is an NE if any player p cannot improve the result (from losing to winning) by changing her strategy alone. Because $p \in \mathrm{Win}(\boldsymbol{\alpha}, \boldsymbol{s})$ is equivalent to $\mathrm{out}(\boldsymbol{s}) \in O_p$, a strategy profile $\boldsymbol{s} \in S$ is an NE for $\boldsymbol{\alpha}$ and S if and only if $\forall p \in P. \forall s_p \in S_p. \mathrm{out}(\boldsymbol{s}[p \mapsto s_p]) \in O_p \implies \mathrm{out}(\boldsymbol{s}) \in O_p$. We write this condition as $Nash(\boldsymbol{s}, \boldsymbol{\alpha}, S)$.

Example 1. Figure 1 shows a 3-player game arena $G = (P, V, (V_p)_{p \in P}, v_0, \Delta)$ where $P = \{0, 1, 2\}$, $V = \{v_0, v_1, v_2\}$, $V_p = \{v_p\}$ $(p \in P)$ and $\Delta = \{(v_i, v_j) \mid i, j \in P, i \neq j\}$. The objective of player p is $O_p = $ Büchi($\{v_{(p+1) \bmod 3}\}$), namely to visit the vertex $v_{(p+1) \bmod 3}$ infinitely often. The objective profile is $\boldsymbol{\alpha} = (O_p)_{p \in P}$. Let $\boldsymbol{s} = (s_p)_{p \in P} \in \mathsf{Pos}$ be the strategy profile over positional strategies where $s_p(h) = v_{(p+1) \bmod 3}$ for all $h \in Hist_p$. Let $\boldsymbol{s}' = (s'_p)_{p \in P} \in \mathsf{Pos}$ be the strategy profile over positional strategies where $s'_0(h_0) = v_1$ and $s'_1(h_1) = s'_2(h_2) = v_0$ for all $h_p \in Hist_p$ $(p \in P)$. It holds that $\mathrm{out}(\boldsymbol{s}) = (v_0 v_1 v_2)^\omega \in O_p$ for all p. Hence, $\mathrm{Win}(\boldsymbol{\alpha}, \boldsymbol{s}) = \{0, 1, 2\}$. On the other hand, it holds that $\mathrm{out}(\boldsymbol{s}') = (v_0 v_1)^\omega \in O_0 \cap O_2$ and $\mathrm{out}(\boldsymbol{s}') \notin O_1$. Hence, $\mathrm{Win}(\boldsymbol{\alpha}, \boldsymbol{s}') = \{0, 2\}$. The strategy profile $\boldsymbol{s}$ is an NE for $\boldsymbol{\alpha}$. The strategy profile $\boldsymbol{s}'$ is not an NE for $\boldsymbol{\alpha}$ because there is a positional strategy $s_1 \in \mathsf{Pos}_1$ of player 1 such that $1 \in \mathrm{Win}(\boldsymbol{\alpha}, \boldsymbol{s}'[1 \mapsto s_1])$.

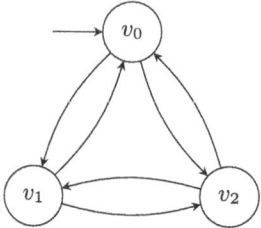

Fig. 1. 3-player game arena with Büchi objectives

The following problem asks if a given strategy profile s satisfies a specification O. We use Lemma 1 to prove the upper bounds of the complexities of verification problems in Sect. 4.

Problem 1. Let G be a game arena, $O \subseteq Play$ be a Muller objective and $S \in \{\mathsf{Pos}, \mathsf{Str}\}$ be a class of strategy profiles. We define the simple verification problem as follows.

$$sVP_S = \{\langle G, s, O \rangle \mid s \in S \wedge \mathrm{out}(s) \in O\}.$$

Lemma 1. sVP_{Pos} *is in* PTIME.

Proof. Let φ be a given Boolean formula representing a Muller objective O (i.e. $O = \mathrm{Muller}(\varphi)$). Because $s \in \mathsf{Pos}$ is a strategy profile over positional strategies, the play $\mathrm{out}(s)$ can be written as $\mathrm{out}(s) = u_0 u^\omega$ for some $u_0 \in V^*$ and $u \in V^+$ such that $u_0 u$ does not contain any vertex twice. Vertices in u are visited infinitely often and vertices not in u are visited only finite times, and thus we can construct the truth assignment $\theta_{\mathrm{out}(s)}$ such that $\theta_{\mathrm{out}(s)}(v) = true$ iff $v \in Inf(\mathrm{out}(s))$ in polynomial time. Simply evaluating φ under $\theta_{\mathrm{out}(s)}$, we can check whether the play satisfies the Muller objective O. □

3   Epistemic Model

In this section, we first review Kripke frame and epistemic model together with the important notion: (epistemic) rationality and common knowledge of rationality and give simple examples. We then propose a new characterization of the notion of common knowledge of rationality based on graph games.

KT5 Kripke Frame

Definition 3. *A KT5 Kripke frame is a pair* $(W, (R_p)_{p \in P})$, *where*

- *P is a finite set of players,*
- *W is a finite set of (possible) worlds, and*
- *$R_p \subseteq W \times W$ is an equivalence relation on W, namely, R_p satisfies*
     (reflexivity) $\forall w \in W. (w, w) \in R_p$,
     (symmetry) $\forall w, w' \in W. ((w, w') \in R_p \implies (w', w) \in R_p)$, *and*

(transitivity) $\forall w_1, w_2, w_3 \in W.$ $((w_1, w_2), (w_2, w_3) \in R_p \implies (w_1, w_3) \in R_p)$.

A Kripke frame expresses the structure of knowledge of players. In the world w, Player p only knows that she is in one of the worlds of $R_p(w)$. In other words, in the world w, Player p cannot distinguish the worlds of $R_p(w)$ with one another.

Knowledge Operator. For a given KT5 Kripke frame $(W, (R_p)_{p \in P})$, we call any subset $E \subseteq W$ an *event*.

Definition 4. *Let $(W, (R_p)_{p \in P})$ be a KT5 Kripke frame and $p \in P$ be a player. The knowledge operator $\mathcal{K}_p : 2^W \to 2^W$, the mutual knowledge operator $\mathcal{MK} : 2^W \to 2^W$ and the common knowledge operator $\mathcal{CK} : 2^W \to 2^W$ are defined as follows.*

$$\mathcal{K}_p(E) = \{w \in W \mid R_p(w) \subseteq E\},$$
$$\mathcal{MK}(E) = \bigcap_{p \in P} \mathcal{K}_p(E), \ and$$
$$\mathcal{CK}(E) = \bigcap_{1 \leq i} \mathcal{MK}^i(E),$$

where $\mathcal{MK}^i$ $(0 \leq i)$ is defined as

$$\mathcal{MK}^0(E) = E, \ and$$
$$\mathcal{MK}^{i+1} E = \mathcal{MK}(\mathcal{MK}^i(E)).$$

Equivalently, we can define $\mathcal{CK}$ as $\mathcal{CK}(E) = \{w \in W \mid R^+(w) \subseteq E\}$ where R^+ is the transitive closure of $\bigcup_{p \in P} R_p$. Note that there is no constant upper bound on the depth of the recursive definition of $\mathcal{CK}$.

Recall that in a world w, she knows only that she is in one of the worlds of $R_p(w)$. If $w \in \mathcal{K}_p(E)$, then $R_p(w) \subseteq E$ holds from the definition of $\mathcal{K}_p$. Hence, in a world $w \in \mathcal{K}_p(E)$, player p knows that she is in one of the worlds of E. When $w \in \mathcal{K}_p(E)$, we say that player p knows the event E occurs in w, or simply p knows E in w. The set $\mathcal{MK}(E)$ is the event such that all players know the event E. If $w \in \mathcal{MK}(E)$, we say that the event E is mutual knowledge in w.

If all players know an event E and all players know that all players know the event E, and all players know that all players know that all players know the event E and so on, we say that E is common knowledge. The set $\mathcal{CK}(E)$ is the event where E is common knowledge. If $w \in \mathcal{CK}(E)$, we say that the event E is common knowledge in w.

Epistemic Model

Definition 5. *Let $G = (P, V, (V_p)_{p \in P}, v_0, \Delta)$ be a game arena and $S \in \{\mathsf{Pos}, \mathsf{Str}\}$ be a class of strategy profiles. An epistemic model for G and S is a tuple $(W, (R_p)_{p \in P}, (\sigma_p)_{p \in P})$ where $(W, (R_p)_{p \in P})$ is a KT5 Kripke frame and $\sigma_p : W \to S$ is a function such that*

$$\forall w, w' \in W. \ ((w, w') \in R_p \implies \sigma_p(w) = \sigma_p(w')). \tag{1}$$

Condition (1) guarantees that each player takes the same strategy in the worlds she cannot distinguish. For a game arena G and a class of strategies $S \in \{\mathsf{Pos}, \mathsf{Str}\}$, let $M(G, S)$ be the set of all epistemic models for G and S.

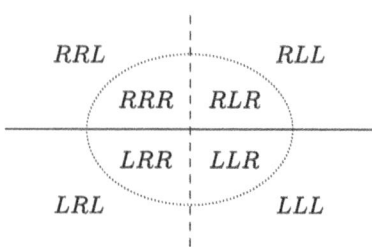

Fig. 2. Equivalence classes in W

Example 2. Let G be a game arena defined in Example 1. Let $s_p^R, s_p^L \in \mathsf{Pos}_p$ be the positional strategies for player p defined as $s_p^R(h) = v_{(p-1) \bmod 3}$ and $s_p^L(h) = v_{(p+1) \bmod 3}$ for all $h \in Hist_p$. Let $M = (W, (R_p)_{p \in P}, \sigma) \in M(G, \mathsf{Pos})$ be an epistemic model for G and Pos, where $W = \{RRR, RRL, RLR, RLL, LRR, LRL, LLR, LLL\}$, $R_p = \{(X_0 X_1 X_2, Y_0 Y_1 Y_2) \mid X_i, Y_i \in \{R, L\}$ for $0 \leq i \leq 2$ and $X_p = Y_p\}$, $\sigma(XYZ) = (s_0^X, s_1^Y, s_2^Z)$ for all $X, Y, Z \in \{R, L\}$. Figure 2 shows the equivalence classes in W. The solid, dashed and densely dotted lines divide W into the equivalence classes of R_0, R_1 and R_2 respectively. Let $E = \{RRR, RRL, RLR, RLL\}$ be the event such that player 0 takes the strategy s_0^R. Then, player 0 knows E in each world of E because $\mathcal{K}_0(E) = E$. On the other hand, players 1 and 2 never know E in any world of W because $\mathcal{K}_1(E) = \mathcal{K}_2(E) = \varnothing$. The event W is both mutual knowledge and common knowledge in all worlds because it holds that $\mathcal{MK}(W) = \mathcal{CK}(W) = W$.

Rationality

Definition 6. *Let $G = (P, V, (V_p)_{p \in P}, v_0, \Delta)$ be a game arena, $\boldsymbol{\alpha}$ be an objective profile, $S \in \{\mathsf{Pos}, \mathsf{Str}\}$ be a class of strategy profiles and $M = (W, (R_p)_{p \in P}, \sigma)$ be an epistemic model for G and S. For a world $w \in W$ and a player $p \in P$, if there is no p's strategy $s_p \in S$ such that*

$$\forall w' \in R_p(w). \; (p \in \mathrm{Win}(\boldsymbol{\alpha}, \sigma(w')) \implies p \in \mathrm{Win}(\boldsymbol{\alpha}, \sigma(w')[p \mapsto s_p])), \, and \quad (2)$$

$$\exists w' \in R_p(w). \; (p \notin \mathrm{Win}(\boldsymbol{\alpha}, \sigma(w')) \wedge p \in \mathrm{Win}(\boldsymbol{\alpha}, \sigma(w')[p \mapsto s_p])), \quad (3)$$

then p is rational[1] *in w.*

We write the set of all worlds where p is rational as $RAT_{G, \boldsymbol{\alpha}, M, S}^p \subseteq W$. The set of all worlds where each player is rational is written as $RAT_{G, \boldsymbol{\alpha}, M, S} = \bigcap_{p \in P} RAT_{G, \boldsymbol{\alpha}, M, S}^p$.

---

[1] The rationality in Definition 6 is called the strong notion of rationality [3].

Characterization of the Notion of Common Knowledge of Rationality

Definition 7. *Let $G = (P, V, (V_p)_{p \in P}, v_0, \Delta)$ be a game arena, α be an objective profile, $S \in \{\mathsf{Pos}, \mathsf{Str}\}$ be a class of strategy profiles. We define a characterization $T_{G,\alpha,S} \subseteq S$ of the notion of common knowledge of rationality for G, α and S as*

$$T_{G,\alpha,S} = \{s \in S \mid \exists M = (W, (R_p)_{p \in P}, \sigma) \in M(G, S).$$
$$\exists w \in W. \ (w \in \mathcal{CK} \ RAT_{G,\alpha,M,S} \wedge \sigma(w) = s)\}.$$

Lemma 2. *Let $T_{G,\alpha,S}$ be a characterization for a game arena $G = (P, V, (V_p)_{p \in P}, v_0, \Delta)$, an objective profile α and a class S of strategy profiles. If $p \in P$ has a winning strategy, then p is a winner, namely $p \in \mathrm{Win}(\alpha, t)$ for all $t \in T_{G,\alpha,S}$.*

Proof. Assume $p \in P$ has a winning strategy. Let t be an arbitrary strategy profile in $T_{G,\alpha,S}$. By the definition of $T_{G,\alpha,S}$, there exist $M = (W, (R_p)_{p \in P}, \sigma) \in M(G, S)$ and $w \in W$ such that $w \in \mathcal{CK} \ RAT_{G,\alpha,M,S}$ and $t = \sigma(w)$. Since $w \in R^+(w)$, $w \in \mathcal{CK} \ RAT_{G,\alpha,M,S}$ implies $w \in RAT_{G,\alpha,M,S}$. If p is a loser under t, namely $p \notin \mathrm{Win}(\alpha, \sigma(w))$, then p is not rational in w because her winning strategy satisfies both conditions (2) and (3) in Definition 6 by letting $w' = w$ in condition (3). This contradicts $w \in RAT_{G,\alpha,M,S}$, and thus, p should win under t. $\qquad \square$

Example 3 (continued). Let G and M be the game arena and the epistemic model respectively, defined in Example 2. Let $\alpha' = (O_p)_{p \in P}$ be an objective profile where $O_p = \mathrm{B\ddot{u}chi}(\{v_p\})$. Then, it holds that $RAT_{G,\alpha',M,\mathsf{Pos}} = W$ because for any world $w \in W$, player p and p's positional strategy $s_p \in \mathsf{Pos}_p$, the condition (2) in Definition 6 holds but (3) does not hold. For example, let $w = RRR$, $p = 0$ and $s_p = s_0^L$. Note that by the structure of G and α', player 0 loses if and only if players 1 and 2 takes s_1^L and s_2^R (regardless of the strategy of player 0). Hence, $0 \in \mathrm{Win}(\alpha', \sigma(w')) \iff 0 \in \mathrm{Win}(\alpha', \sigma(w')[0 \mapsto s_0^L])$ for all $w' \in R_0(RRR)$. By $RAT_{G,\alpha',M,\mathsf{Pos}} = W$, it is easy to see that $\mathcal{CK} \ RAT_{G,\alpha',M,\mathsf{Pos}} = W$ from the structure of M, and hence $T_{G,\alpha',\mathsf{Pos}} = \{\sigma(w) \mid w \in W\} = \mathsf{Pos}$.

Restriction of Epistemic Models. So far, we have made no assumptions about the size of an epistemic model and hence there could be an epistemic model whose size is extremely large. An epistemic model represents a structure of information that players have. It is unnatural to assume that players can use extremely large information within a limited time or a limited computation power. Therefore, we assume that there is a polynomial $p(n)$ such that the size of a given epistemic model is not greater than $p(n)$ where n is the size of a given game arena.

Let G be a game arena and $S \in \{\mathsf{Pos}, \mathsf{Str}\}$ be a class of strategy profiles. We write the set of all epistemic models for G and S whose size is not greater than $p(n)$ for some polynomial p as $M_{\mathsf{P}}(G, S)$ where n is the size of G. Let α be an objective profile. We also define a characterization $T_{\mathsf{P},G,\alpha,S} \subseteq S$ as

$$T_{\mathsf{P},G,\alpha,S} = \{s \in S \mid \exists M = (W, (R_p)_{p \in P}, \sigma) \in M_{\mathsf{P}}(G, S).$$
$$\exists w \in W. \ (w \in \mathcal{CK} \ RAT_{G,\alpha,M,S} \wedge \sigma(w) = s)\}.$$

4 Verification Problems with Common Knowledge of Rationality

We define three types of rational verification problems. The first two of them are defined based on epistemic rationality while the last one is defined based on Nash equilibrium (NE). The second problem is a variant of the first problem, where the size of an epistemic model is not greater than a polynomial size of a game arena. We start with the analysis of the last problem because NE is easier to analyze than epistemic rationality.

Problem 2. We define *verification problems with common knowledge of rationality (VPCKR)* as

$$VPCKR_S = \{\langle G, \boldsymbol{\alpha}, O \rangle \mid \forall \boldsymbol{t} \in T_{G,\boldsymbol{\alpha},S}. \text{ out}(\boldsymbol{t}) \in O\},$$

$$VPCKR_{\mathsf{P},S} = \{\langle G, \boldsymbol{\alpha}, O \rangle \mid \forall \boldsymbol{t} \in T_{\mathsf{P},G,\boldsymbol{\alpha},S}. \text{ out}(\boldsymbol{t}) \in O\}, \text{ and}$$

$$VPNash_S = \{\langle G, \boldsymbol{\alpha}, O \rangle \mid \forall \boldsymbol{s} \in S. \ Nash(\boldsymbol{s}, \boldsymbol{\alpha}, S) \implies \text{out}(\boldsymbol{s}) \in O\}$$

where $G = (P, V, (V_p)_{p \in P}, v_0, \Delta)$ is a game arena, $\boldsymbol{\alpha}$ is an objective profile over Muller objectives, $O \subseteq Play$ is a specification given by a Muller objective and $S \in \{\mathsf{Pos}, \mathsf{Str}\}$ is a class of strategy profiles.

Example 4 (continued). Let G and $\boldsymbol{\alpha}' = (O_p)_{p \in P}$ be the game arena and the objective profile, respectively defined in Example 3. Let O be the specification defined as $O = \bigcap_{p \in P} O_p$. Recall that $T_{G,\boldsymbol{\alpha}',\mathsf{Pos}} = \mathsf{Pos}$. Then, $\langle G, \boldsymbol{\alpha}', O \rangle \notin VPCKR_{\mathsf{Pos}}$ because there is the strategy profile $\boldsymbol{s_3} = (s_0^R, s_1^R, s_2^L) \in T_{G,\boldsymbol{\alpha}',\mathsf{Pos}}$ such that $\text{out}(\boldsymbol{s_3}) \notin O$.

Note that $VPCKR_{\mathsf{P},S}$ is *not* a restricted problem of $VPCKR_S$, because the fact that $\langle G, \boldsymbol{\alpha}, O \rangle \notin VPCKR_S$ (i.e. there is some $\boldsymbol{t} \in T_{G,\boldsymbol{\alpha},S}$ that satisfies $\text{out}(\boldsymbol{t}) \notin O$) gives no information on whether every $\boldsymbol{t} \in T_{\mathsf{P},G,\boldsymbol{\alpha},S}$ satisfies $\text{out}(\boldsymbol{t}) \in O$ or not. For the same reason, $VPNash_S$ is not a restricted problem of $VPCKR_S$ or $VPCKR_{\mathsf{P},S}$. On the other hand, we can say that $VPCKR_S \subseteq VPCKR_{\mathsf{P},S} \subseteq VPNash_S$ holds, because every NE belongs to $T_{\mathsf{P},G,\boldsymbol{\alpha},S}$[2] and $T_{\mathsf{P},G,\boldsymbol{\alpha},S} \subseteq T_{G,\boldsymbol{\alpha},S}$. Also note that $VPCKR_{\mathsf{Pos}}$, $VPCKR_{\mathsf{P},\mathsf{Pos}}$, and $VPNash_{\mathsf{Pos}}$ are not restricted problems of $VPCKR_{\mathsf{Str}}$, $VPCKR_{\mathsf{P},\mathsf{Str}}$, and $VPNash_{\mathsf{Str}}$, respectively. Moreover, because $\boldsymbol{t} \in T_{G,\boldsymbol{\alpha},\mathsf{Pos}}$ does not imply $\boldsymbol{t} \in T_{G,\boldsymbol{\alpha},\mathsf{Str}}$, $VPCKR_{\mathsf{Str}} \not\subseteq VPCKR_{\mathsf{Pos}}$ in general. (For the same reason, $VPCKR_{\mathsf{P},\mathsf{Str}} \not\subseteq VPCKR_{\mathsf{P},\mathsf{Pos}}$ and $VPNash_{\mathsf{Str}} \not\subseteq VPNash_{\mathsf{Pos}}$ in general.)

Before investigating the complexity of $VPCKR_{\mathsf{P},S}$ and $VPCKR_S$, we mention the complexity of $VPNash_S$. As described in Introduction, $VPNash_S$ is closely related to rational synthesis (RS), and with the class of Muller objectives (which is closed under negation and the negation does not cause exponential blow-up), we can easily show that the complexity of RS with the class S of strategy profiles is the same as that of $\overline{VPNash_S}$. By the results of [9], we have the following proposition for $VPNash_{\mathsf{Str}}$.

---

[2] For every NE $\boldsymbol{s} \in S$, the epistemic model with a single world w where $\sigma(w) = \boldsymbol{s}$ satisfies $w \in \mathcal{CK} \, RAT_{G,\boldsymbol{\alpha},M,S}$.

Proposition 1. *VPNash$_{\mathsf{Str}}$ is PSPACE-complete.*

Although the complexity of the same problem with positional strategies was not studied in [9], we can show that *VPNash$_{\mathsf{Pos}}$* is Π_2^P-complete as follows.

Lemma 3. *VPNash$_{\mathsf{Pos}}$ is Π_2^P-hard.*

Proof. We reduce $\forall\exists$SAT to *VPNash$_{\mathsf{Pos}}$*. Let $\varphi = \forall x_1 \ldots x_n \exists y_1 \ldots y_m \, \psi$ be an instance of $\forall\exists$SAT, where $x_1, \ldots, x_n, y_1, \ldots, y_m$ are variables and ψ is a Boolean formula over them. From φ, we construct an instance $\langle G, \alpha, O \rangle$ of *VPNash$_{\mathsf{Pos}}$* where $G = (\{A, E\}, V_A \cup V_E, (V_A, V_E), a_1, \Delta)$ as follows.

$$V_A = \{a_1, \ldots, a_n, x_1, \ldots, x_n, \overline{x_1}, \ldots, \overline{x_n}\},$$
$$V_E = \{e_1, \ldots, e_m, y_1, \ldots, x_m, \overline{y_1}, \ldots, \overline{y_m}\},$$
$$\Delta = \{(a_i, u) \mid 1 \le i \le n, \ u \in \{x_i, \overline{x_i}\}\}$$
$$\cup \{(u, a_{i+1}) \mid 1 \le i < n, \ u \in \{x_i, \overline{x_i}\}\} \cup \{(u, e_1) \mid u \in \{x_n, \overline{x_n}\}\}$$
$$\cup \{(e_i, u) \mid 1 \le i \le n, \ u \in \{y_i, \overline{y_i}\}\}$$
$$\cup \{(u, e_{i+1}) \mid 1 \le i < n, \ u \in \{y_i, \overline{y_i}\}\} \cup \{(u, a_1) \mid u \in \{y_m, \overline{y_m}\}\},$$
$$\alpha = (O_A, O_E) \text{ where } O_A = true \text{ and } O_E = \psi, \text{ and}$$
$$O = \psi.$$

Figure 3 shows the game arena obtained from a formula over x_1, x_2 and y_1. Note that we regard a Boolean formula ψ as a Muller objective. For example, a formula $\psi = x_1 \vee \overline{x_2}$ is considered as the Muller objective such that a player whose objective is ψ wins if the play visits vertex x_1 infinitely often or the play visits x_2 only finite times.

By the structure of G, we can consider every strategy profile $s \in \mathsf{Pos}$ over positional strategies as a truth assignment to the variables in φ; choosing x_i (resp. $\overline{x_i}$) as the next vertex at vertex a_i corresponds to letting $x_i = true$ (resp. $x_i = false$). The same for y_i and $\overline{y_i}$. The play out(s) contains the chosen vertices infinitely many times while it does not contain any unchosen vertex. Therefore, out(s) satisfies ψ as a Muller objective if and only if ψ is true under the truth assignment represented by s.

We show that $\varphi \in \forall\exists$SAT $\iff$ $\langle G, \alpha, O \rangle \in$ *VPNash$_{\mathsf{Pos}}$*.

($\implies$) Assume that $\varphi \in \forall\exists$SAT. We have to show $\forall s \in \mathsf{Pos}$. $Nash(s, \alpha, \mathsf{Pos})$ $\implies$ out(s) $\in O$. Assume that $s = (s_A, s_E) \in \mathsf{Pos}$ and $Nash(s, \alpha, \mathsf{Pos})$. Since $\varphi \in \forall\exists$SAT, for the truth assignment represented by s_A, there must exist a truth assignment to $y_1, \ldots, y_m$ that makes ψ true. Let s'_E denote the positional strategy of E corresponding to this assignment; hence, out($s[E \mapsto s'_E]$) $\in O_E$. On the other hand, by the definition of NE, either out(s) $\in O_E$ or out($s[E \mapsto s'_E]$) $\notin O_E$ should hold for any positional strategy s'_E of E. As shown above, the latter does not hold. Therefore, the former holds and thus out(s) $\in O$ since $O = O_E$.

($\impliedby$) Assume that $\forall s \in \mathsf{Pos}$. $Nash(s, \alpha, \mathsf{Pos})$ $\implies$ out(s) $\in O$. Let s_A be an arbitrary positional strategy of A. We have to show that for s_A, there exists a positional strategy s_E of E such that the truth assignment corresponding to (s_A, s_E) makes ψ true. Let s_E be an arbitrary chosen positional strategy of E

and let $s = (s_A, s_E)$. By the assumption, out$(s) \in O$ holds or $Nash(s, \alpha, \mathsf{Pos})$ does not hold. If out$(s) \in O$ holds, then s_E is just the desired strategy that makes ψ true. If $Nash(s, \alpha, \mathsf{Pos})$ does not hold, then there exist a player p and a positional strategy s' of p that satisfy out$(s) \notin O_p$ and out$(s[p \mapsto s']) \in O_p$. We have $p = E$ because out$(s) \notin O_A$ never holds. Since out$(s[E \mapsto s']) \in O_E$, s' is the desired strategy that makes ψ true.   □

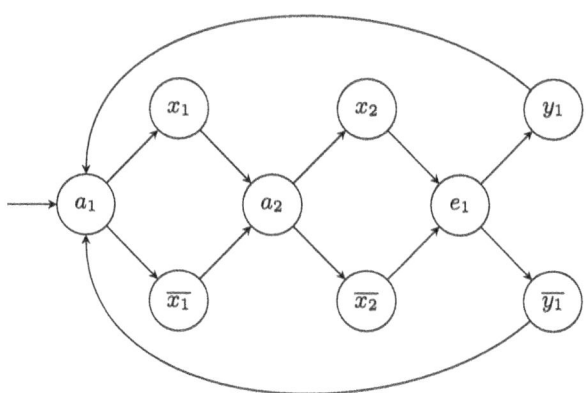

Fig. 3. The game arena constructed from a formula having x_1, x_2 and y_1

Lemma 4. *VPNash$_{\mathsf{Pos}}$ is in Π_2^{P}.*

Proof. By Lemma 1, deciding whether out$(s) \in O$ is in P for a given game, a Muller objective O, and a strategy profile s over positional strategies. Deciding whether $Nash(s, \alpha, \mathsf{Pos})$ for a given game and s is in coNP: Guess a player p and a positional strategy s_p of p, and check whether out$(s) \notin O_p$ and out$(s[p \mapsto s_p]) \in O_p$. Let A be an oracle of this problem. Using A, we can construct a non-deterministic polynomial-time oracle Turing machine for deciding whether $\langle G, \alpha, O \rangle \notin VPNash_{\mathsf{Pos}}$: Guess s and check whether $Nash(s, \alpha, \mathsf{Pos})$ and out$(s) \notin O$. Therefore, $VPNash_{\mathsf{Pos}}$ is in coNP$^{\mathsf{NP}} = \Pi_2^{\mathsf{P}}$.   □

Theorem 1. *VPNash$_{\mathsf{Pos}}$ is Π_2^{P}-complete.*

Proof. By Lemmas 3 and 4.   □

Next, let us consider the complexity of $VPCKR_S$ and $VPCKR_{\mathsf{P},S}$. In this paper, we concentrate on the complexity of $VPCKR_{\mathsf{Pos}}$ and $VPCKR_{\mathsf{P},\mathsf{Pos}}$. For $VPCKR_{\mathsf{P},\mathsf{Pos}}$, we can show that it is coNP-hard and in Π_2^{P} as follows.

Theorem 2. *VPCKR$_{\mathsf{P},\mathsf{Pos}}$ is coNP-hard.*

Proof. We reduce $\overline{\mathsf{SAT}}$, the complement of the satisfiability problem, to $VPCKR_{\mathsf{P,Pos}}$. Let φ be a Boolean formula given as an instance of $\overline{\mathsf{SAT}}$, where $x_1, \ldots x_n$ are variables of φ. From φ, we construct an instance $\langle G, \boldsymbol{\alpha}, O \rangle$ of $VPCKR_{\mathsf{P,Pos}}$ where $G = (\{p\}, V, (V), v_1, \Delta)$ as follows.

$$
\begin{aligned}
V &= \{v_1, \ldots, v_n, x_1, \ldots, x_n, \overline{x_1}, \ldots, \overline{x_n}\}, \\
\Delta &= \{(v_i, u) \mid 1 \le i \le n, \, u \in \{x_i, \overline{x_i}\}\} \\
&\quad \cup \{(u, v_{i+1}) \mid 1 \le i < n, \, u \in \{x_i, \overline{x_i}\}\} \\
&\quad \cup \{(u, v_1) \mid u \in \{x_i, \overline{x_i}\}\}, \\
\boldsymbol{\alpha} &= (O_p) \text{ where } O_p = \varphi, \text{ and} \\
O &= \neg \varphi.
\end{aligned}
$$

We regard a Boolean formula φ as a Muller objective and consider every strategy profile $\boldsymbol{s} \in \mathsf{Pos}$ over positional strategies as a truth assignment to the variables in φ in the same way as the proof of Lemma 3.

We show that $\varphi \in \overline{\mathsf{SAT}} \iff \langle G, \boldsymbol{\alpha}, O \rangle \in VPCKR_{\mathsf{P,Pos}}$.

($\Longrightarrow$) Assume $\varphi \in \overline{\mathsf{SAT}}$. Because φ is unsatisfiable, any strategy profile $\boldsymbol{s} \in \mathsf{Pos}$ satisfies $\mathrm{out}(\boldsymbol{s}) \in O \; (= \neg\varphi)$. Therefore, $\forall t \in T_{\mathsf{P},G,\boldsymbol{\alpha},\mathsf{Pos}}.\ \mathrm{out}(t) \in O$ holds.

($\Longleftarrow$) Assume $\forall t \in T_{\mathsf{P},G,\boldsymbol{\alpha},\mathsf{Pos}}.\ \mathrm{out}(t) \in O$. Note that $\varphi \in \overline{\mathsf{SAT}}$ is equivalent to $\forall \boldsymbol{s} \in \mathsf{Pos}.\ \mathrm{out}(\boldsymbol{s}) \in O$. We show this by contradiction. Suppose $\boldsymbol{s} \in \mathsf{Pos}$ and $\mathrm{out}(\boldsymbol{s}) \notin O$. Consider an epistemic model $M = (\{w\}, (R_p)_{p \in P}, \boldsymbol{\sigma})$ where $R_p = \{(w,w)\}$ and $\boldsymbol{\sigma}(w) = \boldsymbol{s}$. Because $\mathrm{out}(\boldsymbol{s}) \notin O$, player p wins in world w. It is easy to see that $w \in \mathcal{CK}\,RAT$ because of the structure of M. Therefore, $\boldsymbol{s} \in T_{\mathsf{P},G,\boldsymbol{\alpha},\mathsf{Pos}}$. By the outer assumption, $\mathrm{out}(\boldsymbol{s}) \in O$, which contradicts the inner assumption $\mathrm{out}(\boldsymbol{s}) \notin O$.   □

Theorem 3. *$VPCKR_{\mathsf{P,Pos}}$ is in Π_2^{P}.*

Proof. In a similar way to the proof of Lemma 4, we can construct a non-deterministic polynomial-time oracle Turing machine for deciding $\overline{VPCKR_{\mathsf{P,Pos}}}$. Deciding whether $w \in \mathcal{CK}\,RAT_{G,\boldsymbol{\alpha},M,\mathsf{Pos}}$ for a given game, an epistemic model $M = (W, (R_p)_{p \in P}, \boldsymbol{\sigma})$ and a world $w \in W$ is in coNP: Guess a world $u \in R^+(w)$, a player p and a positional strategy $s_p \in \mathsf{Pos}_p$ of p, and check both conditions (2) and (3) in Definition 6 substituting u for w. A non-deterministic polynomial-time oracle Turing machine for deciding whether $\langle G, \boldsymbol{\alpha}, O \rangle \notin VPCKR_{\mathsf{P,Pos}}$ is as follows: Guess an epistemic model $M = (W, (R_p)_{p \in P}, \boldsymbol{\sigma}) \in M_{\mathsf{P}}(G, S)$ and a world $w \in W$, and check whether $w \in \mathcal{CK}\,RAT_{G,\boldsymbol{\alpha},M,\mathsf{Pos}}$ and $\mathrm{out}(\boldsymbol{\sigma}(w)) \notin O$. Note that because the size of M is not greater than some polynomial of the size of G, the construction of M takes only polynomial time. Therefore, $VPCKR_{\mathsf{P,Pos}}$ is in $\mathrm{coNP}^{\mathrm{NP}} = \Pi_2^{\mathsf{P}}$.   □

For $VPCKR_{\mathsf{Pos}}$, we can show that it is Σ_2^{P}-hard and in $\mathrm{coNEXP}^{\mathrm{NP}}$ as follows.

Theorem 4. *VPCKR*$_\text{Pos}$ *is* Σ_2^P-*hard.*

Proof. We reduce ∃∀SAT to *VPCKR*$_\text{Pos}$. Let $\varphi = \exists y_1 \ldots y_m \, \forall x_1 \ldots x_n \, \psi$ be an instance of ∃∀SAT. From φ, we construct an instance $\langle G, \alpha, O \rangle$ of *VPCKR*$_\text{Pos}$ where G is the same game arena as in the proof of Lemma 3 and $O = \psi$ and α consists of $O_A = \neg\psi$ and $O_E = \psi$. As described in the proof of Lemma 3, there is a one-to-one correspondence between the strategy profiles in Pos and the truth assignments to the variables in φ, and player E wins under a strategy profile s if and only if ψ is true under the truth assignment corresponding to s. Therefore by the structure of φ, φ is true if and only if E has a winning strategy.

We show that $\varphi \in$ ∃∀SAT $\iff \langle G, \alpha, O \rangle \in$ *VPCKR*$_\text{Pos}$.

($\implies$) As mentioned above, $\varphi \in$ ∃∀SAT implies E has a winning strategy. By Lemma 2, E wins for every $t \in T_{G,\alpha,\text{Pos}}$; i.e., $\forall t \in T_{G,\alpha,\text{Pos}}$. out$(t) \in O_E$ ($= O$).

($\impliedby$) Assume that $\varphi \notin$ ∃∀SAT; that is, E has no winning strategy. If A has a winning strategy s_A, then any strategy profile $s \in$ Pos where A takes s_A is an NE. Since every NE belongs to $T_{G,\alpha,\text{Pos}}$ and A wins under s, it holds that $s \in T_{G,\alpha,\text{Pos}}$ and out$(t) \notin O$. Therefore, $\langle G, \alpha, O \rangle \notin$ *VPCKR*$_\text{Pos}$.

Consider the case where neither A nor B has a winning strategy. Let T^∞ be the subset of strategy profiles obtained by the following iterative procedure called the *iterated deletion of inferior profiles* (IDIP) [3, Def. 9.8]: For a subset X of strategy profiles and its member $s = (s_p)_{p \in P} \in X$, s is *inferior relative to* X if there exist a player p and p's strategy $t_p \in$ Pos$_p$ such that

1. out$(s) \notin O_p \land$ out$(s[p \mapsto t_p]) \in O_p$, and
2. out$(s') \in O_p \implies$ out$(s'[p \mapsto t_p]) \in O_p$ for every $s' = (s'_p)_{p \in P} \in X$ such that $s'_p = s_p$.

Let $T^0 =$ Pos. T^{i+1} is the set obtained from T^i by removing all strategy profiles inferior relative to T^i. We repeat this construction until there is no inferior strategy profiles. Since Pos is finite, this procedure always halts. Moreover, since neither A nor B has a winning strategy and the game is zero-sum, there must exist a strategy profile $s \in$ Pos remaining in T^∞ that satisfies out$(s) \notin O_E$ ($= O$). As shown in [3, Proposition 9.4 (B)], $s \in T^\infty$ also belongs to $T_{G,\alpha,\text{Pos}}$. Therefore, $\langle G, \alpha, O \rangle \notin$ *VPCKR*$_\text{Pos}$.   □

Theorem 5. *VPCKR*$_\text{Pos}$ *is in co*NEXP$^\text{NP}$.

Proof. For a subset X of Pos, let $M(X) = (W, (R_p)_{p \in P}, \sigma)$ be an epistemic model where $W = X$ and $\sigma(s) = s$ for all $s \in X$, and $R_p = \{(w_1, w_2) \mid \sigma_p(w_1) = \sigma_p(w_2)\}$ for $p \in P$. Using this construction of an epistemic model from a subset of strategy profiles, we can construct a non-deterministic exponential-time oracle Turing machine for deciding $\overline{VPCKR_\text{Pos}}$ as follows: Let $\langle G, \alpha, O \rangle$ be a given instance of *VPCKR*$_\text{Pos}$. Guess a subset $T \subseteq$ Pos and $t \in T$, and construct $M(T)$. Then, check whether t (as a world of $M(T)$) satisfies $t \in \mathcal{CK}\,RAT_{G,\alpha,M(T),\text{Pos}}$ and out$(t) \notin O$.

As mentioned in the proof of Theorem 3, deciding whether $t \in \mathcal{CK}\,RAT$ for given $M(T)$ and t is in coNP. The above Turing machine uses an NP oracle to decide $t \in \mathcal{CK}\, RAT$. Since the size of T and $M(T)$ is exponential to the size of G in general, guessing T and constructing $M(T)$ take exponential time. Deciding whether $\mathrm{out}(t) \notin O$ is in P by Lemma 1 and is not dominant.

If the answer of the Turing machine is *yes*, then obviously $t \in T_{G,\alpha,\mathsf{Pos}}$ and thus $\langle G, \alpha, O \rangle \in \overline{VPCKR_{\mathsf{Pos}}}$. On the other hand, [3, Proposition 9.4] and its proof say that the subset T^∞ of strategy profiles obtained by the IDIP procedure [3, Def. 9.8] satisfies $T^\infty = T_{G,\alpha,\mathsf{Pos}}$, and every world w of the epistemic model $M(T^\infty)$ satisfies $w \in \mathcal{CK}\, RAT_{G,\alpha,M(T^\infty),\mathsf{Pos}}$. Hence, we do not need to consider epistemic models other than $M(T)$ for $T \subseteq \mathsf{Pos}$. Therefore, if the answer of the above Turing machine is *no*, then we can conclude that $\langle G, \alpha, O \rangle \in VPCKR_{\mathsf{Pos}}$.

$\square$

5   Conclusion

We introduced an epistemic approach to rational verification. We defined rational verification problems $VPCKR_S$, $VPCKR_{\mathsf{P},S}$ and $VPNash_S$ based on common knowledge of rationality and Nash equilibrium. The problem $VPCKR_{\mathsf{P},S}$ is a variant of $VPCKR_S$ where the size of an epistemic model is not greater than $p(n)$ for some polynomial p and the size n of a given game arena. The problem $VPNash_S$ asks whether each Nash equilibrium satisfies given specification. Then, we analyzed the complexities of these problems shown. Table 1 summarizes the complexities of the problems.

In this paper, we consider only for the $S = \mathsf{Pos}$ case. Analysing above problems for other S such as the class of the finite memory strategies is future work. Our epistemic model based on KT5 Kripke frame is the knowledge based setting. Hence, if a player knows E in a world w, then E actually occurs in w. There is another setting called belief based setting. In belief based setting, even if a player knows E in w, E doesn't necessarily occur in w. Studying belief based setting is also future work.

References

1. Bloem, R., Chatterjee, K., Jobstmann, B.: Graph games and reactive synthesis. In: Clarke, E., Henzinger, T., Veith, H., Bloem, R. (eds.) Handbook of Model Checking, pp. 921–962. Springer, Cham (2018). https://doi.org/10.1007/978-3-319-10575-8_27
2. Clarke, E.M., Grumberg, O., Peled, D.A.: Model Checking. MIT Press, Cambridge (2001)
3. Bonanno, G.: Epistemic foundations of game theory. In: van Ditmarsch, H. et al. (eds.) Handbook of Epistemic Logic, chap. 9, pp. 411–450, College Publications (2015)
4. Büchi, J.R., Landweber, L.H.: Solving sequential conditions by finite-state strategies. Trans. Am. Math. Soc. **138**, 295–311 (1969)
5. Pnueli, A., Rosner, R.: On the synthesis of a reactive module. In: 16th ACM Symposium on Principles of Programming Languages (POPL 1989), pp. 179–190 (1989)

6. Fisman, D., Kupferman, O., Lustig, Y.: Rational synthesis. In: Esparza, J., Majumdar, R. (eds.) TACAS 2010. LNCS, vol. 6015, pp. 190–204. Springer, Heidelberg (2010). https://doi.org/10.1007/978-3-642-12002-2_16

7. Gutierrez, J., Najib, M., Perelli, G., Wooldridge, M.: On the complexity of rational verification. Ann. Math. Artif. Intell. **91**, 409–430 (2023)

8. Ummels, M.: The complexity of nash equilibria in infinite multiplayer games. In: Amadio, R. (ed.) FoSSaCS 2008. LNCS, vol. 4962, pp. 20–34. Springer, Heidelberg (2008). https://doi.org/10.1007/978-3-540-78499-9_3

9. Condurache, R., Filiot, E., Gentilini, R., Raskin, J.-F.: The complexity of rational synthesis. In: 43rd International Colloquium on Automata, Languages, and Programming (ICALP 2016). LIPIcs, vol. 55, pp. 121:1–121:15 (2016)

10. Kremer, S., Raskin, J.-F.: A game-based verification of non-repudiation and fair exchange protocols. In: Larsen, K.G., Nielsen, M. (eds.) CONCUR 2001. LNCS, vol. 2154, pp. 551–565. Springer, Heidelberg (2001). https://doi.org/10.1007/3-540-44685-0_37

11. Chatterjee, K., Raman, V.: Synthesizing protocols for digital contract signing. In: Kuncak, V., Rybalchenko, A. (eds.) VMCAI 2012. LNCS, vol. 7148, pp. 152–168. Springer, Heidelberg (2012). https://doi.org/10.1007/978-3-642-27940-9_11

12. Kupferman, O., Perelli, G., Vardi, M.: Synthesis with rational environments. Ann. Math. Artif. Intell. **78**(1), 3–20 (2016)

13. Kupferman, O., Shenwald, N.: The complexity of LTL rational synthesis. In: TACAS 2022. LNCS, vol. 13243, pp. 25–45. Springer, Cham (2022). https://doi.org/10.1007/978-3-030-99524-9_2

14. Bruyère, V., Raskin, J.-F., Tamines, C.: Pareto-rational verification. In: 33rd International Conference on Concurrency Theory (CONCUR 2022). LIPIcs.CONCUR.2022, pp. 33:1–33:20 (2022)

15. Brice, L., Raskin, J.-F., van den Bogaard, M.: Rational verification for Nash and subgame-perfect equilibria in graph games. In: 48th International Symposium on Mathematical Foundations of Computer Science (MFCS 2023), pp. 26:1–26:15 (2023)

16. Aumann, R., Brandenburger, A.: Epistemic conditions for Nash equilibrium. Econometrica J. Econom. Soc. 1161–1180 (1995)

17. Polak, B.: Epistemic conditions for Nash equilibrium, and common knowledge of rationality. Econonetrica **67**(3), 673–676 (1999)

Process Calculi

Reversibility in Process Calculi with Nondeterminism and Probabilities

Marco Bernardo[(✉)] and Claudio A. Mezzina

Dipartimento di Scienze Pure e Applicate, Università di Urbino, Urbino, Italy
`marco.bernardo@uniurb.it`

Abstract. A reversible system features not only forward computations, but also backward computations along which the effects of forward ones can be undone by starting from the last performed action. According to causal reversibility, an executed action can be undone provided that all the actions it caused have been undone already. We investigate causal reversibility in a nondeterministic and probabilistic setting by adapting the framework of Phillips and Ulidowski to define a reversible calculus in which action transitions and probabilistic transitions alternate in the style of Hansson and Jonsson. We show that the calculus meets causal reversibility through a suitable variant of the technique of Lanese, Phillips, and Ulidowski that ensures the proper forward and backward interplay of nondeterminism and probabilities. The use of the calculus is illustrated on a quantum computing example.

1 Introduction

Reversible computing has the potential of achieving lower energy consumption because irreversible manipulation of information must be accompanied by an entropy increase due to heat dissipation [25, 2, 7, 16]. Its applications encompass biochemical reaction modeling [37, 38], parallel discrete-event simulation [34, 41], fault-tolerant systems [11, 48, 26, 47], concurrent program debugging [17, 28], robotics [30], control theory [45], and wireless communications [45].

Reversibility in a computing system has to do with the possibility of reverting actions starting from the last performed one. In a concurrent system there may not be a total order over executed actions, hence the last performed action may not be uniquely identifiable. This led to the introduction of the notion of causal reversibility [10], according to which a previously executed action can be undone provided that all of its consequences, if any, have been undone beforehand.

In the process algebraic setting, two approaches have been developed to deal with causal reversibility. The dynamic one of [10, 24] attaches external stack-based memories to process terms so as to store executed actions and discarded subprocesses. A single transition relation is present, where transitions can be labeled with forward or backward actions. In contrast, the static one of [36] makes all process algebraic operators static – in particular action prefix and choice – so that executed actions and discarded subprocesses are kept within

© The Author(s), under exclusive license to Springer Nature Switzerland AG 2025
C. Anutariya and M. M. Bonsangue (Eds.): ICTAC 2024, LNCS 15373, pp. 251–271, 2025.
https://doi.org/10.1007/978-3-031-77019-7_15

the syntax. There are two separate transition relations, a forward one and a backward one. The two approaches have been shown to be equivalent in terms of labeled transition system isomorphism [27] and the common properties they exploit to ensure causal reversibility have been systematically classified in [29].

The approach of [36, 29] is adequate to study reversibility on basic process calculi and state-transition graphs in the nondeterministic case. Recently we have addressed its adoption in the presence of quantitative information. While it smoothly applies to stochastically timed calculi, for which both causal reversibility and time reversibility [22] have been investigated in [5, 4], in the case of deterministically timed calculi its use requires a careful treatment of delays as well as time additivity, laziness, and maximal progress as shown in [6].

In this paper we address reversibility for untimed calculi featuring both nondeterminism and probabilities and show that the approach of [36, 29] has to be adapted again, in a way different from [6]. An example of application of such reversible calculi is randomized dining philosophers [31], in which a philosopher may revoke the choice of the first chopstick if the second one is not available (possibly within a short amount of time like in [4]). A different example is given by speculative consumers [39], where to boost parallelism a consumer can probabilistically predict a value on the basis of which to launch a computation, which has to be undone if the guessed value is different from the one sent later by the producer. Yet another example is the smart contract rollback vulnerability [9]; for instance, in a lottery a smart contract makes a probabilistic choice to draft the winning ticket, but an attacker may try to revert the transaction in the case that the purchased ticket is different from the winning one [15].

There are several probabilistic state-transition models that can be used as a basis for our reversible calculus. A limited form of nondeterminism is allowed within reactive models [18], which correspond to Markov decision processes [13] and Rabin probabilistic automata [40]. Like in generative models [18], which correspond to action-labeled discrete-time Markov chains [23], each transition is labeled with an action and an execution probability, but probabilities are enforced only among transitions labeled with the same action. Therefore, in every state a nondeterministic selection is made among transitions labeled with different actions, then a probabilistic selection takes place inside the set of transitions labeled with that action.

Internal nondeterminism, i.e., nondeterministic choices among transitions labeled with the same action, is supported by Segala simple probabilistic automata [42]. In this model every transition is labeled only with an action and goes from a state to a probability distribution over states. In every state the transition to be executed is selected nondeterministically, then the reached state is selected probabilistically among those in the support of the target probability distribution of the chosen transition.

That combination of probability and nondeterminism is called nonalternating to distinguish it from the alternating one of [19]. In the latter model, states are divided into nondeterministic and probabilistic, with transitions being classified as action transitions, which are labeled with an action and go from a nondeterministic state to a probabilistic one, and probabilistic transitions, which are labeled with a probability and go from a probabilistic state to a nondeterministic one. A more flexible variant, called non-strictly alternating model [35], admits action transitions between two nondeterministic states too.

Both the non-alternating model and the alternating one – whose relationships have been studied in [44] – encompass nondeterministic models, generative models, and reactive models as special cases. Since branching bisimulation semantics plays a fundamental role in reversible systems [12, 3, 14, 15], in this paper we adopt the non-strictly alternating model because in [1] a probabilistic branching bisimulation congruence has been developed for it along with equational and logical characterizations and a polynomial-time decision procedure. In the non-alternating model, for which branching bisimilarity has been just defined in [43], weak variants of bisimulation semantics are more involved because, to achieve transitivity, they require that a single transition be matched by a convex combination of several transitions, corresponding to the use of randomized schedulers; decision procedures can be found in [8, 46].

The first contribution of this paper (Sect. 2) is to show how the general method for reversing process calculi of [36] can be applied to the nondeterministic and probabilistic case based on the non-strictly alternating model. The following adaptations are needed, which are different from those in [6]:

– Similar to executed actions, which have to be decorated with communication keys to know who synchronized with whom when building the backward transition relation [36], probabilistic selections have to be decorated with keys to avoid wrong pairings in the backward direction when they have been performed on both sides of a nondeterministic choice or a parallel composition.
– To comply with the adopted model, in which the forward transitions departing from a state are all either action transitions or probabilistic transitions, like in the forward-only calculus of [1] probabilistic selections have to be made before nondeterministic ones when going forward. As a consequence, a probabilistic selection cannot resolve nondeterministic choices or decide which subprocess advances in a parallel composition. This adds a technical challenge to the definition of the operational semantic rules with respect to [36], as nondeterministic selections – including those among concurrent actions – have to be revoked before probabilistic ones when going backward.

The second contribution (Sect. 4) is to prove that the resulting calculus meets causal reversibility. This is accomplished through notions of [10] and the technique of [29], which however cannot be applied as they are:

– Conflicting transitions, from which concurrent transitions [10] are then derived, and causal equivalence [10], which is needed to identify computations that differ for the order of concurrent action transitions, have to be extended with additional conditions specific to probabilistic transitions.
– The square property for concurrent transitions, on which the technique of [29] relies to obtain causal reversibility, has to be revised to deal with extended squares that include probabilistic transitions as well.

The paper also features an application of the resulting calculus to a quantum computing example (Sect. 3) and some directions for future work (Sect. 5).

2   Reversible Probabilistic Process Calculus

In this section we present the syntax and the semantics of RPPC – Reversible Probabilistic Process Calculus, which is inspired by the process calculi in [20, 1] and tailored for a reversible setting according to the static approach of [36].

Table 1. Syntax of forward (top) and reversible (bottom) processes ($. > {}_p\oplus > + > \|_L$)

$$
\begin{array}{l}
F, G ::= \underline{0} \mid a \, . \, F \mid F \,{}_p{\oplus}\, G \mid F + G \mid F\|_L G \\
R, S ::= F \mid a[i] \, . \, R \mid R \,{}_{[i]p}{\oplus}\, S \mid R \,{}_p{\oplus}_{[i]}\, S \mid R + S \mid R\|_L S
\end{array}
$$

The syntax of RPPC is shown in Table 1 (along with operator precedence). A standard *forward process* F describes the future behavior and is one of the following: the terminated process $\underline{0}$; the action-prefixed process $a \, . \, F$, which is able to perform action $a \in \mathcal{A}$ and then continues as process F, with action set $\mathcal{A}$ including τ as unobservable action; the probabilistic choice $F \,{}_p{\oplus}\, G$, where F is selected with probability $p \in \mathbb{R}_{]0,1[}$ while G is selected with probability $1 - p$; the nondeterministic choice $F + G$, which is resolved based on the actions executable by F and G; or the parallel composition $F\|_L G$, where processes F and G execute in parallel and must synchronize only on actions in $L \subseteq \mathcal{A} \setminus \{\tau\}$.

While in [20] there is a strict alternation between nondeterministic processes like $N = \sum_{h \in H} a_h \, . \, P_h$ and probabilistic processes like $P = \bigoplus_{h \in H} \langle p_h \rangle \, . \, N_h$, as in [1] we stipulate for our more liberal syntax that probabilistic choices have to be resolved *before* nondeterministic ones when going forward, so that every process either executes actions or makes probabilistic selections and no consecutive probabilistic transitions are possible. Thus, similar to time determinism in [6], a probabilistic selection cannot resolve nondeterministic choices or decide who advances in a parallel composition. When each subprocess of a nondeterministic choice or a parallel composition makes a probabilistic selection, the corresponding probabilities are then multiplied at the level of the entire process.

A *reversible process* R includes the past behavior. The syntax of reversible processes differs from the one of forward processes due to the fact that, in the former, actions and probabilities may be decorated. As in [36], an action is decorated with a *communication key* i belonging to a countable set $\mathcal{K}$. A process of the form $a[i] \, . \, R$ expresses that in the past it synchronized with the environment on a and this synchronization was identified by key i. Keys are thus attached only to executed actions and, as we will see, are necessary to remember who synchronized with whom when undoing actions; keys could be omitted in the absence of parallel composition. Processes $R \,{}_{[i]p}{\oplus}\, S$ and $R \,{}_p{\oplus}_{[i]}\, S$ indicate that in the past a probabilistic selection was made in favor of the left or the right subprocess, respectively. We will see that communication keys are needed to avoid wrong pairings of probabilistic selections in the backward direction; keys could be omitted in the absence of nondeterministic choice and parallel composition.

We denote by $\mathcal{P}$ the set of processes generated by the productions for R in Table 1, while we use predicate $\mathtt{std}(\_)$ to identify the standard forward processes that can be derived from the productions for F in the same table. For example, $a \cdot (b \cdot \underline{0}_{\,0.5} \oplus c \cdot \underline{0})$ is a standard forward process that can execute action a and then probabilistically selects between doing action b or doing action c, while $a[i] \cdot (b \cdot \underline{0}_{\,[j]0.5} \oplus c \cdot \underline{0})$ is a reversible process that can either undo the probabilistic selection in favor of b (key j) and then action a (key i), or perform action b. Note that $a \cdot (b \cdot \underline{0}_{\,[j]0.5} \oplus c \cdot \underline{0})$ and $a \cdot (b[i] \cdot \underline{0}_{\,0.5} \oplus c \cdot \underline{0})$ are not in $\mathcal{P}$ as a future action or probabilistic selection cannot precede a past one in the description of a process.

Let $\mathcal{A_K} = \mathcal{A} \times \mathcal{K}$ and $\mathbb{R}_\mathcal{K} = \mathbb{R}_{]0,1[} \times \mathcal{K}$, with $\mathcal{L} = \mathcal{A_K} \cup \mathbb{R}_\mathcal{K}$ ranged over by ℓ. The semantics for RPPC is the labeled transition system $(\mathcal{P}, \mathcal{L}, \longmapsto)$. The transition relation $\longmapsto \,\subseteq\, \mathcal{P} \times \mathcal{L} \times \mathcal{P}$ is given by $\longmapsto \,=\, \longrightarrow \cup \dashrightarrow$ where in turn the *forward transition relation* is given by $\longrightarrow \,=\, \longrightarrow_\mathtt{a} \cup \longrightarrow_\mathtt{p}$ and the *backward transition relation* is given by $\dashrightarrow \,=\, \dashrightarrow_\mathtt{a} \cup \dashrightarrow_\mathtt{p}$. In the definitions of the transition relations, we make use of the set $\mathtt{key}_\mathtt{a}(R)$ of action keys and of the set $\mathtt{key}_\mathtt{p}(R)$ of probabilistic selection keys occurring in $R \in \mathcal{P}$:

$$
\begin{aligned}
\mathtt{key}_\mathtt{a}(F) &= \emptyset & \mathtt{key}_\mathtt{p}(F) &= \emptyset \\
\mathtt{key}_\mathtt{a}(a[i] \cdot R) &= \{i\} \cup \mathtt{key}_\mathtt{a}(R) & \mathtt{key}_\mathtt{p}(a[i] \cdot R) &= \mathtt{key}_\mathtt{p}(R) \\
\mathtt{key}_\mathtt{a}(R_{\,[i]p} \oplus S) &= \mathtt{key}_\mathtt{a}(R) & \mathtt{key}_\mathtt{p}(R_{\,[i]p} \oplus S) &= \{i\} \cup \mathtt{key}_\mathtt{p}(R) \\
\mathtt{key}_\mathtt{a}(R_{\,p} \oplus_{[i]} S) &= \mathtt{key}_\mathtt{a}(S) & \mathtt{key}_\mathtt{p}(R_{\,p} \oplus_{[i]} S) &= \{i\} \cup \mathtt{key}_\mathtt{p}(S) \\
\mathtt{key}_\mathtt{a}(R + S) &= \mathtt{key}_\mathtt{a}(R) \cup \mathtt{key}_\mathtt{a}(S) & \mathtt{key}_\mathtt{p}(R + S) &= \mathtt{key}_\mathtt{p}(R) \cup \mathtt{key}_\mathtt{p}(S) \\
\mathtt{key}_\mathtt{a}(R\|_L S) &= \mathtt{key}_\mathtt{a}(R) \cup \mathtt{key}_\mathtt{a}(S) & \mathtt{key}_\mathtt{p}(R\|_L S) &= \mathtt{key}_\mathtt{p}(R) \cup \mathtt{key}_\mathtt{p}(S)
\end{aligned}
$$

as well as of predicate $\mathtt{npa}(\_)$ to establish whether the considered process $R \in \mathcal{P}$ contains no past actions (note that $\mathtt{std}(R)$ ensures $\mathtt{npa}(R)$):

$$
\begin{aligned}
\mathtt{npa}(F) &= \mathtt{true} & \mathtt{npa}(a[i] \cdot R) &= \mathtt{false} \\
\mathtt{npa}(R_{\,[i]p} \oplus S) &= \mathtt{npa}(R) & \mathtt{npa}(R_{\,p} \oplus_{[i]} S) &= \mathtt{npa}(S) \\
\mathtt{npa}(R + S) &= \mathtt{npa}(R) \wedge \mathtt{npa}(S) & \mathtt{npa}(R\|_L S) &= \mathtt{npa}(R) \wedge \mathtt{npa}(S)
\end{aligned}
$$

The *action transition relations* $\longrightarrow_\mathtt{a} \,\subseteq\, \mathcal{P} \times \mathcal{A_K} \times \mathcal{P}$ and $\dashrightarrow_\mathtt{a} \,\subseteq\, \mathcal{P} \times \mathcal{A_K} \times \mathcal{P}$ are the least relations respectively induced by the forward rules in the left part of Table 2 and by the backward rules in the right part of the same table.

Rule ACT1 handles processes of the form $a \cdot F$, where F is written as R subject to $\mathtt{std}(R)$. In addition to transforming the action prefix into a transition label, it generates a key i that is bound to action a thus yielding the label $a[i]$. As can be noted, according to [36] the prefix is not discarded by the application of the rule, instead it becomes a key-storing part of the target process that is necessary to offer again that action after rolling back. Rule ACT1$^\bullet$ reverts action $a[i]$ of process $a[i] \cdot R$ provided that R is a standard process, which ensures that $a[i]$ is the only executed action that is left to undo.

Table 2. Operational semantic rules for RPPC action transitions

$$(\text{ACT1}) \ \frac{\texttt{std}(R)}{u \,.\, R \xrightarrow{a[i]}_{\mathbf{a}} a[i] \,.\, R} \qquad\qquad (\text{ACT1}^\bullet) \ \frac{\texttt{std}(R)}{a[i] \,.\, R \dashrightarrow^{a[i]}_{\mathbf{a}} a \,.\, R}$$

$$(\text{ACT2}) \ \frac{R \xrightarrow{b[j]}_{\mathbf{a}} R' \quad j \neq i}{a[i] \,.\, R \xrightarrow{b[j]}_{\mathbf{a}} a[i] \,.\, R'} \qquad\qquad (\text{ACT2}^\bullet) \ \frac{R \dashrightarrow^{b[j]}_{\mathbf{a}} R' \quad j \neq i}{a[i] \,.\, R \dashrightarrow^{b[j]}_{\mathbf{a}} a[i] \,.\, R'}$$

$$(\text{ACT3}) \ \frac{R \xrightarrow{b[j]}_{\mathbf{a}} R'}{R \,_{[i]p}{\oplus}\, S \xrightarrow{b[j]}_{\mathbf{a}} R' \,_{[i]p}{\oplus}\, S} \qquad\qquad (\text{ACT3}^\bullet) \ \frac{R \dashrightarrow^{b[j]}_{\mathbf{a}} R'}{R \,_{[i]p}{\oplus}\, S \dashrightarrow^{b[j]}_{\mathbf{a}} R' \,_{[i]p}{\oplus}\, S}$$

$$(\text{CHO}) \ \frac{R \xrightarrow{a[i]}_{\mathbf{a}} R' \quad \texttt{npa}(S) \quad S \not\to_{\mathbf{p}}}{R + S \xrightarrow{a[i]}_{\mathbf{a}} R' + S} \qquad (\text{CHO}^\bullet) \ \frac{R \dashrightarrow^{a[i]}_{\mathbf{a}} R' \quad \texttt{npa}(S) \quad S \not\to_{\mathbf{p}}}{R + S \dashrightarrow^{a[i]}_{\mathbf{a}} R' + S}$$

$$(\text{PAR}) \ \frac{\begin{array}{c} R \xrightarrow{a[i]}_{\mathbf{a}} R' \quad a \notin L \quad i \notin \texttt{key}_{\mathbf{a}}(S) \\ S \not\to_{\mathbf{p}} \end{array}}{R\|_L S \xrightarrow{a[i]}_{\mathbf{a}} R'\|_L S} \quad (\text{PAR}^\bullet) \ \frac{\begin{array}{c} R \dashrightarrow^{a[i]}_{\mathbf{a}} R' \quad a \notin L \quad i \notin \texttt{key}_{\mathbf{a}}(S) \\ S \not\to_{\mathbf{p}} \end{array}}{R\|_L S \dashrightarrow^{a[i]}_{\mathbf{a}} R'\|_L S}$$

$$(\text{COO}) \ \frac{R \xrightarrow{a[i]}_{\mathbf{a}} R' \quad S \xrightarrow{a[i]}_{\mathbf{a}} S' \quad a \in L}{R\|_L S \xrightarrow{a[i]}_{\mathbf{a}} R'\|_L S'} \quad (\text{COO}^\bullet) \ \frac{R \dashrightarrow^{a[i]}_{\mathbf{a}} R' \quad S \dashrightarrow^{a[i]}_{\mathbf{a}} S' \quad a \in L}{R\|_L S \dashrightarrow^{a[i]}_{\mathbf{a}} R'\|_L S'}$$

The presence of rules ACT2 and ACT2$^\bullet$ is motivated by the fact that rule ACT1 does not discard the executed action from the process it generates. In particular, rule ACT2 allows a process $a[i] \,.\, R$ to execute if R itself can execute, provided that the action performed by R picks a key j different from i so that all the action prefixes in a sequence are decorated with distinct keys. Rule ACT2$^\bullet$ simply propagates the execution of backward actions from inner subprocesses that are not standard by preserving key uniqueness, in such a way that executed actions are undone from the most recent one to the least recent one.

Rules ACT3 and ACT3$^\bullet$, along with their omitted symmetric variants for $R \,_{p}{\oplus}_{[i]}\, S$ (in which S has been selected with probability $1-p$), play an analogous propagating role for a resolved probabilistic choice. Note that executed actions and resolved probabilistic choices are not required to feature different keys.

Unlike the classical rules for nondeterministic choice [33], according to [36] rule CHO does not discard the part of the overall process that has not contributed to the executed action. If process R does an action, say $a[i]$, and becomes R', then the entire process $R + S$ becomes $R' + S$ as the information about $+ S$, where S contains no past actions, is necessary for offering again the original choice after rolling back. Once the choice is made, only the non-standard process R' can proceed further because process S – which is standard or contains resolved probabilistic choices – constitutes a dead context of R'. Moreover, since we have stipulated that probabilistic choices have to be resolved before nondeterministic ones when going forward, $R+S$ can perform $a[i]$ and become $R'+S$ if S has no probabilistic transitions, which is denoted by $S \not\to_{\mathbf{p}}$. Rule CHO$^\bullet$ has precisely the same structure as rule CHO, but deals with the backward transition relation; if R' is standard, then the dead context S will come into play again. The symmetric variants of CHO and CHO$^\bullet$, in which it is S to move, are omitted. Note that, in order to apply CHO (resp. CHO$^\bullet$) or its symmetric variant, at least one of R and S must contain no past actions, meaning that it is impossible for two processes containing past actions to execute if they are composed by a choice operator.

The semantics of parallel composition is inspired by [21]. Rule PAR allows process R within $R\|_L S$ to individually perform an action $a[i]$ provided $a \notin L$. It is also checked that the executing action is bound to a key $i \notin \mathsf{key}_\mathsf{a}(S)$, thus ensuring the uniqueness of communication keys across parallel composition too. Moreover, since we have stipulated that, when going forward, probabilistic choices have to be resolved before nondeterministic ones (including those arising from action interleaving), it is further verified that S has no probabilistic transitions. Rule PAR$^\bullet$ has the same structure as PAR; their symmetric variants are omitted. Rules COO and COO$^\bullet$ instead allow both R and S to move by synchronizing on any action in the set L as long as the communication key is the same on both sides. The resulting cooperation action has the same name and the same key as the two synchronizing actions.

To illustrate the need of communication keys [36], consider the standard forward process $(a \,.\, F_1 \|_\emptyset a \,.\, F_2) \|_{\{a\}} (a \,.\, F_3 \|_\emptyset a \,.\, F_4)$, which may evolve to either the reversible process $(a[i] \,.\, F_1 \|_\emptyset a[j] \,.\, F_2) \|_{\{a\}} (a[i] \,.\, F_3 \|_\emptyset a[j] \,.\, F_4)$ or the reversible process $(a[i] \,.\, F_1 \|_\emptyset a[j] \,.\, F_2) \|_{\{a\}} (a[j] \,.\, F_3 \|_\emptyset a[i] \,.\, F_4)$ after performing a forward $a[i]$-transition followed by a forward $a[j]$-transition. When going backward, in the absence of the two distinct communication keys i and j we do not know that the a preceding F_1 (resp. F_2) synchronized with the a preceding F_3 (resp. F_4) in the first case or the a preceding F_4 (resp. F_3) in the second case.

The *probabilistic transition relations* $\longrightarrow_\mathsf{p} \subseteq \mathcal{P} \times \mathbb{R}_\mathcal{K} \times \mathcal{P}$ and $\dashrightarrow_\mathsf{p} \subseteq \mathcal{P} \times \mathbb{R}_\mathcal{K} \times \mathcal{P}$ are the least relations respectively induced by the forward rules in the left part of Table 3 and by the backward rules in the right part of the same table. Each backward probabilistic transition is conventionally labeled with the same probability as the corresponding forward transition; note however that this probabilistic value is meaningful only in the forward direction.

Rules PSEL1 and PSEL2 handle probabilistic selections between standard processes. The former rule describes the case in which R has no probabilistic choices, hence the probability of selecting R is simply p. The latter rule describes the case in which R has probabilistic choices, so that p is multiplied by the probability of selecting R'. To enable reversibility, in both rules the probability associated with the operator is decorated with a unique key and the subprocess that has not been selected is not discarded. Rules PSEL1$^\bullet$ and PSEL2$^\bullet$ are the backward counterparts. The symmetric variants for $R\,_p\oplus_{[i]}\,S$ (in which S has been selected with probability $1 - p$) are omitted. For processes like $\underline{0}\,_{0.5}\oplus\,\underline{0}$ two distinct transitions $\underline{0}\,_{0.5}\oplus\,\underline{0} \xrightarrow{\;(0.5)^{[i]}\;}_\mathsf{p} \underline{0}\,_{[i]0.5}\oplus\,\underline{0}$ and $\underline{0}\,_{0.5}\oplus\,\underline{0} \xrightarrow{\;(0.5)^{[i]}\;}_\mathsf{p} \underline{0}\,_{0.5}\oplus_{[i]}\,\underline{0}$ are generated thanks to decorations in distinct positions within the two target processes, thus avoiding to resort to multisets of probabilistic transitions [20].

Table 3. Operational semantic rules for RPPC probabilistic transitions

$$(\text{PSEL1}) \quad \frac{\text{std}(R) \quad \text{std}(S) \quad R \not\rightarrow_{\text{p}}}{R\,_p{\oplus}\,S \xrightarrow{\ (p)^{[i]}\ }_{\text{p}} R\,_{[i]p}{\oplus}\,S} \qquad (\text{PSEL1}^{\bullet}) \quad \frac{\text{std}(R) \quad \text{std}(S) \quad R \not\rightarrow_{\text{p}}}{R\,_{[i]p}{\oplus}\,S \dashrightarrow^{\ (p)^{[i]}\ }_{\text{p}} R\,_p{\oplus}\,S}$$

$$(\text{PSEL2}) \quad \frac{R \xrightarrow{\ (q)^{[j]}\ }_{\text{p}} R' \quad \text{std}(R) \quad \text{std}(S) \quad i \notin \text{key}_{\text{p}}(R')}{R\,_p{\oplus}\,S \xrightarrow{\ (p\cdot q)^{[i]}\ }_{\text{p}} R'\,_{[i]p}{\oplus}\,S} \qquad (\text{PSEL2}^{\bullet}) \quad \frac{R \dashrightarrow^{\ (q)^{[j]}\ }_{\text{p}} R' \quad \text{std}(R') \quad \text{std}(S) \quad i \notin \text{key}_{\text{p}}(R)}{R\,_{[i]p}{\oplus}\,S \dashrightarrow^{\ (p\cdot q)^{[i]}\ }_{\text{p}} R'\,_p{\oplus}\,S}$$

$$(\text{PSEL3}) \quad \frac{R \xrightarrow{\ (q)^{[j]}\ }_{\text{p}} R' \quad \neg\text{std}(R) \quad j \neq i}{R\,_{[i]p}{\oplus}\,S \xrightarrow{\ (q)^{[j]}\ }_{\text{p}} R'\,_{[i]p}{\oplus}\,S} \qquad (\text{PSEL3}^{\bullet}) \quad \frac{R \dashrightarrow^{\ (q)^{[j]}\ }_{\text{p}} R' \quad \neg\text{std}(R') \quad j \neq i}{R\,_{[i]p}{\oplus}\,S \dashrightarrow^{\ (q)^{[j]}\ }_{\text{p}} R'\,_{[i]p}{\oplus}\,S}$$

$$(\text{PSEL4}) \quad \frac{R \xrightarrow{\ (q)^{[j]}\ }_{\text{p}} R'}{a[i]\,.\,R \xrightarrow{\ (q)^{[j]}\ }_{\text{p}} a[i]\,.\,R'} \qquad (\text{PSEL4}^{\bullet}) \quad \frac{R \dashrightarrow^{\ (q)^{[j]}\ }_{\text{p}} R'}{a[i]\,.\,R \dashrightarrow^{\ (q)^{[j]}\ }_{\text{p}} a[i]\,.\,R'}$$

$$(\text{PCHO1}) \quad \frac{R \xrightarrow{\ (p)^{[i]}\ }_{\text{p}} R' \quad i \notin \text{key}_{\text{p}}(S) \quad \text{npa}(S) \quad S \not\rightarrow_{\text{p}}}{R + S \xrightarrow{\ (p)^{[i]}\ }_{\text{p}} R' + S} \qquad (\text{PCHO1}^{\bullet}) \quad \frac{R \dashrightarrow^{\ (p)^{[i]}\ }_{\text{p}} R' \quad i \notin \text{key}_{\text{p}}(S) \quad \text{npa}(S) \quad S \not\rightarrow_{\text{p}}}{R + S \dashrightarrow^{\ (p)^{[i]}\ }_{\text{p}} R' + S}$$

$$(\text{PCHO2}) \quad \frac{R \xrightarrow{\ (p)^{[i]}\ }_{\text{p}} R' \quad S \xrightarrow{\ (q)^{[i]}\ }_{\text{p}} S'}{R + S \xrightarrow{\ (p\cdot q)^{[i]}\ }_{\text{p}} R' + S'} \qquad (\text{PCHO2}^{\bullet}) \quad \frac{R \dashrightarrow^{\ (p)^{[i]}\ }_{\text{p}} R' \quad S \dashrightarrow^{\ (q)^{[i]}\ }_{\text{p}} S'}{R + S \dashrightarrow^{\ (p\cdot q)^{[i]}\ }_{\text{p}} R' + S'}$$

$$(\text{PPAR}) \quad \frac{R \xrightarrow{\ (p)^{[i]}\ }_{\text{p}} R' \quad i \notin \text{key}_{\text{p}}(S) \quad S \not\rightarrow_{\text{p}}}{R\|_L S \xrightarrow{\ (p)^{[i]}\ }_{\text{p}} R'\|_L S} \qquad (\text{PPAR}^{\bullet}) \quad \frac{R \dashrightarrow^{\ (p)^{[i]}\ }_{\text{p}} R' \quad i \notin \text{key}_{\text{p}}(S) \quad S \not\rightarrow_{\text{p}} \quad \text{npa}(S) \vee \neg\text{npa}(R)}{R\|_L S \dashrightarrow^{\ (p)^{[i]}\ }_{\text{p}} R'\|_L S}$$

$$(\text{PCOO}) \quad \frac{R \xrightarrow{\ (p)^{[i]}\ }_{\text{p}} R' \quad S \xrightarrow{\ (q)^{[i]}\ }_{\text{p}} S'}{R\|_L S \xrightarrow{\ (p\cdot q)^{[i]}\ }_{\text{p}} R'\|_L S'} \qquad (\text{PCOO}^{\bullet}) \quad \frac{R \dashrightarrow^{\ (p)^{[i]}\ }_{\text{p}} R' \quad S \dashrightarrow^{\ (q)^{[i]}\ }_{\text{p}} S'}{R\|_L S \dashrightarrow^{\ (p\cdot q)^{[i]}\ }_{\text{p}} R'\|_L S'}$$

Rules PSEL3 and PSEL3$^{\bullet}$ propagate probabilistic selections in the context of resolved probabilistic choices followed by executed actions; their symmetric variants are omitted. Rules PSEL4 and PSEL4$^{\bullet}$ propagate probabilistic selections in the context of executed actions only. We remind that executed actions and resolved probabilistic choices are not required to feature different keys.

Rule PCHO1 represents a probabilistic selection made within a nondeterministic choice by R alone as $S \not\rightarrow_{\text{p}}$, provided that S contains no past actions and key i does not occur in S, with PCHO1$^{\bullet}$ being its backward counterpart. Their symmetric variants are omitted. Note that, as a consequence of the fact that probabilistic choices have to be resolved before nondeterministic choices when going forward, nondeterministic choices have to be revoked before probabilistic choices when going backward. For instance, $(a\,.\,\underline{0}\,_p{\oplus}\,b\,.\,\underline{0}) + c\,.\,\underline{0}$ first resolves the probabilistic choice thus becoming e.g. $(a\,.\,\underline{0}\,_{[i]p}{\oplus}\,b\,.\,\underline{0}) + c\,.\,\underline{0}$ and then can perform e.g. c thus evolving to $(a\,.\,\underline{0}\,_{[i]p}{\oplus}\,b\,.\,\underline{0}) + c[j]\,.\,\underline{0}$, where the probabilistic choice cannot be revoked – otherwise $(a.\underline{0}_p\oplus b.\underline{0}) + c[j].\underline{0}$ would be reached that cannot be encountered when going forward – thanks to the **npa** constraint.

Rule PCHO2 expresses instead the fact that, since a probabilistic selection cannot decide which subprocess is chosen in a nondeterministic choice, if each subprocess of a nondeterministic choice makes a probabilistic selection then the two selections are synchronized and the corresponding probabilities are multiplied. Rule PCHO2$^\bullet$ plays the corresponding role in the backward direction.

Likewise, rule PPAR represents a probabilistic selection made within a parallel composition by R alone as $S \not\rightarrow_p$, provided that key i does not occur in S, with PPAR$^\bullet$ being its backward counterpart. Their symmetric variants are omitted. Note that PPAR$^\bullet$ additionally requires $\mathbf{npa}(S) \vee \neg\mathbf{npa}(R)$. The $\mathbf{npa}(S)$ part stems from the fact that nondeterministic choices, including those between two interleaving actions in a parallel composition, have to be revoked before probabilistic choices when going backward. As an example, $(a.\underline{0}_p\oplus \quad b.\underline{0})\|_\emptyset c.\underline{0}$ first resolves the probabilistic choice thus becoming e.g. $(a.\underline{0}_{[i]p}\oplus b.\underline{0})\|_\emptyset c.\underline{0}$ and then can perform e.g. c thus evolving to $(a.\underline{0}_{[i]p}\oplus b.\underline{0})\|_\emptyset c[j].\underline{0}$, where the probabilistic choice cannot be revoked – otherwise $(a.\underline{0}_p\oplus b.\underline{0})\|_\emptyset c[j].\underline{0}$ would be reached that cannot be encountered when going forward – thanks to the additional constraint. The $\neg\mathbf{npa}(R)$ part is needed when two probabilistic choices are preceded by two interleaving actions like in $a_1.(b.\underline{0}_p\oplus c.\underline{0})\|_\emptyset a_2.(d.\underline{0}_q\oplus e.\underline{0})$. While going forward this can reach e.g. $a_1[i_1].(b.\underline{0}_{[j_1]p}\oplus c.\underline{0})\|_\emptyset a_2[i_2].(d.\underline{0}_q\oplus_{[j_2]} e.\underline{0})$, from which it must be possible to revoke either probabilistic choice.

Rule PCOO represents instead the fact that, since a probabilistic selection cannot decide which subprocess advances in a parallel composition, if each subprocess of a parallel composition makes a probabilistic selection then the two selections are synchronized and the corresponding probabilities are multiplied. Rule PCOO$^\bullet$ plays the corresponding role in the backward direction.

To illustrate the need of communication keys also for probabilistic choices (not in [36]), consider the standard forward process $(a.\underline{0}_p\oplus b.\underline{0})\|_\emptyset(c.\underline{0}_q\oplus d.\underline{0})$, which may evolve to one of the following four reversible processes:

- $(a.\underline{0}_{[i]p}\oplus b.\underline{0})\|_\emptyset(c.\underline{0}_{[i]q}\oplus d.\underline{0})$ with probability $p\cdot q$.
- $(a.\underline{0}_{[i]p}\oplus b.\underline{0})\|_\emptyset(c.\underline{0}_q\oplus_{[i]} d.\underline{0})$ with probability $p\cdot(1-q)$.
- $(a.\underline{0}_p\oplus_{[i]} b.\underline{0})\|_\emptyset(c.\underline{0}_{[i]q}\oplus d.\underline{0})$ with probability $(1-p)\cdot q$.
- $(a.\underline{0}_p\oplus_{[i]} b.\underline{0})\|_\emptyset(c.\underline{0}_q\oplus_{[i]} d.\underline{0})$ with probability $(1-p)\cdot(1-q)$.

When going backward, in the absence of communication key i we do not know which subprocess of the probabilistic choice on the left of $\|_\emptyset$ was combined with which subprocess of the probabilistic choice on the right of $\|_\emptyset$.

It may be argued that what really matters is the position of the key with respect to the probabilistic parameter, hence a uniform decoration within every occurrence of the probabilistic choice operator – e.g., $_{\langle p}\oplus$ and $_{p\rangle}\oplus$ – would suffice. However, consider the standard forward process $a.(b.\underline{0}_p\oplus c.\underline{0}) \# (d.\underline{0}_q\oplus e.\underline{0})$ where $\# \in \{+, \|_\emptyset\}$. The only initial option is resolving the probabilistic choice on the right, thus reaching for instance

$a . (b . \underline{0}_p \oplus c . \underline{0}) \# (d . \underline{0}_{[i]q} \oplus e . \underline{0})$. Then suppose that a is executed, which can only be followed by resolving the probabilistic choice on the left, which yields for instance $a[j] . (b . \underline{0}_{p \oplus [k]} c . \underline{0}) \# (d . \underline{0}_{[i]q} \oplus e . \underline{0})$. Now, in the backward direction, the two probabilistic selections cannot be undone together – thus reaching the inconsistent $a[j] . (b . \underline{0}_p \oplus c . \underline{0}) \# (d . \underline{0}_q \oplus e . \underline{0})$ – because $i \neq k$ and hence PCHO2$^\bullet$ and PCOO$^\bullet$ are not applicable.

Process syntax prevents future actions or probabilistic selections from preceding past ones as well as both sides of a probabilistic choice from being simultaneously selected. However, these are not the only necessary limitations, because not all the processes generated by the considered grammar are semantically meaningful. In the case of a nondeterministic choice at least one of the two subprocesses has to contain no past actions (but can contain resolved probabilistic choices), hence for instance $a[i] . \underline{0} + b[j] . \underline{0}$ is not admissible as it indicates that both branches have been selected. Moreover, key uniqueness must be enforced within processes featuring executed actions or resolved probabilistic choices, so for example $a[i] . b[i] . \underline{0}$, $a[i] . \underline{0} \|_\emptyset b[i] . \underline{0}$, $F_1{}_{[i]p} \oplus F_2{}_{[i]q} \oplus F_3$, and $\underline{0}_{p \oplus [i]} a[j] . F \# a[j] . (F_1{}_{[i]q} \oplus F_2)$ where $\# \in \{+, \|_{\{a\}}\}$ are not admissible either.

In the following we thus consider only *reachable processes*, whose set we denote by $\mathbb{P}$. They include processes from which a computation can start, i.e., standard forward processes, as well as processes that can be derived from the previous ones via finitely many applications of the semantic rules. Given a reachable process $R \in \mathbb{P}$, if $\mathrm{npa}(R)$ then $\mathtt{key}_a(R) = \emptyset$ while $\mathtt{key}_a(R') \neq \emptyset$ for any other process R' reachable from R in which at least one of the actions occurring in R has been executed, as that action has been equipped with a key inside R'.

We conclude by discussing some properties of the resulting labeled transition system $(\mathbb{P}, \mathcal{L}, \longmapsto)$, where we recall that $\longmapsto = \longrightarrow \cup \dashrightarrow$, $\longrightarrow = \longrightarrow_a \cup \longrightarrow_p$, and $\dashrightarrow = \dashrightarrow_a \cup \dashrightarrow_p$. First of all, we observe that forward probabilistic transitions across a parallel composition are combined with each other into single transitions by rule PCOO in the same way as nested probabilistic choices yield a single forward probabilistic transition by rule PSEL2 and its symmetric variant. Therefore, every state reached by a forward probabilistic transition cannot have forward probabilistic transitions and hence the labeled transition system cannot feature squares composed of forward probabilistic transitions, whereas it can contain squares made out of forward action transitions due to the interleaving of concurrent actions. As an example consider again $(a . \underline{0} \oplus_p b . \underline{0}) \|_\emptyset (c . \underline{0} \oplus_q d . \underline{0})$, whose underlying labeled transition system is depicted in Fig. 1 up to keys.

Secondly, when focusing only on the forward transition relation $\longrightarrow = \longrightarrow_a \cup \longrightarrow_p$, the labeled transition system is consistent with the non-strict variant [35] of the alternating model [20]. This means that in every state all the forward transitions are either action transitions, in which case the state is nondeterministic, or probabilistic transitions, in which case the state is probabilistic. The alternation is not strict because, while a probabilistic state can reach via forward transitions only nondeterministic states due to rule PSEL2 and its symmetric variant as well as rule PCOO, a nondeterministic state can reach via forward transitions either probabilistic states or other nondeterministic states. In contrast, a state can

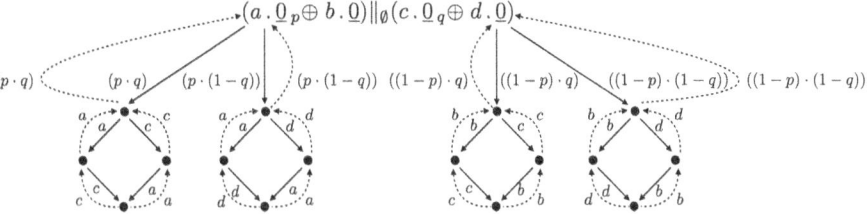

Fig. 1. Labeled transition system underlying $(a.\underline{0}_p \oplus b.\underline{0}) \|_\emptyset (c.\underline{0}_q \oplus d.\underline{0})$

have both backward action transitions and backward probabilistic transitions. This may happen when transitions arising from probabilistic selections are involved in squares along with action transitions stemming from the interleaving of concurrent actions. For instance consider $a.(c.\underline{0}_p \oplus \underline{0}) \|_\emptyset b.\underline{0}$, whose underlying labeled transition system is depicted in Fig. 2, and look at the rectangle with action and probabilistic transitions on the right as well as its bottommost state.

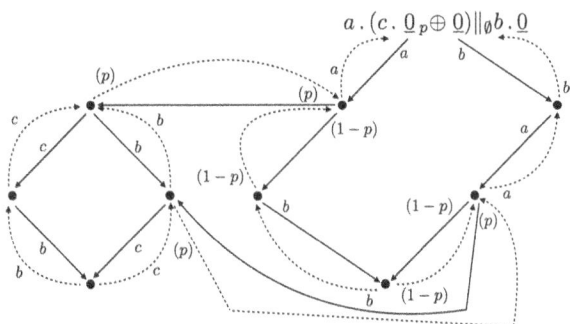

Fig. 2. Labeled transition system underlying $a.(c.\underline{0}_p \oplus \underline{0}) \|_\emptyset b.\underline{0}$

3   Example: Applying RPPC to Quantum Computing

A quantum bit, or qubit, is a physical system with two basis states conventionally denoted by $|0\rangle$ and $|1\rangle$, which correspond to one-bit classical values. According to quantum theory, a general state of a quantum system is a superposition or linear combination of basis states. For instance, a qubit has state $\alpha|0\rangle + \beta|1\rangle$ where $\alpha, \beta \in \mathbb{C}$ satisfy $|\alpha|^2 + |\beta|^2 = 1$. In RPPC we can model a qubit as:

$$Q = m.(z_p \oplus o)$$

where m stands for measurement, z for zero, and o for one. Measuring its value destroys superposition and yields 0 with probability $p = |\alpha|^2$ and 1 with probability $1 - p = |\beta|^2$, leaving the system in state $|0\rangle$ or $|1\rangle$ respectively.

Tensor product is used to represent systems made out of several qubits. For example, a 2-qubit system has basis states $|00\rangle$, $|01\rangle$, $|10\rangle$, $|11\rangle$. Its general state is $\alpha|00\rangle + \beta|01\rangle + \gamma|10\rangle + \delta|11\rangle$ where $|\alpha|^2 + |\beta|^2 + |\gamma|^2 + |\delta|^2 = 1$. Measuring the first (resp. second) qubit only yields 0 with probability $|\alpha|^2 + |\beta|^2$ (resp. $|\alpha|^2 + |\gamma|^2$) and 1 with probability $|\gamma|^2 + |\delta|^2$ (resp. $|\beta|^2 + |\delta|^2$), leaving the system in state $\frac{1}{\sqrt{|\alpha|^2+|\beta|^2}}(\alpha|00\rangle + \beta|01\rangle)$ or state $\frac{1}{\sqrt{|\gamma|^2+|\delta|^2}}(\gamma|10\rangle + \delta|11\rangle)$ (resp. in state $\frac{1}{\sqrt{|\alpha|^2+|\gamma|^2}}(\alpha|00\rangle + \gamma|10\rangle)$ or state $\frac{1}{\sqrt{|\beta|^2+|\delta|^2}}(\beta|01\rangle + \delta|11\rangle)$) respectively.

If both qubits are measured simultaneously, then the possible results are 0, 1, 2, 3 with corresponding probabilities $|\alpha|^2$, $|\beta|^2$, $|\gamma|^2$, $|\delta|^2$ and states $|00\rangle$, $|01\rangle$, $|10\rangle$, $|11\rangle$, respectively. This can be modeled in RPPC as follows:

$$QQ = m \, . \, (z \, . \, (z_{q_1} \oplus o)_p \oplus o \, . \, (z_{q_2} \oplus o))$$

where $p \cdot q_1 = |\alpha|^2$, $p \cdot (1 - q_1) = |\beta|^2$, $(1 - p) \cdot q_2 = |\gamma|^2$, $(1 - p) \cdot (1 - q_2) = |\delta|^2$.

In a closed quantum system, all the operations on qubits are reversible. A common example of such an operation is the quantum controlled-NOT gate, or CNOT gate. This gate acts on two qubits, often called the control qubit and the target qubit. The CNOT gate flips the state of the target qubit if and only if the control qubit is in state $|1\rangle$. It is reversible because it is a unitary operation, meaning that it can be undone by applying the same operation again, like NOT on classical bits. The truth table of CNOT is as follows:

control input	target input	control output	target output
$|0\rangle$	$|0\rangle$	$|0\rangle$	$|0\rangle$
$|0\rangle$	$|1\rangle$	$|0\rangle$	$|1\rangle$
$|1\rangle$	$|0\rangle$	$|1\rangle$	$|1\rangle$
$|1\rangle$	$|1\rangle$	$|1\rangle$	$|0\rangle$

We can model a CNOT gate in RPPC as follows, where we use primes to distinguish output bits from input ones:

$$CNOT = m \, . \, (z \, . \, z \, . \, z' \, . \, z' + z \, . \, o \, . \, z' \, . \, o' + o \, . \, z \, . \, o' \, . \, o' + o \, . \, o \, . \, o' \, . \, z')$$

and then apply it to the 2-qubit system as follows:

$$QQ\|_L CNOT$$

where $L = \{m, z, o\}$. The following execution takes place when the input is $|10\rangle$ – o and z are executed – in which case $|11\rangle$ is returned – o' and z' are executed:

$$\xrightarrow{\;m[1]\;}_a\; m[1].(z.(z_{q_1}\oplus o)\,_p\oplus o.(z_{q_2}\oplus o))\|_L$$
$$m[1].(z.z.z'.z' + z.o.z'.o' + o.z.o'.o' + o.o.o'.z')$$

$$\xrightarrow{\;(1-p)^{[2]}\;}_p\; m[1].(z.(z_{q_1}\oplus o)\,_p\oplus_{[2]} o.(z_{q_2}\oplus o))\|_L$$
$$m[1].(z.z.z'.z' + z.o.z'.o' + o.z.o'.o' + o.o.o'.z')$$

$$\xrightarrow{\;o[3]\;}_a\; m[1].(z.(z_{q_1}\oplus o)\,_p\oplus_{[2]} o[3].(z_{q_2}\oplus o))\|_L$$
$$m[1].(z.z.z'.z' + z.o.z'.o' + o[3].z.o'.o' + o.o.o'.z')$$

$$\xrightarrow{\;(q_2)^{[4]}\;}_p\; m[1].(z.(z_{q_1}\oplus o)\,_p\oplus_{[2]} o[3].(z_{[4]q_2}\oplus o))\|_L$$
$$m[1].(z.z.z'.z' + z.o.z'.o' + o[3].z.o'.o' + o.o.o'.z')$$

$$\xrightarrow{\;z[5]\;}_a\; m[1].(z.(z_{q_1}\oplus o)\,_p\oplus_{[2]} o[3].(z[5]_{q_2[4]}\oplus o))\|_L$$
$$m[1].(z.z.z'.z' + z.o.z'.o' + o[3].z[5].o'.o' + o.o.o'.z')$$

$$\xrightarrow{\;o'[6]\;}_a\xrightarrow{\;o'[7]\;}_a\; m[1].(z.(z_{q_1}\oplus o)\,_p\oplus_{[2]} o[3].(z[5]_{q_2[4]}\oplus o))\|_L$$
$$m[1].(z.z.z'.z' + z.o.z'.o' + o[3].z[5].o'[6].o'[7] + o.o.o'.z')$$

where action and selection keys are all distinct for the sake of readability.

Note that when performing $o[3]$ process $CNOT$ may wrongly select the fourth branch of its nondeterministic choice, i.e., $o.o.o'.z'$, thus resulting in the following computation that cannot be completed in the forward direction:

$$m[1].(z.(z_{q_1}\oplus o)\,_p\oplus_{[2]} o.(z_{q_2}\oplus o))\|_L$$
$$m[1].(z.z.z'.z' + z.o.z'.o' + o.z.o'.o' + o.o.o'.z')$$

$$\xrightarrow{\;o[3]\;}_a\; m[1].(z.(z_{q_1}\oplus o)\,_p\oplus_{[2]} o[3].(z_{q_2}\oplus o))\|_L$$
$$m[1].(z.z.z'.z' + z.o.z'.o' + o.z.o'.o' + o[3].o.o'.z')$$

$$\xrightarrow{\;(q_2)^{[4]}\;}_p\; m[1].(z.(z_{q_1}\oplus o)\,_p\oplus_{[2]} o[3].(z_{[4]q_2}\oplus o))\|_L$$
$$m[1].(z.z.z'.z' + z.o.z'.o' + o.z.o'.o' + o[3].o.o'.z')$$

This can be undone – in favor of the third branch of the aforementioned nondeterministic choice, i.e., $o.z.o'.z'$ – thanks to the fact RPPC is reversible:

$$m[1].(z.(z_{q_1}\oplus o)\,_p\oplus_{[2]} o[3].(z_{[4]q_2}\oplus o))\|_L$$
$$m[1].(z.z.z'.z' + z.o.z'.o' + o.z.o'.o' + o[3].o.o'.z')$$

$$\dashrightarrow{\;(q_2)^{[4]}\;}_p\; m[1].(z.(z_{q_1}\oplus o)\,_p\oplus_{[2]} o[3].(z_{q_2}\oplus o))\|_L$$
$$m[1].(z.z.z'.z' + z.o.z'.o' + o.z.o'.o' + o[3].o.o'.z')$$

$$\dashrightarrow{\;o[3]\;}_a\; m[1].(z.(z_{q_1}\oplus o)\,_p\oplus_{[2]} o.(z_{q_2}\oplus o))\|_L$$
$$m[1].(z.z.z'.z' + z.o.z'.o' + o.z.o'.o' + o.o.o'.z')$$

Since our calculus is fully reversible, i.e., every action can be undone in RPPC, even m can be reverted although measurement is known to be an irreversible operation in quantum computing. To amend this, following [11] we should see m as an irreversible action, to which only forward semantic rules are applicable.

4   Causal Reversibility of RPPC

We now prove the causal reversibility of RPPC. This means that each reach-able process of RPPC is able to backtrack *correctly*, i.e., without encountering previously inaccessible states, and *flexibly*, i.e., along any path that is causally equivalent to the one undertaken in the forward direction. This is accomplished through the notion of concurrent transitions of [10] and the technique of [29].

A necessary condition for reversibility is the *loop property* [10, 36, 29]. It establishes that each executed action can be undone and that each undone action can be redone, which in our setting needs to be extended to probabilistic selections. Therefore, when considering the states associated with two reachable processes, either there is no transition between them, or there is a pair of iden-tically labeled transitions such that one is a forward transition from the first to the second state while the other is a backward transition from the second to the first state.

Proposition 1 (loop property). *Let* $R, S \in \mathbb{P}$ *and* $\ell \in \mathcal{L} = \mathcal{A}_\mathcal{K} \cup \mathbb{R}_\mathcal{K}$. *Then* $R \xrightarrow{\ell} S$ *iff* $S \dashrightarrow^{\ell} R$. ∎

Given a transition $\theta : R \xmapsto{\ell} S$ with $R, S \in \mathbb{P}$, we call R the *source* of θ and S its *target*. If θ is a forward transition, i.e., $\theta : R \xrightarrow{\ell} S$, we denote by $\bar{\theta} : S \dashrightarrow^{\ell} R$ the corresponding backward transition. Two transitions are said to be *coinitial* if they have the same source and *cofinal* if they have the same target. Two tran-sitions are *composable* when the target of the first transition coincides with the source of the second transition. A finite sequence of pairwise composable tran-sitions is called a *path*. We use ε for the empty path and ω to range over paths, with $|\omega|$ denoting the length of ω, i.e., the number of transitions constituting ω. When ω is a forward path, we denote by $\overline{\omega}$ the corresponding backward path, where the order of the transitions is reversed. The notions of source, target, coini-tiality, cofinality, and composability naturally extend to paths. We indicate with $\omega_1 \omega_2$ the composition of the two paths ω_1 and ω_2 when they are composable.

Before specifying when two transitions are concurrent [10], we need to present the notion of process context along with the set of causes – identified by action and probabilistic keys – leading to a given communication key.

A *process context* is a process with a hole • in it, generated by the grammar:

$$\mathcal{C} ::= \bullet \mid a[i] . \mathcal{C} \mid \mathcal{C}_{[i]p} \oplus R \mid R_{p \oplus [i]} \mathcal{C} \mid \mathcal{C} + R \mid R + \mathcal{C} \mid \mathcal{C} \|_L R \mid R \|_L \mathcal{C}$$

We write $\mathcal{C}[S]$ to denote the process obtained by replacing the hole in $\mathcal{C}$ with S.

The *causal set* $\mathsf{cau}(R, i)$ of $R \in \mathbb{P}$ until $i \in \mathcal{K}$ under $\mathsf{key}_a(R) \cap \mathsf{key}_p(R) = \emptyset$ is inductively defined as:

$$\mathsf{cau}(F, i) = \emptyset$$

$$\mathsf{cau}(a[j].R, i) = \begin{cases} \emptyset & \text{if } j = i \text{ or } i \notin \mathsf{key}_a(R) \cup \mathsf{key}_p(R) \\ \{j\} \cup \mathsf{cau}(R, i) & \text{otherwise} \end{cases}$$

$$\mathsf{cau}(R_{[j]p} \oplus S, i) = \begin{cases} \emptyset & \text{if } j = i \text{ or } i \notin \mathsf{key}_a(R) \cup \mathsf{key}_p(R) \\ \{j\} \cup \mathsf{cau}(R, i) & \text{otherwise} \end{cases}$$

$$\mathsf{cau}(R_{p \oplus [j]} S, i) = \begin{cases} \emptyset & \text{if } j = i \text{ or } i \notin \mathsf{key}_a(S) \cup \mathsf{key}_p(S) \\ \{j\} \cup \mathsf{cau}(S, i) & \text{otherwise} \end{cases}$$

$$\mathsf{cau}(R + S, i) = \mathsf{cau}(R, i) \cup \mathsf{cau}(S, i)$$
$$\mathsf{cau}(R \|_L S, i) = \mathsf{cau}(R, i) \cup \mathsf{cau}(S, i)$$

If $i \in \mathsf{key}_a(R) \cup \mathsf{key}_p(R)$, then $\mathsf{cau}(R, i)$ represents the set of keys in R that caused i, with $\mathsf{cau}(R, i) \subset \mathsf{key}_a(R) \cup \mathsf{key}_p(R)$ as on the one hand $i \notin \mathsf{cau}(R, i)$ and on the other hand keys that are not causally related to i are not considered. Key j causes key i if it appears before i in R, i.e., if i is inside the scope of j.

We are now in a position to define, for coinitial transitions, what we mean by concurrent transitions on the basis of the notion of conflicting transitions. As in previous work, the first condition below tells that a forward transition is in conflict with a coinitial backward one whenever the latter tries to undo a cause of the key of the former (with abuse of notation the key is made explicit next to ℓ), while the second one deems as conflictual two action transitions respectively generated by the two subprocesses of a nondeterministic choice. The further third condition is an adaptation of the previous one to the probabilistic case. Since probabilistic choices have to be resolved before nondeterministic ones, there can never be conflicts between action transitions and probabilistic transitions.

Definition 1 (conflicting and concurrent transitions). *Two coinitial transitions θ_1 and θ_2 from a process $R \in \mathbb{P}$ are in conflict if one of the following conditions holds, otherwise they are said to be concurrent:*

- $\theta_1 : R \xrightarrow{\ell_1[i]} S_1$ *and* $\theta_2 : R \xdashrightarrow{\ell_2[j]} S_2$ *with* $j \in \mathsf{cau}(S_1, i)$.
- $R = \mathcal{C}[F_1 + F_2]$ *with* θ_k *deriving in R from* $F_k \xrightarrow{a_k[i_k]}_a S_k$ *for* $k = 1, 2$.
- $R = \mathcal{C}[F_1 {}_p\oplus F_2]$ *with* θ_k *deriving in R from* $F_k \xrightarrow{(p_k)[i_k]}_p S_k$ *for* $k = 1, 2$. ∎

We prove causal reversibility by adapting the technique of [29], according to which causal consistency stems from the *square property* – which amounts to concurrent transitions being confluent – *backward transitions independence* – which generalizes the concept of backward determinism used for reversible sequential languages [49] – and *past well foundedness* – which ensures that reachable processes have a finite past.

Before proving the three properties, as for the classical definition of square property [29] we have to deal with the fact that probabilistic choices take precedence over nondeterministic ones in the forward direction. Hence, even if from a process there are two transitions coming from the two subprocesses of a parallel composition, we have to determine whether either reached process can directly perform the other transition to close the square, or it has to first resolve probabilistic choices. Once such choices have been resolved, the remaining transition can be done thus closing the square. For example, consider $a \,.\, (c \,.\, \underline{0}_p \oplus \underline{0}) \|_{\emptyset} b \,.\, \underline{0}$ depicted in Fig. 2. It can initially perform an a-action and a b-action, but if a is done then a probabilistic choice is enabled. Hence, before doing b, the process has to first resolve the probabilistic choice and only then it can proceed with b. On the other hand, if the process does b first, then it can immediately do a, but in order to reach the same process as the left path it also has to resolve the probabilistic choice. As an analogous though more extended example of square, consider the one originated from $a_1 \,.\, (b \,.\, \underline{0}_p \oplus c \,.\, \underline{0}) \|_{\emptyset} a_2 \,.\, (d \,.\, \underline{0}_q \oplus e \,.\, \underline{0})$. These cases are handled by the second and the third clauses below.

Lemma 1 (square property). *Let $\theta_1 : R \xrightarrow{\ell_1} S_1$ and $\theta_2 : R \xrightarrow{\ell_2} S_2$ be two coinitial transitions from a process $R \in \mathbb{P}$. If θ_1 and θ_2 are concurrent, then one of the following holds:*

- *If $S_1 \not\rightarrow_p$ and $S_2 \not\rightarrow_p$ then there exist two cofinal transitions $\theta_2' : S_1 \xrightarrow{\ell_2} S$ and $\theta_1' : S_2 \xrightarrow{\ell_1} S$ with $S \in \mathbb{P}$.*
- *If $S_1 \not\rightarrow_p$ and $S_2 \rightarrow_p$ then there exist two cofinal paths $\omega_2' : S_1 \xrightarrow{\ell_2} S_p \xrightarrow{\ell_p} S$ and $\omega_1' : S_2 \xrightarrow{\ell_p} S_p \xrightarrow{\ell_1} S$ with $S_p, S \in \mathbb{P}$.*
- *If $S_1 \rightarrow_p$ and $S_2 \rightarrow_p$ then there exist two cofinal paths $\omega_2' : S_1 \xrightarrow{\ell_p} S_p^1 \xrightarrow{\ell_2} S_q^1 \xrightarrow{\ell_q} S$ and $\omega_1' : S_2 \xrightarrow{\ell_q} S_q^2 \xrightarrow{\ell_1} S_p^2 \xrightarrow{\ell_p} S$ with $S_p^1, S_p^2, S_q^1, S_q^2, S \in \mathbb{P}$.* ∎

Lemma 2 (backward transitions independence). *Let $R \in \mathbb{P}$. Then two coinitial backward transitions $\theta_1 : R \dashrightarrow^{\ell_1} S_1$ and $\theta_2 : R \dashrightarrow^{\ell_2} S_2$ are concurrent.* ∎

Lemma 3 (past well foundedness). *Let $R_0 \in \mathbb{P}$. Then there is no infinite sequence of backward transitions such that $R_i \dashrightarrow^{\ell_i} R_{i+1}$ for all $i \in \mathbb{N}$.* ∎

Following [10, 32], we also define a notion of *causal equivalence* over paths. In addition to identifying the composition of a transition and its inverse with the empty path, it abstracts from the order of concurrent action and probabilistic transitions. In this way, paths obtained by swapping the order of those transitions are identified with each other.

Since probabilistic choices take precedence over nondeterministic ones in the forward direction, a swap between two concurrency action transitions is not always possible, unless all probabilistic choices have been made. More precisely, after opening a square, it may be the case that, in order to close it, the process has to first resolve some probabilistic choices. This is rendered by the third and fourth clauses in the definition below. For example, if we consider again process $a \,.\, (c \,.\, \underline{0}_p \oplus \underline{0}) \|_{\emptyset} b \,.\, \underline{0}$ in Fig. 2, we have that the action transitions a and b are concurrent and coinitial. If we take the left path, then after doing a the process has to resolve the probabilistic choice. Suppose it decides for the right branch, which is labeled with $(1 - p)$. Then a process is reached in which b can be done. On the other hand, if we take the right path, we have that the process can do b followed by a but then again, in order to close the square, it has to resolve the probabilistic choice; if it decides for $(1 - p)$ the same process as the left path is reached. Therefore the two paths can be considered as causally equivalent. Something similar happens along the more extended square originating from $a_1 . (b . \underline{0}\ {}_p\oplus c . \underline{0}) \|_\emptyset a_2 . (d . \underline{0}\ {}_q\oplus e . \underline{0})$.

Definition 2 (causal equivalence). *Causal equivalence* $\asymp$ *is the smallest equivalence relation over paths that is closed under composition and satisfies the following clauses:*

1. $\theta_1\theta'_2 \asymp \theta_2\theta'_1$ *for every two coinitial concurrent action transitions* $\theta_1 : R \xrightarrow{\ell_1} R_1$
   and $\theta_2 : R \xrightarrow{\ell_2} R_2$ *and every two cofinal action transitions* $\theta'_2 : R_1 \xrightarrow{\ell_2} S$ *and*
   $\theta'_1 : R_2 \xrightarrow{\ell_1} S$ *respectively composable with the previous ones.*
2. $\theta\bar{\theta} \asymp \varepsilon$ *and* $\bar{\theta}\theta \asymp \varepsilon$ *for every transition* θ.
3. $\theta_1\theta_p\theta'_2 \asymp \theta_2\theta'_1\theta'_p$ *for every two coinitial concurrent action transitions* $\theta_1 : R \xrightarrow{\ell_1}$
   R_1 *and* $\theta_2 : R \xrightarrow{\ell_2} R_2$, *every probabilistic transition* $\theta_p : R_1 \xrightarrow{\ell_p} R'_1$, *and every*
   two cofinal transitions $\theta'_2 : R'_1 \xrightarrow{\ell_2} S$ *and* $\theta'_p : R'_2 \xrightarrow{\ell_p} S$, *with* $\theta'_1 : R_2 \xrightarrow{\ell_p} R'_2$.
4. $\theta_1\theta_p\theta'_2\theta'_q \asymp \theta_2\theta_q\theta'_1\theta'_p$ *for every two coinitial concurrent action transitions* $\theta_1 :$
   $R \xrightarrow{\ell_1} R_1$ *and* $\theta_2 : R \xrightarrow{\ell_2} R_2$, *every two probabilistic transitions* $\theta_p : R_1 \xrightarrow{\ell_p} R'_1$
   and $\theta_q : R_2 \xrightarrow{\ell_q} R'_2$, *and every two cofinal transitions* $\theta'_q : R'_2 \xrightarrow{\ell_q} S$ *and*
   $\theta'_p : R'_1 \xrightarrow{\ell_p} S$, *with* $\theta'_1 : R_2 \xrightarrow{\ell_1} R'_2$ *and* $\theta'_2 : R_1 \xrightarrow{\ell_2} R'_1$. ∎

The further property below, called the *parabolic lemma* in [29], states that every path can be seen as a backward path followed by a forward path. As observed in [10], up to causal equivalence one can always reach for the maximum freedom of choice among transitions by going backward and only then going forward (not the other way around). Intuitively, computations can be viewed as parabolas: the system first draws potential energy from its memory by undoing all the executed actions and then restarts. The proof of the parabolic lemma has to account for the presence of probabilistic transitions.

Lemma 4 (parabolic lemma). *For each path* ω, *there exist two forward paths* ω_1 *and* ω_2 *such that* $\omega \asymp \overline{\omega_1}\omega_2$ *and* $|\omega_1| + |\omega_2| \leq |\omega|$. ∎

We conclude by obtaining a property called *causal consistency* in [29], which establishes that being coinitial and cofinal is necessary and sufficient in order for two paths to be causally equivalent, i.e., to contain concurrent action and probabilistic transitions in different orders (swap) or to be one the empty path and the other a transition followed by its reverse (cancelation).

Theorem 1 (causal consistency). *Let* ω_1 *and* ω_2 *be two paths. Then* $\omega_1 \asymp \omega_2$ *iff* ω_1 *and* ω_2 *are both coinitial and cofinal.* ∎

Theorem 1 shows that causal equivalence characterizes a space for admissible rollbacks that are (i) correct as they do not lead to states not reachable by any forward path and (ii) flexible enough to allow undo operations to be rearranged with respect to the order in which the undone concurrent actions and probabilistic transitions were originally performed. This implies that the states reached by any backward path could be reached by performing forward paths only. Thus, we can conclude that RPPC meets causal reversibility.

5   Conclusions

In this paper we have studied causal reversibility [10] of nondeterministic and probabilistic process calculi in the non-strictly alternating model [20,35]. The syntax and operational semantics have been defined by suitably adapting the method of [36], while causal reversibility has been demonstrated by suitably adapting the technique of [29], thus extending results developed in the fully nondeterministic setting.

As future work, similar to the stochastically timed case [5,4], for our reversible probabilistic calculus we plan to study behavioral equivalences as well as time reversibility [22] and its possible relationships with causal reversibility.

Acknowledgments. This work has been supported by the Italian MUR PRIN 2020 project *NiRvAna*, the Italian MUR PRIN 2022 project *DeKLA*, the French ANR project *DCore*, and the Italian INdAM-GNCS project *RISICO*.

References

1. Andova, S., Georgievska, S., Trcka, N.: Branching bisimulation congruence for probabilistic systems. Theor. Comput. Sci. **413**, 58–72 (2012)
2. Bennett, C.H.: Logical reversibility of computation. IBM J. Res. Dev. **17**, 525–532 (1973)
3. Bernardo, M., Esposito, A.: Modal logic characterizations of forward, reverse, and forward-reverse bisimilarities. In: Proceedings of the 14th International Symposium on Games, Automata, Logics, and Formal Verification (GANDALF 2023). EPTCS, vol. 390, pp. 67–81 (2023)
4. Bernardo, M., Lanese, I., Marin, A., Mezzina, C.A., Rossi, S., Sacerdoti Coen, C.: Causal reversibility implies time reversibility. In: Jansen, N., Tribastone, M. (eds.) QEST 2023. LNCS, vol. 14287, pp. 270–287. Springer, Cham (2023). https://doi.org/10.1007/978-3-031-43835-6_19
5. Bernardo, M., Mezzina, C.A.: Bridging causal reversibility and time reversibility: a stochastic process algebraic approach. Logical Methods Comput. Sci. **19(2)**, 6:1–6:27 (2023)
6. Bernardo, M., Mezzina, C.A.: Causal reversibility for timed process calculi with lazy/eager durationless actions and time additivity. In: Petrucci, L., Sproston, J. (eds.) FORMATS 2023. LNCS, vol. 14138, pp. 15–32. Springer, Cham (2023). https://doi.org/10.1007/978-3-031-42626-1_2

7. Bérut, A., Arakelyan, A., Petrosyan, A., Ciliberto, S., Dillenschneider, R., Lutz, E.: Experimental verification of Landauer's principle linking information and thermodynamics. Nature **483**, 187–189 (2012)
8. Cattani, S., Segala, R.: Decision algorithms for probabilistic bisimulation. In: Brim, L., Křetínský, M., Kučera, A., Jančar, P. (eds.) CONCUR 2002. LNCS, vol. 2421, pp. 371–386. Springer, Heidelberg (2002). https://doi.org/10.1007/3-540-45694-5_25
9. Chatterjee, K., Goharshady, A.K., Pourdamghani, A.: Probabilistic smart contracts: secure randomness on the blockchain. In: Proceedings of the 1st IEEE International Conference on Blockchain and Cryptocurrency (ICBC 2019), pp. 403–412. IEEE-CS Press (2019)
10. Danos, V., Krivine, J.: Reversible communicating systems. In: Gardner, P., Yoshida, N. (eds.) CONCUR 2004. LNCS, vol. 3170, pp. 292–307. Springer, Heidelberg (2004). https://doi.org/10.1007/978-3-540-28644-8_19
11. Danos, V., Krivine, J.: Transactions in RCCS. In: Abadi, M., de Alfaro, L. (eds.) CONCUR 2005. LNCS, vol. 3653, pp. 398–412. Springer, Heidelberg (2005). https://doi.org/10.1007/11539452_31
12. De Nicola, R., Montanari, U., Vaandrager, F.: Back and forth bisimulations. In: Baeten, J.C.M., Klop, J.W. (eds.) CONCUR 1990. LNCS, vol. 458, pp. 152–165. Springer, Heidelberg (1990). https://doi.org/10.1007/BFb0039058
13. Derman, C.: Finite State Markovian Decision Processes. Academic Press (1970)
14. Esposito, A., Aldini, A., Bernardo, M.: Branching bisimulation semantics enables noninterference analysis of reversible systems. In: Huisman, M., Ravara, A. (eds.) FORTE 2023. LNCS, vol. 13910, pp. 57–74. Springer, Cham (2023). https://doi.org/10.1007/978-3-031-35355-0_5
15. Esposito, A., Aldini, A., Bernardo, M.: Noninterference analysis of reversible probabilistic systems. In: Castiglioni, V., Francalanza, A. (eds.) FORTE 2024. LNCS, vol. 14678, pp. 39–59. Springer, Cham (2024). https://doi.org/10.1007/978-3-031-62645-6_3
16. Frank, M.P.: Physical foundations of Landauer's principle. In: Kari, J., Ulidowski, I. (eds.) RC 2018. LNCS, vol. 11106, pp. 3–33. Springer, Cham (2018). https://doi.org/10.1007/978-3-319-99498-7_1
17. Giachino, E., Lanese, I., Mezzina, C.A.: Causal-consistent reversible debugging. In: Gnesi, S., Rensink, A. (eds.) FASE 2014. LNCS, vol. 8411, pp. 370–384. Springer, Heidelberg (2014). https://doi.org/10.1007/978-3-642-54804-8_26
18. van Glabbeek, R.J., Smolka, S.A., Steffen, B.: Reactive, generative and stratified models of probabilistic processes. Inf. Comput. **121**, 59–80 (1995)
19. Hansson, H.: Time and probability in formal design of distributed systems. Ph.D. thesis (1992)
20. Hansson, H., Jonsson, B.: A calculus for communicating systems with time and probabilities. In: Proceedings of the 11th IEEE Real-Time Systems Symposium (RTSS 1990), pp. 278–287. IEEE-CS Press (1990)
21. Hoare, C.A.R.: Communicating Sequential Processes. Prentice Hall (1985)
22. Kelly, F.P.: Reversibility and Stochastic Networks. Wiley, Hoboken (1979)
23. Kemeny, J.G., Snell, J.L.: Finite Markov Chains. Van Nostrand (1960)
24. Krivine, J.: A verification technique for reversible process algebra. In: Glück, R., Yokoyama, T. (eds.) RC 2012. LNCS, vol. 7581, pp. 204–217. Springer, Heidelberg (2013). https://doi.org/10.1007/978-3-642-36315-3_17
25. Landauer, R.: Irreversibility and heat generation in the computing process. IBM J. Res. Dev. **5**, 183–191 (1961)

26. Lanese, I., Lienhardt, M., Mezzina, C.A., Schmitt, A., Stefani, J.-B.: Concurrent flexible reversibility. In: Felleisen, M., Gardner, P. (eds.) ESOP 2013. LNCS, vol. 7792, pp. 370–390. Springer, Heidelberg (2013). https://doi.org/10.1007/978-3-642-37036-6_21

27. Lanese, I., Medić, D., Mezzina, C.A.: Static versus dynamic reversibility in CCS. Acta Informatica **58**, 1–34 (2021)

28. Lanese, I., Nishida, N., Palacios, A., Vidal, G.: CauDEr: a causal-consistent reversible debugger for erlang. In: Gallagher, J.P., Sulzmann, M. (eds.) FLOPS 2018. LNCS, vol. 10818, pp. 247–263. Springer, Cham (2018). https://doi.org/10.1007/978-3-319-90686-7_16

29. Lanese, I., Phillips, I., Ulidowski, I.: An axiomatic theory for reversible computation. ACM Trans. Comput. Logic **25**(2), 11:1–11:40 (2024)

30. Laursen, J.S., Ellekilde, L.P., Schultz, U.P.: Modelling reversible execution of robotic assembly. Robotica **36**, 625–654 (2018)

31. Lehmann, D., Rabin, M.O.: On the advantage of free choice: A symmetric and fully distributed solution to the dining philosophers problem. In: Proceedings of the 8th ACM Symposium on Principles of Programming Languages (POPL 1981), pp. 133–138. ACM Press (1981)

32. Lévy, J.J.: An algebraic interpretation of the $\lambda\beta K$-calculus; and an application of a labelled λ-calculus. Theor. Comput. Sci. **2**, 97–114 (1976)

33. Milner, R.: Communication and Concurrency. Prentice Hall (1989)

34. Perumalla, K.S., Park, A.J.: Reverse computation for rollback-based fault tolerance in large parallel systems - evaluating the potential gains and systems effects. Clust. Comput. **17**, 303–313 (2014)

35. Philippou, A., Lee, I., Sokolsky, O.: Weak bisimulation for probabilistic systems. In: Palamidessi, C. (ed.) CONCUR 2000. LNCS, vol. 1877, pp. 334–349. Springer, Heidelberg (2000). https://doi.org/10.1007/3-540-44618-4_25

36. Phillips, I., Ulidowski, I.: Reversing algebraic process calculi. J. Logic Algebraic Program. **73**, 70–96 (2007)

37. Phillips, I., Ulidowski, I., Yuen, S.: A reversible process calculus and the modelling of the ERK signalling pathway. In: Glück, R., Yokoyama, T. (eds.) RC 2012. LNCS, vol. 7581, pp. 218–232. Springer, Heidelberg (2013). https://doi.org/10.1007/978-3-642-36315-3_18

38. Pinna, G.M.: Reversing steps in membrane systems computations. In: Gheorghe, M., Rozenberg, G., Salomaa, A., Zandron, C. (eds.) CMC 2017. LNCS, vol. 10725, pp. 245–261. Springer, Cham (2018). https://doi.org/10.1007/978-3-319-73359-3_16

39. Prabhu, P., Ramalingam, G., Vaswani, K.: Safe programmable speculative parallelism. In: Proceedings of the 31st ACM Conference on Programming Language Design and Implementation (PLDI 2010), pp. 50–61. ACM Press (2010)

40. Rabin, M.O.: Probabilistic automata. Inf. Control **6**, 230–245 (1963)

41. Schordan, M., Oppelstrup, T., Jefferson, D.R., Barnes, P.D., Jr.: Generation of reversible C++ code for optimistic parallel discrete event simulation. N. Gener. Comput. **36**, 257–280 (2018)

42. Segala, R.: Modeling and verification of randomized distributed real-time systems. Ph.D. thesis (1995)

43. Segala, R., Lynch, N.: Probabilistic simulations for probabilistic processes. In: Jonsson, B., Parrow, J. (eds.) CONCUR 1994. LNCS, vol. 836, pp. 481–496. Springer, Heidelberg (1994). https://doi.org/10.1007/978-3-540-48654-1_35

44. Segala, R., Turrini, A.: Comparative analysis of bisimulation relations on alternating and non-alternating probabilistic models. In: Proceedings of the 2nd International Conference on the Quantitative Evaluation of Systems (QEST 2005), pp. 44–53. IEEE-CS Press (2005)

45. Siljak, H., Psara, K., Philippou, A.: Distributed antenna selection for massive MIMO using reversing Petri nets. IEEE Wirel. Commun. Lett. **8**, 1427–1430 (2019)

46. Turrini, A., Hermanns, H.: Polynomial time decision algorithms for probabilistic automata. Inf. Comput. **244**, 134–171 (2015)

47. Vassor, M., Stefani, J.-B.: Checkpoint/rollback vs causally-consistent reversibility. In: Kari, J., Ulidowski, I. (eds.) RC 2018. LNCS, vol. 11106, pp. 286–303. Springer, Cham (2018). https://doi.org/10.1007/978-3-319-99498-7_20

48. de Vries, E., Koutavas, V., Hennessy, M.: Communicating transactions. In: Gastin, P., Laroussinie, F. (eds.) CONCUR 2010. LNCS, vol. 6269, pp. 569–583. Springer, Heidelberg (2010). https://doi.org/10.1007/978-3-642-15375-4_39

49. Yokoyama, T., Glück, R.: A reversible programming language and its invertible self-interpreter. In: Proceedings of the 13th ACM Workshop on Partial Evaluation and Semantics-based Program Manipulation (PEPM 2007), pp. 144–153. ACM Press (2007)

A Theory of Proc-Omata—and Proof Methods for Process Architectures

Benoît Ballenghien⬤ and Burkhart Wolff[(✉)]⬤

LMF, Université Paris-Saclay, Paris, France
benoit.ballenghien@universite-paris-saclay.fr, wolff@lmf.cnrs.fr

Abstract. This work is based on Isabelle/HOL-CSP 2.0, a shallow embedding of the failure-divergence model of denotational semantics proposed by Hoare, Roscoe and Brookes in the eighties. In several ways, HOL-CSP is actually an extension of the original setting in the sense that it admits higher-order processes and infinite alphabets.

In this paper, we present a particular sub-class of CSP processes which we call Proc-Omata, a fantastic beast between processes and functional automata. For this class of processes, particular proof techniques can be applied allowing for reasoning over unbounded families of sub-processes and similar architectural compositions.

We develop the basic theory of deterministic terminating and non-terminating Proc-Omata, both their relation to conventional CSP processes as well as possible transformation operations on them. As an application of Proc-Omata theory, we demonstrate the use of so-called compactification theorems that pave the way, for example, to proofs over process rings of arbitrary size.

Keywords: Process-Algebra · Concurrency · Automata · Computational Models · Theorem Proving · Isabelle/HOL · CSP

1 Introduction

Communicating Sequential Processes (CSP) is a language to specify and verify patterns of interaction of concurrent systems. Together with CCS and LOTOS, it belongs to the family of *process algebras*. CSP's rich theory comprises denotational, operational and algebraic semantics.

The theory of CSP was first described in 1978 by Tony Hoare, and detailed in a book in 1985 [15], but has since evolved substantially [7,8,27]. The denotational semantics of CSP is described by a fully abstract model of behaviour designed to be *compositional*: a process P encompasses all possible behaviours, i. e. sets of *traces* annotated by additional information that allow to reason over

- deadlocks (the resulting semantic domain is called *failure semantics F*)
- and additionally livelocks (the *failure/divergence semantics FD*).

© The Author(s), under exclusive license to Springer Nature Switzerland AG 2025
C. Anutariya and M. M. Bonsangue (Eds.): ICTAC 2024, LNCS 15373, pp. 272–289, 2025.
https://doi.org/10.1007/978-3-031-77019-7_16

Several attempts have been undertaken to formalize this fairly complex theory, notably [16, 19, 24, 32]. The presented work here is based on HOL-CSP [3, 4, 6, 29, 31], a shallow embedding of the denotational and operational semantics theory in the proof-assistant Isabelle/HOL. HOL-CSP is in several ways not only a formalization, but a generalization of the original setting:

- type 'a trace is constructed over an arbitrary type 'a in HOL, paving the way for events carrying dense-time, vector-spaces, etc.[1],
- in general, HOL-CSP attempts to remove finiteness-restrictions, and
- the semantic domain is encapsulated in the type 'a process belonging to the class of *complete partial orders* (cpo's). Process patterns are functions in higher-order logic (HOL), and thus first-class citizens.

In this paper, we present the formal theory of Proc-Omata built on top of HOL-CSP. Proc-Omata are a sub-class of CSP processes, that have an extremely simple process structure but possess a functional automata [22, 23] inside which can have an infinite state and communication alphabet. For certain process-patterns such as an i-indexed family of interleaving processes ||| i $\in$# M. P i, it is possible to convert this pattern into a Proc-Omaton provided that the P i can be converted into Proc-Omata. Since this construction is possible for index-sets M of arbitrary size, this paves the way for proofs of properties such as deadlock or livelock freeness over process-patterns. The key-instruments of this constructions are a particular form of equations we call *compactification theorems* that we formally prove correct in this paper.

Functional automata consist of a transition function τ coming in two flavors; non-terminating and potentially terminating ones.

Now, a Proc-Omaton has the general form of a CSP process schema:
$$\mu \ X. \ (\lambda\sigma. \ \Box e \in \varepsilon \ A \ \sigma \rightarrow F \ (\tau \ A \ \sigma \ e) \ X)$$
where μ is the recursion operator over process functions (here: parameterized over an internal state σ), $\Box$ a choice-operator ranging over a set of events, τ A is the transition function of the automaton A, ε A σ computes the set of events for which A is *enabled* (ready to make a transition) in the state σ and the function F depends on whether A is non-terminating or potentially terminating (see Sect. 3 and Sect. 4). In all cases, the resulting fixed point is a function of type '$\sigma \Rightarrow$ 'e process. When P is a Proc-Omaton, classic CSP theory gives us from some state σ the definitions for the set of *traces* $\mathcal{T}$ (P σ), the set of *failures* $\mathcal{F}$ (P σ) and the set of *divergences* $\mathcal{D}$ (P σ). The latter is always empty: Proc-Omata have no divergences.

At first glance, one might think that this concept is too restrictive to be useful in practice. A closer look reveals that the contrary is actually the case, as the following example illustrates:

Example 1. *Consider the Collatz Process:*

$$\text{Collatz} \equiv \mu \ X. \ (\lambda n. \ \ (\Box x \in \{0, 1\} \cap \{n\} \rightarrow \text{SKIP})$$
$$\Box \ (\Box x \in (\text{Even} - \{0\}) \cap \{n\} \rightarrow X \ (x \ \text{div} \ 2))$$
$$\Box \ (\Box x \in (\text{Odd} - \{1\}) \cap \{n\} \rightarrow X \ (3 * x + 1)))$$

---

[1] Or even differential equations as in cyber-physical system models [11].

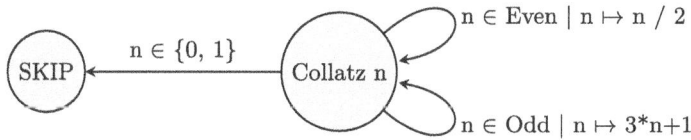

Fig. 1. The Collatz Function seen as Process

Note that the Collatz function is unknown to be terminating; a standard definition in HOL as a recursive function is therefore out of reach. This example shows, however, that it is perfectly possible to represent the Collatz process as a recursive HOL-CSP process, since HOL-CSP is built for modeling potentially non-terminating computations. Figure 1 represents its behaviour as a symbolic Labelled Transition System (LTS), which has the format of an extended finite state machine (EFSM) where the underlying Proc-Omaton is potentially terminating (see Sect. 4). The resulting Proc-Omaton transition definitions are a tedious but direct translation of the symbolic LTS above:

τ Collatz_A $\Diamond$ e = $\Diamond$

τ Collatz_A $\lfloor$n$\rfloor$ e = (if n = e then if n $\in$ {0, 1} then $\lfloor\Diamond\rfloor$
                        else if even n then $\lfloor\lfloor$n div 2$\rfloor\rfloor$
                            else $\lfloor\lfloor$3 * n + 1$\rfloor\rfloor$ else $\Diamond$)

where $\Diamond$ and $\lfloor\_\rfloor$ are a notation for None *and* Some *of the 'a option-type.*

The example above gives rise to a particular proof-methodology which is depicted in Fig. 2 and Fig. 3. First, we construct a Proc-Omaton and prove that it is equivalent to the initial process; this *conversion* proof can be done via fixed point induction (see Theorem 2) or sometimes by model-checking. Second, we apply the aforementioned compactification theorems over Proc-Omata which trades so to speak the complexity of the underlying LTS of the process into the complexity of the data space of the automaton. Third, we can prove properties over the compactified Proc-Omaton by classical invariant reasoning.

We proceed as follows. After an introduction to "classic" CSP and our extension HOL-CSP and HOL-CSPM in Isabelle/HOL, we present the core-constructions of this paper: formal definitions of terminating and non-terminating Proc-Omata, a number of basic and advanced theorems over them, and the compactification theorems allowing to internalize compositions of Proc-Omata. Finally we illustrate this with some examples.

HOL-CSP [31] and HOL-CSPM [3] are published in the Archive of Formal Proofs AFP. Wrt. the session HOL-CSP_Proc-Omata see the developer version https://gitlab.lisn.upsaclay.fr/burkhart.wolff/hol-csp2.0/. Note that our formal theories cover also non-deterministic versions of Proc-Omata; however, their detailed presentation is out of scope of this paper due to space limitations.

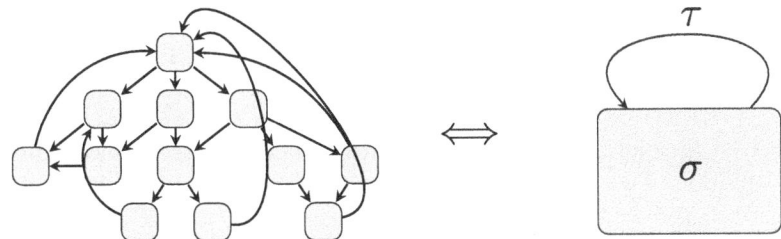

Fig. 2. Conversion of an LTS

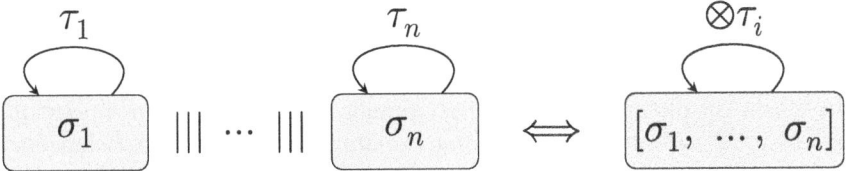

Fig. 3. Compactification

2 Background

2.1 Classic CSP Syntax

At a glance, the fragment of the classic CSP core language we will be using in this paper reads as follows:

P ::= SKIP | STOP | P □ P' | P ⊓ P' | P [A] P' | P ; P' | P \ A
     | a → P | □a ∈ A → P a | Renaming P g | μ X. f X

SKIP signals termination and STOP denotes a deadlock.

Two choice operators are distinguished: the *external* one _□_ forces a process "to follow" whatever its context requires and the *internal* one _⊓_ imposes on the context of a process "to follow" the non-deterministic choices made.

The later is generalized to unbounded non-determinism: ⊓a ∈ A. P a where A may be infinite at the price of loosing continuity (which has no incidence here since non-deterministic versions of Proc-Omata are out of scope of this paper).

From the former and the prefix operator a → P which signals a (where a is an element of a set Σ of events) and continues with P, the multi-prefix deterministic choice □a∈A → P a is constructed. When events are tagged with *channels*, i. e.Σ = CHANNELS × DATA, syntactic sugar like c?x→P x or c!x→P x is added; the former reads intuitively as "x is read from channel c" while the latter means "x is sent into c" (where c ∈ CHANNELS and x ∈ DATA).

The sequential composition P ; P' behaves first like P and, once it has successfully terminated, like P'. We denote by P \ A the process obtained from P after hiding the events of the set A. Similarly, Renaming P g is a process in which each event e of P was renamed in g(e).

The fixed point μ X. f X operator provides a solution to P $=$ f P (but requires precautions, see Sect. 2.4). The synchronized product P [A] P' is a primitive for all communication. It is abbreviated as P ||| P' when A $= \emptyset$ (interleaving) or P || P' when A $=$ UNIV (parallel), where UNIV :: 'a set is the universal set over the type 'a. Last but not least, the multi-prefix non-deterministic choice appearing in the definition of deadlock freeness (cf Theorem 4) is simply defined as $\sqcap$a $\in$ A $\rightarrow$ P a $= \sqcap$a $\in$ A. a $\rightarrow$ P a.

2.2   Classic CSP Semantics

The denotational semantics (following [27]) comes in three layers: the *trace model*, the *(stable) failures model* and the *failure/divergence model*.

In the trace semantics model, the behaviour of a process P is denoted by a prefix-closed set of traces, denoted $\mathcal{T}$ P, similar to the well-known concept of a "language of an automata". Since traces are finite lists and infinite behaviour is therefore represented via the set of approximations, an additional element tick (written ✓) is used to represent explicit termination signalized by SKIP. Obviously, ✓ should only appear at the end of a trace (i. e. traces are front_tickFree).

It is impossible to distinguish external and internal non-determinism in the trace model since the traces of both operators are just the union of their argument traces. To be more discriminant, [7] proposed the failure semantics model, where traces were annotated with a set of *refusals*, i. e. sets of events a process can *not* engage in. This leads to the notion of a *failure* (t, X) $\in \mathcal{F}$ P which is a pair of a trace t and a set of refusals X. Finally, [7] enriched the semantic domain of CSP with one more element, the set of *divergences* (written $\mathcal{D}$ P), in order to distinguish deadlocks from livelocks[2]. In the failure divergence model, the semantic domain consists of a pair of failures and divergences, where the latter are traces to situations where livelocks may occur.

While Hoare Logics is a framework to reason over terminating calculations, CSP and process refinement are designed to reason over non-terminating ones. Several variants of refinement were considered, but the most important one is the failure-divergence refinement:

$$P \sqsubseteq_{FD} Q \equiv \mathcal{F} P \supseteq \mathcal{F} Q \wedge \mathcal{D} P \supseteq \mathcal{D} Q$$

It turns out that beyond common protocol refinement proofs and test problems, many properties such as deadlock or livelock freeness can be expressed via a refinement statement. Moreover, this is a partial order, thus allowing proofs by double refinement.

2.3   Theories in Isabelle and HOL

Isabelle is a major interactive proof assistant implementing higher-order logic (HOL). As an LCF style theorem prover, it is based on a small logical core

---

[2] Also called *infinite internal chatter* as occurring in processes like μ x. a $\rightarrow$ x $\setminus$ {a}.

(kernel) to increase the trustworthiness of proofs. The Isabelle distribution comes with a number of library theories constructed solely from definitional axioms; among them theories for sets, lists, arithmetics, and analysis.

A particularly relevant library-theory is HOLCF Scott domain theory [21,28] providing a particular type class for *pointed complete partial orders* 'a, i.e. the class of types 'a which posses a least element ⊥ and a complete partial order _⊑_. The type-system uses type-classes to infer automatically that if 'b is a pcpo, then the function space 'a ⇒ 'b is also a pcpo.

For types of pcpo, HOLCF provides a theory of *continuity*, the concept of *admissibility*, the *fixed point induction* and the *least fixed point operator* μ x. f x.

2.4   Isabelle/HOL-CSP

Isabelle/HOL-CSP is a shallow embedding of CSP in HOL based on the traditional semantic domain described by nine well-formedness conditions (that we omit here) over the three semantic functions $\mathcal{T}$ :: 'a process ⇒ 'a trace set, $\mathcal{F}$ :: 'a process ⇒ 'a failure set and $\mathcal{D}$ :: 'a process ⇒ 'a trace set expressing well behaviour for processes. The core of HOL-CSP is to encapsulate wellformedness into a type definition. This is achieved by via the specification construct:

$$\text{typedef 'a process} = \text{"}\{P :: \text{'a process}_0 \,.\, \text{is\_process P}\}\text{"}$$

creating a new type which is isomorphic to the subset of 'a process$_0$'es satisfying the predicate is_process capturing the well-formedness conditions, where 'a process$_0$ is an abbreviation for 'a failure set × 'a divergence set. Subsequently, we define each CSP operator in terms of 'a process$_0$ and lift them to 'a process by proving the preservation of the is_process-invariant (thus formalizing [27]). The preservation even holds for arbitrary (possibly infinite) sets A in the generalisations □x∈A → P x resp. ⊓x∈A → P x. Note that both use higher-order abstract syntax and have the type 'a set ⇒ ('a ⇒ 'a process) ⇒ 'a process.

In order to give semantics to the fixed point operator (and thus access to the theory HOLCF), it is shown that 'a process belongs to the type class pcpo, which also gives higher-order functions over processes a pcpo structure. Recall that Scott domains provides semantics for the fixed point operator μ X. f X only under the condition that f is continuous wrt. a complete partial ordering. Since the natural ordering _ ⊑$_{FD}$ _ is too weak for this purpose, Roscoe and Brookes [25] proposed a complete *process ordering* P ⊑ Q which is stronger, i.e. P ⊑ Q ⟹ P ⊑$_{FD}$ Q, and yet ensures completeness at least for general read and write operations (see session HOL-CSP for technical details). With this ordering, the following core theorem is established:

Theorem 1 (Continuity). *Almost every operator ⊗ is continuous i.e.:*

$$\text{cont f} \Longrightarrow \text{cont g} \Longrightarrow \text{cont}(\lambda x.\,(\text{f x}) \otimes (\text{g x}))$$

Based on the lemma that ⊑$_{FD}$ is admissible for the fixed point induction, when f is continuous we have an induction rule of the following form:

Theorem 2 (Fixed-point Inductions). *For continuous functions f, we have:*

$$C \perp \sqsubseteq_{FD} Q \Longrightarrow (\bigwedge x.\ C\ x \sqsubseteq_{FD} Q \Longrightarrow C\ (f\ x) \sqsubseteq_{FD} Q) \Longrightarrow C\ (\mu\ X.\ f\ X) \sqsubseteq_{FD} Q$$

Proposition 1 (CSP-Algebra). *HOL-CSP provides about 200 rules derived from the denotational semantics, be it monotonicities or equalities, constituting what is often called the "algebraic semantics" in the literature. We show here only the small collection:*

$$P \,\square\, Q = Q \,\square\, P \qquad P \,\square\, P = P \qquad P \,\square\, (Q \,\square\, R) = (P \,\square\, Q) \,\square\, R$$
$$\square x{\in}A \cup B \to P\ x = (\square a{\in}A \to P\ a) \,\square\, (\square b{\in}B \to P\ b)$$
$$(\forall y.\ c\ y \in S) \Longrightarrow c?x \to P\ x\ [\![S]\!]\ c?x \to Q\ x = c?x \to (P\ x\ [\![S]\!]\ Q\ x)$$
$$\forall y.\ c\ y \notin B \Longrightarrow c!a \to P \setminus B = c!a \to (P \setminus B)$$
$$c\ a \in B \Longrightarrow c!a \to P \setminus B = P \setminus B \qquad\qquad\qquad \text{etc.}$$

The theories HOL-CSP and HOL-CSPM [3] also add a number of extensions of the original language. This includes the generalization of synchronization indexed by a multiset M: $[\![S]\!]i \in\!\#\ M.\ P\ i$, the generalization of sequential composition indexed by a list L: $SEQ\ l \in@\ L.\ P\ i$, etc.

3   Deterministic Proc-Omata

3.1   Motivations

Refinements proofs can quickly become counter-intuitive and fastidious, especially when modeling concurrent systems built from iterative architectural compositions[3]. We propose a certain subclass of CSP processes Proc-Omata to which many processes occurring in practice can be equivalently represented.

We start with another example, a simple counter of two events communicated by the environment:

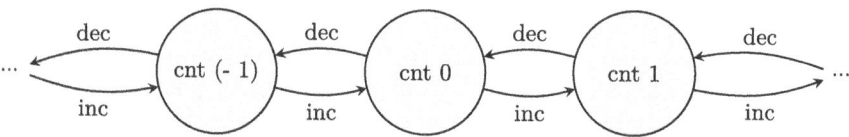

Fig. 4. LTS for the integer counter example

---

[3] In the CSP literature, the synchronous product P $[\![S]\!]$ Q, Hiding P \ S and Renaming were called the *architectural composition operators*.

Example 2 (Counter for integers). *Given two distinct events* inc *(increase)*
and dec *(decrease), we can define a counter for integers as follows:*

cnt ≡ μ X. (λn. (inc → X (n + 1)) □ (dec → X (n - 1)))

Note that if inc *and* dec *are of type* 'a, *the fixed point operator acts on a*
function *of type* int ⇒ 'a process*; and since* 'a process *belongs to the type class* cpo,
this implies that int ⇒ 'a process *also belongs to the* cpo *class. Thus, type inference*
establishes that the least fixed point exists (and by proving that this process has
no divergence, one could also establish that such a fixed point is unique) or in
other words that cnt *is well defined. This results in a process function of type* int
⇒ 'a process *that is parameterized in the initial state, something we could call a*
higher-order process. To rephrase this, we have defined for each integer a process
whose relationship to the others can be illustrated by the LTS in Fig. 4. Note that
its non-symbolic presentation makes the state-space infinite.

From algebraic properties of Mprefix and Det in HOL-CSP (cf Proposition 1),
and relying on the fact that inc and dec are distinct, we can rewrite our counter
process as follows:

cnt = (μ X. (λn. □e∈{dec, inc} → (if e = inc then X (n + 1) else X (n - 1))))

This example gives the intuition of what is a deterministic Proc-Omaton: a
fixed point within which there is only one step given by a multi-prefix deterministic choice.

3.2   Formal Definitions

We capture the intuition of the example above, by a formal definition of our
notion of a deterministic *Proc-Omaton*: it is a higher-order process canonically
associated with a functional automaton [23]. Let us first define a deterministic
automaton by a *record* in Isabelle/HOL.

Definition 1 (Abstract syntax of a deterministic automaton).

$$\text{record } (\text{'}\sigma, \text{'e}) \ A_d = \tau :: \langle \text{'}\sigma \Rightarrow \text{'e} \Rightarrow \text{'}\sigma \text{ option} \rangle$$

This command creates the record named A_d, of type ('σ, 'e) A_d ('σ and 'e being
of course polymorphic), and τ is the name of the record's field.

Intuitively 'σ is the type of the states and 'e the type of the transitions.

Isabelle/HOL records support a limited form of object-orientation; records
are *extensible* (i. e. new fields my be added, while theorems established over an
extensible record remain valid for the extensions). We will exploit this feature
in the following.

We now provide the formal definitions of enableness, reachability set and
Proc-Omaton associated with an automaton.

Definition 2 (Enableness). *Let* A *be an automaton of type* ('σ, 'e) A_d; *its transition function is accessible via by* τ A. *From this, we derive the following notion:*

$$\varepsilon \ A \ \sigma \equiv \{e \mid \tau \ A \ \sigma \ e \neq \Diamond\}$$

Definition 3 (Reachability set of an automaton).

> inductive_set $\mathcal{R}_d$ :: ‹('σ, 'e) A_d ⇒ 'σ ⇒ 'σ set› (‹$\mathcal{R}_d$›)
>   for A :: ‹('σ, 'e) A_d› and σ :: 'σ
> where init : ‹σ ∈ $\mathcal{R}_d$ A σ›
> | step : ‹σ' ∈ $\mathcal{R}_d$ A s ⟹ ⌊σ'⌋ = τ A σ e ⟹ σ' ∈ $\mathcal{R}_d$ A σ›

Definition 4 (Deterministic Proc-Omata). *To an automaton* A *we associate a parametric process that we call a "Proc-Omaton". It is a function of type* 'σ ⇒ 'e process *that we denote by:*

$$P[\![A]\!]_d \equiv \mu \ X. \ (\lambda\sigma. \ \Box \ e \in \varepsilon \ A \ \sigma \rightarrow X \ (\lceil \tau \ A \ \sigma \ e \rceil))$$

where ⌈y::'a option⌉ *denotes the* x::'a *such that* y = ⌊x⌋ *when* y ≠ ◇.

Example 3 (Proc-Omata for the integer counter). *We associate to the process* cnt *presented in Example 2 the deterministic automaton:*

A ≡ (|τ = λn e. if e = inc then ⌊n + 1⌋ else if e = dec then ⌊n - 1⌋ else ◇|)

and prove that cnt n = $P[\![A]\!]_d$ n.

When applying the operational rules of CSP to processes [4], our intuition that process proceeds by transiting between several "states" can be made explicit. In this paper, we use a simpler construction that just requires that they exist and are explicitly accessible.

3.3   Properties of Proc-Omata

As mentioned earlier, a deterministic Proc-Omaton can be seen as a way of accessing the states of the process from which we built an automaton. This paves the way for using the underlying automaton for establishing indirectly properties about processes. The following formally proven results constitute bridges between CSP and automata theory.

The first notable thing is that the step function is continuous. We can consequently unfold the fixed point, leading to our first property.

Proposition 2 (Unfolding). $P[\![A]\!]_d \ \sigma = \Box \ e \in \varepsilon \ A \ \sigma \rightarrow P[\![A]\!]_d \ \lceil \tau \ A \ \sigma \ e \rceil$

Theorem 3 (Termination). non_terminating ($P[\![A]\!]_d \ \sigma$)
where non_terminating *is a predicate over processes expressing that no trace is ending normally with* ✓.

The notion of reachability set defined earlier Definition 3 leads to the two following characterizations.

Theorem 4 (Deadlock). deadlock_free $(P[\![A]\!]_d \, \sigma) = (\forall \sigma' \in \mathcal{R}_d \, A \, \sigma. \, \varepsilon \, A \, \sigma' \neq \emptyset)$ *where* deadlock_free *is a predicate over processes defined as*

   deadlock_free P $\equiv (\mu \, X. \, \sqcap e \in UNIV \rightarrow X) \sqsubseteq_{FD} P$

expressing that "P *can always make progress".*

Theorem 5 (Alphabet). events_of $(P[\![A]\!]_d \, \sigma) = \bigcup \, (\varepsilon \, A \, ' \, \mathcal{R}_d \, A \, \sigma)$ *where* events_of P *is the alphabet of the process* P.

Finally, an interesting yet not too surprising property is that deterministic Proc-Omata correspond to deterministic processes. This concept is defined in the CSP theory such that no continuation of a trace can be in a refusals set associated to it, i. e.deterministic P $\equiv \forall s \, e. \, s \, @ \, [e] \in \mathcal{T} \, P \longrightarrow (s, \{e\}) \notin \mathcal{F} \, P.$

Since such processes are maximal for the $(\sqsubseteq_{FD})$ ordering, we only have to establish the following refinement for proving the equality.

Theorem 6 (Deterministic equality). $P[\![A]\!]_d \, \sigma \sqsubseteq_{FD} P \Longrightarrow P = P[\![A]\!]_d \, \sigma$

Thus, establishing the core of the Proc-Omata theory requires some work, indeed. Now comes the benefit: the general theorems for compactification.

3.4   Compactification of Synchronization

It turns out that the Proc-Omata behave very well in synchronization contexts. The main idea is that given two deterministic automaton A_1 and A_2 of type $('\sigma, \, 'e) \, A_d$ and a synchronization set E (of type $'e$ set), we *construct* a new deterministic automaton $A_0 \,_d \otimes [\![E]\!]_{bin} \, A_1$ of type $('\sigma$ list, $'e) \, A_d$ such that

   $P[\![A_0]\!]_d \, \sigma_0 \, [\![E]\!] \, P[\![A_1]\!]_d \, \sigma_1 = P[\![A_0 \,_d \otimes [\![E]\!]_{bin} \, A_1]\!]_d \, [\sigma_0, \sigma_1]$

under some assumptions on enableness independence that we will discuss later. We omit the formal definition of this binary operator here (which is essentially a translation of the synchronization behavior into the automaton product), but we draw the reader's attention to the choice of $'\sigma$ list instead of $'\sigma \times '\sigma$. This is so that we can inductively generalize the product, leading to what we call a compactification theorem.

Theorem 7 (Compactification of Synchronization). *Assuming* $|\sigma s| = |\sigma A|$ *and a generalization of the hypothesis of independence on the enableness:*

$$[\![E]\!] \, (\sigma, \, A) \in \# mset \, (zip \, \sigma s \, \sigma A). \, P[\![A]\!]_d \, \sigma = P[\![_d \bigotimes [\![E]\!] \, \sigma A]\!]_d \, \sigma s$$

If we say that this generalization from the binary to the n-ary case is intuitive, this does by no means imply that the underlying proofs are straight-forward; this part of the Proc-Omata theory took about 1500 lines of definitions and dense proofs in Isabelle/HOL, in short because synchronization gives rise to many cases to be dealt with during the proof by double refinement.

The importance of Theorem 7 lies in the fact that an iterative synchronization of an arbitrary number of Proc-Omata can be reconstructed into a Proc-Omaton, paving the way for invariant proof techniques in combination with what we evoked in Sect. 3.3.

Note that the order in which the Proc-Omata appears is arbitrary, but we have to track the associated state, and this is why the zip function seems to appear from nowhere.

Some basic ideas of this result already appeared in [30] from 2020. But instead of one transition function τ, the enableness ε had also to be defined independently (rather than having it as a derived concept). This made the construction more difficult to understand, and obscured the compactification result that was hidden inside a proof for a particular example. Moreover, only the case $E = \emptyset$ and $E = $ UNIV i. e. interleaving and parallelism had been discussed, while the above form of the compactification is suited for arbitrary synchronization sets.

As mentioned earlier, our result is always available as soon as we have the independence assumption on the enableness (we write the binary version here):

$$\forall \sigma_0' \in \mathcal{R}_d \ A_0 \ \sigma_0. \ \forall \sigma_1' \in \mathcal{R}_d \ A_1 \ \sigma_1. \ \varepsilon \ A_0 \ \sigma_0' \cap \varepsilon \ A_1 \ \sigma_1' \subseteq E$$

This is necessary if we want to remain with deterministic automata, because otherwise the synchronization would not be a deterministic process anymore.

4   Potentially Terminating Proc-Omata

In this section, we discuss a variant of Proc-Omata as introduced in Sect. 3, which were non_terminating automata. They may deadlock, but never gracefully terminate with SKIP. However, since this may be useful for numerous applications, we have extended our definitions to cope with this kind of situation. We will concentrate a few key-results of the deterministic case.

4.1   Formal Definitions

Actually our records have an additional field: $\mathcal{S}_F$, the set of final states.

Definition 5 (Abstract syntax of a deterministic automaton). *We add an additional field in the record with the concept of a final state, i. e. a state representing that* SKIP *has been reached:*

$$\text{record } ('\sigma, \ 'e) \ A_d = \tau :: \langle '\sigma \Rightarrow 'e \Rightarrow '\sigma \text{ option} \rangle \ \mathcal{S}_F :: \langle '\sigma \text{ set} \rangle$$

Definition 6 (Deterministic SKIP-Proc-Omata). *The process scheme corresponding to a SKIP-Proc-Omaton reads as follows:*

$$P_{SKIP}[\![A]\!]_d \equiv \mu \ X. \ (\lambda\sigma. \text{ if } \sigma \in \mathcal{S}_F \ A \text{ then SKIP else } \Box e \in \varepsilon \ A \ \sigma \to X \ \lceil \tau \ A \ \sigma \ e \rceil)$$

Note that the Collatz process shown in Example 1 can be expressed as a Proc-Omaton of this variant. This definition naturally generalizes Sect. 3.2, which is a special case $\mathcal{S}_F \ A = \emptyset$. Such a fixed point can be unfolded in the same way as in Proposition 2.

4.2   Properties of Potentially Terminating Proc-Omata

These new versions of Proc-Omata enjoy almost the same properties as the previous ones, except that we now have to consider the possibility of termination with SKIP. The counterparts of Theorem 3, Theorem 6 and Theorem 4 are as follows:

non_terminating $(P_{SKIP}[\![A]\!]_d \; \sigma) = (S_F \; A \cap R_d \; A \; \sigma = \emptyset)$

$P_{SKIP}[\![A]\!]_d \; \sigma \sqsubseteq_{FD} P \Longrightarrow P = P_{SKIP}[\![A]\!]_d \; \sigma$

fin_states_not_enabled A $\Longrightarrow$
deadlock_free$_{SKIP}$ $(P_{SKIP}[\![A]\!]_d \; \sigma) = (\forall \sigma' \in R_d \; A \; \sigma. \; \sigma' \in S_F \; A \vee \varepsilon \; A \; \sigma' \neq \emptyset)$

The latter theorem requires some explanation. deadlock_free$_{SKIP}$ P is a predicate on P meaning that P is either always making progress, either terminating with SKIP. For establishing this result we need an additional assumption: fin_states_not_enabled A stipulating that $\varepsilon \; A \; \sigma = \emptyset$ as soon as $\sigma \in S_F \; A$.

However, the most important result is the fact that we have managed to extend the compactification of synchronization to such variants of Proc-Omata. Admittedly, these rules have more the format of program transformation rules (what they are) which are geared towards mechanization.

Theorem 8 (General Compactification of Synchronization). *The generalized form is technically quite dense, but this is due to the fact that it requires a fairly large number of applicability conditions. We assume:*

- $|\sigma s| = |\sigma A|$
- $\forall A \in set \; \sigma A$. fin_states_not_enabled A
- $\forall i < |\sigma A|. \; \forall j < |\sigma A|. \; i \neq j \longrightarrow$ det_indep_enabl $\sigma A_{[i]} \; \sigma s_{[i]} \; E \; \sigma A_{[j]} \; \sigma s_{[j]}$.

Thus $[\![E]\!] \; (\sigma, A) \in \#mset \; (zip \; \sigma s \; \sigma A)$. $P_{SKIP}[\![A]\!]_d \; \sigma = P_{SKIP}[\![d \bigotimes [\![E]\!] \; \sigma A]\!]_d \; \sigma s$.

4.3   Compactification of Sequential Composition

The extension of our formalization for allowing potentially terminating Proc-Omata was actually motivated by the fact that SKIP is the neutral element for the sequential composition i. e.P ; SKIP = P and SKIP ; P = P. This makes it possible to split big architectures into smaller sub-components, which can potentially be Proc-Omata. But why should we only consider the binary case? For the MultiSeq operator, we proved a compactification theorem in the same philosophy as Theorem 8.

Theorem 9 (General Compactification of Sequential composition). *Again, the generalized form is technically quite dense. We assume:*

- $\sigma A \neq []$
- $|\sigma s| = |\sigma A|$
- fin_states_not_enabled (last σA).

Thus SEQ $(\sigma, A) \in @zip \; \sigma s \; \sigma A$. $P_{SKIP}[\![A]\!]_d \; \sigma = P_{SKIP}[\![d \bigotimes ; \sigma A]\!]_d \; \sigma s$.

5   Examples

5.1   Bounded Buffer

Let us first start with an example where conversion is immediate. Using a fixed point we define a bounded buffer such that for every n and L:

BBuf n L =
(n < N) & (input?x → BBuf (n + 1) (L @ [x])) □
(0 < n) & (output!hd L → BBuf (n - 1) (tl L))

   where:

 − n is a nat and L an 'a list
 − the maximal size N of the buffer is non negative
 − input and output are channels
 − P & c is just an abbreviation for if c then P else STOP.

   We prove that this example can be easily "procomatized" with the following transition function:

λ(n, L) e.
   case e of input x $\Rightarrow$ if n < N then $\lfloor$(n + 1, L @ [x])$\rfloor$ else $\Diamond$
   | output x $\Rightarrow$ if 0 < n $\wedge$ hd L = x then $\lfloor$(n - 1, tl L)$\rfloor$ else $\Diamond$

From this it is straightforward to conclude that BBuf 0 [] is deadlock_free, and we can more generally use it inside an architecture with other Proc-Omata.

5.2   Dining Philosophers

A good illustration of the power of Proc-Omata reasoning is the paradigmatic Dining Philosophers example, first introduced by Dijkstra in 1965 and reformulated to the present form by Hoare [15]. The problem has been tackled by many model checkers, who routinely solve this problem up to say 15 philosophers before giving up due to state explosion.
   The problem assumes that N philosophers—with N an **arbitrary** number— are dining around a round table, each one sharing his right and left fork with his left and right neighbour respectively. However, philosophers need two forks to actually eat, a naive strategy to just grab both forks may therefore result in a deadlock.
   In the following, we present a formalization in HOL-CSP. We start to define the *channels* by a datatype:

   datatype dining_event = picks nat nat | putsdown nat nat

   Based on these events, we construct a number of simple processes representing right-handed philosophers (they pick the fork to the right first), a left-handed philosopher, and forks:

Definition 7 (Basic Processes).

RPHIL i $\equiv$ μ X. picks i i $\rightarrow$ picks i ((i - 1) mod N) $\rightarrow$
$\qquad\qquad$ putsdown i ((i - 1) mod N) $\rightarrow$ putsdown i i $\rightarrow$ X

LPHIL0 $\equiv$ μ X. picks 0 (N - 1) $\rightarrow$ picks 0 0 $\rightarrow$
$\qquad\qquad\qquad$ putsdown 0 0 $\rightarrow$ putsdown 0 (N - 1) $\rightarrow$ X

FORK i $\equiv$ μ X. $\quad$ (picks i i $\rightarrow$ putsdown i i $\rightarrow$ x)
$\qquad\qquad\quad$ $\square$ (picks ((i + 1) mod N) i $\rightarrow$ putsdown ((i + 1) mod N) i $\rightarrow$ X)

Using the architectural operator multi-interleave, philosophers and forks are "wired together" as follows:

Definition 8 (Architecture of right-handed Dining Philosophers).

$$RPHILS \equiv ||| \ i \in \# \ mset \ [0..<N]. \ RPHIL \ i$$
$$RPHILS' \equiv ||| \ i \in \# \ mset \ [1..<N]. \ RPHIL \ i$$
$$FORKS \equiv ||| \ i \in \# \ mset \ [0..<N]. \ FORK \ i$$
$$RDINING = FORKS \ || \ RPHILS$$

Reasoning about a potential deadlock for such a system can be difficult: you do not really know where to start in the ring. But it is straightforward to construct for the simple processes of Definition 7 equivalent deterministic Proc-Omata. In more details, this can be achieved for the forks and the right-handed philosophers. With the appropriate definitions we prove FORK i = P[[fork_A i]]$_d$ 0 and RPHIL i = P[[rphil_A i]]$_d$ 0. Finally, using the compactification Theorem 7, we obtain a big Proc-Omaton equivalent to RDINING.

We show that ([1 ... 1],[1 ... 1]) (both lists length N) is reachable from the initial state ([0 ... 0],[0 ... 0]), and that in this state our big Proc-Omaton has its enableness empty. (This corresponds to the situation where each philosopher has picked his right fork, thus no left fork is available). With the characterization Theorem 4, we have proven that RDINING deadlocks for any N > 1.

By modifying the construction to DINING = (FORKS || (LPHIL0 ||| RPHILS')) i. e. replacing the first right-handed philosopher by a left-handed one, we can again compactify, and prove by invariant on the Proc-Omaton for DINING that every reachable state is enabled, which results with Theorem 4 in deadlock_free DINING.

We emphasize, again, that these proofs are independent from N and that the fully formalized proofs for e.g. deadlock_free DINING can be found in session HOL-CSP_Proc-Omata.

5.3   Copy Buffer with a Queue

Even if a process is not completely convertible in a Proc-Omaton, the technique may be applicable for crucial sub-problems. Let us consider a copy buffer with a queue where the data transmitted by the sender is stored until the recipient actually receives it. The queue may have arbitrary size *and* be parameterized over an arbitrary type 'a.

Again, we define the channels of the process via a datatype:

$$\text{datatype 'a chan} = \text{left 'a} \mid \text{enqueue 'a} \mid \text{dequeue 'a} \mid \text{right 'a}$$

Definition 9 (Definitions for a Queue Buffer). *The definition of the Queue-Buffer is as follows:*

$$\text{send} \equiv \mu\ X.\ \text{left?x} \rightarrow \text{enqueue!x} \rightarrow X$$

$$\text{rec} \equiv \mu\ X.\ \text{dequeue?x} \rightarrow \text{right!x} \rightarrow X$$

$$\text{queue} \equiv \mu\ X.(\lambda L.\ (\text{enqueue?x} \rightarrow X\ (x\ \#\ L))$$
$$\Box(\text{if}\ L = []\ \text{then STOP else dequeue!last}\ L \rightarrow X\ (\text{butlast}\ L)))$$

$$\text{QueueBuffer\_pre}\ L \equiv \text{send}\ [\![\text{range enqueue}]\!]\ (\text{queue}\ L\ [\![\text{range dequeue}]\!]\ \text{rec})$$

$$\text{QueueBuffer}\ L \equiv \text{QueueBuffer\_pre}\ L \setminus \text{range enqueue} \cup \text{range dequeue}$$

We can write send, rec and queue as Proc-Omata without much difficulty, and treat therefore QueueBuffer_pre with compactification. As a consequence of Theorem 4, we immediately obtain that QueueBuffer_pre is deadlock free by establishing that enableness is always non-empty. Because of the Hiding operator, however, the entire QueueBuffer can not be converted. Fortunately, for the obtained Proc-Omaton for QueueBuffer_pre, we can still apply a fixed point induction where we let the state free variable. This allows us to look only one step ahead and prove relatively easily that QueueBuffer is deadlock free.

6   Related Work

The theory of CSP has attracted a lot of interest since the eighties and nineties, both as a theoretical device as well as a modelling language to analyze complex concurrent systems. Not surprisingly, numerous formalisation attempts have been undertaken with the advent of powerful interactive proof assistants. This ranges from pioneering work in HOL4 [9], fragments of operational semantics as in [24] and [16] and first attempts towards a symbolically working tool [12,17–19]. Our CSP background theory contained in [3,5,6,29,31] represents to our knowledge the most comprehensive formal treatment of the theory of CSP (cf. [4] for a more in-depth comparison over existing approaches).

Parametric verification attracted a lot of interest, in particular in model-checking communities, in order to overcome the obvious limitations of finite models. This applies for stochastic model-checking [13], linear time model-checking [2], or protocol verifiers [10,14] just to cite a few out of a plethora of publications.

Attempts for parametric model-checking can also be found in the closer related field of process algebras. Notably [1,20,26] attempted to find process characterizations to generalise finite results to infinite ones by *data-independence*. Roscoe developed a data independent technology to verify security protocols modelled with CSP/FDR, which allows the node to call infinite fresh values for nonces, thus infinite sequence of operations [26]. We'd like to object that our approach, albeit having the apparent drawback to be based on interactive theorem proving, achieves similar or even more general results with finally lesser effort[4].

7   Conclusion

We presented a formalization of Proc-Omata and the cornerstones of their theory. The interest in Proc-Omata lays in the fact that they may serve as a bridge between process algebras and automata theory. They can be seen as a compromise: by conceding a certain expressiveness, we obtain powerful proof techniques by reusing product-automata constructions and their properties. We actually presented several motivations and variants with increasing levels of abstraction before giving an overview of the key results: the compactification theorems geared at process synchronization families.

We illustrated this with three examples: the bounded buffer, where the conversion to Proc-Omaton is straightforward, the Dining Philosophers where the situation of a parameterized unbounded ring of processes fits our theory perfectly, and the queue buffer where Proc-Omata-techniques can at least be used for critical sub-components.

Our construction motivates several lines of future research:

- automated conversion of processes in their Proc-Omata counterpart
- the extension of our theory to non-deterministic Proc-Omata
- generalizations to more operators and process patterns, e. g. interleaving and sequencing for reordering theorems,
- more proof automation by connecting to external tools (model checkers, simulators)
- automated synthesis of invariants as in CEGAR, Cubicle, or Kind 2.

---

[4] Our version of the random-number generator can be found in [4].

References

1. An, J., Zhang, L., You, C.: The design and implementation of data independence in the CSP model of security protocol. Adv. Mater. Res. **915–916**, 1386–1392 (2014). https://doi.org/10.4028/www.scientific.net/AMR.915-916.1386

2. André, É., Nguyen, H.G., Petrucci, L., Sun, J.: Parametric model checking timed automata under non-zenoness assumption. In: Barrett, C., Davies, M., Kahsai, T. (eds.) NFM 2017. LNCS, vol. 10227, pp. 35–51. Springer, Cham (2017). https://doi.org/10.1007/978-3-319-57288-8_3

3. Ballenghien, B., Taha, S., Wolff, B.: HOL-CSPM - architectural operators for HOL-CSP. Arch. Formal Proofs **2023** (2023). https://www.isa-afp.org/entries/HOL-CSPM.html

4. Ballenghien, B., Wolff, B.: An operational semantics in Isabelle/HOL-CSP. In: Bertot, Y., Kutsia, T., Norrish, M. (eds.) 15th International Conference on Interactive Theorem Proving, ITP 2024. LIPIcs, vol. 309, pp. 29:1–29:18. Schloss Dagstuhl - Leibniz-Zentrum für Informatik (2024). https://doi.org/10.4230/LIPIcs.ITP.2023.29

5. Ballenghien, B., Wolff, B.: An operational semantics in Isabelle/HOL-CSP. In: Bertot, Y., Kutsia, T., Norrish, M. (eds.) 15th International Conference on Interactive Theorem Proving, ITP 2024, 9–14 September 2024, Tbilisi, Georgia. LIPIcs, vol. 309, pp. 7:1–7:18. Schloss Dagstuhl - Leibniz-Zentrum für Informatik (2024). https://doi.org/10.4230/LIPICS.ITP.2024.7

6. Ballenghien, B., Wolff, B.: Operational semantics formally proven in HOL-CSP. Archive of Formal Proofs (2023). https://isa-afp.org/entries/HOL-CSP_OpSem.html

7. Brookes, S.D., Hoare, C.A.R., Roscoe, A.W.: A theory of communicating sequential processes. J. ACM **31**(3), 560–599 (1984)

8. Brookes, S.D., Roscoe, A.W.: An improved failures model for communicating processes. In: Brookes, S.D., Roscoe, A.W., Winskel, G. (eds.) CONCURRENCY 1984. LNCS, vol. 197, pp. 281–305. Springer, Heidelberg (1985). https://doi.org/10.1007/3-540-15670-4_14

9. Camilleri, A.J.: A higher order logic mechanization of the CSP failure-divergence semantics. In: Birtwistle, G. (ed.) IV Higher Order Workshop, Banff 1990, pp. 123–150. Springer, London (1991). https://doi.org/10.1007/978-1-4471-3182-3_9

10. Conchon, S., Delzanno, G., Ferrando, A.: Declarative parameterized verification of distributed protocols via the cubicle model checker. Fundam. Informaticae **178**(4), 347–378 (2021). https://doi.org/10.3233/FI-2021-2010

11. Crisafulli, P., Taha, S., Wolff, B.: Modeling and analysing cyber-physical systems in HOL-CSP. Robotics Auton. Syst. **170**, 104549 (2023). https://doi.org/10.1016/J.ROBOT.2023.104549

12. da Silva Carvalho de Freitas, C.A.: A theory for communicating, sequential processes in Coq (2020). https://api.semanticscholar.org/CorpusID:259373665

13. Hahn, E.M., Hermanns, H., Wachter, B., Zhang, L.: PARAM: a model checker for parametric Markov models. In: Touili, T., Cook, B., Jackson, P. (eds.) CAV 2010. LNCS, vol. 6174, pp. 660–664. Springer, Heidelberg (2010). https://doi.org/10.1007/978-3-642-14295-6_56

14. Hess, A.V., Mödersheim, S.A., Brucker, A.D.: Stateful protocol composition in Isabelle/HOL. ACM Trans. Priv. Secur. **26**(3), 25:1–25:36 (2023). https://doi.org/10.1145/3577020

15. Hoare, C.A.R.: Communicating Sequential Processes. Prentice-Hall Inc., Upper Saddle River (1985)

16. Igried, B., Setzer, A.: Programming with monadic CSP-style processes in dependent type theory. In: Proceedings of the 1st International Workshop on Type-Driven Development, TyDe 2016, pp. 28–38. Association for Computing Machinery, New York (2016). https://doi.org/10.1145/2976022.2976032

17. Igried, B., Setzer, A.: Trace and stable failures semantics for CSP-AGDA. arXiv preprint arXiv:1709.04714 (2017)

18. Isobe, Y., Roggenbach, M.: A complete axiomatic semantics for the CSP stable-failures model. In: CONCUR 2006 - Concurrency Theory, 17th International Conference, Bonn, Germany, 27–30 August 2006, pp. 158–172 (2006)

19. Isobe, Y., Roggenbach, M.: CSP-prover: a proof tool for the verification of scalable concurrent systems. Inf. Media Technol. **5**(1), 32–39 (2010). https://doi.org/10.11185/imt.5.32

20. Lazic, R.S.: A semantic study of data-independence with applications to the mechanical verification of concurren. Ph.D. thesis, University of Oxford (1999)

21. Müller, O., Nipkow, T., von Oheimb, D., Slotosch, O.: HOLCF = HOL + LCF. J-FP **9**(2), 191–223 (1999). https://doi.org/10.1017/S095679689900341X

22. Nipkow, T.: Verified lexical analysis. In: Grundy, J., Newey, M. (eds.) TPHOLs 1998. LNCS, vol. 1479, pp. 1–15. Springer, Heidelberg (1998). https://doi.org/10.1007/BFb0055126

23. Nipkow, T.: Functional automata. Arch. Formal Proofs **2004** (2004). https://www.isa-afp.org/entries/Functional-Automata.shtml

24. Noce, P.: Conservation of CSP noninterference security under sequential composition. Archive of Formal Proofs (2016). https://www.isa-afp.org/entries/Noninterference_Sequential_Composition.shtml

25. Roscoe, A.W.: An alternative order for the failures model. J. Log. Comput. **2**, 557–577 (1992)

26. Roscoe, A.W., Broadfoot, P.J.: Proving security protocols with model checkers by data independence techniques. J. Comput. Secur. **7**(1), 147–190 (1999)

27. Roscoe, A.: Theory and Practice of Concurrency. Prentice Hall, Hoboken (1997)

28. Scott, D.: Continuous lattices. In: Lawvere, F.W. (ed.) Toposes, Algebraic Geometry and Logic. LNM, vol. 274, pp. 97–136. Springer, Heidelberg (1972). https://doi.org/10.1007/BFb0073967

29. Taha, S., Wolff, B., Ye, L.: The HOL-CSP refinement toolkit. Arch. Formal Proofs **2020** (2020). https://www.isa-afp.org/entries/CSP_RefTK.html

30. Taha, S., Wolff, B., Ye, L.: Philosophers may dine - definitively! In: Dongol, B., Troubitsyna, E. (eds.) IFM 2020. LNCS, vol. 12546, pp. 419–439. Springer, Cham (2020). https://doi.org/10.1007/978-3-030-63461-2_23

31. Taha, S., Ye, L., Wolff, B.: HOL-CSP Version 2.0. Archive of Formal Proofs (2019). http://isa-afp.org/entries/HOL-CSP.html

32. Tej, H., Wolff, B.: A corrected failure-divergence model for CSP in Isabelle/HOL. In: Fitzgerald, J., Jones, C.B., Lucas, P. (eds.) FME 1997. LNCS, vol. 1313, pp. 318–337. Springer, Heidelberg (1997). https://doi.org/10.1007/3-540-63533-5_17

Formal Foundations for Efficient Simulation of MOM Systems: The Refinement Calculus for Object-Oriented Event-Graphs

Sini Chen[1], Huibiao Zhu[1(✉)], Ran Li[2], Lili Xiao[3], Jiapeng Wang[1], Ning Ge[4], and Xinbin Cao[4]

[1] East China Normal University, Shanghai, China
hbzhu@sei.ecnu.edu.cn
[2] Nanjing University of Information Science and Technology, Nanjing, China
[3] Donghua University, Shanghai, China
[4] Beihang University, Beijing, China

Abstract. The rise of Industry 4.0 has spurred a growing need for smart, interconnected production systems and supply chains in manufacturing. In this context, the seamless integration of Manufacturing Operations Management (MOM) practices is crucial for ensuring operational efficiency, product quality, and regulatory compliance across the manufacturing life-cycle. This paper presents a formal foundation for the Object-Oriented Event-Graph (OOEG) language, which aims to enable efficient simulation within the MOM architecture. At the core of this work is the proposal and formal definition of a new OOEG language, named Refinement Calculus for Object-Oriented Event-Graph (rCOE), and we explore the language's operational semantics. This rigorous semantics specification provides a solid theoretical underpinning for the OOEG language, facilitating precise formalization and simulation of complex manufacturing processes. To demonstrate the practical applicability of the proposed approach, we present a real-world case study within the aviation manufacturing domain, focusing on the partial assembly phase.

Keywords: Manufacturing Operations Management (MOM) · Object-Oriented Event Graph (OOEG) · Operational Semantics · Simulation · Formalization

1 Introduction

Characterized by the fusion of digital technologies and automation, Industry 4.0 revolutionizes traditional manufacturing practices to create smart, interconnected production systems and supply chains [19]. This paradigm shift seeks to boost efficiency, productivity, and flexibility, while fostering innovation and satisfying evolving customer demands. [17]. In this dynamic and highly regulated

C. Anutariya and M. M. Bonsangue (Eds.): ICTAC 2024, LNCS 15373, pp. 290–309, 2025.
https://doi.org/10.1007/978-3-031-77019-7_17

sector, seamless integration of Manufacturing Operations Management (MOM) practices [9,14,15] is indispensable for ensuring operational efficiency, product quality, and regulatory compliance throughout the manufacturing life cycle.

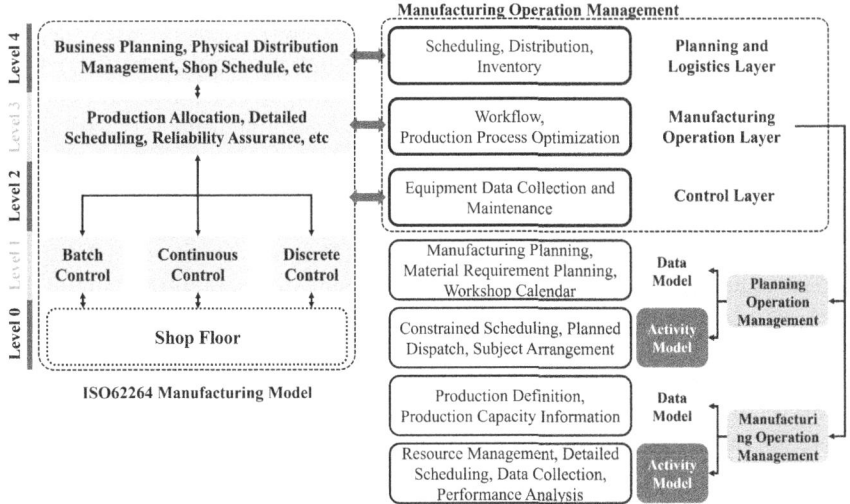

Fig. 1. The ISO62264 Manufacturing Model with accordance to the MOM architecture.

The MOM architecture has a tight correlation with the International Standard ISA-95/ISO-62264, also known as the Enterprise-Control System Integration [2]. It serves as a guiding beacon for organizations to foster seamless communication and interoperability across various levels of the manufacturing hierarchy [5,11,21]. The correspondence between MOM and the ISA-95/ISO-62264 model is illustrated in Fig. 1. The Manufacturing Operations Layer (MOL), corresponding to level 3 in the ISA-95/ISO-62264 model, manages production workflows, advanced scheduling, and resource allocation. To address the need for a user-friendly, well-defined, and adaptable requirement language [16] in this context, this paper proposes a formalism to support the creation of rigorous, mathematical models within the MOL. This formalization can enable simulation, analysis, and optimization, helping to identify and eliminate potential issues or bottlenecks in the manufacturing workflow.

While general-purpose modeling languages like Unified Modeling Language (UML) [10] and System Modeling Language (SysML) [6] offer robust expressive capabilities, they lack an intuitive and independent sub-graph tailored to portray production lines in manufacturing, leading to ambiguity as enterprises may adopt vaired modeling elements for the same concept. Conversely, domain-specific languages such as Business Process Model and Notation (BPMN) [3] and Manufacturing Execution System Modeling Language (MES-ML) [23] provide extensive symbol systems and specialized tools, but their steep learning curve can be cumbersome.

In this paper, we adopt the Object-Oriented Event Graph (OOEG) [20] formalism for simulating production lines, offering a straightforward and effective modeling approach tailored for OO simulation. Within the MOL, both the Planning Operations Management and the Manufacturing Operations Management can be decomposed into a data model and an activity model. By aligning the Physical Class Diagram (PCD) and Event Class Diagram (ECD) with the data model and empowering the event graph to encapsulate the activity model, OOEG emerges as an exemplary requirement language well-suited for production line simulations. It performs as a completion of the UML diagrams set, with which systems are described by linking components analogously to the real factory.

Despite the suitability for production simulation, OOEG exhibits certain limitations in practice. So far, OOEG lacks formal foundations, which is critical for requirement analysis in manufacturing [7]. Varying interpretations of language elements by different stakeholders can result in errors during simulation, impacting subsequent real-world production processes. Additionally, the absence of simulation tools poses a challenge, impeding the seamless implementation and widespread adoption of OOEG in practical manufacturing settings.

This paper establishes a formal foundation for the OOEG through the proposition of a codified representation named Refinement Calculus for Object-Oriented Event-Graph (rCOE) and the precise definition of its operational semantics, drawing inspiration from the well-established Refinement Calculus for Object Systems (rCOS) [8]. Compared to the OOEG's graphic presentation, which provides intuitive understanding, the rCOE offers precision and computability. By minimizing ambiguity and accurately representing the underlying concepts, the rCOE formalism becomes more readily processed by computers. Moreover, the rCOE's operational semantics serves as a foundation for defining corresponding tool implementations using rewriting logic. We demonstrate the approach through a real-world unclassified case study within the aviation manufacturing domain, particularly focusing on the assembly stage, and discuss translating the rCOE semantics into executable implementations.

The subsequent sections of this paper unfold as follows: Sect. 2 provides an overview to the foundational elements. Section 3 and 4 present a comprehensive elucidation of the proposed language, covering its syntax and semantics. Section 5 demonstrates the application of this language through a real-world case study within the avionic manufacturing industry. Finally, Sect. 6 concludes the paper and discusses potential future expansions and enhancements.

2   Background

This section provides concise introductions to the key foundations underlying our work, rCOS and OOEG.

2.1   Refinement Calculus for Object Systems

The Refinement Calculus for Object Systems (rCOS) provides a mathematical characterization of fundamental Object-Oriented (OO) concepts [13]. By integrating support for both high-level design patterns and low-level refactoring, rCOS enables developers to effectively model and analyze complex design patterns, while also facilitating the systematic improvement and evolution of software systems through iterative refactoring [12]. As a result, rCOS is well adapted in software engineering for modeling and verifying OO systems [4].

The syntax of rCOS is defined in the manner of Backus Normal Form (BNF), and here is a snippet of the class declaration. This indicates that a class declaration consists of: the class keyword, the class name C, an optional extends clause specifying the base class, and a body containing a set of attributes As and a set of methods Ms. The BNF notation succinctly captures the structure of a class declaration, including the optional inheritance relationship and the composition of attributes and methods within the class body.

$$\langle cdecl \rangle ::= class\ C\ [extends\ C]\{\langle As \rangle; \langle Ms \rangle\}$$

This paper presents an extension to the rCOS framework tailored to the features of OOEG, aimed at enhancing its capabilities in modeling and analyzing complex object-oriented systems, with a focus on manufacturing processes.

2.2 Object-Oriented Event Graph

As an evolution of the traditional Event-Based modeling formalism [1], the Object-Oriented Event Graph (OOEG) provides a visual representation of objects and the events that trigger changes in their states [20]. By introducing a modularized representation of physical knowledge, OOEG enables more coherent description of object interactions that correspond to real-world physical entities.

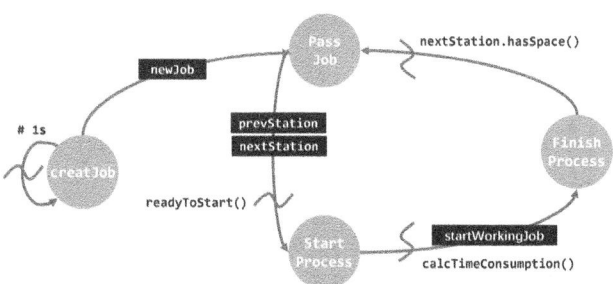

Fig. 2. OOEG Construction

The OOEG modeling paradigm comprises three key components. The **UML Physical Class Diagram (PCD)** establishes a parallelism between the simulation model and the underlying physical/enterprise system. The **UML Event Class Diagram (ECD)** provides facilities for creating and scheduling events within the simulation, mirroring corresponding business/enterprise concepts.

And the **Object-Oriented Event Graph (OOEG)** encapsulates the dynamic system behavior, extended to cater to OO simulation models.

Figure 2 is an example of a typical OOEG describing one production assembly line at coarse granularity. Each node represents an *event*, and each edge corresponds to a *scheduling operation*. Curly symbols on edges denote *guard conditions*, e.g., the Passing event can only be scheduled when *nextStation.hasSpace()* evaluates to *true*. Boxes on edges indicate *parameters* being passed. Multiple instances of events are allowed to be executed in parallel.

While this visual formalism provides an intuitive way to model the interactions and dependencies between various production events and activities, however, in this paper, we propose a codified representation named rCOE. Through the proposition of rCOE and its operational semantics, we aim to minimize ambiguity and accurately represent the underlying concepts.

3   Syntax

In this section, we propose the rCOE modeling language, inspired by rCOS [22], to formally describe the OOEG's characteristics in a symbolic manner that captures its inherent OO nature. The syntax of rCOE is presented in Table 1.

Table 1. Syntax of rCOE

Structure		
Declarations	$classDef$	$::= \ class \ C_{derive} \ extends \ C_{base}\{attrDef \bullet methDef\}$
	$attrDef$	$::= \ T \ x; \ | \ T \ x; \ attrDef \ | \ \epsilon$
	$methDef$	$::= \ T \ m(params; vars)\{s\}$
		$| \ T \ m(params; vars)\{s\} \ \bullet \ methDef \ | \ \epsilon$
Expressions	le	$::= \ x \ | \ le.a$
	ie	$::= \ int \ | \ ie \ + \ ie \ | \ ie \ - \ ie \ | \ ie \ * \ ie \ | \ ie \ / \ ie$
	be	$::= \ bool \ | \ ie \ < \ ie \ | \ ie \leq ie \ | \ ie \ > \ ie \ | \ ie \ \geq \ ie$
		$| \ ie \ == \ ie \ | \ ie \neq ie \ | \ be \ \&\& \ be \ | \ be \ || \ be \ | \ \neg be$
	e	$::= \ be \ | \ ie \ | \ self \ | \ null \ | \ (T)e \ | \ e.a$
Commands	s	$::= \ skip; \ | \ T \ x; \ | \ le \ := \ e; \ | \ new(T); \ | \ c1; c2;$
		$| \ c_1 \lhd be \rhd c_2 \ | \ be * c \ | \ e.m(params, \ vals); \ | \ return \ e;$
	$main$	$::= \ ||_{1..n} \ @\langle guard \rangle \ \langle event \rangle \ (params, \ vals)$
	$guard$	$::= \ be \ | \ \delta t \ | \ be \ \wedge \ \delta t \ | \ be \ \vee \ \delta t \ | \ cancel$
	$event$	$::= \ s \ | \ event \ \bullet \ s$
Type	$params$	$::= \ T \ x \ | \ T \ x \ \bullet \ params \ | \ \epsilon$
	$vals$	$::= \ x \ | \ x \ \bullet \ vals \ | \ \epsilon$

3.1   Declarations

The majority of definitions retains equivalence with those found in rCOS. The class declaration consists of three parts. The outermost layer records the type of the class C_{derive} and the parent class type C_{base}, while the body section consists of a set of attributes $attrDef$ and functions $methDef$. Both elements can be empty, as denoted by the symbol ϵ.

However, a notable difference emerges in the definition of a method. Instead of relying on the parameter rps as in rCOS, a single return type T now explicitly specifies the return value. This modification aligns the syntax more closely with the conventions commonly used in programming languages, facilitating the design of concise type systems.

3.2   Expressions

We have undertaken an additional refinement of the expression e, differentiating it to bool expression be and int expression ie. The primary motivation is to provide a more precise definition for primary types, which is crucial for the subsequent formalization of expression evaluation and assignment. While the syntax could be expanded to include additional primary types like real and string, we omit them here for simplicity and clarity.

Additionally, we introduce the notion of le from rCOS to represent expressions that can appear on the left-hand side of a statement. This includes local variables x, which hold values for both primitive and reference types, as well as object attributes $le.a$. We then form the concept of expressions e that require immediate evaluation upon their appearance, encompassing the previously defined ie, be and le expressions, while also incorporating the $self$ reference, $null$ reference, type casting, and attribute access.

3.3   Commands

The rCOE syntax for sequential programs is straightforward. $skip$ represents a dummy transition, $T\ x$ declares a local variable of type T, $le := e$ denotes assignment, and $new(T)$ creates a new object of type T. The fundamental control flow constructs are defined as $c_1; c_2$, $c_1 \lhd be \rhd c_2$ and $be * c$, correspond to sequential composition, conditional choice and iteration respectively.

Compared to the rCOS syntax, a notable difference emerges in method calls. Combining the method call statement and return statement, we substitute the original $e.m(e; le; le)$ statement in rCOS. These modifications align the OOEG syntax more closely with the conventions commonly found in mainstream programming languages, facilitating the design of more concise and readable models.

To showcase the event-driven characteristics, we introduce three new components within this block: $main$, $guard$, and $event$. The entire simulation is viewed as a collection of events executing in parallel, as defined in $main$. Each event consists of a $guard$ condition (edges), an $event$ itself (nodes), and a set of parameters (labels on edges). Specifically, a guard is a combination of time elapsed δt and boolean expressions *be*. An event can only be scheduled to join the parallel execution if the guard condition is satisfied. Upon event completion, a schedule function updates the global events. If the guard evaluates to *cancel*, the next event is removed from the future events.

3.4   Type System

Unlike rCOS's extrinsic type system, our rCOE methodology embeds type information directly into the syntax. This built-in type system ensures type-safety as an integral part of language processing, eliminating the need for a separate type checker. The formal parameters *params* and actual parameters *vals* used in method invocations are type information that has not been defined yet.

Our rCOE type system considers several key aspects. Concerning **Type Declaration**, the syntax provides explicit type definitions for function return values, formal parameters, variables, and inheritance. Type information is maintained in the global state using class-level type stacks that reflect the inheritance hierarchy. During execution, **Type Compatibility and Conversion** are straightforward inspections using the type stacks and the separated local/global environments. Similarly, to handle **Scope and Name Resolution**, rCOE introduces a sequence of stacks to maintain local environments under function calls, enabling correct identification and resolution of variables, functions, and types within their scopes. Most importantly, rCOE establishes a premise for utilizing **Polymorphism**. Each object reference stores the declared type and the actual type in the environment. Method invocation searches the actual type and its ancestors following inheritance order until a matching parameter is found.

4   Operational Semantics for rCOE

We will build the operational semantics in a gradual manner, commencing with the configuration structure and progressing towards the dynamic transitions. Due to page limitations, the **complete operational semantics of rCOE** is available in the GitHub repository[1]. In this paper, we focus on a subset of representative rules for detailed explanation, resulting in non-continuous rule numbers. Please refer to the GitHub documentation for the complete definitions.

4.1   Configuration Structures

To capture state changes during execution, a typical manufacturing system in the OOEG formalism consists: A global environment *gEnv* storing class information and objects, a set of parallel executing events *eEnv* each with its own local environments *lEnv* and behaviors, and an auxiliary environment *auxEnv* to record temporary information. To better illustrate the structure of the configuration, we have summarized it as Fig. 3.

---

[1] https://github.com/celine-celine/Operational-Semantics-for-rCOE.

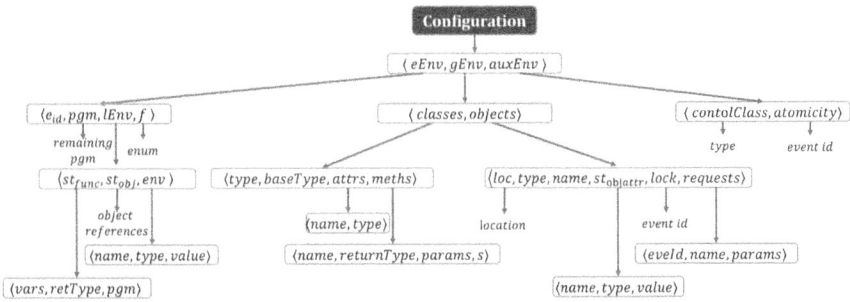

Fig. 3. Structure of configuration.

gEnv. The global state should maintain comprehensive information about class definitions and objects, which are shared resources among various events.

The **Class Structure** is defined in the form of a quadruple $class ::= \langle\, type, baseType, attrs, meths\,\rangle$. The quadruple comprises the current type $type$, the $baseType$ maintaining inheritance relations as a stack, the $attrs$ recording the names and types of a list of attributes $attr ::= \langle\, name, type\,\rangle$, and the $meths$ detailing each method $meth ::= \langle\, name, returnType, params, s\,\rangle$. The set of all class definitions forms the configuration $Classes$.

An **Object Structure** can be portrayed as a six-tuple in the form $object ::= \langle\, \hat{loc}, type, name, st_{objattr}, lock, requests\,\rangle$. When an object is created, it is assigned a virtual address $\hat{loc}$. The $type$ records the actual type of the object. The $lock$ value indicates whether the object has been locked by synchronized method call from event i, corresponding to the event's unique identifier, and if it evaluates to -1, the object is free. Further, $request$ keeps track of pending requests including $request ::= \langle\, eveId, methodName, params\,\rangle$.

Notably, given the polymorphic nature of OO programming, we model the attributes of each object as a stack structure $st_{objattr}$. The hierarchy of this stack directly corresponds to inheritance relationship, with each layer recording the attribute information $attr ::= \langle\, name, type, value\,\rangle$. When accessing one object attribute, the first step is to determine the declared type of the object reference. The relevant attribute information can then be accessed or updated by traversing the corresponding hierarchy in the property stack.

eEnv. The overarching configuration of the executing program is a set of *parallel executing events*, each depicted as $eEnv ::= \{\langle\, e_{id}, pgm, lEnv, f\,\rangle\}$, with e_{id} signifies the unique event identifier, the pgm delineates the residual program of event i. The local environment $lEnv$ of an event is compositely defined by st_{func}, st_{obj}, and env, which will be elaborated upon in the subsequent section on function call semantics. Finally, the f variable enumerates the concurrent status of events, including *running*, *waiting*, *pending*, and *terminated*.

AuxEnv. Auxiliary variables are included to monitor the control flow. The semantic model includes two auxiliary configurations: $controlClass$ to identify the current class being declared in the declaration phase, and $atomicity$ to coordinate scheduling during the execution phase.

4.2   Static Semantics

Class declarations form the static semantic base. According to our definition of syntax, all classes are declared before executing the event. We assign a special event e_0 structured as $\langle e_0,\ classDef,\ lEnv,\ running \rangle$.

Notations. For convenience, Table 2 and Table 3 provide the symbols and functions used in this paper.

Table 2. Main symbols used in operational semantics of rCOE.

Symbol	Implication
$config \longrightarrow config'$	After executing a transition, the configuration transits to $config'$
$config \xrightarrow{b} config'$	The transition is taken only if the b evaluates to true
$A \oplus \{B \cup C\}$	Take set element B from set A, and substitute B with the union of B and C
$A \oplus \{b \rightarrow c\}$	Take element b from set A, and set the value of b to c
$A[b]$	Get element b from set A

Declarations. The declaration of a class entails the invocation of three distinct transition rules. Foremost, the fundamental information of a class, encompassing its name and base type, are appended to the global environment, as captured by the rule $(decl-1)$.

$(decl-1)\ \langle\ \langle\ e_0,\ class\ C_{derive}\ extends\ C_{base}\ \{...\},\ lEnv,\ running \rangle,\ gEnv,\ auxEnv \rangle$
$\qquad \longrightarrow \langle\ \langle\ e_0,\ \{...\},\ lEnv,\ running\ \rangle,$
$\qquad\qquad gEnv \oplus \{\ Classes \cup \{\langle\ C_{derive},\ findAncestors(C_{base}).push(C_{base}),\ \emptyset,\ \emptyset\ )\}\ \},$
$\qquad\qquad auxEnv \oplus \{controlClass \rightarrow C_{derive}\}\rangle$

Subsequently, a set of attributes are defined within the class scope, as denoted by the rule $(decl-2)$. The following specification of a set of methods which we omit here is similar. Finally, upon the completion of the declaration process,

Table 3. Auxiliary functions used in operational semantics of rCOE.

Function	Effect
$findAncestors(t)$	From the $Classes$ collection in the global environment $gEnv$, the type stack of a parameter t can be retrieved, with default $Object$
$location(e)$	The location of the referenced object e is retrieved
$val(e)$	The concrete value of the primary expression e is calculated
$cmd(m)$	From the $Classes$ collection in the global environment $gEnv$, the body of a method m can be retrieved
$mat(ps, vs)$	Check if the types of formal parameters ps and actual parameters vs are compatible. If they are, assign the value of the vs to ps and store it as the local environment of the event in env
$stack.push(e)$	Push element e on top of the stack
$stack.pop()$	Pop the top element from the stack
$stack.top()$	Read the top element from the stack
$typeOf(e)$	Return the current declared type of e
$subType(T_1, T_2)$	Return if the two types are compatible according to subtyping

we remove the specialized event from the event pool by setting its status to *terminated*, and proceed to schedule the remaining events.

$$(decl-2) \; \langle \, \langle \, e_0, \; T \; x;, \; lEnv, \; running \, \rangle, \; gEnv, \; auxEnv \, \rangle$$
$$\longrightarrow \langle \, \langle \, e_0, \; \epsilon, \; lEnv, \; running \, \rangle, \; gEnv[Classes] \oplus \{\langle \, auxEnv[controlClass],$$
$$typeStack, \; attrs \rightarrow attrs \cup \{\langle \, x, \; T \, \rangle\}, \; \emptyset\}, \; auxEnv \, \rangle$$

It is worth emphasizing that upon declaring a new class, we first invoke the $findAncestors$ function to ascertain whether the putative parent class has been declared, then push the base class onto the type stack. The final component, $controlClass$, serves as an auxiliary attribute to designate the class currently undergoing the declaration process, thereby facilitating the proper storage of attributes and methods. The $\oplus$ operator signifies the act of modifying the existing configuration. For instance, in rule $(decl-2)$, an attribute x of type T is declared within the $controlClass$. In correspondence, we amend the configuration by retrieving the class named $controlClass$ from the $Classes$ collection, and performing a union to incorporate the novel attribute into the $attrs$.

4.3 Dynamic Semantics

Variable Creation. The process to *new* an object is intuitive. According to our syntax, the *new* operation is regarded as an expression, thus the evaluation of the new operation returns the allocated $\hat{loc}$. We place an abstraction on the process of allocation, by making an assumption that all variables, primary or object, all take one space. The name remains empty, and will be initialized once it is assigned to a type-adapted variable. Moreover, the initial values of attributes of an object is the same as defined in its class, with initial values set to empty by function $init()$.

$$(\text{new} - 1) \langle \langle e_{id}, new(C), lEnv, running \rangle, gEnv, auxEnv \rangle$$
$$\longrightarrow \langle \langle e_{id}, \hat{loc}, lEnv, running \rangle,$$
$$gEnv \oplus \{Objects \cup \{\langle \hat{loc}, C, \emptyset, st_{objattr}[C].init(), -1, null \rangle\}\}, auxEnv \rangle$$

Declaring a local variable for both primary and reference types is identical - simply adding the new variable to the local environment will suffice. Here, T represents the declared type for references.

$$(\text{var} - 1) \langle \langle e_{id}, T \; x;, lEnv, running \rangle, gEnv, auxEnv \rangle$$
$$\longrightarrow \langle \langle e_{id}, \epsilon, lEnv \oplus \{env \cup \{\langle x, T, null \rangle\}\}, running \rangle, gEnv, auxEnv \rangle$$

Expression Evaluation. Given that our language encompasses both primary and object types, a well-defined evaluation semantics for expressions is fundamental in facilitating subsequent assignment and access operations. In this paper, we stipulate that for expressions of primary types, we return the calculated value, whereas for expressions of object types, we return a reference, which is the memory address of the object instance.

$$(\text{eval} - 1) \langle \langle e_{id}, null, lEnv, running \rangle, gEnv, auxEnv \rangle$$
$$\longrightarrow \langle \langle e_{id}, -1, lEnv, running \rangle, gEnv, auxEnv \rangle$$
$$(\text{eval} - 2) \langle \langle e_{id}, this, lEnv, running \rangle, gEnv, auxEnv \rangle$$
$$\longrightarrow \langle \langle e_{id}, location(lEnv[st_{obj}] . top()), lEnv, running \rangle, gEnv, auxEnv \rangle$$

The initial pair of transition rules handles the *null* and *this* reference respectively. In the case of *null*, we assign a dedicated location -1 to denote the absence of a valid value within the address space. For *this*, we retrieve the current object instance by accessing the top of the st_{obj} stack, using the $location(object)$ auxiliary function. The st_{obj} here maintained within the event's local environment preserves the invocation chain of object methods.

$$(\text{eval} - 3) \langle \langle e_{id}, be, lEnv, running \rangle, gEnv, auxEnv \rangle$$
$$\longrightarrow \langle \langle e_{id}, val(be), lEnv, running \rangle, gEnv, auxEnv \rangle$$

The next pair of transition rules pertains to the evaluation of expressions of primary types. An auxiliary $val()$ function is designed to facilitate the computation of these expressions to their final values. All variable identifiers appearing within bool and int expressions are resolved by performing a lookup within the *env* structure maintained in the local environment $lEnv$ of the current event. The evaluation of *be* is given in rule $(eval - 3)$ and the one of *ie* is similar.

$$(\text{eval} - 5) \; \langle \, \langle \, e_{id}, \; (T)e, \; lEnv, \; running \, \rangle, \; gEnv, \; auxEnv \, \rangle$$
$$\longrightarrow \langle \, \langle \, e_{id}, \; lEnv[env][e][value], lEnv[env] \; \oplus \; \{e[type] \to T\} \,, \; running \, \rangle,$$
$$gEnv, \; auxEnv \, \rangle \quad \text{if } subtype(T, \; typeof(e)) \; == \; true$$

The $(eval - 5)$ transition rule specifically addresses type casting expressions. The evaluation depends upon the compatibility of the expression's original type and the target type. We employ an auxiliary $subtype()$ to determine the sub-typing relationship between the two types, and another auxiliary $typeof()$ to retrieve the type of an expression. If the types are deemed incompatible, the event will be terminated abnormally by setting its status to *terminated*. Otherwise, we will switch the declared type of the reference to that type T without modifying the object type in the storage, in order to reflect the polymorphism feature.

$$(\text{eval} - 6) \; \langle \, \langle \, e_{id}, \; e.a, \; lEnv, \; running \, \rangle, \; gEnv, \; auxEnv \, \rangle$$
$$\longrightarrow \langle \, \langle \, e_{id}, \; loc.val(a), \; lEnv, \; running \, \rangle, \; gEnv, \; auxEnv \, \rangle$$
$$\text{if } typeof(e.a) \; == \; int \text{ or } typeof(e.a) \; == \; bool$$

The $(eval - 6)$ rule governs the object attribute access. Given the resolved object location of *e*, we diverge based on the attribute type: For primitive attributes, we directly retrieve the value from the attribute stack $st_{objattr}$. It is noteworthy that due to polymorphism, we must first check the declared type of the object reference from *env*, then consult the $st_{objattr}$ structure to locate the correct attribute list, and read the final value from it. For object attributes, is analogous, we similarly consult the attribute stack, but return the address of the attribute rather than its evaluated value.

Assignment. Aligned with our expression evaluation strategy, assignment statements are based on the target type. For primary types, the value is directly modified within the local environment. In contrast, for object types, we employ a shallow copy strategy, assigning the object's address rather than the object itself.

$$(\text{assn} - 2) \; \langle \, \langle \, e_{id}, \; le := loc;, \; lEnv, \; running \, \rangle, \; gEnv, \; auxEnv \, \rangle$$
$$\longrightarrow \langle \, \langle \, e_{id}, \; \epsilon, \; lEnv[env] \; \oplus \; \{ le[value] \to loc\}, \; running \, \rangle, \; gEnv, \; auxEnv \, \rangle$$
$$\text{if } subtype(typeof(le), \; typeof(loc)) \; == \; true$$

We manage the read and write operations of local variables by maintaining two distinct function call stacks to preserve the temporary local environment *env*. This ensures that, during execution, the variables accessed by each event, whether they are references or values, are properly stored within the env structure. Consequently, for the assignment of each local variable, we search for and modify the variable through the env structure. Rule $(assn-2)$ specify the assignment of reference, rule for concrete values is alike.

$$(\text{assn} - 3) \; \langle \; \langle \; e_{id}, \; o.a := e;, \; lEnv, \; running \; \rangle, \; gEnv, \; auxEnv \; \rangle$$
$$\longrightarrow \langle \; \langle \; e_{id}, \; \epsilon, \; lEnv, \; running \; \rangle,$$
$$gEnv \; \oplus \{Objects[o][type][a][value] \rightarrow val(e)\}, \; auxEnv \; \rangle$$
$$\text{if } typeof(o.a) \; == \; int \text{ or } typeof(o.a) \; == \; bool$$

Furthermore, for the assignment of global variables, specifically attributes of objects, we must modify the relevant parameters of the corresponding object o in the global $Objects$ environment. As shown in $(assn-3)$, we first locate the position of o within the $Objects$. We then check the current type $type$ of the object, retrieve the list of attributes corresponding to that type, and assign the desired value to the appropriate variable a within the attribute list.

Function Call. Function calls in our approach follow rCOS design principles, categorizing them as synchronized or non-synchronized, aligned with Java style. Additionally, to define the type system, we mandate that each function call must conclude with a return statement.

$$(\text{func} - 1) \; \langle \; \langle \; e_{id}, \; o.m(params, vals);, \; lEnv, \; running \; \rangle, \; gEnv, \; auxEnv \; \rangle$$
$$\longrightarrow \; \langle \; \langle \; e_{id}, \; cmd(m), \; lEnv \oplus \{st_{func} \rightarrow st_{func}.push(env), \; st_{obj} \rightarrow$$
$$st_{obj}.push(o), \; env \rightarrow mat(params, vals)\}, \; running \; \rangle, \; gEnv, \; auxEnv \; \rangle$$
$$(\text{func} - 2) \; \langle \; \langle \; e_{id}, \; o.m(params, vals);, \; lEnv, \; running \; \rangle, \; gEnv, \; auxEnv \; \rangle$$
$$\longrightarrow \; \langle \; \langle \; e_{id}, \; o.m(params, vals);, \; lEnv, \; waiting \; \rangle,$$
$$gEnv[Objects] \oplus \{\langle \; loc, \; type, \; o, \; st, \; locked, \; requests \cup \{e_{id}\}\rangle\}, \; auxEnv \; \rangle$$

The first pair of transition rules correspond to non-synchronized function calls. In the $(func-1)$ rule, an event e_{id} attempts to invoke the method m on the object o. In this case, where o is a free object, the function call is successful, and the control flow transfers to o. To characterize the transfer of control flow, we push the current local environment into the st_{func} stack, along with the remaining code to be executed and the expected return value of m. We then extract the function body from the $Classes$ structure using the auxiliary $cmd(m)$ function. This extracted code will be the continuation of execution. Additionally, we push the current class o onto the st_{obj} stack to denote the fact that the control flow has now transitioned to reside within o. Furthermore, we define the auxiliary $mat(params, vals)$ function to bind the formal and actual parameters of the method, which are local variables in the new local environment env.

Conversely, if the object o is currently occupied by another event, the current event e_{id} will be set to the $waiting$ status. The attempt to call method m is then recorded in the $requests$ structure associated with o.

The synchronized and non-synchronized function calls are highly similar, with the sole distinction that if the synchronized function call is successfully executed, the object o where method m is located will be locked by the invoking event, and the *locked* field of o will be set to e_{id}.

$$(\text{func} - 5) \; \langle \, \langle \, e_{id}, \; return \; e;, \; lEnv, \; running \, \rangle, \; gEnv, \; auxEnv \, \rangle$$
$$\longrightarrow \langle \, \langle \, e_{id}, \; e, \; lEnv \oplus \{$$
$$st_{func} \to st_{func}.pop(), \; st_{obj} \to st_{obj}.pop(), \; env \to st_{func}.top()\}, running \rangle,$$
$$gEnv[Objects] \oplus \{\langle \, loc, \; type, \; o, \; st, \; lock \to \emptyset, \; requests \, \rangle\}, \; auxEnv \, \rangle$$

Finally, both the function calls will culminate in a return statement. To recover the local environment during the process of transferring the control flow back to the caller, we first get the top element from the st_{func} stack, overwrite the env with its variables, and perform type checking based on the values of T and e. If the type check succeeds, the return statement will be simply rewritten to e. Thereafter, we pop the top elements from both the st_{func} and st_{obj} stacks. Finally, the *locked* field is set back to empty, as shown in rule $(func - 5)$.

Schedule Operation. Pursuant to the rules of OOEG, at the termination of an event, a following event will be explicitly invoked. In order to analyze the scheduling operation, we first define the triggering mechanism for the *guard* condition. The guard condition is a composite of boolean conditions and time delay conditions. If the guard condition is fired, we set its status from *pending* to *running*, extract the program pgm to be executed, and initialize its local environment in a manner analogous to function invocation.

$$(\text{guar} - 1) \; \langle \, \langle \, e_{id}, \; @\langle guard \rangle \langle pgm \rangle \langle ps, vs \rangle, \; \langle \emptyset, \; \emptyset, \; \emptyset \rangle, \; pending \, \rangle, \; gEnv, \; auxEnv \, \rangle$$
$$\longrightarrow \langle \, \langle \, e_{id}, \; pgm, \; lEnv \oplus \{env \to mat(ps, vs)\}, \; running \, \rangle, \; gEnv, \; auxEnv \, \rangle$$

The scheduling operation encompasses both the standard scheduling of the upcoming event as well as the cancellation of an event. For the normal scheduling, as denoted in rule $(sch - 1)$, we simply add the event to the ρ configuration with the event status set to *pending*, awaiting the triggering of its guard condition. For the cancellation operation, as denoted in rule $(sch - 2)$, we modify the status of the event with id $event$ in ρ to *terminated* to signify that it has been canceled.

$$(\text{sch} - 1) \; \langle \, \langle \, e_{id}, \; schedule(nextEvent), \; lEnv, \; running \, \rangle, \; gEnv, \; auxEnv \, \rangle$$
$$\longrightarrow \langle \, \langle \, e_{id}, \; \epsilon, \; lEnv, \; terminated \, \rangle \cup$$
$$\langle \, nextEvent, \; @\langle guard \rangle \langle pgm \rangle \langle ps, vs \rangle, \; lEnv', \; pending \, \rangle, \; gEnv, \; auxEnv \, \rangle$$
$$(\text{sch} - 2) \; \langle \, \langle \, e_{id}, \; cancel(event), \; lEnv, \; running \, \rangle, \; gEnv, \; auxEnv \, \rangle$$
$$\longrightarrow \langle \, eEnv \oplus \{\langle \, e_{id}, \; \epsilon, \; lEnv, \; running \to terminated \, \rangle,$$
$$\langle event, \; pgm, \; \emptyset, \; \emptyset, \; \emptyset, \; pending \to terminated \, \rangle\}, \; gEnv, \; auxEnv \, \rangle$$

Control Flow. The semantics of sequential compositions, conditional statements, and loop statements in this paper are analogous to those found in traditional programming languages, and we have retained the corresponding characterizations within the rCOS operational semantics. For parallel operations, we have defined more detailed rules, and thus have dedicated a separate sub-chapter to the semantics of parallel statements.

The selection of branches in parallel composition is an essential scheduling operation. Atomic operations hold the highest priority in the scheduling process. Once an atomic operation commences, it will not be interrupted by the environment, implying that no other events will be scheduled during the execution of the atomic operation.

$$(para-1) \ \langle \ \langle \ e_{id}, \ <pgm>, \ lEnv, \ running \ \rangle, \ gEnv, \ auxEnv \ \rangle$$
$$\longrightarrow \langle \ \langle \ e_{id}, \ pgm >, \ lEnv, \ running \ \rangle, \ gEnv, \ auxEnv \oplus \{atomicity \rightarrow e_{id}\} \ \rangle$$
$$(para-2) \ \langle \ eEnv_1, \ gEnv, \ \langle \emptyset, \ e_1 \rangle \ \rangle \longrightarrow \langle \ eEnv_1', \ gEnv, \ \langle \emptyset, \ e_1 \rangle \ \rangle$$
$$\overline{\langle \ eEnv_1 \ || \ eEnv_2, \ gEnv, \ \langle \emptyset, \ e_1 \rangle \ \rangle \longrightarrow \langle \ eEnv_1' \ || \ eEnv_2, \ gEnv, \ \langle \emptyset, \ e_1 \rangle \ \rangle}$$

The first three parallel rules address atomic actions. An atomic action is denoted in the form $< \cdots >$, and when encountering the $<$ symbol, we set the *atomicity* field to the id e_{id1} of the current event, as shown in rule $(para-1)$. During the execution of atomic statements, we consistently select the branch holding the *atomicity*, as depicted in rule $(para-2)$. Finally, an atomic action is properly terminated with the *atomicity* field set back to empty.

The second priority in the scheduling process is regular program operations, and the lowest priority is time elapse. Consequently, there are three distinct scenarios. If both programs are ordinary program statements, a non-deterministic selection is made. If one of the branches is a time elapse operation, the other branch is preferred for execution. If both sides are delayed operations, then the synchronization delay is 1 second, as denoted in rule $(para-6)$. This scheduling strategy can be extended to the selection of parallel execution branches for multiple events.

$$(para-6) \ \langle \ \langle \ e_{id1}, \ \delta t_1, \ lEnv_1, \ running \ \rangle \ ||$$
$$\langle \ e_{id2}, \ \delta t_2, \ lEnv_2, \ running \ \rangle, \ gEnv, \ \langle \emptyset, \ atomicity \rangle \ \rangle$$
$$\longrightarrow \langle \ \langle \ e_{id1}, \ \delta(t_1 - 1), \ lEnv_1, \ running \ \rangle \ ||$$
$$\langle \ e_{id2}, \ \delta(t_2 - 1), \ lEnv_2, \ running \ \rangle, \ gEnv, \ \langle \emptyset, \ atomicity \rangle \ \rangle$$

5   Application of rCOE in Production Line

5.1   Preliminaries of Production Line in Aerospace Manufacturing

In the overall process of **Assembly**, we extract the subprocess of *Tail Wing Reception and Alignment* and examine the process in greater detail. In aviation manufacturing industries, requirements are distributed in the form of a series of *Assembly Operation (AO)* to different workshops. Here, we extract one exemplary *AO* shown in Fig. 4.

AO: Vertical tail receiving and inspection
AO number: 10110-150-C03-0021
Affiliated Section: 10110-150-505
Affiliated Workstation: 10110-150-50501-004

Process Number	Process Name	Process Detail	Inspect	Type	Certs	Certed	Factory	Station
00	Preparation	Verify materials based on the supporting material list	√	Authorized	×	×	150	2
05	Acceptance	According to the requirements of "xx", check whether the vertical tail edge has sharp burrs and whether the appearance is complete	×	×	HTC001 HTC003	√	150	3
10	Final Inspection	Receiving completed materials for inspection	√	Specialized	×	×	150	4

Supporting materials: [Components] Vertical tail

Fig. 4. Partial description of AO:10110-150-C03-0021.

A typical *AO* file includes multiple processes, but for the sake of conciseness, we have retained only a subset that is sufficient to showcase the characteristics of rCOE. The AO provides a clear and unified representation of the task execution, including details such as the description, inspection, location, required materials, etc. This structure aligns closely with the object-oriented paradigm.

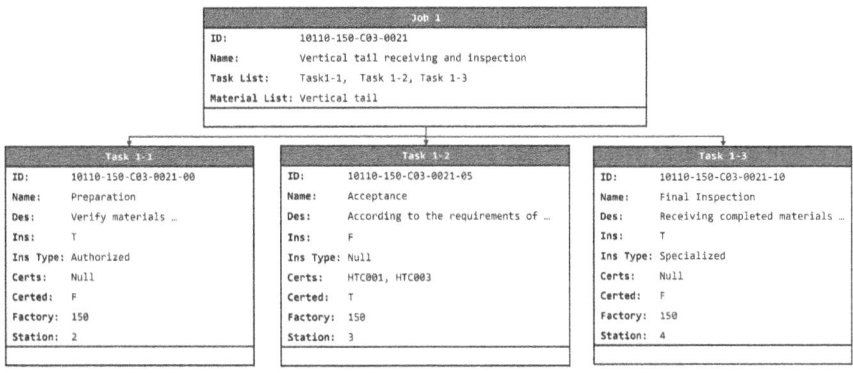

Fig. 5. PCD Construction of AO:10110-150-C03-0021

We can construct Physical Class Diagrams (PCDs) based on the *AO*, one such example is given in Fig. 5. The correspondence is highly intuitive. Each sub-process of an *AO* is constructed as a *Task* in the *PCD*, and a Job is an aggregation of a set of *Tasks*. Apart from the Jobs, we also need to give PCD models to the physical assets of the factory, which can be modeled similarly.

As for the construction of Event Classs Diagram (ECD) and OOEG (shown in Fig. 2), we will continue to use the simplified design from the references [18] with slight revision. Create Job Event simulate the arrival of *AO*s to the shop floor. Passing Job Event is responsible for checking whether the unfinished *JOB*s can be distributed to the corresponding workstations for operation. Start Processing Event denotes the actual implementation of work in the factory. And finally, Finish Processing Event is an interim event for the next round of passing.

5.2   Simulation

In the simulation execution section, we selected representative scenarios from both static and dynamic semantics, incorporating as many inference rules as possible to clearly demonstrate the application of rCOE semantics.

With the PCD at hand, we can apply rCOE to describe the static semantics. For example, we may construct the declaration of *Job* as "$\langle\langle$ *e0, class Job extends Objects* $\{...\}$, *lEnv, running* $\rangle$, *gEnv, auxEnv*$\rangle$". In Fig. 6, we demonstrate the declaration of *Station* from the PCD describing the physical assets of the factory, covering the majority of rules in the static semantics as well as the guard triggering rule.   Moreover, in Fig. 7, we present

```
1 <<e0, @<#0><class Station extends Object{...}><empty>, <empty,empty,empty>,pending>,gEnv, auxEnv>
2 -(guar-1)-> <<e0, class Station extends Object {...},lEnv, running>, gEnv, auxEnv>
3 -(decl-1)-> <<e0, int id; , lEnv, running>, gEnv`, auxEnv`>
4 -(decl-2)-> <<e0, ... , lEnv, running>, gEnv``, auxEnv`>
5 -(...other attribute declarations) -> <<e0, bool hasSpace(){...} , lEnv, running>, gEnv```, auxEnv`>
6 -(decl-3)-> <<e0, ... , lEnv, running>, gEnv````, auxEnv`>
7 -(...other method declarations) -> <<e0, epsilon, lEnv, running>, gEnv`````, auxEnv`>
8 //Configuration after one Class Declaration:
9 <eEnv,<<type:Station, bastType:Object,
10           attrs:<<int,id>, <List,standList>, <List,waiting>, <List,idle>>,
11           meths: <hasSpace, bool, empty, if(!idle.isEmpty){...}...>
12           >,..., objects>, auxEnv>
```

Fig. 6. Simulating execution within static semantics: class declaration.

the scenario of two events executing in parallel, covering the predominant genre of dynamic rules. In this example, we have selected the scenario where two *Job*s are executed concurrently, *Job*1 (10110-150-C03-0021, corresponding to Fig. 5) and *Job*2 (10110-150-C03-0021, omitted). Event "*e1*" demonstrates the interme-diate process of the *PassJob* event with parameter *Job*1. At this juncture, the *updateReference*() method will be invoked to facilitate the distribution of *Job*s to individual *Station*s based on the remaining tasks. Similarly, event "*e2*" illus-trates the intermediate process of the *StartProcess* event for *Job*2, calculating the process time of the current *Task* and waiting for the processing time to be elapsed.

```
1 <<e1, myTask.updateReference() ,<empty,empty,<Task, myTask, task1>>, running>                    ||
2 <<e2, int procTime;, <empty,empty, <Station, myStation, station2>>, running>, gEnv, auxEnv>
3 (para-4)-->
4 <<e1, myTask.updateReference() ,<empty,empty,<Task, myTask, task1>>, running>                    ||
5 <<e2, int procTime;, <empty,empty, <<Station, myStation, station2>,<int, procTime, empty>>>, running>,
  gEnv, auxEnv>
6 (seq-1)-->
7 <<e1, myTask.updateReference() ,<empty,empty,<Task, myTask, task1>>, running>                    ||
8 <<e2, procTime = myStand.calcProcessingTime();, <empty,empty, <<Station, myStation, station2>, <int,
  procTime, empty>>>, running>, gEnv, auxEnv>
9 (func-1)-->
10 <<e1, myTask.updateReference() ,<empty,empty,<Task, myTask, task1>>, running>                   ||
11 <<e2, cmd(myStand.calcProcessingTime()), <<<Station, myStation, station2>, <int, procTime, empty>>,
   myStand, empty>, running>, gEnv, auxEnv>
12 (...calculating)-->
13 <<e1, myTask.updateReference() ,<empty,empty,<Task, myTask, task1>>, running>                   ||
14 <<e2, return 10;, <<<Station, myStation, station2>,<int, procTime, empty>>, myStand, empty >, running>,
   gEnv, auxEnv>
15 (func-5)->
16 <<e1, myTask.updateReference() ,<empty,empty,<Task, myTask, task1>>, running>                   ||
17 <<e2, procTime = 5;, <empty,empty, <<Station, myStation, station2>,<int, procTime, empty>>>, running>,
   gEnv, auxEnv>
18 (assn-1)-->
19 <<e1, myTask.updateReference() ,<empty,empty,<Task, myTask, task1>>, running>                   ||
20 <<e2, epsilon, <empty,empty, <<Station, myStation, station2>,<int, procTime, 5>>>, running>, gEnv, auxEnv>
21 (seq-1)-->
22 <<e1, myTask.updateReference() ,<empty,empty,<Task, myTask, task1>>, running>                   ||
23 <<e2, #procTime, <empty,empty, <<Station, myStation, station2>,<int, procTime, 5>>>, running>, gEnv,
   auxEnv>
24 (eval-1)-->
25 <<e1, myTask.updateReference() ,<empty,empty,<Task, myTask, task1>>, running>                   ||
26 <<e2, #8, <empty,empty, <<Station, myStation, station2>,<int, procTime, 5>>>, running>, gEnv, auxEnv>
27 (para-5)-->
28 <<e1, int currStationIndex = currStation.id; ,<<Task, myTask, task1>, myTask, empty>, running>   ||
29 <<e2, #8, <empty,empty, <<Station, myStation, station2>,<int, procTime, >, running>, gEnv, auxEnv>
```

Fig. 7. Simulating execution within dynamic semantics: parallel execution.

6   Conclusion and Future Work

This paper proposes a formal calculus, rCOE, based on rCOS and OOEG principles to provide an intuitive, well-defined requirement language for manufacturing. The operational semantics for rCOE provides rigorous and unambiguous interpretation of OOEG and lays the foundation for future design of tools. The real-world case study demonstrates the formalism's practical applicability.

Future work will focus on both theoretical and practical aspects. Theoretically, we aim to extend the semantics and enhance the language's expressiveness to cover requirements beyond planning and production, such as logistics. Practically, we are implementing the operational semantics using rewriting logic to automate simulation and broaden its applicability to more stakeholders.

Acknowledgements.. This work was partially supported by the National Key Research and Development Program of China (No. 2022YFB3305102), the National Natural Science Foundation of China (No. 62032024), the "Digital Silk Road" Shanghai International Joint Lab of Trustworthy Intelligent Software (No. 22510750100), Shanghai Trusted Industry Internet Software Collaborative Innovation Center, the Natural Science Foundation of the Jiangsu Higher Education Institutions of China (No. 24KJB520018), the Startup Foundation for Introducing Talent of NUIST (No. 2024r035), the Automatic Software Generation and Intelligent Service Key Laboratory of Sichuan Province (No. CUIT-SAG202306).

References

1. Buss, A.: Basic event graph modeling. Simul. News Europe **31**(1), 1–6 (2001)
2. Chen, D.: Enterprise-control system integration–an international standard. Int. J. Prod. Res. **43**(20), 4335–4357 (2005)
3. Compagnucci, I., Corradini, F., Fornari, F., Re, B.: Trends on the usage of BPMN 2.0 from publicly available repositories. In: Buchmann, R.A., Polini, A., Johansson, B., Karagiannis, D. (eds.) BIR 2021. LNBIP, vol. 430, pp. 84–99. Springer, Cham (2021). https://doi.org/10.1007/978-3-030-87205-2_6
4. Dong, R., Faber, J., Ke, W., Liu, Z.: rCOS: defining meanings of component-based software architectures. In: Liu, Z., Woodcock, J., Zhu, H. (eds.) Unifying Theories of Programming and Formal Engineering Methods. LNCS, vol. 8050, pp. 1–66. Springer, Heidelberg (2013). https://doi.org/10.1007/978-3-642-39721-9_1
5. Firmansyah, A.: Design of manufacturing operation management system (MOMS) for gas processing facility using ISA 95 standard. Ph.D. thesis, Sepuluh Nopember Institute of Technology (2023)
6. Herber, D.R., Narsinghani, J.B., Eftekhari-Shahroudi, K.: Model-based structured requirements in SysML. In: SysCon2022, pp. 1–8. IEEE (2022)
7. Huisman, M., Gurov, D., Malkis, A.: Formal methods: from academia to industrial practice. a travel guide. arXiv preprint arXiv:2002.07279 (2020)
8. Jifeng, H., Li, X., Liu, Z.: rCOS: a refinement calculus of object systems. Theor. Comput. Sci. **365**(1–2), 109–142 (2006)
9. Kletti, J.: Manufacturing Execution Systems–MES. Springer, Cham (2007)
10. Koç, H., Erdoğan, A.M., Barjakly, Y., Peker, S.: UML diagrams in software engineering research: a systematic literature review. In: Proceedings, vol. 74, p. 13. MDPI (2021)
11. Li, C., Mantravadi, S., Schou, C., Nielsen, H., Madsen, O., Møller, C.: An ISA-95 based middle data layer for data standardization—enhancing systems interoperability for factory automation. In: Weißgraeber, P., Heieck, F., Ackermann, C. (eds.) Advances in Automotive Production Technology – Theory and Application. A, pp. 187–194. Springer, Heidelberg (2021). https://doi.org/10.1007/978-3-662-62962-8_22
12. Liu, Z.: Linking formal methods in software development. In: Bowen, J.P., Li, Q., Xu, Q. (eds.) Theories of Programming and Formal Methods. LNCS, vol. 14080, pp. 52–84. Springer, Cham (2023). https://doi.org/10.1007/978-3-031-40436-8_3
13. Liu, Z., Jifeng, H., Li, X.: rCOS: refinement of component and object systems. In: de Boer, F.S., Bonsangue, M.M., Graf, S., de Roever, W.-P. (eds.) FMCO 2004. LNCS, vol. 3657, pp. 183–221. Springer, Heidelberg (2005). https://doi.org/10.1007/11561163_9
14. Mantravadi, S., Møller, C., Chen, L., Schnyder, R.: Design choices for next-generation IIoT-connected MES/MOM: an empirical study on smart factories. Robot. Comput.-Integrated Manuf. **73**, 102225 (2022)
15. Mantravadi, S., Srai, J.S., Møller, C.: Application of MES/MOM for industry 4.0 supply chains: a cross-case analysis. Comput. Ind. **148**, 103907 (2023)
16. Mažeika, D., Butleris, R.: Integrating security requirements engineering into MBSE: profile and guidelines. Secur. Commun. Netw. **2020**(1), 5137625 (2020)
17. Obermayer, N., Csizmadia, T., Hargitai, D.M.: Influence of industry 4.0 technologies on corporate operation and performance management from human aspects. Meditari Accountancy Res. **30**(4), 1027–1049 (2022)

18. Singamneni, S., Yifan, L., Hewitt, A., Chalk, R., Thomas, W., Jordison, D.: Additive manufacturing for the aircraft industry: a review. J. Aeronaut. Aerosp. Eng **8**(1), 351–371 (2019)
19. Singh, A., Madaan, G., Hr, S., Kumar, A.: Smart manufacturing systems: a futuristics roadmap towards application of industry 4.0 technologies. Int. J. Comput. Integrated Manuf. **36**(3), 411–428 (2023)
20. Tiacci, L.: Object-oriented event-graph modeling formalism to simulate manufacturing systems in the industry 4.0 era. Simul. Model. Pract. Theory **99**, 102027 (2020)
21. Wagner, P., Hansch, G., Konrad, C., John, K.H., Bauer, J., Franke, J.: Applicability of security standards for operational technology by SMEs and large enterprises. In: ETFA2020, vol. 1, pp. 1544–1551. IEEE (2020)
22. Wang, Z., Yu, X., Pu, G., Feng, L., Zhu, H., He, J.: Execution semantics for rCOS. In: 2008 15th Asia-Pacific Software Engineering Conference, pp. 119–126. IEEE (2008)
23. Weißenberger, B., Flad, S., Chen, X., Rösch, S., Voigt, T., Vogel-Heuser, B.: Model driven engineering of manufacturing execution systems using a formal specification. In: ETFA2015, pp. 1–8. IEEE (2015)

Verification and Reasoning

Type Safety for Isabelle/Solidity

Billy Thornton[(✉)] [iD] and Diego Marmsoler[(✉)] [iD]

Department of Computer Science, The Innovation Centre, University of Exeter,
Exeter EX4 4RN, UK
bt319@exeter.ac.uk, d.marmsoler@exeter.ac.uk

Abstract. Smart contracts are programs stored on the blockchain that
are often developed in a high-level programming language, the most popular of which is Solidity. Smart contracts are used to automate financial
transactions; thus, bugs can lead to large financial losses. In previous
works, we developed a formalization of Solidity in Isabelle/HOL, which
can be used to verify the properties of Solidity smart contracts. This
formalization features untyped stores, where the types are inferred using
a type environment. It is currently unclear whether our semantics can
cause type inconsistencies between stores and their environments. With
this work we address this problem by formalizing the notion of type
safety for untyped stores and verifying that our semantics preserve this
property. The formalization and proofs were verified using Isabelle/HOL.
Our results guarantee that our semantics are type safe and the proofs can
be used to simplify the verification process for the properties of Solidity
smart contracts.

Keywords: Type Safety · Smart Contracts · Solidity · Program
Verification · Isabelle/Solidity

1 Introduction

Blockchain [23] is a novel technology for providing decentralised and openly
accessible ledgers without the need of a trusted third party. Originally designed
to support cryptocurrencies, blockchain have been used in a wide range of applications, such as *finance* [17], *healthcare* [5], *land management* [10], *business process management* [22], and even *identity management* [30].

Blockchain ecosystems have been rapidly evolving, with *smart contracts*
being one of the primary innovations. Smart contracts are digital contracts used
to automate transactions on the blockchain once pre-defined conditions are met.
For instance, a payment for an item might be released instantly once the buyer
and seller have met all specified parameters for a deal. Every day, hundreds of
thousands of new contracts are deployed managing millions of dollars' worth of
transactions [29].

Smart contracts consist of non-modifiable code which is deployed to the
blockchain and which can be executed by sending a special transaction to it.
Smart contracts are usually developed in a high-level programming language,

C. Anutariya and M. M. Bonsangue (Eds.): ICTAC 2024, LNCS 15373, pp. 313–330, 2025.
https://doi.org/10.1007/978-3-031-77019-7_18

the most popular of which is *Solidity* [14]. Currently, 90% of all smart contracts are developed using Solidity [18] and, according to a 2023 survey, Solidity is by far the most popular language used by blockchain developers [4].

As with every computer program, smart contracts may contain bugs which can be exploited. However, since smart contracts are often used to automate financial transactions, such exploits may result in huge economic losses. In general, it is estimated that since 2019, more than $5B was stolen due to vulnerabilities in smart contracts [11].

The high impact of vulnerabilities in smart contracts, together with the fact that once deployed to the blockchain, they cannot be updated or removed easily, makes it important to "get them right" before they are deployed. Consequently, there has been a growing amount of work to verify smart contracts (see [3] for an overview). There is, however, a lack of work which focuses on the analysis of Solidity and in particular its type safety.

Thus, with the following work we formalize and verify type safety for Isabelle/Solidity [19–21], a formalization of Solidity in Isabelle [24]. To this end, we provide the following contributions:

– We provide a formal definition of type safety in the context of Isabelle/Solidity (Sect. 3). The definition highlights different aspects of type safety in our context, such as type consistency, structural consistency, and contract properties.
– We verify that the semantics of Isabelle/Solidity preserves type safety (Sect. 4). In particular the verification of pointer structures available in Solidity was challenging and is discussed in more detail.

All of our work is mechanized in Isabelle and the formalization and verification of type safety consists of around 7 000 lines of Isabelle/Isar code.

In the following, we first provide a brief introduction into Isabelle/Solidity in Sect. 2. Then, in Sect. 3 we discuss our definition of type safety and in Sect. 4 its verification. We then discuss related work in Sect. 5 and conclude the paper with a discussion of results in Sect. 6.

2 Isabelle/Solidity

Our formalisation of the type safety of Solidity is based on the denotational semantics of Solidity described in [19–21] which we summarize in this section. Isabelle/Solidity is developed using higher-order logic with inductive data types [7]. To this end, we use **bold** font for types and *italics* for type constructors. We shall also use

$$\mathbf{type}_\perp \stackrel{\text{def}}{=} \perp \cup \{x_\perp \mid x \in \mathbf{type}\}$$

to denote the type which adds a distinct element $\perp$ to the elements of **type**. Sometimes we shall use

$$\mathbf{type} \rightharpoonup \mathbf{type} \stackrel{\text{def}}{=} \mathbf{type} \rightarrow \mathbf{type}_\perp$$

to denote the type of partial functions. For such a function f we shall use $dom(f)$ to denote its domain.

2.1 Value Types

Our version of Solidity supports four basic data types, called *value types*:

$$\textbf{Types} \quad ::= \quad TBool \mid TAddr \mid TSInt(\textbf{Nat}) \mid TUInt(\textbf{Nat})$$

TBool denotes boolean values and *TAddr* denotes addresses. We also support *signed* and *unsigned* integers from 8 to 256 bits in steps of 8. Thus, $TSInt(b)$ and $TUInt(b)$ denote signed and unsigned integers of bit size b. In Solidity, raw data is encoded and stored in hexadecimal format, however, to simplify the computation of locations for reference types, we use the string representation of values for raw data in our model. Thus, type **Valuetype** is actually just a synonym for type **String**, and it is used to represent the data of value types in the store. In addition, we write $\lfloor v \rfloor$ and $\lceil v \rceil$ to convert the value v of a basic data type to and from a string representation, respectively.

2.2 Stores and Reference Types

We use strings to model the addresses of storage cells to simplify the computation of locations for reference types. Thus, type **Loc** denotes these types of strings and is used to represent storage locations. We can then model a general store for values of type v as a parametric data type:

$$\textbf{Store}(v) \quad \overset{\text{def}}{=} \quad (\textbf{Loc} \rightharpoonup v) \times \textbf{Nat}$$

A store consists of a (finite) mapping to assign values of type v to locations, and in addition, it holds a pointer to the next free location. In the following we denote the mapping of a store s with $mapping(s)$ and we use $toploc(s)$ to denote its top location. We shall also use functions

$$accessStore(l, s) \quad \overset{\text{def}}{=} \quad mapping(s)(l)$$
$$updateStore(l, val, s) \quad \overset{\text{def}}{=} \quad s[mapping \mapsto mapping(s)[l \mapsto val]]$$

to access and update a location l of a store s.

Computing Storage Locations. Solidity computes storage locations for reference types by combining the address of the reference type variable with the corresponding index and hashing the result using the Keccak hash function [8]. In our model, the location of the storage cell which holds the value of an element ix of a reference type which is stored at location loc is obtained by concatenating ix with loc separated by a dot:

$$h(loc, \; ix) \quad \overset{\text{def}}{=} \quad ix + \text{"."} + loc \tag{1}$$

Stack. The *stack* stores the values for variables which can either be concrete values (for value type variables) or pointers to either memory, calldata, or storage (for reference type variables). Thus, a stack can be modelled as a store which can contain four different types of values:

$$\textbf{Stackvalue} \quad ::= \quad \textit{Simple}(\textbf{Valuetype}) \mid \textit{Memptr}(\textbf{Loc}) \mid \textit{CDptr}(\textbf{Loc}) \mid \textit{Stoptr}(\textbf{Loc})$$

$$\textbf{Stack} \quad \overset{\text{def}}{=} \quad \textbf{Store}(\textbf{Stackvalue})$$

Memory, Calldata, and Storage. Solidity supports three additional stores for storing the value of *reference types*. While *memory* and *calldata* support only arrays, *storage* also supports mappings:

$$\textbf{MTypes} \quad ::= \quad \textit{MTValue}(\textbf{Types}) \mid \textit{MTArray}(\textbf{Nat}, \textbf{MTypes})$$

$$\textbf{STypes} \quad ::= \quad \textit{STValue}(\textbf{Types})$$
$$\mid \textit{STArray}(\textbf{Nat}, \textbf{STypes}) \mid \textit{STMap}(\textbf{Types}, \textbf{STypes})$$

The internal organization of the three stores differ fundamentally. While memory and calldata use pointer structures to organize the values of reference types, storage values are accessed directly by computing the corresponding location. Thus, we model memory and calldata as stores which can contain two different types of values:

$$\textbf{Memoryvalue} \quad ::= \quad \textit{Value}(\textbf{Valuetype}) \mid \textit{Pointer}(\textbf{Loc})$$

$$\textbf{Memory} \quad \overset{\text{def}}{=} \quad \textbf{Store}(\textbf{Memoryvalue})$$

$$\textbf{Calldata} \quad \overset{\text{def}}{=} \quad \textbf{Memory}$$

Storage, on the other hand is modelled as a simple mapping from locations to value types:

$$\textbf{Storage} \quad \overset{\text{def}}{=} \quad \textbf{Loc} \rightharpoonup \textbf{Valuetype}$$

Storage access is non-strict, which means that access to an undefined storage cell returns a default value. To this end, we first define a function

$$\textit{ival} : \textbf{Types} \rightarrow \textbf{Valuetype}$$

which returns a default value for each value type. Then, we can define a corresponding access function for storage:

$$\textit{accessStorage} : \textbf{Types} \times \textbf{Loc} \times \textbf{Storage} \rightarrow \textbf{Valuetype}$$

$$\textit{accessStorage}(t, l, s) \overset{\text{def}}{=} \begin{cases} v, & \text{if } s(l) = v_\perp \\ \textit{ival}(t), & \text{if } s(l) = \perp \end{cases}$$

Our model also provides several functions to copy structures between different stores. For example,

$$cp_m^m : \textbf{Loc} \times \textbf{Loc} \times \textbf{Int} \times \textbf{MTypes} \times \textbf{Memory} \times \textbf{Memory} \rightarrow \textbf{Memory}_\perp$$

$$cp_m^m(l_s, l_d, x, t, m_s, m_d) \overset{\text{def}}{=} \textit{iter}'(\lambda i, m. \; \textit{cprec}_m^m(h(l_s, \lfloor i \rfloor), h(l_d, \lfloor i \rfloor), t, m_s, m), m_d, x)$$

can be used to copy x elements of type t from location l_s of memory/calldata m_s to location l_d of memory/calldata m_d. In the above definition $iter'$ is a function which executes a given function several times and accumulates its results.

States. A state of a Solidity program consists of the balances of the accounts, as well as the current configuration of the different stores and the remaining amount of gas (an abstract unit of computation):

$$\textbf{State} \stackrel{\text{def}}{=} (\textbf{Address} \rightarrow \textbf{Accounts}) \times (\textbf{Address} \rightarrow \textbf{Storage})$$
$$\times \textbf{Memory} \times \textbf{Stack} \times \textbf{Nat}$$

Note that each address has its own storage. In the following, we use $acc(st)$, $sto(st)$, $mem(st)$, $sck(st)$, and $gas(st)$ to access the account, storage, memory, stack, and gas component of state st. Moreover, we shall use

$$st(\!|\mathrm{acc} := a, \mathrm{sto} := s \, \mathrm{mem} := m, \mathrm{sck} := k, \mathrm{gas} := g|\!)$$

to update the gas, account, stack, memory, and storage, of state st to g, a, k, m, and s, respectively.

2.3   Environments

Variables are always interpreted w.r.t. an environment that assigns them types and denotable-values (denvalues). They can be either a stack reference or storage reference, which denote the value of the variable, and refer to either a valuetype or a complex data type in one of the stores.

$$\begin{aligned}\textbf{Type} \quad ::= \quad & Value(\textbf{Types}) \mid Calldata(\textbf{MTypes}) \\ & \mid Memory(\textbf{MTypes}) \mid Storage(\textbf{STypes}) \\ \textbf{Denvalue} \quad ::= \quad & Stackloc(\textbf{Loc}) \mid Storeloc(\textbf{Loc}) \end{aligned}$$

In addition to the type and value of variables, an environment contains the address of the executing contract, the address triggering the execution, and the amount of money sent with it:

$$\textbf{Environment} \stackrel{\text{def}}{=} \textbf{Address} \times \textbf{Address} \times \textbf{Valuetype}$$
$$\times (\textbf{Identifier} \rightharpoonup \textbf{Type} \times \textbf{Denvalue})$$

We use $address(env)$, $sender(env)$, $svalue(env)$, $denvalue(env)$ to denote the address, sender, obtained funds, and denvalue of an environment env.

To support the creation of fresh environments our model provides a function

$$empty : \textbf{Address} \times \textbf{Identifier} \times \textbf{Address} \times \textbf{Valuetype} \rightarrow \textbf{Environment}$$

where $empty(a, c, s, v)$ creates a fresh environment with address a, contract c, sender s, value v, and empty type/denvalue.

To help with the declaration of new variables, our model provides a function

$$decl : \textbf{Identifier} \times \textbf{Type} \times (\textbf{Stackvalue} \times \textbf{Type})_\perp \times \textbf{Bool} \times \textbf{Calldata} \times \textbf{Memory}$$
$$\times\ (\textbf{Address} \times \textbf{Storage}) \times \textbf{Calldata} \times \textbf{Memory} \times \textbf{Stack} \times \textbf{Environment}$$
$$\rightharpoonup (\textbf{Calldata} \times \textbf{Memory} \times \textbf{Stack} \times \textbf{Environment})$$

The idea is that $decl(id, tp, val_\perp, copy, cd, mem, sto, c, m, k, e) = (c_l, m_l, k_l, e_l)_\perp$ creates a new environment e_l and corresponding calldata c_l, memory m_l, and stack k_l from an existing environment e with calldata c, memory m, and stack k. The new environment includes a new variable id of type tp initialized with an optional value val. In the case where val is $\perp$, id is initialized with a default value. $copy$ is a flag that indicates whether memory should be copied from the mem parameter. Copying is required, for example, during external method calls. cd, mem, sto are the original calldata, memory, and storage, respectively, which are used as the sources.

2.4 Expressions and Statements

Expressions. Our subset of Solidity supports basic logical and arithmetic operations over signed and unsigned integers of various bit sizes. Moreover, it allows referencing elements of complex data types, creating addresses, querying the balances of addresses, or obtaining the address of the currently executing contract. Finally, it allows calling internal and external functions and obtaining the address that triggered the current execution and the value which was sent with it.

The corresponding syntax of expressions is given by a data type **E** defined as follows:

$$\textbf{B} ::= 8 \mid 16 \mid \ldots \mid 256$$
$$\textbf{L} ::= Id(\textbf{Identifier}) \mid Ref(\textbf{Identifier}, [\textbf{E}])$$
$$\textbf{E} ::= SInt(\textbf{B}, \textbf{Int}) \mid UInt(\textbf{B}, \textbf{Int}) \mid \textbf{E}+\textbf{E} \mid \textbf{E}-\textbf{E}$$
$$\mid\ True \mid False \mid \textbf{E}==\textbf{E} \mid \textbf{E}<\textbf{E} \mid \neg\textbf{E} \mid \textbf{E}\wedge\textbf{E} \mid \textbf{E}\vee\textbf{E}$$
$$\mid\ Address(\textbf{String}) \mid Balance(\textbf{E}) \mid L(\textbf{L}) \mid This \mid Sender \mid Value$$
$$\mid\ Call(\textbf{Identifier}, [\textbf{E}]) \mid ECall(\textbf{E}, \textbf{Identifier}, [\textbf{E}]) \mid Contracts$$

where **String** denotes the type of strings, **Identifier** is just a synonym for **String**, and $[a]$ denotes a list of elements of type a.

Our model also provides a formal semantics for expressions. It is given in the form of a function $expr(exp, ev, cd, st)$ which maps an expression, environment, calldata and state to a well defined result state. This result state can be either a normal state (N) for case where an expression terminates correctly and (E) otherwise.

Statements. The syntax of statements is given by datatype **S** defined as follows:

$$\mathbf{S} ::= Skip \mid \mathbf{L} = \mathbf{E} \mid \mathbf{S} \mathbin{;} \mathbf{S} \mid Ite(\mathbf{E}, \mathbf{S}, \mathbf{S}) \mid While(\mathbf{E}, \mathbf{S}) \mid Transfer(\mathbf{E}, \mathbf{E})$$
$$\mid Block((\mathbf{Identifier} \times \mathbf{Type} \times E_\perp), \mathbf{S}) \mid \mathrm{New}(\mathbf{Identifier}, [\mathbf{E}], \mathbf{E})$$
$$\mid Invoke(\mathbf{Identifier}, [\mathbf{E}]) \mid External(\mathbf{E}, \mathbf{Identifier}, [\mathbf{E}], \mathbf{E})$$

Again, our model provides a formal semantic for statements in the form of a function $stmt(sm, ev, cd, st)$, which maps a statement, environment, calldata, and state to a well defined result state.

One statement which is of particular interest for this work is assignments which alter the stores. Assignments are special in Isabelle/Solidity when complex data types, such as arrays, are involved. In particular, if the left- and right-hand sides are both located in memory, then the assignment only changes the pointer. However, if one of the two is storage and the other is memory, then the assignment executes an actual copy.

3   Defining Type Safety

We define type safety of Solidity over contract environments and their respective stores. A given environment ev is considered type safe with respect to a set of accounts acc, a stack sck, a memory mem, a storage sto and a calldata cd if they satisfy the following function:

$$TypeSafe(ev, acc, sck, mem, sto, cd) \;\overset{\mathrm{def}}{=}\; TypeConsistency(ev, sck, mem, cd, sto)$$
$$\wedge\, UniqStLocs(denvalue(ev)) \;\wedge CompPnts(sck, sto(address(ev)), denvalue(ev))$$
$$\wedge CompPnts(sck, mem, denvalue(ev)) \wedge CompPnts(sck, cd, denvalue(ev))$$
$$\wedge LessTLocs(sck) \wedge LessTLocs(mem) \wedge LessTLocs(cd)$$
$$\wedge SafeCont(sto, \mathbf{Env_P}) \;\wedge MNoPrefxs(\mathbf{Env_P}) \;\wedge VBalT(acc)$$
$$\wedge VSTypes(svalue(ev))$$

3.1   Type Consistency

Type consistency is the key property we consider when defining type safety and its definition requires considering two key components. The stores contained within the state, which contain the values of variables (Sect. 2.2), and the *denvalue* of the environment, which is its type environment and maps their variables to their store locations and types (Sect. 2.3).

Type consistency of an environment and a state's stores requires that the types of the variables specified in *denvalue* are consistent with their actual values in the stores. Recall that the **Valuetype**, which represent the values which are stored, is synonymous with the **String** type (Sect. 2.1). As a result of this our storage model is very generalized with all the contents being of **String** type. Thus, in our context, type consistency can only guarantee that the content of a given store location (associated with a variable in the *denvalue*) can be correctly interpreted to a value of its type. Notably this means that locations which have become disconnected from the *denvalue*, floating pointers, are not checked. However, this is not a problem for our semantics as these values should not be accessible using the statements and expressions we currently

Type Consistency of Value Types. To determine whether a given string value conforms to a given type we define the function

$$TypeCon : \textbf{Types} \times \textbf{Valuetype} \rightarrow \textbf{Bool}, \text{ where}$$

$$TypeCon(t, v) \stackrel{\text{def}}{=} \begin{cases} (v = \text{``}True\text{''} \vee v = \text{``}False\text{''}) & \text{if } t = TBool \\ \text{``.''} \notin v & \text{if } t = TAddr \\ \boxed{1} & \text{if } t = TUInt(b) \\ \boxed{2} & \text{if } t = TSInt(b) \end{cases}$$

$$\boxed{1} = \lceil v \rceil \geq 0 \wedge \lceil v \rceil < 2^b \wedge \lfloor \lceil v \rceil \rfloor = v$$
$$\boxed{2} = \lceil v \rceil \geq -(2^{b-1}) \wedge \lceil v \rceil < 2^{b-1} \wedge \lfloor \lceil v \rceil \rfloor = v$$

The cases where type t is a boolean or address are trivial, in the case of booleans we require the string v to be either "*True*" or "*False*" and for addresses we just require that the address does not contain a "." to prevent conflicts with our memory address indexing method. For unsigned integers, the integer representation of v must be greater than or equal to 0 and must also be less than the maximum value that can be represented by the bit size b. Similarly, unsigned integers must fall between the minimum and maximum values which can be supported by size b. In addition to the size constraint there is an additional property that string representations of integers must hold. Converting v to an integer and then back to a string must remain the same. The reason for this is that Solidity does not allow numeric values with preceding zeros, but this restriction is not present for our stores which only operate over **Valuetype**. It is therefore possible to have the string "0001" in a store. This property of TypeCon prevents this for type consistent stores.

Type Consistency of Reference Types. In addition to the value types we also support *reference types*. These types include memory, calldata and storage arrays and also storage maps. The concept of verifying these types is much the same, involving traversing the structure of the reference type to check every **Valuetype** element it contains. The major difference is with the traversal mechanism as memory and calldata support pointers while storage accesses locations directly.

Note that we only consider a *reference type* structure to be type consistent if all of its elements are type consistent. We do not allow for partial conformity. We also do not consider partially initialized arrays to be type safe, this is because Solidity initializes all arrays with default values on declaration and thus every location of an array must have a value.

The function *MCon* is defined to check the type consistency for memory and calldata arrays for a type t, memory (or calldata) m and location *loc*.

$MCon : \textbf{MTypes} \times \textbf{Memory} \times \textbf{Loc} \rightarrow \textbf{Bool}$, where

$$MCon(t, m, loc) \stackrel{\text{def}}{=} \begin{cases} \boxed{1} & \text{if } t = MTValue(typ) \\ \boxed{2} & \text{if } t = MTArray(len, subTyp) \end{cases}$$

$$\boxed{1} = \begin{cases} TypeCon(t, v) & \text{if } accessStore(loc, m) = Value(v) \\ False & \text{otherwise} \end{cases}$$

$$\boxed{2} = \forall i < \text{ len} \begin{cases} subTyp = MTValue(t') & \text{if } accessStore(h(loc, i), m) \\ \wedge TypeCon(t', v) & = Value(v) \\ subTyp = MTArray(len', subTyp') & \text{if } accessStore(h(loc, i), m) \\ \wedge MCon(subTyp', m, ptrLoc) & = Pointer(ptrLoc) \\ False & \text{otherwise} \end{cases}$$

MCon first distinguishes between whether the type being examined is an *MTArray* or an *MTValue*. In the *MTValue* case, the string value v located at *loc* in m is retrieved. If this is a **Valuetype**, then the v is checked against type t using *TypeCon*. If the accessed value is not a **Valuetype**, for example a *Pointer*, *MCon* returns false. The reason for this is that, while a *Pointer* is a **String** in the store, it is not considered a valid value, instead indicating the address prefix of the next array. For the *MTArray* case the *loc* which is passed to *MCon* represents the prefix location for all elements in the array to be checked. We access each element individually using a location hash (Eq. 1), where the index i is limited to be less than the length of the array *len*, due to the zero indexing of arrays. If the accessed value v is a **Valuetype**, then the subtype of the array, must be an *MTValue* and *TypeCon* must hold. Otherwise, if the accessed value is a *Pointer* to the start of the next sub array, the subType must be an *MTArray* type and each index of this sub array must satisfy *MCon*. Finally, if accessing the index returns nothing, then *MCon* returns false. This prohibits both null pointers and also partially initialized arrays.

To verify storage locations, a similar function *SCon* is defined:

$SCon : \textbf{STypes} \times \textbf{Loc} \times \textbf{Storage} \rightarrow \textbf{Bool}$, where

$$SCon(t, loc, stor) \stackrel{\text{def}}{=} \begin{cases} \boxed{1} & \text{if } t = (STValue\ typ) \\ \boxed{2} & \text{if } t = (STArray\ len\ subTyp) \\ \boxed{3} & \text{if } t = (STMap\ keyT\ subTyp) \end{cases}$$

$\boxed{1} = TypeCon(typ, accessStorage(typ, loc, stor))$

$\boxed{2} = \forall i < len.SCon(subTyp, (h\ loc\ i), stor)$

$\boxed{3} = \forall i::string.(typeCon\ keyT\ i) \implies SCon(subTyp, (hloci), stor)$

For the array case, *SCon* operates similarly to *MCon*, however, as storage does not use pointers to reference structures there is no need to look up a pointer before indexing the array. The case for *STValues* is also similar to *MCon*, however, there is no need to check the return of *accessStorage* as it will always return either an existing value or the default value of the type *typ* which is type consistent by construction. Mappings (*STMap*) are unique to storage and support mappings from a key to a value. The key can be any value but must conform to the key type (*keyT*). Additionally, a key must always have a value. Thus, *STMaps* are considered type consistent if *TSSCon* holds for all key values i, which conform to *keyT*.

Type Consistency of Environments and Stores. Finally, the following function determines whether the values in a set of stores are type consistent with an environment.

$$TypeConsistency : \textbf{Environment} \times \textbf{Stackvalue} \times$$
$$\textbf{Memory} \times \textbf{Calldata} \times \textbf{Storage} \to \textbf{Bool}, \text{ where}$$

$$TypeConsistency(ev, sck, mem, cd, stor) \stackrel{\text{def}}{=}$$
$$\forall (t, l) \in range(denvalue(ev)) \implies$$
$$\begin{cases} \boxed{1} & \text{if } l = Stackloc(loc) \\ t = Storage(typ) \wedge SCon(typ, ptr, stor(address(ev))) & \text{if } l = Storeloc(loc) \end{cases}$$

Type consistency checks the types t and locations l for all the variables stored within the range of the *denvalue* of the environment *ev*. We then distinguish between variables which are referenced from the stack and those stored in storage. For locations on the stack we do the following:

$$\boxed{1} = \begin{cases} t & = Value(typ) \wedge TypeCon(loc, typ) \\ & \quad \text{if } accessStore(loc, sck) = Simple(val) \\ t & = Memory(typ) \wedge MCon(typ, mem, ptr) \\ & \quad \text{if } accessStore(loc, sck) = Memptr(ptr) \\ t & = Calldata(typ) \wedge MCon(typ, cd, ptr) \\ & \quad \text{if } accessStore(loc, sck) = CDptr(ptr) \\ t & = Storage(typ) \wedge SCon(typ, ptr, stor(address(ev))) \\ & \quad \text{if } accessStore(loc, sck) = Stoptr(ptr) \end{cases}$$

First, we look up the corresponding value from the stack using l and then further distinguish between four cases. In the case where a *Simple* element is stored, the corresponding type t must be a *Value* type. The string value *val* is then checked against the type *typ* using *TypeCon*. Alternatively, the l could correspond to a pointer *ptr* for a *reference type*. In these cases, t must be one of the store types and correspond to the same store as *ptr*. Moreover, the structure of the *ptr* in the store must correspond to the type which is checked using the appropriate function. Note that in the case of storage pointer, the storage for the current contract, which is using ev, is used $stor(address(ev))$. The process is similar for cases where l is a storage location. The only difference is that we do not need to reference a pointer before checking the structure with $SCon$ as the location points to storage directly.

3.2   Structural Consistency

In addition to ensuring that the stores are consistent with each entry in the type environment, it is also important to ensure that the type environment is consistent with itself and the layout of the store. To ensure this, we have a number of properties to ensure that structual consistency is maintained.

This includes ensuring that if two variables in the denvalue point to the same stack location, then their types must be the same ($UniqStLocs$). Further, there must be consistency between the stack and the stores ($CompPnts$). If two variables with different $Stacklocs$ contain pointers to the same store and the pointers have the same location or are sublocations of one another then their types must be the same or compatible. This is true for pointers to all three stores. We also enforce that memory, calldata and stacks must not contain any values at locations which are greater than the top location of the store ($LessTLocs$).

3.3   Contract Related Properties

Smart contracts can have member variables which are always stored in storage (using **STypes**). When a contract is initialized these member variables are loaded into the store and their references are added to the type environment. Therefore, we require that all contracts in the contract environment **Env$_P$** must have type consistent member variables ($SafeCont$) with respect to their stores. Additionally, member variables should not reference each other, as when they are defined in Solidity (before the contract is created), this would not be possible ($MNoPrefxs$). Contracts also have a balance which stores the current amount of cryptocurrency associated with a contract and a $evalue$ which represents the funds sent to the contract at the time of a contract call. We require that both of these values must conform to an appropriate type ($VBalT$, $VSTypes$).

4   Verifying Type Safety

Type safety of Solidity can primarily be violated in one of two ways: A statement or expression changes the values in the stores, i.e. assignments. A statement or expression alters the denvalue, i.e. a new variable is declared or a new environment is created.

Statements are the primary way in which these alterations may occur and so we must verify that the type safety of the environment is preserved after each statement. Resulting in the following lemma:

Lemma 1 (TypeSafe_Statements).

$$TypeSafe(ev, acc(st), sck(st), mem(st), sto(st), cd) \wedge \tag{2}$$
$$stmt(smt, ev, cd, st) = N((), st') \tag{3}$$
$$\implies TypeSafe(ev, acc(st'), sck(st'), mem(st'), sto(st'), cd) \tag{4}$$

Given an environment ev which is type safe with respect to the accounts, stack, memory and storage of a state st and of calldata cd (Eq. 2). Then, for every statement which terminates normally and returns an updated state st' (Eq. 3), ev remains type safe with respect to the stores in the new st' and the original calldata cd, which remains un-changed (Eq. 4).

Proof. The proof is by induction over the statements with arbitrary st'. For non-trivial cases each statement is then proven by constructing a series of abstract states which follow the definition of the current statement while demonstrating that each state preserves type safety. □

Statements rely on expressions when working with variables in the state. Thus, we also proved the following lemma:

Lemma 2 (TypeSafe_Expressions).

$$TypeSafe(ev, acc(st), sck(st), mem(st), sto(st), cd) \wedge \tag{5}$$
$$expr(exp, ev, cd, st, g) = N((v, t), g') \implies \tag{6}$$
$$\begin{cases} TypeCon(loc, typ) \wedge v = Simple & if\ t = Value(typ) \\ MCon(typ, mem(st), ptr) \wedge v = Memptr & if\ t = Memory(typ) \\ MCon(typ, cd, ptr) \wedge v = CDptr & if\ t = Calldata(typ) \\ SCon(typ, ptr, sto(st)(address(ev))) \wedge v = Stoptr & if\ t = Storage(typ) \end{cases} \tag{7}$$

Given a type safe environment ev (Eq. 5), the lemma states that for an expression exp which terminates normally and returns a value v and type t (Eq. 6), v is indeed a compatible string representation for a variable of type t (Eq. 7).

Proof. Similar to TypeSafe_Statements, this lemma is proven by induction over the expressions and shown for each case. □

In the following we discuss some of the more complex aspects of the proof.

4.1   Verifying Memory/Calldata Reference Types

If a location containing a simple value type is altered, the only requirement is to show that the new value is consistent with the type of the location in the denvalue. However, for arrays the requirements are more complex. The reason for this is that not only is it necessary to verify the location that has changed is consistent, it is also necessary to check that any variables that may reference the location also remain consistent.

One particularly interesting case is when assigning a memory array with a calldata array as a value. During this process the array is copied from calldata to memory. This is handled by the function cp_m^m discussed in Sect. 2.2. Thus, we needed to verify that cp_m^m does not violate type safety (We verified similar properties for all other copy functions).

To demonstate that executing cp_m^m does not violate type safety it is only necessary to show that the segment of the destination memory which is altered by cp_m^m is *MCon*. Essentially, this requires showing that the result of cp_m^m is *MCon* for the structure that has been copied at the location in the destination it was copied to. To this end, we verified the following lemma.

Lemma 3 (MCon_cpm2m).

$$MCon(MTArray(x,t), ms, ls) \ \wedge \ x > 0 \ \wedge \qquad\qquad (8)$$

$$cp_m^m(ls, ld, x, t, ms, md) = updM \ \wedge \qquad\qquad (9)$$

$$\implies \ MCon(MTArray(x,t)aa, updM, ld) \qquad\qquad (10)$$

Equation 8 establishes that the source memory/calldata store ms is *MCon* with respect to an *MTArray* type of length x and subtype t at the prefix location ls. Further, x is a nat greater than zero, as array lengths must be greater than zero. Equation 9 then states that cp_m^m, which copies the sub-elements of the $MTArray(x,t)$ from ms to the destination memory (or calldata) md to location ld, terminates normally and returns an updated memory/calldata $updM$. Finally, Eq. 10 shows that $updM$ is *MCon* with respect to the $MTArray(x,t)$, but at the destination location ld.

Proof. As cp_m^m is a mutually recursive definition using $iter'$ and $cprec_m^m$ we first expand the definition of cp_m^m. We then perform induction over the length of the x which are all the indices of the source array being copied. For the non-trivial case $(x > 0)$ we then apply structural induction over the **MTypes** (t). For cases where t is a further *MTArray* we again apply an additional induction over the sub-arrays length for $iter'$. The intuition here is that if $cprec_m^m$ correctly reconstructs a copy of the source structure, and that structure was *MCon* in the source, then the structure should also be *MCon* in the destination.   □

4.2   Internal and External Method Calls

Internal and External method calls (*ECall*, *Call*) are another interesting aspect of the verification. When calling external methods, a new state is created with an empty stack and memory, and a new environment with a new denvalue in which the external contracts member variables are loaded. This state and environment are then used to load the method parameters, using *load* and *decl*.

The result of this loading process is then used to execute the method body. As method bodies are defined using expressions, Lemma 2 can be used to show that their return values are type consistent. However, in order to use Lemma 2, we must show that the environment and stores being used for the execution of the method body are type safe.

To verify that the new environment is type safe we proved three lemmas: $ffoldInitTypeSafe$ which confirms that the fresh environment is type safe, and $TypeSafeDecl$ and $TypeSafeLoad$ which verify that the environment remains type safe after the variables have been loaded. The lemma $ffoldInitTypeSafe$ is trivial as an environment with only contract member variables is by definition type safe, and so we will focus on $TypeSafeDecl$ and $TypeSafeLoad$.

Lemma 4 (TypeSafeLoad).

$$TypeSafe(lev0, acc(lst), sck(lst), mem(lst), sto(lst), lcd0) \land \tag{11}$$

$$TypeSafe(lev, acc(lst), lk, lm, sto(lst), lcd) \land \tag{12}$$

$$\forall locs\ typs.\ \neg\ lcp \implies MCon(tp, mem(lst), locs) \implies MCon(tp, lm, locs) \tag{13}$$

$$(\forall ev\ cd\ k\ m\ g'.$$
$$load(lcp, lis, lxs, lev0, lcd0, lk, lm, lev, lcd, lst, lg) = \mathrm{N}((ev, cd, k, m), g')$$
$$\implies\ TypeSafe(ev, acc(lst), k, m, sto(lst), cd)) \tag{14}$$

Equation 11 and Eq. 12 state that the source and destination environments are type safe with respect to the accounts, stack, memory and storage of a state lst and of calldata $lcd0$ and lcd respectively. Equation 13 states that for internal method calls, where a copy is not taking place ($\neg\ lcp$), all locations and types which are $MCon$ for the source memory are also $MCon$ for the destination memory. Finally, equation Eq. 14 states that for results of $load$ which terminate in a N state, $load$ returns an environment ev which is $TypeSafe$ with respect to the returned calldata cd, stack k, memory m and the storage and accounts of lst.

Proof. The proof is by induction over the elements of the list of variables to be loaded (lis). The base case (empty list) is trivial as the destination elements $lev\ lcd\ lm\ lk$ are returned. For the inductive case it is necessary to show that after the current head of the list is loaded using $decl$ the resultant environment is type safe, this is verified using Lemma 5. When using the $TypeSafeDecl$ lemma we pass the assumptions of $TypeSafeLoad$. In addition to the knowledge that the current value and type (v, t'') being declared (the head of list lxs) is the result of an expression and so is typeCon using Lemma 2.   □

Lemma 5 (TypeSafeDecl).

$$TypeSafeLoad(amms) \land \tag{15}$$

$$\forall ts.t_p \neq \mathbf{Storage}(ts) \land \tag{16}$$

$$decl(i_p, t_p, (v, t''), lcp, lcd, mem(lst), (sto(lst)address(lev0)), (lcd0, lm, lk, lev0))$$
$$= \mathrm{N}((e, c', k', m'), g') \tag{17}$$

$$\implies\ TypeSafe(e, acc(lst), k', m', sto(lst), c') \land \tag{18}$$

$$(\forall locs\ typs.\ \neg\ lcp \implies MCon(tp, mem(lst), locs) \implies MCon(tp, m', locs)) \tag{19}$$

As decl is called from the context of load, we pass the assumptions of *TypeSafeLoad* to *TypeSafeDecl* (Eq. 15). In addition, Eq. 16 establishes that the type being added to the denvalue t_p is not a **Storage** type. Then, Eq. 17 requires that *decl* terminates in a N state and returns an environment e calldata c', stack k' and memory k'. Equation 18 concludes that e is *TypeSafe* with respect to k', c', m', and the accounts and storage of the source state *lst*. Finally, Eq. 19 states that for internal method calls all locations and types which are *MCon* in the source memory $mem(lst)$ are also *MCon* in the resultant memory m'.

Proof. The proof for *TypeSafeDecl* is a case split over the outcome of *decl*. Trivial cases such as when t_p is a **Valuetype** are proven by unfolding the definitions and more complex cases, such as declaring array types are handled using the MCon_cp(m/s)2 m lemmas which ensures the changes being made are MCon. ☐

5   Related Work

Verification of Type Safety in Isabelle. Type safety has been formalized and verified in Isabelle. One famous example is the formalization and verification of the soundness of a static type system for IMP [25]. In addition, there have been verification of type safety aspects for real programming languages in Isabelle, such as Java [27], C++ [28], ecc. Compared to traditional programming languages, Solidity provides some specialized features, such as the different types of stores. Thus, by providing a formalization of type safety for Solidity we complement this line of research.

Formalizations of Solidity. Another line of research which is related to our work concerns formalizations of Solidity. As outlined by Almakhour et al. [3] and Tolmach et al. [26], there is a growing amount of research investigating the formalization of Solidity. Early work in this area was done by Bhargavan et al. [9] who describe an approach to map a Solidity contract to F* where it can then be verified. TinySol [6] and Featherweight Solidity [12], on the other hand, are two calculi formalizing some core features of Solidity. Crosara et al. [13] describe an operational semantics for a subset of Solidity. Moreover, Ahrendt and Bubel describe SolidiKeY [2], a formalization of a subset of Solidity in the KeY tool [1] to verify data integrity for smart contracts. In addition, Jiao et al. [15,16], provide a formalization of Solidity in $\mathbb{K}$. While all of these works focus on the formalization of Solidity, none of them investigate type safety aspects.

Verification of type safety for Solidity. Crafa et al. [12] investigate soundness of a static type system for Featherweight Solidity (a formalization of a subset of Soldity). In their work, they identify problems with the Solidity type system and propose an alternative one. Our work differs in two main aspects from their work. First, they focus on the verification of soundness of the base types of Solidity, with our work we also focus on verifying consistency of the complex types, such as, memory arrays and their pointer structures. Second, FS is a restricted subset of Solidity which lacks many features of modern Solidity. For example FS does not support the various types of stores which are available to a Solidity program and which pose a particular challenge to the verification of type safety.

6   Conclusion

With this paper we describe our work on a type-safe version of Solidity. To this end, we first provide a formalization of type-safety for Solidity programs. Then we verify that our semantics of Solidity preserves type-safety in Isabelle.

Technical Challenges. One of the key technical challenges in verifying type safety for Solidity is the complexity of the different stores and the pointer/addressing scheme used for reference types in Solidity. This is even more pronounced when verifying the type safety of statements such as Assign, which have many cases and a semantics which changes dependent on the storage types involved. We found that the interactions between the different stores made deriving properties for type safe environments very difficult and that verification of those properties required the largest amount of the proof effort.

   We have covered some of the more complex aspects in this paper. The formalization of the *MCon* and *SCon* properties which are able to check the type consistency of memory and storage reference types. We also examined the verification effort for ensuring the type consistency of copying between the different stores (Lemma 3) and declaring and loading new states and environments which contain reference types (Lemma 4, Lemma 5).

Type Issues in Isabelle/Solidity. While we did not identify any type issues of Solidity as a language for our definition of type safety however we did detect a number of issues in our formalization. In total, we found 13 issues with our formalization, 12 of these were related to missing type checks without which the type safety of the environment could be violated. The remaining issue was a bug in the operation of the semantics. Importantly 10 of the 13 issues were related to functions which operated over reference types, demonstrating the complexity of these types. To highlight some of these issues:

- $cprec_m^m$ did not correctly traverse the pointer structure of the source memory/calldata. While we accessed the pointers from the store we did not use those pointers as the prefix for the next indexed location. As a result any pointer which did not point to itself would not have been reached.
- *Call* was able to accept storage reference types as parameters. This is prohibited in Solidity.
- *decl* did not verify that the type of the variable being declared in storage matched the type of the value being added to the *denvalue*. This would result in mismatched types between the stores and the *denvalue*.

Future Work. The type system discussed in this paper uses untyped stores in combination with a typing environment and can only be checked at runtime. Thus, future work should focus on the development of a static, strongly typed, type system which can also be checked at compile time.

Acknowledgments. We thank the anonymous reviewers of ICTAC 2024 for their careful reading and constructive comments to improve an earlier version of this paper.

This work was supported by the Engineering and Physical Sciences Research Council [grant number EP/X027619/1].

References

1. Ahrendt, W., Beckert, B., Bubel, R., Hähnle, R., Schmitt, P.H., Ulbrich, M.: Deductive Software Verification-the Key Book, vol. 10001. Springer, Cham (2016). https://doi.org/10.1007/978-3-319-49812-6

2. Ahrendt, W., Bubel, R.: Functional verification of smart contracts via strong data integrity. In: Margaria, T., Steffen, B. (eds.) ISoLA 2020. LNCS, vol. 12478, pp. 9–24. Springer, Cham (2020). https://doi.org/10.1007/978-3-030-61467-6_2

3. Almakhour, M., Sliman, L., Samhat, A.E., Mellouk, A.: Verification of smart contracts: a survey. Pervasive Mob. Comput. **67**, 101227 (2020). https://doi.org/10.1016/j.pmcj.2020.101227

4. Authors, S.: Solidity developer survey 2023 results (2024). https://soliditylang.org/blog/2024/04/03/solidity-developer-survey-2023-results/

5. Azaria, A., Ekblaw, A., Vieira, T., Lippman, A.: MedRec: using blockchain for medical data access and permission management. In: 2016 2nd International Conference on Open and Big Data (OBD), pp. 25–30 (2016). https://doi.org/10.1109/OBD.2016.11

6. Bartoletti, M., Galletta, L., Murgia, M.: A minimal core calculus for solidity contracts. In: Pérez-Solà, C., Navarro-Arribas, G., Biryukov, A., Garcia-Alfaro, J. (eds.) DPM/CBT -2019. LNCS, vol. 11737, pp. 233–243. Springer, Cham (2019). https://doi.org/10.1007/978-3-030-31500-9_15

7. Berghofer, S., Wenzel, M.: Inductive datatypes in HOL — lessons learned in formallogic engineering. In: Bertot, Y., Dowek, G., Théry, L., Hirschowitz, A., Paulin, C. (eds.) TPHOLs 1999. LNCS, vol. 1690, pp. 19–36. Springer, Heidelberg (1999). https://doi.org/10.1007/3-540-48256-3_3

8. Bertoni, G., Daemen, J., Peeters, M., Van Assche, G.: Keccak. In: Johansson, T., Nguyen, P.Q. (eds.) EUROCRYPT 2013. LNCS, vol. 7881, pp. 313–314. Springer, Heidelberg (2013). https://doi.org/10.1007/978-3-642-38348-9_19

9. Bhargavan, K., et al.: Formal verification of smart contracts: Short paper. In: Programming Languages and Analysis for Security, pp. 91–96. PLAS, ACM (2016).https://doi.org/10.1145/2993600.2993611

10. Chavez-Dreyfuss, G.: Sweden tests blockchain technology for land registry. https://www.reuters.com/article/us-sweden-blockchain-idUSKCN0Z22KV. Accessed 18 Apr 2023

11. Clegg, P., Jevans, D.: Cryptocurrency crime and anti-money laundering report. Technical report, CipherTrace (2021)

12. Crafa, S., Di Pirro, M., Zucca, E.: Is solidity solid enough? In: Bracciali, A., Clark, J., Pintore, F., Rønne, P.B., Sala, M. (eds.) FC 2019. LNCS, vol. 11599, pp. 138–153. Springer, Cham (2020). https://doi.org/10.1007/978-3-030-43725-1_11

13. Crosara, M., Centurino, G., Arceri, V.: Towards an operational semantics for solidity. In: van Rooyen, J., Buro, S., Campion, M., Pasqua, M. (eds.) VALID, pp. 1–6. IARIA (2019)

14. Ethereum: Solidity. https://docs.soliditylang.org/. Accessed 04 May 2023

15. Jiao, J., Kan, S., Lin, S.W., Sanan, D., Liu, Y., Sun, J.: Semantic understanding of smart contracts: executable operational semantics of Solidity. In: SP, pp. 1695–1712. IEEE (2020). https://doi.org/10.1109/SP40000.2020.00066

16. Jiao, J., Lin, S.-W., Sun, J.: A generalized formal semantic framework for smart contracts. In: FASE 2020. LNCS, vol. 12076, pp. 75–96. Springer, Cham (2020). https://doi.org/10.1007/978-3-030-45234-6_4

17. Kelly, J.: Banks adopting blockchain 'dramatically faster' than expected: IBM (2016). https://www.reuters.com/article/us-tech-blockchain-ibm-idUSKCN11Y28D. Accessed 04 May 2023

18. Llama, D.: TVL breakdown by smart contract language (2024). https://defillama.com/languages

19. Marmsoler, D., Brucker, A.D.: A denotational semantics of solidity in Isabelle/HOL. In: Calinescu, R., Păsăreanu, C.S. (eds.) SEFM 2021. LNCS, vol. 13085, pp. 403–422. Springer, Cham (2021). https://doi.org/10.1007/978-3-030-92124-8_23

20. Marmsoler, D., Brucker, A.D.: Conformance testing of formal semantics using grammar-based fuzzing. In: Kovács, L., Meinke, K. (eds.) TAP 2022. LNCS, vol. 13361, pp. 106–125. Springer, Cham (2022). https://doi.org/10.1007/978-3-031-09827-7_7

21. Marmsoler, D., Brucker, A.D.: Isabelle/solidity:a deep embedding of solidity in isabelle/hol. Archive of Formal Proofs (2022). https://isa-afp.org/entries/Solidity.html, Formal proof development

22. Mendling, J., et al.: Blockchains for business process management - challenges and opportunities. ACM Trans. Manage. Inf. Syst. 9(1) (2018).https://doi.org/10.1145/3183367

23. Nakamoto, S.: Bitcoin: a peer-to-peer electronic cash system (2008). https://doi.org/10.2139/ssrn.3440802

24. Nipkow, T., Paulson, L.C., Wenzel, M.: Isabelle/HOL: a proof assistant for higher-order logic (2002). https://doi.org/10.1007/3-540-45949-9

25. Nipkow, T., Klein, G.: Concrete Semantics: With Isabelle/HOL. Springer, Cham (2014). https://doi.org/10.1007/978-3-319-10542-0

26. Tolmach, P., Li, Y., Lin, S.W., Liu, Y., Li, Z.: A survey of smart contract formal specification and verification. ACM Comput. Surv. 54(7) (2021). https://doi.org/10.1145/3464421

27. von Oheimb, D., Nipkow, T.: Machine-checking the java specification: proving type-safety. In: Alves-Foss, J. (ed.) Formal Syntax and Semantics of Java. LNCS, vol. 1523, pp. 119–156. Springer, Heidelberg (1999). https://doi.org/10.1007/3-540-48737-9_4

28. Wasserrab, D., Nipkow, T., Snelting, G., Tip, F.: An operational semantics and type safety proof for multiple inheritance in c++. In: Proceedings of the 21st Annual ACM SIGPLAN Conference on Object-Oriented Programming Systems, Languages, and Applications, pp. 345–362 (2006).https://doi.org/10.1145/1167515.1167503

29. YCharts.com: Ethereum transactions per day. https://ycharts.com/indicators/ethereum_transactions_per_day. Accessed 04 May 2024

30. Yurcan, B.: How blockchain fits into the future of digital identity (2016). https://fintechranking.com/2016/04/10/how-blockchain-fits-into-the-future-of-digital-identity/

History-Based Reasoning About Behavioral Subtyping

Jinting Bian[1,2(✉)] , Hans-Dieter A. Hiep[1,2] , and Frank S. de Boer[1,2]

[1] Leiden Institute of Advanced Computer Science (LIACS), Leiden, The Netherlands
jintingbian@163.com
[2] CWI, Science Park 123, 1098 XG Amsterdam, The Netherlands
{hdh,frb}@cwi.nl

Abstract. We introduce a new history-based proof-theory for reasoning about behavioral subtyping in class and interface hierarchies. Our approach is based on a semantic definition of types in terms of sets of sequences of method calls and returns, so-called histories.Behavioral subtyping is then naturally defined semantically as a set-theoretic subset relation between sets of histories, modulo a *projection relation* that captures the syntactic subtype relation. The main contribution is a Hoare-style proof theory for the specification and verification of the behavioral subtyping relation in terms of histories, abstracting from the underlying implementation.Through the use of a banking example we show the practical applicability of our approach.

Open Science. Includes a source code artifact [8].

Keywords: Software verification · Behavioral subtyping · History-based reasoning · Object-oriented programming

1 Introduction

The *programming to interfaces* discipline is one of the most important principles in software engineering. This methodology allows the developer of client code to abstract away from internal implementation details, such as object state, thereby aiding modular program development. Type hierarchies support this principle in object-oriented design by allowing the declaration of new subtypes that inherit properties and behaviors from their supertypes, while also providing the flexibility to add or override specific features as needed. The concept of *behavioral subtyping* (which refers to subtyping based on behavior, in contrast to nominal subtyping and structural subtyping [1]) ensures that in clients one should be able to replace the use of a supertype by a subtype without causing unexpected behavior [18,25]. This concept is employed in object-oriented programming to ensure software maintainability and robustness.

Histories, as defined in our previous work [17], are sequences of method calls performed on the object. We define the semantics of a type as a set of histories, thus abstracting from the underlying state/implementation. This allows one to define the behavioral subtype relation semantically as a subset relation between

© The Author(s), under exclusive license to Springer Nature Switzerland AG 2025
C. Anutariya and M. M. Bonsangue (Eds.): ICTAC 2024, LNCS 15373, pp. 331–349, 2025.
https://doi.org/10.1007/978-3-031-77019-7_19

sets of histories, modulo a projection relation between histories that correspond with the syntactic definition of the subtype relation. For the specification and verification of the behavioral subtype relation, we introduce method contracts using Hoare triples that involve suitable user-defined abstractions over histories, called *attributes*. We discuss behavioral subtyping in three settings: class-class inheritance, class-interface inheritance, as well as interface-interface inheritance.

There exists a large body of research on behavioral subtyping [3,4,10,15], starting from the seminal work by Liskov and Wing [24], who point out that a subtype must adhere to the behavioral contracts of its supertype. To define the subtype relation, they introduced an *abstraction function* that maps the state of each subtype to a state of its corresponding supertype. The soundness of the substitution principle follows from two conditions: the precondition of the supertype implies the precondition of the subtype, and the postcondition of the subtype implies the postcondition of the supertype. The pre/postconditions of the subtype speak of the state of the subtype, whereas the pre/postconditions of the supertype speak of a different state: so the abstraction function takes a state of the subtype and maps it to a state of the supertype in such a way that these conditions hold. Is worth mentioning that in Liskov and Wing's work, they introduce a notion of *history constraint*, which is different from our notion of a history. Their history refers to temporal properties of objects, which are used to declare a relationship between pre-states and post-states preserved by any method of a type [19]. Leavens and Weih [20,22,23] present a technique for the modular reasoning about object-oriented programs, called *supertype abstraction*, which allows adding behavioral subtypes without reverification. However, their method is based on the assumption that each specified subtype relation consti-tutes a behavioral subtype. Demonstrating such behavioral subtyping requires again the use of an abstraction function. Although there have been several logics for the reasoning about object-oriented programs including a notion of behavioral subtyping [5,11–14,27,30,31], they are all based on the abstraction function. In the field of refinement calculus [6,7,26], which focuses on the stepwise transfor-mation of an abstract specification into an executable implementation, one also uses the abstraction functions. These functions help in mapping implementation to specification, ensuring that each refinement step is correct.

In contrast to the above related work, the history-based reasoning approach in this paper avoids formulating ad hoc abstraction functions between different state-based implementations. Instead, it is based on a general semantic definition of the behavioral sub-type relation as a subset relation between sets of histories modulo a projection relation. Further, our proof method is based on the use of suitable user-defined history abstractions which allows for a modular verification of the proof obligations. Finally, our approach is applicable to both interfaces and classes, and allows reasoning about behavioral subtyping in settings that are typically absent in most related studies [16,20,28,32].

The paper is intentionally written to introduce and motivate a new idea rather than to work out all the formal details. We discuss the methodology of history-based behavioral subtyping in Sect. 2. Our specification methods are presented in the context of history and attributes. In Sect. 3, we use a banking example to illustrate our approach. We provide only informal proofs for three particular sub-type relations: interface-interface, interface-class, and class-class. The part of this example is proven using the KeY theorem prover [2] and Isabelle/HOL [29]. The verification workflow is based on our previous work [9]. The workflow consists of three steps: step 1 is formalizing ADTs in Isabelle/HOL, step 2 is using ADTs in JML specification, and step 3 is verifying behavioral subtyping based on the supertype and subtype specification, which we discussed separately in Sects. 3.1, 3.2, and 3.3.

2 Methodology

In object-oriented programming, a method signature consists of a list of param-eter types and a return type. An interface contains a set of method signatures. A class consists of a set of field declarations and a set of method declarations.

The type hierarchy for classes and interfaces in languages with a nominal type system can be declared as below:

> **interface** I [**extends** $I_1, I_2, \ldots, I_n$]
> **class** C' [**extends** C] [**implements** $I_1, I_2, \ldots, I_n$]

An interface can extend zero or more interfaces, which is known as interface inheritance. When one interface extends another, it inherits all of the methods defined in its super interfaces, but it can also add new methods of its own. A class can inherit from multiple interfaces, by providing implementations for all methods defined in the interfaces. However, a class can only inherit from a *single* class. This is due to the fact that class inheritance is typically used for defining the (memory) structure of a class. Allowing multiple inheritance of classes can potentially lead to conflicts among class invariants [21] and ambiguity, as exemplified by the so-called diamond problem [33].

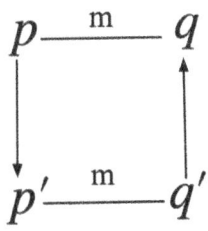

Fig. 1. The behavioral notion of subtyping.

The basic behavioral notion of subtyping dis-cussed in [24] is shown in Fig. 1. A Hoare triple specification, denoted as $\{p\}$ m $\{q\}$, consists of a method m, a precondition p that describes the object state before the method is executed, and a postcondition q that describes the expected object state after the method is executed. In Fig. 1, we have $\{p\}$ m $\{q\}$ on top and $\{p'\}$ m $\{q'\}$ below, which represent the supertype and subtype spec-ification of m, respectively, where m is a method inherited by the subtype from the supertype.

From the perspective of a client, we ensure before a method call that the precondition of the supertype holds, so that after dynamic dispatch where we jump to the implementation of the subtype, we also need the precondition of the corresponding method in the subtype holds. After the execution of the subtype method finishes, it reaches the postcondition of the subtype's method. This postcondition should also imply the postcondition of the method in the supertype, since the client assumes that the postcondition of the supertype holds after the method returns. Moreover, if both types are classes then the invariant of the supertype must be preserved in the subtype.

However, typically the precondition and postcondition, given in some specification language, are intrinsically state-based and as such are not directly suitable for the specification of a state-hiding interface. In history-based reasoning, we introduce the concept of a history that can be seen as the most general abstraction of the state space of an interface. There are two approaches: the executable history-based (EHB) approach [17], and the logical history-based (LHB) approach [9]. In the former approach, histories become part of the run-time environment and are encoded as objects. In the latter approach, histories do not exist at run-time and are only introduced as bookkeeping devices for reasoning, similar to ghost variables. We proceed with the latter approach. In the LHB approach, histories are modeled as elements of an abstract data type (ADT). This means histories are immutable and inaccessible: no program can modify or even inspect a history value.

A history is a sequence of events. Every method is represented by a corresponding event type, that records the types of the parameters and the type of the return value. For technical convenience, we only regard normal returns from method calls as events. For each class and interface, we introduce a history type by defining it as an inductive data type of sequences of events.

Following the information hiding principle, we assume an object encapsulates its own state. This means that other objects can not directly access its fields; instead, they must call methods, such as getter and setter, to access fields. Consequently, each object can enforce invariants over its own fields and its state can be completely determined by the sequence of method calls invoked on the object. Attributes are user-defined abstractions of histories that are in general defined inductively over the history. These attributes are used in method specifications to specify the intended behavior of implementations, and by using attributes the method specifications do not depend on the (hidden) state of an object.

The overall approach in history-based reasoning can be summarized by the following diagram, see Fig. 2. We will provide more details on each of the components in Fig. 2.

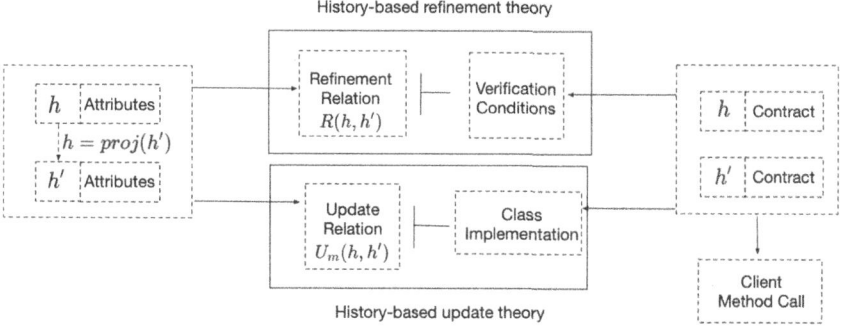

Fig. 2. History-based reasoning about behavioral subtyping. In the refinement relation $R(h, h')$, h represents the history of the supertype and h' represents the history of the subtype. In the relation $U_m(h, h')$ h' is intended to result from an update of the history h by a call of m.

History-Based Refinement Theory. To establish that the behavioral subtype relation holds between two types, we define a set of proof obligations between the preconditions and postconditions of methods inherited by a subtype. For a modular verification of these proof obligations we introduce a methodology that consists of two parts: verification of the refinement relation and, separately, verification of the proof obligations generated from method specifications, assuming the refinement relation. The method specifications refer to the attributes of the associated history. They are abstract from the inductive definition of the history and its attributes. The *refinement relation* on the other hand captures logically the relationship between attributes of *different* histories, namely the histories of the supertype and the subtype. The axioms of the refinement relation itself, as a logical theory, should be established as logical consequences of the inductive definitions of the attributes and the projection relation.

Our overall approach is based on the basic assumption that a history h of a supertype can be obtained as a projection of the subtype history h', formalized by $h = proj(h')$. The projection is defined as the subsequence of the subtype history h' that only includes the events of methods that are inherited from the supertype. This assumption can be justified as follows. When a method from a subtype that inherits from a supertype in the hierarchy is called, updates are made to both the histories of supertype and subtype. For methods only present in the subtype, updates are made only to the history of the subtype, while that of the supertype remains unchanged. This design choice is intentional to avoid the potential issues that may occur if the subtype is cast to the supertype. More general approaches, where the history of a subtype can be simulated by the history of a supertype, will be left for future work. For any given histories h and h', where h is a projection of h', the user-defined refinement relation $R(h, h')$ describes a logical relation between the attributes of h and h', *abstracting* from their inductive definitions. Note that attributes in general may have different meanings when interpreted by the history of a supertype or by the history of a subtype.

The proof obligations, also called verification conditions, for interface-interface refinement, interface-class refinement and class-class refinement are shown below. For a supertype, h represents the history of the supertype, p represents the precondition and q represents the postcondition. For a subtype, h' represents the history of the subtype, p' represents the precondition and q' represents the postcondition. For classes, Inv and Inv' denote the superclass and the subclass invariant, respectively. Class invariants in general describe a (logical) relation between the fields of a class and the attributes of the associated class. In proving the verification conditions for the pre- and postconditions of the inherited methods, the refinement relation is assumed. It should be noted that, by using the logical consequence relation $\vdash$, the history variables h and h' are implicitly universally quantified (on both sides of $\vdash$). The refinement relation itself involves a separate proof obligation which is formulated by

$$h = proj(h') \rightarrow R(h, h')$$

That is, the logical relation between the attributes of the histories of the supertype and the subtype should follow from the projection relation and their inductive definitions.

Verification Condition IIR (Interface-Interface Refinement).

$$R(h, h') \vdash (p \rightarrow p') \quad \text{and} \quad R(h, h') \vdash (q' \rightarrow q)$$

Verification Condition ICR (Interface-Class Refinement).

$$R(h, h') \vdash (p \wedge Inv' \rightarrow p') \quad \text{and} \quad R(h, h') \vdash (q' \wedge Inv' \rightarrow q)$$

Verification Condition CCR (Class-Class Refinement).

$$R(h, h') \vdash (Inv' \rightarrow Inv) \text{ and}$$
$$R(h, h') \vdash (p \wedge Inv' \rightarrow p') \text{ and } R(h, h') \vdash (q' \wedge Inv' \rightarrow q)$$

Verifying Method Calls and Method Implementations. In the usual manner, method calls are verified in terms of the corresponding method specification (as determined by the *static* type of the callee expression). This involves the usual substitution of the formal parameter by the actual parameter. More specifically, a method specification $\{p\}\ m(\bar{u})\ \{q\}$ can be instantiated to a method call $x = y.m(\bar{e})$ by substituting **this** with the calling object y and the method parameters $\bar{u}$ with the actual arguments $\bar{e}$ in the preconditions and postconditions. The method call rule is formalized as below:

$$\{p[y/this, \bar{e}/\bar{u}]\}\ x = y.m(\bar{e})\ \{q[y/this, \bar{e}/\bar{u}]\}$$

Here $[y/this, \bar{e}/\bar{u}]$ describes the context switch from callee to the caller: $\bar{u}$ are the formal parameters of method m, the variable y denotes the callee and $\bar{e}$

are the actual parameters call by y. We assume the formal parameters do not change during the method call and that the actual parameters are pure.

To validate the postcondition of a method body, which specifies the corresponding update of the associated history, we assume in the following method implementation rule a logical *update relation* $U_m(h, g)$ between the attributes of the updated history h and the 'old' history g.

Rule 1 (Method Implementation Rule). Given the method definition $\{p\}\, m\, \{q\}$, the body S of m, and the class invariant Inv, we have the rule

$$\frac{\{p \wedge Inv\}\; S\; \{r\}\quad U_m(h, g) \vdash r \to (q \wedge Inv)}{\{p\}\, m\, \{q\}}$$

This rule thus allows one to abstract from the inductive definitions of the history attributes in the validation of the method body. The logical *update relation* $U_m(h, g)$ between the attributes of the updated history h and the 'old' history g, then can be established separately as a logical consequence of $h = Cons(m(\bar{x}, \mathbf{result}), g)$ which directly describes the relation between the updated history and the old one in terms of their sequence structure. Here $\bar{x}$ are the actual parameters and **result** is the return value. The **result** variable here may either be *null* (indicating no return value) or contain a return value. $Cons$ indicating that the history is composed of an event (in this rule is the $m(\bar{x}, \mathbf{result})$) as its head and another history (in this rule is the g) as its tail.

3   Case study

In this section, we introduce a banking example to illustrate the methodology discussed in Sect. 2. This example features a type hierarchy, which allows us to demonstrate our ideas effectively. It also presents some interesting challenges that occur in real-world programs, such as how to enforce protocol at the interface level where we have no access to the underlying state. We also consider some real-world scenarios, like how to extend functionality in existing programs. We implemented the case study by defining the ADTs in Isabelle/HOL, and used ADTs in the specification and KeY proof for Java programs.

In the banking example, we have two interfaces. The `Saving` interface, as shown in Listing 1, specifies methods for depositing an integer amount into the account and for retrieving the current balance. The `Payment` interface (Listing 2) defines two new methods: the `query` method and the `withdraw` method. The `query` method is used to check whether there are sufficient funds in the account before each `withdraw` method.

```
interface Saving {
    void deposit(int i);
    int getbalance();}
```

Listing 1. The `Saving` interface.

```
interface Payment extends Saving {
    boolean query(int i);
    void withdraw();}
```

Listing 2. The `Payment` interface.

The method signatures of the interface are designed to allow for the expression of the intended protocol. The protocol for the `Payment` interface stipulates that the `withdraw` method can only be invoked when the return value of the `query` is true. This protocol is designed to protect the interface from executing invalid withdrawal operations that could potentially lead to errors in the system (e.g. by calling `withdraw` multiple times without having enough balance).

We have three classes for our example. The `Account` class (Listing 3) implements the methods defined in the `Saving` interface.

```
class Account implements Saving {
    int balance; // field
    void deposit(int i) { balance=balance + i; }
    int getbalance() { return balance; } }
```

Listing 3. The `Account` class.

The `Credit` class (Listing 4) permits withdrawals even if the balance is insufficient. In the `Credit` class, the `query` method always returns true.

```
class Credit implements Payment {
    int request = −1; int balance;
    void deposit(int i) { balance=balance + i; }
    int getbalance() { return balance; }
    boolean query(int i) { request = i; return true; }
    void withdraw() { balance = balance − request; request = −1; } }
```

Listing 4. The `Credit` class.

In contrast, the `Debit` class (Listing 5) allows withdrawals only if the account has sufficient funds. Specifically, the return value of the `query` method is true if and only if the balance is greater than or equal to the argument.

```
class Debit extends Account implements Payment {
    int request = −1;
    boolean query(int i) {
        if (balance ≥ i) { request = i; return true; } else return false; }
    void withdraw() { balance = balance − request; request = −1; } }
```

Listing 5. The `Debit` class.

3.1   History-Based reasoning

We discuss how we formalize ADTs for the banking example. This step is completed in Isabelle/HoL. We define data types (using the **datatype** command) and functions (using the **fun** command) to logically model domain-specific knowledge of the Java program that we want to verify. These definitions can defined using polymorphic type parameters.

The data types *events* contain the method name, the actual parameter values, and the output value (which is the final argument of the event) of a method call. The events are designed to be generic and do not contain information about the caller. This design choice makes events useful for a general history-based theory that is related to the caller. With regard to methods, there are methods like `deposit` that take an integer as a parameter but have no return value, whereas the `getbalance` method takes no input parameters but returns an integer. To distinguish between the input type and output type, we use a unit type **void** to represent the absence of a meaningful value. As discussed above, each subtype includes the events that are inherited from its supertype. For example, the definitions of the events for the interfaces in our running example are as follows:

$$\textbf{datatype } saveEvent = deposit(\textbf{int}, \textbf{void}) \mid balance(\textbf{void}, \textbf{int})$$
$$\textbf{datatype } payEvent = deposit(\textbf{int}, \textbf{void}) \mid balance(\textbf{void}, \textbf{int}) \mid$$
$$query(\textbf{int}, \textbf{bool}) \mid withdraw(\textbf{void}, \textbf{void})$$

The concept of *history* is formally defined as an inductive data type of a sequence of events. Rather than employing temporal logic or formalizing history as an indexed set of events, we find that inductive data types offer a more convenient approach for defining attributes by induction and are easier to integrate with theorem provers in general. Thus, we introduce the history as a parameterized inductive datatype:

$$\textbf{datatype } history(\alpha) = Empty \mid Cons(\alpha, history(\alpha))$$

The type parameter α corresponds to the type of event occurring in the history, such as *saveEvent* and *payEvent*. For example, we can instantiate the parameter by the datatype *saveEvent* to obtain the histories for the `Saving` interface, which is represented as *history(saveEvent)*. The history data type uses the constructors *Empty* and *Cons*, indicating that the history is either empty or composed of an event as its head and another history as its tail. When a new event is added, the new event, along with its argument and return type, becomes the head of the history, while the old history turns to become the tail. The history is generated in reverse order, which means that the last generated event appears at the start of the sequence.

The *amount* attribute, defined below, denotes the total amount of money in a given account. Intuitively, it serves as a snapshot representation of the interface's 'contents' at a particular instant. In the `Saving` interface, *amount* is defined inductively over the structure of the saving history, as shown below: a successful deposit increases the amount of money according to the value of the provided argument. We use *null* to represent a constant of type **void**.

$$\textbf{fun } amount : history(saveEvent) \Rightarrow \textbf{int}$$
$$amount(Empty) = 0$$
$$amount(Cons(deposit(i, null), h)) = amount(h) + i$$
$$amount(Cons(balance(null, i), h)) = amount(h)$$

Attributes of history are treated similarly as "fields" in a class. To be specific, attributes defined by a supertype can be freely used and reinterpreted by its subtype. In our case, we redefine the *amount* attribute based on the payment history, taking the new methods `query` and `withdraw` into account.

$$\textbf{fun } amount : history(payEvent) \Rightarrow \textbf{int}$$
$$amount(Empty) = 0$$
$$amount(Cons(deposit(i, null), h)) = amount(h) + i$$
$$amount(Cons(balance(null, i), h)) = amount(h)$$
$$amount(Cons(query(i, b), h)) = amount(h)$$
$$amount(Cons(withdraw(null, null), h)) =$$
$$amount(h) - (ready(h) ? take(h) : 0)$$

We define attributes *ready* and *take* as follows: given a history, *ready* checks whether the previous query event has returned **true**, and if so, *take* returns the parameter of `query` method.

$$\textbf{fun } ready : history(payEvent) \Rightarrow \textbf{boolean}$$
$$ready(Empty) = \textbf{false}$$
$$ready(Cons(query(i, b), h)) = b$$
$$ready(Cons(withdraw(null, null), h)) = \textbf{false}$$
$$ready(Cons(e, h)) = ready(h)$$
$$\textbf{fun } take : history(payEvent) \Rightarrow \textbf{int}$$
$$take(Empty) = -1$$
$$take(Cons(query(i, b), h)) = (b ? i : -1)$$
$$take(Cons(withdraw(null, null), h)) = -1$$
$$take(Cons(e, h)) = take(h)$$

In the last clause, e is any event of *payEvent* not specified in the clauses above.

For the full Isabelle theory of banking example, we refer the reader to the artifact accompanying this paper [8]. This artifact also includes the proof files for the example discussed later.

3.2   History-Based Specification

We now formulate contracts for the methods of interface and class, making use of histories and their attributes defined in Sect. 3.1. By overloading field access notation, we can treat the attributes of a history associated with **this** like how we would treat an unqualified field. For example, when considering the *amount* defined in the `Saving` interface, we can use syntactic sugar to simplify $amount(h)$ where h is of type *history(saveEvent)* to just *amount* within the `Saving` interface. For external objects, we can explicitly indicate the object of which the corresponding history is taken in an attribute. Listing 6 shows a concrete example: suppose we would add a default method `transfer` to the `Payment` interface, that performs a withdrawal and immediately transfers the amount to the given `Saving` instance, then the postcondition illustrates that the amount of (the history of) **this** decreases, while the amount of (the history of) the receiver increases. Moreover, this example illustrates why hiding the concrete structure of a history from specifications is useful: while the default implementation does not record *transfer* as an event in the history of `Payment` and instead records the events which are used by the default implementation (in our case *withdraw*), non-default implementations do record a *transfer* event, thus have a different structure of the history.

// Transfer money from this Payment account to the given Saving account
$\{ready = \textbf{true} \wedge take = \texttt{i}\}$
default void `transfer`(**int** i, `Saving` s) { `withdraw`(); `s.deposit`(i); }
$\{(\texttt{s} \neq \textbf{this} \rightarrow amount = \textbf{old}(amount) - \texttt{i} \wedge \texttt{s}.amount = \textbf{old}(\texttt{s}.amount) + \texttt{i}) \wedge$
$(\texttt{s} = \textbf{this} \rightarrow amount = \textbf{old}(amount))\}$

Listing 6. An example to specify the object of a history explicitly.

To avoid introducing a logical *freeze* variable, which would capture the history as it were in the pre-state, we use the notation **old** as a logical operation on terms to denote the attribute value evaluated in the pre-state of the method call, where **old** distributes over pure operations such as arithmetical functions. In the postcondition, *amount* in our example refers to the amount after the method call, while **old**(*amount*) represents the amount before the method call.

An interface specification includes the name of the interface being specified and the method signatures that the interface provides along with their respective precondition and postcondition. Listing 7 illustrates the use of the history attribute in the specification of the `Saving` interface.

Specification(`Saving`) =
($\{\texttt{i} \geq 0\}$ **void** `deposit`(**int** i) $\{amount = \textbf{old}(amount) + \texttt{i}\}$,
 $\{\textbf{true}\}$ **int** `getbalance`() $\{amount = \textbf{old}(amount) \wedge \textbf{result} = amount\}$)

Listing 7. The specification of the `Saving` interface in terms of attribute *amount*.

The special variable **result** in the postcondition captures the return value of a method.

The specification of the `Payment` interface in terms of the attribute *amount* is shown in Listing 8.

Specification(`Payment`) =
($\{\texttt{i} \geq 0\}$ **void** `deposit`(**int** i) $\{amount = \textbf{old}(amount) + \texttt{i}\}$,
 $\{\textbf{true}\}$ **int** `getbalance`() $\{amount = \textbf{old}(amount) \wedge \textbf{result} = amount\}$,
 $\{\texttt{i} \geq 0\}$ **boolean** `query`(**int** i) $\{amount = \textbf{old}(amount) \wedge$
                         $\textbf{result} = ready \wedge (ready \rightarrow take = \texttt{i})\}$,
 $\{ready\}$ **void** `withdraw`() $\{amount = \textbf{old}(amount - take) \wedge \neg ready)$

Listing 8. The specification of the `Payment` interface in terms of attributes *amount*.

One should observe that the return value of the query method remains unspecified, thereby leaving design decisions open for subtypes and implementors. Two implementations can be considered: a credit account (the specification see Listing 10) and a debit account (the specification see Listing 11). It is not possible to further specify the result in the Payment interface in a way that is compatible with both subtypes.

In addition to the type name and method specifications, a class specification may also contain the *class invariant*. The method specifications of a class are described in terms of both fields and history attributes. The specification of the Account class is shown in Listing 9.

Specification(Account) =
(balance = *amount* ∧ balance ≥ 0, // *class invariant*
{i ≥ 0} **void** deposit(**int** i) {balance = **old**(balance)+i},
{**true**} **int** getbalance() {balance = **old**(balance) ∧ **result** = balance})

Listing 9. The specification of the Account class.

The specification of the Credit class and the specification of the Debit class are present in Listings 10 and 11, respectively.

Specification(Credit) =
(balance = *amount* ∧ request = *take* // *class invariant*
{i≥0} **void** deposit(**int** i) {balance = **old**(balance)+i},
{**true**} **int** getbalance() {balance = **old**(balance) ∧ **result** = balance},
{i≥0} **boolean** query(**int** i) {balance = **old**(balance) ∧
                              result = **true** ∧ request = i},
{request ≠ −1} **void** withdraw() {request = −1 ∧
                              balance = **old**(balance−request)})

Listing 10. The specification of the Credit class.

The value of **result** for the query method is explicitly specified in the classes Debit and Credit that implement the interface. Specifically, for the Credit class, **result** is unconditionally true. Conversely, for the Debit class, **result** is true when and only when the *balance* ≥ *i*. Note that these two conditions are not compatible: no debit object can be considered as a credit object.

Specification(Debit) =
(balance = *amount* ∧ request = *take* ∧ balance ≥ 0 ∧ balance ≥ request,
{i ≥ 0} **void** deposit(i) {balance = **old**(balance)+i},
{**true**} **int** getbalance() {balance = **old**(balance) ∧ **result** = balance},
{i≥0} **boolean** query(i) {balance = **old**(balance) ∧ request = i ∧
                        result=(balance≥i)},
{balance ≥ request ∧ request ≠ −1} **void** withdraw()
                        {request = −1 ∧ balance = **old**(balance−request)})

Listing 11. The specification of the Debit class.

The preconditions and postconditions effectively specify protocols for methods. For instance, the `withdraw` method should only be invoked following a valid query. In both the `withdraw` method in the `Debit` and `Credit` class, we impose the precondition constraint $request \neq -1$. When dealing with an interface method where we have no access to the underlying state, such as in the `Payment` interface (Listing 8), the protocol can be describe using the attribute of history, specifically the *ready* attribute. This allows us to capture the return value of a previous query, abstracting from the underlying implementation.

3.3   Behavioral Subtyping

We now discuss verifying the behavioral subtyping in the context of the banking example. The verifying process follows the steps discussed in Sect. 2, which involves formulating refinement theory, generating verification conditions, and reasoning about behavioral subtyping.

Let us start with interface-interface refinement. The example we provide is the `deposit` method in the `Saving` interface (Listing 7) and its subtype, the `Payment` interface (Listing 8). First, we consider formulating the refinement relation. For user-defined refinement relation $R(h, h')$, h is of type $history(saveEvent)$, and h' is of type $history(payEvent)$, we can get $R(h, h')$ through the definition of *amount* for both the `Saving` and `Payment` interfaces, as provided below: every time the `withdraw` is called within the `Payment` interface and returns a *true* value, the *amount* attribute defined on the `Payment` history will decrease. To reflect this behavior, we introduce a new attribute, *withdrawamount*, to accumulate the total amount successfully withdrawn:

$$\textbf{fun } withdrawamount : history(payEvent) \Rightarrow \textbf{int}$$
$$withdrawamount(Empty) = 0$$
$$withdrawamount(Cons(withdraw(null, null), h)) =$$
$$withdrawamount(h) + (ready(h) ? take(h) : 0)$$
$$withdrawamount(Cons(e, h)) = withdrawamount(h)$$

In the last clause, e is any *payEvent* not mentioned above.

Due to the introduction of the new attributes, we need to modify the method specification to capture the behavior of the interface. In this example, the method within the `Payment` interface requires modification for the introduction of attribute *withdrawamount*, as illustrated in Listing 12.

Specification(`Payment`) =
({i≥0} **void** deposit(i) {*amount*=**old**(*amount*)+i ∧
                    withdrawamount=**old**(*withdrawamount*)}, ...)

Listing 12. The update `deposit` method specification for the `Payment` interface. The specifications for other methods within the `Payment` interface have also been revised.

For $h : history(saveEvent)$ and $h' : history(payEvent)$, we can formulate the refinement relation as follows:

$$R(h, h') \overset{\text{def}}{\equiv} amount(h) = amount(h') + withdrawamount(h')$$

We generate verification conditions based on **Verification Condition IIR** principle. We first consider the implication between the preconditions of both types, where i serves as the actual parameter of the `deposit` method. The proof seems straightforward: $i \geq 0 \rightarrow i \geq 0$ is trivial. But what about postcondition $amount = \mathbf{old}(amount) + i \rightarrow amount = \mathbf{old}(amount) + i$? We cannot directly prove this due to the attribute $amount$ of the `Saving` history is different from the attribute $amount$ of the `Payment` history, as $amount$ definition given in before. Even though attribute names may be identical, their definitions are specific to and can differ between different histories.

Instead, by de-sugaring and renaming the attribute, we explicitly get the $amount$ of h, which is of type $history(saveEvent)$, and h', which is of type $history(payEvent)$. Since **old** distributes over pure operations, the designation of an attribute with the keyword **old** means to take the attribute of the old history, that is, the history prior to the method call. Thus, the expression $\mathbf{old}(amount(h'))$ is equivalent to $amount(\mathbf{old}(h'))$. We now have to show:

$$amount(h') = amount(\mathbf{old}(h')) + i \rightarrow amount(h) = amount(\mathbf{old}(h)) + i$$

However, the verification condition remains unproven because there is a lack of knowledge about the internal structure of the history and the definition of the attributes. To solve this issue, we use the *refinement relation* which allows us to relate the histories of supertype and subtype, and then we can further relate predicates about the supertype to those about the subtype and vice versa. By eliminating the universal quantified for h and h', we can get the refinement relation for the history in the state where the method call started for free, that is $R(\mathbf{old}(h), \mathbf{old}(h'))$. We then can simply prove this verification condition:

$$
\begin{aligned}
amount(h') = amount(\mathbf{old}(h')) + i \;\wedge \\
withdrawamount(h') = withdrawamount(\mathbf{old}(h')) \wedge \\
amount(h) = amount(h') + withdrawamount(h') \;\wedge \\
amount(\mathbf{old}(h)) = amount(\mathbf{old}(h')) + withdrawamount(\mathbf{old}(h')) \\
\downarrow \\
amount(h) = amount(\mathbf{old}(h)) + i
\end{aligned}
$$

The refinement for interface and class needs to take into account the class invariants. The specific example of interface-class refinement is the precondition of the `withdraw` method of the `Payment` interface and its subclass, the `Debit` class. In this case, the `Debit` class fully inherits from the `Payment` interface. Thus, the refinement relation between them is as follows:

$$R(h, h') \overset{\text{def}}{\equiv} ready(h) = ready(h') \wedge amount(h) = amount(h')$$

The parameter h is an instance of the datatype $history(payEvent)$, and the parameter h' is an instance of the datatype $history(debitEvent)$.

We can derive the following precondition implication from their specifications (Listings 8 and 11) based on **Verfication Condition ICR** principle:

$$ready(h) \wedge ready(h) = ready(h') \wedge amount(h) = amount(h')$$
$$\texttt{balance} \geq 0 \wedge \texttt{balance} = amount(h') \wedge$$
$$\texttt{request} = \texttt{take(h')} \wedge \texttt{balance} \geq \texttt{request}$$
$$\downarrow$$
$$\texttt{balance} \geq \texttt{request} \wedge \texttt{request} \neq -1$$

One can see that only the refinement relation is not sufficient to solve the verification condition (the first line of verification condition). The class invariant of the Debit class contains $\texttt{balance} = amount$ and $\texttt{request} = take$ which relates the attributes $amount$ and $take$ to the fields $\texttt{balance}$ and $\texttt{request}$. By assuming the refinement relation, we also need the class invariant (shown in Listing 11): according to the definition of the attribute, if $ready$ returns true, then $take \neq -1$.

The refinement relation between two classes needs to consider the use of class invariants in both the superclass and the subclass. In the banking example, an invariant property of the Account class is that its balance is always greater or equal to zero. The Credit class allows one to withdraw money even if the balance is negative, so the Credit class cannot be a subclass of the Account class. Conversely, the Debit class inherits invariants from the specification of the Account class and also has its own invariants, as outlined in Listing 11.

In most cases, the designer of the example or system has the flexibility to decide at what level a method should be placed, but it needs to be careful if the subtype wants to be the behavioral subtype. For instance, the Payment interface introduces two new methods: query and withdraw. One potential approach is to define the withdraw method within the Payment interface and introduce the query method exclusively as an addition to the Debit implementation. However, this approach clashes with behavioral subtyping, which requires the implication as follows to hold: $ready \rightarrow \texttt{balance} \geq \texttt{request} \wedge \texttt{request} \neq -1$, but $ready$ cannot be given a sensible meaning at the level of the Payment interface without the query method. Thus, as a designer, we define the query method in the supertype.

From a developer's perspective, another important consideration is how to extend the functionality of a program. For example, with the increasing need for security, the system may require an additional step: entering the pin code to verify whether the person withdrawing money is legitimate. Instead of modifying the existing Payment interface, a new sub-interface, named Security, can be defined. This sub-interface would include a new attribute, pin, designed to capture the entered pin code. Thus, in the query method, the subtype need to add a new precondition to verify the correctness of the pin code. Benefiting from our approach, we do not need to reconstruct abstract functions for each state, but only formulate refinement relations between the new type and its supertypes and subtypes to ensure behavioral subtyping.

We exemplify the method call rule through a client-side example: the verification of the check method, as shown in Listing 13.

```
class ClientExample{
  {true}
  int check(Saving s){ int i = s.getbalance(); return i;}
  {result = s.amount ∧ s.amount = old(s.amount)}

  {j≥0}
  int myAccount(Account a, int j){
  a.deposit(j); int r = check(a); return r;}
  {result = a.amount ∧ a.amount = old(a.amount)+j}}
```

Listing 13. Client code that illustrate the method call rule.

At the beginning of the method, its precondition is assumed. To verify the call to check method, we rely on the specification of the callee, in this case, the Saving interface (with specifications provided in Listing 7). By substituting the implicit receiver **this** with the Saving interface, we can assume the postcondition hold.

$$\{\mathbf{true}\}\ \mathbf{result} = this.\text{check}(\text{Saving s})\ \{\mathbf{result} = s.amount\}$$

The technique for method call verification relies on the method specification, which uses the attributes and fields to describe the behavior of the method. The verification of clients based on those method specifications leaves histories uninterpreted, thereby eliminating the need to prove the correctness of the method's implementation each time the method is called. For myAccount method, the verification of the method call is independent of the implementation of the argument. This means that only the specification given in the Account is accessible (specifications provided in Listing 9). We can prove the postcondition of the myAccount method by referring to the history of the Account class and its definition of the attribute *amount*.

A specific example of method implementation we can consider the deposit method in the Account class, as shown in Listing 14.

```
class Account implements Saving {
balance ≥ 0 ∧ balance = amount, //invariant
{i≥0} void deposit(i){balance=balance+i;}{balance=old(balance)+i}
...}
```

Listing 14. The deposit implementation in the Account class.

One verification condition involves reasoning about the class invariant balance = *amount* should hold before and after the method deposit call. We verify the deposit method is correct with respect to the contract. How can we show the attribute *amount* also changed without knowing the internal structure of the history and the attribute definition? Within the implementing class, the history is defined by the field **this**, which is updated during the method call with a newly created history that involves the new event: the deposit event.

Attributes are used to map the history to a particular value, with the update of the history, the value of the attribute also changed.

For this example, we can establish the update relation $U_m(h, g)$ in terms of the attributes as below. Here the 'old' history is g and the updated history h is replaced by $Cons(deposit(i, null), g)$, then can be established separately as a logical consequence of: $amount(Cons(deposit(i, null), g)) = amount(g) + \texttt{i}$, which directly describes the relation between the updated history and the old one in terms of their sequence structure. This can be verified by unfolding the $amount$ definition. We provide a manual translation as $amount = \mathbf{old}(amount) + \texttt{i}$, so it can be used in the verification condition. One can prove the class invariant by showing that both the class field and attribute increase accordingly.

4   Conclusion

The main contribution of this paper is a Hoare-style proof theory for the specification and verification of the behavioral subtyping relation in terms of histories, allowing consistent program specification at different abstraction levels. We showed how our refinement approach can be effectively employed to rationalize various kinds of refinements in terms of projection relation: from interface to interface, interface to class and class to class. Moreover, we applied our approach to verifying method calls as well as class implementation. Our banking example served as a practical guide, showcasing the value of our approach in realistic scenarios. Although the traditional reasoning approach using abstraction functions can verify class-class refinement, our history-based reasoning approach, based on the refinement relation, is simpler and more general. Additionally, our methodology enables us to reason about interface-based behavioral subtyping, which notably cannot be achieved using the traditional approach. While our discussion is guided by banking example, our approach is applicable to any type hierarchy.

This work simplifies the workflow by clearly distinguishing between the role of the designer of the example, who deals with attributes, and the role of the verifier, who handles verification conditions. This distinction facilitates the verification of complex examples. Designers can not only define attributes but also provide the grounding to confirm the realizability of the theory. The verifier's assumptions are based on the refinement relation provided by the designer, which can be used to prove the verification conditions generated for behavioral subtyping.

The history-based reasoning approach is suitable for method inheritance, method overriding, and methods explicitly defined within the subtype itself [25]. When a method is inherited, the subtype simply inherits the same specification as the method in its supertype. For method overriding, a subtype that overrides its supertype's method must adhere to the behavioral subtyping rule. For method overloading, the method in the subtype may have a different signature compared to the methods of the same name in its supertype. We can treat this as the subtype defining a new method, which is independent of the supertype's method.

Moving forward, our next step is to apply history-based reasoning approach to the verification of widely used software libraries, such as the Java Collection

Framework. Benefiting from our novel approach, we can follow the hierarchy structure to systematically analyze and verify the behavioral subtyping relations between each class and interface.

References

1. AbdelGawad, M.A.: Why Nominal-Typing Matters in OOP (2016). arXiv preprint arXiv:1606.03809
2. Ahrendt, W., Beckert, B., Bubel, R., Hähnle, R., Schmitt, P.H., Ulbrich, M. (eds.): Deductive Software Verification - The KeY Book. LNCS, vol. 10001. Springer (2016)
3. America, P.: Inheritance and subtyping in a parallel object-oriented language. In: Bézivin, J., Hullot, J.-M., Cointe, P., Lieberman, H. (eds.) ECOOP 1987. LNCS, vol. 276, pp. 234–242. Springer, Heidelberg (1987). https://doi.org/10.1007/3-540-47891-4_22
4. America, P.: Designing an object-oriented programming language with behavioural subtyping. In: Foundations of Object-Oriented Languages: REX School/Workshop Noordwijkerhout, The Netherlands, May 28-June 1, 1990 Proceedings. LNCS, vol. 489, pp. 60–90. Springer (1991)
5. Ancona, D., Franceschini, L., Ferrando, A., Mascardi, V.: Rml: theory and practice of a domain specific language for runtime verification. Sci. Comput. Program. **205**, 102610 (2021)
6. Back, R.J., Wright, J.: Refinement Calculus: a Systematic Introduction. Springer Science & Business Media (2012)
7. Back, R.: On correct refinement of programs. J. Comput. Syst. Sci. **23**(1), 49–68 (1981)
8. Bian, J., Hiep, H.A., de Boer, F.S.: History-based reasoning about behavioral subtyping: proof fiels. Zenodo (2024). https://doi.org/10.5281/zenodo.10998227
9. Bian, J., Hiep, H.A., de Boer, F.S., de Gouw, S.: Integrating ADTs in KeY and their application to history-based reasoning. In: Formal Methods: 24th International Symposium, FM 2021, Virtual Event, November 20–26, 2021, Proceedings 24. LNCS, vol. 13047, pp. 255–272. Springer (2021)
10. Bruce, K.B., Wegner, P.: An algebraic model of sybtypes in object-oriented languages (draft). ACM Sigplan Notices **21**(10), 163–172 (1986)
11. Bubel, R., Gurov, D., Hähnle, R., Scaletta, M.: Trace-based deductive verification. In: LPAR, pp. 73–95 (2023)
12. Chen, F., Roşu, G.: Mop: an efficient and generic runtime verification framework. In: Proceedings of the 22nd Annual ACM SIGPLAN Conference on Object-Oriented Programming Systems, Languages and Applications, pp. 569–588 (2007)
13. Cheon, Y., Perumandla, A.: Specifying and checking method call sequences of java programs. Software Qual. J. **15**, 7–25 (2007)
14. Colombo, C., Pace, G.J., Schneider, G.: Larva–safer monitoring of real-time java programs (tool paper). In: 2009 Seventh IEEE International Conference on Software Engineering and Formal Methods, pp. 33–37. IEEE (2009)
15. Dhara, K.K., Leavens, G.T.: Forcing behavioral subtyping through specification inheritance. In: Proceedings of IEEE 18th International Conference on Software Engineering, pp. 258–267. IEEE (1996)
16. Goldsack, S., Kent, S.: A type-theoretic basis for an object-oriented refinement calculus. In: Formal Methods and Object Technology, pp. 317–335. Springer (1996)

17. Hiep, H.-D.A., Bian, J., de Boer, F.S., de Gouw, S.: History-based specification and verification of java collections in key. In: Dongol, B., Troubitsyna, E. (eds.) IFM 2020. LNCS, vol. 12546, pp. 199–217. Springer, Cham (2020). https://doi.org/10.1007/978-3-030-63461-2_11

18. Leavens, G.T.: Introduction to the literature on object-oriented design, programming, and languages. ACM SIGPLAN OOPS Messenger **2**(4), 40–53 (1991)

19. Leavens, G.T.: JML's rich, inherited specifications for behavioral subtypes. In: Formal Methods and Software Engineering: 8th International Conference on Formal Engineering Methods, ICFEM 2006, Macao, China, November 1–3, 2006. Proceedings 8. LNCS, vol. 4260, pp. 2–34. Springer (2006)

20. Leavens, G.T., Naumann, D.A.: Behavioral subtyping, specification inheritance, and modular reasoning. ACM Trans. Program. Lang. Syst. (TOPLAS) **37**(4), 1–88 (2015)

21. Leavens, G.T., Poll, E., Clifton, C., Cheon, Y., Ruby, C., Cok, D., Müller, P., Kiniry, J., Chalin, P., Zimmerman, D.M., et al.: JML reference manual (2008)

22. Leavens, G.T., Weihl, W.E.: Reasoning about object-oriented programs that use subtypes. In: Proceedings of the European Conference on Object-Oriented Programming on Object-Oriented Programming Systems, Languages, and Applications, pp. 212–223 (1990)

23. Leavens, G.T., Weihl, W.E.: Specification and verification of object-oriented programs using supertype abstraction. Acta Informatica **32**(8), 705–778 (1995)

24. Liskov, B.H., Wing, J.M.: A behavioral notion of subtyping. ACM Trans. Program. Lang. Syst. (TOPLAS) **16**(6), 1811–1841 (1994)

25. Meyer, B.: Object-Oriented Software Construction, vol. 2. Prentice Hall, Englewood Cliffs (1997)

26. Morgan, C.: Programming from Specifications. Prentice-Hall Inc. (1990)

27. Müller, P. (ed.): Modular Specification and Verification of Object-Oriented Programs. LNCS, vol. 2262. Springer, Heidelberg (2002). https://doi.org/10.1007/3-540-45651-1

28. Müller, P., Poetzsch-Heffter, A., Leavens, G.T.: Modular invariants for layered object structures. Sci. Comput. Program. **62**(3), 253–286 (2006)

29. Nipkow, T., Wenzel, M., Paulson, L.C. (eds.): Isabelle/HOL. LNCS, vol. 2283. Springer, Heidelberg (2002). https://doi.org/10.1007/3-540-45949-9

30. Parkinson, M.J.: Local reasoning for Java. University of Cambridge, Computer Laboratory, Tech. rep. (2005)

31. Pierik, C.: Validation Techniques for Object-Oriented Proof Outlines. Ph.D. thesis, Utrecht University (2006)

32. Reus, B.: Modular semantics and logics of classes. In: Baaz, M., Makowsky, J.A. (eds.) CSL 2003. LNCS, vol. 2803, pp. 456–469. Springer, Heidelberg (2003). https://doi.org/10.1007/978-3-540-45220-1_37

33. Snyder, A.: Encapsulation and inheritance in object-oriented programming languages. SIGPLAN Not. **21**(11), 38–45 (1986)

Switched Systems in Coq for Modeling Periodic Controllers

Andrei Aleksandrov[1,2]([⊠])[iD] and Kim Völlinger[2][iD]

[1] Fraunhofer Institute for Open Communication Systems FOKUS, Berlin, Germany
[2] Technische Universität Berlin, Berlin, Germany
`andrei.aleksandrov@fokus.fraunhofer.de`, `voellinger@tu-berlin.de`

Abstract. Switched systems (i.e. systems switching between a finite set of continuous systems) are an important subclass of hybrid systems, expressive enough for a wide range of systems. This paper introduces the first formalization of switched systems in the proof assistant Coq – a step towards building verified controllers in Coq. We define switched systems and the trajectories they induce while prioritizing verification. Moreover, we offer a specialized formalization for the efficient modeling of periodic controllers. Finally, we illustrate the formalization by modeling and verifying an air filter.

Keywords: Switched Systems · Control Theory · Interactive Theorem Proving · Coq · Modeling · Verification

1 Introduction

A switched system consists of two ingredients: (1) a finite set of continuous-time subsystems called *modes* (e.g. a car's acceleration), and (2) a discrete procedure switching between the modes called *switching signal* (e.g. going from acceleration to braking) [15]. Switched systems are an important subclass of hybrid systems, as they are simple and yet expressive enough for a wide range of systems. As such, they are studied abundantly in domains such as energy systems, unmanned marine vehicles, epidemics, chemical processes or drones.

In this paper, we present the first formalization of switched systems in the proof assistant Coq [30] – a step towards building verified controllers and safe cyber-physical systems in Coq. In particular, we define switched systems and their induced trajectories in Coq while prioritizing verification. The trajectories are expressed as ordinary differential equations (ODEs). We consider the exact computation of ODE solutions using ODE solvers for reasoning. That is why, the formalization incorporates a (dependent) type called `ModeSolver`, specifically designed to facilitate the verification of ODE solvers. The `ModeSolver` acts like a function contract, enforcing any implementation of an ODE solver to yield valid solutions. As a matter of proving techniques, we examine induction on trajectories in Coq. Further, for the pivotal subclass of periodic controllers, we present a specialized formalization for efficient modeling. Finally, we illustrate

© The Author(s), under exclusive license to Springer Nature Switzerland AG 2025
C. Anutariya and M. M. Bonsangue (Eds.): ICTAC 2024, LNCS 15373, pp. 350–367, 2025.
https://doi.org/10.1007/978-3-031-77019-7_20

the formalization on the example of an air filter for which we verify that it keeps the dust level below a certain threshold.

To our knowledge, only a single formalization specifically dedicated to switched systems exists in any proof assistant [29], namely KeYmaera X [13]. We give a detailed comparison in Sect. 5.

Contributions. To sum up, this paper presents the following contributions with the corresponding Coq code available on GitHub[1]:

1. an inductive definition of switched systems (Sect. 3.2);
2. a specialized formalization of switched systems to ease the modeling of periodic controllers (Sect. 3.3);
3. as a proof technique, induction on the trajectories switched systems induce, and the dependent type, ModeSolver to facilitate the verification of ODE solvers for trajectories (Sect. 3.4); and
4. as a showcase of the formalization, the modelling and verification of an air filter (Sect. 4).

2 Preliminaries

2.1 Proof Assistant Coq

We use the proof assistant Coq (version 8.15.2) that provides a functional language with dependent types for proving and programming [30]. We employ the library Coquelicot [7] (version 3.4.0) with Riemann integration (RInt), a matrix formalization, and vectors colvec [3] for real analysis. Coq's axiomatic reals are tailored to proving with built-in proof automation, e.g. the tautology solvers lra and nra for linear and nonlinear real arithmetic.

2.2 Switched Systems

A switched system consists of finitely many continuous subsystems, represented as modes, and a discrete procedure switching between them, represented as a switching signal:

Definition 1 (Switched System [15]**).** Let $M = \{0, \ldots, p\}$ with $p \in \mathbb{N}$ be a set of *mode indices*, $n \in \mathbb{N}$ the dimension of the system, $f_i(x) : \mathbb{R}^n \to \mathbb{R}^n$ for $i \in M$ the *modes*, and $\sigma : D \to M$ the *switching signal* with domain $D \subseteq \mathbb{R}$. A *switched system* is a collection of *modes* f_i together with a left-continuous piecewise constant *switching signal* σ.[2]

---

[1] https://github.com/verinncoq/switched-systems-coq.
[2] Textbook definitions of switching signals [15] are mostly right-continuous. This difference does not affect the resulting trajectory but simplifies technical proofs in Coq.

Trajectories. A switched system induces several *trajectories*, representing the behavior of this switched system, which reduces to a unique trajectory given an initial point and time:

Definition 2 ((Carathéodory) Trajectory [15]**).** For an initial point $x_0 \in \mathbb{R}^n$ and time $t_0 \in \mathbb{R}$, a switching system defines a *trajectory* $x(t)$ by the following equation: $x(t) = x_0 + \int_{t_0}^{t} f_{\sigma(t)}(x(t))dt$.

Note that for some systems, a trajectory may diverge to infinity in a finite time. This phenomenon is called *blow-up* of a trajectory.

Switched Signals as Sequences. Any switching signal $\sigma(t)$ is representable by a (possibly infinite) sequence $S_\sigma = [\ldots, (t_{-1}, m_{-1}), (t_0, m_0), (t_1, m_1), \ldots]$ of pairs (t_i, m_i) of a time t_i and mode m_i with S_σ being sorted in an ascending order by time t_i [33]. Given S_σ, we can reconstruct a switching signal $\sigma(t)$ by the following rule: $\sigma(t) = m_i$, if $t_i \leq t < t_{i+1}$. We assume the domain of a switching signal to be restricted from the left (i.e. $D = [t_0, \infty)$) such that $S_\sigma = [(t_0, m_0), (t_1, m_1), \ldots]$. We call a pair $(t_i, m_i) \in S_\sigma$ a *switch*, and denote a subsequence of switches $(t_i, m_i) \in S_\sigma$ with $t_i < t$ as $S_\sigma(t) = [(t_0, m_0), \ldots, (t_k, m_k)]$. Note that in order to truthfully represent a switching signal, a sequence has to at least capture all mode changes. Further, each switching signal can be represented by several sequences. Such a sequence can have an infinite amount of switches in finite time, for example $S_\sigma^n = (\sum_{i=1}^{n} \frac{1}{2^i}, m_{(n \mod 2)})$ for $S_\sigma = [S_\sigma^1, S_\sigma^2, \ldots]$ contains infinitely many switches in the time interval $[0, 2]$.

ODE Solvers. Note that between mode changes (i.e. an interval $t \in (t_i, t_{i+1}) \subseteq \mathbb{R}$ such that $\sigma(t) = c$ is constant), the trajectory equation reduces to an ODE system $x'(t) = f_c(x(t))$ with $t \in (t_i, t_{i+1})$. ODE solvers are often employed to compute a trajectory in this case, enabling computation of and reasoning about trajectories. There are several solving techniques for different types of ODEs that can be implemented in a solver, e.g. linear ODEs [18].

Periodic Controllers. An important subclass of switched systems are periodically triggered controllers operating in a continuous system. A periodic controller can be represented by a function $c(t_i)$ returning a mode index m_i every Δ_t time unit. Hence, such a controller produces a sequence $S_\sigma = \{(t_0, m_0), (t_0 + \Delta_t, c(t_0 + \Delta_t)), (t_0 + \Delta_t \cdot 2, c(t_0 + \Delta_t \cdot 2)), \ldots\}$, representing a switching signal with the domain $D = [t_0, \infty)$. The continuous system in which the controller acts is represented as modes. Periodic controllers are also known as *fixed dwell time systems* [16].

3 Results of the Coq Formalization of Switched Systems

For the Coq code of this Section, see file switched_systems.v. We present the formalization of switched systems in Coq by starting with a running example (Sect. 3.1), followed by the definition of switched systems such that induction is enabled (Sect. 3.2). Further, we propose a specialization of switched systems tailored to periodic controllers (Sect. 3.3). We follow up by a recursive definition of trajectories for which again induction is supported (Sect. 3.4) and a dependent type that facilitates verifying ODE solvers for trajectories (Sect. 3.4). In the follow-up Sect. 4, we showcase the formalization on a more elaborated example than the running example of this Section.

3.1   Running Example

We introduce a switched system that develops along two modes, representing drifts in opposite directions each with constant speed. We denote the system's trajectory as $x(t) \in \mathbb{R}^2$ and define two modes:

$$f_0(x) = \begin{bmatrix} 2 \\ 1 \end{bmatrix} \text{ and } f_1(x) = \begin{bmatrix} -2 \\ -1 \end{bmatrix}$$

The controller's task then is to keep the system state within a cycle while being exposed to the side drifts. More concretely, the controller brings the trajectory as close to the surface $x_2 + 2x_1 = 0$ as possible, realized by switching between the two modes:

$$control([x_1, x_2]^T) = \begin{cases} f_1 & x_2 + 2x_1 > 0 \\ f_0 & x_2 + 2x_1 \leq 0 \end{cases}$$

We assume the controller to be periodically triggered and revisit this example once we introduced the specialized formalization for periodic controllers in Sect. 3.3.

3.2   Enabling Induction on Switched Systems

We define a `SwitchedSystem` consisting of modes and a switching signal:

```
Structure SwitchedSystem : Type := BuildSwitchedSystem {
  dimension: nat;
  modes: list (colvec dimension → colvec dimension);
  switching_signal: InductiveSwitchingSignal;
  ...}.
```

To enhance the readability, we omit some details in the shown code (e.g. propositions to be proven for a correct-by-construction instance) and indicate the absence by three dots. For a `SwitchedSystem`, a user is required to prove that a `switching_signal` always selects a valid mode.

We enable induction on switching signals by enforcing that in any interval $(-\infty, t] \subset \mathbb{R}$, there is a finite number of switches, and further by using the sequence representation of a switching signal S_σ that supports induction over its members:

```
Structure InductiveSwitchingSignal := BuildSwitchingSignal {
  is_switch_descriptor: (R * nat) → Prop;
```

```
switch_count: R → nat;
compute_prev_switch: R → (R * nat);
...}.
```

A user is required to define the following three functions: the predicate is
_switch_descriptor stating that a switch (t_i, m_i) is contained in the sequence
S_σ allowing for quantification over switches, the function switch_count return-
ing $|S_\sigma(t)|$ for each input time $t \in \mathbb{R}$, and the function compute_prev_switch
computing a previous switch $(t_i, m_i) \in S_\sigma$ if it exists. For simplification, we omit
five propositions from the structure that ensure the consistent interplay between
these three functions. A user must prove that no two switches happen at the
same time, that switch_count increases by exactly one with each switch and
remains constant if a switch does not appear, that the function compute_prev
_switch behaves functionally correct and that a starting time t_0 exists with no
switch appearing before it.

Further, the function switches_until computes the sequence $S_\sigma(t)$ of all
switches before t using a helper function generate_switches:

```
Fixpoint generate_switches (count: nat) (t:R) (s: SwitchedSystem) :=
  let prev_switch_f := (compute_prev_switch (switching_signal s)) in
  match count with
  | 0 ⇒ [] | S n ⇒ let (t_prev, m_prev) := prev_switch_f t in
  (t_prev, m_prev) :: generate_switches n t_prev s
  end.
```

```
Definition switches_until (t: R) (s: SwitchedSystem) :=
  generate_switches ((switch_count (switching_signal s)) t) t s.
```

Crucially for reasoning, the fixpoint generate_switches enables induction
on switch_count(t) which is not possible on real-valued time itself. Thus, general results about switched systems can be proven by induction using this fixpoint.

Discussion. We enabled induction over switched systems by a restriction to
finite switches in any interval $(-\infty, t]$, and by the fixpoint computation of $S_\sigma(t)$.
The imposed restriction on switching signals prevents us from encoding some
switched systems. An extension to infinite switches in finite time can be achieved
by using a co-inductive type with the disadvantage that the proof complexity
would increase.

3.3   Periodic Controllers

A pivotal subclass of switched systems are controllers that are periodically triggered and that operate in a continuous system. For efficient modeling of this
important subclass, we present a specialized representation of a periodic controller:

```
Structure PeriodicController := MakePeriodicController {
  control_func: R → nat;
```

```
period: R;
period_greater_zero: period > 0;
start: R; }.
```

The control function `control_func` represents a time-dependent decision procedure triggered at `start` for the first time and then periodically after each `period`. A function `periodic_controller_to_switching_signal` then converts each periodic controller into an instance of an `InductiveSwitchingSignal`. The structure `PeriodicController` simplifies the construction of switching signals; however, a simple proof is required that the control function `control_func` returns a valid mode index.

A benefit of using `PeriodicController` though is the reduction of the overall proof burden. For each instance of a switching signal, five proofs must be supplied to verify it being correct-by-construction[3]. In contrast, for periodic controllers, none of these proofs is needed.

Modeling the Running Example as a Periodic Controller. We model the modes of the running example (see Sect. 3.1) as functions over column vectors `colvec`:

```
Definition mode0 (x: colvec 2) := [[2], [1]].
Definition mode1 (x: colvec 2) := [[−2], [−1]].
```

Further, we encode the following control law into a switching signal:

```
Definition example_control_func (current_x: colvec 2): nat :=
  let x1 := coeff_colvec 0 current_x 0 in
  let x2 := coeff_colvec 0 current_x 1 in
  match cond_positivity (x2 + 2 * x1) with
  | true  ⇒ 1%nat
  | false ⇒ 0%nat
  end.
```

Note that the function `cond_positivity` checks whether its real-valued argument is greater or equal to zero. The control function is assumed to be triggered periodically. We construct the periodic controller, convert it to a switching signal, and subsequently, define the switched system:

```
Parameter observable_trajectory: R → colvec 2.
```

```
Definition example_controller :=
  MakePeriodicController
    (fun t ⇒ example_control_func (observable_trajectory t))
    example_period example_period_greater_zero example_t0.
```

```
Definition example_switching_signal :=
  periodic_controller_to_switching_signal example_controller.
```

```
Definition example_switched_system :=
```

---

[3] These proofs result out of parts of the definition of `InductiveSwitchingSignal` that are omitted in this paper.

```
BuildSwitchedSystem 2
  example_modes
  example_switching_signal
  example_signal_selects_modes.
```

For the construction, we have to take into account that the controller depends on the system's trajectory which in turn does not exist unless an instance of `SwitchedSystem` is constructed. The dependency of a switching signal on the resulting trajectory is a general challenge of switching systems independent from the chosen formalization. That is why, we assume a trajectory `observable _trajectory`, and, in the following Section, replace it by the actual trajectory.

Discussion. A periodic controller can be conveniently represented as a switching signal, and its construction is less tedious in Coq than the construction of a generic switching signal, as the correct-by-construction proof burden is reduced. The formalization applies to systems where (1) the underlying dynamic system is purely continuous with (2) a parameter set from a discrete domain controlled by (3) a Coq-representable control function $c : \mathbb{R} \to M$ triggered periodically.

3.4 Trajectories of Switched Systems in Coq

We turn to a switched system's trajectory expressed as a sum of integrals corresponding to ODEs. We start by examining different real number libraries we can choose from in Coq and their impact on ODE solving.

On the Choice of Reals in Coq. When selecting a library for real numbers in Coq, there is a compromise to choose. While MathComp-Analysis [2] is a new library that supports Lebesgue integration, it lacks automation and is difficult to use for those unfamiliar with measure theory. Coquelicot [7] is working with the simpler Riemann integration and provides not only many lemmas for integrals but also a derivation tactic that partially automates proofs with integrals. As a drawback, Coquelicot lacks a basic ODE formalization, which in turn can be found then in CoRN [19]. CoRN introduces its own type of constructive reals though which comes with some hurdles, especially in the construction of discontinuous functions that are necessary for switching signals [8].

In the end, we choose Coquelicot due to its compatibility with the standard library, and its diverse lemmas and partial automation. By that choice, we loose access to the Picard-Lindelöf theorem [19] that guarantees the existence of ODE solutions. To circumvent this problem, we introduce a dependent type, namely `ModeSolver`, that is required to provide a solution for a trajectory.

Mode Solvers. For a mode $f_i : \mathbb{R}^n \to \mathbb{R}^n$, the induced ODE system is $x'(t) = f_i(x(t))$. By considering an initial point x^* and time t^*, the ODE system transforms to the integral $x(t) = x^* + \int_{t^*}^{t} f_i(x(t))dt$, representing the part without mode changes of the trajectory during an interval (t^*, t_{end}). In Coq, this integral for a `mode`, an initial time `t_from` and an initial point `x_t_from` reads as:

```
solution t =
    Mplus (RInt_multi (fun tau ⇒ mode (solution tau)) t_from t) x_t_from.
```

We define a predicate is_mode_solution that is satisfied if the solution is an actual ODE solution, and a dependent type ModeSolver working as a function contract by enforcing the existence of an ODE solver for each mode. Each instance can encapsulate a different solver, e.g. one for linear ODEs [18]. Once a solver is implemented in Coq, the ModeSolver type enforces specific proof obligations. If these are proven, an instance of ModeSolver is verified to correctly solve the according ODE systems. Hence, the ModeSolver type does not take away the proof burden from a user, but structures the verification of any ODE solver in a canonical way.

Importantly, the ModeSolver type allows us to reason about trajectories even if an ODE solution is infeasible to compute, as the existence of a mode solver can be assumed as part of the verification hypothesis. Further, the ModeSolver type allows for trajectories to be expressed as fixpoints which in turn enables induction on trajectories.

Mode Solver for the Running Example. The simplicity of the running example allows for a simple ODE solver in Coq, as the two solutions for the ODE systems induced by the modes are:

$$x_{f_0}(t) = x_0 + \begin{bmatrix} 2t \\ t \end{bmatrix}, x_{f_1}(t) = x_0 + \begin{bmatrix} -2t \\ t \end{bmatrix}$$

With x_{f_0} working analogously, we encode x_{f_1} in Coq and construct a solver:

```
Definition mode1_solution (t: R) (x_init: colvec 2): colvec 2 :=
    [[−2∗t + coeff_colvec 0 x_init 0], [−t + coeff_colvec 0 x_init 1]].
...
Definition example_mode_solver_implementation
    (mode_idx: nat)
    (t_from: R)
    (x_t_from: colvec 2): R → colvec 2 :=
    match mode_idx with
    | 0 ⇒ (fun t ⇒ mode0_solution (t − t_from) x_t_from)
    | 1 ⇒ (fun t ⇒ mode1_solution (t − t_from) x_t_from)
    | _ ⇒ (fun t ⇒ null_vector 2)
    end.
```

We prove that the encoded ODE solutions are correct, mostly by solving integrals in Coq with lemmas from the Coquelicot library:

```
Theorem example_mode_solver_correct:
forall mode_idx t_from x_t_from,
is_mode_solution example_switched_system mode_idx t_from x_t_from
    (example_mode_solver_implementation mode_idx t_from x_t_from).
```

Using this theorem, we construct an instance of the ModeSolver type:

```
Definition example_mode_solver: ModeSolver example_switched_system :=
        exist _ example_mode_solver_implementation example_mode_solver_correct.
```

Computation of Trajectories. Given a switched system s and a `solver`, we can construct the system's trajectory by using its switches. By Definition 2, the trajectory is the integral $x(t) = x_0 + \int_{t_0}^{t} f_{\sigma(t)} x(t) dt$. Using the subsequence $S_\sigma(t) = \{(t_0, m_0), \ldots, (t_k, m_k)\}$, we can rewrite the trajectory as the sum

$$x(t) = x_0 + \sum_{i=0}^{k-1} \int_{t_i}^{t_{i+1}} f_{m_i}(x(t)) dt + \int_{t_k}^{t} f_{m_k}(x(t)) dt$$

We use this rewriting to define the trajectory as a function `trajectory` that computes the last integral in the equation above and calls a recursive function `trajectory_on_switches` to compute the general sum in the trajectory equation using a mode solver. The function `trajectory_on_switches` is a fixpoint operating on a list received from the fixpoint `switches_until`. We previously discussed this function for its crucial role in reasoning, as it enables induction. Hence, reasoning by induction is preserved. Conceptually, the sum is split into two functions as follows:

$$x(t) = \overbrace{x_0 + \underbrace{\sum_{i=0}^{k-1} \int_{t_i}^{t_{i+1}} f_{m_i}(x(t)) dt}_{\text{trajectory\_on\_switches (switches\_until } t)} + \int_{t_k}^{t} f_{m_k}(x(t)) dt}^{\text{trajectory } t}$$

Note that in the case when a trajectory blow-up happens, a valid trajectory would not exist as the integral in the Definition 2 would diverge. As defined in Coquelicot, the result of a diverging integral is always zero. This discrepancy can be mitigated in future works.

Computation of the Trajectory of the Running Example. For illustration, we express the value of the trajectory at a time t for the running example:

```
trajectory example_switched_system initial_point example_mode_solver t
```

Induction on Trajectories. Induction on trajectories is enabled by the recursive fixpoint `trajectory_on_switches`. However, for a induction step, it is convenient to convert `trajectory_on_switches` back to `trajectory`. Hence, to make induction proofs more feasible, we prove the lemma `trajectory_induction_lemma`:

```
Lemma trajectory_induction_lemma:
...
trajectory_on_switches s (switches_until t_next s) initial_point mode_solver
= trajectory s initial_point mode_solver t.
```

Importantly, this lemma only holds if t and t_next are times of mode changes with no other mode change existing between them. Mathematically speaking, this lemma states the following for $(t_i, m_i) \in S_\sigma$:

$$x(t_k) = \underbrace{x_0 + \sum_{i=0}^{k-1} \int_{t_i}^{t_{i+1}} f_{m_i}(x(t))dt}_{\text{trajectory\_on\_switches (switches\_until } t_{k+1})} =$$

$$\underbrace{\underbrace{x_0 + \sum_{i=0}^{k-2} \int_{t_i}^{t_{i+1}} f_{m_i}(x(t))dt}_{\text{trajectory\_on\_switches (switches\_until } t_k)} + \int_{t_{k-1}}^{t_k} f_{m_k}(x(t))dt}_{\text{trajectory } t_k}$$

Verification of the Running Example. For the running example, we show by induction that the trajectory is periodic, starting at the initial point $x_0 = [1, 0.5]^T$, and use the trajectory at $t \in (-\infty, 2]$ as a base case for induction:

```
Definition initial_point: colvec 2 := [[1], [0.5]].
```

```
Theorem trajectory_until_0:
  forall t, (t < 0) →
  trajectory switched_example initial_point example_mode_solver t
    = initial_point.
```

```
Theorem trajectory_0_1:
  forall t, let traj_f :=
    trajectory example_switched_system initial_point example_mode_solver in
    observable_trajectory = traj_f →
    (0 <= t <= 1) → traj_f t = [[−2 ∗ t + 1], [−t + 0.5]].
```

```
Theorem trajectory_1_2:
  forall t, let traj_t :=
    trajectory example_switched_system initial_point example_mode_solver in
    observable_trajectory = traj_t →
    (1 < t <= 2) → traj_t t = [[2 ∗ t − 3], [t − 1.5]].
```

Note that the assumption observable_trajectory = traj_f in each theorem fixes the value of the assumed parameter to the actual trajectory of the switched system. All three proofs involve unfolding definitions of the trajectory, using the mode solver, and applying tactics for real numbers. Subsequently, we verify that the controller moves the system state periodically between two endpoints of the cycle:

```
Theorem example_trajectory_cycle:
  forall i,
    let traj_t := trajectory example_switched_system
          initial_point example_mode_solver in
    observable_trajectory = traj_t →
    (traj_t (INR (2 ∗ i)%nat) = initial_point ∧
     traj_t (INR (2 ∗ i + 1)%nat) = limit_cycle_point).
```

We prove this theorem by induction on i. Note that i is a natural number and must be converted to a real using the INR function. For i = 0, we use trajectory_0_1 and trajectory_1_2. The induction hypothesis then assumes the system state to be in the trajectory cycle for times 2 * i and 2 * i + 1. For the induction step, we use the trajectory_induction_lemma apart from the induction hypothesis, and finish up by unfolding solvers and solving the resulting equations.

Discussion. The behavior of a switched system is described by trajectories that depend on modes encoding the continuous dynamics. ODE solvers typed by ModeSolver represent verified solutions of ODE systems and can be instantiated for ODE systems using any existing algorithm or known solution. Given a mode solver, we can compute trajectories in Coq. Further, induction on trajectories is enabled by fixpoints throughout the formalization and additionally supported by the lemma trajectory_induction_lemma.

With the running example, we demonstrated that by using induction we reduced a proof about the system behavior for all $t \in R$ to two main cases with proofs about two subsets of the trajectory. The first being for $t \in (-\infty, \ldots, 2]$ and the second for $t \in [2 \cdot (i+1), \ldots, 2 \cdot (i+1) + 1]$. Due to the simple dynamics of the running example, we could create a complete mode solver and use it to prove both cases. Additionally, we showed that controllers can exhibit trajectory-dependent behavior by assuming observable trajectories and later on replace them with the actual trajectories.

4 Example: Modeling and Verifying an Air Filter

We model a controller for an air filter and verify that it keeps the pollutants concentration below a certain threshold.

4.1 Modeling of an Air Filter

An air filter reduces the concentration of pollutants in the air, as used for improving the air quality indoors [5] or preventing virus outbreaks in hospitals [22]. The code for this example is in the file air_filter.v. As a technical remark, in the following formalization, we use the functions toReal and toColvec for the conversion between reals and column vectors of length one, i.e. scalars.

First, we model pollutants in a room as presented in [11] but deviate by summarizing parameters:

```
Definition air_filter_model (C: colvec 1) (FullOutflow: R): colvec 1
   := toColvec (Inflow − FullOutflow * toReal C).
```

The concentration of pollutants in a room is proportional to the Inflow of pollutants, which is assumed to be constant, and inversely proportional to the FullOutflow ratio multiplied with the current pollutant concentration C. We split FullOutflow into Outflow and Filtered pollutants, and construct two modes for when the filter is turned on or off:

```
Definition mode_filter_off (C: colvec 1): colvec 1
    := air_filter_model C Outflow.
Definition mode_filter_on (C: colvec 1): colvec 1
    := air_filter_model C (Outflow + Filtered).
```

Inflow, Outflow and Filtered are assumed to be strictly positive. The core of the periodic air filter controller is the following function:

```
Definition air_filter_controller_func (C: colvec 1): nat :=
    if cond_positivity (Target − toReal C) then 0 else 1 .
```

The controller receives the parameter Target, representing an allowed maximum concentration of pollutants in the air. If the concentration gets too high, the controller turns the filter on. Otherwise the filter is turned off to save energy. The controller is formalized as a PeriodicController that is periodically triggered every 0.1 time unit.

4.2   Verification of an Air Filter

In the following, we prove that the air filter has an *invariant region* that the trajectory of pollutant concentration will not leave. To be able to reason about the trajectories, we first develop a ModeSolver for the filter's modes by encoding and verifying a solution for the ODE system induced by the air_filter_model:

```
Definition general_mode_solution (t: R) (t_init: R) (C_init: colvec 1)
    (FullOutflow: R) : colvec 1 := toColvec ((
      (toReal C_init − Inflow/FullOutflow)/ exp (− FullOutflow * t_init )) *
            exp (− FullOutflow * t) + (Inflow/FullOutflow)).
```

Further, we introduce the assumption that the filter actually has the physical ability to reach the Target:

```
Hypothesis (Hfilter_useful: Inflow / (Outflow + Filtered) <= Target).
```

We then define the invariant region of interest as follows:

```
Definition in_invariant_region (x: colvec 1) : Prop :=
    toReal x <= toReal (mode_off_solution period 0 (toColvec Target)).
```

The definition states the pollutant concentration to be bounded from above by a value derived from the following situation. Assuming the concentration is exactly Target, the controller decides to disable the filter and follow mode _filter_off for one period (0.1 time units). The concentration reached after this period is the upper bound for pollutant concentration. Finally, we verify the air filter by proving the following theorem in Coq:

```
Theorem air_filter_keeps_concentration:
    forall C_init, let filter_traj_t :=
      trajectory air_filter_switched_system C_init air_filter_mode_solver in
        Cobserved = filter_traj_t → in_invariant_region C_init →
          forall t, t > 0 → in_invariant_region (filter_traj_t t).
```

The theorem states that if the initial pollutant concentration C_init is in the invariant region then the entire trajectory of the system is in the invariant region. Note that Cobserved expresses the controller dependency on the observable concentration trajectory. The proof of the theorem is structured by lemmas in_invariant_region_mode_off and in_invariant_region_mode_on prove necessary conditions for the system modes to stay in the invariant region for a single period.

Further, the lemma air_filter_switches_invariant lifts the results from a single-period lemma stating that all switches lie in the invariant region. The proof is done by applying trajectory_induction_lemma and relating controller decisions with the behavior of the trajectory in a single period in the induction step. The proof of the theorem itself extends the statement of air_filter _switches_invariant from switches only to the entire trajectory.

Discussion. The example of the air filter showcases that we can model and verify controllers in low-dimensional systems with simple mode solutions. The existing tactics and theories in Coq already allow for proofs that involve non-trivial real-valued algebraic expressions with integrals and exponential functions. The proof scripts of this example are still unnecessarily lengthy due to a lack of automation – a direction of future improvements.

5   Related Work

Hybrid systems – a superclass of switched systems – have a long history of formal verification, focusing on properties such as decidability [23], stability [9] or reachability [4] and on verification techniques such as model checking [12] or deductive verification in proof assistants, e.g. KeYmaera X [13,29], Isabelle [10], Event-B [20] or Coq [26,27]. Switched systems, as a subclass of hybrid systems, have a large body of research in the area of control theory [32]. We are not aware of any formalization of switched systems in the proof assistant Coq. Notably, there is a formalization in Coq of hybrid systems based on the Temporal Logic of Actions [26]. In contrast to our contribution, this formalization considers discrete-time systems, while this paper's focus is strictly on continuous-time models. To the best of our knowledge, only a single formalization specifically dedicated to switched systems exists in any proof assistant [29], namely KeYmaera X [13].

Comparison with the Switched System Formalization in KeYmaera X. We highlight significant aspects that differentiate the presented formalization from the one in KeYmaera X:

1. **Formalizing Switched Systems.** As a foundation, KeYmaera X implements differential dynamic logic to model hybrid systems in general, and their subclass switched systems in particular. Basing the conceptually simpler switched systems on differential dynamic logic allows them to be part of the eco-system of KeYmaera X. As a consequence, the representation of

switched systems deviates significantly from their classic representation in control theory. For example, KeYmaera X does not have a concept of a switching signal and uses ODE evolution domains instead. To help users to model their switched systems, KeYmaera X provides a separate interface allowing users to enter modes with a DSL for describing switching behaviors.

In contrast, this paper's formalization evolves around the classical textbook definitions of switched systems [15]. For instance, by removing the technical details tailored to verification in Coq from the type `SwitchedSystem` such as the correct-by-construction proof obligations, the type resolves to a list of modes together with a switching signal – a direct implementation of Definition 1. The encoding of trajectories, as a sum of integrals, is easily traced back to Definition 2.

2. **Reasoning on Switched Systems.** The two formalization approaches come with different means of reasoning on switched systems. KeYmaera X, as a special purpose proof assistant for hybrid systems, offers inductive reasoning with differential invariants and ghosts. The switched systems formalization profits from the general reasoning techniques in KeYmaera X.

This paper's formalization offers inductive reasoning and profits from Coq's built-in proof automation, e.g. on real arithmetic by the tactics `lra` and `nra` as well as `auto_derive` for integrals, enabling the verification of switched systems such as the illustrated air filter. However, as discussed as part of future work (Sect. 6), more proof automation tailored to switched systems is desirable. The most popular reasoning method for (stable) switched systems, applied when computing ODE solutions is hard, is the Lyapunov method. For purely continuous systems, Lyapunov functions are already formalized in Coq [27] but need to be extended to serve the presented formalization, following another conceptual direction for reasoning techniques than KeYmaera X.

3. **Reduced Trust Base.** Both proof assistants, KeYmaera X and Coq, come with a small trust base (i.e. the unverified code base) and are considered trustworthy tools. However, the two switched system formalizations differ in their trust base. KeYmaera X implements differential dynamic logic with a small base of axioms (relying on definitions of ODEs and real numbers), proven on paper and confirmed in several interactive theorem provers to be sound [6,24]. In contrast, the presented Coq formalization inherits meta-properties from Coq's type theory and therefore, does not require a separate soundness proof at all. While the existence and uniqueness of ODE solutions is guaranteed in KeYmaera X by restricting the space of possible ODEs [25], the Coq formalization does not make such assumptions, but shifts the proof burden to the user.

Most importantly, KeYmaera X relies on external computations in a computer algebra system which considerably enlarges the trust base of the formalization. This paper's formalization, on the contrary, relies only on Coq libraries, allowing to solve simple integrals without any external tool. As a consequence, this paper's formalization has a reduced trust base in comparison to the one in KeYmaera X, but cannot immediately achieve the techniques available in KeYmaera X by external solvers.

4. **Use of a General-purpose Proof Assistant.** The used proof assistants differ considerably by KeYmaera X being specifcally designed to deal with hybrid systems, while Coq is one of the most used *general-purpose* proof assistants. Both eco-systems come with their benefits. The advantage of integrating switched systems in a general-purpose proof assistant is the abundance of other theories available beyond hybrid systems, e.g. floating-point numbers [21], probability theory [28], distributed systems [14], or cryptography [1]. Combining these theories with the formalization of this paper, allows us to tackle a large class of cyber-physical systems. By using `InductiveSwitchedSystem`, any Coq function can be turned into a controller. For instance, in an example provided in the code[4], we use a neural network [3] as a periodic controller to model a common reinforcement learning benchmark. Due to the general nature and popularity of Coq, one can combine different theories without extending the trust base.

6   Conclusion

This paper presents the first formalization of switched systems in Coq which represents a significant step towards building verified controllers and safe cyber-physical systems in Coq.

6.1   Summary

The presented formalization of switched systems evolves around their classical textbook definitions with verification in Coq in mind. As a proof technique, the formalization enables inductive reasoning over switched systems and the trajectories they induce. We defined trajectories as a sum of ODE solutions such that the definition applies to any instance of `SwitchedSystem` and is computable by the terminating function `trajectory`. Moreover, we introduced the dependent type `ModeSolver` that structures the verification of ODE solvers for induced trajectories, and circumvents the missing ODE existence theorem of Picard-Lindelöf in the Coq.

Furthermore, we presented a specialized formalization of switched systems tailored to efficient modeling and verification of periodically triggered controllers in Coq – an important subclass of switched systems.

Finally, we illustrated the formalization of switched systems on the example of an air filter for which we verified that it keeps the concentration of pollutants in the air below a certain threshold.

---

[4] See the file inverted_pendulum.v.

6.2   Future Work

Proof Automation. We see several directions for more proof automation such as tailored low-level tactics, the further integration of results from the theory of switched systems and the creation of ODE solvers for known classes of ODEs, e.g. linear ODE systems in Coq. Further, in the case where computing ODE solutions is hard, the most popular reasoning method for switched systems is the Lyapunov method. For purely continuous systems, Lyapunov functions are formalized in Coq [27] using Coquelicot. The Lyapunov method for switched systems could be integrated in Coq by first completing and extending the existing stability results in Coq and applying them to switched systems. Note that in [27] the ODE existence theorem of Picard-Lindelöf is assumed without a proof.

Extending the Class of Switched Systems. The presented switched systems are restricted to have only a finite amount of switches in a time interval $(-\infty, t]$ for any $t \in \mathbb{R}$. Using co-inductive instead of inductive types allows for infinite switching in finite time but with the price of complicating proofs. Furthermore, statements about uncontrolled switching are, in theory, possible in the presented formalization by using theorems that quantify over all possible inductive switching signals. However, we expect that additional developments are needed to conveniently prove such statements. Another important subclass of switched systems besides periodically triggered controllers are event-triggered controllers. A specialized formalization of switched systems tailored to efficient modeling and verification for this class is therefore desirable.

Import of Switched System Models. Furthermore, an admirable feature is the ability to import switched system models from other sources into Coq, e.g. from Simulink as possible in KeYmaera X [17], or the verification of controllers written in the language C by building up on the verification system based on the verified C compiler CompCert [31].

References

1. Abate, C., et al.: SSProve: a foundational framework for modular cryptographic proofs in COQ. In: 2021 IEEE 34th Computer Security Foundations Symposium (CSF), pp. 1–15. IEEE (2021)
2. Affeldt, R., Cohen, C.: Measure construction by extension in dependent type theory with application to integration. J. Autom. Reason. **67**(3), 28 (2023)
3. Aleksandrov, A., Völlinger, K.: Formalizing piecewise affine activation functions of neural networks in COQ. In: Rozier, K.Y., Chaudhuri, S. (eds.) NFM 2023. LNCS, vol. 13903, pp. 62–78. Springer, Cham (2023). https://doi.org/10.1007/978-3-031-33170-1_4
4. Althoff, M., Frehse, G., Girard, A.: Set propagation techniques for reachability analysis. Ann. Rev. Control, Robot. Auton. Syst. **4**, 369–395 (2021)
5. Belias, E., Licina, D.: Outdoor PM2. 5 air filtration: optimising indoor air quality and energy. Build. Cities **3**(1), 186–203 (2022)

6. Bohrer, R., Rahli, V., Vukotic, I., Völp, M., Platzer, A.: Formally verified differential dynamic logic. In: Proceedings of the 6th ACM SIGPLAN Conference on Certified Programs and Proofs, pp. 208–221 (2017)
7. Boldo, S., Lelay, C., Melquiond, G.: Coquelicot: a user-friendly library of real analysis for Coq. Math. Comput. Sci. **9**(1), 41–62 (2015)
8. Boldo, S., Lelay, C., Melquiond, G.: Formalization of real analysis: a survey of proof assistants and libraries. Math. Struct. Comput. Sci. **26**(7), 1196–1233 (2016)
9. Chen, X., Liu, Y., Jiang, B., Lu, J.: Exponential stability of nonlinear switched systems with hybrid delayed impulses. Int. J. Robust Nonlinear Control **33**(5), 2971–2985 (2023)
10. Crisafulli, P., Taha, S., Wolff, B.: Modeling and analysing cyber-physical systems in HOL-CSP. Robot. Auton. Syst. **170**, 104549 (2023)
11. Dong, Q., Long, E.: Establishment of mathematical model for indoor particle pollutant concentration change and suggestions on the use of air filters. In: MEMAT 2022; 2nd International Conference on Mechanical Engineering, Intelligent Manufacturing and Automation Technology, pp. 1–3. VDE (2022)
12. Fränzle, M., Herde, C.: HySAT: an efficient proof engine for bounded model checking of hybrid systems. Formal Methods Syst. Des. **30**, 179–198 (2007)
13. Fulton, N., Mitsch, S., Quesel, J.-D., Völp, M., Platzer, A.: KeYmaera X: an axiomatic tactical theorem prover for hybrid systems. In: Felty, A.P., Middeldorp, A. (eds.) CADE 2015. LNCS (LNAI), vol. 9195, pp. 527–538. Springer, Cham (2015). https://doi.org/10.1007/978-3-319-21401-6_36
14. Gondelman, L., Hinrichsen, J.K., Pereira, M., Timany, A., Birkedal, L.: Verifying reliable network components in a distributed separation logic with dependent separation protocols. Proc. ACM Programm. Lang. **7**(ICFP), 847–877 (2023)
15. Liberzon, D.: Basic concepts. In: Switching in Systems and Control, pp. 3–15. Birkhäuser Boston, Boston, MA (2003)
16. Liberzon, D.: Stability under constrained switching. In: Switching in Systems and Control, pp. 53–71. Birkhäuser Boston, Boston, MA (2003)
17. Liebrenz, T., Herber, P., Glesner, S.: Deductive verification of hybrid control systems modeled in simulink with KeYmaera X. In: Sun, J., Sun, M. (eds.) ICFEM 2018. LNCS, vol. 11232, pp. 89–105. Springer, Cham (2018). https://doi.org/10.1007/978-3-030-02450-5_6
18. Logemann, H., Ryan, E.P.: Linear Differential Equations, pp. 21–64. Springer, London (2014)
19. Makarov, E., Spitters, B.: The picard algorithm for ordinary differential equations in Coq. In: Blazy, S., Paulin-Mohring, C., Pichardie, D. (eds.) ITP 2013. LNCS, vol. 7998, pp. 463–468. Springer, Heidelberg (2013). https://doi.org/10.1007/978-3-642-39634-2_34
20. Mammar, A., Afendi, M., Laleau, R.: Modeling and proving hybrid programs with event-b: an approach by generalization and instantiation. Sci. Comput. Program. **222**, 102856 (2022)
21. Martin-Dorel, É., Melquiond, G., Roux, P.: Enabling floating-point arithmetic in the coq proof assistant. J. Autom. Reason. **67**(4), 33 (2023)
22. Mousavi, E.S., Kananizadeh, N., Martinello, R.A., Sherman, J.D.: COVID-19 outbreak and hospital air quality: a systematic review of evidence on air filtration and recirculation. Environ. Sci. Technol. **55**(7), 4134–4147 (2021)
23. de Oliveira Oliveira, M., Tveretina, O.: Mortality and edge-to-edge reachability are decidable on surfaces. In: 25th ACM International Conference on Hybrid Systems: Computation and Control, pp. 1–10 (2022)

24. Platzer, A.: A complete uniform substitution calculus for differential dynamic logic. J. Autom. Reason. **59**(2), 219–265 (2016). https://doi.org/10.1007/s10817-016-9385-1
25. Platzer, A., Tan, Y.K.: Differential equation invariance axiomatization. J. ACM (JACM) **67**(1), 1–66 (2020)
26. Ricketts, D., Malecha, G., Alvarez, M.M., Gowda, V., Lerner, S.: Towards verification of hybrid systems in a foundational proof assistant. In: 2015 ACM/IEEE International Conference on Formal Methods and Models for Codesign (MEMOCODE), pp. 248–257. IEEE (2015)
27. Rouhling, D.: A formal proof in Coq of a control function for the inverted pendulum. In: Proceedings of the 7th ACM SIGPLAN International Conference on Certified Programs and Proofs, pp. 28–41 (2018)
28. Shinnar, A., Trager, B.: General probability in coq. In: 2022 52nd Annual IEEE/IFIP International Conference on Dependable Systems and Networks Workshops (DSN-W), pp. 70–71. IEEE (2022)
29. Tan, Y.K., Mitsch, S., Platzer, A.: Verifying switched system stability with logic. In: 25th ACM International Conference on Hybrid Systems: Computation and Control, pp. 1–11 (2022)
30. T.C.D., Team: The Coq Proof Assistant (2022). https://doi.org/10.5281/zenodo.7313584
31. Verified Software Toolchain. https://vst.cs.princeton.edu
32. Wei, Y., Jia, S., Liu, K.: A survey on anti-disturbance control of switched systems with input saturation. Syst. Sci. Control Eng. **8**(1), 241–248 (2020)
33. Zhu, F., Antsaklis, P.J.: Optimal control of hybrid switched systems: a brief survey. Discrete Event Dyn. Syst. **25**, 345–364 (2015)

A Quantum-Inspired Mechanical Method for Proving of Ramsey's Theorem by Symbolic Computation over the Finite Field $GF(2)$

Zhenbing Zeng[1,2(✉)]⒟, Jian Lu[2]⒟, and Liangyu Chen[3]⒟

[1] Shandong Xiehe University, Ji'nan 250109, Shandong, China
[2] Department of Mathematics, Shanghai University, Shanghai 200444, China
zbzeng@shu.edu.cn, lujian@picb.ac.cn
[3] East China Normal University, Software Engineering Institute, Shanghai 200062, China
lychen@sei.ecnu.edu.cn

Abstract. This paper presents a quantum-inspired method for proving Ramsey's theorem using symbolic computation on conventional computers, an improvement of the classical Ramsey's theorem, and a mechanized proof of $R(3,4) = 9$ implemented by symbolic computation on the finite field $GF(2)$.

Keywords: Ramsey theorem · Mechanized proof · Symbolic computation · Complete graph · Combinatorial geometry

1 Introduction

In 1929, Frank P. Ramsey published an article "On a Problem of Formal Logic" [1] in which he studied the decidability of a class of problems (now known as the Bernays-Schönfinkel-Ramsey class or Effectively Propositional Logic) in first-order logic and the spectrum of these logical propositions [2]. One of the theorems in this article, which is now generally stated as: Given a complete graph K_n with n vertices and edges colored red or blue, there must be a 3-vertex complete subgraph K_3 of the same color (i.e., all edges are either red or blue). Figure 1 shows that this assertion is not true for the complete graph K_5. Ramsey's result later became a basic theorem in combinatorics and has generalized to other situations: for any number of colors c and given integers $n_1, n_2, \ldots, n_c$, there exists an integer $R(n_1, n_2, \ldots, n_c)$ such that any complete graph K with $R(n_1, n_2, \ldots, n_c)$ vertices, colored with c different colors (numbered $1, 2, \ldots, c$), will always have a color i such that K contains a complete subgraph with n_i

This work is supported by NSFC (No. 62272416), the National Key Research Project of China (No. 2023YFA1009402) and National Education Sciences Planning Project (grant number BCA240048).

vertices, all of whose edges are colored i. $R(n_1, n_2, \ldots, n_c)$ is called a Ramsey number. Ramsey's theorem has also been extended to the case of infinite graphs.

Ramsey's theorem is an important result in combinatorics and a cornerstone for studying decidability problems. This theorem has important implications for the study of the termination of programs, such as the intuitive proof of the termination of programs containing while-loop statements given by S. Berardi and S. Steila in [3] using an intuitionistic variant of Ramsey's theorem.

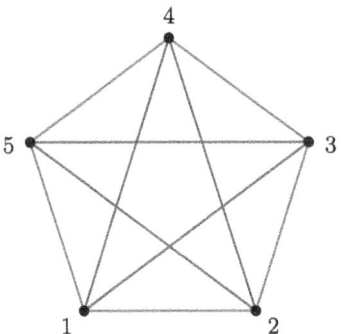

Fig. 1. A 2-coloring of K_5 without monochromatic K_3.

In the case of $c = 2$ (coloring the edges with red and blue or 0 and 1), due to symmetry, it is easy to see that $R(m, n) = R(n, m)$. Using mathematical induction, it can be proven that the upper bound of $R(r, s)$ is:

$$R(r, s) \leq R(r - 1, s) + R(r, s - 1). \tag{1}$$

Further, from this formula, it can be proven that:

$$R(r, s) \leq \binom{r + s - 2}{r - 1}. \tag{2}$$

In particular, for sufficiently large $r = s$, we have

$$R(s, s) \leq (1 + o(1)) \cdot 4^{s-1}/\sqrt{\pi s}. \tag{3}$$

Recently, an exponential improvement of the above upper bound of the Ramsey number has been obtained recently by Campos et al. in [4]:

$$R(s, s) \leq (4 - \varepsilon)^s, \quad \varepsilon = 1/2^7. \tag{4}$$

For lower bound of $R(s, s)$, Paul Erdős [5] in 1947 got following result:

$$R(s, s) \geq (1 + o(1)) \cdot \frac{s \cdot 2^{s/2}}{\sqrt{2e}}, \tag{5}$$

which shows that the lower bound of Ramsey numbers increases exponentially, and therefore, the calculation of $R(r, s)$ using exhaustive search would be very difficult. The only proven accurate results of Ramsey numbers are $R(2, s)$ (which is trivial to prove for any integer s) and 9 cases of non-trivial results, namely R(3,s) (for integers $3 \leq s \leq 9$) and $R(4, 4)$ and $R(4, 5)$. The results are listed in Table 1.

Table 1. The 9 known non-trivial Ramsey numbers

r	3	3	3	3	3	3	3	4	4
s	3	4	5	6	7	8	9	4	5
$R(r, s)$	6	9	14	18	23	28	36	18	25

Here $R(4, 5) = 25$ was proved by B. McKay and S. Radziszowski in 1995 [6]. For $R(5, 5)$, the best known result is

$$43 \leq R(5, 5) \leq 48, \tag{6}$$

here the lower bound was obtained by G. Exoo in 1989 [7], and the upper bound was obtained by Angeltveit and McKay in 2018 [8].

Computing $R(r, s)$ by using exhaustive search on a computer is equivalent to test all $2^{n(n-1)/2}$ colorings of the edges of the complete graph K_n for n from small to large, to see if it contains a purely red K_r subgraph or a purely blue K_s subgraph. Formula (5) shows that this brute-force algorithm has an exponential complexity on a classical electronic computer. In contrast, a quantum computer can represent 2^k states using k qubits, which can significantly accelerate the calculation of Ramsey numbers on a quantum computer. In 2012, F. Gaitan and L. Clark transformed the calculation of Ramsey numbers into the following combinatorial optimization problem in [9]: using a binary sequence $a = z_1 z_2 \cdots z_L$ ($L = n(n-1)/2$) to represent a 2-coloring of an n-vertex complete graph, for any integers x and y, calculate the number of single-coloring complete subgraphs (x-cliques) K_x containing x vertices $C_x^n(a)$ and the number of y-independent sets $I_y^n(a)$ in the graph. They defined an "energy function" as follows:

$$h_{x,y}^n(a) = C_x^n(a) + I_y^n(a), \tag{7}$$

which satisfies the following property for all 2^L binary sequences $a = z_1 z_2 \cdots z_L$: if $n < R(x, y)$, then $\min_a h_{x,y}^n(a) = 0$, and if $n \geq R(x, y)$, then $h_{x,y}^n(a) > 0$. Then they used the L quantum vector $|\varphi\rangle = |z_1 z_2 \cdots z_L\rangle$ to represent all 2^L different coloring schemes. In this way, the Hamiltonian H_p of the Ramsey number calculation problem is defined as follows:

$$H_p |z_1 z_2 \cdots z_L\rangle = h_{x,y}^n |z_1 z_2 \cdots z_L\rangle. \tag{8}$$

Thus, $H_p |\varphi\rangle = 0$ if and only if there exists a coloring scheme $z_1 z_2 \cdots z_L$ that contains neither a complete subgraph with x vertices nor a y-independent set.

Gaitan and Clark used the adiabatic quantum evolution method to construct an algorithm for solving the above combinatorial optimization, and simulated the correctness of the method for calculating Ramsey numbers for $R(3,3) = 6$ and $R(2,s) = 2$ (when $5 \leq s \leq 7$). In the proof of $R(2,7) = 7$, they had used $(1/2) \times 7 \times 6 = 21$ qubits. In general, the number of qubits required to detect the problem $R(r,s) \overset{?}{=} N$ is larger than or equal to the number of edges $N(N-1)/2$ of the complete graph K_N. Gaitan and Clark also proved that the complexity of verifying Ramsey numbers using a quantum computer belongs to the Quantum Merlin Arthur (QMA) class of problems.

H. Wang [10] gave another quantum algorithm for solving Ramsey numbers by constructing a probe qubit that couples the original problem with the register (including L qubits to represent chromatic schemes and one additional qubit) to check the energy level of the Hamiltonian, and decide the probability of the correctness of $N = R(x,y)$ through observing the resonance in the whole system of the $L + 2$ qubits.

In 2012, Z. Bian et al. [11] verified the problem of $R(2,8) = 8$ on the D-Wave One quantum computer. The calculation used 84 qubits, of which 28 (corresponding to the number of edges of K_8) were used for calculation, and the rest were used for error checking, with a total time of 2.70 billion milliseconds (equivalent to 75 hours).

At present, there is no news of using these machines to calculate $R(5,5)$. Since the number of edges contained in a complete graph of 48 vertices is $(1/2) \times 48 \times 47 = 1128$, theoretically, this means that the system for calculating $R(5,5)$ would need more than a thousand of qubits. According to reports in June 2022, D-Wave delivered a prototype of Next-Generation Advantage2, whose number of qubits exceeded 500. They also expected that in 2023-2024, the full Advantage2 system will be available, which will have more than 7,000 qubits with a new qubit design, and therefore, it should be enough to solve $R(5,5)$ in the coming two years. Since the current known range for $R(6,6)$ is 102 to 165 [12,13], the quantum computers that can solve this problem would require over 5,000 to 13,500 qubits.

Inspired by quantum algorithms for computing Ramsey numbers, J. Lu and Z. Zeng presented a mechanized proof of $R(3,3) = 6$ using symbolic computation on conventional computers in [14] in Chinese. A sketch for proving the more difficult result $R(3,4) = 9$ is also described in the Chinese article. Analogous to functions $C_x^n(a)$ and $I_y^n(a)$ mentioned in previous, two polynomials $J_x^n(z_1, z_2, \ldots, z_L), I_y^n(z_1, z_2, \ldots, z_L)$ have been constructed for checking whether or not a coloring scheme $z_1 z_2 \cdots z_L$ of the complete graph K_n contains a 0-coloring subgraph of x vertices or an 1-coloring independent set of y vertices, and their multiplication $H(n,x,y) = J_x^n(z) \times I_y^n(z)$ is used to analogize the Hamiltonian in the quantum algorithms. Unlike quantum algorithms, this method detects the minimum integer n for which $H(n,x,y) \equiv 0$ through exact symbolic computation, so it obtain the determination result of the Ramsey number $R(x,y)$. Note that in quantum algorithms published so far for calculating Ramsey numbers, the final step for observing energy levels is done with a probability close to 1, therefore, it can only observe the results that are true with high probability [15].

In this paper, we shall extend method of [14] to prove a stronger version of the classical theorem of Ramsey, which states that for any complete graph of six vertices whose edges are arbitrarily colored by two colors (say, blue and red), there are at least two monochromatic triangles, namely, two blue subgraphs K_3, or two red subgraphs K_3, or one blue and one red subgraph K_3. We will also give a new mechanized proof of $R(3,4) = 9$ by using simple numerical manipulation for polynomial computation over the finite field $GF(2)$. The paper is organized as follows. In Sect. 2 we introduce the characteristic polynomials that acts as analogous of the Hamiltonian in quantum computation. In Sect. 3 we prove the improvement of Ramsey theorem. In Sect. 4 we give a mechanized proof of $R(3,4) = 9$. Section 5 is a brief summary.

2   Algebraization for Mechanical Proofs of Ramsey's Theorem

Let $V = \{1, 2, \ldots, n\}$ be the vertex set of the complete graph K_n, and (i, j) be the edge between vertex i and j, $x_{ij} \in \{0, 1\}$ represent the color of the edge (i, j), where $x_{ij} = 0$ if the edge (i, j) is colored red, and $x_{ij} = 1$ if the edge (i, j) is colored blue. For convenience, we assume that $i < j$ in x_{ij}. Let

$$(x_{12}, x_{13}, \ldots, x_{n-1,n}) = (x_{12}, x_{13}, \ldots, x_{1n}, x_{23}, \ldots, x_{2n}, \ldots, \ldots, x_{n-1,n})$$

be the sorted list of the $n(n-1)/2$ variables x_{ij} for $1 \leq i < j \leq n$. In this section, we construct a polynomial $H = H_{r,s}(x_{12}, x_{13}, \ldots, x_{n-1,n})$ for given r, s over the finite field $GF(2)$ that satisfies $H \equiv 0$ for any natural number n with $n \geq R(r, s)$. For this, we first define the following two polynomials by

$$f_r : \{0,1\}^{\frac{1}{2}r(r-1)} \longrightarrow \mathbb{Z}, \ f_r(z_1, z_2, \ldots, z_{r(r-1)/2}) = z_1 + z_2 + \cdots + z_{r(r-1)/2}, \quad (9)$$

and

$$g_s : \{0,1\}^{\frac{1}{2}s(s-1)} \longrightarrow \mathbb{Z}, \ g_s(z_1, z_2, \ldots, z_{s(s-1)/2}) = 1 - z_1 z_2 \cdots z_{s(s-1)/2}. \quad (10)$$

Then the following result can be easily proved.

Theorem 1. ([14].) *Let $\{1, 2, \ldots, n\}$ be the vertices of the complete graph K_n and $(x_{12}, x_{13}, ..., x_{n-1,n}) \in \{0,1\}^{n(n-1)/2}$ a 2-coloring chromatic scheme of K_n. Assume that $1 \leq i_1 < i_2 < \cdots < i_r \leq n$, $1 \leq j_1 < j_2 < \cdots < j_s \leq n$. Then*

(1). The coloring of all edges in the complete subgraph $K_r(i_1, i_2, \ldots, i_r)$ with vertex set $\{i_1, i_2, \ldots, i_r\}$ is red if and only if $f_r(x_{i_1 i_2}, x_{i_1 i_3}, \ldots, x_{i_{r-1} i_r}) = 0$;

(2). The coloring of all edges in the complete subgraph $K_s(j_1, j_2, \ldots, j_s)$ with vertex set $\{j_1, j_2, \ldots, j_s\}$ is blue if and only if $g_s(x_{j_1 j_2}, x_{j_1 j_3}, \ldots, x_{j_{s-1} j_s}) = 0$.

Proof. The two statements are true according to the definitions of the functions f_r and g_s.   □

To see the property of f_r, g_s intuitively, we may observe the example of the coloring of the complete graph K_5 in Fig. 1, where

$$x_{12} = x_{23} = x_{34} = x_{34} = x_{15} = 0, \quad x_{13} = x_{14} = x_{24} = x_{25} = x_{35} = 1.$$

Thus, for $K_3(1, 2, 4)$, the subgraph formed by vertices numbered by $1, 2, 4$, we have

$$f_3(x_{12}, x_{14}, x_{24}) = 0 + 1 + 1 = 2, \quad g_3(x_{12}, x_{14}, x_{24}) = 1 - 0 \times 1 \times 1 = 1.$$

Multiplying the values of chromatic functions $f_3(x_{ij}, x_{jk}, x_{ik}), g_3(x_{ij}, x_{jk}, x_{ik})$ for all 10 complete subgraphs $K_3(i, j, k)$ with vertices numbered by i, j, k ($1 \leq i < j < k \leq 5$), we get

$$\prod_{1 \leq i < j < k \leq 5} f_3(x_{ij}, x_{jk}, x_{ik}) = 32, \qquad \prod_{1 \leq i < j < k \leq 5} g_3(x_{ij}, x_{jk}, x_{ik}) = 1.$$

According to Theorem 1, the above two equalities imply that no 3-vertex complete subgraph in the coloring scheme in Fig. 1 is monochromatic. Therefore, $R(3, 3) > 5$. For any general coloring scheme of K_5, represented by 10 variables $(x_{12}, x_{13}, \ldots, x_{45})$, we can calculate the following polynomials

$$
\begin{aligned}
I &= \prod_{1 \leq i < j < k \leq 5} g_3(x_{ij}, x_{jk}, x_{ik}) \\
&= 1 - x_{12}x_{13}x_{14} - x_{12}x_{13}x_{15} - \cdots - x_{34}x_{35}x_{45} \\
&\quad + \cdots + 4x_{12}x_{13} \cdots x_{15}x_{23} \cdots x_{45}, \tag{11} \\
J &= \prod_{1 \leq i < j < k \leq 5} f_3(x_{ij}, x_{jk}, x_{ik}) \\
&= 3(x_{12}x_{13}x_{23} \cdot x_{45} + x_{12}x_{14}x_{24} \cdot x_{35} + \cdots + x_{34}x_{35}x_{45} \cdot x_{12}) \\
&\quad + \cdots + 60x_{12}x_{13} \cdots x_{15}x_{23} \cdots x_{45}, \tag{12}
\end{aligned}
$$

here I, J have 187 and 388 monomials, respectively. Notice $x_{ij} \in \{0, 1\}$, and $x^k = x$ is valid for all $x = x_{ij}$ and any integer $k > 0$, so I, J are multi-linear, i.e., the degree regarded to each variable is 1. Moreover, using symbolic computation we can check that, after simplification, the product of I and J contains 218 monomials as below:

$$I \times J = 32x_{12}x_{13}x_{24}x_{35}x_{45} + 32x_{12}x_{14}x_{23}x_{35}x_{45} + \cdots - 384x_{12}x_{13} \cdots x_{15}x_{23} \cdots x_{45},$$

hence it is not identified to the zero polynomial.

Remark 1. By solving the equation

$$I(x_{12}, x_{13}, \ldots, x_{45}) \times J(x_{12}, x_{13}, \ldots, x_{45}) \neq 0, \tag{13}$$

we can find all 2-coloring chromatic scheme of K_5 that has neither a triangle whose three edges are red nor a triangle whose three edges are blue (we call such colored graph a $K(3, 3, 5)$ graph). Actually, this easily derives that, in the sense of graph automorphism, any $K(3, 3, 5)$ graph can be reduced to the coloring shown in Fig. 1. See [14] for a detailed discussion.

In view of Theorem 1, for general n, r, s, if $H = J_r^n \times I_s^n$ is not equal to the zero polynomial, then there exists at least one 2-coloring chromatic scheme of K_n, that contains neither a 0-coloring complete subgraph K_r, nor a 1-coloring complete subgraph K_s. Now we can construct the analogue of the Hamiltonian of quantum computing as follows.

Theorem 2. ([14]). *Assume that* $\{1, 2, \ldots, n\}$ *is the set of vertices of a complete graph* K_n, $x_{ij}(1 \leq i < j \leq n)$ *are* $n(n-1)/2$ *indeterminate, taking value from* $\{0, 1\}$, *and the vector* $(x_{12}, x_{13}, \ldots, x_{1n}, x_{23}, \ldots, x_{2n}, \ldots, x_{n-1,n}) \in \{0, 1\}$ *represents a 2-coloring chromatic scheme of* K_n. *Let* $1 \leq r, s \leq n$, *and* J_r^n, I_s^n *be polynomials defined by:*

$$J_r^n := J(x_{12}, x_{13}, \ldots, x_{n-1,n}) = \prod_{1 \leq i_1 < i_2 < \cdots < i_r \leq n} f_r(x_{i_1 i_2}, x_{i_1 i_3}, \ldots, x_{i_{r-1} i_r}),$$

$$I_s^n := I(x_{12}, x_{13}, \ldots, x_{n-1,n}) = \prod_{1 \leq j_1 < j_2 < \cdots < j_s \leq n} g_s(x_{j_1 j_2}, x_{j_1 j_3}, \ldots, x_{j_{s-1} j_s}).$$

Let $H := J_r^n \times I_s^n$. *Then for any* $n \geq R(r, s)$,

$$H \equiv 0 \mod (x^2 - x),$$

i.e., H *is the zero polynomial after simplification. Here, the modulus computation* mod $(x^2 - x)$ *is done over all variables* x_{ij} $(1 \leq i < j \leq n)$, *which equals to the remainder of* H *divided by polynomials* $x_{ij}^2 - x_{ij}$ $(1 \leq i < j \leq n)$.

For convenience of English readers, we shall give a brief proof to the above theorem. We need the following well-known classical result.

Lemma 1. *For any polynomial* $P(y_1, y_2, \ldots, y_N)$ *of* N *variables, if* $\deg(P, y_i) = d_i$ *and each* Y_i *is a set of* $d_i + 1$ *different real numbers for* $i = 1, 2, \ldots, N$, *then*

$$P|_{Y_1 \times Y_2 \times \cdots \times Y_N} = 0 \Longrightarrow P(y_1, y_2, \ldots, y_N) = 0 \text{ for all } y_1, y_2, \ldots, y_N \in R.$$

$\square$

Proof of Theorem 2. According to the definition of Ramsey number $R(r, s)$, it is clear that for any integer $n \geq R(r, s)$, and every chromatic scheme of K_n:

$$(x_{12}, x_{13}, \ldots, x_{1n}, x_{23}, \ldots, x_{2n}, \ldots, x_{n-1,n}) \in \{0, 1\}^{\frac{1}{2} n(n-1)},$$

either there is a subset $1 \leq i_1 < i_2 < \cdots < i_r \leq n$, so that the complete subgraph $K_r(i_1, i_2, \ldots, i_r)$ determined by the r-vertices $i_1, i_2, \ldots, i_r$ is colored by the color 0 (red), which implies that

$$f_r(x_{i_1 i_2}, x_{i_1 i_3}, \ldots, x_{i_{r-1} i_r}) = 0, \tag{14}$$

and therefore, $J_r^n = 0$; or there is a subset $1 \leq j_1 < j_2 < \cdots < j_s \leq n$, such that

$$g_s(x_{j_1 j_2}, x_{j_1 j_3}, \ldots, x_{j_{s-1} j_s}) = 0, \tag{15}$$

and therefore $J_s^n = 0$. In both cases, we have

$$H(x_{12}, x_{13}, \ldots x_{n-1,n}) = J \times I = 0. \tag{16}$$

That means, the values of the polynomial $H(x_{12}, x_{13}, \ldots, x_{n-1,n})$ on the grid

$$\underbrace{\{0, 1\} \times \{0, 1\} \times \cdots \times \{0, 1\}}_{\frac{1}{2}n(n-1)}$$

are constantly equal to 0. Notice that the polynomial $H(x_{12}, x_{13}, \ldots, x_{n-1,n})$ has been simplified under relation $x_{ij}^2 = x_{ij}$ ($1 \le i < j \le n$), so the highest degree of each x_{ij} in it is at most 1. Apply Lemma 1 we assert $H(x_{12}, x_{13}, \ldots, x_{n-1,n}) \equiv 0$: □

Let the integer n increase from small to large, expand the polynomial $H(n) := H = J_r^n \times I_s^n$ and simplify the result using $x^2 = x$, if we observe that $H(n-1) \ne 0$ and $H(n) \equiv 0$, then we can assert that $R(s, r) = n$ according to Theorem 2. In this way, we have transformed the computing problem of $R(s, r)$ to a problem of multiplication expanding and simplification over $GF(2)$.

Now using symbolic computation, a proof of the classical Ramsey theorem, i.e., $R(3, 3) = 6$, can be derived in a mechanical way. The crucial work is to expand and simplify the following polynomials I, J and their product $I \times J$ over $GF(2)$:

$$J(V) = \prod_{1 \le i < j < k \le 6} (x_{ij} + x_{jk} + x_{ik})$$

$$= 9 \sum_{\substack{1 \le i < j < k \le 6}} \prod_{\substack{1 \le i_1 < l_2 \le 6 \\ l_1, l_2 \ne i, j, k}} x_{l_1 l_2} \cdot x_{ij} x_{ik} x_{jk} + \cdots + 26250768 \prod_{1 \le i < j \le 6} x_{ij}, \tag{17}$$

$$I(V) = \prod_{1 \le i < j < k \le 6} (1 - x_{ij} x_{jk} x_{ik})$$

$$= 1 - \sum_{1 \le i < j < k \le 6} x_{ij} x_{ik} x_{jk} - \cdots - 3 \prod_{1 \le i < j \le 6} x_{ij}, \tag{18}$$

where V represents a 2-coloring chromatic scheme on K_6:

$$V = (x_{12}, x_{13}, \ldots, x_{16}, x_{23}, \ldots, x_{26}, x_{34}, \ldots, \ldots, x_{56}) \in \{0, 1\}^{15}.$$

In the reduced form of J has $5,789$ monomials, the highest degree of which is 15, and the lowest degree is 6, in the reduced form of I has $5,395$ monomials, the highest degree of which is also 15. For the product $tmesJ$, using symbolic computation to expand the multiplication, and again using $x_{ij}^2 = x_{ij}$ ($1 \le i < j \le 10$) to simplify the result, one obtain $H \equiv 0$ finally, which implies that $R(3, 3) \le 6$. Combining the fact $R(3, 3) > 5$, we complete the proof of the classical Ramsey's theorem.

3   An Improvement of Ramsey Theorem

Ramsey theorem has the following simple corollary: Assume the complete graph K_9 of 9 vertices $\{1, 2, \ldots, 9\}$ is colored by two colors, say, blue and red, then, from vertices $\{1, 2, \ldots, 6\}$ one can find one mono-chromatic triangle, say, the triangle formed by vertices $1, 2, 3$, then in complete subgraph K_6 formed by vertices $4, 5, \ldots, 9$, one can find another mono-chromatic triangle, say $4, 5, 6$. Therefore, there are at least two mono-chromatic triangle in any 2-coloring chromatic scheme of K_9 (the two triangles may be colored by one same color or two different colors). A curious question is, find the smallest n, so that every 2-coloring chromatic K_n has above property. For convenience, we shall write this number as $R_2(3, 3)$. In this section we use the symbolic computation method to prove that $R_2(3, 3)$ is also 6. Namely, we have the following result.

Theorem 3. $R_2(3, 3) = 6$, *i.e., for any 2-coloring chromatic scheme*

$$V = (x_{12}, x_{13}, \ldots, x_{16}, x_{23}, \ldots, x_{26}, x_{34}, \ldots, , \ldots, x_{56})$$

of the complete graph K_6, there exist $1 \leq i < j < k \leq 6, 1 \leq i' < j' < k' \leq 6$ so that $(i, j, k) \neq (i', j', k')$, and both (i, j, k) and (i', j', k') are colored by single color.

Proof. Assume $\{1, 2, 3, 4, 5, 6\}$ is the set of vertices of the complete graph K_6. According to the Ramsey theorem, there exist $1 \leq i < j < k \leq 6$ so that the triangle (i, j, k) is colored by single color. Without loss of generality, we may assume that $(i, j, k) = (1, 2, 3)$, and $x_{12} = x_{23} = x_{13} = 1$, i.e., the triangle $(1, 2, 3)$ is colored by blue. We are going to prove that among the rest $\binom{6}{3} - 1 = 19$ triangles, there exists at least one triangle colored by single color. Let

$$F_{i,j,k} := f_3(x_{ij}, x_{jk}, x_{ik}) = x_{ij} + x_{jk} + x_{ik}, \tag{19}$$
$$G_{i,j,k} := g_3(x_{ij}, x_{jk}, x_{ik}) = 1 - x_{ij}x_{jk}x_{ik}, \tag{20}$$

be defined for $1 \leq i < j < k \leq 5$. Let $SB30$ be the following set of substitution rules:

$$\{x_{12}^2 = x_{12}, x_{12}^3 = x_{12}, x_{12}^4 = x_{12}, \ldots, x_{45}^2 = x_{45}, x_{45}^3 = x_{45}, x_{45}^4 = x_{45}\},$$

Write a short Maple program $\mathtt{mult}(P, Q)$ as below:

$$\mathtt{mult}(P, Q) := \mathtt{subs}(SB30, \mathtt{expand}(P \cdot Q)),$$

which applies the Maple built-in function $\mathtt{expand}(P \cdot Q)$ to compute the multiplication of two multivariate polynomials P and Q which variables take value in $\{0, 1\}$, and then simplify the result by doing substitution $SB30$. Then, we have

$$F_{1,2,3} = 3, \quad F_{1,2,4} = 1 + x_{24} + x_{14},$$
$$F_{1,2,5} = 1 + x_{25} + x_{15}, \quad F_{1,2,6} = 1 + x_{26} + x_{16},$$
$$\cdots,$$
$$F_{3,5,6} = x_{35} + x_{56} + x_{36}, \quad F_{4,5,6} = x_{45} + x_{56} + x_{46},$$

and

$$G_{1,2,3} = 0, \ G_{1,2,4} = 1 - x_{24} \cdot x_{14},$$
$$G_{1,2,5} = 1 - x_{25} \cdot x_{15}, \ G_{1,2,6} = 1 - x_{26} \cdot x_{16},$$
$$\cdots,$$
$$G_{3,5,6} = 1 - x_{35} \cdot x_{56} \cdot x_{36}, \ G_{4,5,6} = 1 - x_{45} \cdot x_{56} \cdot x_{46}.$$

Let

$$J' = \mathtt{mult}(F_{1,2,4}, \mathtt{mult}(F_{1,2,5}, \mathtt{mult}(F_{1,2,6}, \mathtt{mult}(F_{1,3,4}, \cdots)))),$$
$$I' = \mathtt{mult}(G_{1,2,4}, \mathtt{mult}(G_{1,2,5}, \mathtt{mult}(G_{1,2,6}, \mathtt{mult}(G_{1,3,4}, \cdots)))).$$

Then, we can observe that J' has $1,536$ monomials, and I' has $1,450$ monomials. Finally, compute $\mathtt{mult}(J', I')$, we get

$$J' \times I' \equiv 0,$$

which means that among the 19 triangles:

$$(1, 2, 4), \ (1, 2, 5), \ (1, 2, 6), \ (1, 3, 4), \ \ldots, \ \ldots, \ (4, 5, 6)$$

there exists at least one mono-chromatic one, as stated in Theorem 3.

Notice that if we assume the first mono-chromatic triangle 123 is colored by red, i.e., $x_{12} = x_{23} = x_{13} = 0$, then we can also construct $F_{i,j,k}, G_{i,j,k}$ for $1 \leq i < j < k \leq 6$ and computer J', I' accordingly. In this way, we can see that J' has only 349 monomials, and I' has 288 monomials, and finally, $J' \times I' \equiv 0$. Which derives Theorem 3 immediately.   □

4   Mechanized Proof of $R(3, 4) = 9$

Using quantum computing, Gaitan et al. [9] and Bian et al. [11] have proved $R(3,3) = 6$ and $R(2, s) = s$ $(s \leq 8)$ where the maximum number of vertices in the complete graph is 8. For computing $R(2, s)$ with our method, the f_2 polynomials are monomials, i.e.,

$$f_2(x_{ij}) = x_{ij}, \ 1 \leq i < j \leq s,$$

therefore the polynomial

$$J = \prod_{1 \leq i < j \leq s} x_{ij}$$

is also a monomial. Meanwhile, we have

$$g_s(K_s) = 1 - \prod_{1 \leq i < j \leq s} x_{ij},$$

and $I = g_s$. It is easy to see that

$$J \times I = \prod_{1 \le i < j \le s} x_{ij} \cdot \left(1 - \prod_{1 \le i < j \le s} x_{ij} \right) = \prod_{1 \le i < j \le s} x_{ij} - \left(\prod_{1 \le i < j \le s} x_{ij} \right)^2 = 0.$$

This shows that the method can also be used to prove the trivial fact $R(2, s) = s$ for any integer $s \ge 2$.

The next simplest case is $R(3, 4) = 9$. To the best knowledge of authors, this problem is not proved on quantum machine yet. In this section we devote to prove this result using symbolic computation on the classical computer. As shown in Fig. 2, the complete graph K_8 can be colored by two colors (red and blue) in a specific way so that it contains no red K_3 and no blue K_4, which means that $R(3, 4) > 8$. In terms of the $0, 1$ representation, the chromatic scheme in Fig. 2 can be represented as

$$x_{ij} = \begin{cases} 0, \text{ if } (i, j) \in \{(1, 2), (2, 3), (3, 4), (4, 5), (5, 6), (6, 7), (7, 8), (8, 1)\} \\ \quad \cup \{(1, 3), (2, 4), (3, 5), (4, 6), (5, 7), (6, 8), (7, 1), (8, 2)\}, \\ 1, \text{ otherwise.} \end{cases}$$

It is easy to verify that

$$f_3(i, j, k) = x_{ij} + x_{jk} + x_{ik} \ge 1, \quad g_4(i, j, k, l) = 1 - x_{ij}\, x_{ik}\, x_{il}\, x_{jk}\, x_{jl}\, x_{kl} = 1$$

for all $K_3(i, j, k)$ and $K_4(i, j, k, l)$, which leads to $H = J \times I \ne 0$.

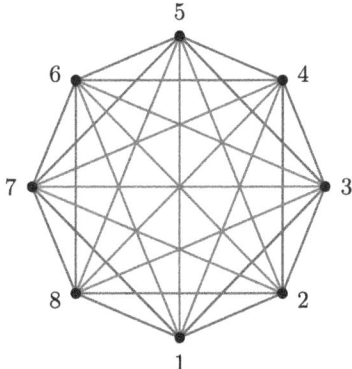

Fig. 2. A 2-coloring of K_8 that contains no red monochromatic K_3 and no blue monochromatic K_4.

Therefore, to prove that $R(3, 4) = 9$, we need only to verify that $H(V) = J_3^9(V) \times I_4^9(V)$ is a zero polynomial after expand and simplification, where

$$V = (x_{12}, x_{13}, \ldots, x_{19}, x_{23}, \ldots, x_{89}) \in \{0, 1\}^{36}$$

represents a general coloring scheme of K_9 (the complete graph with 9 vertices), with $x_{ij} = 0$ for red edges and $x_{ij} = 1$ for blue edges, and the polynomials $J_3^9(V), I_4^9(V)$ are defined by

$$J_3^9(V) := \prod_{1 \le i < j < k \le 9} F_{i,j,k}, \quad I_4^9(V) := \prod_{1 \le i < j < k < l \le 9} G_{i,j,k,l}, \qquad (21)$$

in which

$$F_{i,j,k} := f_3(x_{ij}, x_{jk}, x_{ik}) = x_{ij} + x_{jk} + x_{ik}, \qquad (22)$$

$$G_{i,j,k,l} := g_4(x_{ij}, x_{ik}, x_{il}, x_{jk}, x_{jl}, x_{kl}) = 1 - x_{ij}\,x_{ik}\,x_{il}\,x_{jk}\,x_{jl}\,x_{kl}. \qquad (23)$$

In the computation experimentation on a computer with Intel Core i7 CPU M620 2.67 GHz (8 GB RAM), the direct expansion of the polynomial $J(V) = J_3^9(V)$ was not completed within 24 hours. Considering that $J(V)$ and $I(V) = I_4^9(V)$ have 36 variables, we need to overcome storage difficulty even if the multiplications and reduction $x^n = x\,(n > 1)$ for $x \in V$ in the expression (21) can be completed in given time. In a rough estimation, the number of monomials of $J(V)$ would be $3^{\binom{9}{3}} = 3^{84} \approx 1.197 \times 10^{40}$ before combining like terms, and it could reach the level of $2^{36} = 6.872 \times 10^{10}$ after simplification, which is out of the storage ability of most laptop computers.

We applied the following two strategies to reduce computational complexities.

1. Rewrite a specific symbolic computation program for polynomial over $GF(2)$. Namely, we used lists of integers to represent multi-linear polynomials and their multiplications over $GF(2)$ in the following way

$$1 - 2x_{12} + 3x_{13}x_{34} \leftrightarrow ((-1), (-2, 12), (3, 13, 34)),$$

$$2x_{12}x_{13} \times (1 - 3x_{13}x_{34}) = 2x_{12}x_{13} - 6x_{12}x_{13}x_{34}$$

$$\leftrightarrow ((2, 12, 13)) \times ((1), (-3, 13, 34)) = ((2, 12, 13), (-6, 12, 13, 34)).$$

2. Divide and Conquer. Namely, we divide the computation problem into 9 smaller calculation tasks, by setting several variables as constants (i.e., 0 or 1) in each sub-task so that it can be processed by symbolic computation and a partial result for that sub-task can be generated, then synthesize the partial results into the final result.

For the Strategy 1 above can be easily implemented in the computer algebra software Maple, so we concentrate to explain the Strategy 2 below. In the first step, we rearrange the chromatic variable V in the following form:

$$x_{12},$$

$$x_{13}, x_{23},$$

$$x_{14}, x_{24}, x_{34},$$

$$\cdots \ \cdots \ \cdots \ \cdots$$

$$x_{18}, x_{28}, x_{38}, \ldots, x_{78},$$

$$x_{19}, x_{29}, x_{39}, \ldots, x_{79}, x_{89} \qquad (24)$$

and rearrange the vertices $1, 2, \ldots, 8$ so that

$$x_{19} = \cdots = x_{k9} = 0, \quad x_{k+1,9} = \cdots, x_{89} = 1, \quad (0 \leq k \leq 8) \tag{25}$$

then divide the original problem for computing $H(V) = J(V) \times I(V)$ into the following 9 sub-problems (P_k) $(k = 0, 1, \ldots, 8)$:

Sub-Problem (P_k): $H = \texttt{mult}(J, I)$ where J and I are defined in (21), and

$$x_{1j} = 0 \, (1 \leq j \leq k), \quad x_{j9} = 1 \, (k+1 \leq j \leq 9).$$

In each task (P_k), we compute the multiplication of some factors of J, I and search certain complete subgraph $K = \{i_1, i_2, \ldots, i_p\}$, formed by p vertices $1 \leq i_1 < i_2 < \cdots < i_p \leq 9$ of K that satisfies $H_K = J_K \times I_K = 0$, here, J_K, I_K are defined as follows:

$$J_K := \prod_{\substack{1 \leq i < j < k \leq 9 \\ i,j,k \in K}} F_{i,j,k}, \quad I_K := \prod_{\substack{1 \leq i < j < k < l \leq 9 \\ i,j,k,l \in K}} G_{i,j,k,l}. \tag{26}$$

Clearly, if K is any complete subgraph of K_9, then H_K is a divisor of H, and therefore, $H_K \equiv 0$ implies that $H \equiv 0$. Thus, to solve each sub-problem we need to find a subgraph K with relatively small number of vertices so that $H_K = 0$. Actually, the existence of such K is guaranteed by human proofs of $R(3, 4) = 9$ (cf. e.g., [16]), the key to implement the mehanized proof by symbolic computation here is to find a K so that the unknowns chromatic variables $V_K = \{x_{ij}, i, j \in K\}$ is as less as possible. So for realizing a symbolic-computation-based proof of $R(3, 4) \leq 9$, our goal in each sub-task (P_k) is to search the satisfied subgraph K over all possible combinations $\{i_1, i_2, \ldots, i_p\}$ for p from 4 to 9, with the priority $9 \in K$, and either $K \subset A = \{1, \ldots, k, 9\}$ or $K \subset B = \{k+1, \ldots, 8, 9\}$. Indeed, this idea is also borrowed from the above mentioned human proof of $R(3, 4) = 9$.

The following theorem summarizes our solution the computation experiments for solving sub-tasks (P_k).

Theorem 4. (1) *When $k = 0, 1, 2$, the subgraph $K_7 = \{3, 4, 5, 6, 7, 8, 9\}$ satisfies $H_{K_7} \equiv 0$;*
  (2) *When $k = 4, 5, 6, 7, 8$, the subgraph $K_5 = \{1, 2, 3, 4, 9\}$ satisfies $H_{K_5} \equiv 0$;*
  (3) *When $k = 3$, at least one of the following three statements is true:*

$$H_{K_4(1,2,3,9)} \equiv 0, \quad H_{K_6(4,5,6,7,8,9)} \equiv 0, \quad H_{K_8(1,2,3,4,5,6,7,8)} \equiv 0.$$

Proof. The three cases in this theorem are built according to computational experiment. Below we describe the searching process of the claimed subgraph for each case and analyze its computational complexity.

In the Case (1), we consider the subgraph $K = K_7$ formed $3, 4, 5, 6, 7, 8, 9$. According to the preassumption (25), the following six among the 21 variables x_{ij} $(3 \leq i < j \leq 9)$ are known in advance:

$$x_{39} = x_{49} = x_{59} = x_{69} = x_{79} = x_{89} = 1, \tag{27}$$

and the other 15 variables are free to take value from $\{0, 1\}$. According to the classical Ramsey theorem $R(3, 3) = 6$, among the six vertices $3, 4, 5, 6, 7, 8$, there exist $(i', j', k') (3 \leq i' < j' < k' \leq 8)$ such that

$$(x_{i'j'} + x_{i'k'} + x_{j'k'}) \cdot (1 - x_{i'j'} x_{i'k'} x_{j'k'}) = 0.$$

Notice that if $x_{i'j'} + x_{i'k'} + x_{j'k'} = 0$, then $x_{i'j'} = x_{i'k'} = x_{j'k'} = 0$, which means that the three edges of the triangle (i', j', k') are colored by the color 0, and naturally,

$$J_K = (x_{i'j'} + x_{i'k'} + x_{j'k'}) \times \prod_{\substack{i,j,k \in K \\ (i,j,k) \neq (i',j',k')}} F_{i,j,k} = 0; \tag{28}$$

if $1 - x_{i'j'} x_{i'k'} x_{j'k'} = 0$, then $x_{i'j'} = x_{i'k'} = x_{j'k'} = 1$, so together with $x_{i'9} = x_{j'9} = x_{k'9} = 1$, we obtain a quadrilateral formed by $i', j', k', 9$, whose four edges and two diagonals are colored by the color 1, and

$$1 - x_{i'j'} x_{i'k'} x_{j'k'} x_{i'9} x_{j'9} x_{k'9} = 0,$$

and therefore,

$$I_K = (1 - x_{i'j'} x_{i'k'} x_{j'k'} x_{i'9} x_{j'9} x_{k'9}) \times \prod_{\substack{i,j,k,l \in K \\ (i,j,k,l) \neq (i',j',k',9)}} G_{i,j,k,l} = 0. \tag{29}$$

Clearly, (28) and (29) imply that $H_K = J_k \times I_K \equiv 0$ in the Case (1). To estimate the complexity of the symbolic computation of H_K in this case, notice that the number of free variables in x_{ij} ($3 \leq i < j \leq 9$) is 15 as indicated, so both space and time complexities are in the similar level of the proof of $R(3, 3) = 6$. Based on this analysis, we straight conducted the symbolic computation of H_K for $K = \{3, 4, 5, 6, 7, 8, 9\}$ under the condition (27) over $GF(2)$ and obtained affirmative result $H_K \equiv 0$.

In the Case (2), we consider the complete subgraph K_5 formed by $1, 2, 3, 4, 9$. In this case, the following 4 of the 10 variable x_{ij} ($i, j \in \{1, 2, 3, 4, 9\}$) are already determined:

$$x_{19} = x_{29} = x_{39} = x_{49} = 0,$$

so the polynomial $H_{K_5} = J_{K_5} \times I_{K_5}$ contains the following factor:

$$x_{12} x_{13} x_{14} x_{23} x_{24} x_{34} \cdot (1 - x_{12} x_{13} x_{14} x_{23} x_{24} x_{34}),$$

which will be reduced to 0 after expansion and substitution using $x_{ij}^2 = x_{ij}$, therefore, H_{K_5} has a zero factor. Obviously, the computational complexity in this case is lower than that of the Case (1). We also did the computation directly and verified that $H_{K_5} \equiv 0$ as claimed.

For the Case (3), we have

$$x_{19} = x_{29} = x_{39} = 0, \quad x_{49} = x_{59} = \cdots = x_{89} = 1. \tag{30}$$

according to the preassumption (25). Let

$$A = \{1, 2, 3, 9\}, \quad B = \{4, 5, 6, 7, 8, 9\}.$$

By computational experiments, neither from A nor from B we had found a subgraph K that satisfies $H_K \equiv 0$. Notice that the complexity of the testing here has not exceeding that of $R(3,3) = 6$ since $\#A = 4$, $\#B = 6$. Thus, we have to search the required subgraph K from larger subset of $\{1, 2, \ldots, 9\}$. To achieve this target we are going to prove the following equivalent statement:

$$\text{not} \left(H_{K_4(1,2,3,9)} \equiv 0 \right) \wedge \text{not} \left(H_{K_6(4,5,6,7,8,9)} \equiv 0 \right) \implies H_{K_8(1,2,3,4,5,6,7,8)} \equiv 0,$$
(31)

for from the following two conditions

$$(3a): \text{not} \left(H_{K_4(1,2,3,9)} \equiv 0 \right), \quad (3b): \text{not} \left(H_{K_6(4,5,6,7,8,9)} \equiv 0 \right),$$

we can fix more variables in the chromatic vector V, naturally, that would significantly reduce the further computation of H_K for larger subgraph K.

Actually, from the condition (3a) we have obtained the following three extra equalities:

$$x_{12} = x_{13} = x_{23} = 1.$$
(32)

Meanwhile, the condition (3b) implies that the complete subgraph formed by $4, 5, 6, 7, 8$ contains neither a triangle that is colored by the color 0 nor a triangle that is colored by the color 1 (otherwise, there will be a four-point subgraph of $\{4, 5, 6, 7, 8, 9\}$ that is colored by the color 1), which is to say that $B \setminus \{9\} = \{4, 5, 6, 7, 8\}$ is a $K(3, 3, 5)$ graph. According to Remark 1 in Sect. 2, under an isometry of B, so without loss of generality we can assume that

$$x_{45} = x_{56} = x_{67} = x_{78} = x_{48} = 1, \quad x_{46} = x_{68} = x_{58} = x_{57} = x_{47} = 0. \quad (33)$$

Thus, under the assumptions (3a) and (3b), the colors of $3 + 5 + 5 = 13$ edges have been determined in the complete graph $K_8 = \{1, 2, 3, 4, 5, 6, 7, 8\}$, and the number of variables in the chromatic scheme of K_8 (hence, the variable number of the polynomial H_{K_8}) is reduced to 15 now. Therefore, H_{K_8} is a product of $\binom{8}{3} = 56$ or less f_3 polynomials and $\binom{8}{4} = 70$ or less g_4 polynomials, where each f_3 is a linear trinomial and g_4 is a binomial of degree 6, defined by (22) and (23), and the polynomials involved in every step of multiplication and elimination have at most $2^{15} = 32,768$ monomials, where in the beginning of the computation, we have put $H_{K_8} = 1$, and in each step we multiply H_{K_8} by one f_3 or one g_4 polynomial and simplify the result using $x^2 = x$ immediately, as we have designed in the specific symbolic computation program for polynomial over $GF(2)$. Based on the above discussion, we have seen that the space and time complexities in symbolic computation of H_{K_8} are also controlled in the level of that for $R(3,3) = 6$, so we have let computer run it directly and finally got the expected result $H_{K_8} \equiv 0$.

Combining the computation for the three cases, we complete the mechanized proof of Theorem 4 on conventional computer.   □

Notice that Theorem 4 proved that for any $k\,(0 \le k \le 8)$, the polynomial $H = J \times I$ has a zero factor. Thus, we have proved $R(3,4) \le 9$ by symbolic computation.

5   Conclusion

Although using computers to calculate Ramsey numbers has a history of over fifty years (see also [17–21]), and recently the quantum computers are also used to prove Ramsey theorem, but the use of symbolic computation for mechanical proof has not been seen in literature before. In this paper we have described a method of proving Ramsey's theorem using symbolic computation, which converts the proof of a combinatorial problem into a polynomial identity testing problem of verifying that a multi-linear polynomial is the zero polynomial, and thus can provide a strict proof of the related combinatorial theorem. Applied the new method we have proved a stronger version of the classical Ramsey theorem. By combining a new implementation of symbolic computation on $GF(2)$ and the divide and conquer technique, we have also given a mechanized proof to $R(3,4) = 9$, which was not proved by quantum computing yet. We hope that this method can be improved by using advanced computers and GPGPU computing, and methods based on the Schwartz-Zippel lemma [22,23] to prove more difficult results like $R(3,5) = 14$ and $R(4,4) = 18$ in future. We had not made any progress in this problem until now.

The authors also hope that the f_r, g_s polynomials constructed in this paper will be helpful in designing the new Hamiltonian for computing Ramsey numbers $R(n_1, n_2, \ldots, n_c)$ for $c \ge 3$ on quantum computers. In particular, for three-color chromatic schemes of complete graph K_n, a known result is $R(3,3,3) = 17$, which is to say, if the complete graph of 17 vertices is colored by three colors (say, red, green, and blue), then, it must have a pure subgraph K_3. The example of a three-colored K_{16} no monochromatic triangle is shown in Fig. 3. To prove this extension of Ramsey's theorem, one way to extend our method would be to use $x_{ij} \in \{-1, 0, 1\}$ to record edge colors, and, for example, to use the following three polynomials

$$f_{-1}(z_1, z_2, \ldots, z_k) = z_1 + z_2 + \ldots + z_k + k,$$
$$f_0(z_1, z_2, \ldots, z_k) = z_1^2 + z_2^2 + \ldots + z_k^2,$$
$$f_1(z_1, z_2, \ldots, z_k) = z_1 + z_2 + \ldots + z_k - k,$$

where $(z_1, z_2, \ldots, z_k) = (x_{12}, x_{13}, \ldots, x_{r-1,r})$, $k = r(r-1)/2$, as characteristic polynomials for representing that a complete subgraph K_r of K_n is monochromatic with a specified color. It seems that an implementation of this computer-algebra-based method involves more computation than that for $R(3,5)$ and $R(4,4)$. We also wonder that if the above three polynomials could help people to reversely design appropriate Hamiltonians for proving the three-color chromatic problems on quantum machines in any way. In best of our knowledge, there is no report on proving three-color chromatic Ramsey's on quantum computers.

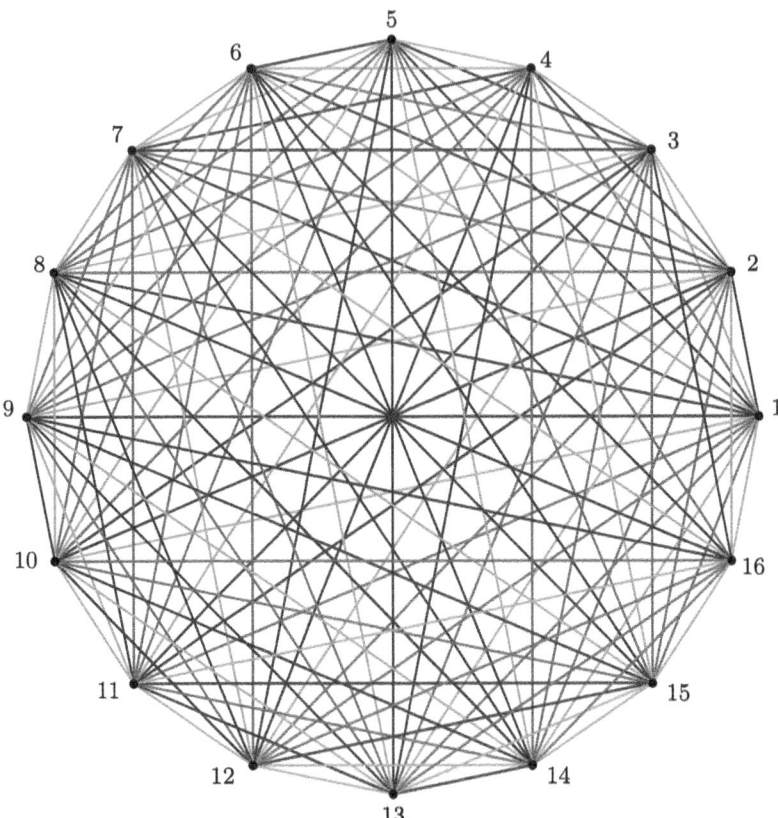

Fig. 3. The three-color chromatic scheme of complete graph K_{16} without any pure K_3 subgraph.

References

1. Ramsey, F.P.: On a problem in formal logic. Proc. Lond. Math. Soc. Ser. 2 **30**(1), 264–286 (1930)
2. Piskac, R., de Moura, L., Bjorner, N.: Deciding effectively propositional logic with equality. Microsoft Res. Tech. Rep. **30**, 264–286 (2008)
3. Berardi, S., Steila, S.: An intuitionistic version of Ramsey's theorem and its use in program termination. Ann. Pure Appl. Logic **166**(12), 1382–1406 (2015)
4. Campos, M., Griffiths, S., Morris, R., Sahasrabudhe, J.: An Exponential Improvement for Diagonal Ramsey (2023). https://arxiv.org/pdf/2303.09521.pdf
5. Erdős, P., Szeckers, G.: A combinatorial problem in geometry. In: Gessel, I., Rota, G.C. (eds.) Classic Papers in Combinatorics. Modern Birkhäuser Classics, Birkhäuser Boston (2009)
6. McKay, B.D., Radziszowski, S.P.: $R(4,5) = 25$. J. Graph Theory **19**(3), 309–322 (1995)
7. Exoo, G.: A lower bound for r(5, 5). J. Graph Theory **13**, 97–98 (1989)
8. Angeltveit, V., McKay, B.: $R(5,5) \leq 48$. J. Graph Theory **89**(1), 5–13 (2018)

9. Gaitan, F., Clark, L.: Ramsey numbers and adiabatic quantum computing. Phys. Rev. Lett. **108**, 010501 (2012)
10. Wang, H., McKay, B.D.: Determining Ramsey numbers on a quantum computer. Phys. Rev. A **93**(3), 032301 (2016)
11. Bian, Z., Chuak, F., Macready, W.G., et al.: Experimental determination of Ramsey numbers. Phys. Rev. Lett. **111**, 130505 (2013)
12. Walker, K.: An upper bound for the Ramsey number $M(5,4)$. J. Comb. Theory Ser. A **11**(1), 1–10 (1971)
13. Mackey, J.: Combinatorial remedies. Ph.D. thesis. Department of Mathematics, University of Hawaii (1994)
14. Lu, J., Zeng, Z.: A mechanical proof of Ramsey's theorem via symbolic computation. J. Syst. Sci. Math. Sci. Chin. Ser. **41**(12), 3311–3323 (2021)
15. Ranjbar, M., Macready, W.G., Clark, L., Gaitan, F.: Generalized Ramsey numbers through adiabatic quantum optimization. Quant. Inf. Process. **15**(9), 3519–3542 (2016). https://doi.org/10.1007/s11128-016-1363-3
16. Barton, L.: Ramsey Theory (2021). https://www.cs.umd.edu/~ gasarch/courses/250/S22/slides/comb/otherpaperkings.pdf
17. Kalbfleisch, J.G., Stanton, R.G.: On the maximal triangle-free edge-chromatic graphs in three colors. J. Comb. Theory **5**, 9–20 (1968)
18. Grinstead, C.M., Roberts, S.M.: On the Ramsey numbers $R(3,8)$ and $R(3,9)$. J. Comb. Theory Ser. B **33**(1), 27–51 (1982)
19. Graham, R.L., Rothschild, B.L., Spencer, J.H.: Ramsey Theory, 2nd edn. Wiley-Interscience (1990)
20. Graham, R.L., Spencer, J.H.: Ramsey theory. Sci. Am. **263**(7), 112–117 (1990)
21. McKay, B.D., Min, Z.K.: The value of the Ramsey number $R(3,8)$. J. Graph Theory **16**, 99–105 (1996)
22. Schwartz, J.T.: Fast probabilistic algorithms for verification of polynomial identities. J. ACM **27**(4), 701–717 (1980)
23. Zippel, R.: Probabilistic algorithms for sparse polynomials. In: Ng, E.W. (ed.) Symbolic and Algebraic Computation. LNCS, vol. 72, pp. 216–226. Springer, Heidelberg (1979). https://doi.org/10.1007/3-540-09519-5_73

Runtime Enforcement with Event Reordering

Ankit Pradhan[1]([⊠])(iD), C. G. Mitun Akil[2], and Srinivas Pinisetty[2](iD)

[1] University of Texas at Austin, Austin, USA
ankpradh@cs.utexas.edu
[2] Indian Institute of Technology Bhubaneswar, Bhubaneswar, India
{20cs01020,spinisetty}@iitbbs.ac.in

Abstract. Embedded systems for low latency safety-critical applications such as autonomous vehicles, space flight systems, large-scale chemical, energy and nuclear systems require formal guarantees on the input received at runtime prior to data processing. A common unintended behavior arising in communication over a network is that packets may arrive out-of-order and typically application layer protocols require underlying transport layer packets to arrive in order to ensure Quality of Service (QoS). In this context, if a processor is available to buffer and check events received over the network for safe execution, it is possible to deploy a Runtime Enforcement (RE) framework to guarantee that the protected system receives input that satisfies a set of formally defined properties. However, most current RE frameworks do not consider the order of events while processing their configured policies which makes them less viable to low latency safety-critical applications. This work proposes a new formal RE paradigm which handles event reordering for any regular property specified as an automaton. We formally define the RE framework, develop an online enforcement algorithm, and prove its correctness. We illustrate that our enforcer implementation is latency-sensitive by reasoning about the influence of out-of-order events in all possible future paths. We analyze the limits of memory utilization for enforcement theoretically for a few classes of regular properties along with extensive performance evaluation across a wide range of input lengths and properties. This includes testing the limits of the latency-sensitive implementation and its practical effectiveness against a safety-critical case-study on smart switches.

Keywords: Runtime Enforcement · Reordering · Radix tree · Smart switch

1 Introduction

The Advent of the Internet of Things (IoT) and proliferation of embedded systems for various safety-critical applications, ranging from autonomous vehicles, space flight systems, smart energy grid and manufacturing systems and heavy chemical and nuclear industries, has led to an increase in security threats due to incorrect configuration or deployment, software or hardware bugs and unforeseen system executions [25]. This has expanded the attack surface, exposing embedded devices to new vulnerabilities and attack vectors.

In this context, the order of inputs received at runtime by these systems can negatively affect the quality of service (QoS) and create contrived usage patterns that can

C. Anutariya and M. M. Bonsangue (Eds.): ICTAC 2024, LNCS 15373, pp. 386–407, 2025.
https://doi.org/10.1007/978-3-031-77019-7_22

be exploited by malicious agents. These inputs are generally delivered over a network (wired or wireless) and are subject to reordering or information loss that needs to be taken care of by the network transport protocol that is relaying the input data. Packet reordering in transport protocols like TCP, UDP or QUIC [9,11,26] has been a bottleneck in many applications and increasingly so in the safety-critical domain wherein the latency-sensitive nature of devices requires them to act on input events received at runtime.

Hence, many applications are in need of formal guarantees at runtime on the sequence of control inputs received over a network so as to ensure a safe execution of the underlying system that needs to be protected. Runtime Enforcement (RE) provides a framework for ensuring that inputs received by the protected system satisfy a set of formally defined properties. An enforcer is an algorithm operating on inputs at runtime and transforming the inputs in a sound, transparent and monotonic manner to comply with a property specified in some formal logic.

1.1   Related Work

Existing RE frameworks have primarily focused on enforcing safety properties [3,22, 24], where the enforcer stops execution upon detecting a violating trace of inputs; regular properties [7,21], real-time [6,17] and reactive properties [16,20] with varying degrees of operational power such as rectifying input sequence by introducing, suppressing, buffering or instantaneously editing events. The compositional RE problem of combining multiple enforcers to enforce all of their individually expressible behaviors has also been addressed [15,18,21].

Most of the above frameworks assume input events arrive in order which is not guaranteed in practical scenarios where packet loss over a network, traffic splitting over multiple links, malfunctioning equipment or even a denial-of-service (DoS) attack can lead to events appearing out-of-order [26]. A recent approach in [1,2] considered the verification problem while the only RE framework that considers reordering of events is [8], however, their approach employs healing (by inserting events) and suppression which can be aggressive and allow any possible reordering since the enforcer may not wait sufficiently long for the true delayed event. Also, it requires multiple parameters, *e.g.* to decide when to switch to healing mode.

1.2   Reordering RE Framework

In this context, we adopt a utilitarian perspective where the enforcer is reactive in a latency-sensitive manner such that there is minimal delay between when a re-ordered event is received and emitted by the enforcer. This makes our approach very different from [8]. We effectively utilize sequence numbers available in most transport protocols [4,5,10,14] to tackle the re-arrangement of the events and verify and correct the ordered sequence as per the policies to be enforced.

Our RE framework for handling event reordering is depicted in Fig. 1. For a regular property specification φ, the reordering enforcement monitor computes the enforced output $E_\varphi(\cdot)$ by processing the input stream $\sigma \in \mathbb{S}^*$ which is a sequence of tuples, each containing an event that can be processed by the property automaton and a sequence

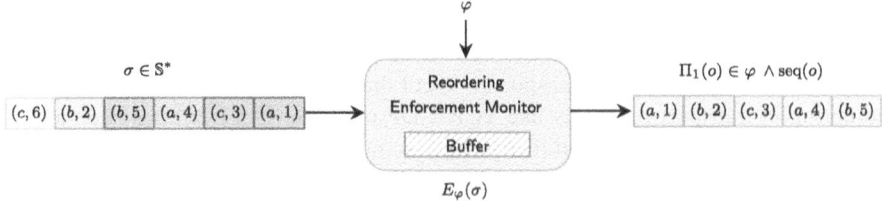

Fig. 1. Runtime Enforcer with Event Reordering

number signifying the intended order. The enforcement monitor leverages an internal buffer to delay received events for both property satisfaction and rearrangement. If the enforcer is able to satisfy property φ on the events in the re-ordered input stream (obtained by projecting the first element $\Pi_1(\cdot)$) and the re-ordered stream is in sequence till that point with no missing events (checked using function $seq(\cdot)$), then the enforcer emits the re-ordered sequence as output. We operate on a threat model where the adversary can rearrange events within a finite horizon (*e.g.* by delaying) and cannot modify the events. This mirrors the out-of-order behavior in transport protocols [26].

1.3 Illustrative Example

To motivate our RE framework, consider a safety-critical application in the context of smart switches. Smart load control switches are devices used in distribution boards of power grids to optimize energy distribution during peak usage or outgoing distribution to specific regions. They handle loads and power generation to ensure grid stability.

These switches act as a demand response system and must handle requests in order to ensure proper load distribution across the grid. Consider the following events recorded from the sensors on the transformers:

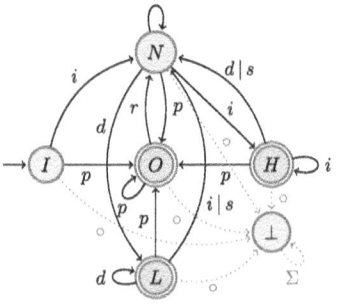

- [INC] i: request to increase the load.
- [DEC] d: request to decrease the load.
- [STB] s: load has stabilized.
- [OUT] p: power outage or faults in the grid.
- [RST] r: power has been restored.

Define $\Sigma = \{i, d, s, p, r\}$ as the set of all events. Sensor events from substations or transformers are relayed to the smart switch that needs to act

Fig. 2. Automaton $\mathcal{A}_{\mathsf{Switch}}$ defining a smart control switch property

on increase/decrease in power generation by shedding/restoring non-critical loads and in power outage scenarios by subsequently relaying corrective actions over the network. This can be modelled by the regular property 'Switch' whose automaton $\mathcal{A}_{\mathsf{Switch}}$ is described in Fig. 2. Here I is the idle state and O is the power outage stage. N, H and L stands for normal, high and low load scenarios. We denote a dead-state (from which no event can transition out) by $\bot$ and $\circ$ transitions from any state q to $\bot$ as the residual actions of state q from Σ that are not explicitly depicted in Fig. 2.

1.4 Our Contributions

We propose a new runtime enforcement framework that handles event reordering in a latency-sensitive manner that is sound and transparent for intended applications in low-latency safety-critical systems. We provide both functional and algorithmic models of the re-ordering enforcer and describe constraints that the enforcer must satisfy to guarantee soundness, transparency and monotonicity. Our latency-sensitive processing technique adapts a traditional Σ–Radix tree for property-based path abstraction which reduces the state-space spanned by merging tree nodes for paths that have similar history. We extensively evaluate the re-ordering enforcer on a wide variety of metrics including running time and memory usage for both short and long streams and for different reordering strategies along with a case study on smart switches.

2 Preliminaries

A (finite) word over a finite alphabet Σ is defined as a finite sequence $\sigma = a_1 a_2 \cdots a_n$ of elements of Σ. The *length* of σ is n and is denoted by $|\sigma|$. The empty word over Σ is denoted by ϵ^Σ, or ϵ when clear from the context. The sets of *all words* and *all non-empty words* are denoted by Σ^* and Σ^+, respectively. A *language* or a *property* over Σ is any subset $\mathcal{L} \subseteq \Sigma^*$.

The *concatenation* of two words σ and σ' is denoted as $\sigma \cdot \sigma'$. A word σ' is a *prefix* of a word σ, denoted as $\sigma' \preccurlyeq \sigma$, whenever there exists a word σ'' such that $\sigma = \sigma' \cdot \sigma''$; conversely σ is said to be an *extension* of σ'.

The set $\mathrm{pref}(\sigma)$ denotes the *set of prefixes* of σ and subsequently, $\mathrm{pref}(\mathcal{L}) \overset{\mathrm{def}}{=} \bigcup_{\sigma \in \mathcal{L}} \mathrm{pref}(\sigma)$ is the set of prefixes of words in $\mathcal{L}$. A language $\mathcal{L}$ is *prefix-closed* if $\mathrm{pref}(\mathcal{L}) = \mathcal{L}$ and *extension-closed* if $\mathcal{L} \cdot \Sigma^* = \mathcal{L}$.

Given an n-tuple of symbols $e = (e_1, \ldots, e_n)$, for $i \in [1, n]$, $\Pi_i(e)$ is the projection of e on its i-th element $(\Pi_i(e) \overset{\mathrm{def}}{=} e_i)$.

A *deterministic & complete automaton* $\mathcal{A} = (Q, q_0, \Sigma, \delta, F)$ is a tuple where, Q is the set of *locations*, $q_0 \in Q$ is the initial location, Σ is the alphabet, $\delta : Q \times \Sigma \to Q$ is the transition function and $F \subseteq Q$ is the set of accepting locations. In the rest of the paper we associate the term automaton to a deterministic & complete automaton.

Function δ is extended to words by setting $\delta(q, \epsilon) = q$, and $\delta(q, a \cdot \sigma) = \delta(\delta(q, a), \sigma)$ recursively. A word σ is *accepted* by $\mathcal{A}$ *starting from location* q if $\delta(q, \sigma) \in F$, and σ is *accepted* by $\mathcal{A}$ if σ is accepted starting from the initial location q_0. The *language* of $\mathcal{A}$, denoted $\mathcal{L}(\mathcal{A})$, is the set of all accepted words from location q_0.

A *regular property* is a language accepted by an automaton. From here on, we consider only regular properties and refer to them as just properties. We also consider two sub-classes of regular properties: safety and co-safety properties. Safety properties are the prefix-closed languages that can be accepted by an automaton. Co-safety properties are the extension-closed languages that can be accepted by an automaton.

Thus, an automaton $\mathcal{A} = (Q, q_0, \Sigma, \delta, F)$ is a *safety* automaton if $\forall a \in \Sigma, q \notin F \implies \delta(q, a) \notin F$, and is a *co-safety* automaton if $\forall a \in \Sigma, q \in F \implies \delta(q, a) \in F$.

The *single dead-state assumption (for safety properties)* states that all non-accepting states of the automaton accepting a safety property can be compressed into one non-accepting dead-state s (also called sink-state) such that $\forall a \in \Sigma, \delta(s, a) = s$.

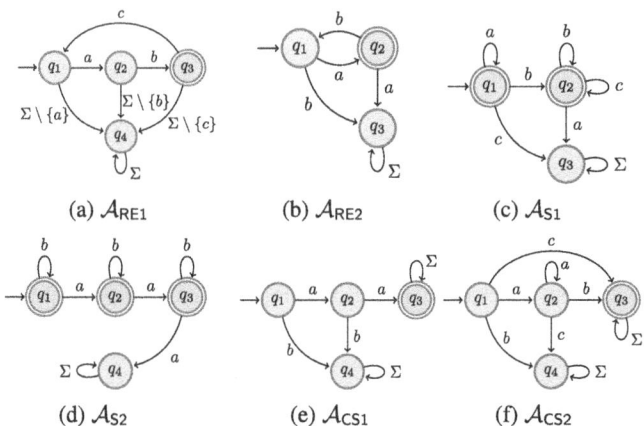

Fig. 3. Automata defining properties RE1, RE2, S1, S2, CS1 and CS2.

Example 1. (Properties defined as automata). Consider the following properties:

- RE1: Event a followed by b and any number of subsequent $c \cdot a \cdot b$ events is accepted.
- RE2: The first event should be an a, immediately followed by zero or more $b \cdot a$ sequences.
- S1: The first event should not be c and after a b occurs, it is forbidden to have an a.
- S2: There can only be at most two a actions.
- CS1: The first two actions should be a.
- CS2: The first event must be c or the sequence must start with one or more a events followed by one b event.

The set of actions for RE1, S1 and CS2 is $\Sigma = \{a, b, c\}$ and RE2, S2 and CS1 is $\Sigma = \{a, b\}$. The automata in Fig. 3 define these properties. Properties RE1 and RE2 are regular properties (that are neither safety nor co-safety), and are defined by automata in Figs. 3a and 3b respectively. Properties S1 and S2 are safety properties defined by safety automata in Figs. 3c and 3d respectively. Properties CS1 and CS2 are co-safety properties defined by co-safety automata in Figs. 3e and 3f respectively.

2.1 Runtime Enforcement for Regular Properties

Several runtime enforcement frameworks exist as already mentioned in the introduction. In this paper, enforcement monitors are synthesized from regular properties modelled as automata [18, 19].

The enforcer considers the system being monitored as a black-box similar to various other RE mechanisms (cf. [7, 12, 17, 18, 22]). Thus, there are no assumptions on the input sequence (which can be any sequence of events over some alphabet Σ). The input-output behavior of an enforcement monitor is specified by an enforcement function. Given a property φ to be monitored, the enforcement function E_φ transforms some input word σ which is possibly incorrect w.r.t. φ. The enforcement mechanism has the ability of blocking events when a violation is detected. The output $E_\varphi(\sigma)$ is a prefix of the input word σ.

Several constraints, namely soundness and transparency, are required on how E_φ transforms words. Details of the constraints, enforcement function definition and the enforcement algorithms can be found in [18,19].

This study considers an enforcement system for regular properties such as [18,19], which prevents the insertion or suppression of events. However, it permits the storage and deferral of some input events (without immediate release) upon detection of a violation. The frameworks in [18,19] consider an enforcer receiving events in order and also do not permit the enforcement mechanism to change the order of events. In this work, we leverage sequence numbers to enable the enforcement mechanism the ability to rearrange events when necessary.

3 Runtime Enforcement with Reordering

This section introduces a runtime enforcement framework with reordering along with constraints on the enforcement mechanism. We formalize the enforcement function, prove its correctness, provide concrete algorithms for implementing the enforcer and conclude with describing how latency-sensitive processing is achieved using a Σ–Radix tree model, algorithms for inserting, modifying and pruning the tree and present theoretical limits on memory utilization for safety and co-safety properties.

3.1 Preliminaries for RE with Reordering

We modify the standard runtime enforcement framework to accept words from an alphabet Σ along with positive integer sequence numbers. Let $\mathbb{S} = \Sigma \times \mathbb{N}$. A (finite) word $\sigma \in \mathbb{S}^*$ is a finite sequence $a_1 \cdots a_n$ where tuple $a_i \in \mathbb{S}$. Let $\varepsilon^\mathbb{S}$ denote the empty word of $\mathbb{S}$ and for consistency, let $\Pi_1(\varepsilon^\mathbb{S}) = \varepsilon$ and $\Pi_2(\varepsilon^\mathbb{S}) = 0$. We abuse notation for Π_i with $i \in \{1,2\}$ to operate on $\sigma = a_1 \cdots a_n \in \mathbb{S}^*$ as $\Pi_1(\sigma) = \Pi_1(a_1) \ldots \Pi_1(a_n)$ generating the event sequence and $\Pi_2(\sigma) = \{\Pi_2(a_1), \ldots, \Pi_2(a_n)\}$ generating the set of corresponding sequence numbers. We associate the terms symbolic and sequential projection with Π_1 and Π_2 respectively. Denote $\sigma_{-1} = a_n$ as the last element of σ and $\sigma \setminus \sigma_i$ removes the ith element of σ where $i \in \{1,2,\ldots n\}$. To avoid ambiguities, if $\sigma = \varepsilon^\mathbb{S}$, then $\sigma_{-1} = \varepsilon^\mathbb{S}$. Let $\max : \mathbb{S}^* \to \mathbb{S}$ be a function that returns an element i from input σ such that for any element $j \in \sigma$ with $j \neq i$, $\Pi_2(i) > \Pi_2(j)$ and $\max(\varepsilon^\mathbb{S}) = \varepsilon^\mathbb{S}$. We use a *distinctness assumption* for sequential projection. For any input sequence $\sigma \in \mathbb{S}^*$, no two elements of σ have the same sequence number.

A function ord : $\mathbb{S}^* \to \mathbb{S}^*$ for sequentially ordering any word $\sigma \in \mathbb{S}^*$ w.r.t. an increasing sequence number and a Boolean function seq : $\mathbb{S}^* \to \{\top, \bot\}$ where $\top, \bot$ are Boolean true and false respectively are defined as follows:

$$\mathrm{ord}(\varepsilon^\mathbb{S}) = \varepsilon^\mathbb{S}$$

$$\mathrm{ord}(\sigma \cdot a) = \begin{cases} \mathrm{ord}(\sigma) \cdot a & \text{if } \Pi_2(\max(\sigma)) < \Pi_2(a), \\ \mathrm{ord}(\sigma \setminus \max(\sigma) \cdot a) \cdot \max(\sigma) & \text{otherwise} \end{cases}$$

$$\mathrm{seq}(\varepsilon^{\mathbb{S}}) \quad = \top$$

$$\mathrm{seq}(\sigma \cdot a) = \begin{cases} \top & \text{if } \mathrm{seq}(\sigma) = \top \wedge \Pi_2(a) - \Pi_2(\sigma_{-1}) = 1, \\ \bot & \text{otherwise.} \end{cases}$$

where $a \in \mathbb{S}$. The function seq returns $\top$ only when all elements of σ are in-order i.e. $\Pi_2(a_{i+1}) = \Pi_2(a_i) + 1$ for $i \in \{1, \ldots, |\sigma| - 1\}$ and there are no missing events. We assume that sequence numbers advance by 1 for presentation simplicity, however, this definition can be easily modified to accommodate packet sequence numbers representing the length of packets or the number of bytes transmitted.

The following lemmas characterize some functional aspects of the $\mathrm{ord}(\cdot)$ and $\mathrm{seq}(\cdot)$ defined above. Lemma 1 states that the function $\mathrm{ord}(\sigma)$ does not edit its input σ by adding or removing elements while Lemma 2 states that if any input σ is in-order, then re-ordering the input does not modify the original input. Detailed proofs are presented in Appendix A.

Lemma 1. $\mathrm{ord}(\cdot)$ *neither adds nor deletes elements, that is,* $|\mathrm{ord}(\sigma)| = |\sigma|$

Lemma 2. *For any* $\sigma \in \mathbb{S}^*$, $\mathrm{seq}(\sigma) = \top \implies \sigma = \mathrm{ord}(\sigma)$

3.2   Enforcement Mechanism Constraints

Similar to the enforcement mechanisms such as [18,19], we consider that the enforcer is allowed to buffer and delay events, inorder to correct the input sequence. In addition, we want the enforcer to be given the ability to re-order events, and thus we revise and define the constraints to take this into account.

Definition 1 (Constraints on the enforcement with reordering). *Given a property* $\varphi \subseteq \Sigma^*$, *the enforcement mechanism behaves as a function* $E_\varphi : \mathbb{S}^* \to \mathbb{S}^*$ *satisfying the following constraints:*

Soundness

$$\forall \sigma \in \mathbb{S}^* : E_\varphi(\sigma) \neq \epsilon^{\mathbb{S}} \implies \Pi_1(E_\varphi(\sigma)) \in \varphi \tag{Snd}$$

Transparency

$$\forall \sigma \in \mathbb{S}^* : E_\varphi(\sigma) \preccurlyeq \mathrm{ord}(\sigma) \wedge \mathrm{seq}(E_\varphi(\sigma)) \tag{Tr1}$$

$$\forall \sigma \in \mathbb{S}^* : \Pi_1(\mathrm{ord}(\sigma)) \in \varphi \wedge \mathrm{seq}(\mathrm{ord}(\sigma)) \implies E_\varphi(\sigma) = \mathrm{ord}(\sigma) \tag{Tr2}$$

Monotonicity

$$\forall \sigma, \sigma' \in \mathbb{S}^* : \mathrm{ord}(\sigma) \preccurlyeq \mathrm{ord}(\sigma') \implies E_\varphi(\sigma) \preccurlyeq E_\varphi(\sigma') \tag{Mon}$$

Soundness (**Snd**) condition conveys that for any input word σ, a non-empty output $E_\varphi(\sigma) \neq \varepsilon^{\mathbb{S}}$ means the first-element projection of the output $\Pi_1(E_\varphi(\sigma))$ must satisfy φ. Transparency (**Tr1** and **Tr2**) expresses how an enforcement mechanism is allowed to correct the input sequence: (**Tr1**) the output word is a sequential prefix of the ordered input, and (**Tr2**) if the symbolic projection of the input word satisfies the property and the input, if ordered, is sequential, the output should be equal to the ordered input. Monotonicity (**Mon**) is related to the online behavior of the enforcement mechanism, that it cannot undo what is already released as output during the incremental computation, and new events can be only appended to the tail of the output.

*Remark 1 (Soundness (**Snd**)).* Using the condition $E_\varphi(\sigma) \neq \varepsilon^{\mathbb{S}}$, we exclude pathological cases such as the enforcer E_φ for some property φ (*e.g.* co-safety) generating output $\varepsilon^{\mathbb{S}} \notin \varphi$. Alternate formalism such as allowing future extensions to satisfy φ can lead to a violation of soundness since the enforcer might get stuck in a non-accepting loop after reading future events [18].

3.3 Enforcement Function

We are now fully equipped to provide a functional definition of the enforcement mechanism with reordering. Recall from Sect. 3.1, $\mathrm{ord}(\cdot)$ arranges the input sequence in order and $\mathrm{seq}(\cdot)$ checks if the input sequence is in order with no missing events.

Definition 2 (Enforcement function). *Given a property $\varphi \subseteq \Sigma^*$, the enforcement function is $E_\varphi : \mathbb{S}^* \to \mathbb{S}^*$, and is defined as $E_\varphi(\sigma) = \Pi_1\big(\mathrm{store}_\varphi(\sigma)\big)$. where $\mathrm{store}_\varphi : \mathbb{S}^* \to \mathbb{S}^* \times \mathbb{S}^*$ is defined as:*

$$\mathrm{store}_\varphi(\varepsilon^{\mathbb{S}}) = (\varepsilon^{\mathbb{S}}, \varepsilon^{\mathbb{S}})$$

$$\mathrm{store}_\varphi(\sigma \cdot a) = \begin{cases} (\sigma^s \cdot \sigma^c \cdot a, \varepsilon^{\mathbb{S}}) & \textit{if } \Pi_1(\sigma^s \cdot \sigma^c \cdot a) \in \varphi \wedge \mathrm{seq}(\sigma^s \cdot \sigma^c \cdot a), \\ (\sigma^s, \sigma^c \cdot a) & \textit{if } \Pi_1(\sigma^s \cdot \sigma^c \cdot a) \notin \varphi \wedge \mathrm{seq}(\sigma^s \cdot \sigma^c \cdot a), \\ (\sigma^s, \sigma^c \cdot a) & \textit{if } \xi \geq 1 \wedge \neg\mathrm{seq}(\sigma^s \cdot \sigma^c \cdot a), \\ \mathrm{store}_\varphi(\sigma^s \cdot \mathrm{ord}(\sigma^c \cdot a)) & \textit{otherwise} \end{cases}$$

with $\mathrm{store}_\varphi(\sigma) = (\sigma^s, \sigma^c)$ and $\xi = \Pi_2(a) - \Pi_2((\sigma^s \cdot \sigma^c)_{-1})$.

Definition 2 builds the output of the enforcement function incrementally and in-order. The store_φ function takes a word over $\mathbb{S}^*$ as input and returns a pair of words over $\mathbb{S}^*$, the first (σ^s) being the output of the enforcement function (extracted by Π_1) and the second (σ^c) representing unprocessed events which are buffered.

Function store_φ is defined inductively. Initially, for empty input $\varepsilon^{\mathbb{S}}$, both σ^s and σ^c are empty. Subsequently, a word σ is read with output and buffer contents as $\mathrm{store}_\varphi(\sigma) = (\sigma_s, \sigma_c)$. After a new event $a \in \mathbb{S}$ is read (received as input), there are four possible cases that the store_φ function chooses from:

- if $\Pi_1(\sigma^s \cdot \sigma^c \cdot a) \in \varphi$ and all events of $\sigma^s \cdot \sigma^c \cdot a$ are in sequence ($\mathrm{seq}(\sigma^s \cdot \sigma^c \cdot a)$ is true), then the buffer content in σ^c can be flushed out along with the new event read a and appended to σ^s, resetting the buffer σ^c to $\varepsilon^{\mathbb{S}}$.
- if $\Pi_1(\sigma^s \cdot \sigma^c \cdot a) \notin \varphi$ and all events of $\sigma^s \cdot \sigma^c \cdot a$ are in sequence ($\mathrm{seq}(\sigma^s \cdot \sigma^c \cdot a)$ is true), then due to the property φ not being satisfied, the output σ^s is left unmodified and the new event read a is appended to the buffer σ^c.
- if all events of $\sigma^s \cdot \sigma^c \cdot a$ are *not* in sequence, then $\xi = \Pi_2(a) - \Pi_2((\sigma^s \cdot \sigma^c)_{-1})$ is computed. If $\xi \geq 1$, the buffer σ^c contains missing events and thus, the new event read a is appended to the buffer σ^c. Note that for $\xi = 1$, this condition gets invoked only when the existing buffer σ^c already has missing events.
- otherwise, the events in $\sigma^s \cdot \sigma^c \cdot a$ are *not* in sequence and $\xi < 0$. Here, the new event read a is an event that has been missing in σ^c, so we invoke $\mathrm{store}_\varphi(\cdot)$ on the new ordered input of $\sigma^s \cdot \mathrm{ord}(\sigma^c \cdot a)$. Here, σ^s is already ordered (and output), so $\mathrm{ord}(\cdot)$ is input $\sigma^c \cdot a$ which inserts a in its correct position in σ^c and checks if the modified order satisfies φ recursively.

To clarify the execution of the reordering enforcer, consider the example presented in Table 1 for the Switch property. We use a short-hand notation for brevity of long sequences. Notice that the inputs are buffered as σ^c until a missing event reveals that the enforcer can emit in step 7 and again in step 9.

Table 1. Example illustrating incremental evaluation of the reordering enforcer for the input $i_1 s_2 s_3 \llcorner s_5 \llcorner i_4 p_7 d_6$ on the property Switch from Fig. 2. For brevity, event $\sigma = (a, i) \in \mathbb{S}$ is depicted as a_i and missing event denoted by $\llcorner$. $\text{seq}(\cdot)_{\text{before}}$ and $\text{seq}(\cdot)_{\text{after}}$ denote whether the output followed by the buffer $\sigma^s \cdot \sigma^c$ is in sequence before the arrival of a new event and after the new event is processed by the enforcer respectively.

	Input σ	Output σ^s	Buffer σ^c	$\text{seq}(\cdot)_{\text{before}}$	$\text{seq}(\cdot)_{\text{after}}$
1	i_1	$\varepsilon^{\mathbb{S}}$	i_1	T	T
2	$i_1 s_2$	$\varepsilon^{\mathbb{S}}$	$i_1 s_2$	T	T
3	$i_1 s_2 s_3$	$\varepsilon^{\mathbb{S}}$	$i_1 s_2 s_3$	T	T
4	$i_1 s_2 s_3 \llcorner s_5$	$\varepsilon^{\mathbb{S}}$	$i_1 s_2 s_3 s_5$	T	$\bot$
5	$i_1 s_2 s_3 \llcorner s_5 \llcorner i_4$	$i_1 s_2 s_3 i_4$	s_5	$\bot$	T
6	$i_1 s_2 s_3 \llcorner s_5 \llcorner i_4 p_7$	$i_1 s_2 s_3 i_4$	$s_5 p_7$	T	$\bot$
7	$i_1 s_2 s_3 \llcorner s_5 \llcorner i_4 p_7 d_6$	$i_1 s_2 s_3 i_4 s_5 d_6 p_7$	$\varepsilon^{\mathbb{S}}$	$\bot$	T

The following proposition captures the satisfaction of the constraints defined in Definition 2 by the re-ordering enforcement function. Detailed proof is presented in Appendix A.

Proposition 1. *Enforcement function as per Definition 2 satisfies the constraints of an enforcement mechanism with reordering as per Definition 1.*

3.4   Enforcement Algorithm

Algorithm 1. Process $\mathcal{A}_\varphi$ up to saturation

1: **procedure** process($\mathcal{A}_\varphi, \sigma^c, q,$ prev)
2:      $q_f \leftarrow q$; $\sigma^m \leftarrow \varepsilon^{\mathbb{S}}$; $\sigma^r \leftarrow \sigma^c$; pc $\leftarrow$ prev
3:      **for** $a \in \sigma^c$ **do**
4:          $q \leftarrow \delta_\varphi(q, a)$
5:          **if** $\Pi_2(a) -$ prev $= 1$ **then**
6:              **if** $q \in F_\varphi$ **then**
7:                  $q_f \leftarrow q$; pc $\leftarrow \Pi_2(a)$
8:                  $\sigma^m \leftarrow \sigma^c_{[1,...,\Pi_2(a)]}$
9:                  $\sigma^r \leftarrow \sigma^c_{[\Pi_2(a)+1,...,|\sigma^c|]}$
10:             **end if**
11:             prev $\leftarrow \Pi_2(a)$
12:         **else**
13:             **break**
14:         **end if**
15:     **end for**
16:     **return** $q_f, \sigma^m, \sigma^r,$ pc
17: **end procedure**

We provide a concrete algorithm for the enforcement function presented in Definition 2. Define the property φ that needs to be enforced using an automaton $\mathcal{A}_\varphi = (Q_\varphi, q_0, \Sigma, \delta_\varphi, F_\varphi)$. Before illustrating the enforcer algorithm, we first describe a sub-procedure 'process' presented in Algorithm 1 which iterates over events in a buffer σ^c and runs the automaton $\mathcal{A}_\varphi$ incrementally from the current state q up till the first missing event is encountered or processes σ^c completely if there are no missing events. This can be viewed as processing up to saturation. The variable 'prev' captures the last index of the previous combined state $\Pi_2((\sigma^s \cdot \sigma^c)_{-1})$. Additionally, process returns the final state q_f that can be emitted by the enforcer E_φ, the maximal emit sequence σ^m that led to an accepting state, rest of the buffer that is not emitted σ^r and the sequence number of the latest emit point pc.

Enforcement Algorithm: Algorithm 2 presents the re-ordering enforcer. It starts by initializing the buffer σ^c to $\varepsilon^{\mathbb{S}}$ and the current state as the start state q_0 of the automaton $\mathcal{A}_\varphi$ along with three tracking variables. 'sequence' is a Boolean ensuring whether the inputs are in sequence, 'last' is an integer tracking the sequence number of the last emitted output and 'missing' list keeps track of sequence numbers of missing events. The enforcement algorithm E_φ, in an online fashion, awaits events (function await()), checks whether the new event is in sequence with what is emitted and whether the automaton reaches a final state $\in F_\varphi$ so that it can emit events from the buffer using emit($\cdot$) (which corresponds to σ^s in Definition 2). The function last-emit($\cdot$) captures the last emitted event needed to compute ξ. If the enforcer receives future events ($\xi > 1$) or the automaton does not reach a final state, it buffers the event and adds sequence numbers to missing list. If the

---

Algorithm 2. Enforcer with reordering $E_\varphi(\mathcal{A}_\varphi)$

1: $\sigma^c \leftarrow \varepsilon^{\mathbb{S}}$; $q \leftarrow q_0$
2: sequence $\leftarrow \top$; last $\leftarrow 0$; missing $\leftarrow \emptyset$
3: **while** true **do**
4:      $a \leftarrow$ await()
5:      $\xi \leftarrow \Pi_2(a) - \Pi_2(\text{last-emit}(\cdot))$
6:      **if** $\xi = 1$ **then**
7:          **if** sequence $\wedge\ \delta_\varphi(q, \sigma^c \cdot a) \in F_\varphi$ **then**
8:              $q \leftarrow \delta_\varphi(q, \sigma^c \cdot a)$
9:              emit($\sigma^c \cdot a$)
10:             $\sigma^c \leftarrow \varepsilon^{\mathbb{S}}$
11:             last $\leftarrow \Pi_2(a)$
12:         **else**
13:             $\sigma^c \leftarrow \sigma^c \cdot a$
14:         **end if**
15:     **else if** $\xi > 1$ **then**
16:         $\sigma^c \leftarrow \sigma^c \cdot a$
17:         sequence $\leftarrow \perp$
18:         missing $\leftarrow$ missing $\cup \{\Pi_2(\sigma^c_{-1}) + 1, ..., \Pi_2(a)\}$
19:     **else**
20:         **if** $\Pi_2(a) \in$ missing **then**
21:             $\sigma^c \leftarrow$ insert-m(σ^c, a)
22:             **if** $\Pi_2(a) = \min($missing$)$ **then**
23:                 $q_f, \sigma^m, \sigma^r,$ pc $\leftarrow$ process($\mathcal{A}_\varphi, \sigma^c, q,$ last)
24:                 **if** $\sigma^m \neq \varepsilon^{\mathbb{S}}$ **then**
25:                     $q \leftarrow q_f$
26:                     emit(σ^m)
27:                     $\sigma^c \leftarrow \sigma^r$
28:                     last $\leftarrow$ pc
29:                 **end if**
30:             **end if**
31:             missing $\leftarrow$ missing $\setminus \Pi_2(a)$
32:             **if** missing $= \emptyset$ **then**
33:                 sequence $\leftarrow \top$
34:             **end if**
35:         **end if**
36:     **end if**
37: **end while**

---

enforcer receives past events, it checks in the missing list and uses an insert-missing procedure to modify the buffer σ^c (insert missing events). In this case, if the new event is the earliest missed event, then the enforcer leverages the process sub-procedure to search for the maximal sequence it can emit and sets all tracking variables appropriately. With optimal choices for different data structures, the runtime of insert-missing procedure can be improved, however, there is a linear overhead of running process after every missing event is received that can lead to instability in the expected running time of the enforcer. In this context, we introduce a latency-sensitive property-based path abstraction approach which modifies a Radix tree [13] to reason over all possible paths corresponding to missing events encountered by the enforcer E_φ and output the maximal sequence that satisfies property φ.

3.5   Latency-Sensitive Processing

For each property φ that needs to be enforced, we define a Σ−Radix tree $\mathcal{R}_\varphi$ as a data structure consisting of nodes with two components: 1) Structural: pointers to parent and child nodes (only the root node has no parent) and 2) Data: a 3-tuple (q, l_e, l_v) where $q \in Q_\varphi$ is a state of the automaton $\mathcal{A}_\varphi$ associated with property φ, an integer $l_e \in \mathbb{N}$ denoting the sequence number of the last emitting event along any path of the tree and a level pointer l_v for ease of access while manipulating $\mathcal{R}_\varphi$. To simplify the discussion, we assume that an efficient implementation of the structural component is available and only focus on the data component that is modified when the enforcer finds events missing or receives previously missed events. An efficient implementation is evaluated in Sect. 4. The 'insert', 'prune' and 'progress' algorithms for manipulating $\mathcal{R}_\varphi$ are presented below.

Algorithm 3. insert($\mathcal{R}_\varphi, m, n$)

1: **if** $m > n$ **then** return
2: **else**
3:    **if** $\mathcal{R}_\varphi(ll) = \emptyset$ **then**
4:        nodes, $l_v \leftarrow (q, \text{last}, 1)$, 1
5:    **else**
6:        nodes, $l_v \leftarrow \mathcal{R}_\varphi(ll)$
7:    **end if**
8:    **for** node $\in$ nodes **do**
9:        $q, l_e \leftarrow$ node
10:       **for** $a \in \Sigma$ **do**
11:           $q' \leftarrow \delta_\varphi(q, a)$
12:           **if** $q' \in F_\varphi$ **then**
13:               node$' \leftarrow (q', m, l_v + 1)$
14:           **else**
15:               node$' \leftarrow (q', l_e, l_v + 1)$
16:           **end if**
17:           **if** node$' \notin \mathcal{R}_\varphi$ **then**
18:               node.child(a) $\leftarrow$ node$'$
19:           **end if**
20:       **end for**
21:    **end for**
22:    insert($\mathcal{R}_\varphi, m + 1, n$)
23: **end if**

Algorithm 4. prune($\mathcal{R}_\varphi, a$)

1: $l_v \leftarrow$ binary-search(missing, $\Pi_2(a)$)
2: nodes $\leftarrow \mathcal{R}_\varphi$.level($l$)
3: **if** $|$nodes$| = 1$ **then**
4:    node $\leftarrow$ nodes[1]
5:    **if** node.parent $= \emptyset$ **then**
6:        node$' \leftarrow$ node.child($\Pi_1(a)$)
7:        node$'$.parent $\leftarrow \emptyset$
8:        $\mathcal{R}_\varphi$.delete-recursive(node)
9:        q_f, pc $\leftarrow \Pi_1$(node$'$), Π_2(node$'$)
10:       $\sigma^m \leftarrow \sigma^c_{[1,...,\Pi_2(\text{node}')]}$
11:       $\sigma^r \leftarrow \sigma^c_{[\Pi_2(\text{node}')+1,...,|\sigma^c|]}$
12:       **return** q_f, σ^m, σ^r, pc
13:    **end if**
14: **end if**
15: **for** node $\in$ nodes **do**
16:    node$' \leftarrow$ node.child($\Pi_1(a)$)
17:    node$'$.parent $\leftarrow$ node.parent
18:    node.parent $\leftarrow \emptyset$
19:    **if** $\delta_\varphi(\Pi_1$(node$'$), $\Pi_1(a)) \in F_\varphi$ **then**
20:        Π_2(node$') \leftarrow \Pi_2(a)$
21:    **end if**
22:    $\mathcal{R}_\varphi$.delete-recursive(node)
23: **end for**

Algorithm 3 (insert) operates only when enforcer E_φ detects missing sequence numbers (Algorithm 2, line 15) and inserts nodes recursively for sequence numbers in the range of m to n. This can be viewed as a pre-processing step in anticipation of actual missed events in the range m to n. $\mathcal{R}_\varphi(ll)$ accesses the last layer of $\mathcal{R}_\varphi$ to insert new nodes. The algorithm then generates and merges all nodes in the same level if the nodes are equal, *i.e.* any 2 nodes with the same 3-tuple are merged. Merge operation signifies that different execution paths may end up in the same state with the same last emitted action and level.

Algorithm 5. progress$(\mathcal{R}_\varphi, a)$

1: nodes, $l_v \leftarrow \mathcal{R}_\varphi(ll)$
2: **for** node $\in$ nodes **do**
3:    $q, l_e \leftarrow$ node
4:    $q' \leftarrow \delta_\varphi(q, \Pi_1(a))$
5:    **if** $q' \in F_\varphi$ **then**
6:       node$' \leftarrow (q', \Pi_2(a), l_v)$
7:    **else**
8:       node$' \leftarrow (q', l_e, l_v)$
9:    **end if**
10:   **if** node$' \notin \mathcal{R}_\varphi$ **then**
11:      node $\leftarrow$ node$'$
12:   **end if**
13: **end for**

Algorithm 4 (prune) operates when the enforcer E_φ receives a missing event $a \in \mathbb{S}$ (Algorithm 2, line 19) and needs to return the last emit point from $\mathcal{R}_\varphi$ in a time-sensitive manner. Due to the structure of $\Sigma-$Radix tree $\mathcal{R}_\varphi$, the prune algorithm needs to perform a binary search on the list of missing events to get the corresponding level pointer l_v, collapse sub-trees if the received event is not the first event and return the last emit event l_e from the root node otherwise. Hence, prune updates the structure and compresses $\mathcal{R}_\varphi$.

Algorithm 5 (progress) operates when an in-sequence event $a \in \mathbb{S}$ is received by the enforcer E_φ (Algorithm 2, line 7) and updates the last level by running 1-step of the automaton $\mathcal{A}_\varphi$ for each of the nodes in the last level. By replacing the last level nodes, progress does not increase the depth of the tree and may merge nodes if equal nodes are found after the 1-step transition. This operation signifies that $\mathcal{R}_\varphi$ is primarily breadth-only and height of $\mathcal{R}_\varphi$ denotes the number of missing events in the buffer σ^c.

Effectively, Algorithms 3 (insert), 5 (progress) and 4 (prune) can run in parallel to the original enforcer E_φ with the only exception of replacing the sub-procedure process with algorithm prune. This method compresses the possible execution paths w.r.t. missing events by aggressive insertion and pruning, thus creating fast inference where the enforcer does not need to run the entire sequence through the automaton after it receives the input. In a way, it computes property-based path abstractions in an online manner when it detects missing events while parallelizing the pruning process. Using the same input trace as in Table 1, consider the events between labels 4 and 7. Figure 4 depicts the tree growth and prune stages over the four sequential events (event 4 is missed, s_5 processed, event 6 is missed and event i_4 is received). Notice that node merging has substantially reduced the number of nodes in the tree.

However, for certain properties, the 'insert' algorithm can create too many nodes and occupy large portion of the processor memory that is hoisting the enforcer. Accommodating the advantages of latency-sensitive processing, it makes sense to specify memory usage bounds so that when memory is available, the enforcer operates in the latency-sensitive processing (LSP) mode by constructing $\mathcal{R}_\varphi$ and when the resources become constrained, it falls back to standard operation (SO) using the sub-procedure 'process'. We characterize these two modes of behavior using $\alpha \sim \beta$ bounds where α is the lower bound and β is the upper bound on memory measured in terms of number of nodes in $\mathcal{R}_\varphi$. These bounds can be specified based on memory availability and requirements of the processor.

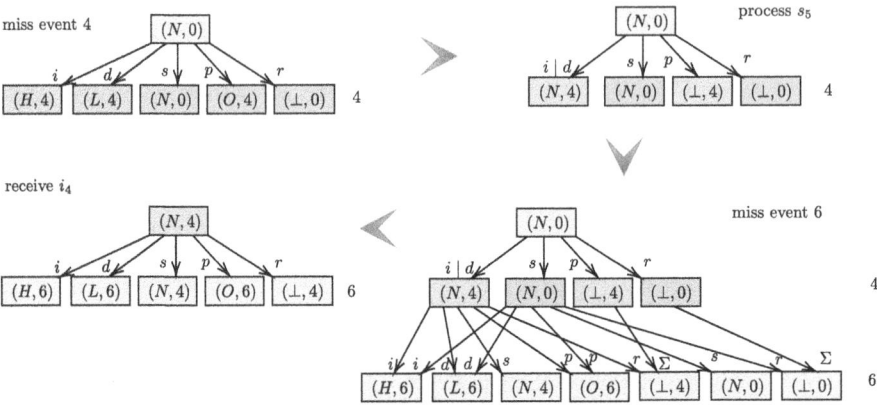

Fig. 4. State of Σ−Radix tree when the re-ordering enforcer processes events between labels 4 and 7 from Table 1 using the latency-sensitive processing.

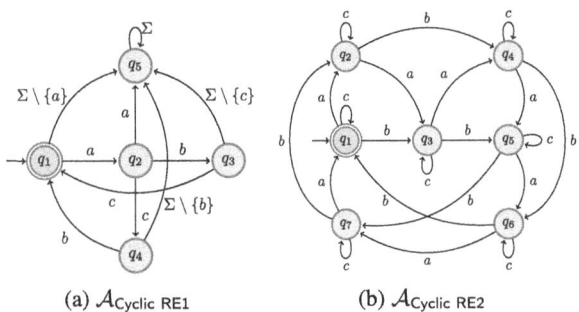

(a) $\mathcal{A}_{\text{Cyclic RE1}}$ (b) $\mathcal{A}_{\text{Cyclic RE2}}$

Fig. 5. Automata defining properties Cyclic RE1 and Cyclic RE2.

Lastly, we theoretically analyze memory usage of Σ−Radix tree $\mathcal{R}_\varphi$. The number of nodes in $\mathcal{R}_\varphi$ is a function of the number of missed events n. For enforcing general regular properties, a coarse upper-bound is exponential $O(\Sigma^n)$ since at each level and for each missing event, a maximum of Σ states can be added and the growth is multiplicative. However, for enforcing safety (on certain assumptions) and co-safety properties (unconditionally), memory growth is linear in the size of missing events as demonstrated by the following theorem.

Theorem 1. *Total memory usage (in terms of number of nodes in $\mathcal{R}_\varphi$) for co-safety properties is $O(n)$ where n is the number of missing events. With the single dead-state assumption, the total memory usage of safety properties is also $O(n)$.*

These bounds can be derived by analyzing the merging pattern in $\mathcal{R}_\varphi$ and showing that a constant number of nodes are added for each missing event in case of safety and co-safety properties. Detailed proof is presented in Appendix A.

4   Evaluation

Performance analysis is conducted in the context of regular, safety, and co-safety properties. We consider the properties illustrated in Sect. 2 Example 1 along with two regular properties with multiple cycles described by their automata models in Fig. 5 for our experiments and comparison (a total of eight properties). We evaluate on two approaches, the standard operation (SO) which uses the process method for re-ordering and second, the latency-sensitive mode (LSP) discussed in Sect. 3.5. We analyse the relationship between the input size and the growth in memory, as well as the impact on the performance of the enforcer with an increase in unordered events. All experiments were conducted on an Intel i7-10510U CPU @ 2.30 GHz, with RAM of 16.0 GB, running on Ubuntu 22.04.3 LTS, 64-bit operating system. Further details along with experimental hyper-parameters are presented in Appendix B.

We develop a trace generator that generates random input traces similar to realistic system execution. This is achieved by using pre-defined arbitrary batches (with fixed batch size) and randomly reordering a fixed percent of events within a batch (referred to as drop percentage alluding to the packet drop behavior of transport protocols).

Subsequently, we analyze the performance of LSP mode and SO mode using seven input traces from the trace generator against each of the eight properties described ear-

Table 2. Average time taken by LSP mode (t_L) and SO mode (t_B) in (milliseconds) for properties RE1, RE2, Cyclic RE1, Cyclic RE2, S1, S2, CS1 and CS2

Property	Input Size	t_L (ms)	t_B (ms)	Property	Input Size	t_L (ms)	t_B (ms)
RE1	2^6	5.92×10^{-1}	2.01×10^{-1}	S1	2^6	8.63×10^{-1}	1.64×10^{-1}
	2^8	2.24×10^0	5.97×10^{-1}		2^8	1.79×10^0	5.70×10^{-1}
	2^{10}	1.00×10^1	4.06×10^0		2^{10}	5.48×10^0	3.82×10^0
	2^{12}	6.51×10^1	3.62×10^1		2^{12}	7.01×10^1	3.75×10^1
	2^{14}	6.98×10^2	5.67×10^2		2^{14}	7.88×10^2	6.20×10^2
	2^{16}	1.23×10^4	1.23×10^4		2^{16}	1.30×10^4	1.60×10^4
	2^{17}	1.05×10^5	1.13×10^5		2^{17}	1.04×10^5	1.10×10^5
RE2	2^6	5.13×10^{-1}	1.78×10^{-1}	S2	2^6	5.64×10^{-1}	2.13×10^{-1}
	2^8	1.93×10^0	6.49×10^{-1}		2^8	1.53×10^0	6.57×10^{-1}
	2^{10}	7.86×10^0	3.89×10^0		2^{10}	1.27×10^1	4.13×10^0
	2^{12}	6.93×10^1	3.65×10^1		2^{12}	7.11×10^1	3.79×10^1
	2^{14}	7.15×10^2	6.12×10^2		2^{14}	7.63×10^2	6.34×10^2
	2^{16}	1.28×10^4	1.33×10^4		2^{16}	1.26×10^4	1.32×10^4
	2^{17}	1.06×10^5	1.09×10^5		2^{17}	1.06×10^5	1.13×10^5
Cyclic RE1	2^6	4.66×10^{-1}	1.74×10^{-1}	CS1	2^6	3.06×10^{-1}	1.87×10^{-1}
	2^8	2.32×10^0	1.09×10^0		2^8	7.45×10^{-1}	7.97×10^{-1}
	2^{10}	1.93×10^1	4.32×10^0		2^{10}	3.17×10^0	3.49×10^0
	2^{12}	7.20×10^1	3.92×10^1		2^{12}	3.87×10^1	4.34×10^1
	2^{14}	7.74×10^2	6.00×10^2		2^{14}	7.03×10^2	7.07×10^2
	2^{16}	1.29×10^4	1.31×10^4		2^{16}	1.36×10^4	1.49×10^4
	2^{17}	1.07×10^5	1.12×10^5		2^{17}	1.09×10^5	1.11×10^5
Cyclic RE2	2^6	9.47×10^{-1}	1.50×10^{-1}	CS2	2^6	2.09×10^{-1}	1.61×10^{-1}
	2^8	2.63×10^0	6.68×10^{-1}		2^8	7.06×10^{-1}	6.97×10^{-1}
	2^{10}	5.01×10^0	3.30×10^0		2^{10}	3.68×10^0	3.96×10^0
	2^{12}	4.94×10^1	5.15×10^1		2^{12}	3.82×10^1	4.00×10^1
	2^{14}	1.24×10^3	6.87×10^2		2^{14}	7.20×10^2	7.30×10^2
	2^{16}	2.59×10^4	1.43×10^4		2^{16}	1.49×10^4	1.74×10^4
	2^{17}	1.26×10^5	1.16×10^5		2^{17}	1.11×10^5	1.32×10^5

lier and report the average run-times in Table 2. LSP mode is more effective than SO mode for long input sequences ($> 30,000$ events), however, both modes are quite comparable in runtime for smaller sequences. Performance is also more significant for co-safety properties compared to other properties which corroborate with the conclusions of Theorem 1.

We also analyze the memory usage patterns of the LSP mode in terms of the number of nodes present in the Σ−Radix tree. While processing each event, tree size can grow and sink depending on the property enforced. We select $\alpha \sim \beta$ limits for constraining the available memory on the processor. Figure 6a captures the memory usage for varying input lengths (in the logarithmic scale). Figures 6b and 6c depict the average memory usage and processing time by varying the drop percentage. We depict exact event localization which presents the event at which the $\alpha \sim \beta$ limits are crossed in Figs. 6d, 6e and 6f for different input sizes. All figures portrayed above are with respect to the Cyclic RE1 property. We conclude that with an increase in input sizes or drop percentage, there is a noticeable increase in memory usage and it is dependent on the relative ordering of events in the input trace (up to randomization).

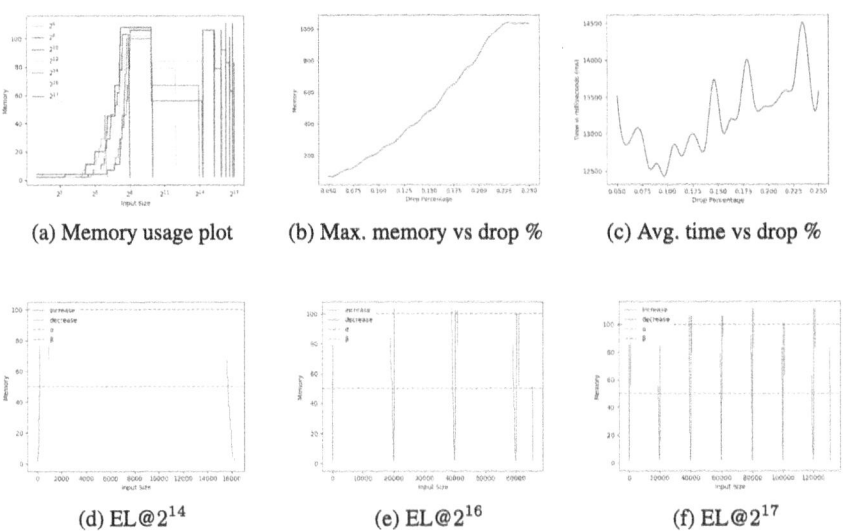

(a) Memory usage plot   (b) Max. memory vs drop %   (c) Avg. time vs drop %

(d) EL@2^{14} (e) EL@2^{16} (f) EL@2^{17}

Fig. 6. Memory usage for various input sizes, memory and time comparison to drop percentage and event localization for different input sizes (EL@<input-size>) for property Cyclic RE1

Evaluating the Smart Control Switch Property (Switch)

In addition to the previously discussed experiments, we also evaluate the smart control Switch property presented in Fig. 2 of the Introduction. LSP mode enforcer configurations were modified with α and β set to a reasonably higher memory limit of 300 and 500 nodes respectively. Results observed for the Switch property as depicted in Table 3 and Fig. 7 were consistent with those obtained in earlier evaluations. The computational benefits of the LSP mode became more pronounced for large input sizes $\geq$30,000. Using

Table 3. Average time taken by LSP mode (t_L) and SO mode (t_B) in (milliseconds) for the safety-critical Switch property

Input Size	t_L (ms)	t_B (ms)
2^6	1.38×10^0	1.58×10^{-1}
2^8	3.89×10^0	5.67×10^{-1}
2^{10}	3.80×10^1	4.37×10^0
2^{12}	1.41×10^2	3.85×10^1
2^{14}	1.11×10^3	6.16×10^2
2^{16}	1.38×10^4	1.57×10^4
2^{17}	1.23×10^5	1.30×10^5

a re-ordering enforcer is an excellent alternative to providing safety via formal guarantees on smart load switches. It can enhance efficiency and reliability in Demand Response Management Systems.

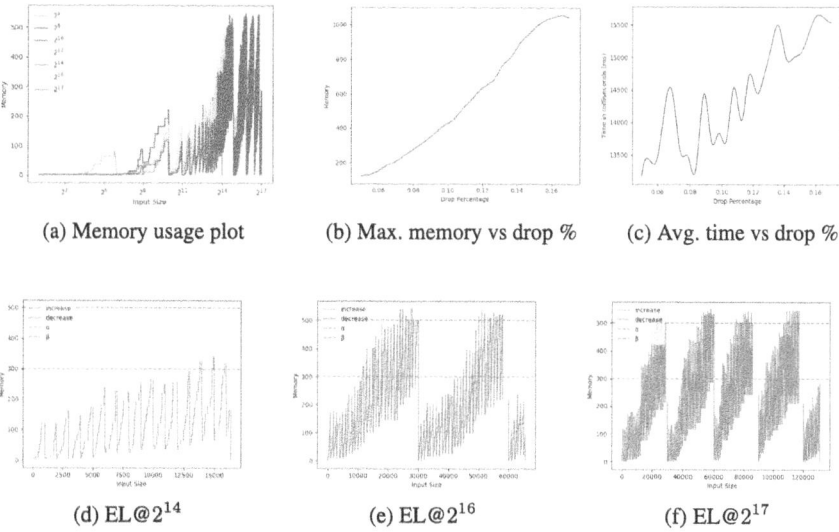

(a) Memory usage plot   (b) Max. memory vs drop %   (c) Avg. time vs drop %

(d) EL@2^{14} (e) EL@2^{16} (f) EL@2^{17}

Fig. 7. Memory usage for various input sizes, memory and time comparison to drop percentage and event localization for different input sizes (EL@<input-size>) for the safety-critical Switch property

5 Conclusion and Future Work

We introduced a new formal RE framework that handles event reordering at runtime in a sound, transparent and monotonic fashion by effectively utilizing sequence numbers available, for instance, in various transport protocols like TCP, UDP, and QUIC. We formalized the enforcement problem with reordering for any regular property

(Sect. 3.2), defined the enforcement function (Sect. 3.3), and provided optimal enforcement algorithms (Sect. 3.4) operating with latency-sensitive processing (Sect. 3.5). We also present a constraint satisfaction proposition and theoretical bounds on memory usage in the LSP mode Σ−Radix tree for safety and co-safety regular properties. The proposed enforcement algorithms are implemented and extensively evaluated over several examples, including an example in safety-critical applications such as smart load control switches (Sect. 4).

For future work, we plan to explore the reordering enforcement problem from a bounded buffer context. This problem has been recently answered in the context of regular enforcement [23], however, event reordering may require a different formulation in this setting since the enforcer has to decide between which events to wait or drop based on how close the buffer is to being full. Another interesting avenue is to build a reordering enforcer that operates on timed properties.

Appendix for Runtime Enforcement with Event Reordering

A   Proofs

Lemma 1. $\mathrm{ord}(\cdot)$ *neither adds nor deletes elements, that is,* $|\mathrm{ord}(\sigma)| = |\sigma|$

Proof. A strong inductive argument on the length of σ suffices.

Induction Basis: By definition, $|\mathrm{ord}(\varepsilon^{\mathbb{S}})| = |\varepsilon^{\mathbb{S}}| = 0$. If $\sigma = a \in \mathbb{S}$, then $\mathrm{ord}(\sigma) = \mathrm{ord}(a) = \mathrm{ord}(\varepsilon^{\mathbb{S}}) \cdot a = a$.

Induction Step: Assume that for all σ with $|\sigma| \leq n \in \mathbb{N}$, $\mathrm{ord}(\cdot)$ neither adds nor deletes elements. Consider $a \in \mathbb{S}$ and define $\sigma' = \sigma \cdot a$. There are two cases for $\mathrm{ord}(\sigma')$, the first of which computes $\mathrm{ord}(\sigma)$. It follows from the inductive argument and the *distinctness assumption* that no additions or deletions were made and $|\mathrm{ord}(\sigma) \cdot a| = n + 1$. The second case computes $\mathrm{ord}(\sigma \setminus \max(\sigma) \cdot a)$ and appends $\max(\sigma)$ to the end. Total length of the output is $((n-1)+1)+1 = n+1$ and the element $\max(\sigma)$ which was removed from σ is added back. Leveraging the same assumptions as before concludes the proof.   □

Lemma 2. *For any* $\sigma \in \mathbb{S}^*$, $\mathrm{seq}(\sigma) = \top \implies \sigma = \mathrm{ord}(\sigma)$

Proof. Due to its recursive definition, $\mathrm{seq}(\sigma) = \top$ for any $\sigma \in \mathbb{S}^*$ implies $\forall i \in \{1, \ldots, |\sigma| - 1\}$, $\Pi_2(\sigma_{i+1}) - \Pi_2(\sigma_i) = 1$. Thus, from the definition of $\mathrm{ord}(\cdot)$, the first branch is always chosen while processing σ which does not change the order of elements in σ. This concludes $\mathrm{ord}(\sigma) = \sigma$.   □

Proposition 1. *Enforcement function as per Definition 2 satisfies the constraints of an enforcement mechanism with reordering as per Definition 1.*

Proof. Using structural induction on the length of input $\sigma \in \mathbb{S}^*$, we get four cases based on the definition of the enforcement function.

Induction Basis: By definition, $E_\varphi(\varepsilon^{\mathbb{S}}) = \Pi_1 \left(\text{store}_\varphi(\varepsilon^{\mathbb{S}}) \right) = \Pi_1 \left((\varepsilon^{\mathbb{S}}, \varepsilon^{\mathbb{S}}) \right) = \varepsilon^{\mathbb{S}}$. Constraints **Snd**, **Tr1**, **Tr2**, and **Mon** are either vacuously or by definition true.

Induction Step: Assume that for all σ with $|\sigma| \leq n \in \mathbb{N}$, the reordering enforcement function $E_\varphi(\sigma)$ satisfies the four constraints of Definition 1 such that $E_\varphi(\sigma) = \Pi_1 \left(\text{store}_\varphi(\sigma) \right) = \Pi_1 \left((\sigma^s, \sigma^c) \right) = \sigma^s$ where $\sigma = \sigma^s \cdot \sigma^c$ and $\Pi_1(\sigma^s) \in \varphi$. Consider $a \in \mathbb{S}$ and the four cases as per definition of E_φ:

- Case $\Pi_1(\sigma^s \cdot \sigma^c \cdot a) \in \varphi \wedge \text{seq}(\sigma^s \cdot \sigma^c \cdot a)$:

  Since $E_\varphi(\sigma \cdot a) = \sigma^s \cdot \sigma^c \cdot a$, **Snd** holds by definition. In case of **Tr1**, we only need to check $E_\varphi(\sigma \cdot a) = \sigma^s \cdot \sigma^c \cdot a \preccurlyeq \text{ord}(\sigma^s \cdot \sigma^c \cdot a)$ which holds due to Lemma 2 since $\text{seq}(\sigma^s \cdot \sigma^c \cdot a)$ is true. Lemma 2 also helps prove **Tr2** since $E_\varphi = \sigma^s \cdot \sigma^c \cdot a = \text{ord}(\sigma^s \cdot \sigma^c \cdot a)$. For **Mon**, let $\text{ord}(\sigma) \preccurlyeq \text{ord}(\sigma \cdot a)$ be true. Then, $E_\varphi(\sigma) = \sigma^s \preccurlyeq \sigma^s \cdot \sigma^c \cdot a = E_\varphi(\sigma \cdot a)$ holds, otherwise, **Mon** is vacuously true.

- Case $\Pi_1(\sigma^s \cdot \sigma^c \cdot a) \notin \varphi \wedge \text{seq}(\sigma^s \cdot \sigma^c \cdot a)$:

  Since $E_\varphi(\sigma \cdot a) = \sigma^s$, **Snd** holds due to inductive hypothesis. For **Tr1**, note that $E_\varphi(\sigma \cdot a) = \sigma^s \preccurlyeq \sigma^s \cdot \sigma^c \cdot a \preccurlyeq \text{ord}(\sigma^s \cdot \sigma^c \cdot a)$ using Lemma 2 and $\text{seq}(\sigma^s \cdot \sigma^c \cdot a) \implies \text{seq}(\sigma^s)$ due to its recursive definition. For **Tr2**, using Lemma 2 on $\Pi_1(\text{ord}(\sigma^s \cdot \sigma^c \cdot a))$ shows that it is vacuously true and similar to the previous case, $E_\varphi(\sigma) = \sigma^s \preccurlyeq \sigma^s = E_\varphi(\sigma \cdot a)$ assuming $\text{ord}(\sigma) \preccurlyeq \text{ord}(\sigma \cdot a)$ proves **Mon**.

- Case $\xi = \Pi_2(a) - \Pi_2((\sigma^s \cdot \sigma^c)_{-1}) \geq 1 \wedge \neg\text{seq}(\sigma^s \cdot \sigma^c \cdot a)$:

  Since $E_\varphi(\sigma \cdot a) = \sigma^s$, **Snd** holds due to inductive hypothesis. For **Tr1**, the corresponding induction hypothesis states $E_\varphi(\sigma) = \sigma^s \preccurlyeq \text{ord}(\sigma) \wedge \text{seq}(E_\varphi(\sigma))$. Since $\xi \geq 1$, $\text{ord}(\sigma \cdot a) = \text{ord}(\sigma) \cdot a$ and thus, $E_\varphi(\sigma \cdot a) = \sigma^s \preccurlyeq \text{ord}(\sigma) \preccurlyeq \text{ord}(\sigma) \cdot a = \text{ord}(\sigma \cdot a)$. Again using the inductive hypothesis, $\text{seq}(E_\varphi(\sigma \cdot a)) = \text{seq}(\sigma^s) = \text{seq}(E_\varphi(\sigma)) = \top$. For **Tr2**, $\xi > 1$ implies $\text{seq}(\text{ord}(\sigma^s \cdot \sigma^c \cdot a)) = \bot$ rendering the statement vacuously true and for $\xi = 1$, $\text{seq}(\text{ord}(\sigma^s \cdot \sigma^c \cdot a)) = \text{seq}(\text{ord}(\sigma^s \cdot \sigma^c)) = \bot$ which follows from the inductive hypothesis for **Tr2**, $\text{seq}(\sigma^s \cdot \sigma^c) = \bot$ and the fact that the output of the $\text{store}_\varphi(\cdot)$ function is ordered. The argument for **Mon** is the same as that of the previous case.

- For the last case, $\xi < 1 \wedge \neg\text{seq}(\sigma^s \cdot \sigma^c \cdot a)$. Due to the distinctness assumption, $\Pi_2(a) \notin \Pi_2(\sigma)$. Consider the set of all finite prefixes $\mathbb{P} = \{\sigma^{c'} \preccurlyeq \text{ord}(\sigma^c \cdot a)\}$. Here $|\mathbb{P}| = |\sigma^c| + 2$ which also includes $\varepsilon^{\mathbb{S}}$. Choose $p \in \mathbb{P}$ of maximum length such that $\Pi_1(\sigma^s \cdot p) \in \varphi \wedge \text{seq}(\sigma^s \cdot p) = \top$. Given the induction hypothesis, $\Pi_1(E_\varphi(\sigma)) = \Pi_1(\sigma^s) \in \varphi$, computing $\Pi_1(E_\varphi(\sigma \cdot a)) = \Pi_1(\Pi_1(\text{store}_\varphi(\sigma^s \cdot \text{ord}(\sigma^c \cdot a)))) = \Pi_1(\sigma^s \cdot p) \in \varphi$ shows **Snd**. The choice of p also ensures that $E_\varphi(\sigma \cdot a) = \sigma^s \cdot p \preccurlyeq \text{ord}(\sigma^s \cdot \sigma^c \cdot a)$ and since $\text{seq}(E_\varphi(\sigma \cdot a)) = \text{seq}(\sigma^s \cdot p) = \top$ by definition, **Tr1** holds. To show **Tr2**, note that the only scenario when $E_\varphi(\sigma) = \text{ord}(\sigma)$ occurs is when $p = \text{ord}(\sigma^c \cdot a)$ otherwise $|E_\varphi(\sigma)| \neq |\text{ord}(\sigma)|$. If $E_\varphi(\sigma) \neq \text{ord}(\sigma)$, $\Pi_1(\sigma^s \cdot \text{ord}(\sigma^c \cdot a)) \notin \varphi$ due to the choice of maximum length prefix p. This implies that $\Pi_1(\text{ord}(\sigma^s \cdot \sigma^c \cdot a)) \notin \varphi$ using a recursive argument on the definition of $\text{ord}(\cdot)$ function. For **Mon**, assuming $\text{ord}(\sigma) \preccurlyeq \text{ord}(\sigma \cdot a)$, $E_\varphi(\sigma) = \sigma^s \preccurlyeq \sigma^s \cdot p = E_\varphi(\sigma \cdot a)$ which concludes the inductive argument. $\square$

Theorem 1. *Total memory usage (in terms of number of nodes in $\mathcal{R}_\varphi$) for co-safety properties is $O(n)$ where n is the number of missing events. With the single dead-state assumption, the total memory usage of safety properties is also $O(n)$.*

Proof. Consider layer l of Σ−Radix tree $\mathcal{R}_\varphi$ with k nodes in that layer. It is possible to partition the set of k nodes into accepting A_l and non-accepting N_l states of magnitude Δ_l and ∇_l respectively such that $\Sigma \supseteq A_l \cup N_l$ and $|\Sigma| \geq \Delta_l + \nabla_l$. Any new missed event with sequence number r invokes Algorithm 3 to insert and merge new nodes for layer $l + 1$. For any state $s \in A_l$, the maximum number of nodes that can be created is $\Delta_{l+1} + \nabla_{l+1} \leq |\Sigma|$ and every other state can be merged with one of these $|\Sigma|$ states. This is possible because $l_e = r − 1$ for any $s \in A_l$ and l_e changes to r for $A_l \rightarrow A_{l+1}$ transitions and $r − 1$ for $A_l \rightarrow N_{l+1}$ which are uniquely determined. This does not hold for transitions from $s \in N$ since l_e can be unique for each state s.

Co-safety Properties: These properties disallow $A_l \rightarrow N_{l+1}$ transitions by definition and thus, for any $s \in N_l$, $l_e = 0$, so uniquely, $N_l \rightarrow A_{l+1}$ transitions add Δ_{l+1} and $N_l \rightarrow N_{l+1}$ transitions (retaining $l_e = 0$) add ∇_{l+1} states respectively. Hence total new states added is $2\Delta_{l+1} + \nabla_{l+1}$ which is a constant.

Safety Properties: These properties disallow $N_l \rightarrow A_{l+1}$ transitions by definition and with the single dead-state assumption, $|N_{l+1}| = 1$ wherein the new node added carries the same last emitting sequence number l_e, so uniquely, total new states added is $\leq \Sigma + 1$ which is a constant.

   In both the above arguments, each missing event adds a layer l and increases the memory usage by a constant number of states. Thus the total memory usage is $O(n)$. □

B   Experimental Details

B.1   Trace Generator for Creating Out-of-Order Events

We develop a trace generator that generates random input traces similar to realistic system execution. We then introduce a re-ordering function to simulate the occurrence of out-of-order events by emulating scenarios where events are dropped and subsequently re-emitted at a later time. The re-ordering function operates on a specified batch-size and drop percentage. The entire input is partitioned into batches, and within each batch, a certain percentage of events are displaced from their original position, randomly re-ordered and appended to the end of the batch. This process effectively disrupts the original sequence of events within each batch. To ensure two levels of event drops we reordered them twice using this method for two different batch-sizes and drop percentages. The first for a batch size of $1{,}000$ and drop percentage 1% and the second for a batch-size was $30{,}000$ and drop percentage 0.05%.

B.2   Experiment 1: Comparative Analysis of Re-Ordering Approaches

This experiment compares the computational performances of the two approaches (SO and LSP) by generating seven ordered input traces of varying sizes using the trace generator. These traces were tested against eight properties described earlier. The performance of the enforcer under both re-ordering approaches is evaluated based on the average run-times, as presented in Table 2. For the LSP approach, α and β were fixed to 50 and 100 respectively.

We note that LSP outperforms SO for input sizes greater than 30,000 events. Performance is also more significant for co-safety properties compared to other properties which corroborates with the conclusions of Theorem 1.

B.3 Experiment 2: Memory Efficiency Analysis of the LSP mode

In this experiment, we analyze the memory efficiency of the LSP mode by measuring the size of the Σ–Radix tree generated for the same properties as in the previous experiment. Tree size is the total number of nodes in the tree while processing each event in the input sequence. We observe growth and shrinkage patterns of the tree by plotting, for each of the eight properties, tree size (or memory usage) against input size in the logarithmic scale as depicted in Fig. 8. Exact event locations that lead to growth and shrinkage in tree sizes are useful in understanding the frequency and nature of tree sizes changes. This is presented for the Cyclic RE1 property in Figs. 6d, 6e and 6f. Note that the $\alpha \sim \beta$ constraints on memory and the randomization in the trace generator determine the maximum number of events that can be missed and the duration for which they can be missed.

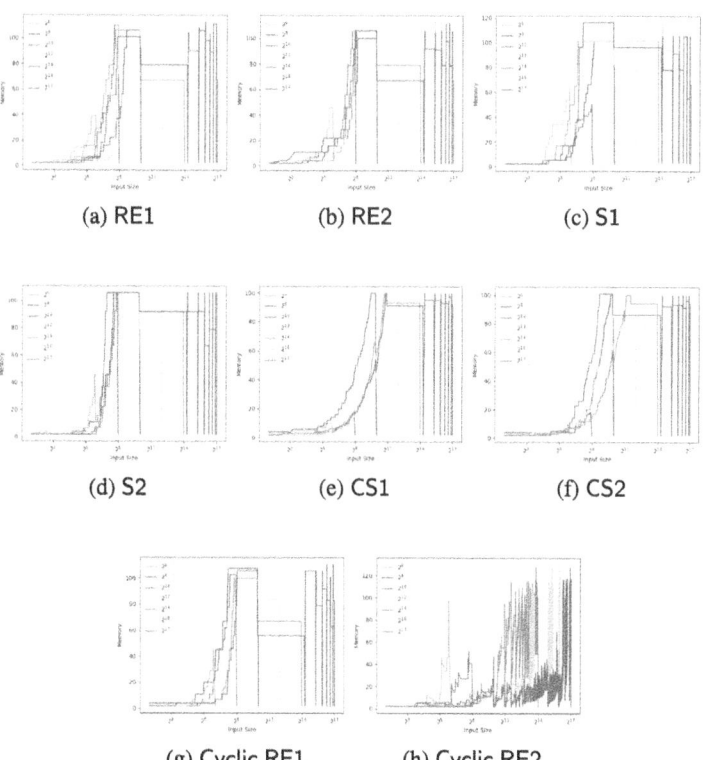

(a) RE1   (b) RE2   (c) S1

(d) S2   (e) CS1   (f) CS2

(g) Cyclic RE1   (h) Cyclic RE2

Fig. 8. Memory usage plots of the LSP mode for varying input sizes measured in terms of tree size

The batch-size is clearly visible, indicating a sharp drop in tree size after each batch, as all missed events were received at the end of the batch (Figs. 8, 6d, 6e and 6f). We also observe that the duration between when the tree size is frozen after crossing $\beta = 100$ and when the tree size drops to or below $\alpha = 50$ is randomized based on re-ordering within the batch.

B.4   Experiment 3: Analysis of Memory Usage and Time Efficiency in Relation to Drop Percentage of LSP mode

This experiment analyzes the relationship between memory usage and processing time with respect to the drop percentage. We test the LSP mode for Cyclic RE1 property with α and β set to 700 and 1000, respectively and input size fixed to 2^{16}. The drop percentage was varied while maintaining a fixed batch size of 20,000 and the maximum overhead memory and average processing time were measured.

The results, which are plotted in Fig. 6b and 6c, show a gradual increase in tree size with increase the drop percentage up to β. A slight increase in time taken was also observed with the increase in drop percentage.

References

1. Basin, D., Klaedtke, F., Zălinescu, E.: Runtime verification of temporal properties over out-of-order data streams. In: Majumdar, R., Kunčak, V. (eds.) CAV 2017. LNCS, vol. 10426, pp. 356–376. Springer, Cham (2017). https://doi.org/10.1007/978-3-319-63387-9_18
2. Basin, D., Klaedtke, F., Zălinescu, E.: Runtime verification over out-of-order streams. ACM Trans. Comput. Logic **21**(1) (2019). https://doi.org/10.1145/3355609
3. Bloem, R., Könighofer, B., Könighofer, R., Wang, C.: Shield synthesis: runtime enforcement for reactive systems. In: Baier, C., Tinelli, C. (eds.) TACAS 2015. LNCS, vol. 9035, pp. 533–548. Springer, Heidelberg (2015). https://doi.org/10.1007/978-3-662-46681-0_51
4. Eddy, W.: Transmission control protocol (TCP). RFC 9293 (2022). https://doi.org/10.17487/RFC9293, https://www.rfc-editor.org/info/rfc9293
5. Eggert, L., Fairhurst, G., Shepherd, G.: UDP usage guidelines. RFC 8085 (2017). https://doi.org/10.17487/RFC8085, https://www.rfc-editor.org/info/rfc8085
6. Falcone, Y., Jéron, T., Marchand, H., Pinisetty, S.: Runtime enforcement of regular timed properties by suppressing and delaying events. Sci. Comput. Program. **123**, 2–41 (2016)
7. Falcone, Y., Mounier, L., Fernandez, J.C., Richier, J.L.: Runtime enforcement monitors: composition, synthesis, and enforcement abilities. Form Methods Syst. Des. **38**(3), 223–262 (2011)
8. Falcone, Y., Salaün, G.: Runtime enforcement with reordering, healing, and suppression. In: Calinescu, R., Păsăreanu, C.S. (eds.) SEFM 2021. LNCS, vol. 13085, pp. 47–65. Springer, Cham (2021). https://doi.org/10.1007/978-3-030-92124-8_3
9. Ghasemirahni, H., et al.: Packet order matters! Improving application performance by deliberately delaying packets. In: 19th USENIX Symposium on Networked Systems Design and Implementation (NSDI 22), pp. 807–827. USENIX Association, Renton (2022). https://www.usenix.org/conference/nsdi22/presentation/ghasemirahni
10. Iyengar, J., Thomson, M.: QUIC: a UDP-based multiplexed and secure transport. RFC 9000 (2021).https://doi.org/10.17487/RFC9000, https://www.rfc-editor.org/info/rfc9000

11. Kakhki, A.M., Jero, S., Choffnes, D., Nita-Rotaru, C., Mislove, A.: Taking a long look at QUIC: an approach for rigorous evaluation of rapidly evolving transport protocols. In: Proceedings of the 2017 Internet Measurement Conference, IMC 2017, pp. 290–303. Association for Computing Machinery, New York (2017). https://doi.org/10.1145/3131365.3131368

12. Ligatti, J., Bauer, L., Walker, D.: Run-time enforcement of nonsafety policies. ACM Trans. Inf. Syst. Secur. 12(3), 19:1–19:41 (2009)

13. Morrison, D.R.: Patricia—practical algorithm to retrieve information coded in alphanumeric. J. ACM 15(4), 514–534 (1968). https://doi.org/10.1145/321479.321481

14. NASA: CCSDS space packet protocol (2020)

15. Panda, A., Baird, A., Pinisetty, S., Roop, P.S.: Incremental security enforcement for cyber-physical systems. IEEE Access 11, 18475–18498 (2023). https://doi.org/10.1109/ACCESS.2023.3246121

16. Pearce, H., Pinisetty, S., Roop, P.S., Kuo, M.M.Y., Ukil, A.: Smart i/o modules for mitigating cyber-physical attacks on industrial control systems. IEEE Trans. Industr. Inf. 16(7), 4659–4669 (2020). https://doi.org/10.1109/TII.2019.2945520

17. Pinisetty, S., Falcone, Y., Jéron, T., Marchand, H., Rollet, A., Nguena Timo, O.: Runtime enforcement of timed properties revisited. Formal Methods Syst. Design 45(3), 381–422 (2014). https://doi.org/10.1007/s10703-014-0215-y

18. Pinisetty, S., Pradhan, A., Roop, P.S., Tripakis, S.: Compositional runtime enforcement revisited. Form Methods Syst. Des. 59, 205–252 (2021). https://doi.org/10.1007/s10703-022-00401-y

19. Pinisetty, S., Preoteasa, V., Tripakis, S., Jéron, T., Falcone, Y., Marchand, H.: Predictive runtime enforcement. Formal Methods Syst. Design 51(1), 154–199 (2017). https://doi.org/10.1007/s10703-017-0271-1

20. Pinisetty, S., Roop, P.S., Smyth, S., Allen, N., Tripakis, S., Hanxleden, R.V.: Runtime enforcement of cyber-physical systems. ACM Trans. Embed. Comput. Syst. 16(5s) (2017). https://doi.org/10.1145/3126500

21. Pinisetty, S., Tripakis, S.: Compositional runtime enforcement. In: Rayadurgam, S., Tkachuk, O. (eds.) NFM 2016. LNCS, vol. 9690, pp. 82–99. Springer, Cham (2016). https://doi.org/10.1007/978-3-319-40648-0_7

22. Schneider, F.B.: Enforceable security policies. ACM Trans. Inf. Syst. Secur. 3(1), 30–50 (2000)

23. Shankar, S., Pradhan, A., Pinisetty, S., Rollet, A., Falcone, Y.: Bounded-memory runtime enforcement with probabilistic and performance analysis. Form Methods Syst. Des. (2024). https://doi.org/10.1007/s10703-024-00446-1

24. Wu, M., Zeng, H., Wang, C.: Synthesizing runtime enforcer of safety properties under burst error. In: Rayadurgam, S., Tkachuk, O. (eds.) NFM 2016. LNCS, vol. 9690, pp. 65–81. Springer, Cham (2016). https://doi.org/10.1007/978-3-319-40648-0_6

25. Yu, T., Sekar, V., Seshan, S., Agarwal, Y., Xu, C.: Handling a trillion (unfixable) flaws on a billion devices: rethinking network security for the internet-of-things. In: Proceedings of the 14th ACM Workshop on Hot Topics in Networks. HotNets-XIV. Association for Computing Machinery, New York (2015). https://doi.org/10.1145/2834050.2834095

26. Zheng, Y., Yu, H., Rexford, J.: Detecting TCP packet reordering in the data plane (2023)

Author Index

© The Editor(s) (if applicable) and The Author(s), under exclusive license
to Springer Nature Switzerland AG 2025
C. Anutariya and M. M. Bonsangue (Eds.): ICTAC 2024, LNCS 15373, pp. 409–410, 2025.
https://doi.org/10.1007/978-3-031-77019-7

GPSR Compliance

The European Union's (EU) General Product Safety Regulation (GPSR) is a set of rules that requires consumer products to be safe and our obligations to ensure this.

If you have any concerns about our products, you can contact us on ProductSafety@springernature.com

In case Publisher is established outside the EU, the EU authorized representative is:

Springer Nature Customer Service Center GmbH
Europaplatz 3
69115 Heidelberg, Germany

The manufacturer's authorised representative in the EU is Springer
Nature Customer Service Centre GmbH, Europaplatz 3, 69115 Heidelberg,
Germany. If you have any concerns regarding our products, please
contact ProductSafety@springernature.com

Printed and bound by CPI Group (UK) Ltd, Croydon, CR0 4YY
06/05/2026
02103968-0001